S0-ARJ-335

Valerie Boyd is arts editor at *The Atlanta Journal-Constitution*. Her articles, essays and reviews have appeared in *Ms.*, *Emerge*, the *Oxford American* and the *Washington Post*. She lives in Atlanta, Georgia.

Praise for *Wrapped in Rainbows*

'After finishing *Wrapped in Rainbows: The Life of Zora Neale Hurston* I wondered which of three words best described it: magnificent, extraordinary or masterpiece. The research and interpretation of events is breathtaking, the writing precise and beautiful. The book takes such a warm, honest, all-encompassing *and wise* view of its subject, that I read it from start to finish as though reading an adventure, and it is on this journey that Boyd, as if born to do so, takes us. However, as I was sifting through superlatives I was visited by a voice that sounded very much like Zora's. That voice dismissed all concern about the praise-song I was planning and seemed content (*profoundly content*) with just one thought: *My name is in my daughters' hands*, it said.

This daughter, Valerie Boyd, has written a biography of Zora Neale Hurston that will be the standard for years to come. Offering vivid splashes of Zora's colorful humor, daring individualism and refreshing insouciance, Boyd has done justice to a dauntless spirit and a heroic life.'

Alice Walker, author of *The Color Purple*

WRAPPED IN RAINBOWS

THE LIFE OF ZORA NEALE HURSTON

Valerie Boyd

Virago

A *Virago* Book
Published by Virago Press 2004
First published in Great Britain by Virago Press 2003

Copyright © Valerie Boyd 2003
Letters of Zora Neale Hurston © Estate of Zora Neale Hurston

The moral right of the author has been asserted

Copyright Acknowledgements on page 588
constitute an extension of this copyright page

All rights reserved.
No part of this publication may be reproduced, stored in a retrieval system,
or transmitted in any form or by any means, without the prior permission
in writing of the publisher, nor be otherwise circulated in any form
of binding or cover other than that in which it is published
and without a similar condition including this condition
being imposed on the subsequent purchaser.

A CIP catalogue record for this book
is available from the British Library

ISBN 1 86049 996 1

Typeset in Goudy Old Style by M Rules
Printed and bound in Great Britain
by Bookmarque Ltd, Croydon, Surrey

Virago Press
An imprint of
Time Warner Book Group UK
Brettenham House
Lancaster Place
London WC2E 7EN

www.virago.co.uk

To Zora Neale Hurston, for choosing me.

And

To Gurumayi Chidvilasananda, my spiritual teacher,
for illuminating every step like the rays of the sun.

Contents

WRAPPED IN RAINBOWS

I have been in Sorrow's kitchen and licked out all the pots.
Then I have stood on the peaky mountain wrapped in rainbows,
with a harp and a sword in my hands.

—Zora Neale Hurston, 1891–1960

CHAPTER 1

Sky Blue Bottoms

There was never quite enough for Zora Neale Hurston in the world she grew up in, so she made up whatever she needed.

In her father's house, on five acres of land in central Florida, young Zora lacked no material comforts. She had eight rooms to roam; a large yard carpeted with Bermuda grass; plenty of playmates; seven siblings; ample amounts of yellow Octagon laundry soap for bathing; two big chinaberry trees for climbing; enough leftover boiled eggs to use as hand grenades on other children; and all the home-cured meat, garden-fresh collard greens, and Mama-made cornbread she could eat.

But Zora had other needs. She needed to know, for instance, what the end of the world was like—"whether it was sort of tucked under like the hem of a dress," as she once wrote, or if it was just "a sharp drop-off into nothingness." One summer day around 1900, when she was about nine years old, Zora decided she ought to walk out to the horizon and see.

She asked a friend, a schoolmate named Carrie Roberts, to go with her. The next morning, bright and soon, Zora and Carrie were to meet by the palmettos near Zora's house to begin their journey to the edge of the world. Daunted by the daring of the thing, Carrie came to tell Zora she couldn't go. That perhaps they should wait until they were big enough to wear long dresses and old enough to stay out past sundown without earning a spanking. Zora pleaded with her friend, but she refused to go. They fought, and Zora went home, she wrote decades later, "and hid under the house with my heartbreak." Still, she recalled, "I did not give up the idea of my journey. I was merely lonesome for someone brave enough to undertake it with me."

Zora decided to put off her trip until she had something to ride on. Then, she reasoned, she could go alone. "So for weeks I saw myself sitting astride of a fine horse," she would remember. "My shoes had sky-blue bottoms to them, and I was riding off to look at the belly-band of the world."

The summer, lush with the fragrance of Florida oranges and the cries of the mockingbirds, surrendered to fall. Then Christmas-time came.

A few days before Christmas that year, Zora's father—John Hurston, a preacher and carpenter—did something unusual. After dinner, he pushed back from the table and asked his children a question. What did they want Santa Claus to bring them? Zora's oldest brothers wanted baseball outfits, she recalled in her autobiography years later. Her younger brothers wanted air rifles. Her big sister wanted patent leather pumps and a belt. Then it was Zora's turn.

"I want a fine black riding horse with white leather saddle and bridles," I told Papa happily.

"You, what?" Papa gasped. "What was dat you said?"

"I said, I want a black saddle horse with . . ."

"A saddle horse!" Papa exploded. "It's a sin and a shame! Lemme tell you something right now, my young lady; you ain't white. Riding horse!! Always trying to wear de big hat! I don't know how you got in this family nohow. You ain't like none of de rest of my young'uns."

"If I can't have no riding horse, I don't want nothing at all," I said stubbornly with my mouth, but inside I was sucking sorrow. My longed-for journey looked impossible.

"I'll riding-horse you, Madam!" Papa shouted and jumped to his feet.

For sassing her father, Zora was bound for a spanking. But she beat her father to the kitchen door and outran him.

Zora got a doll for Christmas. "Since Papa would not buy me a saddle horse," she remembered, "I made me one up."

Within the elastic bounds of her imagination, Zora became an adventurer, taking frequent jaunts on her fictitious saddle horse.

"No one around me knew how often I rode my prancing horse," she recalled, "nor the things I saw in far places."

This was a harbinger of events to come.

Zora's mother, Lucy Potts Hurston, understood her daughter's singular needs—or at least her need to make up the things she did not, could not, have. So Lucy tried to give her baby girl plenty of dreamtime. Zora often found refuge—a place to read and think and listen to her "inside urges"—in her mother's room. There, she also found a welcome retreat from her father, who seemed to believe it was his job to break Zora's impudent spirit, before it was broken—inevitably, he felt, and much more harshly—by the lurking white world.

So Lucy and John Hurston saw Zora's prodigious imagination differently. In fact, they saw a lot of things differently. It hadn't always been that way.

When Lucy Ann Potts and John Hurston started courting, in the early 1880s, they only had eyes for each other. The way Zora Hurston told the story, the way it was always told to her, the first time John saw Lucy was on a Sunday morning in Notasulga, Alabama.

Notasulga is a blink of a town, just six miles north of the more famous Tuskegee, located in eastern Alabama not far from the Georgia border. Despite its diminutiveness (fourteen square miles), Notasulga straddles two counties, Macon and Lee. It is a town surrounded by creeks—creeks with names like Red, Wolf, Chinquapin, Chowocle, and Uphapee.

John grew up "over the creek," Hurston once wrote. If she knew which one, she didn't say. What she did say, though, was that being an over-the-creek Negro was the same, in any other town, as being from the wrong side of the railroad tracks. Over-the-creek Negroes were notoriously poor: they lived from hand to mouth and from one white man's plantation to another. But what made others regard them with such disdain was that they also seemed poor in pride, living in rundown conditions with no apparent ambition to better themselves.

John Hurston, however, ached with ambition. So he found his way to Macedonia Baptist Church, on the right side of the creek, and his eyes lighted on Lucy Potts, who sang treble in the choir. Pecan brown and all of ninety pounds, Lucy must have seemed to John the perfect complement to his two hundred pounds of high-yellow muscle. John's golden skin, gray-green eyes, powerful build, and handsome features weren't lost on Lucy, either. By the time John started sneaking her love notes hidden in the pages of the Baptist hymnal, Lucy had already asked her neighbors about him, already knew his name and his over-the-creek pedigree.

John's parents, Alfred and Amy Hurston, both had known slavery. Alfred had been born in Georgia and Amy in Alabama. By 1880, just seventeen years after Emancipation, they'd made a home for themselves and their nine children—ranging from six-month-old Alfred Jr. to eighteen-year-old John—on the Lee County side of Notasulga. That year, Alfred and Amy reported their ages as forty-six and thirty-eight. A census taker identified Alfred as a mulatto, which might explain why John's skin was "bee-stung yaller," as Lucy put it. (The Notasulga rumor mill provided another explanation: that John himself was a mulatto, the bastard son of a certain white man.)

Lucy's parents, Richard and Sarah Potts, also had been born into slavery, both in Georgia. After freedom came, they settled in the neighboring state of Alabama. Richard Potts had managed to become a landowner in Notasulga, and in 1880 the sixty-five-year-old farmer's household included his fifty-year-old wife, their four children, and two grandchildren. Lucy was the Potts's youngest child. So, perhaps understandably, the relatively well-to-do Potts family was not pleased when Lucy announced she was marrying John—an over-the-creek Negro five years her senior.

Despite her parents' opposition, on the second day of February in 1882, Lucy left the Potts's farm and set out for her wedding—alone. Convinced that Lucy was throwing herself away and disgracing the family by marrying John, Sarah Potts refused to attend the wedding. Most of the family followed suit, declining to witness Lucy's "great come-down in the world." Seeing his daughter's determination, though, Richard Potts decided he didn't want Lucy walking the two miles by herself. So he hitched up his wagon and carried her to the small ceremony, where Lucy and John were married by the Rev. J. Pollard. The bride had just turned sixteen a little more than a month earlier, on December 31. On New Year's Day, the groom had turned twenty-one.

On their wedding night, the young couple basked in the beguiling glimmer of first love. In her novel *Jonah's Gourd Vine*, Hurston evoked the evening this way:

When [Lucy] rode off beside John at last she said, "John Buddy, look lak de moon is givin' sunshine."

He toted her inside the house and held her in his arms infant-wise for a long time. "Lucy, don't you worry 'bout yo' folks, hear? Ahm gointer be uh father and uh mother tuh you. You jes' look tuh me, girl chile. Jes' you put yo' 'pendence in me. Ah means tuh prop you up on eve'y leanin' side."

John took Lucy to the only home he could provide at that time—a small cabin on a white man's plantation in Notasulga, where the young couple worked as sharecroppers. Lucy and John were not invited to settle on her parents' five acres. Richard Potts might have been more welcoming to the couple, but it wasn't solely up to him. Sarah Potts would have none of John Hurston. She never got over losing Lucy to "dat yaller bastard"—her way of referring to her son-in-law for many years to come.

Once, a few years after her wedding night, Lucy had a craving for some of the clingstone peaches on her parents' farm. Her yearning was so intense, she walked for miles to get a few. Creating a makeshift basket, Lucy was holding the corners of her apron with one hand and picking peaches with the other when her mother saw her and ordered her off the place.

Her mother's persistent opposition aside, Lucy soon settled into her new life with John and immediately got down to the business of making babies. In November 1882, just nine months after John and Lucy said their vows, Lucy gave birth to their first child—a boy they named Hezekiah Robert, a mouthful of a name that his siblings would soon reduce to "Bob." A second son, Isaac, was born ten months later, but he didn't survive early childhood. Two more healthy sons followed—John Cornelius and Richard William.

When, in December 1889, Lucy finally gave birth to a girl, Sarah Emmeline—named for Lucy's mother and older sister—John was delighted. For several years, he had wished for a daughter. So when Sarah finally arrived, a bit underweight but healthy, John was joyous. He doted on his daughter, changing her, washing her diapers, and coochie-cooing her every move. When Sarah was old enough to express her wishes, they didn't go unheeded. "What was it Papa's

girl-baby wanted to eat? She wanted two dolls instead of one? Bless
her little heart!"

If John's first-born daughter was his favorite child, his second
daughter was to be his least favorite. "It seems that one daughter was
all that he figured he could stand," Zora Hurston once wrote.
Apparently John wanted "plenty more sons, but no more girl babies
to wear out shoes and bring in nothing."

Nature, however, gave John little say in the matter. When Lucy's
water broke on January 7, 1891, John was out of town.

No other adults were around, either. It was hog-killing time, and
most folks were off helping neighbors butcher and pack away meat
for the rest of the year. As every farmer knew, the optimal time for
the slaughter was between December and February, but the coldest
days were the best ones. Since they had no refrigerators, farmers
had to rely on frigid temperatures to keep their freshly butchered
meat from spoiling before they could pack it with preserving salt. A
crisp, cold day like this one was perfect for the ritual. That Tuesday
morning, whole families had bundled up and trudged off to assist
their neighbors. There was enough work for everyone: the men
would kill and cut, the children would fetch buckets of water to
clean the meat, and the women would salt it down and pack it away.
They would withhold a bit from storage, though, and cook it right
then, repaying their neighbors' kindness with dinner and a mess of
meat to take home.

As her Notasulga neighbors relished one another's company and
savored their freshly killed feast, Lucy struggled with the eager-for-
life child demanding release from her womb.

From the beginning, Zora was ahead of her time. Lucy knew
she was due soon, but she didn't expect the baby to come so suddenly. The way Zora told the story—"this is all hear-say," she
warned—Lucy sent one of her older children to find Aunt Judy, the
midwife, who had gone to a hog-killing in a neighboring town. But
Lucy's ready-for-the-world baby girl could not wait. She rushed
out on her own, and all Lucy could do was lie there, too weak to
reach down for the newborn. Lucy's only consolation was the
child's cacophonous cries, which let her know the baby at least had
healthy lungs.

A neighbor, a white man, was passing through, perhaps to drop off some fresh meat to Lucy and her children, as Hurston later speculated, or perhaps in search of Negroes to help with his hogs. The baby's plentiful lungpower compelled the man to push the door open to see what all the fuss was about. Once he saw what the situation was, "he took out his Barlow knife and cut the navel cord," Zora was to write, "then he did the best he could about other things." When the midwife arrived, the baby had been sponged off and was resting quietly in her mother's arms.

The white man got no thanks from Aunt Judy for his act of heroism. The midwife "grumbled for years about it," Zora once said. "She complained that the cord had not been cut just right, and the belly-band had not been put on tight enough. She was mighty scared I was going to have a weak back, and that I would have trouble holding my water until I reached puberty. I did."

Within a few days, the baby had been named Zora Neal Lee Hurston, according to the family record page of the Bible that Lucy and John passed down to future Hurstons. Exactly where the name came from is a minor mystery. "Lee" might have been a nod to the county in which the child was born; "Neal" and "Zora" are harder to figure. Perhaps, as Hurston later wrote, a friend of Lucy's, a Mrs. Neal, contributed her name to the mix and chose the newborn's unusual first name. "Perhaps she had read it somewhere," Hurston once mused, "or somebody back in those woods was smoking Turkish cigarettes." In any case, Zora never used the name "Lee." And, if the family Bible is accepted as gospel, somewhere down the line, she must have added the final "e" to "Neal," having found the name in need of some embellishment.

For the birth and naming of his second daughter, John Hurston was absent. He had become a fairly successful carpenter by now and was often away on business. Then, too, John had begun to want more than the Notasulga life could offer him. So he occasionally left his wife and children at home while he explored life beyond eastern Alabama's cramping borders. At the time of Zora's birth, he had been away for months.

The way the story goes, the way Zora always heard it, when John got the news that he was the papa of a new baby girl, he threatened to cut his own throat.

The threat was never a serious one, of course, just John's

histrionic way of responding to what he considered bad news. Still, when she was a full-grown woman, Zora Hurston said of her father: "I don't think he ever got over the trick he felt that I played on him by getting born a girl, and while he was off from home at that."

CHAPTER 2

A Pure Negro Town

While Zora was being born, her father was off contemplating perhaps the single most important and most auspicious decision he would ever make. For his fifth surviving child—the one who'd just bellowed her arrival—the decision John was about to make would be crucial to her development as a woman and as a writer.

But John did not know that then. All he knew was that life in Notasulga was "crushing to his ambition," that he needed to go someplace where he could rise to the occasion of his own life.

Eatonville, Florida, was such a place. When John happened upon the town, just four miles east of Orlando, he must have sensed that it was fertile with possibility. Oranges, tangerines, and grapefruits hung invitingly from tree after tree, shameless in their ripeness. Spanish moss hugged the town like a warm gray quilt. And slews of Florida sunshine kissed John's face with a tan and beckoned him to stay a while.

Eatonville was—and is—an all-black town. Not "the black backside of an average town," Hurston once wrote, but "a pure Negro town—charter, mayor, council, town marshal and all."

John's discovery of Eatonville was purely accidental, as Hurston told it in *Jonah's Gourd Vine*. He was ambling about, looking for an appealing place to move his family, when he met another traveler. The man was bound for Sanford, Florida, and invited John to come along. Once there, he told John about a nearby Negro town.

John was astonished. "You mean uh whole town uh nothin' but colored folks?" he asked his friend. "Who bosses it, den?"

"Dey bosses it deyself."

"You mean dey runnin' de town 'thout de white folks?"

"Sho is. Eben got uh mayor and corporation."

"Ah sho wants tuh see dat sight."

When John first walked into Eatonville, it was not only a pure Negro town, but also a *new* Negro town, having been formed only a few years before, in 1887. That year, on August 15, twenty-seven black men had met and voted to incorporate Eatonville—making it one of the first incorporated all-black municipalities in the country.

At least two of these men, Joe Clarke and Tony Taylor, had already gained some experience in government. Curiously, the city that gave these men their early political training had as many white citizens as black. That town was Maitland, Florida, just a mile from Eatonville. It's fair to say that Eatonville was a spin-off from Maitland. So, for a true understanding of Eatonville's beginnings, Maitland must have its say.

Maitland's history began about twenty years before Eatonville's. Just after the Civil War, a few white men who had been officers in the Union Army decided to stake their futures in the unsettled country of central Florida. The shores of Lake Maitland were lovely and seemed as good a place to settle as any. "The terrain was as flat as a table" and free from troublesome rocks. Roads could be made simply by driving wagons back and forth over the walking trail, which ran for several miles between Maitland and Orlando. The roadmakers didn't even bother to cut down the numerous pine trees and oaks; they just curved their roads around the formidable trees, making the paths look as if they had been laid out by prankish rattlesnakes—of which Maitland had no shortage. The town's early settlers persuaded friends from the North to join them in this potential paradise, and soon, affluent, educated whites were coming from as far away as Michigan and Minnesota.

The area was attracting other settlers, as well: Newly freed slaves from as far west as Mississippi and as far north as the Carolinas also flocked to Maitland. The Negroes were needed to clear the land and build houses, so they found profitable employment and good relations with Maitland's whites.

While white settlers erected large estates on the shores of Lake Maitland, the black settlers built shacks around St. John's Hole, soon to be renamed Lake Lily. Only a half mile wide, St. John's Hole was perfectly round and a perfect place for black women to wash clothes and catch fish for dinner, while their men earned a living by cutting new ground, building houses for white settlers, and planting the groves that would give Orange County its name.

There was plenty for any able-bodied worker to do. As former slaves in neighboring states heard about the boom in central Florida, the black population swelled. "No more backbending over rows of cotton; no more fear of the fury of Reconstruction. Good pay, sympathetic white folks and cheap land, soft to the touch of a plow. Relatives and friends were sent for."

In 1884, the people of Maitland—black and white together— began to consider a formal city government. Maitland was incorporated that year, and when it was time to hold an election, the Negroes had just as many votes as the whites. Tony Taylor, a black man, became the first mayor of Maitland, and Joe Clarke, once described as "a 200-pound, dark-complexioned Georgia Negro," won out as town marshal. This may have been an unexpected turn of events for the white citizens of Maitland, but no one voiced any formal objections, so the Negro mayor and town marshal, along with the white city council, took office peacefully and served a yearlong term without incident.

By 1887, though, the black settlers of Maitland, under the outspoken leadership of Joe Clarke, had become eager to start their own town. The crumbling, yellowed records of the period don't reveal why the freedmen suddenly wanted to break away from an economically stable and racially harmonious town to begin their own municipal venture. Perhaps a racial fissure was erupting just under the surface of the historical record. Or perhaps the Negroes' motherwit made them suspect that the white Maitlanders, sympathetic though they were, eventually might seek to put a cap on black ambition—a glass ceiling of sorts. Enterprising men like Tony Taylor and Joe Clarke clearly wanted to have a big voice not just for a one-year term, but for a lifetime. Given the realities of racism, an all-black town was more likely to provide them with a consistent and level playing field for their dreams.

Immediately after the Civil War, Clarke, then a young man in his twenties, had tried to establish a town for freedmen in another part of Florida. But no whites would sell him any land.

Yet when Clarke broached the idea of an all-black town with Lewis Lawrence, a white New York philanthropist who'd settled in Maitland, he found a receptive audience. Several years before, in 1881, Lawrence had purchased twenty-two acres from Josiah Eaton, another white Maitlander. Lawrence then donated ten of those acres to the black community for a place of worship. To distinguish it from the white church, they called it "the African Methodist Church." Later, they added Lawrence's name to the title, canonizing him in the process, and the church became the St. Lawrence African Methodist Episcopal Church.

As for the other land acquired in his 1881 transaction with Eaton, Lawrence sold the remaining twelve acres to Joe Clarke. Those acres formed the foundation for Eatonville. In short order, Clarke and other black leaders bought more than one hundred acres from Lewis Lawrence, Josiah Eaton (for whom the town was named, at Lawrence's suggestion), and other whites in Maitland. Clarke then resold the land in small parcels to black settlers, who paid for their chunks of America in manageable installments. Most families bought forty-by-one-hundred-foot lots for their homes, and those who could afford to do so bought additional acres for vegetable gardens or orange groves. In this way—lot by lot, acre by acre—Eatonville was born, just three and a half years before the child who would become its most famous daughter.

At Eatonville's incorporation meeting on August 15, 1887, Joe Clarke was made an alderman. Columbus H. Boger, a minister who'd moved to the area from Jacksonville, was elected Eatonville's first mayor. Under Boger's leadership, Eatonville developed all the essential elements of a thriving community: a post office and a general store (both owned by Clarke), a school, a library, and even a town newspaper, *The Eatonville Speaker*.

By the time John Hurston strode into this promised land, around 1890, Eatonville had established a second church—one with a name that must have struck a responsive chord in him. It was called Macedonia Baptist, the same as the church in Notasulga where John had first met Lucy. Both Macedonia and St. Lawrence had strong

Sunday schools that provided a spiritual foundation for the children of Eatonville. The town also had a school—the only one for Negroes in central Florida—that offered plenty of book learning as well as useful trades.

Many of Eatonville's women worked in the orange groves or hired out as cooks or maids for white families in Maitland. Men found year-round employment as citrus workers, yardmen, or construction helpers. Eatonville and Maitland were still being built from the ground up, so John expected he'd find an abundance of carpentry work in the area.

Then, too, Eatonville seemed to be the kind of place where a man like John could stretch out his limbs without the irritation of some plantation boss's foot on his neck. Booker T. Washington, perhaps the era's greatest advocate of black enterprise, observed that in black-governed towns like Eatonville, "Negroes are made to feel the responsibilities of citizenship in ways they cannot be made to feel them elsewhere. If they make mistakes, they, at least, have an opportunity to profit by them. In such a town individuals who have executive ability and initiative have an opportunity to discover themselves and find out what they can do."

In an all-black town like Eatonville, racism was no excuse for failure. Here, individuals could sink or swim on their own merits. If you were cream, you'd rise to the top. If you were a bottom-dweller, you'd find your place. If you were a skunk, you'd stink up the place—and be rapidly run out of town, as all lawbreakers were.

So John decided to settle in Eatonville, "the city of five lakes, three croquet courts, three hundred brown skins, three hundred good swimmers, plenty guavas, two schools, and no jail-house," as Zora Hurston would later describe it. John was there for about a year before he sent money for Lucy and the children to join him.

John met Lucy at the train depot in Maitland with a wagon and a team of horses he'd borrowed from a prosperous neighbor. "He wouldn't let her walk down the coach steps, but held wide his arms and made her jump into his bosom," as Hurston later told it. The meager possessions Lucy brought from Notasulga—her feather bed, a battered tin trunk, and some hand-sewn quilts—didn't fill up the wagon. But, as John proudly drove the mile to Eatonville, the buggy brimmed with love and laughter.

That night John went to the woods and filled several burlap bags with Spanish moss for the older children to sleep on. John and Lucy put the baby on the feather mattress with them. They didn't have much in their small cabin that night, but the family was together, and Lucy was happy. "Lucy sniffed sweet air laden with night-blooming jasmine and wished that she had been born in this climate," Zora Hurston wrote of her mother. "She seemed to herself to be coming home. This was where she was meant to be."

CHAPTER 3

Mama's Child

At Lucy's urging, John soon went to Joe Clarke's general store to purchase a plot of land. He had become so successful at his carpentry business that he could afford five acres, on which he built an eight-room house. Two chinaberry trees guarded the front gate of the Hurston home, and Cape jasmine bushes lined the walks, intoxicating passersby with their fragrant white blooms.

The two-story house stood in the heart of Eatonville, within easy walking distance of Macedonia Baptist and the Hungerford School, where the oldest children, Bob and John Cornelius, were promptly enrolled. The younger ones learned their ABCs and other fundamentals at home from Lucy, who believed education was an indispensable stepping-stone for her children.

Lucy's youngest child, meanwhile, had no interest in stepping-stones. Zora was a reluctant walker, refusing to even try until she was more than a year old. Even then, she had to be roused by an overbearing farm animal. The way Zora told the story, Lucy was preparing collard greens for the family's supper. When she went to the nearby spring to give the greens a thorough washing, Lucy left Zora sitting on the floor with a piece of cornbread to keep her quiet.

A few minutes later, Lucy heard her baby screaming. She rushed back and saw that a hog had entered the house. She must have been terrified, since hogs are notorious for eating *anything*, including human flesh. The hog, however, had no interest in Lucy's child; it was busily nuzzling at the crumbs of cornbread Zora had dropped on the floor. "But I was not taking this thing sitting down," Zora was to write. "I had been placed by a chair, and when my mother got inside the door, I had pulled myself up by that chair and was getting around it right smart."

After that incident, "with no more suggestions from the sow or anybody else," Zora had no further reticence about walking. "The strangest thing about it was that once I found the use of my feet, they took to wandering," she wrote decades later. "I always wanted to go. I would wander off in the woods all alone, following some inside urge to go places. This alarmed my mother a great deal. She used to say that she believed a woman who was an enemy of hers had sprinkled 'travel dust' around the doorstep the day I was born. That was the only explanation she could find."

Travel dust or not, Lucy needn't have worried about Zora. As she made her way through girlhood and beyond, Zora always remembered a choice piece of folk wisdom that black women have whispered in their children's ears, or sung out loud, for generations: "Wherever you go, you must never forget your way home."

For Zora Hurston, Eatonville was always home. Throughout her life, she would claim Eatonville as her birthplace and refer to it as her "native village." Because she was so young when her family moved to Eatonville, perhaps her parents never told her she was actually born in Notasulga, Alabama. Or perhaps she was told, but considered it an insignificant detail not worth repeating. In any case, she never mentioned Notasulga as part of her personal geography. When, as a successful writer in New York, Hurston would speak of going "down home" for a visit, Notasulga never crossed her mind. Always, she meant Eatonville.

Essentially everything that Zora Hurston would grow up to write, and to believe, had its genesis in Eatonville. The setting of her earliest childhood memories and the site of her coming of age, Eatonville was where Hurston received her first lessons in individualism and her first immersion in community.

Here, she saw black folks in all their folly and all their glory. She witnessed silly fights between neighbors that left them mute with one another for months. Then, too, she once watched her father load his rifle and stalk off into the dark woods, along with the other men of the village, prepared to defend a neighbor against racist violence, or die in the attempt.

Anywhere Zora looked, she could see the evidence of black achievement. She could look toward town hall and see black men, including her father, formulating the laws that governed Eatonville. She could look to the Sunday schools of both the town's churches and see black women, including her mother, directing the Christian curricula. She could look to the porch of Joe Clarke's store and see black men and women passing worlds through their mouths in the form of colorful, engaging stories.

Yet Zora Hurston quickly came to reject the idea of "race achievement." "Races have never done anything," she would write well into her adulthood. "What seems race achievement is the work of individuals." And, as her Eatonville experience taught her, "all clumps of people turn out to be individuals on close inspection."

For individuals to admire, young Zora didn't have to look any farther than her own home.

Lucy Hurston was a talented seamstress who sewed for the community and taught in Macedonia's Sunday school. She also became the driving force behind her husband's growing success.

John Hurston had always been a man of ambition, but Lucy urged him to action. Describing her parents' differing temperaments, Hurston once wrote: "He could put his potentialities to sleep and be happy in the laugh of the day. He could do next year, or never, what Mama would have insisted must be done today."

Soon after settling in Eatonville, Lucy encouraged John to answer an inner calling to become a minister. It had all started the first time John prayed aloud in a quiet church, according to Hurston. When the "empty house threw back his resonant tones like a guitar box," John was enchanted by the sound of his own voice calling God's name. "Dat sho sound good," John exulted. "If mah voice sound *dat* good de first time Ah ever prayed in de church house, it sho won't be de las'."

Others, too, were impressed by the sound of John's voice when he lifted it up in prayer. So when he announced that God had called him to preach, Macedonia Baptist and Eatonville at large roared their approval. "His trial sermon had to be preached in a larger church—so many people wanted to hear him. He had a church to pastor before the hands had been laid on his head."

In 1893, John became the pastor of Zion Hope Baptist Church in Sanford, about twenty miles east of Eatonville. As the church's membership swelled monthly, John acquired a nickname that honored his powerful pulpit presence: He was called "God's Battle-Axe." The Reverend Hurston would stretch wide his arms in a dramatic gesture and boom his favorite greeting: "Welcome ye lovers of Jesus. Our doors are open. Come!"

That same year, in March, Lucy gave birth to another child, Clifford Joel. Two more sons soon followed: Benjamin Franklin, born in December 1895, and Everett Edward, in October 1898.

For his six sons and two daughters, John was an excellent provider. A large vegetable garden ensured the Hurston children were never hungry. The town's lakes furnished them with their fill of fish, and the dining room pantry was crowded with jars of guava jelly and peach and pear preserves. Homegrown chickens found their way to the dinner table often, and the children had all the eggs they wanted. "It was a common thing for us smaller children to fill the iron tea-kettle full of eggs and boil them," Zora would recall, "and lay around in the yard and eat them until we were full. Any leftover boiled eggs could always be used for missiles."

The Hurston children had plenty of playmates for target practice. On any given summer evening, dozens of Eatonville children came to play hide-and-seek and other boisterous games with Zora and her siblings, who, by the end of the century, ranged in age from toddlers to teens.

Lucy and John also entertained frequent visitors—preachers, Sunday school workers, and friends. Overnight guests were given John's bedroom, fresh water from the pump, sweet soap and store-bought towels from the round-topped trunk in Lucy's room—rather than the bleached-out meal sacks the family usually used for bath towels.

For her children, Lucy's room was the center of the world. After supper, they would pile in to do their homework. Lucy helped them all past long division and parsing sentences, but that was as far as her own education allowed her to go. Then she turned over the younger children to their big brother, Bob. Lucy would sit in her rocking chair during these tutoring sessions, her disciplining gaze ensuring that the little ones obeyed Bob and remained focused on their lessons.

"Jump at de sun," Lucy dared her children. "We might not land on the sun," Zora remembered her mother saying, "but at least we would get off the ground."

John was less optimistic. Though he shared Lucy's commitment to educating the children, he objected to filling their heads with lofty, unattainable dreams. "It did not do for Negroes to have too much spirit," he believed.

Given this criterion, Zora continued to disappoint her father. Having inherited her mother's spunky temperament, Zora was too spirited and too mouthy for her own good, John felt. He predicted a dire future for her, as Zora recalled: "The white folks were not going to stand for it. I was going to be hung before I got grown. Somebody was going to blow me down for my sassy tongue. Mama was going to suck sorrow for not beating my temper out of me before it was too late."

Lucy acknowledged that Zora was "impudent and given to talking back," but she refused to "squinch" her daughter's spirit, as Zora wrote, "for fear that I would turn out to be a mealy-mouthed rag doll by the time I got grown."

From all indications, John himself was not a meek, mealy-mouthed Negro, yet he wanted his children to be schooled in humility. He wanted them to know when and how to defer to whites because he knew that just beyond the borders of Eatonville loomed a large white world—one that he expected would be hostile to a Negro girl as saucy as Zora.

Zora's sister, Sarah, had a milder disposition. "She would always get along," John believed. Why couldn't Zora be more like her? When John would put this question to Lucy, she would answer: "Zora is my young'un, and Sarah is yours. . . . You leave her alone. I'll tend to her when I figger she needs it."

So, with Lucy's tacit permission, John continued to dote on his older daughter—and to largely ignore his younger one, except to chastise her. For Zora, Lucy's loving attention appeared to fill any void created by the absence of John's gaze. And Zora never seemed to blame her sister for their father's favoritism—particularly after she found a way to take advantage of the situation: "If the rest of us wanted to sneak jelly or preserves and get off without a licking, the thing to do was to get Sarah in on it," she recalled. "Papa might ignore the whipping-purge that Mama was organizing until he found that Sarah was mixed up in it." Then he would hastily put down the newspaper he might be reading and say to Lucy, "Dat'll do! Dat'll do, Lulu! I can't stand all dat racket around de place."

Zora added: "I have seen Papa actually snatch the switch out of Mama's hand when she got to Sarah."

For Lucy and John, spanking was a common method of discipline—a deeply ingrained practice not just in the Hurston household but in many black households in Eatonville and beyond. Though spanking was simply a fact of life for her as a child, Zora later came to view corporal punishment as an unfortunate legacy of slavery: Black parents had learned to keep their children in line the same way white slavers kept slaves in their place—through violence, or the threat of it. In her novel *Jonah's Gourd Vine*, Hurston has one of her characters, a former slave, delivering an impassioned speech about honoring black children: "We black folks don't love our chillun. We couldn't do it when we wuz in slavery. We borned 'em but dat didn't make 'em ourn. Dey b'longed tuh old Massa. 'Twan't no use in treasurin' other folkses property. It wuz liable tuh be took away any day. But we's free folks now. De big bell done rung! Us chillun is ourn. Ah doan know, mebbe hit'll take some of us generations, but us got tuh 'gin tuh practise on treasurin' our younguns. . . . Ah don't want 'em knocked and 'buked."

John expressed no such reservations about whipping his children, but he would never strike Sarah. If Lucy spanked John's favorite child, Zora noted, "Sarah was certain to get some sort of a present on Monday when Papa came back from Sanford," where he spent weekends as pastor of Zion Hope.

"Papa delighted in putting the finest and the softest shoes on her dainty feet," Zora wrote of her sister, "the fluffiest white organdy dresses with the stiffest ribbon sashes."

As Sarah sashayed in her frilly dresses—fitting well into the delicate image John had constructed for his girl children—Zora became an acceptable playmate among the neighborhood boys. The reason was simple, she recalled: "I was the one girl who could take a good pummeling without running home to tell." Zora had discovered, by playing with Sarah and other girls, that she was unusually strong. "I had no way of judging the force of my playful blows, and so I was always hurting somebody," she remembered. "Then they would say I meant to hurt, and go home and leave me. Everything was all right, however, when I played with boys."

Yet Zora's parents disapproved of this cross-gender play. "It was not ladylike for girls to play with boys," Zora was told. "No matter how young you were, no good could come of the thing. . . . What was wrong with my doll-babies? Why couldn't I sit still and make my dolls some clothes?"

For a roughhousing child like Zora, dolls were a bore. "Dolls caught the devil around me," she remembered. Christmas dolls "got into fights and leaked sawdust before New Year's. They jumped off the barn and tried to drown themselves in the lake," she wrote. "Perhaps the dolls bought for me looked too different from the ones I made up myself. The dolls I made up in my mind did everything. Those store-bought things had to be toted and helped around. Without knowing it, I wanted action."

Too rough for sustained play with other girls, and prohibited from playing with boys, Zora became a bit of a loner, comfortable with her own company. "I was driven inward," she would recall. "I lived an exciting life unseen."

With no more than a discarded shuck of corn, a cake of soap found in Lucy's dresser drawer, and a corn cob rescued from the kitchen waste pile, Zora would amuse herself for months. In her favorite play spot, under the house, she imagined the elaborate lives of Miss Corn-Shuck, Mr. Sweet Smell, and the conniving Miss Corn-Cob, directing them through dramatic plot twists—and beginning her own life as a storyteller.

Though only thirteen months older than Zora, Sarah was given much more sophisticated toys. For her tenth birthday, John surprised Sarah with a parlor organ shipped from Jacksonville, and he saw to it that she had music lessons. "It did not matter that she was not interested in music, it was part of his pride," Zora wrote. "When I begged for music lessons, I was told to dry up before he bust the hide on my back."

Zora's father often threatened her with such harsh words. "Behind Mama's rocking chair was a good place to be in times like that," Zora recalled. "Papa was not going to hit Mama. . . . When people teased him about Mama being the boss, he would say he could break her of her headstrong ways if he wanted to, but she was so little that he couldn't find any place to hit her."

As the twentieth century dawned, black women were becoming leaders in the national women's suffrage movement and making unprecedented progress in business. Booker T. Washington's National Negro Business League, for instance, reported that in 1900 there were "160 black female physicians, seven dentists, ten lawyers, 164 ministers," and numerous black women journalists, writers, and artists.

In Eatonville, however, the blossoming women's movement was barely a bud. It wasn't uncommon, in those days, for men to sit on the porch of Joe Clarke's store and brag about beating their wives. Lucy's brother Jim, for instance, "maintained that if a woman had anything big enough to sit on, she had something big enough to hit on," Hurston would recall. Zora's Uncle Jim scoffed at men like John, who preferred not to strong-arm women.

John defended his choice with an odd blend of gallantry and bigotry: "What's de use of me taking my fist to a poor weakly thing like a woman? Anyhow, you got to submit yourself to 'em, so there ain't no use in beating on 'em and then have to go back and beg 'em pardon."

John never hit Lucy, as far as Zora remembered. But he did threaten her. "On two occasions," Hurston would write, "I heard my father threaten to kill my mother if she ever started towards the gate to leave him."

In the first incident, John had become outraged when he heard Lucy say, rather casually, that if he wasn't willing to provide for her and her children, "there was another man over the fence waiting for his job." That expression was a common folk saying, as Hurston recounted, and John undoubtedly had heard other women say it. But he was incensed at hearing it from Lucy. "She definitely understood, before he got through carrying on," Hurston wrote elliptically, "that the saying was not for her lips."

On the occasion of the second threat, John and Lucy were headed for a party with another couple. John suggested they exchange partners for the evening: John would escort his friend's wife, and his friend would be Lucy's escort. Lucy reluctantly agreed, but then she seemed to enjoy the experiment more than John thought she should.

The night ended with John leaving the other woman at the party to follow Lucy and her escort home. He marched Lucy into the house, Hurston remembered, "with the muzzle of his Winchester rifle in her back."

John's apparent insecurity about losing Lucy's fidelity was likely a projection, rooted in guilt over his own unfaithfulness.

The Rev. John Hurston was a man of the spirit, but he also was a man of the flesh. And, despite his Bible's admonitions against adultery, he was often attracted to the flesh of women other than his wife. As pastor of Zion Hope Baptist, John usually spent weekends in Sanford, twenty miles from home. With eight children to care for, Lucy rarely had the mobility to travel with him. In addition to his regular ministry, John was often called to conduct revival meetings throughout Florida. A handsome, charismatic preacher, he also was frequently invited to minister to the physical needs of the state's women.

Lucy knew about John's amours. Here's how Zora Hurston imagined her mother's conflicted feelings the first time she recognized John's betrayal: "She was glad to see him in his new suits that his congregation proudly bestowed upon him without his asking. She loved to see him the center of admiring groups. She loved to hear him spoken of as 'The Battle-Axe.' She even loved his primitive poetry and his magnificent pulpit gestures, but, even so, a little cold feeling impinged upon her antennae. There was another woman."

John's current affair would end after a short while, usually with no intervention on Lucy's part, and husband and wife would grow closer for a time. Then Lucy would feel the familiar coldness in the pit of her stomach again, alerting her that John was involved with yet another woman. As Hurston put it, "There came other times of cold feelings and times of triumphs. Only the coldnesses grew numerous."

Sometimes Lucy challenged John about his philandering. Young Zora watched these confrontations with some bewilderment and tried to stay out of the path of John's embarrassed anger—which could easily turn on her. "Every time Mama cornered him about some of his doings, he used to threaten to wring a chair over her head. She never even took notice of the threat to answer. She just went right on asking questions about his doings and then answering

them herself until Papa slammed out of the house looking like he had
been whipped all over with peach hickories," Hurston would recall.
"But I had better not let out a giggle at such times, or it would be just
too bad."

Part of the reason John's anger could so easily turn on his baby
daughter was that he saw in Zora's face a clear reflection of his own.
"I looked more like him than any child in the house," Zora once said.
Looking at Zora was like looking in a mirror, and John did not like
what he saw. So he often struck out at the mirror—his ire for Zora
largely a reflection of his own self-contempt, perhaps left over from
his days and years as an over-the-creek Negro.

By almost any measure, John had become a success. Yet somehow
he couldn't seem to shake his lingering feelings of unworthiness.
The men on the porch of Joe Clarke's store teasingly called John "a
wife-made man"—one whose prosperity was largely the result of his
wife's efforts. He knew there was some truth to this label, and he
seemed simultaneously to love and resent Lucy for it. John fled from
his disconcerting feelings into the validating arms of various
women—women who idolized him in ways that Lucy no longer
could.

As Hurston put it, "My mother took her over-the-creek man and
bare-knuckled him from brogans to broadcloth, and I am certain that
he was proud of the change, in public. But in the house, he might
have always felt over-the-creek, and because that was not the statue
he had made for himself to look at, he resented it. But then, you
cannot blame my mother too much if she did not see him as his
entranced congregations did. The one who makes the idols never
worships them, however tenderly he might have molded the clay."

Conjecture on the reasons for John's infidelity could run as wild as
John himself did. Surely, Lucy had her theories. Zora Hurston, as an
adult, even offered her own sarcastic speculations: "Maybe he was
just born before his time. There was nothing then to hinder impulses.
They didn't have these zippers on pants in those days, guaranteed to
stay locked no matter what the strain. From what I can learn, those
button-up flies were mighty tricky and betraying."

Hurston's biting humor barely masks the pain she must have felt
in witnessing her father repeatedly betray the mother she adored.

Still, despite John's obvious weaknesses—including his tenacious inability to fully embrace her—Zora found much to appreciate about her father. "I know that I did love him in a way, and that I admired many things about him," she would write. "He had a poetry about him that I loved. That had made him a successful preacher. He could hit ninety-seven out of a hundred with a gun. He could swim Lake Maitland from Maitland to Winter Park, and no man in the village could put my father's shoulders to the ground."

Zora and her siblings were awed by John's sheer physical prowess. In some ways, their father seemed invincible. "We had seen him bring down bears and panthers with his gun, and chin the bar more times than any man in competing distance. He had to our knowledge licked two men who Mama told him needed to be licked," Zora Hurston wrote. "All that part was just fine with me. But I was Mama's child."

CHAPTER 4

Glints and Gleams

The relationship between Lucy and John Hurston was as complex and inexplicable as love itself. Certainly, it was too complicated to be grasped by a child—even one as precocious as Zora.

Zora Hurston never fully understood her mother's allegiance to her father, and she certainly would grow up to make very different choices in her own relationships. Even in retrospect, as a rather worldly woman, Hurston seemed to have only a feeble understanding of what kept her parents together. "I know that my mother was very unhappy at times, but neither of them ever made any move to call the thing off," she wrote in her autobiography. "So, looking back, I take it that Papa and Mama, in spite of his meanderings, were really in love."

As a child, Zora had little choice but to throw up her hands at her parents' sometimes puzzling relationship. She found refuge from the confusions of her childhood—an irascible, unfaithful father, an inscrutably loyal mother—by retreating into the controllable surety of her own imagination.

Zora imagined, for instance, that she was the moon's favorite child. "For a long time I gloated over the happy secret that when I played outdoors in the moonlight, the moon followed me, whichever way I ran," she would recall. "The moon was so happy when I came out to play that it ran shining and shouting after me like a pretty puppy dog. The other children didn't count."

Yet, just as Lucy Hurston faced the reality of her husband's infidelity, Zora soon came to know the unfaithfulness of the moon. Her friend Carrie Roberts broke the news to her: The moon—the same one that Zora claimed as her own—followed only *her*, Carrie insisted. "We disputed the matter with hot jealousy," Zora remembered, "and nothing would do but we must run a race to prove which one the moon was loving."

The girls counted to three in unison, then tore out in opposite directions—but each alleged the moon followed her alone. Since the results of the race were inconclusive, Zora and Carrie temporarily parted company, angered by each other's claims on the moon's affections. "When the other children found out what the quarrel was about, they laughed it off. They told me the moon always followed them," Zora recalled.

"The unfaithfulness of the moon hurt me deeply. . . . But after a while, I ceased to ache over the moon's many loves. I found comfort in the fact that though I was not the moon's exclusive friend, I was still among those who showed the moon which way to go," Hurston mused many years later. Then she added more pointedly: "That was my earliest conscious hint that the world didn't tilt under my footfalls, nor careen over one-sided just to make me glad."

Still, there were many glad moments—idyllic days of adventure and discovery. Zora's favorite place for viewing the distant, beckoning horizon—"the most interesting thing that I saw," as she put it—was atop one of the chinaberry trees in her front yard. For a less pastoral view, she perched herself on top of the gatepost. The road to Orlando ran past the Hurstons' front gate and Zora eagerly observed the parade of carriages the route hosted. "The movement made me glad to see it," she would recall.

Having spent virtually her entire life in an all-black town, Zora was especially curious about the whites who passed through Eatonville, and naive about the boundaries that were supposed to divide the races. Often, she flagged down white travelers and invited herself on their trips, asking: "Don't you want me to go a piece of the way with you?"

Usually the travelers welcomed her wide-eyed company. "I know now that I must have caused a great deal of amusement among them," Hurston wrote in her autobiography, "but my self-assurance

must have carried the point, for I was always invited to come along."
She would ride up the road for a half mile or so, then walk back
home. When her parents would find out about her unauthorized
adventures, Zora would be disciplined sharply, as she recalled.

Zora's maternal grandmother, Sarah Potts, had reconciled with
Lucy, for the most part, and visited the Hurston home often after her
husband's death in the late 1880s. Having experienced slavery—a
time when white brutality toward black people was commonplace—
Grandma Potts found Zora's conduct inconceivable, and dangerous.
"Git down offa dat gate post!" she would order Zora. "Setting up dere
looking dem white folks right in de face! They's gowine to lynch you,
yet. And don't stand in dat doorway gazing out at 'em neither. Youse
too brazen to live long."

Despite spankings and reprimands, Zora continued to take her
occasional trips beyond the borders—both actual and racial—of
Eatonville. "I felt no fear of white faces," she would recall. "The
Southern whites in the neighborhood were very friendly and kind,
and so I failed to realize that I was any different from them, in spite
of the fact that my own village had done its best to impress upon me
that white faces were something to fear and be awed by."

Zora and her classmates were accustomed to the periodic presence of white faces in their classrooms at the Robert Hungerford
Normal and Industrial School, which was named for the deceased
son of its benefactors, Edward and Anna Hungerford. The
Hungerford School frequently hosted visits by white northerners,
who seemed to find the idea of a Negro school curious and compelling.

The school's founders, Russell and Mary Calhoun, both had
attended the famous Tuskegee Institute in Alabama, not far from
John and Lucy's hometown of Notasulga. The Calhouns had used
Tuskegee as a model when they founded the Hungerford School, in
1889, to provide academic and vocational training for Negro children in central Florida. They even named the school's first building,
housing classrooms and administrative offices, for their Tuskegee
mentor: It was called Booker T. Washington Hall. (Washington himself was an active supporter of the school, responsible for a $400 gift
during Hungerford's fledgling years.)

The Calhouns welcomed all visitors, hoping the Hungerford

School might elicit the same kind of acclaim—and financial support—that Tuskegee enjoyed. Usually, visitors gave the Calhouns a day's notice, and Eatonville's children "would be cautioned to put on shoes, comb our heads, and see to ears and fingernails," as Zora recalled. The next day, the children would be lined up in the corridors of Washington Hall for inspection. Any child who showed up with uncombed hair, waxy ears, or dirty fingernails was spanked and sent home.

To welcome visitors, the children usually sang a hastily rehearsed Negro spiritual—just what patronizing guests would want to hear from the mouths of colored babes. Mr. Calhoun himself would lead the song, Zora remembered, and "Mrs. Calhoun always stood in the back, with a palmetto switch in her hand as a squelcher. We were all little angels for the duration, because we'd better be."

One afternoon in the early 1900s, though, two white visitors arrived unannounced. Mr. Calhoun called upon Zora's fifth-grade class to read for the ladies. Zora was barefoot that day, and she and her classmates stood to read for the visitors on feet and legs that were dusty from outdoor play. Here's how she remembered it:

We stood up in the usual line, and opened to the lesson. It was the story of Pluto and Persephone. It was new and hard to the class in general, and Mr. Calhoun was very uncomfortable as the readers stumbled along, spelling out words with their lips, and in mumbling undertones before they exposed them experimentally to the teacher's ears.

Then it came to me. I was fifth or sixth down the line. The story was not new to me, because I had read my reader through from lid to lid, the first week that Papa had bought it for me. . . . Some of the stories, I had reread several times, and this Greco-Roman myth was one of my favorites. I was exalted by it, and that is the way I read my paragraph.

Mr. Calhoun smiled his approval at Zora's reading and nodded for her to continue. She read the story to the end and was invited to meet the visitors after class. Based on Hurston's recollection of the event, it's likely the white visitors were Episcopalian educators or missionaries from Minnesota. In any case, the women shook Zora's hand and patted her head appreciatively, if condescendingly.

"They asked me if I loved school, and I lied that I did. There was *some* truth in it, because I liked geography and reading, and I liked to play at recess time," Zora recalled. "Whoever it was invented writing

and arithmetic got no thanks from me. Neither did I like the arrangement where the teacher could sit up there with a palmetto stem and
lick me whenever he saw fit. I hated things I couldn't do anything
about. But I knew better than to bring that up right there, so I said
yes, I *loved* school."

Duly delighted, the women invited Zora to visit them at the Park
House Hotel in Maitland. Mr. Calhoun sent a note to Zora's parents
detailing the invitation. On the appointed afternoon, Zora left school
an hour early and went home to a tub of Octagon soap suds Lucy
had prepared for her. Lucy made sure her daughter's ears were
scrubbed and that her shoes were on the right feet, Zora recalled.
"My sandy hair sported a red ribbon to match my red and white
checked gingham dress, starched until it could stand alone."

Zora's big brother John Cornelius walked the mile with her to
Maitland and waited for her at the hotel gate. Zora went in to see the
women alone.

This was a milestone in young Zora's life. It was a school-
sanctioned, Mama-supported opportunity to do what she had
secretly sought to do in hitching rides with strangers: to travel
beyond Eatonville's borders, yes, but also to assert herself in the
world as an individual—independent of her family.

Inside the hotel, in the affable eyes of the visiting educators, Zora
was not standing in her older sister's shadow. She was not the
Reverend Hurston's least favorite child. She was not even Lucy's
baby girl. She was just Zora, free to be as inventive and impressive as
she dared to be.

Zora succeeded in impressing the white women and was roundly
rewarded for her intellectual aptitude. The women offered her exotic
snacks, like stuffed dates and candied ginger. They asked her to read
for them once more, and invited her outside to take her photograph.
They then sent her on her way with approving smiles and a mysterious present—a cylinder wrapped in colorful paper and tied with
ribbon.

Zora's big brother insisted on carrying the heavy package for her,
and when they got home with the gift, Lucy let Zora open it.
"Perhaps I shall never experience such joy again. The nearest thing
to that moment was the telegram accepting my first book," Hurston
wrote decades later. "One hundred goldy-new pennies rolled out of

the cylinder. Their gleam lit up the world. It was not avarice that moved me. It was the beauty of the thing. I stood on the mountain. Mama let me play with my pennies for a while, then put them away for me to keep."

The gifts kept coming. The next day, the women sent Zora an Episcopal hymnbook, a copy of *The Swiss Family Robinson*, and a book of fairy tales. A month or so later, Zora received a large box stuffed with books and clothes.

Of the clothes, she found a red coat and its matching red tam most appealing. "The clothes were not new," Zora noted, "but they were very good. I shone like the morning sun."

The books were an even greater illuminator. By then, Zora's hungry mind had already consumed everything in her family's small library—including "the Doctor Book, which my mother thought she had hidden securely from my eyes," Zora recalled, and as much of the Bible as she was interested in. She preferred rugged Old Testament figures like David, yet she was drawn to the lovely New Testament language of Luke and Paul. Zora and her playmate Carrie Roberts also "spent long afternoons reading what Moses told the Hebrews not to do in Leviticus," Zora remembered. "In that way I found out a number of things the old folks would not have told me. Not knowing what we were actually reading, we got a lot of praise from our elders for our devotion to the Bible."

The box from Minnesota, however, introduced Zora to a whole new world of books worthy of devotion. "In that box," she recalled, "was Gulliver's Travels, Grimm's Fairy Tales, Dick Whittington, Greek and Roman Myths, and best of all, Norse Tales."

The box contained other books that Zora found less compelling—"thin books about this and that sweet and gentle little girl who gave up her heart to Christ and good works." Zora was indifferent to these docile heroines. Instead, she was enamored of characters who exhibited strength and who thirsted for knowledge. She particularly loved "the great and good Odin, who went down to the well of knowledge to drink, and was told that the price of a drink from that fountain was an eye. Odin drank deeply, then plucked out one eye without a murmur and handed it to the grizzly keeper, and walked away. That held majesty for me," Hurston would remember.

"Of the Greeks, Hercules moved me most," she recalled. "I

followed him eagerly on his tasks. The story of the choice of Hercules
as a boy when he met Pleasure and Duty, and put his hand in that of
Duty and followed her steep way to the blue hills of fame and glory,
which she pointed out at the end, moved me profoundly. I resolved
to be like him."

Zora's vow to emulate Hercules and her other literary heroes did
not release her from her household chores, nor from the mundane-
ness of her own life, as she saw it. "Stew beef, fried fatback and
morning grits were no ambrosia from Valhalla. Raking back yards
and carrying out chamber pots were not the tasks of Hercules. I
wanted to be away from drabness and to stretch my limbs in some
mighty struggle," she recounted.

Zora's early exposure to literature, then, intensified her childhood
angst and made her chafe at the confines of her own limited life. "In
a way this early reading gave me great anguish through all my childhood and adolescence," she later acknowledged. "My soul was with
the gods and my body in the village."

The village, however, also had its instructions to impart. While
Zora nurtured her longing for adventure through her reading and
through her geography lessons at the Hungerford School, she
received an equally important education on the porch of Joe Clarke's
store—"the heart and spring of the town," as she called it.

Children, of course, were not allowed to sit around the porch and
listen to grown folks talk. But whenever Zora was sent to the
store, just down the road from her house, she managed to drag her
feet enough to catch an earful of the "adult double talk" she gradually came to understand.

She would hear, for instance, veiled references to young women
who'd been "ruint"; flirtatious banter between the sexes; brags about
male potency; and plentiful gossip about supposedly clandestine love
affairs. "There were no discreet nuances of life on Joe Clarke's
porch," Hurston would recall. "There was open kindnesses, anger,
hate, love, envy and its kinfolks, but all emotions were naked, and
nakedly arrived at."

As Zora ambled toward adolescence, the occasional risqué porch
story piqued her curiosity. Yet what she really loved to hear were the
folktales. When Eatonville's men—and, sometimes, women—held
their "lying sessions," Zora recalled, "God, Devil, Brer Rabbit, Brer

Fox, Sis Cat, Brer Bear, Lion, Tiger, Buzzard, and all the wood folk walked and talked like natural men."

On the porch owned and presided over by Joe Clarke—who had become Eatonville's second mayor, in 1900—Zora was first exposed to the storytelling genius of the people of her community. There, she heard tales about how black folks got their color, learned why there were Methodists and Baptists, and heard poetic theories on why God gave men and women different strengths. There, Zora absorbed phrases that would later find their way into her own stories— trumphant phrases, such as "I got a rainbow wrapped and tied around my shoulder," as well as those expressing defeat: "My heart was beneath my knees, and my knees in some lonesome valley."

There, on the store porch, Zora learned what would become the primary language of her own literature, the vital force of her life as a storyteller. She learned this language—these phrases and stories and nuances—by heart. Which is to say she learned them irrevocably— not as memorized information to be recounted by rote, but as an essential part of who she was, and who she was to become.

As much as she could, Zora lingered near the porch and listened, she explained years later, "while Mama waited on me for sugar or coffee to finish off dinner, until she lifted her voice over the tree tops in a way to let me know that her patience was gone: 'You Zora-a-a! If you don't come here, you better!' That had a promise of peach hickories in it, and I would have to leave."

The stories followed Zora home. In 1902, when she was eleven years old, her father became pastor of Macedonia Baptist in Eatonville, while still maintaining his ministry at Zion Hope in Sanford. John Hurston also was moderator of the South Florida Baptist Association, and scores of preachers would visit the Hurston home just before the association's periodic meetings. After they'd conducted their business, Zora recalled, the ministers would hold a big storytelling session on the Hurstons' front porch, poking good-natured fun at preachers, congregations, and sinners alike.

Eatonville's air was refreshed by these stories, and Zora inhaled deeply, imbibing this living text until it became no different from who she was.

To many of Eatonville's children, this proliferation of stories—or "lies," as some folks called them—might have seemed ordinary, or even tiring. But these tales of God, the Devil, the animals, and the elements fueled Zora's own inventiveness. "Life took on a bigger perimeter by expanding on these things," she recalled. "I picked up glints and gleams out of what I heard and stored it away to turn it to my own uses."

The earliest stories Zora remembered creating were, like many of the porch stories, inspired by nature. One afternoon, for example, Zora rushed in from outdoor play to tell her mother that the lake had invited her for a walk. "Well, I stepped out on the lake and walked all over it," Zora told Lucy. "It didn't even wet my feet. I could see all the fish and things swimming around under me, and they all said hello, but none of them bothered me. Wasn't that nice?"

Lucy agreed that it was. But Lucy's visiting mother, Sarah Potts, glared at her granddaughter "like open-faced hell," as Zora recalled, and lit into Lucy: "You hear dat young'un stand up here and lie like dat? And you ain't doing nothing to break her of it? Grab her! Wring her coat tails over her head and wear out a handful of peach hickories on her back-side!"

Lucy indulgently defended her daughter. "Oh, she's just playing."

"Playing! Why dat lil' heifer is lying just as fast as a horse can trot. Stop her! Wear her back-side out. I bet if I lay my hands on her she'll stop it. . . ."

Sarah Potts blamed John Hurston for what she perceived as Zora's wayward ways: Zora was "the spitting image of dat good-for-nothing yaller bastard," Hurston recalled her grandmother saying, "the punishment God put on Mama for marrying Papa. I ought to be thrown in the hogslops, that's what."

Yet, ironically, in their shared abhorrence for Zora's flights of fancy, Sarah Potts and John Hurston had finally found common ground. John, too, wanted to take a switch to Zora and break her of her fanciful spirit. But, Zora recalled, "my mother was always standing between us."

Lucy never tried to break Zora of the storytelling habit. "She'd listen sometimes," Zora recalled, "and sometimes she wouldn't. But she never seemed displeased."

Since Lucy largely ignored Sarah Potts's child-rearing advice, Zora was able to disregard her grandmother's curses as well and cling to the covertness of her rich inner life. "How was she going to tell what

I was doing inside? I could keep my inventions to myself," Zora reasoned, "which was what I did most of the time."

Keeping her stories to herself, though, carried its own price. Having no one with whom to revel in her own inventiveness, Zora developed a lonesomeness that would become her lifelong companion. This was especially true after the visions began.

Sometime during her childhood—she never specified when—Zora Hurston began to have visions of events to come. One day, while hiding out from a spanking, she fell into a strange and unfamiliar sleep. In this state, she saw moments from her future flash before her, "just disconnected scene after scene with blank spaces in between," as she would recall. "I knew they were all true, a preview of things to come, and my soul writhed in agony and shrunk away," Hurston wrote. "But I knew there was no shrinking. These things had to be."

After the last image flickered and fled, Zora walked away from this prescient dream shaken and changed:

I had knowledge before its time. I knew my fate. I knew that I would be an orphan and homeless, I knew that while I was still helpless, that the comforting circle of my family would be broken, and that I would have to wander cold and friendless until I had served my time. I would stand beside a dark pool of water and see a huge fish move slowly away at a time when I would be somehow in the depth of despair. I would hurry to catch a train, with doubts and fears driving me and seek solace in a place and fail to find it when I arrived, then cross many tracks to board the train again. I knew that a house, a shot-gun built house that needed a new coat of white paint, held torture for me, but I must go. I saw deep love betrayed, but I must feel and know it. There was no turning back. And last of all, I would come to a big house. Two women waited there for me. I could not see their faces, but I knew one to be young and one to be old. One of them was arranging some queer-shaped flowers such as I had never seen. When I had come to these women, then I would be at the end of my pilgrimage, but not the end of my life. Then I would know peace and love and what goes with those things, and not before.

These ominous visions would return periodically, without warning. Zora would go to bed, and the scenes—always the same—would flash before her, sometimes for two or three consecutive nights, sometimes separated by weeks or months.

Afraid of being dismissed as a liar or shunned for her strangeness, Zora never told anyone about the prophetic visions—not even her mother. Instinctively, Zora knew there was nothing anyone could do to fend the visions off, or to spare her from the fate they promised. "I consider that my real childhood ended with the coming of the pronouncements," Hurston wrote years later. "True, I played, fought and studied with other children, but always I stood apart within. . . . A cosmic loneliness was my shadow."

This shadow grew larger and more menacing with each sunset, as the first of the visions hurried to deliver on its promise of unwanted things.

CHAPTER 5

Sundown

On days when the Florida sky was the right shade of blue and the wind breathed softly on the nape of her neck, Zora would retreat into the woods near her house for a bit of solitude. Embraced by the forest, she'd nibble on sweet oat stalks and listen to the lofty, long-leaf pine trees whispering among themselves.

Over the years, she became especially friendly with one tall tree. "I named it 'the loving pine,'" Zora Hurston would remember. "Finally all of my playmates called it that too. I used to take a seat at the foot of that tree and play for hours without any other toys. We talked about everything in my world."

Zora might have been sitting at the foot of the loving pine on September 18, 1904, when she noticed a buzz of activity at her house. "I noted a number of women going inside Mama's room and staying. It looked strange," Zora recalled. "So I went on in."

Even before she made her way to the door, Zora, at age thirteen, could sense that the buzz was not one of excitement, but of melancholy and fear. Something else was in the air that day, too—something unfamiliar, elusive, and hard to identify.

When Zora pushed her way into Lucy's room, she was able to call this elusive something by its name: Death.

On this day, Hurston wrote many years later, "Death stirred from his platform in his secret place in our yard, and came inside the house."

Zora knew her mother had been sick. "She kept getting thinner and thinner and her chest cold never got any better," Hurston would recall. "I knew she was ailing, but she was always frail, so I did not take it too much to heart. . . . Finally, she took to bed."

Lucy Hurston's persistent sickness had followed her home from a recent visit to Alabama. She had gone there, according to Zora's memory, to be with her dying sister during her sister's last days. Lucy only had one sister, as far as records show. She was a year older than Lucy. Census takers called her Emeline; Zora called her Aunt Dinky.

"Aunt Dinky had lasted on for two months after Mama got there," Zora remembered, "and so Mama had stayed on till the last."

Losing her sister took its toll on Lucy, but other matters seemed to trouble her as well. During her trip to Alabama, Lucy apparently had become depressed about the mysterious murder, years earlier, of her nephew Jimmie. From Hurston's account, it's not clear whether Jimmie was Aunt Dinky's son or the son of one of Lucy's brothers. What is clear, though, is that Jimmie had met a violent death under circumstances that may have had racial undertones.

"He went to a party and started home," Hurston would later recollect. "The next morning his headless body was found beside the railroad track. There was no blood, so the train couldn't have killed him. This had happened before I was born. . . . He was my mother's favorite nephew and she took it hard. She had probably numbed over her misery, but going back there seemed to freshen up her grief."

Some Negroes in Alabama whispered that Jimmie had been shot by a white man accidentally, and then beheaded to hide the wound. Rumor had it that the shooter had been waiting to ambush his enemy—another white man he expected to pass by. It was dark, and the attacker shot at the first footsteps he heard. When he discovered he'd killed Jimmie instead of his intended victim, Hurston explained, the white man "forced a certain Negro to help him move the body to the railroad track without the head, so that it would look as if he had been run over by the train. Anyway, that is what the Negro wrote back after he had moved to Texas years later."

Aware of the racism in Alabama at the time, Hurston concluded: "There was never any move to prove the charge, for obvious reasons. Mama took the whole thing very hard."

Other worries gnawed at Lucy, too. Though she and her mother had long been on speaking terms again, just below the surface, it seemed that Sarah Potts had never quite forgiven Lucy for marrying John more than twenty years before.

This lingering resentment became evident after Aunt Dinky's death, when Lucy suggested that the Potts farm in Notasulga be sold and the profits divided among the remaining family members. Although Sarah Potts no longer lived on the old place, she refused to sell it. She was not going to let Lucy take any money from the Pottses' Alabama acres back to John Hurston in Florida. "Mama could just go on back to that yaller rascal she had married like she came," Zora understood her grandmother to say.

Meanwhile, Lucy's "yaller rascal" of a husband persisted in his extramarital affairs, apparently with no less relish and with no more remorse. John's ongoing infidelity must have weighed heavily on Lucy's heart, and on her health.

Then, too, Lucy had undergone the physical demands of birthing nine children, another factor that likely contributed to her declining health. She also had shouldered the primary responsibility of raising the eight surviving children, who, in September 1904, ranged from twenty-one-year-old Bob to five-year-old Everett.

Though Lucy was a relatively young woman—just a few months shy of her thirty-ninth birthday—she had begun to speak of death often. Still, Zora would recall, "I could not conceive of Mama actually dying." So on that Sunday, September 18, when Lucy called Zora to her bedside to give her certain instructions, Zora indulged her mother, agreeing without question to everything she asked of her.

In the South of Zora's youth, several superstitions about death held sway. It was customary, for example, to remove the pillow from beneath a dying person's head to ensure an easier demise. Folk wisdom demanded that mourners cover the face of a clock in the death room because it would never run again if the dying person glanced at it. The looking glass was also to be covered, folks said, because if the dying person looked into it, the mirror would never cast any more reflections. And if anyone else saw his reflection in the mirror at the moment of death, he would be death's next victim. Church members were turned to die with their feet facing east—they also were buried that way—so that they would arise in the afterlife with their faces to the rising sun.

Lucy did not want these superstitions to have any say in her final moments. So she asked her baby girl to see to it that these death rites were not performed. "I was not to let them take the pillow from under her head until she was dead. The clock was not to be covered, nor the looking-glass," Zora Hurston would recall. "She trusted me to see to it that these things were not done."

Zora promised—never questioning why Lucy wanted to defy her community's accepted ceremonies for greeting death; never imagining that she would have to fight her father and much of Eatonville to try to keep her vow to her mother; never fathoming that death would come so soon.

But on that same day, near sundown, Zora joined the procession of women entering, and not exiting, Lucy's room. "Papa was standing at the foot of the bed looking down on my mother, who was breathing hard," Hurston would remember. "As I crowded in, they lifted up the bed and turned it around so that Mama's eyes would face the east. I thought that she looked to me as the head of the bed was reversed. Her mouth was slightly open, but her breathing took up so much of her strength that she could not talk. But she looked at me, or so I felt, to speak for her. She depended on me for a voice."

Hurston recounted what happened next in crushing detail:

Somebody reached for the clock, while Mrs. Mattie Clarke put her hand to the pillow to take it away.

"Don't!" I cried out. "Don't take the pillow from under Mama's head! She said she didn't want it moved!"

I made to stop Mrs. Mattie, but Papa pulled me away. Others were trying to silence me. I could see the huge drop of sweat collected in the hollow at Mama's elbow and it hurt me so. They were covering the clock and the mirror.

"Don't cover up that clock! Leave that looking-glass like it is! Lemme put Mama's pillow back where it was!"

But Papa held me tight and the others frowned me down. Mama was still rasping out the last morsel of her life. I think she was trying to say something, and I think she was trying to speak to me. What was she trying to tell me? What wouldn't I give to know! Perhaps she was telling me that it was better for the pillow to be moved so that she could die easy, as they said. Perhaps she was accusing me of weakness and failure in carrying out her last wish. I do not know. I shall never know.

Just then, Death finished his prowling through the house on his padded

*feet and entered the room. He bowed to Mama in his way, and she made
her manners and left us to act out our ceremonies over unimportant things.*

The moment of Lucy's death would haunt Zora for decades to
come. "In the midst of play, in wakeful moments after midnight, on
the way home from parties, and even in the classroom during lectures. My thoughts would escape occasionally from their confines
and stare me down," she would write.

As an adult, Hurston certainly understood that the promise she'd
made her mother was impossible to keep under the circumstances.
John Hurston and most of Eatonville's citizens comported themselves according to a common code of moral principles and folkways,
which included certain rituals for the dying. The adults of Eatonville
would not—could not—allow an adolescent to upset the community's mores. Still, Zora was deeply scarred by this incident—
particularly by her own voicelessness, her own powerlessness to
honor her last vow to her beloved mother.

"That moment was the end of a phase in my life. I was old before
my time with grief of loss, of failure, of remorse of failure," Hurston
would write. "No matter what the others did, my mother had put her
trust in me. She had felt that I could and would carry out her wishes,
and I had not. And then in that sunset time, I failed her. It seemed
as she died that the sun went down on purpose to flee away from
me."

As the sun slipped below the horizon, the women of Eatonville
washed Lucy's body and dressed it for her funeral, which would take
place the next day at Macedonia Baptist Church. The warm climate
and the absence of embalming methods necessitated a swift burial.
The women stretched Lucy's body out on the smooth, wooden slab
the family used as an ironing board. This night, it would serve as a
cooling board, the place where the body—no longer home to a
warm, living spirit—grew cold as it awaited burial. Lucy's body, laid
out in the parlor, was draped with a white sheet that rustled gently in
the breeze from the open windows.

This is how her oldest son found her when he arrived home, too
tardy to say good-bye. Bob was away at school in Jacksonville, 135
miles away, and he had been sent for when Lucy's illness worsened.
By the time he got home, though, his mama was already dead. "Bob's
grief was awful when he realized he was too late," Zora recalled. "He

could not conceive at first that nothing could be done to straighten things out."

Lucy's other children also did their weeping. As Zora put it, "We were all grubby bales of misery, huddled about lamps."

John Hurston cried, too. Pacing through the house, "from the kitchen to the front porch and back again," as Zora recalled, "he kept saying, 'Poor thing! She suffered so much.'" For Zora, this was an odd statement to hear her father make. "I do not know what he meant by that. It could have been love and pity for her suffering ending at last," Zora later wrote. Then, more cynically, she added: "It could have been remorse mixed with relief."

Zora wanted to know exactly what her father was feeling. "I have often wished I had been old enough at the time to look into Papa's heart that night," she would write. "If I could know what that moment meant to him, I could have set my compass towards him and been sure."

If there was ever a moment to rescue and recover the love lost between John Hurston and his younger girl, this was it. If John could have somehow let Zora know that his heart was as broken by Lucy's death as hers was, he might have changed the course of his family's history. But John failed to seize the moment, failed to embrace Zora, failed to express his emotions in a way that let her know, unequivocally, that he had loved Lucy and that he was sorry she was gone.

Grappling with his own grief, John no doubt did the best he could. But it wasn't enough for Zora. In his failure to comfort her, and to express his own pain, John alienated his daughter even further.

Lucy Potts Hurston had been Zora's anchor, her protector, her confidante. Lucy was the one who'd been guiding Zora through adolescence and preparing to usher her into adulthood. Lucy was the one who'd been teaching her all the things every colored girl ought to know, as the novelist Toni Morrison has put it, the one who had recited Zora's growing-up litany: "Pull up your socks. . . . Your slip is showin. Your hem is out. Come back in here and iron that collar. Hush your mouth. Comb your head. Get up from there and make that bed. Put on the meat. Take out the trash. Vaseline get rid of that ash."

Lucy died at precisely the time when Zora needed a mama to teach her how to be a woman. Losing Lucy this way hurtled Zora into an emotional autonomy that, though reluctant at first, helped to make her into the fiercely independent woman she was fast becoming.

Looking back, Zora Hurston would remember her mother's death as the moment her own girlhood ended. "That hour began my wanderings," she would write. "Not so much in geography, but in time. Then not so much in time as in spirit."

CHAPTER 6

Aftermath

The day after Lucy died, a neighbor, Sam Moseley, hitched his two finest horses to the wagon that would carry her to Macedonia Baptist Church for the last time. John Hurston and his eight sobbing children walked after the wagon, Zora would remember. "The village came behind and filled the little church with weeping and wildflowers."

The community also filled the church with song: "There is rest for the weary," the people of Eatonville sang through their tears. The death of Lucy Potts Hurston—the pastor's wife, a woman so young and vital—moved them, and it reminded them of their own vulnerability to Old Death's prowl. So they brought colorful bouquets of flowers gathered in the woods, they lifted their voices in melodious entreaties to God, and they let their tears flow freely and fully.

Zora wept, too, for her mother, for her own remorse, for her unknown future. But Zora's tears tumbled out of her eyes through a veil of stubborn disbelief. Perhaps some mistake had been made. Perhaps Old Death had taken the wrong girl's mama. At last, Zora would recall, "the finality of the thing came to me fully when the earth began to thud on the coffin."

The uncontestable finality of death—its insistence on having the last word—pained Zora deeply. Mute with grief, Zora and Sarah and their brothers did not talk that night about their pain. Instead, they all sat in Lucy's parlor, the older ones singing hymns, the younger ones whimpering in their misery. None of them, however, had any way of knowing it might be their last opportunity to discuss their feelings, no way of anticipating the dispersing effect Lucy's death would have on her family. "That night, all of Mama's children were assembled together for the last time on earth," Hurston wrote decades later.

"Mama died at sundown and changed a world. That is, the world which had been built out of her body and her heart. Even the physical aspects fell apart with a suddenness that was startling."

The day after the funeral, Bob went back to school in Jacksonville, and Sarah, who was almost fifteen, went with him. It's impossible to know what the ensuing days were like for Zora, how alone and small she must have felt standing in the doorway of her mama's room, the feather bed mocking her with its emptiness, the rocking chair stunned into stillness.

With Lucy gone forever, and Sarah on her way to a new life in Jacksonville, Zora was the only female presence in her father's house, and she soon realized she'd have to manage her grief alone. Modern-day psychologists might say this was as tragic as the mother loss itself. In her well-respected book, *Motherless Daughters*, Hope Edelman notes: "The loss of a parent during childhood is one of the most stressful life-cycle events an individual can face, but without a forum for discussing her feelings, the motherless daughter finds little validation for the magnitude of her loss. And without this recognition, she feels like a feminine pariah, apart and alone."

Further, Edelman reports: "Researchers have found that children who lose a parent need two conditions to continue to thrive: a stable surviving parent or other caregiver to meet their emotional needs and the opportunity to release their feelings."

Zora had neither. John Hurston had not been able, or willing, to meet Zora's emotional needs even with Lucy as a partner. There was little he could do now, beyond being the good provider he'd always been. But for suddenly motherless daughters, Edelman stresses, "sheer physical care isn't enough."

With Lucy no longer there to stand between them, Zora and John Hurston's relationship further deteriorated. Theirs was "a love-*hurt* relationship," one Hurston scholar has suggested, "a matter of unrequited love." Even in this moment of shared loss, John was not capable of returning his daughter's now-unmoored love. Or, if he was, she was not capable of feeling it, too hurt by all that had gone on before. In Zora's memory of this lonely aftermath, her father was absent, both emotionally and physically: "Papa was away from home a great deal," she wrote vaguely, "so two weeks later, I was on my way to Jacksonville, too."

Perhaps overwhelmed by the prospect of taking care of a girl-child, particularly one he'd never gotten along with, John enrolled Zora at Florida Baptist Academy, the school that Bob, and now Sarah, attended. The academy had been founded about a dozen years before, in 1892, at Bethel Baptist Institutional Church. Through his work with the South Florida Baptist Association, John likely knew the school's founders and early presidents, the Rev. M. W. Gilbert and the Rev. J. T. Brown. The objectives of the school—among them, to help the student "choose goals realistically in the light of his noblest motives, abilities, and limitations"—complemented John's own ambitions for his children. The school's president, N. W. Collier, was widely known as a disciplinarian who commanded respect from his students even while inspiring them to achieve. The academy would be good for Zora, her father believed.

To arrive in Jacksonville by morning, Zora had to travel to Maitland to catch the midnight train. All the possessions she'd accumulated in her thirteen years, and all the necessary things for school, fit easily into what she remembered as "a little, humped-up, shabby-backed trunk," loaded into the open carriage by her third-oldest brother, Richard William, whom everyone called Dick. With a lantern illuminating the way, Dick settled in to drive the buckboard for the mile to Maitland.

About halfway there, as they approached a certain curve in the road near a lake, Zora realized that the first of her ominous visions had come true. "I had seen myself upon that curve at night leaving the village home, bowed with grief that was more than common," she recalled. "As it all flashed back to me, I started violently for a minute, then I moved closer beside Dick as if he could shield me from the others that were to come."

When Dick asked what was wrong, Zora, still afraid to reveal her secret visions to anyone, told him she thought she'd heard some rustling near the lake. Four years her senior, Dick laughed at his little sister's skittishness and soon safely deposited her on the train bound for Jacksonville.

The morning she arrived, Hurston would remember, was "the very day that I became colored." Up until then, she had just been Zora. In all-black Eatonville, and even in the surrounding white neighborhoods, Zora had learned to revel in her individuality, her *me*-ness, while still being part of a larger community, one that valued her singularity, her *Zora*-ness, yet considered her no more or less valuable than anyone else. She was "their Zora," as she put it. "I belonged to them, to the nearby hotels, to the county—everybody's Zora."

In Jacksonville, however, she was anonymous, belonging to no one. And certain things in the city seemed to conspire against her: segregated streetcars, unfriendly stores, and white people who exhibited what Zora called "funny ways." In Jacksonville, she was not rewarded with a piece of candy or a bag of crackers just for walking into a store, as she was at Joe Clarke's.

Eatonville and its neighboring white communities were too tiny to need streetcars, segregated or otherwise. And Zora apparently had taken no notice of discriminatory practices among whites in the area. Her parents' experiences may have been different, but from Zora's child's-eye view, her corner of the world was a bastion of racial health and harmony. Jacksonville was only 135 miles from her home-place, but to young Zora, it was a distant land. "Jacksonville," she wrote cryptically, "made me know that I was a little colored girl."

More specifically, Jacksonville's privations sought to teach Zora, and others like her, that she was neither white nor male—and there-fore certain experiences, privileges, and triumphs were beyond her grasp. In other words, the goal of this powerful system of dispossession and segregation was to make sure she knew her place.

But that was part of the problem: Zora *had* no place. Her home as she knew it, so centered as it was on Lucy, was gone. Even at her new school, she felt displaced and alone. "School in Jacksonville was one of those twilight things," she later wrote. "It was not dark, but it lacked the bold sunlight that I craved. I worshipped two of my teachers and loved gingersnaps with cheese, and sour pickles. But I was deprived of the loving pine, the lakes, the wild violets in the woods and the animals I used to know. No more holding down first base on the team with my brothers and their friends. Just a jagged hole where my home used to be."

At Florida Baptist Academy, Zora's academic aptitude far outpaced her social skills. She welcomed the opportunity to focus on her lessons rather than on her loss. "Lessons had never worried me," she said, "though arithmetic still seemed an unnecessary evil."

As in Eatonville, however, Zora's habit of talking back to authority figures landed her in trouble. Though her immediate teachers were pleased with her work, those who ran study hour and prayer meetings labeled Zora as sassy—a word her father had often used for her—and asked big brother Bob to speak with her a few times. Occasional spankings were also part of the school's disciplinary strategy.

The "lickings," as she called them, didn't bother Zora as much as her outcast status among the other girls, many of whom were slightly older than she was, between the ages of fifteen and eighteen. (Sarah turned fifteen in December 1904, during their first school term, and Zora reached fourteen the following January.)

Though academically advanced, Zora was socially inept in this new environment. To her classmates, she was a bother—a kid sister with no sophistication about boys, conversation, or fashion. "My underskirt was hanging, for instance. Why didn't I go some place and fix it? My head looked like a hoo-raw's nest. Why didn't I go comb it? If I took time enough to match my stockings, I wouldn't have time to be trying to listen in on grown folk's business," the older girls advised.

Sarah was having adjustment problems, too. She not only missed her mother, but she also missed her beloved father and her baby brother Everett, who'd become her primary responsibility during Lucy's illness. So a few months after Zora's arrival in Jacksonville, Sarah said she was sick and wanted to go home. Though Sarah surely was only suffering from a bout of homesickness, John Hurston indulged his older daughter, as he'd always done, and arranged for her to leave Florida Baptist Academy and return to Eatonville.

"In a week or two after she left me in Jacksonville," Zora remembered, "she wrote back that Papa had married again. That hurt us all, somehow."

John Hurston's second wedding took place on February 12, 1905, less than five full months after Lucy's death. If Lucy had lived, she and John would have been celebrating their twenty-third anniversary that same month. The woman John married, Mattie Moge, hadn't yet lived twenty-three years. At age twenty, she was just six years older than Zora—and younger than John's oldest son.

John, now forty-four, hadn't traveled far to find his new bride: Mattie was from Oviedo, just fourteen miles from Eatonville. Her nearby origins and the swiftness of the marriage led Zora and her older siblings—as well as Eatonville's gossips—to suspect that Mattie had been John's lover even while Lucy was alive. This added to the Hurston children's resentment of Mattie, a reaction that was rather predictable to everyone except, evidently, Mattie and John. "No warning bell inside of her caused her to question the wisdom of an arrangement made over so many fundamental stumbling stones," Zora Hurston wrote of her stepmother. "My father certainly could not see the consequences, for he had never had to consider them too seriously. Mama had always been there to do that."

If Eatonville, and particularly the members of Macedonia Baptist, disparaged the Reverend Hurston's new marriage, as Zora would later dramatize in her first novel, John used his houseful of children to defend himself against wagging tongues: "Ah got dese li'l chillun and somebody got tuh see after 'em," he bargained.

Accepting John's new marriage was hardest for Sarah, Zora believed, because of her closeness to her father. Shortly after she moved back home, Sarah commented disapprovingly of the marriage happening so soon after Lucy's death. The new Mrs. Hurston, perhaps resenting John's obvious soft spot for Sarah, became outraged by Sarah's newfound insolence—so furious, in fact, that she insisted John put Sarah out of the house. Mattie also demanded that John whip Sarah, as Zora recalled.

John Hurston had never raised his hand to Sarah. Yet, according to Zora's account, John complied with Mattie's command and struck his favorite child. Heartbroken, "Sarah just married and went down on the Manatee River to live. She took Everett with her," Zora reported.

Sarah's new husband, John Robert Mack, was nearly ten years her senior, in his midtwenties. Having grown up in virtually landlocked Gainesville, he was eager to take his bride to the state's western shore, where the Gulf of Mexico kisses the Tampa Bay. There, in the small town of Palmetto, just below St. Petersburg and the invitingly named Sun City, he found steady work as a longshoreman. John Mack also was, like John Hurston, a Baptist minister.

Zora hardly had time to react to her sister's surprising news. Perhaps feeling a little grateful to be geographically removed from the chaos at home, Zora immersed herself in her studies in Jacksonville and persisted with her uncertain efforts at negotiating her new social terrain. "I had gotten used to the grits and gravy for breakfast, had found out how not to be bored at prayer-meeting—you could always write notes if you didn't go to sleep—and how to poke fun at acidulated disciplinarians," she would recall. "I had generally made a sort of adjustment."

Then the turmoil at home reached out and touched her. One day, a school administrator called Zora into her office to tell her that her room and board had not been paid. Zora was asked what she was going to do about it. Dumbstruck, young Zora had no idea. The administrator went on to berate the Rev. John Hurston and to call the befuddled teenager into her office every few days and ask her what she was going to do. "After a while she did not call me in," Zora remembered, "she would just yell out of the window to where I might be playing in the yard. That used to keep me shrunk up inside."

Zora finished the school year at Florida Baptist Academy by scrubbing the stairs every Saturday, cleaning the pantry, and helping in the kitchen after classes. She also managed to win a citywide spelling bee, beating out students at all the other Negro schools in Jacksonville. "I received an atlas of the world and a Bible as prizes," she recalled, "besides so much lemonade and cake that I told President Collier that I could feel it coming through my skin. He had such a big laugh that I made up my mind to hurry up and get grown and marry him."

Decades later, Zora Hurston would devote a page and a half of her autobiography to her girlhood crush on President Collier. If not for this, it would be easy to dismiss Zora's girlish musings about Collier, but they are significant because they seem to represent her first romantic longings.

Her infatuation with Collier was innocent and safe enough because he took no notice of her. "He acted like he was satisfied with some stale, old, decrepit woman of twenty-five or so. It used to drive me mad," Zora recollected with self-mocking humor. "I comforted myself with the thought that he would cry his eyes out when I would suddenly appear before him, tall and beautiful and disdainful and make him beg me for a whole week before I would give in and marry him, and of course fire all of those old half-dead teachers who were hanging around him."

Hers was an elaborate romantic fantasy: Zora even wrote letters to herself from Collier, and then answered those letters with her own love missives.

This passionate love affair, all in Zora's head, came to an abrupt end when Collier spanked her for an ill-advised practical joke—placing a cold, rain-soaked brick at the foot of the bed of a teacher, one of the overseers of study hour. "I made up my mind to get even. I *wouldn't* marry him now, no matter how hard he begged me," Zora recalled with mock indignation. "Insult me, would he? Turning up *my* dress like I was some child!"

Hurston was lighthearted and good-humored when she recounted this story. Yet it's likely that her feelings ran deeper than she revealed, or even admitted to herself. It's not unusual after the death of a beloved parent for a child to turn to another adult for comfort and love. Transference is what psychologists call this coping mechanism. Edelman explains: "A child who loses a parent can't exist alone emotionally without significant cost. She'd be left in what Anna Freud called the 'no-man's land of affection,' isolated and withdrawn from everyone and with an impaired ability to attach to other people in the future. So instead of detaching from her lost mother, a daughter may try to quickly and directly transfer her feelings of dependency, her needs, and her expectations onto the nearest available adult."

During adolescence, that time of galloping hormones, a mourning daughter might seek a romantic target for her love: a boyfriend or, in Sarah's case, a young groom. For Zora, President Collier seems to have unwittingly played this role, at least for a time.

Still, Zora longed for her mother. Once, when she and the other girls of the school were lined up two by two and taken for a walk, Zora saw a woman sitting on a porch who looked like Lucy. Her thoughts went wild: "Maybe it *was* Mama! Maybe she was not dead at all. They had made some mistake. Mama had gone off to

Jacksonville and they thought she was dead. The woman was sitting in a rocking chair just like Mama always did. It must be Mama! But before I came abreast of the porch in my rigid place in line, the woman got up and went inside," Zora remembered. "I wanted to stop and go in. But I didn't even breathe my hope to anyone. I made up my mind to run away someday and find the house and let Mama know where I was. But before I did, the hope that the woman really was my mother passed. I accepted my bereavement."

Just as Zora began to accept that she was a motherless child, she became, for all practical purposes, a fatherless one as well. The school year ended "in a blaze of programs, cantatas and speeches," she recalled, "and trunks went bumping downstairs." Bob left hurriedly to take a job. Zora was instructed to stay at school until her father sent for her.

"I kept looking out of the window so that I could see Papa when he came up the walk to the office. But nobody came for me," Zora would write. "Weeks passed, and then a letter came. Papa said that the school could adopt me. . . . It was crumbling news for me."

The school had no place for Zora, she was told by the second in command, the same sharp-tongued administrator who'd yelled Zora's financial distresses out the window for all her classmates to hear. On this day, though, "she seemed to speak a little softer than usual, and in half-finished sentences, as if she had her tender parts to hide," Zora would recall. "She took out her purse and handed me some money. She was going to pay my way home by the boat, and I must tell my father to send her her dollar and a half."

Zora enjoyed the trip down the St. Johns River on a side-wheeler dubbed *City of Jacksonville*. When she stood on deck, she found that the thick green curtain of trees along the river shut out the sights and sounds of the city, making her feel as if the river, the chugging boat, and her own roiling thoughts were all that was left of the world.

Inside the steamboat, she happily experienced sensory overload: plush red carpet, white-clad waiters bustling about, the incessant rattle of dishes, shiny lights overhead, and all kinds of people, including a group of turpentine workers eating out of shoe boxes and singing between sips from a common bottle. Zora didn't have a shoe-box meal, but a mulatto waiter noticed the teenager was traveling alone. He made sure Zora was well fed, furtively sending her to the back of the steamboat with chicken and steak sandwiches and slabs of pie and cake.

The next day, the boat docked at Sanford, where Zora got off to take the train to Maitland. The porter, a member of Zion Hope, the church that John Hurston pastored in Sanford, recognized the preacher's daughter and sat beside her when he wasn't busy.

Yet Zora didn't receive such a warm welcome at her father's house, "which was no longer home," as she put it. "The very walls were gummy with gloom. Too much went on to take the task of telling it." Though Zora was tight-lipped about all that occurred during her homecoming, she did report finding her younger brothers in "ragged, dirty clothes," living off "hit-and-miss meals." She concluded: "Papa's children were in his way, because they were too much trouble to his wife."

The worst affront came when Zora discovered her stepmother sleeping in Lucy's feather bed, which Lucy had verbally bequeathed to Zora. This bed was "the one thing which Mama had brought from her father's house," Zora noted. "To see this interloper piled up in my mother's bed was too much for me to bear. I had to do something."

With help from her brothers, Zora took the mattress off the bed. At this, a showdown ensued. The new Mrs. Hurston, faced with surliness from yet another Hurston girl, called upon her husband to discipline his daughter. Zora wasn't too old for a good whipping, Mattie believed, and that might be just what she needed to settle the question of the bed's ownership. But Zora stood her ground, and her brothers, particularly John Cornelius, backed her up. "Actual bloodshed seemed inevitable for a moment," Zora recalled. "John and Papa stood face to face, and Papa had an open knife in his hand. Then he looked his defiant son in the eyes and dropped his hand. He just told John to leave home."

Zora had won the bed, but she'd lost a good deal of respect for her father. "His well-cut broadcloth, Stetson hats, hand-made alligator-skin shoes and walking stick had earned him the title of Big Nigger with his children. Behind his back, of course," Zora once wrote. Now, John Hurston seemed to shrink before his daughter's eyes: "Papa's shoulders began to get tired. He didn't rear back and strut like he used to. . . . He just walked along. It didn't take him near so long to put on his hat."

After John Hurston demanded that his second-oldest son, his namesake, leave his house, Zora's esteem for her father—what little remained—plummeted. Zora soon left home, too.

Lucy Potts Hurston had always been strong enough, and far-sighted enough, to push Zora out into the world. And with her final act—the dying itself—she had done just that.

When Lucy's daughter left home this time, it began a long period of "vagrancy," as she called it—a haunted time that Zora Neale Hurston would later attempt to expunge from the record of her life.

CHAPTER 7

The Wander Years

Dark shadows cloak this part of Hurston's history, making facts and dates difficult to decipher. What she publicly recounted about this period was vague and confusing, and, in fact, seemed contrived to conceal rather than to reveal. No other witnesses to this era of her life have emerged, so we only have Hurston's account—and a few taciturn public records—with which to reconstruct these crucial years.

Here's what we know: When Zora Hurston walked out of her father's house sometime in late 1905, she realized that the wresting of her mama's bed from her stepmother's grasp was what folks called a hollow victory. When the kitchen door slammed behind her, echoing her exit, she didn't feel particularly defiant or triumphant. Instead she felt orphaned and lonesome, even dispossessed.

Though her earlier prescient visions seemed to indicate that she had the gift (or burden) of foreknowledge, Zora's powers were limited. She could not predict what the next few years would bring: the discovery that an internal ache could be just as chronic and painful as any external hardships.

"So my second vision picture came to be. I had seen myself homeless and uncared for," she would later write. "There was a chill about that picture which used to wake me up shivering. I had always thought I would be in some lone, arctic wasteland with no one under the sound of my voice." But Zora soon came to know that the rugged terrain she was destined to traverse was within: "I found the cold, and desolate solitude, and earless silences, but I discovered all that geography was within me. It only needed time to reveal it."

During the next five years, 1906 to 1911, all this inner geography would make itself plain.

According to her own account, Zora went to live with relatives and friends of the family, most likely in Eatonville or nearby Sanford. John Hurston probably made these arrangements himself, believing that the only way to keep peace in his home was to have only one woman in it. And that woman, clearly, had to be his wife. He considered sending Zora back to school in Jacksonville, no doubt, understanding as he did the importance of education. But education—particularly at a good private school like Florida Baptist Academy—was expensive, and, naturally, it was more crucial for his six sons than for his two daughters. Sarah had eschewed education and stepped into womanhood rather briskly; maybe Zora would follow her example. But until she found someone to marry, her father reasoned, Zora could take a room with a good family, church members perhaps, not too far from home.

In the black community at that time, particularly in a place like Eatonville, there were few true orphans. If, for example, a child suddenly lost her parents to that early-twentieth-century scourge, tuberculosis, or to some other plague of nature, the women and men of the community would rally to help provide that child with food and shelter.

Of course, no natural disaster had left Zora looking for a place to live, but folks also understood domestic disasters. They recalled how close Zora had been to her mama, and they could only imagine what her papa's expeditious marriage to Mattie Moge had cost her. They weren't sure what, exactly, had made the girl walk away from her father's five acres, but they sensed that what she needed now was a little tenderness. So some good neighbors agreed to let the teenager stay with them for a while. They knew Lucy Hurston, God rest her soul, would have done the same for any one of their children, had the situation been reversed.

Still, despite this active kindness, Zora felt "bare and bony of comfort and love." Steeped in grief, she could only focus on absence—the absence of her mother's guiding hand, the absence of her siblings' laughter, the absence of books to read and time to read them. "I was miserable," she recalled, "and no doubt made others miserable around me, because they could not see what was the matter with me, and I had no part in what interested them."

What interested Zora was school, but since she was lacking money of her own as well as her father's support, school became an intermittent indulgence. Public school was an option, but just barely. In the early 1900s, few black public schools in the South provided anything beyond basic agricultural and industrial training, particularly at the high school level. And conditions were often poor: 64 percent of black schools in the South were staffed by only one teacher, 19 percent by two teachers. The average public expenditure for education for a white child was $10.82; for a black child, it was $4.01.

Even if Zora could have seen past these obstacles, she still would have needed money for books and school supplies. Yet the people she lived with didn't share her passion for book learning. Of course, education had its place, but "people who had no parents could not afford to sit around on school benches wearing out what clothes they had."

By her own admission, Zora was not comfortable to have around. She was disconsolate—and none too humble. Thus, she often clashed with her hosts and was then shifted to another home. Zora recognized her poor attitude was contributing to her nomadic existence, but she felt powerless to change it. "A child in my place ought to realize I was lucky to have a roof over my head and anything to eat at all," adults told Zora. "And from their point of view, they were right," she conceded. "From mine, my stomach pains were the least of my sufferings. I wanted what they could not conceive of. I could not reveal myself for lack of expression, and then for lack of hope of understanding, even if I could have found the words."

What Zora wanted, but could not yet express, was what she'd always wanted, from the first moment she'd picked up a book and been transported to another time and place. She wanted not only books to read, but the kind of life that could fill a book. She wanted to stride beyond the perimeters of small-town Florida and beyond the parameters of a small black life. She wanted education and excitement and adventure. She wanted a big life.

What she needed was a job. By this time, Zora was fifteen years old, considered, in those days, a young woman, not a little girl. As such, she was expected to contribute to the coffers of whatever household she occupied. After all, more than 40 percent of all black females over age ten were at work in the early 1900s (compared with 16 percent of white girls). Given this rough reality, Zora gradually began to attempt to support herself. But her youth—and her particularly youthful appearance—made even menial work hard to come by.

Standing on a potential employer's doorstep with her arms locked behind her back in that classic pose of self-effacement, insecurity, and supplication, Zora must have looked *interesting*, at the very least: She was big-boned but lean from a recent dearth of second helpings. Her sandy hair tamed into a couple of thick braids, she appeared intelligent around the mouth, melancholy around the eyes. Or was it the other way around? In any case, white southerners generally were not inclined to hire a black housekeeper because she looked like she had an interesting story to tell. "Housewives would open the door at my ring and look me over," Zora would recall. "No, they wanted some one old enough to be responsible. No, they wanted some one strong enough to do the work, and so on like that. Did my mother know I was out looking for work? Sometimes in bed at night I would ask myself that very question and wonder."

Occasionally, one of the housewives would like Zora's looks—the determined set of her mouth perhaps—and give her a chance at a job. Her employers were not often pleased, however, because Zora was more interested in perusing their books than in dusting and dishwashing.

Still, she managed to make a meager living out of a string of such jobs, mostly cleaning and looking after children for an average wage of about two dollars a week—the equivalent of only about thirty-seven dollars today. As the years rushed by, Zora, renting rooms from various landladies, likely moved farther away from Eatonville, back up the St. Johns River toward Jacksonville, where she still pinned her hopes for returning to school.

She also was drawn to Jacksonville because her two oldest brothers, Bob and John Cornelius, lived there. Following his ejection from his father's home, John Cornelius had moved to Jacksonville, rented a room at a boardinghouse, and quickly advanced to foreman in a fish house. Bob had moved to the same lodging house and become a nurse at the local Negro hospital.

In her autobiography, written decades later, Hurston failed to detail specific events of this period—her "five haunted years"—but she did suggest it was a time of significant internal development. These were the years when Lucy's baby girl became a woman. If this maturation process involved a sexual coming of age, Zora didn't say. She did, however, recall a story that revealed her maturing capacity to behave wisely in adult situations, including sexual ones.

In one of her many jobs as a maid, Zora worked in a frowning house of unsmiling people in a town she didn't name. The woman of the house, Mrs. Moncrief, was sick, and her husband was sick and tired of his wife and his life. He urged Zora to become his concubine and run away with him to Canada. She later admitted: "It did sound grand if he would just pay my way up there and he go some place else. . . . But he didn't seem to have but one ear, and it couldn't hear a thing but 'yes.' So every morning, I hated to go back to that house, but I hated more to go home at night."

At dusk Zora would find Mr. Moncrief waiting by her door, as if he were entitled to her as he was to all the privileges of being a white man in a country run by people like him. Zora was mum about whether or not she gave in to her predator's sexual advances, but she implied she had little choice: "Finally, I got over being timid of his being the boss and just told him not to bother me. He laughed at that. Then I said that I would tell his wife, and he laughed again. The very next night he was waiting for me."

Mr. Moncrief's behavior, onerous as it was, was completely commonplace. No white man had to fear prosecution for sexually attacking a black woman in the South. And for any black woman doing domestic work in a white home, the threat of sexual assault—from the man of the house or his sons—was a well-known hazard of the job.

Zora did tell Mrs. Moncrief about her husband's behavior, but to no avail. "Right then," Hurston would recall, "I learned a lesson to carry with me through life. I'll never tell another wife." Mrs. Moncrief cried and poured her heart out to Zora about the anguish of being an unwanted wife. Zora was sympathetic to the white woman's pain, but she had her own problems. The whole experience left her feeling shamed and somehow at fault ("I wanted to run out of there and hide and never let anybody see me again," she later said), not to mention afraid for her future.

The next day Mr. Moncrief confronted her about going to his wife, but he wasn't especially angry, just insistent that Zora accompany him northward in a few days. "He went on down the steps and I ran inside to pack up my few things," she remembered. "In an hour I had moved. He came for me the next night, I was told, and tried to search the house to see if the landlady had tried to block him by telling a lie. He could not conceive of my not wanting to go with him."

A few weeks later, Zora heard that Mr. Moncrief had skipped town accompanied by another young black woman, who apparently was more eager than Zora to flee the South, regardless of the cost.

Zora never went back to the house to see the wife, nor to collect her pay. She was out of a job again. She would get into and out of many more. She just wasn't suited, it seemed, for this line of work.

During these years of "aimless wandering," as she saw them, Zora Hurston became familiar with the blessings and burdens of solitude, intimate with every shade of loneliness, and well acquainted with the oppressive odor of poverty. "There is something about poverty that smells like death," she would write. "Dead dreams dropping off the heart like leaves in a dry season and rotting around the feet; impulses smothered too long in the fetid air of underground caves. The soul lives in a sickly air. People can be slave-ships in shoes."

Zora surely went hungry many days, a new experience for someone who had grown up in the abundant embrace of Eatonville. But a different kind of hunger was enslaving and consuming her: "I wanted family love and peace and a resting place. I wanted books and school," she would remember. "When I saw more fortunate people of my own age on their way to and from school, I would cry inside and be depressed for days, until I learned how to mash down on my feelings and numb them for a spell. I felt crowded in on, and hope was beginning to waver."

Just as hopelessness poised itself to take a permanent seat in Zora's heart, she heard from her brother Dick. He had married recently and invited Zora to come to Sanford to live with him and his wife. Zora was a bit reluctant to move back so close to Eatonville, but when

Dick sent her a ticket, she became hopeful about returning to school and agreed to give Sanford a try.

Regardless of how Zora may have depicted it later, her father's abandonment of her was not total. The Rev. John Hurston was, despite everything, a man of conscience and good will. He no doubt felt remorseful about the gaping chasm that separated him from his daughter. Then, too, he probably heard Lucy's spirit whispering in his ear, urging him to right his relationship with Zora. So when he found out she was staying in Sanford with Dick, he insisted that Zora come home.

This was a mistake. Within a month after she moved back into her father's house, Zora's resentment toward her stepmother, having festered for several years, erupted.

Sigmund Freud—who had coined the term "psychoanalysis" about fifteen years before, in 1896—might have argued that Zora's rage toward her stepmother had a deeper root: that she was actually angry with her mother for abandoning her, as orphaned children often are. Yet Zora found it inappropriate, sacrilege even, to express any outrage toward her deceased mother. In fact, in death, Lucy Hurston was elevated even more in Zora's memory as the archetypal Good Mother. And any unreconciled anger Zora may have felt toward Lucy found a convenient target in Mattie Moge Hurston, who, in Zora's mind, was the epitome of the Evil Stepmother.

This was the same evil stepmother who, six years before, had prompted John Hurston to strike his favorite child, Sarah, thus breaking her heart, Zora felt, and driving her into an early marriage. This was the same evil stepmother, in Zora's view, who had encouraged cowardice to flourish in her father, causing him to drag around "like a stepped-on worm."

All this history, this compounded fury, was lurking at the back of Zora's throat like bile one Monday morning when she and her stepmother exchanged unpleasant words. As Zora remembered it, Mattie called her "a sassy, impudent heifer." For Zora, this was a familiar and not altogether untrue charge, so it didn't rankle her as much as what happened next. According to Zora's account, Mattie then threw a bottle at her head. "The bottle came sailing slowly through the air and missed me easily," Zora remembered. "She never should have missed."

Zora, now twenty years old, had been practically fending for herself ever since her father had married Mattie. Given all that she'd experienced in the past few years, Zora considered herself a woman, not a child to be threatened or spanked, especially not by Mattie, who was just six years her senior. To Zora, Mattie's misdirected bottle was the first blow in a fight between equals, between two young women with obviously irreconcilable differences.

"I didn't have any thoughts to speak of," Hurston would recall. "Just the fierce instinct of flesh on flesh. . . . Consequences be damned! If I died, let me die with my hands soaked in her blood. . . . That is the way I went into the fight, and that is the way I fought it."

Zora pinned Mattie against a wall and pounded her face with unrelenting fists. Mattie fought back, but Zora's unswerving hatred of her stepmother was an indefatigable opponent. "She scratched and clawed at me," Zora remembered, "but I felt nothing at all. In a few seconds, she gave up. I could see her face when she realized that I meant to kill her. She spat on my dress, then, and did what she could to cover up from my renewed fury."

John Hurston was stunned. He knew Zora had grown up fighting with boys, much to his dismay, but he was utterly incapacitated when he realized that the fight now taking place in his home was such an unequal pairing, that Mattie's scratching and hair pulling seemed to have no effect on his maddened daughter. As Zora recalled, her father "wept and fiddled in the door and asked me to stop, while [Mattie's] head was traveling between my fist and the wall, and I wished that my fist had weighed a ton."

A neighbor, a friend of Mattie's, was roused by the ruckus and tried to intervene. Zora greeted her with a hatchet flying through the air and striking a wall close to the woman's head. This was enough to make the neighbor flee, alerting the community, in urgent yells, that Zora had gone crazy.

In a sense, Zora *had* gone crazy, willing to jeopardize her future by giving in to a savage smelting of outrage, desperation, and grief that she had never fully expressed. "I was so mad when I saw my adversary sagging to the floor I didn't know what to do," Zora recalled. "I began to scream with rage. I had not beaten more than two years out of her yet. I made up my mind to stomp her, but at last, Papa came to, and pulled me away."

By pulling Zora away, John Hurston performed an act of heroism that would reverberate for generations. He not only saved Mattie's life, but Zora's as well, salvaging her for an eminent future that neither the father, the daughter, nor the battered stepmother could have fathomed in that hour of round despair.

Mattie was bruised and bloodied, as Zora had intended. Yet Zora emerged from the melee with no more than a few scratches on her arms and neck, she reported, and a wad of Mattie's spit on her dress.

Zora had won the fight, obviously, but she had lost something, too—something like control. She had lost hold of herself in the heat of the moment, yes, but she had also lost hold of her life, such as it was. The actual loss had taken place years earlier, when Old Death had suddenly snatched away her mother. But the reality of how much her life had since spiraled out of control was no more evident than it was at that moment, as Zora's heaving breath sought a resting place in the aftermath of this almost-fatal brawl.

In her attack on Mattie, Zora had exhibited a capacity for rage that was shocking, even to a man as world-wise as John Hurston. Certainly, there was no place for Zora in his house, and any hope of reconciliation between father and daughter had vanished.

Zora soon vanished as well, going not back to Dick's home in Sanford, but to another unnamed town to find yet another servile job that insulted her intelligence and mocked her potential. Yet she felt compelled to get as far away from Eatonville as her scant resources would allow. "I could not bear the air for miles around," she would recall. "It was too personal and pressing, and humid with memories of what used to be."

CHAPTER 8

Lost and Found

To say that Zora Neale Hurston vanished following her alter-cation with her stepmother isn't merely metaphor. She not only vanished from Eatonville but also from the public record. Exhaustive searches of archives from this period have unearthed no census listing, no city directory entry, no school file, no marriage license and no hospital report. The only known record of Hurston from this time is a listing in a church directory, but that would come later.

In 1911, it was relatively easy for someone, particularly a black woman, to evade history's recording gaze. If not legally linked to a man, as daughter or wife, black women did not count in some ways—at least to the people who did the official counting. Few black women owned property, for instance, and they were not allowed to vote, although black men had won that right in 1870, with the pas-sage of the Fifteenth Amendment. In the early part of the twentieth century, however, women—black and white—were still fighting for this fundamental right.

Yet Hurston's vanishing act wasn't just a matter of poor record keeping or official indifference to black women's lives. Her disap-pearance from the public record also seems symbolic of how removed from herself she must have felt at the time. In a sense, she was lost, and she would not reappear on the public record until she'd found herself again.

Years later, Hurston would use this dearth of documents to her advantage. But in 1911, when Zora again left the home that Lucy had built, and that, in her mind, Mattie had destroyed, she was not consciously trying to evade the record keepers. She was only in search of a home, a room, anything of her own.

To this end, Zora drifted to another Florida town looking for a job. She found something arguably more valuable: a battered edition of Milton's complete works, including *Paradise Lost*, its title speaking directly to her own experience. This volume, yellowed and backless when Zora plucked it from a pile of garbage, was a much-needed respite from the dreariness of her life. When she was supposed to be job hunting, Zora would instead find a cool place to stretch out in the woods where she could read the book—slowly, so she could understand the words. Zora "luxuriated in Milton's syllables and rhythms," she later recalled, "without ever having heard that Milton was one of the greatest poets of the world. I read it because I liked it."

Zora eventually also found a job—in a doctor's office, where she answered the telephone and performed various other office duties. This was easy work compared with the chores of a maid. Zora became "so interested and useful," as she put it, that the doctor encouraged her to consider training as a practical nurse.

After a short time working at the doctor's office, however, Zora heard from her brother Bob, who was now studying to become a doctor himself at Meharry Medical College in Nashville, Tennessee. In the post-Reconstruction era, when health conditions among freed slaves had been utterly dismal, several medical schools had been founded to train black doctors. By 1912, only two remained open: Howard University Medical School in Washington, D.C., and Meharry, which had been founded in 1876. Bob was soon to graduate from this venerable institution, and he wanted Zora to come and help his wife with their three young children while he set up his medical practice. In exchange, Bob would send Zora to school.

Zora was ecstatic at the thought of having a home again, of being with family, of returning to the classroom. She packed hurriedly and was soon bound for Tennessee. "When I got on the train, I said goodbye—not to anybody in particular," she would remember, "but to the town, to loneliness, to defeat and frustration, to shabby living, to sterile houses and numbed pangs, to the kind of people I had no wish to know; to an era."

That evening's sunset tattooed itself on Zora's memory. "I shall never forget how the red ball of the sun hung on the horizon and raced along with the train for a short space," she later wrote, "and then plunged below the belly-band of the earth. There have been other suns that set in significance for me, but *that* sun! It was a bookmark in the pages of a life."

While Bob finished medical school, Zora lived with him and his wife, Wilhemina—along with their children, George, Wilhemina, and newborn Hezekiah Robert Jr.—in the Black Bottom neighborhood of Nashville. The area was so named because of its complexion and economic status. The soon-to-be-famous dance called the black bottom—which required dancers to slap their backsides while hopping forward and backward, stamping their feet and gyrating their hips—was born in jook joints not far from where the Hurstons lived. It's likely that Zora, who would write about this dance's origins years later, saw the black bottom performed at the jooks (and may have danced it herself a time or two)—that is, if Bob allowed her to visit any of the neighborhood's pleasure houses.

At age twenty-one, Zora certainly was interested in such diversions, but Bob had always taken his role as big brother seriously and was a bit of a disciplinarian. A studio portrait taken in Nashville in 1912—the first known photo of Zora Neale Hurston—hints at the family's dynamics. Wilhemina is seated and holding her infant son in her lap. Bob stands next to his wife, one hand resting protectively on her shoulder. On the other side, Zora stands next to and slightly behind her sister-in-law. Thick braids graze Zora's shoulders, giving her a Native American look, and she wears a long white dress. Her hands are clasped behind her back, as if in servitude, and she is unsmiling.

Indeed, Zora was disappointed at how her move to Tennessee had turned out. Her brother had taken her for a walk one day soon after her arrival and explained that he couldn't enroll her in school right away. She was needed to work around the house first, particularly since Wilhemina had just birthed a third child. But Bob vowed he would send her back to school soon.

"That did not make me happy at all," Zora would admit. "I wanted to get through high school. I had a way of life inside me and I wanted it with a want that was twisting me. And now, it seemed I was just as far off as before. I was not even going to get paid for working this time, and no time off. But on the other hand, I was with my beloved brother, and the children were adorable! I was soon wrapped up in them head over heels."

After graduating from Meharry in 1913, Bob moved his family, including Zora, to Memphis. This city on the western edge of Tennessee was a popular gateway for black southerners headed north—or west—during what would become known as the Great Migration, which had begun in 1910. There, Bob set up a storefront office, developed a thriving medical practice, and bought a home. The two-story house was in the Scott Street neighborhood, a close-knit community of upwardly mobile Negroes who'd decided to settle in bustling Memphis rather than continue north.

Zora was more comfortable, materially, than she'd been since her idyllic childhood in Eatonville. Bob had the financial means to provide for her, and the family love she'd been craving was at hand. Yet she still was not happy. Zora felt that Bob expected too much of her: she was to get up early every morning and make a fire in the kitchen without waking anyone; she was to do most of the housework while her sister-in-law convalesced. It was as if Bob had employed Zora as a maid—but with no pay and, worse, with no school in sight.

Zora swiftly grew impatient with this arrangement. "My brother was acting as if I were the father of those children, instead of himself," she would write. "There was much more," she added, but declined to detail other conflicts. Yet the central source of discord was apparent: Bob, hardworking and disciplined, expected the same from his baby sister. As the oldest of eight children, he also could be something of a taskmaster, as his mama had taught him to be. In the decade following their mother's death, however, Zora had grown from the sassy, strong-willed girl Bob once knew into an independent-minded young woman, and she chafed at her brother's efforts to govern her.

Soon, she fled. By 1914, Zora was back in Jacksonville, living with her brother John Cornelius and his wife, Blanche, at 1663 Evergreen Avenue. That year she was listed, along with the couple, in the directory of Bethel Baptist Institutional Church—the same church at which the Florida Baptist Academy, her former school, had been founded. Zora had journeyed to Jacksonville not just to elude Bob's authority but also with the hope of returning to the academy and finishing high school.

This was not to be. Yet what happened next is the most mysterious gap in the narrative of Hurston's life.

From the time she was a little girl, dogged by clairvoyant visions of her future, Zora knew that (in her words) "a house, a shot-gun built house that needed a new coat of white paint, held torture for me, but I must go. I saw deep love betrayed, but I must feel and know it. There was no turning back." Sometime around 1914 or 1915—and probably somewhere between Memphis and Jacksonville—Zora went to this foreseen house and lived to tell about it, but never did.

The one sentence she would publicly utter about this episode was placed out of chronological order in her autobiography, in what appeared to be a deliberate attempt to confuse. The only thing this tight-lipped sentence divulged was that by 1915 or so, her most menacing vision—the one of "the house that needed paint, that had threatened me with so much suffering that I used to sit up in bed sodden with agony"—had come true.

Surely, this shotgun house was not Bob's substantial two-story home in Memphis. And surely, Zora did not meet with misery at the Jacksonville home of John Cornelius and Blanche, a couple she would remain close to all her life.

What—or who—was the source of her torment? The speculating mind always wanders to the likelihood that Zora Hurston was in a pernicious relationship with a physically or emotionally abusive man. Perhaps a man similar to the characters she would later write about so knowingly, like Sykes Jones in her short story "Sweat" or Logan Killicks in her novel *Their Eyes Were Watching God*. It's highly conceivable that Zora, recalcitrant and restless in her early twenties, left her brothers' homes to set up housekeeping with a man for whom she felt "deep love," as foretold in her vision, and that this love was betrayed by the man's behavior. More than likely it was a common-law arrangement, which would account for the absence of a marriage record.

That no one knows exactly what occurred during this period says much about Hurston's ability to be discreet and guarded about her personal life. It also is a testament to her talent for surviving. No matter the details, it's clear that Zora suffered horribly during this buried time, so much so that she would never speak directly about her anguish or its causes. That she could walk out of this torture-filled house, that she could emerge from this shadowy time and grow into the woman she would become, speaks volumes.

Regardless of what happened in the unpainted house, Hurston's tenure there was short-lived. Deep love or not, she at some point recollected a piece of advice her mother had given her during her dying days. In addition to admonishing Zora to get an education, Lucy had told her: "Don't you love nobody better'n you do yo'self. Do, you'll be dying befo' yo' time is out." Remembering this, no doubt, Zora found her way out of the shotgun house.

Though Hurston virtually hid this fact in her autobiography, a careful reading reveals that this house—not Bob's home in Memphis—is the one she fled to join a traveling theater troupe and get on with her life.

With help from a friend, and wearing a new blue poplin dress ("to my own self, I never did look so pretty before," she said), Zora landed a job as lady's maid to the lead singer of a Gilbert and Sullivan repertoire company. Her new boss, a blonde whom Zora identified only as "Miss M," was about Zora's age. Because of Zora's youthful countenance, however, Miss M believed her newly hired maid to be a teenager. Zora, now twenty-four years old, did not dispute Miss M's misperception.

The singer offered to pay ten dollars a week—about $160 by today's standards—plus expenses. "I almost fell over," Zora recalled. "It wouldn't take long for me to own a bank at that rate," she thought, feeling fortunate not just because the pay was nearly five times better than she was accustomed to earning, but also because Miss M was kind and playful. In addition, Zora's primary duties—caring for Miss M's clothes and cosmetics, and helping her to get dressed for performances—were easily manageable.

Zora also was instantly smitten by the stage: The sights, the sounds, the backstage atmosphere enchanted her. "Everything was pleasing and exciting," she would remember. "If there was any more Heaven than this, I didn't want to see it."

When the company was ready to move on to the next town, Miss M asked Zora to travel with her, advancing her salary so she could buy a presentable piece of luggage. To go in it, Zora purchased a comb, a brush, a toothbrush, toothpaste, and two handkerchiefs. She further stuffed her new suitcase with newspapers, to prevent her few things from rattling.

Ever since her days perched on the gatepost in front of her home in Eatonville, Zora had longed for this—the opportunity to go out into the world to seek and see.

During the Great Migration, between 1910 and 1930, tens of thousands of Negroes left the segregated South—to see the world, like Zora, and to seek freedom from poverty and other crippling circumstances. Many settled in midwestern and northern states, giving up farms and fields for city lights. They migrated not just for better economic opportunity, but also to escape racist violence, which often manifested for black men as lynching, for black women as rape. For women, domestic violence also was a common motivator.

Typically, men and women migrated in different ways. Single men often worked their way north, sometimes staying in one location for a few years before progressing onward. Unattached women, on the other hand, usually traveled the entire distance in one trip, since women traveling alone faced greater perils. Thus, migrating women often had relatives in northern cities who sent them train fare, gave them places to stay, helped them find jobs.

Largely lacking these things, Zora had been migrating like a man. And she had not gotten any farther north than Memphis, and there only with Bob's help. But Zora was not drawn so much by the pull northward, as by the pull toward school, wherever it might lead her. Her new job empowered her to continue her pilgrimage with a measure of protection. She didn't have a specific destination in mind—and no kin waiting to receive her—but at least she wasn't traveling alone.

"I was the only Negro around," Zora reported of her association with the Gilbert and Sullivan players. "But that did not worry me in the least. I had no chance to be lonesome, because the company welcomed me like, or as, a new play-pretty."

The thirty or so young company members treated Zora like a favorite toy not just because she was black, but because she was green. She was new to the theater world, and generally thought to be younger than she was. She was a perfect target for practical jokes, often with sexual or racial undertones. Yet these backstage gags seemed to Zora part of a necessary and good-natured initiation ritual.

The racial jokes—one was about blondes, brunettes, and "burnt-ettes"—discouraged Zora from being overly sensitive about race, she reasoned. The teasing, racial and otherwise, also taught her "that you are bound to be jostled in the 'crowded street of life.' That in itself need not be dangerous unless you have the open razors of personal vanity in your pants pockets," she would write. "The passers-by don't hurt you, but if you go around like that, they make you hurt yourself."

Zora quickly learned to take a joke without getting her feelings hurt, and she remembered what she already knew—about signifying, specifying, playing the dozens—from growing up in Eatonville. In this way, she became a popular prankster and wag herself. "I was a Southerner," she pointed out, "and had the map of Dixie on my tongue." Mostly northerners, the actors and singers found Zora's way of speaking, particularly her backcountry idioms, humorous and engaging.

Back in Eatonville, where Zora was bequeathed her primary language, rich with image and flavor, it was common—"drylongso," as the folk would say—"to hear somebody called a mullet-headed, mule-eared, wall-eyed, hog-nosed, gator-faced, shad-mouthed, screw-necked, goat-bellied, puzzle-gutted, camel-backed, butt-sprung, battle-hammed, knock-kneed, razor-legged, box-ankled, shovel-footed, unmated so and so!" For the theatrical-minded northerners in the troupe, however, Zora's Negro way of saying whatever she had to say was fresh and delightful. "They teased me all the time just to hear me talk," she would remember. "But there was no malice in it. If I got mad and spoke my piece, they liked it even better. I was stuffed with ice cream sodas and coca-cola."

There were other perks, as well. Miss M paid for Zora to take a manicuring course, and she practiced on everyone until she'd become quite skilled at it. By the time the novelty of having their very own pet Negro had worn off, the company members found Zora indispensable—as manicurist, maid, and confidante. ("I just happened to be there when they released their inside dreams," she explained.)

Zora's time on the road with the troupe was the closest she'd gotten to school in nearly a decade. She was able to read good books gruffly loaned to her by the company's tenor, a Harvard man. Just from being an observant backstage denizen, she received quite an education in music, particularly in light opera. She also became deeply interested in theater, seeing firsthand its power to entertain, and to move.

Just as important, Zora lived communally among a variety pack of white people—Anglo-Saxon, Irish, and Jewish—who were demystified and humanized in her eyes as a result of proximity. The daughter of all-black Eatonville confirmed what she'd long suspected—that white people were remarkably similar to the black men and women she knew so well and carried in her heart, on her tongue, under her skin: Some were wholly admirable, a few were abhorrent; most were somewhere in between. This notable discovery enabled Zora to develop an enduring "approach to racial understanding," as she called it, an attitude that would inform her behavior and philosophy on race relations forever.

After about a year and a half with the company—and trips through Massachusetts, Pennsylvania, Connecticut, and Virginia, among other places—Miss M told Zora she was getting married and leaving the stage. She encouraged Zora to quit the business, too, and go back to school. On a tour stop in Baltimore, Miss M gave Zora a hug, a little cash, and a pocketful of warm wishes for her future. "That was the way we parted," Zora recalled. "I had been with her for eighteen months and though neither of us realized it, I had been in school all that time. I had loosened up in every joint and expanded in every direction."

A matured Zora Hurston had developed a confidence in herself, in her capabilities, that was beyond sassy bravado. "Working with these people," she noted, "I had been sitting by a warm fire for a year and a half and gotten used to the feel of peace." Now, she wanted more of it—peace, that is, and education, too. Zora would recall: "I took a firm grip on the only weapon I had—hope, and set my feet."

CHAPTER 9

Rebirth

I n Baltimore—scenically situated on the Patapsco River, leading into the expansive Chesapeake Bay—Zora experienced an optimism she had not felt in years. This city by the bay seemed a perfect place for regenerating her life.

Baltimore had suffered great devastation in 1904 just as Zora had, with the loss of her mother and the subsequent disintegration of her family. In February of that year, seventy blocks in the heart of the city's business district had been destroyed by fire. By 1917, when Zora arrived, Baltimore had largely rebuilt its downtown from the ashes, just as she had begun to reconstruct her life.

Yet Zora was still without one of the fundamental building blocks: money. At her previous salary of ten dollars a week, she could have saved a substantial amount, if she had received it. "But theatrical salaries being so uncertain," she explained, "I did not get mine half the time." When Miss M had not been able to pay, Zora hadn't worried because she always had a place to stay and plenty of food. But to take care of herself, she now needed money.

Zora soon found a job as a waitress at a restaurant where men routinely paid a quarter for a meal, left her a nickel tip, then tried to take her home. Zora was unmoved. "I was not worrying so much about virtue," she would remember. "The thing just did not call me. There was neither the beauty of love, nor material advantage in it for me. After all, what is the use of having swine without pearls?"

Zora resented "those presumptuous cut-eye looks," she recalled, "and supposed to be accidental touches on the thigh to see how I took to things." She did not take so well to being pursued and patronized by these men, but the ones who did appeal to Zora had no interest in dating a waitress. "Some educated men sat and talked about the things I was interested in," she noted, "but if I seemed to listen, looked at me as much to say, 'What would that mean to you?'"

Given the dismal prospects, Zora dismissed the idea of romance and focused on the job at hand. She could be a competent waitress when she put her mind to it, but most often her thoughts dwelled on other matters, such as returning to school.

Before she found her way into a classroom, however, Zora found herself in a hospital. Illness demanded that she have her appendix removed immediately, so she went to the free ward of Maryland General Hospital. Though Zora claimed she did not fear death— "nobody would miss me very much, and I had no treasures to leave behind me"—she took her appendicitis seriously enough to place a wager with God. "I bet God that if I lived," she remembered, "I would try to find out the vague directions whispered in my ears and find the road it seemed I must follow."

After recovering from surgery, Zora returned to waiting tables and trying to save money for school, goading herself when necessary by recollecting her vow to God. At one point, she operated a confectionery—a place to purchase cigarettes, soft drinks, and other sundries—out of the house she shared on Pennsylvania Avenue with another entrepreneurial hopeful, Martha Tucker. This enterprise, listed in the 1917 Baltimore City Directory as Hurston and Tucker, was in a busy black commercial and residential district. Zora's sister, Sarah, newly migrated to Baltimore, would soon operate a dining establishment out of her home in the same neighborhood.

Zora and Sarah apparently never lived together during this time because Zora disliked her brother-in-law, John Mack. Specifically, Zora objected to the way he treated Sarah. Years later, she would lament the fact that her sister was still "struggling along" with Mack, for whom Zora "wished a short sickness and a quick funeral." Still, despite the ways their lives had diverged, the sisters were glad to be reunited; in a few years, Sarah would name her daughter after Zora.

During this early time in Baltimore, however, the women were concentrating on making their business ventures work, with little success on Zora's part. "I was only jumping up and down in my own foot-tracks," she admitted. "I tried several other things but always I had that feeling that you have in a dream of trying to run, and sinking to your knees at every step in soft sticky mud. . . . How to pull out?"

For Zora, the answer was the same as always: school. So, she would recall, "I just went." Her return to school, however, was not as simple as she made it sound. If it had been, she could have returned years earlier. The difference, in 1917, was that Zora had become too frustrated to continue to play by the rules. "I got tired of trying to get the money to go," she allowed. "My clothes were practically gone. Nickeling and dimering along was not getting me anywhere."

Though she made her frustration plain, here's what Hurston left out of the story: In a quiet act of revolution, in a city where few people knew her history, she decided to subvert the rules. The Maryland Code—the document that codified the state's general laws—provided for free admission to public schools for "all colored youths between six and twenty years of age." In 1917, Zora was twenty-six years old. In order to qualify for free schooling, she shaved ten years off her life, telling Baltimore school officials her year of birth was 1901.

Zora chose 1901 most likely because it was easy to remember by association with her actual birth year, 1891. In addition, she had no idea how long it might take her to finish school. By choosing to present herself as sixteen years old (as opposed to eighteen or nineteen, for example), she bought some extra time in case she needed it.

Zora already had learned, from her experience with the Gilbert and Sullivan troupe, that she could pass for much younger than she was. She also had discovered various benefits to playing the young ingenue. Starting in 1917, Zora Neale Hurston would almost always present herself as at least ten years younger than she was. Thus 1917, the year she went back to school, marked Hurston's rebirth—the moment she was reborn, by her own imaginative labor, as the woman she was to become.

Zora made this backward leap, from twenty-six to sixteen, with little compunction and with only a slight nod to vanity. Granted, she might have been embarrassed to be a twenty-six-year-old high school student, but beyond that, presenting herself as a teenager was a matter of necessity. Lopping a decade off her life seemed to Zora the only way she could do what she had promised Lucy Hurston and God she would do—essentially, to have the courage to live the life of her dreams. Finishing high school was a critical first step toward this exalted end.

Becoming sixteen again also gave Zora a chance to reclaim her lost youth. Her educational development had been stunted after her mother's death. And instead of attending to all the rituals of adolescence, she had spent her teenage years in a peripatetic search for solace and stability. Now, she bargained, she would be able to experience all those things, educational and social, that she had missed.

Besides, telling the truth about her age not only would have barred her from free schooling, it also would have raised uncomfortable questions: "If you're twenty-six now and still trying to finish high school," officials or classmates might have asked, "what were you doing when you were sixteen?" How would she have explained her mama's death and the ten-year abyss—the servile jobs, the aimless wandering, the shotgun house, the rank poverty—that followed?

"So I went to the night high school in Baltimore," Hurston wrote elliptically, "and that did something for my soul."

Her most influential teacher there, Dwight O. W. Holmes, did not question Zora's background. "He never asked me anything about myself," she recalled, "but he looked at me and toned his voice in such a way that I felt he knew all about me. His whole manner said, 'No matter about the difficulties past and present, step on it!'"

Noticing her innate intelligence and her determination to get through school, Holmes stopped Zora after class one evening and complimented her work. And once, while reading aloud from Samuel Taylor Coleridge's *Kubla Khan*, Holmes seemed to direct his stream of words at Zora. As a result, she saw all the writer meant for her to see, she noted, "and infinite cosmic things besides." Zora also felt a renewed courage rising up within herself: "This was my world, I said to myself, and I shall be in it, and surrounded by it, if it is the last thing I do on God's green dirt-ball."

Powered by this conviction, in September 1917, Zora Hurston enrolled in college preparatory classes at Morgan Academy, the high school division of Morgan College (now Morgan State University).

Zora's success at night school—in the classroom as well as with her ruse—gave her the confidence to try this elite black prep school. After an examination, she was given credit for some high school work and assigned to the class of 1920. Recognizing that Zora "had no money and no family to refer to," as she put it—and also seeing her promise as a scholar—Dean William Pickens and his wife found Zora a job that would enable her to attend Morgan.

Zora gladly went to work at the home of Dr. Baldwin, a white clergyman and trustee at the school. His wife had a broken hip and needed someone to do the housework and to help her get dressed and in and out of bed. Zora worked there mainly in the mornings and at night; her days were kept open for classes. In addition to a tuition waiver, the pay was room and board and two dollars a week. And, unlike previous employers, the Baldwins didn't mind Zora's interest in their library. "I acted as if the books would run away," she recalled. If she found a poem she particularly liked, Zora—having grown so accustomed to furtive reading—would memorize it overnight, as if she'd never get a chance to read it again.

The majority of her classmates at Morgan were "good-looking, well-dressed girls from Baltimore's best Negro families." And the six boys in the class "were in demand in town and on campus," Zora noted. "And here I was, with my face looking like it had been chopped out of a knot of pine wood with a hatchet on somebody's off day, sitting up in the middle of all this pretty." Zora was being self-deprecating to a fault. Obviously, she had the youthful good looks to pass for a teenager. With her secret-keeping grin and frank eyes, she was a lovely young woman—her nutmeg-colored skin the perfect middle ground between John Hurston's custard complexion and Lucy Hurston's chocolate brown.

With only one dress, a change of underwear, and a pair of tan oxfords, Zora took her place in her eighteen-person class of "pretty girls and snappy boys," as she saw them. Raised with a sense of egalitarianism that was characteristic of the small Negro middle class, Zora's well-heeled peers did not seem to look down on her because of her lack of clothes. "Sometimes somebody would ask me, 'Zora, what do you think you'll wear to school tomorrow?' I'd humor the joke and describe what I was going to wear. But let a program or a get-together come along, and all the girls in the class would be backing me off in a corner, or writing me notes offering to lend me something to wear."

Zora and her girlfriends prided themselves on dating Morgan's college men. Zora dated a college senior, who, at twenty-one or twenty-two years old, would have been closer to her own age than any date she could have found in the high school division.

Zora's classmates evidently did not suspect she was a decade older than most of them. Some teachers, however, seemed to sense an uncommon maturity in Zora. When the English and history teachers had to be absent, for example, they put Zora in charge. "Once I had the history classes for nearly a month and had to be excused from my other classes," she recalled. "At times like that, my classmates were perfectly respectful to me until the bell rang. Then how they would poke fun at my serious face while I was teaching!"

Predictably, Zora did well in history and English. She also was competent in science and music—scoring 81 and 79, respectively, for the 1917–1918 school year. In arithmetic, she squeaked by with a 74. "I did not do well in mathematics," she admitted. "Why should A minus B? Who the devil was X anyway? I could not even imagine."

Despite being mathematically challenged, Zora was finally happy. She had not known this level of contentment since her halcyon days in Eatonville. "The atmosphere made me feel right," she said of Morgan. "I was at last doing the things I wanted to do. Every new thing I learned in school made me happy."

In the summer of 1918, just as she was finishing up the school year, something happened that threatened to mar Zora's happiness. Her father recently had moved to Memphis, where he was in close contact with his oldest son, Bob. Not long after Zora's fight with her stepmother, John Hurston had been elected mayor of Eatonville, serving from 1912 until 1916. After finishing his term, John had begun to follow the same Jacksonville–Memphis trajectory as his children. In 1916, he had become pastor of Friendship Baptist Church in Jacksonville and had lived on church property. His youngest child, eighteen-year-old Everett, also had moved to Jacksonville, where he lived with his big brother John Cornelius in his stable home on Evergreen Avenue. The Reverend Hurston was not listed as married in the documents that chronicled his move, so it doesn't appear that Mattie accompanied him to Jacksonville.

By 1918, Zora's father was in Memphis. There, he died when a train crashed into his car. "The engine struck the car squarely and hurled it about like a toy," Zora later imagined. "John was thrown out and lay perfectly still. Only his foot twitched a little." John Hurston was fifty-seven years old.

Zora hardly reacted to her father's death, not even traveling south for the funeral. She was too busy plotting her next move—to Washington, D.C., to attend Howard University.

In a sense, John Hurston's death liberated Zora—from the pain of her past as well as from the burden of her family's history. Despite her constant battles with her father (or perhaps because of them), there had always been a part of her that wanted to please him, if only in defiance of what she believed his prevailing notion of her to be. With John Hurston dead, and her siblings engrossed in their own lives, Zora now had no one to answer to but herself, no one back home in Eatonville to make proud or to make ashamed. Now that the two who had made her were gone, Zora Neale Hurston was free to remake herself, wholeheartedly and without looking back.

CHAPTER 10

Hopeful at Howard

Zora Hurston never thought she'd make it to Howard University, "the capstone of Negro education in the world," as she called it. Certainly during the hungry years after her mother's death, the idea of one day attending Howard—or any university—was nothing more than a pipe dream, too painful to seriously yearn for. In those days, higher education for Negroes was a rarefied thing: in 1917, only 2,132 black people were enrolled in college nationwide.

Although Zora believed Howard University was beyond her reach, and planned instead to stay at Morgan to pursue her college degree, a suggestion from a Morgan visitor changed her mind. The providential comment was made by Howard student May Miller, daughter of Dr. Kelly Miller, a Howard dean. May Miller met Zora on a visit to Morgan Academy to see her cousins, Bernice and Gwendolyn Hughes, who were friends of Zora's. After the young women had spent several hours together, as Zora recalled, May turned to her and said: "Zora, you are Howard material. Why don't you come to Howard?"

America's largest black university, Howard had been founded in 1867 in the nation's capital, less than three miles from the White House. With the goal of educating black students intellectually, morally, and socially, the university's founders modeled its curriculum on those of the leading white colleges in the North, emphasizing what might be called a classical education. In the early 1900s, for instance, Howard required of graduates four years of Latin and two years of Greek.

Zora knew all about Howard's reputation for scholastic excellence. She knew that it was for Negroes what Harvard was for whites, and that it was a gathering place for "Negro money, beauty, and prestige," as she put it. She also had heard about the elegant clothes Howard students wore and the elite fraternities and sororities that held sway on campus. Zora believed Howard was out of her league, and said so. But her friends, believing otherwise, tamped down Zora's doubts and stoked her ambition.

With their encouragement, Zora withdrew from Morgan in June 1918 and that summer moved to Washington to find a job that would help her finance her Howard education.

In short order, she was working as a waitress at the Cosmos Club in downtown's Lafayette Square. Established in 1878, the Cosmos Club was a social headquarters for Washington's intellectual aristocracy, which meant its membership was open exclusively to white males. Women and black people were welcome only as servants.

Among the men who gathered there frequently to play billiards and order drinks from the cherry-wood bar were 1906 Nobel Peace Prize winner Theodore Roosevelt and British writer Rudyard Kipling, a 1907 Nobel laureate whose work Zora enjoyed. Its walls lined with portraits of such imposing white men, its ceilings weighted with ornate chandeliers, the Cosmos Club was a comfortable place for its privileged members to relax and exchange ideas.

Yet for Zora—rendered invisible there by her race and gender— the Cosmos Club was just a way station to her own dreams. She worked there only long enough to scrape up the necessary funds for her first quarter's tuition at Howard.

When she went to register, Zora was disappointed to learn that her year at Morgan had not fully prepared her for Howard University. She would have to make up some classes—and some skills—before she could enroll in the college department, she was told. Deflated, Zora considered abandoning her hopes for a Howard education. But she ran into her old night school advocate, Dwight O. W. Holmes, who was now teaching there; he encouraged her to make up whatever she lacked by taking preparatory classes at Howard Academy.

On December 2, 1918, listing 1663 Evergreen Avenue in

Jacksonville as the address of her parent or guardian, Zora enrolled in the academy, where she took classes in history, Latin, English, and physical geography. After finishing her preparatory coursework, Zora finally earned her high school diploma in May 1919 from Howard Academy. She went directly into college classes that fall.

At her first college assembly, Zora was moved by the stately music, the platform packed with distinguished faculty, and the hundreds of students standing shoulder to shoulder with her. Misty-eyed, she whispered to the spirit of Howard University: "You have taken me in. I am a tiny bit of your greatness. I swear to you that I shall never make you ashamed of me."

Zora's first quarter at the university was unremarkable: she earned Bs in English and Spanish and a D in Greek. In her second quarter, she aced her English class, merited a B in public speaking, and got Cs in Greek and Spanish. For the next year—despite that she was working to put herself through school—Zora never let any grade slip below a C, so grateful was she to be at Howard. Every time an assembly at the chapel closed with the singing of the alma mater, Zora was awash with pride: "My soul stood on tiptoe and stretched up to take in all that it meant," she would remember. "So I was careful to do my class work and be worthy to stand there under the shadow of the hovering spirit of Howard. I felt the ladder under my feet."

If Zora stood precariously on this ladder, it was partly because she was attempting to balance school and work. Using the skills she'd acquired during her Gilbert and Sullivan days, Zora got a job as a manicurist at a black-owned barbershop that served a white clientele. George Robinson was the entrepreneur behind this shop at 1410 G Street, and he owned several others in downtown Washington, as well as an uptown barbershop for black clients.

Despite the G Street shop's strict policy of serving whites only, Zora admired Mr. Robinson's achievements and his willingness to help any fellow Negro with ambition. "He had no education himself, but he was for it," Zora noted. "He would give any Howard University student a job in his shops if they could qualify, even if it was only a few hours a week." Mr. Robinson arranged for Zora to work from 3:30 every afternoon to 8:30 in the evening. That schedule left her mornings open for classes, her nights for homework.

The barbershop was near the National Press Club, the Treasury

Building, and the Capitol and was frequented by journalists, bankers, and lawmakers. "I learned things from holding the hands of men like that," Zora quipped.

Because she was "safe," Zora reasoned, these men of power talked freely around her—about backstairs maneuverings at the White House, about the inner workings of Congress, about secret romantic liaisons. In the minds of such self-important men, discussing national affairs or personal intimacies with a black woman, a manicurist, was probably tantamount to confiding in a family pet. Zora came to understand this, despite the men's flattering remarks about her trustworthiness: "I know that my discretion really didn't matter. They were relieving their pent-up frustrations where it could do no harm," she observed. "If I told, nobody would have believed me anyway."

From these white men, Zora learned some fundamentals of politics and power. From the black men who worked with her at the barbershop, she learned other things.

The shop's ten Negro barbers and three porters were plainspoken men aiming to make a decent living through honest work. They weren't much different from John Hurston, Joe Clarke, Sam Moseley, and the other men whose big voices still echoed in Zora's ears, despite the long distance she'd traveled from Eatonville. Like the journalists, bankers, and lawmakers they catered to, these barbers and porters had opinions, too, on world affairs, race relations, and national politics. They also had clandestine affairs, unfulfilled aspirations, and their own stories, funny and poignant, to tell. Zora listened to their stories, and to their language, just as she had listened to the storytellers on the porch of Joe Clarke's store back home—imbibing every image, every inflection.

Sometimes, though, this urbanized equivalent of Joe Clarke's porch was not enough. Sometimes Zora found herself pining for Eatonville. One of her earliest known works, a poem penned in 1919, is called "Home." Stiff with the classical education she was absorbing at Howard, the poem nevertheless bore witness to Zora's nostalgia for Eatonville, romanticized by the power and selectivity of memory. Zora began:

> I know a place that is full of light,
> That is full of dreams and visions bright;

> Where pleasing fancy loves to roam
> And picture me once more at home.

Beneath the typewritten poem, she scribbled an explanatory note: "Just a bubbling over of a melancholy heart—momentarily."

An English major, Zora was beginning to express her emotions on paper frequently. Like many budding writers, she started with poetry, and the poems she wrote during her first couple of years at Howard were as mawkish as those of any college student anywhere. A few were clever little trifles, like "'Twas the Night After Lobster," written in July 1919. Most, however, seemed to focus on that ubiquitous preoccupation called love:

> Who has not felt the fire of youth?
> Nor heard the call of spring?
> Nor read the lines of love and truth
> In arms and lips that cling?

These nascent love poems had titles like "Longin'" (written, interestingly, in an exaggerated Negro dialect) and "Thou Art Mine" (written, apparently, with classical aspirations). Clearly Zora was trying to find her voice through these early poetic efforts. Yet she soon would forsake poetry and seek her voice elsewhere, with much greater success.

Some of Zora's early love verses, however, could well have been composed with a particular young man in mind. In 1920, she met Herbert Arnold Sheen, the handsome son of a Methodist minister. Sheen was twenty-three and Zora was twenty-nine, though still presenting herself as a decade younger. Born in 1897, Sheen had graduated from high school in Decatur, Illinois, in 1916. Having arrived at Howard University after a short stint with the Students Army Training Corps in World War I, he was an industrious student who could play pool almost as well as he could play piano. Like Zora, Sheen was working his way through Howard, mainly as a hotel and boardinghouse waiter.

Though Zora and Sheen were both preachers' kids, "neither one of us was very religious," he recalled. And they each valued the other's more secular qualities: "She wasn't narrow-minded," he observed. And of Sheen, Zora noted, "He could stomp a piano out of this world, sing a fair baritone and dance beautifully." With these irresistible attributes, Sheen drew Zora's attention instantly. "He noticed me, too," Zora would remember, "and I was carried away. For the first time since my mother's death, there was someone who felt really close and warm to me." In no time, Zora Hurston and Herbert Sheen were "palling around together," as he put it, on a regular basis.

Both convivial personalities, the couple maintained a busy social schedule despite their work and school obligations. By now most of Zora's barbershop customers knew she was a student and tipped her generously. Averaging twelve to fifteen dollars a week, she no longer sported the one-dress wardrobe from her days at Morgan. In contrast, Zora was becoming a stylish dresser, favoring chic hats, long dresses, and dramatic colors. In photos from this period, her mouth is wide and laced with mirth; her head is no longer pitched at a supplicant's angle. Her eager eyes warmly embrace the camera rather than shrink from it, and her hands are in front of her, as if she is confident in what she has to give.

Zora's expanded wardrobe and expansive personality served her well in Howard social circles, which largely revolved around the black Greek-letter system. Black sororities and fraternities were not only popular social outlets but also boasted a tradition of service to the community. In addition, sororities offered their members some semblance of sisterhood, of family—a notion that Zora naturally found appealing. Although her friend May Miller was a member of the prestigious Alpha Kappa Alpha sisterhood—founded in 1908 at Howard as the first sorority for black women—Zora joined the upstart Zeta Phi Beta sorority, which was organized on Howard's campus in January 1920.

"There were these three sororities," explained one of Hurston's Howard acquaintances, Ophelia Settle Egypt. "The AKAs (who really could dress beautifully) . . . the Deltas (light skinned) . . . [and] the Zetas (it didn't matter how you looked as long as you had brains). . . . I had enough brains to get into Zeta. Zora Neale Hurston was there and she was a Zeta." Still, even among a group of women reputed to be brainy, Zora stood apart. "She was older than we were, I think. . . . And then she was sort of a loner," Egypt recalled. "But she was brilliant, and she was writing even then. . . .

But we always thought of her as a rather odd person. She was just too brainy for us."

Zora's uncommon intellect found a satisfying forum, however, when she joined May Miller on the staff of *The Stylus*, the annual journal published by Howard's literary club. Also called the Stylus, the club had been founded in 1915 by English and drama professor Montgomery Gregory and philosophy professor Alain Locke, with the purpose of "stimulating and producing authors and artists within the race." Membership was gained through semiannual competitions. "The persons producing the best manuscripts during these competitions," the Howard yearbook explained, were "duly elected to membership in the club."

Using their hard-won Stylus affiliations as calling cards, May and Zora became regulars at a popular literary salon hosted by Washington poet Georgia Douglas Johnson. In the living room of her home on S Street, Johnson served cake and wine to a freewheeling, intergenerational group of the gifted, the famous, and the wannabe famous. They called themselves the Saturday Nighters, and they included playwright Marita Bonner, poets Sterling Brown, Waring Cuney, and Angelina Grimke, as well as writers like Jean Toomer, Rudolph Fisher, and Richard Bruce Nugent. NAACP executive secretary James Weldon Johnson and W.E.B. Du Bois, editor of the NAACP's magazine, *The Crisis*, often came to officiate as senior sages. (Their elder statesmen status was well-earned: Back in 1900, Johnson had written the words for "Lift Ev'ry Voice and Sing," which soon became known as the Negro National Anthem, and in 1912 he had anonymously published an acclaimed novel, *The Autobiography of an Ex-Colored Man*. Meanwhile, Du Bois's 1903 book of essays, *The Souls of Black Folk*, already had become a classic.) Stylus founder Alain Locke usually attended the salon as well.

Though Zora acknowledged Locke as "the presiding genius" at her Stylus meetings, she considered Lorenzo Dow Turner her most influential teacher at Howard. Head of the English department, Turner was a handsome young Harvard graduate who had an impressive command of his subject. "Listening to him," Zora recalled, "I decided that I must be an English teacher and lean over my desk and discourse on the 18th-Century poets, and explain the roots of the modern novel."

But Zora's Saturday evenings on S Street were starting to make her feel that she could do more than teach about great writing. Perhaps, she thought, she could actually produce some herself.

In May 1921, Hurston published a poem, "O Night," in *The Stylus*. More notably, in the same issue she published her first short story, "John Redding Goes to Sea."

Set in an unnamed Florida village obviously modeled on Eatonville, it is the story of John Redding, "a queer child" who dreams of sailing down the St. Johns River to the horizon. John's mother, Matty, believes her son has such strange ambitions because an enemy sprinkled "travel dust" around her door at the time of his birth, to make him run away from her. John's father, Alfred, thinks differently: "Matty, a man doan need no travel dust tuh make 'im wanter hit de road. It jes' comes natcheral fuh er man tuh travel." As John grows older, his wanderlust intensifies, and he vows to leave. Yet his mother refuses to give her blessing. John is further hindered by marriage, as his new bride is no more supportive than his mother is. After a frustrating evening trying to convince both women to let him go, John joins other village men in an emergency effort to fortify the St. Johns bridge against an impending storm. The storm causes the river to rise almost as high as the bridge on which the men are suspended. Traveling downstream as fast as a train, three dislodged pine trees strike the bridge, killing John. In a final act of perverse justice, he is carried away by a piece of timber toward the horizon and his long-dreamed-of sea.

This story contains a hodgepodge of autobiographical elements: As a child, Zora always dreamed of the horizon and felt the urge to wander, which her mother blamed on travel dust sprinkled on the doorstep by an enemy. And the story's names are directly from Zora's family tree: John was her father, Alfred was his father.

Hurston flipped the genders in "John Redding Goes to Sea": John finds understanding in his father, while Zora found encouragement in her mother. The other parent—the one of the opposite sex as the child—is the naysayer: In Zora's life, it was her father; in "John Redding," it's the mother, who, curiously, has the same name as Zora's reviled stepmother.

Hurston transferred her own wanderlust—which Alfred labels as a naturally *male* characteristic—onto John Redding, who is at least partly based on her father, himself an inveterate wanderer. Thus Zora revealed how much she saw herself as similar to John Hurston, rather than different from him. Indeed this short story represented Zora's earliest attempt to make sense of her father's life, and death, through fiction. This was a challenge she would return to later in her career.

The story contains other themes Hurston would revisit as well: She treated Matty's belief in superstitions and signs, for instance, respectfully rather than mockingly. When a screech owl alights on the roof during the storm—a sure sign of death, according to the folk beliefs of the rural village—even Alfred, a nonbeliever, invokes a countermeasure. The world of hoodoo—of charms and counter-charms—was an essential part of Zora's childhood. So in her first short story, she presented black people's faith in such supernatural phenomena sympathetically, without a trace of sensationalism or derision. She would continue this approach throughout her career.

Similarly, the story's language disclosed Hurston's delight in the southern black vernacular voice. The poetic dialect of John, Alfred, and Matty, Hurston's first published characters, would become a hallmark of her work, precisely because it was the language of Eatonville, authentically and lovingly re-created.

As this short story suggests, Hurston was beginning to move away from emulating the European models of literature so highly heralded at Howard and elsewhere. What's missing from the story, as one critic has concisely pointed out, is "Hurston's fully developed use of dialect, mature mastery of metaphor, and distinctive, humor-laden voice." Yet, despite any amateurish flaws, "John Redding Goes to Sea" illustrates that Hurston was on the verge of an epiphany: She had begun to realize that the lives—and the language—of ordinary black country folk had enormous literary potential.

Soon after "John Redding" was published, Zora Hurston and Herbert Sheen experienced the first of several long separations that would characterize their relationship. That summer Sheen joined a crew of college student waiters to work in the resort town of Seabright, New Jersey. There he met an affluent New York physician who offered him a job as a live-in butler, with the promise that he could finish his studies at New York's Columbia University. Sheen invited one of his sisters, Genevieve, to leave Washington and join him in New York as the family's cook.

This arrangement was cut short, however, on January 1, 1922, when Genevieve's husband killed her—Washington's first murder of the year. Sheen assumed the sorrowful duty of accompanying her body back home to Decatur, Illinois. Zora, who had been close to Genevieve, "did a lot for the family" during this difficult period, Sheen recollected decades later. Taking care of the necessary legal business in Washington, Zora handled "a lot of the legwork," as Sheen recalled, endearing herself to him, and to his family, irrevocably.

Later that year, Hurston's interest in writing poetry had its last gasp: she published three poems in *Negro World,* the newspaper of the Universal Negro Improvement Association, marking the first and final time her poetry was published nationally. (A short while later, Zora asked Georgia Douglas Johnson, whom she called a "soulful poet," to pass on a bit of verse to a mutual friend, with this caveat: "She knows I am not trying to be a poet so she won't think that I think it's poetry.")

In the 1923 Howard University yearbook, Zora contributed a couple of tongue-in-cheek pieces: "A Chapter From the Book of Life" and "An Academic Nightmare." She was listed as a member of the Stylus, Zeta Phi Beta, and the Howard Players—the campus theatrical company. "Zora's greatest ambition," the yearbook divulged, "is to establish herself in Greenwich Village where she may write stories and poems and live an unrestrained Bohemian."

Next to the students' class photos were printed their personal mottoes. Sharing the page with Zora were classmates who had chosen cliched quotes such as, "If at first you don't succeed, try, try again." Or, "Where there is a will, there is a way." In contrast, Zora's quote was disarmingly personal—and resounding with the optimism she so keenly felt: "I have a heart with room for every joy."

CHAPTER 11

Drenched in Light

The autumn of 1923 was Zora Hurston's last term at Howard University. Though her spirits were high, her grades were faltering. That year she made As in the subjects that interested her and flunked the classes that bored her, such as physical education. In the spring, she got an F in Spanish, withdrew from her physics class, but aced geology. The following quarter, her A in geology slipped to a D. After the holiday break, when 1924 dawned, Zora did not enroll in classes. "I was out on account of illness," she later explained, "and by the time that was over, I did not have money for my tuition."

Yet Zora still was listed as a student in the 1924 Washington City Directory, which noted that she was living at the "colored" YWCA on Rhode Island Avenue, just a couple of miles from Howard's campus. Zora continued to think of herself as a student, one who was simply sitting out a couple of quarters. By this point, however, she also thought of herself as a writer. If anyone else doubted Zora's vocation—which was revolutionary at a time when most black women labored as maids, cooks, or washerwomen—they needed only to read her short story, "Drenched in Light," published in a 1924 issue of *Opportunity*, the magazine of the National Urban League.

Opportunity: A Journal of Negro Life had been launched in New York in January 1923, with an intention "to lay bare Negro life as it is." The publication's founders wanted to expose and explore the race problem in a more reflective and academic style than the two other leading black magazines of the day, *The Crisis* and *The Messenger*.

W.E.B. Du Bois edited *The Crisis*, which had been founded in 1910. He used the magazine—an organ of the National Association for the Advancement of Colored People—to relentlessly decry racial injustice and violence. "When the magazine would report an NAACP investigation of a lynching," one scholar observed, "its pages almost smelled of burning flesh." Yet the publishers of *The Messenger*, established seven years later, claimed that theirs was "The Only Radical Negro Magazine in America." Founders A. Philip Randolph and Chandler Owen wanted to compete with Du Bois as the most militant and uncompromising champions of Negro equality. *Opportunity*, meanwhile, also sought to advocate the Negro cause, but in a way that reflected the Urban League's tendency toward diplomacy and gradualism, rather than in the protest tradition of the NAACP.

The editors of each of these magazines agreed that an important aspect of their missions was to encourage Negroes' efforts in the arts, and to give black writers publishing outlets for their work. In this regard, Langston Hughes's first nationally published poem, "The Negro Speaks of Rivers," appeared in *The Crisis* in June 1921. And *The Messenger* published early work by Claude McKay, who was, along with Hughes, a leading light of what would become known as the Harlem Renaissance.

Until the middle of 1924, however, *Opportunity*'s articles were more sociological commentary than literature. The magazine's editor, Charles S. Johnson, was a sociologist, and he filled *Opportunity*'s early issues with scholarly studies by young black social scientists like Ralph Bunche and E. Franklin Frazier, and with reports by white anthropologists like Melville Herskovits and Franz Boas. In the magazine's second year, though, Johnson veered the monthly *Opportunity* in a different direction, applying its motto—"Not Alms but Opportunity"—most rigorously to the arts. As one historian has noted: "He was primarily responsible for making *Opportunity* . . . the most important medium of the Harlem Renaissance, even as he also used it to publicize the results of social research."

This shift—and arguably the Harlem Renaissance itself—had its formal genesis on March 21, 1924. Earlier in the month, Charles S.

Johnson had invited a dozen young black writers—including Jean Toomer, Langston Hughes, Countee Cullen, Gwendolyn Bennett, and Eric Walrond—to attend a dinner at the New York Civic Club. Johnson's original idea was to celebrate the recent publication of *There Is Confusion*, a novel by Jessie Fauset, literary editor of *The Crisis* and one of the midwives of the burgeoning New Negro movement. But the dinner quickly became a sort of coming-out party for the younger generation of Negro writers.

Ironically, the two writers who would emerge as the movement's most enduring voices were absent: Langston Hughes was in Paris; and Zora Hurston, still in Washington, was not even invited to what turned out to be the dress rehearsal for the Harlem Renaissance.

Still, about 110 people—including white writers Eugene O'Neill and H. L. Mencken, along with several white publishers—attended the dinner. The New York Civic Club, on Twelfth Street near Fifth Avenue, was the only upper-echelon club in the city without color or gender barriers, the only place where black and white intellectuals could gather in common conversation.

On that particular evening, the conversation was inspired. Charles S. Johnson declared master of ceremonies Alain Locke "the dean" of the New Negro movement. Du Bois addressed the new generation as a representative of the old guard of black writers, as did James Weldon Johnson. And Carl Van Doren, editor of the mainstream *Century* magazine, issued something of an invitational challenge: "What American literature decidedly needs at this moment is color, music, gusto, the free expression of gay or desperate moods," he said. "If the Negroes are not in a position to contribute these items, I do not know what Americans are."

Following up on Van Doren's statement, Paul Kellogg, editor of *Survey Graphic* (a magazine that had previously seemed oblivious to Negroes), privately approached Johnson with an offer to publish an issue of his magazine devoted entirely to exploring "the progressive spirit of contemporary Negro life." The evening also catalyzed the formation of a Black Writers' Guild, whose members included Cullen, Fauset, and Walrond. In this way, the New Negro movement, later known as the Harlem Renaissance, was formally launched. And Charles S. Johnson, through *Opportunity*, was destined to play a crucial role in making the Renaissance flourish.

Decades later, Langston Hughes would remember that Johnson, a masterful organizer and motivator, "did more to encourage and develop Negro writers during the 1920s than anyone else in America." Hurston would agree: The "so-called Negro Renaissance was his work," she said of Johnson, "and only his hush-mouth nature has caused it to be attributed to many others."

Chief among those others was Alain Locke, whose own role in shepherding the younger generation of writers cannot be diminished. A Harvard Ph.D. and Oxford's first black Rhodes scholar, Locke relished the transforming power of art and envisioned Harlem as a cultural mecca for fashioning a fresh and unprecedented black image.

Locke's own image had been carefully cultivated, first by his parents—Philadelphia teachers who instilled in him a passion for literature and "the duty to be cultured"—and then by Locke himself. With his scrupulously tailored suits, frail frame, high-pitched voice, and brisk pace, Locke shuttled back and forth between Washington (where he still taught at Howard) and Harlem, where he served as the "press agent," in Charles S. Johnson's words, for the Negro Renaissance.

Foppish and homosexual, Locke was known to take a special interest in the careers of attractive and intelligent young men like Countee Cullen and Langston Hughes. On the other hand, he was notorious at Howard for warning female students on the first day of class that they would likely receive Cs, regardless of their ability. "Although Locke rarely saw promise in young women," as one observer put it, "he detected talent" in Stylus member Zora Neale Hurston. With her natural aptitude as a storyteller and her proletarian Eatonville background, Hurston clearly had something of value to offer to the blossoming Renaissance. Specifically, as historian Steven Watson has pointed out, "she could provide the connection to the black folk heritage that Locke considered essential to the creation of a New Negro literature." In the fall of 1924, Locke recommended her work to Johnson. On the strength of "John Redding Goes to Sea," Johnson wrote to Zora, inviting her to submit material to *Opportunity*.

The story she sent, "Drenched in Light," was published in *Opportunity*'s December 1924 issue. Her first nationally published short story, it was Hurston's second serious attempt to translate the rural black experience into literature. And it contained some important elements that "John Redding Goes to Sea" lacked—namely, a fairly sophisticated use of metaphor and dialect and an exuberant sense of humor.

"Drenched in Light" was Hurston's unapologetic tribute to the impudent, unrefined child she once had been. The story explores a day in the life of Isis Watts, a playful, fun-loving little girl whose favorite pastime is sitting atop the gatepost in front of her Eatonville house and gleefully hailing travelers. As a result, "everybody in the country, white and colored, knew little Isis Watts, the joyful."

Isis's grandmother has the challenging job of disciplining this strong-willed child, who engages in various behaviors that Grandma Potts finds annoying. In addition to brazenly greeting passersby, Isis plays with boys, sits with her legs flung open—and, sin of sins, whistles. She even embarks on a mischievous though well-intentioned mission to give her grandmother a shave while she sleeps. Grandma Potts wakes up in the nick of time, and Isis, fearful of the spanking to come, crawls under the house. She is drawn out of her hiding place, however, by the sound of a marching band. Isis follows the musicians to a carnival, then quickly doubles back home for Grandma's new red tablecloth, the perfect embellishment for her torn and dirty dress. Grandma Potts soon finds Isis dancing before a gaping crowd at the carnival, her new tablecloth dragging in the dust. Seeing her furious grandmother, Isis bolts into the woods and dramatically vows to drown herself in the creek.

She is stopped by a more interesting proposal: the opportunity to ride in a motor car with some of the white people who'd enjoyed her dancing at the carnival. The white men in the car are indifferent to the little brown girl's chatter, but the woman is kind and enchanted with Isis. When they arrive at the girl's home, the woman is reluctant to part with her. She placates a still-angry Grandma Potts by giving her five dollars for the one-dollar tablecloth. "I want her to go on to the hotel and dance in that table-cloth for me," the white woman explains. "I want brightness and this Isis is joy itself, why she's drenched in light!" Barely hiding her pride, Grandma Potts agrees to let Isis go, and "Isis, for the first time in her life, felt herself appreciated and danced up and down in an ecstasy of joy for a minute."

"Drenched in Light" isn't so much a plot-driven story as it is a self-portrait—an extended character sketch of Isis Watts, clearly Zora Neale Hurston's embodied memory of her own girl-self. Zora's identification with Isis was total: In her imagination, Isis wore golden slippers with blue bottoms and rode white horses to the horizon, just as Zora had done in her own childhood dreams. Hurston even gave Isis a harsh-mouthed grandmother like her own, with the very same name.

The name Hurston chose for her fictional doppelgänger is even more intriguing, symbolically speaking. In Egyptian mythology, Isis was a woman who possessed words of healing power. She used her magic to trick Ra, the Creator, into revealing his secret name and was then elevated to become the most revered goddess of Egypt. Associated with the color red, Isis was considered the most powerful magician in the universe, and she was intelligent and inventive—both attributes Hurston assigned to the fictional Isis of Eatonville. Meanwhile, the young author took the character's last name, Watts, from the word for the primary unit of measuring light and power, an unambiguous indicator of the value Hurston placed on Isis's incandescent spirit and, consequently, on her own.

Almost completely autobiographical, "Drenched in Light"—Hurston's opening statement, so to speak, to a national audience—was a bold declaration of identity, individuality, and independence. While the New Negroes in Harlem were pondering the questions of who they were, where they came from, and how they wished to be perceived by virtue of their literature, "Drenched in Light" revealed that Zora Hurston of Eatonville already had considered these questions. And she had come to a definitive conclusion: She wanted only to be herself.

Zora's ambition escalated with each success. After "Drenched in Light" was published in *Opportunity*, her confidence in her writing—and in Eatonville as a valid wellspring for literature—mounted. Charles S. Johnson, meanwhile, was impressed enough with Hurston's writing that he urged her to consider a move to New York, where the New Negro movement was in full flower.

With Harlem beckoning, Zora convinced herself that if she could just muster the money, she could complete her college education in

New York as well as she could at Howard. She then took a leap of faith—or a jump at the sun, as her mother might have called it: The first week of January 1925, Zora Neale Hurston moved to New York City, as she recalled, with a dollar and fifty cents in her purse, "no job, no friends, and a lot of hope."

Just as important as her hope—and far more valuable than her buck fifty—Zora had "Drenched in Light" on her résumé, as well as a small suitcase of other short stories and plays she'd been working on. So armed, she made her way to the office of the National Urban League, on East Twenty-third Street, and asked for Dr. Charles S. Johnson. The sociologist and editor was accustomed to such visits from enthusiastic young writers. He often helped them find places to stay and gave them important addresses and phone numbers to get started.

The most significant of these addresses was 580 St. Nicholas Avenue, a well-appointed building in the Sugar Hill district, where affluent Harlemites had begun to settle. The 580 building counted well-paid singer Ethel Waters among its tenants, and it also was home to Ethel Ray, Johnson's secretary, and her roommates, Regina Anderson and Louella Tucker. In this trio's relatively plush Harlem flat, writers like Countee Cullen, Langston Hughes, and Jean Toomer had found a comfortable couch, free food, and the company of others like them. The same welcome, Johnson assured Zora, was waiting there for her.

The son of a minister, Johnson had been raised in a middle-class environment and had earned his doctorate at the University of Chicago. He wore elegant double-breasted suits and handsome round-rimmed glasses, and he was, as one writer remembered, "a terrifically warm person." As he'd done for so many before her, Johnson greeted Zora not only with the practical information she needed to get settled, but also with a gentle, paternal smile. (That same week, on January 7, Zora celebrated her thirty-fourth birthday. Despite Johnson's paternal instincts—and Zora's ready acceptance of them— she was two years older than he was. But no one knew.) During Zora's early days in New York, Johnson and his wife often invited her to dinner at their house, and Mrs. Johnson frequently offered her money for carfare.

Given this warm welcome, Eatonville's daughter immediately felt at home in Harlem, where, as one writer recalled, it was absolutely "fun to be a Negro." Harlem in 1925 was a place where being black was not a burden but an act of beauty, not a liability but a state of grace. Strolling down Seventh Avenue, Zora marveled at her neighbors: many were helpful, some were haughty, yet all were exceedingly hopeful. Sometimes Zora felt so comfortable in this nearly all-Negro milieu, her blackness simply disappeared: "At certain times I have no race, I am *me*," she observed. "When I set my hat at a certain angle and saunter down Seventh Avenue, Harlem City, feeling as snooty as the lions in front of the Forty-Second Street Library, for instance." In Harlem, the sense of *me*-ness that Zora had felt so profoundly as a child in Eatonville—the freedom to thrive as an individual within the embrace of community—was fully restored.

When Zora was in the mood for people watching, she knew the intersection of Seventh Avenue and 135th Street was Harlem's gatepost, offering an unparalleled view. Just around the corner was James Weldon Johnson's house and, next door, the home of pianist Fats Waller. Broadway star Florence Mills lived a couple of blocks away. And just down Seventh Avenue, at 131st Street, was "The Corner," an open-air site where musicians routinely hung out with their instruments, sweetening Harlem's already intoxicating atmosphere with the new-sprung music that would name the age: jazz.

Also at the corner of 131st Street and Seventh Avenue was the famous Tree of Hope, "an aging elm that was Harlem's talisman and labor exchange," as historian David Levering Lewis has described it. Rubbing the tree's bark brought success, according to Harlem legend. And if the rub itself didn't work, the tree was also a grapevine—the best place to hear about the latest job openings, particularly in the arts. "At one time or another," Lewis reported, "almost every actor, singer or musician in Harlem found work after a vigil under the Tree of Hope." Never one to balk at superstition, Zora surely paid a visit to the Tree of Hope shortly after her uptown arrival. She likely gave its bark a vigorous and sanguine rub, whispering her womanish dreams to Harlem's old elm the same way she had shared her girlhood longings with Eatonville's "loving pine."

For Zora, and others like her, anything—including a magical tree—seemed possible above 125th Street. And there was always so much to do: lectures and plays at the 135th Street YMCA, poetry

readings and book discussions at the 135th Street library, performances at the Lincoln and Lafayette theaters, and parties at the
Renaissance Ballroom and the Rockland Palace.

For those with little money to spend, like Zora, a quarter could
buy admittance into many a rent party. These raucous parties were
most often held on Saturday and Thursday nights, when domestics—or "kitchen mechanics," in Harlemese—usually had the
evening off. But a serious seeker could find a "chitterling party" or a
"break-down," as they were also called, almost any night of the week.
Everyone knew the deal: pay a dime to fifty cents for admission—to
help your host pay the rent, literally—then slip into the red-lit parlor
and have yourself a high-heel time, as Zora would put it.

These parties became a Harlem institution and an economic
necessity. Harlem's rents were twelve to thirty dollars a month higher
than in other areas of the city, although black New Yorkers earned
lower salaries than their white counterparts. In the mid-1920s, thirty
dollars was a significant chunk of money, equal to about $300 today.
Still, a 1924 Urban League study found that Negroes paid from 40
percent to 60 percent higher rents than white people for the same
class of apartments—and segregated housing practices did not give
black folks the option to just move out of Harlem and into more
affordable New York neighborhoods. As a result, the average Harlem
resident spent an astonishing 40 percent of his or her income on
rent. Thus, rent parties—thoroughly embraced by the community—
helped to keep many Harlemites afloat.

At the liveliest rent parties, professional musicians—even big
names like Fats Waller and Duke Ellington—would show up after
their paid gigs and, through their inspired playing, incite a black
bottom contest or a Charleston frenzy. Harlemized renditions of the
jook-joint parties common throughout the South, these "flop-
wallies"—or "struts," as musicians called them—reminded Zora and
her fellow Harlem newcomers of their rural roots. Rent party menus,
for example, always featured the cuisine of the black South: rice and
black-eyed peas, collard greens, potato salad, and, of course, the
national bird of Negro America, chicken. Also on the menu: hot
music and a diverse crowd of cool people. "You would see all kinds of
people making the party scene," recalled Willie "the Lion" Smith, a
noted pianist who regularly played at rent parties. "Formally dressed

society folks from downtown, policemen, painters, carpenters, mechanics, truckmen in their workingmen's clothes, gamblers, lesbians, and entertainers of all kinds. The parties were recommended to newly arrived single gals as the place to go to get acquainted."

Newly arrived and technically single (if she didn't count her long-distance romance with Herbert Sheen, now in medical school in Chicago), Zora gamely attended her share of Harlem rent parties. She rarely drank—despite Prohibition, rent parties were usually well lubricated—but she loved to dance. And she was, in the oral tradition of Eatonville, a gifted raconteur. Frequently at the parties she attended, Zora commanded center stage by regaling everyone with down-home stories—signed, sealed, and animatedly delivered straight from Joe Clarke's porch. "Almost before you knew it, she had gotten into a story," fellow writer Arna Bontemps recalled. Added Sterling Brown: "When Zora was there, she *was* the party." Exhausted and satisfied, Zora often tumbled out of these parties at the brink of dawn, after bumping elbows with her co-revelers all night, dancing until her legs were wobbly, and helping a neighbor stay a step ahead of the landlord.

The following Sunday evening might find her dancing to a less secular beat at one of Harlem's storefront churches. Zora liked to attend sanctified churches ("where all of the members are saints—they admit it," she chuckled) because the rousing music and dramatic sermons reminded her of home. Often at these services, which were "*most* primitive," as Zora once put it, everyone was expected to contribute to the collective effort to make a joyful noise unto the Lord—with a drum, a rattle, or their own two feet.

As Zora settled into Harlem's rhythms, the special Negro issue of the *Survey Graphic* appeared, trumpeting "Harlem: Mecca of the New Negro." Guest-edited by Alain Locke, the magazine briefly addressed Harlemites' housing challenges and other aspects of the so-called Negro problem in an article titled "Ambushed in the City: The Grim Side of Harlem." Mostly, however, the special edition focused on Harlem's vibrant culture. This apparently was a wise editorial choice: The March 1925 *Survey Graphic* became the most widely read issue in the magazine's history, selling out two printings—more than 42,000 copies.

On the magazine's cover was a drawing by white artist Winold

Reiss of tenor Roland Hayes; on the back cover, one of handsome
Harlem bachelor Harold Jackman, identified only as "A College
Lad." The special edition featured articles by the New Negro movement's forefathers—Du Bois, NAACP officer and novelist Walter
White, Charles S. Johnson, and James Weldon Johnson. More significantly, the magazine included pages of contributions from the
newer Negroes: Countee Cullen, Langston Hughes, Claude McKay
(who'd become an expatriate in Paris), and Jean Toomer (whose
Cane had been published in 1923).

Of the younger generation of writers, only two women were represented in *Survey Graphic*: poets Angelina Grimke and Anne
Spencer. Yet the magazine featured an essay by Elise Johnson
McDougald called "The Double Task: The Struggle of Negro
Women for Sex and Race Emancipation." "In Harlem, more than
anywhere else," asserted the social worker and educator, "the Negro
woman is free from the cruder handicaps of primitive household
hardships and the grosser forms of sex and race subjugation. Here she
has considerable opportunity to measure her powers in the intellectual and industrial fields of the great city."

This optimistic proclamation notwithstanding, the women of the
New Negro movement were conspicuously underrepresented in
Survey Graphic—perhaps because Locke, once called "a certified
misogynist," was its editor. Under his stewardship, the magazine's
New Negro issue published nothing by any of the movement's rising
female stars—not a word from Gwendolyn Bennett, Marita Bonner,
Nella Larsen, or Zora Neale Hurston.

The next major literary event of the year, on May 1, was a bit
more inclusive. The previous fall, Charles S. Johnson had announced
that *Opportunity* magazine was launching a literary contest, offering
cash prizes for the best short stories, plays, poems, and essays. His
announcement prompted more than seven hundred submissions.

The following spring, 316 people showed up at the corner of Fifth
Avenue and Twenty-fourth Street to witness the conferring of
honors. Johnson had been advertising the awards dinner, at the Fifth
Avenue Restaurant, for months. He had collected close to $800 in
prize money, and he'd assembled an estimable, racially balanced
roster of judges: among them, best-selling novelist Fannie Hurst,
Carl Van Doren, Eugene O'Neill, Alain Locke, and James Weldon

Johnson. Other notables rounded out the guest list, including young singer-actor Paul Robeson, wealthy heiress A'Lelia Walker, philanthropist and Barnard College trustee Annie Nathan Meyer, and former *New York Times* music critic Carl Van Vechten. The menu was far less impressive: chicken, mashed potatoes, and green peas. Still, the evening went off without a hitch, ending with the announcement that Harlem businessman Casper Holstein had vowed to finance more awards. (Uptown insiders knew Holstein could well afford it: he was king of the Harlem numbers racket.) As a reporter for the *New York Herald Tribune* declared in the next day's paper, the awards dinner was "a novel sight." "White critics, whom everybody knows, Negro writers whom nobody knew—meeting on common ground."

If there were any New Negro writers Zora had not yet met, she met them at the May 1 awards dinner. All the present and future luminaries of the Harlem Renaissance were there, and many of them won prizes. Hughes and Cullen locked up the poetry category: Hughes earned first place (for "The Weary Blues"), Cullen won second, and the rivals shared the third-place award. Meanwhile, E. Franklin Frazier and Sterling Brown placed first and second in the essay competition.

The winner of the most prizes that evening, however, was Zora Neale Hurston. The earthy Harlem newcomer turned heads and raised eyebrows as she claimed a second-place fiction award for her short story "Spunk," a second-place prize in drama for her play *Color Struck*, and two honorable mentions—for her short story "Black Death" and for a play called *Spears*. Each of her second-place honors carried a thirty-five-dollar cash prize, which provided a welcome boost to Zora's income as well as to her profile.

The names of the writers who beat out Hurston for first place that night would soon be forgotten by Harlemites and by history itself. (John Matheus won first place in the short story category, and G. D. Lipscomb won first place for drama.) But the name of the second-place winner buzzed on tongues all night, and for days and years to come.

Lest anyone forget her, Zora made a wholly memorable entrance at a party following the awards dinner. In deference to the cool temperature that evening, she wore a long, richly colored scarf draped across her shoulders. As she strode into the room—jammed with writers and arts patrons, black and white—Zora flung the colorful scarf around her neck with a dramatic flourish and bellowed a reminder of the title of her winning play: *"Coloooooor Struuckkkk!"* Her exultant entrance literally stopped the party for a moment, just as she had intended. In this way, Zora Neale Hurston made it known that a bright and powerful presence had arrived.

CHAPTER 12

Enter the Negrotarians

Zora's flamboyant gesture at the *Opportunity* after-party could have angered her competitors, alienated her peers, or frightened off potential patrons. It apparently did none of the above. Instead it seemed to have an opposite, endearing effect. "Zora Neale Hurston is a clever girl, isn't she?" Langston Hughes soon wrote. "I would like to know her." At least one person, however, *was* put off by Hurston's immodesty: Paul Robeson's wife, Eslanda, confided to her diary the next day that she liked Zora "less and less the more I see of her." But most people at the party were favorably impressed by Zora's playful, scarf-flinging entrance—and even Essie Robeson's dislike would not endure. In time, Hurston's bold self-introduction to New York's glitterati would become legend—one of the dozens of "Zora stories" that her friends would recount, over the years, to illustrate her bodacious charm.

Zora was "an original," as Arna Bontemps put it. "She was very outgoing. In any group she was the center of attention. . . . She really was not a showoff but she just drew attention in that way," he remembered. "In appearance, Zora was a pleasant, ordinary, brown-skinned young woman. Not stunning, about average—a little above average—in appearance. But she had an ease and somehow projected herself very well orally. . . . She didn't seem pushy or offensive in any way, but she somehow drew attention."

By all accounts, Zora Neale Hurston possessed a quality that enabled her to walk into a roomful of strangers and, a few minutes and a few stories later, leave them so completely charmed and so utterly impressed that they sometimes found themselves offering to help her in any way they could. Among those she thus impressed on the evening of May 1 were three people who had the power to help her immensely: Barnard College founder Annie Nathan Meyer, popular author Fannie Hurst, and novelist and man-about-town Carl Van Vechten. All three would become major champions of Hurston's talent and instrumental forces in the development of her career.

Zora soon coined a term for people like them—influential whites who supported the New Negro movement and who took an interest in black life itself. Because their philanthropic interests had a distinct racial angle, they were not merely humanitarians, in Zora's view. Instead, she called them "Negrotarians."

Zora caught the attention of this particular trio of Negrotarians with little conscious guile, simply by being herself. What they saw of her at the *Opportunity* dinner convinced them that she was a brilliant young woman, luminous with intellectual and artistic promise. Within months, Zora had become a regular at Carl Van Vechten's frequent interracial parties, and he had declared her "one of the most amusing people" he'd ever met. His friend Fannie Hurst concurred. Zora had "the gift," she once said, "of walking into hearts."

Annie Nathan Meyer's response to Zora's "gift" was swift and sensible: She approached her after the awards dinner and offered her a slot at Barnard, an independent women's college affiliated with Columbia University.

Meyer had played a critical role in the founding of Barnard in 1889. Years before, as a Columbia University student, she had been disappointed to learn that the collegiate coursework offered to women was not as rigorous as the standard education for male students. Infuriated by this inequity, she had resolved to create an entire college for women in New York City. Within a few years, she had personally obtained much of the funding for the school through donations from her husband, Dr. Alfred Meyer, and from the likes of John D. Rockefeller.

Once Barnard was on firm footing, Meyer established her own career as a writer and soon became one of several Jewish philanthropists who offered a generous flow of cash to black organizations and causes. Others of this ilk included Urban League backer Julius

Rosenwald (chief stockholder in Sears, Roebuck & Company), as well as Amy, Joel, and Arthur Spingarn, who provided years of financial support to the NAACP. These Jewish Negrotarians were not just curious about black life or intrigued by what some might have considered an exotic culture; rather, they were committed to black uplift, and their philanthropy was effusive. Commented one observer: "Being of use to the Negro was becoming virtually a specialty of the second most abused Americans of the early twentieth century."

By 1925, when she met Zora, Annie Nathan Meyer was a well-ensconced Barnard trustee who felt it was time for the college to become a bit more colorful. And Zora Hurston seemed to have gumption and genius in equal measure—the perfect combination, Meyer believed, for crossing Barnard's color barrier.

For her part, Zora relished the thought of attending Barnard—not because she wanted to become a racial pioneer, but because she wanted to finish school. In fact, she seemed to barely think about the discomfort she might feel as Barnard's only black student. (Zora was poised to step into a minuscule circle: of the thirteen thousand or so black people enrolled in college nationwide in the mid-1920s, fewer than three hundred of them attended white schools.) If she considered the racial consequences at all, she was undaunted by them. Eager to complete her college education, Zora wrote to Meyer less than two weeks after they met to tell her she had requested her transcript from Howard University. She also let Meyer know she was conscious of all that was at stake: "I am tremendously encouraged now. My typewriter is clicking away till all hours of the night," Zora began cheerfully. "I am striving desperately for a toe-hold on the world. You see, your interest keys me up wonderfully—I <u>must not let you</u> be disappointed in me."

With her underlined words, Zora placed the onus on herself, yet she still conveyed to Meyer how very important this opportunity was to her. Meyer could look at Zora and see a young woman with a future so bright it made her squint. But even squinting, she could not see the struggles of Zora's past or the depths from which she had risen. Zora could have told Meyer all about the dark tunnel she'd had to travel through; instead she only said this: "It is mighty cold comfort to do things if nobody cares whether you succeed or not. It is terribly delightful to me to have someone fearing with me and hoping for me, let alone working to make some of my dreams come true."

Meyer was sufficiently moved by Zora's words to spend the summer trying to help her get the funds she needed for Barnard's tuition. Despite Zora's undistinguished transcript from Howard, Barnard's dean, Virginia Gildersleeve, admitted her after an interview in which she found her "an interesting person" who was "distinctly promising." Zora's record, however, did not warrant a scholarship, so Gildersleeve urged Meyer to look elsewhere for Zora's tuition money—$320, the equivalent of about $3,000 in today's currency. "Do you think you could get, from some outside persons interested in the Negro race, money for a special scholarship in her case?" Gildersleeve asked Meyer.

Zora and Meyer spent the next few months casting about for funds. They asked for help from a range of sources, including Carl Van Vechten (who had secured a publishing contract for Langston Hughes within eighteen days of the *Opportunity* dinner) and Poro Company founder Annie Pope Malone, a wealthy Negro who'd earned her riches developing and marketing a line of black beauty products.

Zora was genuinely grateful for Meyer's efforts on her behalf. Having struggled alone for the past twenty years for an education, she viewed Meyer's interest in her as a blessing. Yet Zora also was well aware of the complexities of relationships between New Negro artists and their Negrotarian patrons—an awareness that had led her to concoct the term "Negrotarian" in the first place. It was difficult, for instance, to know what Meyer wanted in return for her kindness. Zora always offered fervent thanks; she also rarely missed an opportunity to point out the disparity between herself and the fifty-eight-year-old Meyer, often signing her letters "your humble and obedient servant," and even occasionally referring to herself, in early notes to Meyer, as "your little pickaninny."

Most contemporary readers, of any race, would find Zora's self-degrading racial references odd, offensive, and unnecessarily obsequious. Yet Meyer, a product of her time, seemed to respond differently. One could argue that Zora was consciously *playing* Meyer, to use a vernacular term, for her own benefit. That is, she was perhaps playing up to any notions of racial superiority Meyer might have held in order to make the older woman feel good about her continued support of a helpless young "pickaninny." Zora admitted (or feigned) ignorance about what she called "white psychology": "I see white people do things, but I don't know that I grasp why they do them," she once told Meyer. Yet, from another perspective, it seems that Zora had a rather sophisticated understanding of "white psychology." She *had* to, in order to get as much help from white people as she got, suggested her contemporary John Henrik Clarke. Zora knew that "if she showed certain scars," Clarke asserted, "she'd get paid for them." In other words, she understood that engaging in a certain kind of racial role-play could be profitable, and she did so with a bittersweet humor.

Whether it was conscious psychological trickery or not, Zora's strategy with Meyer worked. In September 1925, with Meyer's support, Zora enrolled in Barnard College as a twenty-six-year-old transfer student, listing her birth year as 1899. As part of her charade, Zora never found it necessary to tell Meyer (or anyone else) that she was really thirty-four years old.

"We wear the mask," black poet Paul Laurence Dunbar had written famously before the turn of the century.

> We wear the mask that grins and lies,
> It hides our cheeks and shades our eyes,—
> This debt we pay to human guile;
> With torn and bleeding hearts we smile,
> And mouth with myriad subtleties.

Zora Hurston—and arguably every other Negro in America—had learned that there were definite benefits to various types of masking. And when she thought it necessary, Hurston could wear the mask— and speak "with myriad subtleties"—as well as anyone.

It's interesting to note that after her first few months as a Barnard student—after she'd gotten what she wanted, cynics might say—Zora dropped all self-deprecating references in her letters to Meyer, as well as her standard closing ("your most humble and obedient servant"). By January, she had discarded that particular mask altogether and changed her customary closing to simply this: "most cordially yours."

*

During her first semester at Barnard, Zora completed an occupational interest form that was required of every new student. Asked to rate her extracurricular interests, she marked dramatics as number one and athletics as number two. She stated that she had previously held jobs as a manicurist and a "social worker"—perhaps a euphemism for domestic worker. (Zora likely anticipated, wisely, that her affluent white classmates would not take too well to the thought of sparring intellectually with someone who might have been their maid.) She noted that she planned to earn her own living expenses while attending Barnard "either as manicurist, social worker or writer. Perhaps sell a manuscript or two."

When responding to a question about her vocational interests after college, Hurston was definitive: She wanted to be a writer. "I have had some small success as a writer and wish above all to succeed at it," she scrawled. "Either teaching or social work will be interesting but consolation prizes."

All indications so far were that Zora Neale Hurston would not have to settle for a consolation prize. Her literary successes were quietly accumulating. The summer before she began her studies at Barnard, Hurston had published a short story, "Magnolia Flower," in the July 1925 issue of the *Spokesman*. In Hurston's fable, a river tells a brook a story of love conquering all. In the process, Hurston again addressed the theme she'd begun to explore in her play *Color Struck*: the self-destructiveness that results from color-based prejudice among black people.

Hurston also had just published an essay in the September 1925 issue of *The Messenger* called "The Hue and Cry About Howard University." According to Hurston's article, students at her former stomping ground had recently protested singing Negro spirituals for Howard's white president, decrying the songs as "low and degrading, being the product of slaves and slavery." They denounced the plaintive songs for their poor grammar, and they pointed out that spirituals were not sung in white universities—as if that were the measure for worthy art. In her essay, Hurston recounted her own years at Howard, when she'd proudly participated in "the sings"—with no shame and with no fear of being snatched back into slavery. Hurston sharply criticized Howard students' negative, embarrassed attitude toward Negro spirituals, defending the songs as authentic and valuable expressions of black folk culture.

Meanwhile, her award-winning story "Spunk"—whose characters were rooted in the same folk culture that birthed the spirituals—had been published a few months before, in the June 1925 issue of *Opportunity*. "Spunk" tells the story of Spunk Banks, a sawmill worker so big and brash that he struts around town with another man's wife. Joe Kanty timidly confronts his wife, Lena, and her new lover, but they persist in their very public affair. Finally, egged on by the men at the village store, Joe attacks Spunk from behind with a razor. Spunk cavalierly kills him and is then haunted by a black bobcat that he believes to be Joe, "sneaked back from Hell." Though Spunk expertly and bravely rides the circle-saw at his job, he is killed when he is pushed into the saw by an unseen hand. With his final breath, he tells a friend that he believes Joe pushed him, and that he intends to find him in the spirit world and seek retribution. "If spirits kin fight," comments one of the men on the store porch, "there's a powerful tussle goin' on somewhere ovah Jordan 'cause Ah b'leeve Joe's ready for Spunk an' ain't skeered anymore— yas, Ah b'leeve Joe pushed 'im mahself."

Though more deftly executed, this story contains all the elements Hurston had exhibited in her earlier short stories: an Eatonville-inspired setting; an ever-evolving use of dialect, metaphor, and humor (this time, it's a goading, communal humor); and a respectful treatment of black folks' belief in spirits and signs.

While the story is more complex than its title might suggest, the title itself likely made an impression on *Opportunity* contest judge Fannie Hurst that was inseparable from her impression of its author. If there was one word to describe the young writer who'd stopped the *Opportunity* after-party with her grand entrance, that word was "spunk."

Hurst had personally handed Zora the second-place award for "Spunk" on May 1, yet the two women apparently did not have any contact in the weeks that followed. Not long after the story was published in *Opportunity*, however, Fannie Hurst wrote to Carl Van Vechten asking for Zora's address. That fall, Zora—who was renting a room on West 139th Street in Harlem—received a letter from Hurst inviting her to tea at her downtown home. Zora excitedly told

Meyer about the invitation, prompting Meyer to offer to ask Fannie Hurst to contribute to Zora's tuition. Zora thought it was a fine idea: "I am sure she would help," she said of Hurst, "but I felt a little 'delicate' about asking her."

At this point, despite a challenging French class, Zora was doing fine academically in her first Barnard semester. Yet she was waging a mighty financial struggle. She had to attend classes until 5:00 P.M. three days a week and had trouble finding a job that matched her academic schedule and afforded her time to study. She owed $117 for her first-term fees, and she'd already spent a small fortune, she told Meyer, for Barnard necessities: "books, gym outfit, shoes, stockings, maps, tennis racquet." The list went on: "I still must get a bathing suit, gloves, and if I am here in the spring, I will need a golf outfit." Overwhelmed by this lengthy slate of expenses, Zora resigned herself to the idea that she might not finish out the school year: "I have thought things over pretty thoroughly and concluded that this term is about all that I can do unless some more of the people to whom I have appealed send in something substantial. . . . All I can do is make the most of this semester and then take a job."

Once, Zora was so broke, she borrowed money from a beggar. The way the story goes, she was penniless but needed to go downtown. On her way to catch the subway, she was stopped by a blind panhandler holding out his cup. Taking some change from the cup for her subway fare, Zora said: "I need money worse than you today. Lend me this! Next time, I'll give it back."

On October 17, when she gave Meyer the go-ahead to write to Fannie Hurst for funds, Zora had only eleven cents to her name. She had recently lost a job because her employer wanted her to report to work at 3:00, but she could not get there most days until 5:30. "So you see," she told Meyer, "there is some justification for my doubts as to whether I can remain [at Barnard]. I must somehow pay my room-rent and I must have food."

This letter seems to have been written on a day when Zora was seeking to rearrange her priorities in life. She had wearied finally of her long struggle for education in the face of destitution. "I have been my own sole support since I was 13 years old," Zora explained. "I've taken some tremendous loss and survived terrific shocks. I am not telling you this in search of sympathy. No melodrama. If I am losing my capacity for shock absorbing, if privation is beginning to terrify me, you will appreciate the situation and see that it isn't cowardice, but that by being pounded so often on the anvil of life I am growing less resilient. Physical suffering unnerves me now."

By the end of the month, however, it appeared that Zora's days of physical suffering were over, at least for a while. Fannie Hurst responded immediately and generously to Meyer's call for help on Zora's behalf. Undoubtedly, Hurst's openhandedness also was a response to the considerable charm Zora must have exhibited at their meeting over tea. By the first week of November, Zora had moved into Fannie Hurst's apartment on West Sixty-seventh Street and had begun working as her secretary, answering her telephone, replying to letters, and running various errands. She also was reading the proofs of Hurst's soon-to-be-bestseller *Appassionata*.

When Barnard's Dean Gildersleeve learned of the famous Fannie Hurst's interest in Zora, Gildersleeve's own regard for Barnard's sole black student suddenly took an upward turn. She told Meyer of a student loan fund that Zora might benefit from, and she reopened the possibility of a scholarship.

Because of her association with Fannie Hurst, Zora also surged in popularity with her previously chilly classmates—some of whom had burst into unkind laughter upon hearing her, a black southerner, reciting French. Post-Hurst, Zora reported, "they don't laugh in French when I recite, and one of those laughers has asked to quiz with me." Zora wanted to believe the laughter had stopped at least partly because her French had improved—not just because she had been hired by one of America's favorite novelists. Of the laughers, she reasoned: "I knew getting mad would not help any, I had to get my lessons so well that their laughter would seem silly."

Though Zora likely underestimated the role her impressive new job played in silencing her classmates' laughter, she was right to take some credit for herself. For the first time in her life, she was competing academically with white students—young women who'd benefited from all sorts of preparatory advantages that simply were not available to her. Yet Zora performed as well as she had during her more attentive days at Howard, and as well as could be expected, considering her financial troubles. With a load of seven classes her first semester, she managed to earn Bs in English and history, and Cs in everything else, including French. She also got a booster shot of confidence: "You see," she told Meyer, "being at Barnard and measuring arms with others known to be strong increases my self love and stiffens my spine."

Zora's job with Fannie Hurst was certainly a stabilizing factor during that first term at Barnard. The exact nature of the Hurst-Hurston financial arrangement remains a mystery, according to Fannie Hurst's meticulous biographer, Brooke Kroeger. "Perhaps Zora bartered secretarial services for room and board. Perhaps Fannie paid part of the tuition debt, which Zora worked off in this manner. Maybe the deal was a straight salary-for-hours arrangement," Kroeger speculated.

Though Zora Hurston and Fannie Hurst apparently never documented their fiscal relationship, they both chronicled their mutual affection. It's easy to understand why they "took a shine" to each other right away, as Hurst put it. Both women were no doubt intrigued by the similarity of their surnames; this alone must have made them feel an immediate and curious kinship. A committed Negrotarian, Fannie Hurst—who kept in her home office a bulky file headed "Negro Matters"—often lent her name to various black organizations. One of her pet projects was the National Health Circle for Colored People, a nurses' association for indigent black southerners. Hurst had become an active supporter of the health circle, and she had recently joined other prominent white literary figures in loudly lauding Harlem's New Negro writers.

To Hurst, Zora Hurston seemed an especially worthy cause. Here was a talented young black woman who exhibited a "blazing zest for life," as Hurst later recalled. Zora seemed "awash in splendor," and the well-off Hurst was more than willing to be of service to an emerging black female author gleaming with such potential.

Hurst was only five years older than Hurston, but because both women lied about their ages, they each assumed the gap was much wider. And Zora gladly played the role of brilliant young protégée to Fannie's role as older, wiser mentor.

With her keen nose for opportunity, Zora immediately grasped the importance of nurturing a relationship with Fannie Hurst, who was, in Zora's words, "a great artist and globe famous." Hurst was indeed a bona fide celebrity. A best-selling author, highly paid screenwriter, frequent radio guest, newspaper columnist, and popular magazine writer (for *McCall's*, *Cosmopolitan*, and *Harper's Bazaar*, among others), Hurst was in a position to open doors for Zora that few others could. And she had a bold sense of style that Zora found appealing. "She knows exactly what goes with her very white skin, black hair and sloe eyes, and she wears it," Zora noted of Hurst, whom she once called "a stunning wench." "I doubt if any woman on earth has gotten better effects than she has with black, white and red. Not only that, she knows how to parade it when she gets it on. She will never be jailed for uglying up a town."

The fondness Zora and Fannie felt for each other lasted long after their formal financial arrangement ended. In fact, Zora's stint as Hurst's secretary was remarkably short-lived—mercifully so, both women might have agreed. Hurst found Zora's secretarial skills atrocious: "Her shorthand was short on legibility, her typing hit-or-miss, mostly the latter, her filing a game of find-the-thimble," Hurst later recalled. For her part, Zora was happy to be relieved of her secretarial duties, particularly typing. "My idea of Hell is that I would all through eternity be typing a book," she told a friend years later.

In early December—after just a month as Fannie Hurst's live-in secretary—Zora moved out, taking a room on West 131st Street in Harlem. "Though the myth holds otherwise," Hurst's biographer concluded, "the month between November 4 and December 6, 1925 seems to have been the full extent of Zora's tenure in an early-day work-study arrangement at the home office of Fannie Hurst."

The women's friendly relationship was by now firmly established, however, and Zora continued to reap the benefits of their ongoing association. Fannie Hurst, it seemed, was Zora's passport to social success among her elite classmates. "The girls at Barnard are perfectly wonderful to me," Zora reported to Meyer a week after she'd moved out of Hurst's apartment. "They literally drag me to the teas on Wednesdays and then behave as if I am the guest of honor—so eager are they to assure me that I am desired there."

She added: "They have urged me to come to the Junior prom at the Ritz-Carlton in Feb. and several girls have offered to exchange dances with me if I will bring a man as light as myself." Rather than take offense on behalf of her darker-skinned brethren, Zora (at least in her letter to Meyer) laughed off her classmates' color-struck racism: "Their frankness on that score is amusing, but not offensive in that dancing is such an intimate thing that it is not unreasonable for a girl to say who she wishes to do it with." On Meyer's advice, Zora decided not to further upset Barnard's status quo by attempting to integrate the prom. "But even if things were different," she judged, "I could not go. Paying $12.50 plus a new frock and shoes and a wrap and all the other things necessary is not my idea of a good time. I am not that 'Ritzy' yet."

Being the only black person at a party (other than her date) was not Zora's idea of a good time, either. She knew it would only make her feel conspicuously black and intractably *different*. Not inferior. Just different, and apart. This was something Zora felt often enough in her academic life to know she did not wish to seek it out in her social life. "I feel most colored when I am thrown against a sharp white background," she once noted. This was, of course, her everyday experience at Barnard: "Among the thousand white persons, I am a dark rock surged upon, overswept by a creamy sea. I am surged upon and overswept, but through it all, I remain myself." And that self preferred a Harlem rent party to a formal dance at the Ritz any day of the week.

Still, even among her black friends, Zora expressed satisfaction with the way Barnard was treating her. "I suppose you want to know how this little piece of darkish meat feels at Barnard," she playfully wrote to Constance Sheen, the sister of her still-long-distance sweetheart, Herbert Sheen. "I am received quite well," Zora bragged. "In fact I am received so well that if someone would come along and try to turn me white I'd be quite peevish at them."

Pursued by the student government president as well as "the Social Register crowd," Zora became "Barnard's sacred black cow," as she put it. She knew she had Fannie Hurst to thank for her fast ascent to fashionableness, and she did: "Partly because you took me under your shelter, I have had no trouble in making friends," she wrote to Hurst. "Your friendship was a tremendous help to me at a critical time. It made both faculty and students <u>see</u> me when I needed seeing."

Hurst offered other support as well, agreeing to take two of Zora's articles and a short story on rounds to the magazine editors with whom she was so well-connected. As Zora's would-be mentor,

Hurst also suggested some changes to the short story, which Zora made reluctantly. "I do not wish to become Hurstized," Zora complained to Meyer. "There would be no point in my being an imitation Fannie Hurst, however faithful the copy, while the world has the real article at hand." Yet Zora knew she could not afford to balk too loudly: "I am very eager to make my bow to the market, and she says she will do all she can for me with her editors. Victory, O Lord!"

In addition to acquainting editors with Zora's work, Hurst introduced her Negro protégée to some of her celebrity friends. At a December 19 party at Fannie's home, for example, Zora shared a box of matches with Fannie, explorer Vilhjalmur Stefansson and novelist Charles Norris. She sent the empty matchbox to Constance Sheen—a Fannie Hurst fan—as a souvenir.

Zora was not entirely seduced by her heady company, however. "They are OFTEN insincere," she said of her new celebrity acquaintances. "Their show of friendship mere patronage." Zora sensed that this moment in history—when budding black writers like herself were so welcomed by the mainstream literati—would be fleeting. "I know it won't last always," she told Constance Sheen, "so I am playing with my toy while I may."

No longer on Hurst's payroll, Zora found another way to eke out an income—by working part-time as a waitress at private dinners and doing some housekeeping work, often for friends of Meyer's. At the same time, Zora was continuing to write. In late 1925, she penned a satirical essay, called "The Emperor Effaces Himself," about Marcus Garvey's imprisonment in February 1925 on a mail-fraud conviction. Though the piece was never published, it was an early example of Hurston's ability to use biting satire to great effect, as well as an example of her impatience with "race leaders" of dubious moral character. With his "wealth of titles," Garvey "had taken the people's money and he was keeping it," Hurston wrote. "That was how he had become the greatest man of his race. Booker T. Washington had achieved some local notice for collecting monies and spending it on a Negro school. It had never occurred to him to keep it. Marcus Garvey was much in advance of the old school of thinkers," she wrote mordantly.

Meanwhile, Hurston's other creative work was going well: Her play *Color Struck* was scheduled to be presented by an upstart theater company in Harlem at the end of the year. And in December, Alain Locke reprinted "Spunk" in *The New Negro*, a book that was roundly hailed as the benchmark anthology of the Harlem Renaissance.

Locke dedicated his volume to "the younger generation," and declared: "Youth speaks, and the voice of the New Negro is heard. What stirs inarticulately in the masses is already vocal upon the lips of the talented few, and the future listens, however the present may shut its ears." While Locke noted that the writers and artists included in the anthology "constitute a new generation not because of years only, but because of a new aesthetic and a new philosophy of life," the term "New Negro," for him, was largely synonymous with youth. Yet several members of "the younger Negro group" were not so young. Although apparently no male writer of the period felt compelled to invent a later birth date, several women did. Zora Hurston, Jessie Fauset, novelist Nella Larsen, and even grande dame Georgia Douglas Johnson all routinely lied about their ages.

On January 7, 1926, Zora quietly marked her thirty-fifth birthday. But since youth was such a valuable commodity in Harlem (and at Barnard, no doubt), she publicly celebrated it as her twenty-fifth, twenty-sixth, or twenty-seventh, depending on how she was counting that year.

As if to coincide with her progressing age, Zora's relationship with Meyer was gradually moving toward maturity as 1926 began. Like a peer, Zora inquired about the progress of Meyer's writing. Meyer, in turn, sent Zora a copy of her play *Black Souls* and asked for her comments—as if Zora were a well-regarded colleague, not an erstwhile "humble and obedient servant."

Shortly after her birthday, Zora interviewed for a Barnard scholarship and in early February, she hastily scribbled the good news on a postcard to Meyer: "I got the scholarship!!!"

Even so, Dean Gildersleeve still harbored reservations about whether Zora was true Barnard material, apparently because she had missed a recent history exam and had run into trouble completing the registration process for her second semester. "I wonder whether we really ought to encourage her to remain in college," Gildersleeve pondered in a letter to Meyer. "Does she get enough out of it to compensate for the difficulty and annoyance of trying to fit in to the administrative machine? We have given her a grant from the scholarship funds, but I feel a little uncertain about her."

Doing well academically was important to Zora, but it wasn't everything. "I felt that I was highly privileged and determined to make the most of it," she later recalled of her time at Barnard. "I did not resolve to be a grind, however, to show the white folks that I had brains. I took it for granted that they knew that. Else, why was I at Barnard?"

Zora was not only at Barnard, she was in New York—in "Harlem City," as she called it. And she discovered much more to do there than coop herself up in Barnard's classrooms. Zora admitted to a friend that she was "just running wild in every direction, trying to see everything at once." She was regularly partying with the New Negroes in Harlem, occasionally going downtown to visit Negrotarians Hurst and Van Vechten, writing short stories and plays, working part-time, *and* attending to her studies.

Meyer admonished Zora that she would do well to abandon her Harlem-centered dreams and distractions and to focus all her attention instead on the rigors and routine of Barnard. In response to her patron's reprimand, Zora acknowledged her huge blunder in missing her history exam. (Having copied down the wrong time, she showed up for the test four hours late, only to be greeted by a classroom full of strangers.) "Your rebuke is just," she wrote to Meyer. "I have been guilty of gross forgetfulness." Yet Zora was hesitant to part with her tendency toward reverie, offering an impassioned defense of her intrepid imagination that sounded like an answer to everyone—starting with her father—who had ever criticized her for having ambition, and for reveling in it. "I shall try to lay my dreaming aside. Try hard," she promised Meyer. "But, Oh, if you knew my dreams! My vaulting ambition! How I constantly live in fancy in seven league boots, taking mighty strides across the world, but conscious all the time of being a mouse on a treadmill. Madness ensues. I am beside myself with chagrin half of the time; the way to the blue hills is not on tortoise back, it seems to me, but on wings. I haven't the wings, and must ride the tortoise."

Surely, Zora could feel her wings sprouting daily, but she feared she was not growing swiftly enough to accommodate her ballooning spirit. "The eagerness, the burning within, I wonder the actual sparks do not fly so that they be seen by all men. Prometheus on his rock, with his liver being consumed as fast as he grows another, is nothing to my dreams. I dream such wonderfully complete ones, so radiant in astral beauty. I have not the power yet to make them come true. They always die," she confided. "But even as they fade, I have others."

CHAPTER 13

Heaven and Earth

Zora Hurston's self-regenerating dreams were not the sort she could simply lay aside, despite her vow to her benefactor. And if there was any place her dreams could come true, it seemed to Zora, that place was Harlem.

After explaining to Meyer how she had missed her history exam (which she soon made up), Zora added this coda: "All this is a reason, not an excuse. There is no excuse for a person who lives on Earth, trying to board in Heaven."

There were moments, in 1926, when Zora and her Harlem compatriots felt as if they *were* boarding in heaven—*Negro* heaven. As writer Arna Bontemps remembered it, Harlem in the mid-1920s was "like a foretaste of paradise."

For Zora and many of her contemporaries, the gate to paradise had been nudged open at the first *Opportunity* awards dinner the previous spring. "It was not a spasm of emotion," affirmed its organizer, Charles S. Johnson. "It was intended as the beginning of something, and so it was." Soon after the *Opportunity* triumph, numerous organizations and individuals had begun to practically throw money at Harlem's New Negroes. As a result, *The Crisis* set up its own literary prizes—with a $600 donation from Negrotarian Amy Spingarn—and held its first awards ceremony in August 1925. In January 1926, the William E. Harmon Foundation followed suit by establishing annual prizes for black achievers in seven categories: literature, music, fine arts, industry, science, education, and race relations. In

February, historian Carter G. Woodson, capitalizing on the Negro's newfound notoriety, instituted Negro History Week (which survives today as Black History Month). Also that February, Langston Hughes's *The Weary Blues* was published by Alfred A. Knopf to critical acclaim. (Though friendly with Hughes, Zora was not a fan of his collection's title poem; most of it, she complained, was "a song I and most southerners have known all our lives.")

Zora was suffering from her own weary blues that month. Charles Boni—of Boni & Liveright (which had recently published *The New Negro*)—contacted her in mid-February about publishing a collection of folktales that he hoped she would compile. But her many activities, her days and nights of "running wild in every direction," had caught up with her, and had left her temporarily spent. "I want to start on it," she said of the proposed folklore collection, "but I have so little time what with making a living and everything." In a February 22 letter to Meyer, Zora's fatigue was so evident, she felt compelled to acknowledge it. "I am a mere hunk of mud today, and so this letter is words. Just words," Zora concluded. "The turnip has no blood."

Meanwhile, rewarding talented black artists continued to be in fashion: In March, Boni & Liveright, determined to root out talent, announced a $1,000 prize for "the best novel on Negro life" by a black author. And in April 1926, the second *Opportunity* awards proved another success for the magazine—and for Hurston, who took home a second-place prize for her short story "Muttsy." Among the other winners were Bontemps, Arthur Huff Fauset (Jessie Fauset's half brother), and Dorothy West, the talented teenage cousin of poet Helene Johnson.

With all this activity, the Negro—particularly the Negro artist—was in vogue, as Langston Hughes put it. And black people from Washington, Philadelphia, Boston, and elsewhere acknowledged that Harlem was the undisputed intellectual core of Negro America, the central bank of black cool. Even the mainstream media recognized that a renaissance was happening in Harlem. "It is the Mecca for those who seek Opportunity with a capital O," the *Saturday Evening Post* declared.

If Harlem was Negro heaven, then Barnard grounded Zora firmly on earth. The geographical distance between Barnard and Harlem was deceptively small: Zora's room at 108 West 131st Street, for instance, was less than two miles from Barnard's campus. Harlem occupied a triangular section of northern Manhattan, bordered to the west by St. Nicholas Avenue—running from 114th Street to 156th Street—and to the east by what soon came to be known as the Harlem River. Barnard also was uptown, at 116th and Broadway. But for most Harlemites, Barnard and its brother school, Columbia— with their tennis, golf, and riding lessons—could not have been farther away.

Zora Hurston, on the other hand, was finding a way to bestride both universes. For her, this business of straddling two disparate worlds—of bridging the gap between intellectual circles (both black and white) and the Negro folk community—was beginning to appeal.

In her second term at Barnard—following an adviser's suggestion that she study fine arts, economics, and anthropology to balance out her English- and history-heavy curriculum—Zora made her way to Schermerhorn Hall on Columbia University's campus. There, in 1899, German émigré Franz Boas had founded the first anthropology department at a U.S. university. Though the department was now a quarter century old, and had inspired several imitators, it remained the most influential anthropology department in the country, due partly to Boas's esteem as the nation's leading anthropologist. Zora found Boas "full of youth and fun," but also a taskmaster. He demanded of his students "facts, not guesses," and he could "pin you down so expertly," Zora recalled, that she and her classmates soon lost the habit of making points that they could not defend.

With guidance from Boas and from Melville Herskovits (a former Boas student who now taught at Columbia), Hurston did her first anthropological fieldwork, measuring the skulls of Harlemites to disprove claims of racial inferiority. In terms of anthropological theory, Boas was a pioneer of cultural relativism, which asserts that human values, far from being universal, vary widely according to different cultural perspectives. All cultures were equally developed and equally worthy of respect, Boas believed, and no race was innately superior to another.

Though measuring heads in Harlem was perhaps a dubious and dangerous intellectual pursuit, Zora was able to do it successfully by relying on something that Eatonville had ingrained in her: a natural feeling of ease in the presence of her people, no matter the task at hand. "Almost nobody else could stop the average Harlemite on Lenox Avenue," Langston Hughes would remember, "and measure his head with a strange-looking, anthropological device and not get bawled out for the attempt, except Zora, who used to stop anyone whose head looked interesting, and measure it."

This measuring Zora did as part of her training in anthropometry— the study of human body measurement for use in anthropological classification and comparison. Immediately, Boas recognized Zora's acumen in anthropometry and other aspects of cultural anthropology and began encouraging her vigorously. "Papa Franz," as Boas's students secretly called him, admonished Zora to "learn as quickly as possible, and be quite accurate" in her research. After her training was complete, Boas assured her, she would be on her own, as Zora noted, "with a glorious career before me, if I make good."

Though Boas was roundly revered by his students (all of whom were white save Zora), she was especially inspired by his intellect and by his interest in her. She seemed to view him, albeit playfully, as something of a father figure. Once, at a department social gathering, Zora boldly brought his nickname out of the hush-hush realms of student banter and into Boas's plain view. Before the entire anthropology department, which included Ruth Benedict and Gladys Reichard, Zora recounted bursting into Boas's office a few days before and asking for "Papa Franz," only to be reprimanded by his secretary with a look that said: "Don't let him hear you say that." Zora now wanted to know what Boas thought of the matter. As the whole department held its collective breath, the venerable Dr. Boas responded with a devilish smile and a playfulness that matched Zora's own: "Of course, Zora is my daughter. Certainly!" he said. "Just one of my missteps, that's all."

Misstep or not, where anthropology was concerned, Zora hung on Boas's every word, reminiscent of the way she had admired, as a girl, her father's physical strength and the poetics of his sermons. "Dr. Boas says . . ." became a common refrain in her letters to friends about her studies. And years later, as a mature artist and scholar, she still would regard Boas as "the King of Kings."

Under his tutelage, Zora Hurston found a new passion—and a new career track—in anthropology. This academic discipline gave her a fresh and valuable lens through which to view her people, as they lived in present-day Harlem and in the Eatonville of her memory. Before she'd ever left Eatonville, Zora had draped black folk culture around her like a magnificent shawl. But it was fitting her "like a tight chemise," as she observed. "I couldn't see it for wearing it. It was only when I was off in college, away from my native surroundings, that I could see myself like somebody else and stand off and look at my garment. Then I had to have the spy-glass of Anthropology to look through at that."

Through the clarifying monocle of anthropology, Hurston looked at the men and women she had known in Eatonville and saw that they were no longer simply skilled storytellers whose down-home "lies" were suffused with deep humor and almost-ancient superstitions. And the black folks in Harlem—those she'd met in the community's sanctified churches, as well as those she'd met at raucous rent parties—were no longer simply ambitious comers who'd fled the brutal poverty of the South to make good in the big city. Hurston now recognized that these people, past and present, had priceless contributions to make to the field of cultural anthropology. They were, all of them, natural phenomena who should be studied as closely as any textbook.

With this realization, Zora found her anthropological studies both demanding and rewarding. Boas could "make people work the hardest with just a look or a word," she later recalled. Yet this hard work helped to ease the boredom Zora was beginning to feel with the routine that Barnard required. "The regular grind at Barnard is beginning to drive me lopsided," she complained in March, soon before her spring break. "Don't be surprised to hear that I have suddenly taken to the woods. I hate routine."

Taking to the woods, in fact, was not an unheard-of path for anthropologists, as Hurston would soon discover. Ever since her girlhood days of longing to explore the horizon, Zora had always been hungry for knowledge and experience. The discipline of anthropology validated her voracious curiosity and soon became a reliable tool that she would regularly employ to satisfy her continuous yearning to see and to know.

To satisfy her longing to express, she had Harlem. There, Zora relished the opportunity to live and work among other black writers and artists. The small, loosely formed gang of literary bohemians that she gravitated toward called themselves "the Niggerati," an inspired moniker that was simultaneously self-mocking and self-glorifying, and sure to shock the stuffy black bourgeoisie. A natural at nomenclature, Zora has been credited with conjuring up the evocative name for the talented and elastic group, which usually included writers Langston Hughes, Wallace Thurman, Gwendolyn Bennett, and Richard Bruce Nugent, artist Aaron Douglas, sculptor Augusta Savage, Harlem schoolteacher Harold Jackman, Harvard Law student John P. Davis, and teacher and actress Dorothy Peterson. The group routinely expanded to also embrace writers Arna Bontemps, Countee Cullen, Helene Johnson, Dorothy West, and a small, ever-evolving crew of other friends and acquaintances.

With these kindred spirits, Zora's Eatonville-bred streak of humor thrived and was appreciated. With them, she could talk freely and philosophically about "our business of dream weaving that we call writing," as she put it. With them, she could talk literature, she could talk politics, or she could talk trash. With them, she could laugh at the mysterious ways of white folks, lament the woes of black folks, and join in that old and complex Negro refrain: "My people, my people!" With them, she could stay up all night telling stories, singing spirituals, or stomping the blues. With them, she could be most fully herself.

Zora's selfhood, one friend felt, was deeply indigenous: "Zora would have been Zora if she'd been an Eskimo," Richard Bruce Nugent proclaimed.

Nugent, once called "the perfumed orchid of the New Negro movement," was slender and handsome. He looked like he might have been Langston Hughes's brother, only he was a bit prettier than Hughes: his eyes were more playful, his lashes more dense, and his lips more lush—and often, it seemed, on the verge of reckless laughter. Among the Niggerati, Nugent recalled, "I was kind of like the errand boy and the court jester. I really had great license to do almost anything because I was the youngest one." Nugent used that license lavishly, frequently romping through the city with no underwear, no socks, and occasionally no shoes, but always with a gold bead adorning one pierced earlobe.

Perhaps the freest spirit in a very free-spirited bunch, he was vaguely interested in writing, drawing, and fashion design. Because such things mattered to him, Nugent remembered, he was impressed with Zora's unconventional sense of style. "Zora had a unique way of being able to dress very stylishly and it wasn't any style at all. But she always looked as though it were. . . . She was one of the few people that I know that wore her clothes instead of her clothes wearing her." This comfort in her clothes, and in her body, was indicative of Zora's innate sense of self, Nugent felt, and a reflection of her singular personality. "She was not the gentle person of Langston, she was not the smart-alecky person of Wallie, she was not the unsure person that I was. She was not the anything that any of the rest of us were. She had these qualities that were hers, and hers alone."

One of those qualities, Nugent assessed, was the ability to comfortably mingle with people of all sorts. Yet Zora also "was very capable of saying exactly what was on her mind," sometimes in a "caustic" way, as he recalled. "She had strong likes and dislikes and she had no hesitancy about making them known. She had the woman's proclivity to say the cutting thing." But with the Niggerati, Zora's bluntness usually won her admiration rather than animosity, Nugent noted. She was, he added, "one of the most alive people" he knew.

Next to Hurston (the self-proclaimed and undisputed "Queen of the Niggerati") and the already popular poet Langston Hughes, the circle's most prominent and vocal member was Wallie Thurman. The twenty-three-year-old writer had arrived in Harlem from Los Angeles on Labor Day 1925, as a friend recalled, "with nothing but his nerve." Thurman became an editor at *The Messenger* and was soon widely regarded—by Hurston, Hughes, and other members of the Niggerati—as a leader among them.

Meanwhile, a more widely recognized black leader, W.E.B. Du Bois, had founded the Krigwa Players under the auspices of the NAACP and *The Crisis*. The group (originally called CRIGWA, an acronym for Crisis Guild of Writers and Artists) was assembled from those who'd sent in manuscripts for *Crisis* literary prizes. Zora was among the early members of Krigwa and apparently played a role in establishing its Little Negro Theatre, though the details of her involvement have been largely lost to history.

As early as June 1925, Zora had envisioned herself as "chief mid-wife" of a New Negro theater company that was "about to be born." She evidently played a lesser role in Du Bois's theatrical venture than she had anticipated, though still a significant one. In a January 1926 letter to Hurston, Du Bois informed her of the New York Public Library's interest in the idea of the Little Theatre, and assured her that "the money difficulty" could be overcome. In a subsequent letter rejecting Zora's play *The Lilac Bush*, Du Bois wrote: "I rather think it is wiser for us who are conducting the Little Theatre this year if possible not to use our own plays. I am afraid it is going to bring criticism." Still, the Little Negro Theatre managed to stage three plays at the 135th Street library in May. On the heels of the Little Theatre's debut, Du Bois, in a *Crisis* editorial, laid down four essential criteria for black theater. It must be: (1) about us, (2) by us, (3) for us, and (4) near us—that is, "in a Negro neighborhood near the mass of ordinary Negro people," he wrote.

In the mid-1920s, however, it was difficult to meet the second criterion. Finding plays by black writers—particularly pieces that met Du Bois's exacting standards for art as propaganda—proved challenging. Thus Du Bois corresponded with Hurston about using some of her plays, including *The First One*, a comedy based on the biblical legend of Ham. Du Bois was interested in producing the "very beautiful" play, as he called it, but he suggested some changes, which Zora agreed to make at once. "Could you, or would you, bring it past my place soon?" she asked him. "In that way, I shall get a visit out of you without your suspecting it."

Despite her chummy correspondence with Du Bois, Zora and others among the Niggerati had begun to object to the esteemed editor's increasingly strident insistence that Negro art be both beautiful and propagandistic. Rejecting the notion of art simply for art's sake, Du Bois had written in a January 1926 *Crisis* editorial: "We want Negro writers to produce beautiful things but we stress the things rather than the beauty." A few months later, he made his position bluntly clear: "I do not care a damn for any art that is not used for propaganda."

The Niggerati felt differently. Propaganda did not often produce great art, they believed, but frequently compromised it. Members of the Niggerati also were growing more and more uncomfortable with the bourgeois, elitist thrust of the art championed by Du Bois. Rather than mimic white American standards and aesthetics (as black journalist George Schuyler had urged in a June 1926 essay in *The Nation*), they envisioned creating art that reflected and spoke to the common element among Negroes—the folk. These people were not among the "Talented Tenth" that Du Bois believed would uplift the race. These masses, pointed out Niggerati sympathizer Arthur Fauset, were the very people that Du Bois and "that crowd" looked down upon—Negroes "who didn't dress properly, whose fingernails were dirty, and who didn't eat properly, and whose English was not good." During their boisterous nights of conversation and song, the Niggerati envisioned an art that reached "the Negro farthest down," as Hurston would put it, and that reflected black people in all their beauty—and in all their ugliness, too. In response to Schuyler's *Nation* piece, "The Negro-Art Hokum," Langston Hughes published a brilliant essay, in *The Nation*'s next issue, called "The Negro Artist and the Racial Mountain." It expressed most eloquently the burgeoning artistic and aesthetic aims of the Niggerati.

Likening himself and his peers to "the blare of Negro jazz bands" and "the bellowing voice of Bessie Smith singing the Blues," Hughes sought to "penetrate the closed ears of the colored near-intellectuals until they listen and perhaps understand." He called for an art that would cause "the smug Negro middle class to turn from their white, respectable, ordinary books and papers to catch a glimmer of their own beauty." And then Hughes set forth the heretofore-unwritten agenda of the Niggerati:

"We younger Negro artists who create now intend to express our individual dark-skinned selves without fear or shame. If white people are pleased we are glad. If they are not, it doesn't matter. We know we are beautiful. And ugly too. The tom-tom cries and the tom-tom laughs. If colored people are pleased we are glad. If they are not, their displeasure doesn't matter either. We build our temples for tomorrow, strong as we know how, and we stand on top of the mountain, free within ourselves."

This bold manifesto—taken up as a battle cry by Hurston and other members of the Niggerati—soon would face its first trial, by fire.

CHAPTER 14

Tinder

The summer of 1926, despite its scorching days and sweltering nights, must have felt to Hurston like a cool cloth applied to a fevered forehead. It gave her a needed break from the intensity of Barnard, where her first year had been more challenging than her easygoing exterior ever betrayed. "This year has been a great trial of endurance for me. I don't mind saying that more than once I have almost said that I couldn't endure," she admitted to a friend.

"I shall hold on," Zora vowed as her summer caesura approached, "but every time I see a cat slinking in an alley—fearing to walk upright lest again she is crushed back into her slink—I shall go to her and acknowledge the sisterhood in spite of the skin."

Zora still was walking upright when the school year ended and summer delivered on its promise of a rest. Despite her flagging stamina, she had not fared so badly in her spring coursework: She merited Bs in anthropology, anthropometry, English, and physical education. In economics, classical civilizations, and French, she earned Cs.

At the end of June, Zora moved out of Harlem and into an apartment at 43 West Sixty-sixth Street, most likely because her summer anthropological job, secured with Boas's support, required her to be more centrally located than a Harlem address allowed. To furnish her new digs, located in a small downtown row of Negro houses, she threw a Zora-ized version of a rent party. It was a "furniture party," and each guest was required to bring a piece. Zora got plenty of lamps and knickknacks, and even a footstool. Though she grumbled a little about not receiving much furniture to sit on—couches and chairs were too big for her carless Harlem friends to haul on the subway—Zora still provided the party meal. It was, as Langston Hughes remembered, "a *hand*-chicken dinner," because nobody brought forks.

"I have been going through all the hells of moving into a flat," Zora noted as she settled into her new apartment, a short walk from Fannie Hurst's place. "I am now in my flat and flattened out by honest but grimy toil."

Zora's summer was not all toil, however. Her apartment quickly became a popular downtown den for the Niggerati, and Zora welcomed them by habitually keeping a pot of something on the stove. "She was always prepared to feed people," Richard Bruce Nugent remembered. On some evenings, when she felt particularly ambitious, Zora would treat her friends to one of her specialties: fried shrimp and okra. And she soon discovered that a pan of gingerbread and a jug of buttermilk could feed a roomful of New Negroes. "It fills 'em up quick so you don't have to give 'em so much," a budget-minded Zora once deadpanned.

Her generosity with food, Nugent believed, was emblematic of a larger, more notable munificence. Perhaps because of the hunger she had experienced not long before, Zora "would know when you were hungry," recalled the chronically broke Nugent. "She always knew when you were and always did something about it. Not just food, but anything that you might be hungry for."

Accordingly, Zora's quarters were always available for friends needing a place to stay (Nugent lived with her for a time) or a place to create ("I wrote at Zora's because she had paper, pencils, and the space," he noted). Her apartment was a spirited open house for artists and the site of frequent spontaneous get-togethers, as one friend recounted. Zora—"all greased curls, bangles, and slashes of red"—usually presided over the festivities with her harmonica and her head full of stories. At other times, though, she worked quietly in the bedroom while her friends partied boisterously in the living room. And occasionally, if she had an appointment, Zora would just leave, announcing that the last one out should lock the door.

Although a festive atmosphere reigned at Zora's apartment, her place was an oasis of calm compared with the Niggerati's hangout in

Harlem—a rooming house at 267 West 136th Street, where the owner provided rent-free rooms to artists. Among its tenants were Wallace Thurman (accompanied by his white male lover) and—in the summer of 1926—Langston Hughes, on break from Lincoln University in Pennsylvania. With both Thurman and Hughes living there, and Zora hopping the uptown subway for frequent visits, "267 House" soon became the Harlem headquarters of the New Negro vanguard. And Hurston and Thurman promptly gave it a new name: "Niggerati Manor."

The rooming house became infamous for its hedonistic happenings. "Those were the days when Niggerati Manor was the talk of the town," recalled Harlemite Theophilus Lewis. Inside, the building was decorated in red and black, with gaudy wicker furniture. To reflect Thurman's sexual interests, brightly painted phalluses adorned the walls. The paintings were courtesy of the flamboyantly homosexual Nugent, one of the habitues of Niggerati Manor—where, the rumor mill claimed, "gin flowed from all the water taps."

Its licentious reputation notwithstanding, the rooming house was the site of some enterprising artistic labor. There, in midsummer, Hurston and Hughes began discussing the possibility of working on a project together, a black opera based on jazz and the blues. While they shared a similar passion for black folk culture and an almost-equal regard for the folk, Langston and Zora would bring diverse strengths to such a collaboration. He'd already garnered experience writing song lyrics for a full-scale Negro revue that was in the works (*O Blues*). And she possessed a knowledge of the black South and its folkways that was unrivaled by any other Renaissance writer. (She was, in fact, the only one from the South. Hughes, for example, had grown up in Kansas, Countee Cullen was from New York, Richard Bruce Nugent and Gwendolyn Bennett had come of age in Washington, and both Arna Bontemps and Wallace Thurman had moved to Harlem from California.) Hurston also had some experience writing for the stage: In 1925, she'd won an *Opportunity* award for her play *Color Struck*; the same year, she'd filed a copyright request for a musical comedy, partially set in Harlem, called *Meet the Mamma*. The musical presumably was never produced or published and its broad humor succeeds only intermittently. Yet it stands as evidence of Hurston's early interest in exploring Negro life in musical theater. Still, Hurston and Hughes made little progress on their proposed folk opera; they became distracted by a more immediate collaborative challenge.

That summer, they began working—along with Thurman, Nugent, Bennett, John P. Davis, and artist Aaron Douglas—to create a magazine that would exemplify the ideals Hughes had set forth in his essay "The Negro Artist and the Racial Mountain." According to Nugent, the magazine was Hughes's idea: "He suggested that maybe someone should start a magazine by, for, and about the Negro to show what we could do." Getting the magazine from idea to publication, however, would be a communal endeavor. The quarterly magazine the Niggerati collectively envisioned would be aesthetically undiluted by sociological issues and propaganda efforts. It would reflect the proletariat rather than the bourgeoisie, and it would challenge the Victorian morality of the Negro establishment. They would call it *Fire!!*

This new magazine would be "purely literary," as Hurston saw it. "The way I look at it," she said, "*The Crisis* is the house organ of the NAACP and *Opportunity* is the same to the Urban League. They are in literature on the side." Zora and her friends hoped that *Fire!!* "would burn up a lot of the old, dead conventional Negro-white ideas of the past," as Hughes recalled. It would prove to the world that the younger Negro artists "were going to do something big and black and wonderful," Nugent felt. "I believe we can run the other magazines ragged," Zora instigated. To serve as editor of *Fire!!*, the group chose Thurman, "the fullest embodiment," as one observer has noted, "of outrageous, amoral independence among them."

Skinny, effeminate, cynical, and overly sensitive about his coal-black skin, Thurman was, according to Hughes, "a strangely brilliant black boy, who had read everything, and whose critical mind could find something wrong with everything he read." Perhaps Thurman's most remarkable quality, Dorothy West remembered, was his deep, resonant voice, "welling up out of his too-frail body and wasting its richness in unprintable recountings." In a group of people as witty, talented, and cocksure as the Niggerati, Thurman, remarkably, was something of a bellwether. As West put it, "Thurman fitted into this crowd like a cap on a bottle of fizz."

Despite his drinking binges, his frequent all-nighters, and his pursuits of public sex (he was arrested in a subway bathroom a few days after arriving in Harlem), Thurman often worked as hard as he played. For those who bought into the notion that an artist's life must be poverty-stricken, intense, and quickly spent, he was a perfect poster boy. For the Niggerati, Thurman—with his keen, California-honed editorial skills, his uncompromising commitment to the folk, and his acrimonious impatience with bourgeois party-line art—was the perfect leader for the *Fire!!* charge.

One of his goals for *Fire!!*, for instance, was to get it banned in Boston. Such a controversy, Thurman believed, would boost sales. So the group brainstormed on what they might include that would be shocking enough to warrant the magazine's prohibition. After a coin toss, they decided Thurman would write about a teen prostitute, and Nugent about a homosexual. *Fire!!*, its founders intended, would reflect black life in all its complexities—the decadent, the divine, and the disconcerting.

In many ways, New York—and particularly Harlem—seemed ripe for a venture as daring as *Fire!!* In the 1920s, America witnessed a shift from Victorian morality to modernist blasphemy. Nowhere was this sea change more evident than in the nation's most powerful city. The capital of American literature, music and theater, New York in the 1920s was a dazzling metropolis of new skyscrapers, instant gratification, and a nonchalant tolerance of debauchery. In some quarters, debauchery and decadence not only were tolerated but enthusiastically encouraged—often under the influence of popular sexologist Sigmund Freud. The father of psychoanalysis, he "sexualized the narrative of Western culture," as one writer has put it, "and no one got the revamped storyline better than his American fans."

In this decade of unprecedented permissiveness, the term "sex appeal" entered the American vocabulary, contraceptives were publicly promoted, advertisers began pandering to subconscious sexual motives, and popular blues songs traded in transparent double entendres. Even milquetoast magazines such as *Good Housekeeping* warned that the sex drive was something to be reckoned with: "If it gets its yearning it is as contented as a nursing infant. If it does not, beware! It will never be stopped except with satisfactions."

In the 1920s—a new age of individuality, tell-all, and technology—few subjects escaped discussion. "This generation was the first in American history to make, buy, and fit into ready-made, exact-sized (rather than 'stock-sized') clothing. Its members patented electric Victrolas, cameras, microphones, radios, and talking pictures and initiated IQ tests, sex education, birth-control clinics, opinion polls, consumer organizations, and syndicated gossip columns," scholar Ann Douglas has catalogued. "Aiming to leave little or nothing to the imagination, they found out more about themselves, how they looked, how they sounded, what they wore, what they said and did, with whom, where, and why, than any previous generation had ever done, and they made of self-knowledge a fad and an industry."

Not only was self-knowledge valued in this brave new world, but so was self-expression—both artistic and sexual. Mae West's *Sex* was the hottest ticket on Broadway in 1926. (Zora saw the raunchy tabloid drama and pronounced it a must-see.) The same year, *The Captive*, a play about a married woman's seduction by a lesbian, briefly scandalized the Great White Way. Meanwhile, dancer and movie star Louise Brooks was hailed in a 1926 magazine profile as the epitome of New York style because she knew how to "BE COOL AND LOOK HOT." Elsewhere, Brooks announced, in crude and certain terms, that her favorite pastimes were drinking and having sex. And she did plenty of both, sometimes very publicly. Her behavior was not uncommon: several white Manhattan cultural figures were known to engage in public sex acts, and many bragged loudly about their private exploits.

For some white sophisticates—seeking distance from their usual circles, either for a dash of discretion or for more "exotic" playmates—Harlem became an uptown playground. Among those who frequented Harlem in the 1920s were William Faulkner, George Gershwin, Charlie Chaplin, Jimmy Durante, Tallulah Bankhead, Muriel Draper, Theodore Dreiser, and Alexander Woollcott. Most of them were "mere sightseers," as Langston Hughes recalled, "faddists temporarily in love with Negro life." Drawn as much by the irresistible blues and jazz as by Harlem's supposedly loose morals, they journeyed uptown in search of the uninhibited ecstasy that some believed was the Negro's natural state. For these white thrill seekers, Harlem—brimming with jazz, sex, and alcohol—represented all that America, in a rebellious mood, wished to be.

"The Negro," historian Steven Watson has observed, "perfectly satisfied progressive America's psychological and intellectual needs of the moment—he represented pagan spirituality in a period of declining religion, native American expressiveness at the time the nation was forging its own aesthetic, and the polymorphous sensuality that exemplified the 1920s' loosening of behavior."

The decade witnessed the rise of Josephine Baker, Paul Robeson, Roland Hayes, Duke Ellington, Ethel Waters, and Louis Armstrong. It signaled the beginning of the blackening of American culture. Or, as crusty white journalist H. L. Mencken so crassly put it, it was "the Coon Age." By the mid-1920s, a kind of Harlemania had set in. "Negro stock is going up," Harlem writer and physician Rudolph Fisher declared, "and everybody's buying."

Leading the white influx into Harlem was cosmopolitan trend-setter Carl Van Vechten. "Sullen-mouthed, silky-haired Author Van Vechten has been playing with Negroes lately," *Time* magazine noticed in 1925. He was "writing prefaces for their poems, having them around the house, going to Harlem." Blond, buck-toothed, and occasionally blundering, Van Vechten nevertheless was widely regarded as one of the hippest white men in America. He was reputedly the first man in New York to wear a wristwatch, and he otherwise set fashion standards in a notably fashionable city. In the 1920s, however, Van Vechten found nothing more fashionable than the Negro.

In a personal crusade to break down the color bar, Van Vechten and his wife, Russian-born actress Fania Marinoff, hosted frequent interracial parties—gatherings that were "*so* Negro that they were reported as a matter of course in the colored society columns," according to Hughes. And when he wasn't hosting mixed-race parties at his luxurious Fifty-fifth Street apartment, Van Vechten—his sterling-silver hip flask in tow—was often in Harlem, where he routinely served as a tour guide for prominent whites slumming uptown.

Mexican artist Miguel Covarrubias, friendly with Zora and others of the Niggerati, drew a caricature of Van Vechten in 1926 with an ink-black face. Tellingly, he called it "A Prediction." Van Vechten's passion for all things black was so all-consuming that his white friends—even fellow Negrotarians like Fannie Hurst—sometimes wearied of hearing about it. In May 1926, for instance, Hurst invited

Van Vechten to a "taboo-tea" in which they would talk about something—*anything*—else. "Taboo—just for once! The Negro," she pleaded.

Some Harlemites, too, were unnerved by Van Vechten's ubiquitous Nordic presence and especially by the herds of whites he ushered uptown. "Harlem is an all-white picnic ground and with no apparent gain to the blacks," Claude McKay groused from his outpost in Europe. Others, like Rudolph Fisher, took a more optimistic approach: "Maybe these Nordics at last have tuned in on our wavelength," he ventured.

Zora seemed rather indifferent to the white presence in Harlem. She didn't mind sharing a table with a white carouser in one of her favorite nightclubs if the visitor was sincerely interested in black culture, as she judged Van Vechten to be. Still, when a white person was "set down in our midst," Zora noted, she became acutely aware of the contrasts between black and white. Listening to the "narcotic harmonies" of a jazz band could move her to a feral inner state: "I dance wildly inside myself; I yell within, I whoop . . . ," Hurston once wrote. "My face is painted red and yellow and my body is painted blue. My pulse is throbbing like a war drum." Eventually the music ended and the jazz shamans wiped their lips and put down their instruments. And, inevitably, when Zora crept back "to the veneer we call civilization," she would be startled to find "the white friend sitting motionless in his seat, smoking calmly," as she observed. "'Good music they have here,' he remarks, drumming the table with his fingertips. Music! The great blobs of purple and red emotion have not touched him. He has only heard what I felt. He is far away and I see him but dimly across the ocean and the continent that have fallen between us," Hurston concluded. "He is so pale with his whiteness then and I am *so* colored."

If Zora met any white people she considered exceptional in this regard, Van Vechten would have been the one. Even so, his headlong infatuation with Harlem was not above reproach. Some Harlemites openly questioned his motives: Van Vechten, despite his marriage, was a "dinge queen"—Harlem slang for a homosexual white man attracted to black men. And nowhere could a dinge queen find more black men to choose from than in the speakeasies of Harlem.

Yet, despite any untoward sexual motives, Van Vechten was "a sincere friend of the Negro," as Richard Bruce Nugent recalled. Abundant evidence backs up Nugent's assessment: Van Vechten served as press agent, vocal champion, generous bank-roller, and trusted confidant for several black intellectuals and artists. He wrote numerous feature articles for *Vanity Fair* lauding the talents of Paul Robeson, Ethel Waters, Bessie Smith, and others. As a result, many of Harlem's brightest stars were devoted to "Carlo," as they called him. Among them, Robeson and Waters, James Weldon Johnson and Walter White of the NAACP, and Niggerati members Hughes, Thurman, and Hurston. "If Carl was a people instead of a person," Zora once said, "I could then say, these are my people."

Van Vechten almost lost his honorary Negro status, however, when his novel *Nigger Heaven* was published in August 1926. The first fictional account of Harlem by a white writer, the novel created a huge controversy while becoming an instant bestseller. With its depictions of common Negroes and Talented Tenth–inspired intellectuals, *Nigger Heaven* divided the black literary community. Many readers couldn't get past the unfortunate title; that it was a play on a common term for the segregated balcony of a theater did little to ease its sting. "Anyone who would call a book *Nigger Heaven* would call a Negro Nigger," *The New York News* opined. Most Harlem Negroes, including Countee Cullen and W.E.B. Du Bois, were deeply offended by the book, which Du Bois called "a blow in the face." Others—including James Weldon Johnson, Walter White, Charles S. Johnson, Wallace Thurman, Langston Hughes, and Zora Hurston— viewed the novel as an accurate reflection of uptown life. "We could find a counterpart in Harlem life for everything Mr. Van Vechten has pictured in his book," James Weldon Johnson defended. It was, if anything, too full of *pro*-Negro propaganda, Hughes suggested. "Colored people can't help but like it," he wrongly predicted.

To the contrary, nothing Van Vechten's supporters said could convince most Harlem Negroes that the book was anything more than "a copyrighted racial slur," as one writer put it. Though the novel was lavishly praised by white readers and critics, someone in Harlem proposed that Van Vechten be hanged in effigy. The managers of Small's Paradise, one of the author's favorite Harlem nightspots, exacted a harsher punishment, in Van Vechten's view: they barred him from entering the club. Other black-owned speakeasies followed suit, and Van Vechten was mortified. After a while, he became desperate enough to defy the ban. To successfully do so, however, he had to have a formidable escort: Zora Neale Hurston.

To be indefinitely banned from Harlem's nightlife would have been close to personal tragedy for Van Vechten, who reveled in nightclubbing and its attendant vices. He had become so noted for his nocturnal forays into Harlem that he was soon immortalized in song. The popular "Go Harlem" (with lyrics by Harlemite Andy Razaf) urged listeners to "go inspectin' like Van Vechten." And the lumbering six-footer had gone inspecting practically everywhere, from NAACP dances at Happy Rhone's nightclub to transvestite costume balls at the Rockland Palace and the Savoy Ballroom.

Van Vechten's image-conscious Negro detractors might not have minded so much if he had only portrayed NAACP dinners and the like in his novel; it was the drag balls that worried them. Put another way, *Nigger Heaven* created such a flurry of controversy partly because it exposed what many black people thought of as "family secrets," as Charles S. Johnson pointed out. Perhaps most notably, the novel gleefully bared the sexual underbelly of Harlem.

During the experimental 1920s, Harlem was known among erotic adventurers for its "buffet flats," house parties where all manner of sexual activity—hetero and homo—was proffered, cafeteria style. Patrons paid a small admittance fee then were free to roam. "They had shows in every room, two women goin' together, a man and a man goin' together . . . and if you interested they do the same thing to you," one Harlemite recalled.

Harlem's sexual sparks were so pervasive that they singed even people who wouldn't be caught dead at a buffet flat. To be sure, the atmosphere was sexually charged at most of the swank uptown dance clubs: Small's, the Savoy Ballroom, and the Rockland Palace. And the mix of swank and bawdy became noticeably bawdier at the working-class speakeasies along "Jungle Alley"—the main drag of nightspots on 133rd Street between Lenox and Seventh Avenues. Bootleg liquor flowed freely in Jungle Alley, and marijuana—Harlemites called it "reefer"—could be purchased at a rate of ten cigarettes for a dollar.

Several Harlem nightclubs, like the Savoy and the Yeahman, catered to sexually diverse crowds—though, as Van Vechten suggested in *Nigger Heaven*, heterosexual patrons sometimes quit a club when they felt uncomfortably outnumbered. Homosexual night-clubs also thrived uptown: the Ubangi featured a female impersonator who bellowed "Hot Nuts, get 'em from the peanut man!" And at the Clam House, lesbian headliner Gladys Bentley, wearing a tuxedo and top hat, playfully sang "Sweet Georgia Brown." "Miss Bentley was an amazing exhibition of musical energy—a large, dark, masculine lady, whose feet pounded the floor while her fingers pounded the keyboard—a perfect piece of African sculpture, ani-mated by her own rhythm," Langston Hughes enthused.

Hughes obviously had paid a visit or two to the Clam House, the most popular nightclub for those "in the life" (one way black gays and lesbians identified themselves then, as now). Many of the men of the Harlem Renaissance, in fact, were gay or bisexual: Alain Locke, Claude McKay, Countee Cullen, Harold Jackman, and Niggerati stalwarts Nugent, Thurman, and possibly Hughes (who was so furtive in his sexuality as to almost seem asexual).

Less is known about the sexual and affectional preferences of the Harlem Renaissance's women. Angelina Grimke wrote poetry that hinted at her lesbianism, but she was perhaps the only female writer of the Renaissance to publicly express any homosexual leanings. Many of Harlem's most popular female performers, however, were known to be bisexuals, if not unalloyed lesbians: Alberta Hunter, Jackie "Moms" Mabley, Ethel Waters, and Bessie Smith, who was reportedly initiated into the life by her mentor, Gertrude "Ma" Rainey. In 1925, Rainey was arrested for a lesbian orgy at her home and bailed out of jail the next morning by Bessie Smith. Rainey par-layed the public scandal into a hit record, "Prove It on Me Blues," a salacious song about a woman-loving woman.

The popularity of Rainey's tune demonstrated that, in the 1920s, bisexuality (especially among women of wealth or fame) was viewed as intriguing and provocative. Harlem housewives even occasionally engaged in lesbian affairs, sometimes openly and with their hus-bands' approval. While out-and-out lesbianism may have been regarded as deviant, bisexuality seemed to suggest a woman was ultrasexy. And many men did not take the lesbian part of bisexuality seriously. In fact, all of the above-named female performers were married at some point. Of course, Harlem gossips suspected that their marriages were covers and that their husbands were gay. Yet, more often than not, these women were just sexually versatile. And they had chosen the right location to exercise their flexibility: Harlem in the 1920s was a place where people of all sexual stripes could find a comfort zone. "You just did what you wanted to do," Nugent recalled. "Nobody was in the closet. There wasn't any closet."

On the frontlines of Harlem's sexual liberalization was wealthy heiress and voluptuary A'Lelia Walker, who also was married—frequently and usually fleetingly. Harlem's "joy-goddess," as Hughes dubbed her, was "a gorgeous dark Amazon" who could afford to look like a queen and sometimes, as Van Vechten accused, act like a tyrant. Often attended by a small harem of handsome women and pretty men—all ladies-in-waiting, Thurman cattily called them—Walker was so wealthy and influential that her private pleasures had the power to sway public opinion in Harlem. She'd inherited a fortune from her mother, Madam C. J. Walker, a former washerwoman whose "Wonderful Hair Grower" had made her one of the wealthiest women in America and a generous philanthropist for black uplift. In the 1920s, A'Lelia (who continued her mother's hair-care business) spent a large chunk of her riches entertaining New York sophisticates, both black and white. Whether held at her extravagant townhouse on 136th Street (less than two blocks from Niggerati Manor) or at Villa Lewaro (her thirty-four-room mansion on the Hudson River), A'Lelia Walker's sumptuous parties were always as crowded as the New York subway at rush hour, Hughes remembered. Though her gatherings usually attracted a wide cross-section of guests, some of her soirees were mostly intellectual and literary; others were "funny parties," as Harlem dancer Mabel Hampton recalled. "There were men and women, straight and gay. They were kinds of orgies. Some people had clothes on, some didn't. People would hug and kiss on pillows and do anything they wanted to do. You could watch if you wanted to. Some came to watch, some came to play."

Just what role Zora Hurston played in the sexually liberal Harlem of the 1920s remains largely unknowable, particularly from a distance of eight decades. She likely attended A'Lelia Walker's literary parties on occasion. And with her penchant for adventure, Hurston also might have attended one of Walker's "funny parties" or even a buffet flat. "Zora would go anywhere, you know—one time at least," Arna Bontemps observed.

As his comment suggests, Hurston was nothing if not adventurous. And she had no trouble handling herself wherever her adventures might take her, even in parlors and speakeasies where roughnecks and would-be womanizers skulked. Once, for instance, Zora was on her way to a party when she found herself alone in an elevator with an aspiring Beau Diddely (a common name in Negro folklore for a ladies' man). The unfortunate fellow made an overly aggressive move, and Zora—decked out in a willowy white dress and a wide-brimmed hat—coldcocked him with a roundhouse right that left him sprawled on the elevator floor. She then calmly stepped over the erstwhile playboy, exited the elevator, and went on to her party.

Clearly, Hurston was an independent woman, one who, for the most part, went wherever she wanted to go and did whatever she wanted to do. It's easy to imagine, then, that Zora was as independent and adventurous sexually as she was in other areas of her life, particularly during a period when sexual exploration was not only tolerated but, in her own constellation of friends, encouraged.

Hurston certainly did not shy away from the unorthodox act. One sunny summer day, Nugent remembered, he and Zora were walking down Seventh Avenue when she suddenly asked him: "Will you walk on the street with me if I smoke a cigarette?" Zora, who preferred Pall Malls, knew that 1920s propriety frowned upon women smoking in public. But Nugent was game. He lit a cigarette for her in front of the Lafayette Theatre, then watched people's reactions in amused amazement. "They stared at this fallen woman, smoking a cigarette on the street in broad daylight," he recalled. Soon, the pair mischievously lit another cigarette, then another. "And so here we go, the fallen woman and the sissy walking down Seventh Avenue smoking cigarettes." Only days later did Nugent realize "that this really was an act of defiance on Zora's part."

The defiant Hurston rubbed shoulders with Harlem's most worldly women, history tells, including Bessie Smith, Jackie Mabley, and Ethel Waters. Hurston and Waters eventually became good friends, according to Hurston's autobiography, in which she devoted several pages to a discussion of "This Ethel Waters."

Tall and slender, Waters had dreamy eyes and a seductive, gap-toothed smile. Once billed as "Sweet Mama Stringbean," she recorded, for Black Swan Records, the 1921 hit "Down Home Blues," with "Oh Daddy" on the flip side. By the mid-1920s, the high-salaried singer and actress was well on her way to becoming one of America's most popular and enduring black stars.

Van Vechten introduced Hurston and Waters at a dinner party in Hurston's honor. "He was fond of her himself," Zora wrote, "and he knew I wanted to get to know her better, so he had persuaded her to come. Carl is given to doing nice things like that."

Hurston spoke lovingly of Waters: "She is shy and you must convince her that she is really wanted before she will open up her tender parts and show you." Though these may be simply innocent words of friendly admiration, Hurston's intimate, almost-homoerotic tone has raised questions recently among gay studies scholars—particularly since Waters's bisexuality has been well documented. Perhaps Hurston (who could wield a witty double-entendre as well as anyone when she wanted to) was being slyly literal, as well as figurative, when she wrote of her closeness with Waters, of their ability to speak for each other, this way: "I am her friend, and her tongue is in my mouth."

Regardless of its nature, the hermetic Hurston-Waters friendship seems to have crested later, in the 1930s and early forties. In 1926, most of Zora's closest friends were homosexual men like Nugent, Thurman, and Van Vechten. With them, she surely went to see Gladys Bentley perform at the Clam House and she no doubt went dancing at the Rockland Palace and other nightclubs where homosexuals and heterosexuals partied side by side.

Zora gave the distinct impression, Bontemps recalled, that she was a free woman. "There was nothing in her that I saw that suggested a love affair in Harlem. She certainly seemed self-sufficient." Noting that Zora did not appear attached to any particular man in the 1920s, Bontemps also acknowledged that she did not seem the type who would abstain from any worldly pleasures.

Though she had a reputation for flamboyance, Zora could be quite guarded about private matters; discretion about any Harlem amours, then, would have been characteristic. Her discretion also would have been warranted by the fact that she was still in a long-distance relationship with Herbert Sheen.

Given the span between New York and Chicago, however, Hurston and Sheen did not necessarily view monogamy as an imperative. "At the time I was going around with Zora, I had so many other girlfriends that it was almost confusing," admitted Sheen, whose kind eyes, princely handsomeness, and bright future in medicine had won him plenty of female admirers. "It was just, you might say, too hard to turn them down. But we never had any difficulties there," he added, citing Zora's broadmindedness. "I don't remember having any difficulties with Zora about this. Zora was always magnanimous; whatever pleased me was all right with her."

Perhaps Zora's magnanimity was a result of her being "wrapped up in her work," as Sheen believed. Or perhaps she also was immersed in an erotic life of her own. If any of Zora's amorous adventures were with women, these experiences only would have contributed to her broadmindedness. And they would have been temporary jaunts: All evidence suggests that Zora's abiding sexual and romantic interests were men. Yet her broad perspective on issues of gender and sexuality—kindled in the sexual tinderbox that was Harlem—would inform her life, and her work, for decades.

Nugent, who was Zora's roommate for a while, viewed her as an extraordinarily multifarious woman—"an integrated person," as he put it—who had the capacity to understand and appreciate human diversity in all its complex forms. Zora certainly knew about—and was comfortable with—Nugent's homosexuality, for example. In turn, Nugent knew that when Zora had certain company, his added presence constituted a crowd. "Whatever I 'knew' about Zora and her loves," he recalled, "didn't mean anything to me except, 'Don't stay too long . . . maybe they want to be alone,' that sort of thing."

Nugent added elliptically: "I knew that Zora was very capable of doing whatever she wanted to do with her life and her body."

CHAPTER 15

Fire and Sweat

In the midst of all their amorous activity, Zora and her *Fire!!* colleagues had a magazine to produce. Each of the seven founders agreed to contribute fifty dollars to finance the first issue, and they also planned to seek sponsors. Law school student John P. Davis was the magazine's business manager, and the outgoing Nugent was selected to handle distribution. The others served as an editorial board, collecting material and contributing their own writing. Thurman, as editor, suggested the kind of work he wanted from each contributor, then they were all left to select their own pieces.

This process worked well: the collaborators experienced no content disagreements at all, according to Nugent. "For artists and writers," Hughes confirmed, "we got along fine and there were no quarrels." Nugent added: "It was really a very fine kind of communal effort in a way." But the fall arrived before the editorial work was completed, and Hughes had to return to school in Pennsylvania, Davis to Harvard, Gwen Bennett to her job on the fine arts faculty at Howard, and Hurston to her studies at Barnard. Thurman made a change during this period, too; he left *The Messenger* for a job at a white magazine, *The World Tomorrow*. Still, he continued to work on *Fire!!*, planning the layout, finding a printer, and selecting the paper—a thick, cream-colored stock, as Hughes remembered, that was "worthy of the drawings of Aaron Douglas," regarded then (and now) as the foremost visual artist of the Harlem Renaissance.

Two days before the magazine was to go to press, however, an actual fire at Zora's apartment almost extinguished *Fire!!* As Nugent recalled, Zora's youngest brother, Everett, was living with her at the time. Though he was not involved with the Niggerati, twenty-eight-year-old Everett was closer in age to most of its members than was Zora. (At thirty-five, she was several years older than the other *Fire!!* contributors, but her colleagues were unsuspecting: "We are all under thirty," one wrote.) The short story Nugent had penned—the piece that was supposed to help get *Fire!!* banned in Boston—was at Zora's place, along with many of Nugent's other belongings. Innocently oblivious, Everett used the short story and some other papers as kindling for a fire. Nugent was devastated—and furious with Everett. Yet Zora somehow managed to defuse the tension, Nugent remembered. "She never made that boy feel bad about it; she never made me think she was minimizing the loss. . . . So I took a roll of toilet paper and several paper bags and got on the subway and wrote the thing over again."

Fire!!—"devoted to younger Negro artists"—finally appeared in November 1926. It sported a dramatic red-and-black cover by Aaron Douglas that evoked ancient Africa as well as modern sensibilities. The foreword announced the magazine's intention to burn "wooden opposition with a cackling chuckle of contempt." And in his intentionally inflammatory editorial, "Fire Burns," Thurman boldly defended persona non grata Carl Van Vechten, who was one of the nine patrons for *Fire!!* Rather than hang the *Nigger Heaven* author in effigy, Thurman suggested, Harlem Negroes should build a statue on the corner of 135th Street and Seventh Avenue to enshrine Van Vechten "for his pseudo-sophisticated, semi-serious, semi-ludicrous effusion about Harlem."

Throughout its forty-eight pages, *Fire!!* broke ranks with the Talented Tenth propagandists by celebrating jazz, blues, uninhibited sexuality, and the natural black beauty of the folk. It was, as one historian has declared, "a flawed, folk-centered masterpiece." Unlike Alain Locke's *The New Negro*, *Fire!!* was not assembled by a single impresario, so it painted a more complex picture of the New Negro vanguard—many of whom were creating at their peak. In a personal letter to introduce *Fire!!*, one of its contributors effectively distilled the group's ethos: "We have no get-rich-quick complexes. . . . We have no axes to grind. . . . We are primarily and intensely devoted to art. We believe that the Negro is fundamentally, essentially different from their Nordic neighbors. We are proud of that difference. We believe these differences to be greater spiritual endowment, greater sensitivity, greater power for artistic expression and appreciation. We believe Negro art should be trained and developed rather than capitalized and exploited. We believe finally that Negro art without Negro patronage is an impossibility."

All the contributors may have shared these collective views, but the works they published in *Fire!!* were remarkably diverse: Helene Johnson's searing poem, "A Southern Road," was about a lynching, and Gwendolyn Bennett's story, "Wedding Day," was about a Negro in Paris. Hughes supplied the magazine with two fine poems (displaying "his usual ability to say nothing in many words," one critic huffed); Countee Cullen and Arna Bontemps each offered a poem; and Hurston contributed her play *Color Struck* and an exceptional short story, "Sweat."

The pieces that got the most attention from reviewers, however, were the two that had been calculated to rile: Thurman's "Cordelia the Crude" and Nugent's lovely, stream-of-consciousness homosexual riff, "Smoke, Lilies and Jade," which he wrote under the pseudonym Richard Bruce, in consideration for his mother. A black critic in Baltimore, labeling the magazine "Effeminate Tommyrot," began his review by snorting: "I have just tossed the first issue of *Fire!!* into the fire." White critics barely noticed the magazine's existence, but those who did were enthusiastic: One white reviewer called *Fire!!* "original in all its aspects." Yet many black people seemed to think it was *too* original. At Craig's restaurant on 135th Street, where the founders of *Fire!!* had sometimes held editorial meetings, they were given the cold shoulder by staff and patrons. And, Hughes reported, "none of the older Negro intellectuals would have anything to do with *Fire!!*" A friend told Cullen that merely mentioning *Fire!!* to Du Bois hurt the redoubtable editor's feelings so much that he fell into a sullen silence. Publicly, Du Bois refrained from commenting on *Fire!!*, but another pillar of the black establishment, literary critic Benjamin Brawley, fumed: "If Uncle Sam ever finds out about it, it will be debarred from the mails."

Though the magazine was never banned from mailboxes (not even in Boston), it did not sell well. The $1 cover price was too hefty for many Harlem readers, who preferred to pass a single copy from hand to hand rather than invest in their own. The proletariat's inability to afford *Fire!!* was not its only problem. "We had no way of getting it distributed to bookstands or news stands," Hughes recalled. "Bruce Nugent took it around New York on foot and some of the Greenwich Village bookshops put it on display, and sold it for us. But then Bruce, who had no job, would collect the money and . . . eat it up before he got back to Harlem."

In the end, *Fire!!* cost nearly $1,000 to produce, close to $10,000 in today's currency. Because only three of the founders could actually afford to contribute their fifty dollars (Zora was not among them), Thurman had to sign a promissory note to get the printer to release all the magazines for distribution. But then hundreds of unsold copies—stored in the basement of a Harlem apartment house—burned in an all-too-ironic fire.

Fire!! was finished after only one issue. And Thurman became personally responsible for the printer's debt. To help defray the bill, Hurston, Hughes, and others sent him money when they could. (An optimistic Zora still was soliciting subscribers in the spring of 1927.) But for the next three or four years, Thurman's paychecks were periodically garnisheed to pay the debt. "*Fire!!* is certainly burning me," he complained.

Still, the inauspicious extinction of *Fire!!* did not break its founders' radical spirits. In less than a year, Thurman would try again with another magazine, *Harlem*. And a headstrong Hurston would write: "I suppose that *Fire!!* has gone to ashes quite, but I still think the idea is good."

Hurston's refusal to give up so easily on *Fire!!* bespeaks her intention to do more than just make "a big, black splash" with the magazine—something Nugent believed several of the other contributors were satisfied to do. "I think that only two, maybe three, of that Niggerati group felt anything more than this surface business of 'how can I make a splash,'" he judged, counting himself among the superficial majority. The exceptions, he said, were Hughes, Thurman, and Hurston. "And I think more than any other people, Zora and Langston were the ones who gave *Fire!!* any of the artistic solidity that it had."

Even if all the magazine's founders did not recognize its historic importance, *Fire!!* was an inspired idea, and much of its content had enduring literary value. The two pieces Hurston contributed to the magazine, in fact, represented the zenith of her literary output during the Harlem Renaissance.

Her play *Color Struck*, which she'd used as her woof ticket at the 1925 *Opportunity* dinner, is ostensibly about a group of Jacksonville Negroes on their way to a statewide cakewalk—a dance contest in which the best dancers, or walkers, literally take the cake, supposedly the biggest one ever baked in Florida. On the surface, the play is a light, folk-centered romp. But *Color Struck* is really about a dark-skinned woman who, as one character puts it, "so despises her own skin that she can't believe any one else could love it." Though it is clearly an apprentice work, *Color Struck* was, for the 1920s, "an idea of searing, complex irony," as one critic has noted.

Hurston's other piece in *Fire!!*, "Sweat," is a story of enormous tension, nuance, and complexity—arguably her finest fiction from the decade. At the story's core is Delia, an Eatonville washerwoman whose fifteen-year marriage to the abusive Sykes has been, as she puts it, an endless cycle of "work and sweat, cry and sweat, pray and sweat." Sykes has begrudged Delia every moment of her work, even while refusing to contribute to the household coffers. Instead, Sykes—apparently feeling emasculated by Delia's financial independence—berates her for the service-oriented nature of her work: "Ah done tole you time and again to keep them white folks' clothes outa dis house," he rages.

Over the years, Sykes has beaten Delia "enough tuh kill three women, let 'lone change they looks," as one of the men in the community observes. Disgusted now by Delia's thin body and haggard appearance—as much a result of his beatings as the physically demanding work his indolence has forced her to do—Sykes casts Delia aside for a more robust mistress, whom he flaunts before Delia and all of Eatonville. Sykes's behavior is so odious that the village men, gathering on the porch of Joe Clarke's store, briefly consider killing him as a community service. Porch philosopher Clarke eloquently sums up the trouble with men like Sykes: "Taint no law on earth dat kin make a man be decent if it ain't in 'im. There's plenty men dat takes a wife lak dey do a joint uh sugar-cane. It's round, juicy an' sweet when dey gits it. But dey squeeze an' grind, squeeze an' grind an' wring tell dey wring every drop uh pleasure dat's in 'em out. When dey's satisfied dat dey is wrung dry, dey treats 'em just lak dey do a cane-chew. Dey thows 'em away. Dey knows whut dey is doin' while dey is at it, an' hates theirselves fuh it but they keeps on hangin' after huh tell she's empty. Den dey hates huh fuh bein' a cane-chew an' in de way."

Rather than simply leave Delia, however, Sykes tries to run her off so that he and his new woman can have the house that Delia's sweat has bought. Delia refuses to be beaten in this way, however, so she and Sykes end up in a bitter standoff. Preying on Delia's obsessive fear of snakes, Sykes one day brings home a six-foot rattler and leaves it in a pen outside the kitchen. Delia pleads with him to take the snake away, but he refuses. This is when Delia, a woman who takes her Christian commitment seriously, first tastes hate: "Ah hates you, Sykes. . . . Ah hates you tuh de same degree dat Ah useter love you. . . . Ah hates yuh lak uh suck-egg dog."

Sykes is so shocked by the venom of Delia's pronouncement that he is unable to respond with his fists. Instead, a few days later, he secretly lets the snake loose in Delia's laundry basket, hoping that either the fear or the snake itself will kill her. When confronted by "ol' satan," as she calls the snake, Delia, despite her blinding terror, manages to escape into the hay barn, where she spends the night. Hurston's minimalist peek into Delia's mind during this long dark night is masterful: "There for an hour or more she lay sprawled upon the hay a gibbering wreck. Finally she grew quiet, and after that, coherent thought. With this, stalked through her a cold, bloody rage. Hours of this. A period of introspection, a space of retrospection, then a mixture of both. Out of this an awful calm."

Full of gin and spite, Sykes comes home early the next morning in search of Delia's body. But before he can strike a match against the darkness, the rattlesnake strikes him. Delia, lying in her flowerbed beneath the window, is a witness to it all. Yet she never warns Sykes or responds to his moans once he's been attacked. Finally, Delia does move toward the door and, even in the midst of her justifiable rage, she is overcome with compassion for Sykes. Then, with a mixture of remorse and relief, she realizes it's too late. Hurston brilliantly brings together all the themes of "Sweat"—the jobless black man's resentment of his working woman, the triumph of good over evil, the hate that hate produces—in the story's final, gripping paragraph: "She saw him on his hands and knees as soon as she reached the door. He crept an inch or two toward her—all that he was able, and she saw his horribly swollen neck and his one open eye shining with hope. A surge of pity too strong to support bore her away from the eye that must, could not, fail to see the tubs. . . . Orlando with its doctors was too far. She could scarcely reach the Chinaberry tree, where she waited in the growing heat while inside she knew the cold river was creeping up and up to extinguish that eye which must know by now that she knew."

Like Hurston's other early fiction, "Sweat" is true to its Eatonville milieu, with the porch sitters witnessing the main story and offering a backdrop of communal wisdom and commentary. Yet "Sweat" is not dependent on the Eatonville scene, and there is no real folklore in the story. Rather than create a showcase for folklore, superstition, and porch humor, as she'd done in some of her earlier fiction, Hurston mined the language and sensibilities of Eatonville to tell a compelling, original story about two damaged human beings. At the same time, "Sweat" is a shrewd variation on the biblical tale of Adam and Eve and the serpent. Ultimately, it is a penetrating exploration of a good woman's struggle against evil, both within and without. And that struggle, though particular to Delia in the story, is familiar to everyone who breathes.

"Sweat" revealed Hurston to be a writer of stunning capabilities when she committed herself to the craft. It also divulged a bit about Zora's views on some of her life's most pressing questions. "Sweat" makes it clear, for instance, that Hurston placed great value on a woman's ability to work and to become financially independent, something she'd been struggling to do for more than half her life by 1926. The story also shows that Zora (still doing a long-distance dance with Herbert Sheen) harbored, at best, an ambivalent attitude toward marriage. She seemed to view it as oppressive, particularly for women, and potentially deadly. These were ideas that Hurston would revisit in later literary efforts.

"Sweat" was the best of several short stories Hurston wrote during the Harlem Renaissance, pieces that charted her steady growth as a literary artist. In the December 1925 issue of *The X-Ray: The Official*

Publication of Zeta Phi Beta Sorority, Hurston had published a short story called "Under the Bridge" that was similar to "Sweat" in its focus on the passions and pains of a particular Florida household. Though Eatonville goes unnamed in this story, Hurston's hometown memories are unmistakably present in the narrative, which brims with the language and lore of the folk. Luke Mimms is a fifty-eight-year-old newlywed torn by love for his nineteen-year-old bride and for his twenty-two-year-old son. The two "young'uns," as he calls them, clearly love each other. But they must refrain from expressing their love because they also both love Luke, a vulnerable and kind man whom Hurston renders tenderly. Theirs is a complicated love triangle, and once Luke consults the local conjure doctor, it cannot help but end tragically.

In contrast, Hurston's short story "Muttsy," which won second place in the 1926 *Opportunity* contest, is an amusing comedy. Published in the August *Opportunity*, it is the tale of Pinkie, a wide-eyed young woman who moves to Harlem from Eatonville and finds herself trapped in the lowdown life of Ma Turner's back parlor, where men and women dance, sing, drink, fight, and live "hotly their intense lives." Interestingly, the language these Harlemites use is just as colorful and country as the language of Eatonville: You can take the Negroes out of the country, Hurston seems to say with a wink, but you can't take the country out of the Negroes. The best gambler and womanizer in the bunch, Muttsy is smitten with Pinkie, the innocent country girl, and vows to get a regular job and give up gambling if she'll marry him. She eventually does, but, in the end, Muttsy—confident that he can keep both his wife and his gambling habit—returns to his back-parlor ways.

The other pieces Hurston published in 1926 were more folklore than fiction. In September, *Forum* published a folktale under her byline called " 'Possum or Pig." It is a classic tale, about John and the Master, that was well known to black storytellers in southern rural communities. Hurston's decision to publish it in the *Forum* suggests that she was engaging in a rather conscious effort to expose black southern folklore to a wider audience—not just through telling the stories at parties, but through publishing them as well, particularly during the Renaissance years, when magazines were eager to showcase Negro material.

To that end, Hurston published a series called "The Eatonville Anthology" in the September, October, and November 1926 issues of *The Messenger*. The anthology is an engaging amalgam of folklore, fiction, and Eatonville history. It gives readers the sense that they are sitting on the porch of Joe Clarke's store listening to a "lying session" unfold—or, better yet, sitting in a Harlem brownstone listening to Zora Hurston pass all of Eatonville through her mouth, and through her memory.

"The Eatonville Anthology" consists of fourteen short tales, connected only by their locale and their language. Snatches of retrospection and reverie from the rural South of Zora's childhood, the stories paint a rather interesting and complex portrait of Eatonville. In several of the tales, for example, women are routinely beaten by their husbands with no comment from the community (or from Hurston). In one story, a wronged wife forces the town vamp to move to Orlando, where, "in a wider sphere, perhaps, her talents as a vamp were appreciated." In another, various Eatonville residents try to poison an annoying, meat-stealing dog, Tippy. When he survives every attempt on his life, Eatonville accepts "the plague of Tippy, reflecting that it has erred in certain matters and is being chastened." In Hurston's portrayal, the people of Eatonville accepted misfortune of all types—bad dogs, town vamps, spousal abuse, poverty—as karmic debts they were bound to pay. Like black folks anywhere of a certain temperament and experience, Hurston seems to say, they made a place for evil in their lives with little grumbling, just as they did for good.

Some of the stories Hurston included in "The Eatonville Anthology" were common folktales, known not just to her, but to many black southerners of her time. Others were specific memories recounted from her youth. All were told economically (one is only a paragraph long) and colorfully. And several of the tales' characters—including Sykes Jones, Jim Merchant, and Joe Clarke—were destined to reappear elsewhere in Hurston's oeuvre. The story of Joe Clarke's meanness toward his wife, for instance, would later find its way into Hurston's novel *Their Eyes Were Watching God*, where she would rename Clarke (Joe Starkes) and place the focus on his wife, whom she would call Janie.

"The Eatonville Anthology" is the literary equivalent of Hurston's animated storytelling sessions at Harlem parties—spontaneous performances that spurred Langston Hughes to declare her the most amusing member of the Niggerati. "Only to reach a wider audience, need she ever write books," he said, "because she is a perfect book of entertainment in herself."

As Hughes's remark suggests, Hurston was considered more raconteur than writer during the Harlem Renaissance. In Nugent's short story in *Fire!!*, for instance, Zora makes an appearance not as a writer, but as a storyteller of glittering gifts: "Zora had shone again . . . her stories . . . she always shone . . . every one was glad when Zora shone."

Well, perhaps not everyone. Some of Zora's friends—particularly Hughes, Thurman, and Bontemps—occasionally grew frustrated with her because they believed she was more interested in entertaining at parties than in creating literature. She dissipated her material, they felt, by telling it, rather than writing it down. In his novel *Infants of the Spring*, the intensely cynical Thurman expressed his exasperation with Zora by creating a dubious character clearly based on her. Sweetie May Carr, the Zora stand-in, "is a short story writer, more noted for her ribald wit and personal effervescence than for any actual literary work," Thurman jeered. "Sweetie May was a master of southern dialect, and an able raconteur, but she was too indifferent to literary creation to transfer to paper that which she told so well."

Even if some of her friends believed she was squandering her talent by sharing her stories freely at parties, Zora felt differently. In Eatonville, she had been steeped in an oral tradition where stories were meant to be enjoyed in a communal setting, not hoarded for one's own gain. She also was confident that she had plenty of stored material to work with, not to mention a fertile imagination. Telling a few stories at a party would not drain her so dry as to wreck her literary career, she contended, waving off her friends' concerns.

Although "Zora showed at *any* party," as one friend recalled, she also was legitimately busy—with the schoolwork she'd resumed at Barnard, with her effort to earn a living (she still occasionally worked as a waitress for private dinners), and with her new love: anthropology.

As Zora flirted more and more with the science of anthropology, she frequently was too busy to apply herself to the art of literature. Literature, she found, required discipline, or perhaps something more like concentration. Certainly, Zora could find the time and the wherewithal to write down the stories she told at parties as she seems to have done with "The Eatonville Anthology." But true literature required something else, something more. When Hurston pulled Eatonville's folklore from her top hat of memory and transferred it directly and respectfully to the page, she proved herself to be a fine folklorist-in-the-making. Yet when she adapted the lore, the language, the landscape, and the personalities of Eatonville for her own uses—and overlaid this raw material with her own ample inventiveness—she proved herself to be a literary artist of superior talent, as a story like "Sweat" shows. And this, of course, took time, concentration and, well, sweat. As Zora worked to finish her studies at Barnard—and as she succumbed more and more to the allure of anthropology—she was not always up for the effort that literature required.

Though Hurston is often thought of today as a Harlem Renaissance writer, she actually did not produce very much literature during the Renaissance, which began to crumble, most historians agree, when the stock market crashed in October 1929. The truth is, she published no books and only a few short stories and plays during the Roaring Twenties. In fact, after "Sweat" and *Color Struck* appeared in *Fire!!* in 1926, Hurston would not publish any more fiction until the 1930s, and only one play—*The First One*, in Charles S. Johnson's 1927 collection *Ebony and Topaz*.

For the remainder of the Harlem Renaissance, Zora Neale Hurston was rarely even in Harlem. Mostly, she was on the road.

CHAPTER 16

Poking and Prying with a Purpose

In the dead of February 1927, Hurston said farewell to Harlem and headed for Florida. Though she would miss polishing off mounds of fried chicken with her New York friends—and settling "the affairs of the world over the bones," as she put it —a higher calling beckoned.

Several weeks before, Franz Boas had summoned Zora into his office to deliver some long-awaited good news: She had received a fellowship to collect Negro folklore in the South. Knowing she only had a few credits to complete before graduating from Barnard, Boas had started looking for fieldwork on Zora's behalf the previous fall. To that end, he'd written to Carter G. Woodson, director of the Association for the Study of Negro Life and History, recommending Hurston for a fellowship. Boas's recommendation initially did not excite Woodson; the Harvard Ph.D. was just as interested in funding a study of Negro banking. But after some negotiating with Boas— and after interviewing Hurston in early December—Woodson decided to grant a $700 fellowship. Elsie Clews Parsons of the American Folklore Society matched Woodson's grant, bringing the total fellowship amount to $1,400. With this sum, Zora Hurston was to spend a little more than six months, from February to August, recording the stories, superstitions, songs, dances, jokes, customs, and mannerisms of the black South.

When Boas asked Hurston where she wanted to work, she did not hesitate: Florida, she told him. The state drew people from all over the country, she reasoned. "So I knew that it was possible for me to get a cross section of the Negro South in the one state. And then I realized that I was new myself, so it looked sensible for me to choose familiar ground." Boas agreed. Devised under his direction, Zora's plan called for her to start in Jacksonville, where she had family, then work her way south through St. Augustine, Palatka, Sanford, Eatonville, and other Florida towns. If time allowed, she would go on to Mobile, in southwest Alabama, and maybe New Orleans, where she expected to find a rich storehouse of conjure lore.

Hurston was elated that Boas felt she was ready to immerse herself in the "formalized curiosity" of research, which she described as "poking and prying with a purpose." Boas, meanwhile, was a little concerned about Zora's lack of modesty—she was "too much impressed with her own accomplishments," he feared. Nevertheless, he was confident that her background and easy manner would help her to "penetrate through that affected demeanor," as he saw it, "by which the Negro excludes the white observer effectively from participating in his true inner life." Zora was, after all, "one of them."

As New York shivered against February's hawkish winds, Zora was happy to arrive in Florida, where she was greeted by "gorgeous sunlight" and "hyacinths by the mile," as she reported to a friend. By February 18, she was in Jacksonville shopping for a car with her brother John Cornelius, who ran a meat market not far from his home on Evergreen Avenue. Zora and John agreed that she should avoid "common carriers" during her southern travels. On these trains, the segregated Negro coaches were often no more than jerry-rigged sections of baggage bins or smoking cars. With their "dirty upholstery and other inconveniences," as Zora mildly put it, the Jim Crow coaches were poorly lighted, poorly ventilated, and sometimes perilous for women traveling alone. It would be much more convenient and comfortable for Zora to have her own car. On this, sister and brother concurred.

They could not agree, however, on what kind of automobile Zora should buy. "My brother plays so safe," she complained to a friend back in New York. "He doesn't lose anything, but he doesn't get any fun either—the terrific kick that comes from taking a chance." Zora wanted to take a chance on a fully equipped 1927 Oakland Coupe. The dealer was asking $870 for it—$300 down and $54.50 per month. There were less expensive models, Zora knew, but "gee, I want <u>that</u> one," she pined. John, meanwhile, was trying to convince his sister that an older, cheaper Ford would be fine and that she'd be foolish to pay more than $300 or so for what she needed—reliable transportation but nothing fancy. "I think so too," Zora admitted, "but don't be surprised if I own that pretty mama by April 1st." Her brother's logic prevailed, though, and Zora eventually settled on a $300 used car—a peppy but practical choice (at only $26.80 a month) that she soon dubbed "Sassy Susie."

One of Sassy Susie's first road trips was to Eatonville. Zora hurried back to her homeplace, she explained, "because I knew that the town was full of material and that I could get it without hurt, harm or danger." As she motored across the Maitland-Eatonville border, Zora saw a group gathered on the porch of Joe Clarke's store, still the epicenter of Eatonville. "I was delighted," Zora recalled. "The town had not changed. Same love of talk and song." At the store, at the modern new gas station, and elsewhere in town, folks greeted Zora warmly: "Well, if it ain't Zora Hurston!" they hooted. Only slightly impressed by her automobile and her imminent Barnard degree, they were nonetheless happy to see that Lucy Hurston's baby girl had turned out to be a fine young woman.

During her visit, Zora's understanding of Eatonville—and all that she'd received from her upbringing there—deepened even further. Back in her hometown's embrace, with the spyglass of anthropology at the ready, Zora fully recognized and appreciated the affirmation that was inherent in a town such as Eatonville, where black culture flourished free from the burdensome, acquisitive white gaze. Eatonville was, as one observer would put it, "like a four-walled room." Self-governing and self-determining, it was markedly different from the places where most of Zora's Harlem Renaissance colleagues had grown up: "rooms with one wall missing, exposing their lives to the white man's intentions and inspection." Indeed, most black Americans hailed from such three-walled rooms, and their lifelong exposure to white interference and disapproval had taken a psychological toll that Zora could hardly imagine. Now, more than ever, she realized that all-black Eatonville was largely untrammeled by racism and its debilitating effects. It was a place (rare in America, Zora now knew) where black people were free from any indoctrination in inferiority. This—along with the language and the lore—was the gift that Eatonville had given her.

Although Zora's return to Eatonville was personally satisfying, it was disappointing to her as an anthropologist. She stayed with a childhood friend, Armetta Jones, and her husband, Ellis. Zora invited the townsfolk over for gingerbread and buttermilk, but she had trouble gathering any substantial folklore—that is, stories, songs, or other material that she didn't already know from her growing-up years in Eatonville. "Folklore is not as easy to collect as it sounds," she learned. Everybody was sufficiently sociable, but Zora had not come for a social visit. She had come instead as a social scientist, and a surreptitious one at that. She was to pay attention not so much to the content of her informants' stories and songs, Boas had instructed, but to their "habitual movements in telling tales," to "their form of diction," and to their "methods of dancing." Zora found it difficult, however, to wear the scientist's hat—to focus so much on form and method—among old friends and in such a known environment. As a result, Eatonville yielded almost no new material. "Oh, I got a few little items. But compared with what I did later," Hurston acknowledged, "not enough to make a flea a waltzing jacket."

After about ten days in Eatonville, Zora moved on to less familiar surroundings, to towns where she did not know anyone. What she did know, though, was that a black woman traveling the back roads of the South alone needed a mighty form of protection. For this, Zora packed a chrome-plated pistol.

Hurston's daring—and the potential danger of her mission—should not be underestimated. She was, of course, vulnerable to rape and the general misogynistic violence that any woman traveling alone might fear at any moment in American history. But there was more: This was 1927—a time when lynchings and other forms of racial barbarity were rampant in the South. Though black men were the usual targets of lynch mobs, by no means were black women safe from such savagery, and Hurston knew she had to be on constant guard. In 1926, the year before her return to the South, at least twenty-three black people had been lynched, up from seventeen in 1925. At the end of 1927, *The Atlanta Constitution* would find it laudable that the state of Georgia made it through the year without a single such murder. Neighboring Florida would not fare so well. Shortly after her arrival, Zora heard a firsthand account of a lynching near Sanford—"but by a million to one chance, the victim survived," a shaken Hurston reported. "Left for dead, he regained consciousness the following day and crawled 4 miles and hid away in a Negro home until he could escape North."

Hearing such gruesome stories, few of Zora's Harlem compatriots—no matter how much they claimed to love the folk—would have braved the southern backwoods, "forsaking the creature comforts of New York," as she put it, "for these shacks that suffice in the sub-tropics." Zora even called the bluff of one friend who pretended he might join her on her journey: "I cannot see you forsaking the classic halls of universities for the songs and tales of camp and road. . . . I challenge you—I dare you—to try it!"

As her dare implied, the South offered few amenities for Negro travelers. Zora became accustomed to pulling Sassy Susie over on deserted roadsides and wading into high grass to relieve a full bladder. After long days of negotiating lonesome roads, she was forced to bypass downtown motels and restaurants—with their rude "whites only" signs—and make her way to black neighborhoods, where she found lodging and food in rooming houses or private homes.

Zora made these concessions to southern injustice because she had no choice. Yet she apparently did so with little resentment—about which she did have a choice. "Sometimes, I feel discriminated against," Zora acknowledged, "but it does not make me angry. It merely astonishes me. How *can* any deny themselves the pleasure of my company! It's beyond me." Zora chose to forgo bitterness, as much as she was able, because she had come to the conclusion sometime earlier that resentment—about her personal history, about America's racial history or current inequities—was beyond useless. It was self-destructive. It was, Zora knew, like drinking poison and expecting the other person—the resented one—to die. And in this case, there was no one *in particular* to resent. Despite its name, which derived from an early minstrel song, Jim Crow was not a person, and it certainly wasn't human. Yet with its strict rules for segregating the races, it was a way of life in the South. Resentment toward it would have been a waste of energy. Still, Zora was not blind—and no matter how many white motels and restaurants she bypassed, she could not evade the cutting looks of "aggressive intolerance" that many white people shot at her. "The poor whites down here have the harshest and most unlovely faces on earth," she decided.

Because looks could not kill, however, Zora resolved to stay the course and focus on the positive, as was her way. In March, she wrote to a friend: "Flowers are gorgeous now, crackers not troubling me at all—hope they don't begin as I go farther down state. I'll be very glad to be back in New York City, however. I am finding interesting people and things and love it all."

In her letters to New York, Zora occasionally included excerpts from her notebook, some of which illustrated the ridiculousness of Jim Crow justice: "A man arrested for 'vacancy' (vagrancy) but when the police found out that he was working, they fined him for carrying concealed cards and attempt to gamble." More often, however, her excerpts limned the resilience of black southern humor and the manifold richness of Negro life. A stingy man, for example, was heard to say, "I wouldn't give a poor, consumpted, crippled crab a crutch to cross the river Jordan." Meanwhile, Hurston recorded an angry, armed woman declaring, "I'm walkin' down de road wid de law in my mouf." A sad person might lament, "I'm so sobbing-hearted." And when calling out a liar, one might say, "Youse a cotton-tail dispute!"

These colorful excerpts notwithstanding, Hurston consistently found it difficult to collect the kind of material Boas wanted. At first, the problem was her approach. "The glamor of Barnard College was still upon me. I dwelt in marble halls," she later conceded. "I knew where the material was all right. But I went about asking, in carefully accented Barnardese, 'Pardon me, but do you know any folk tales or folk songs?' The men and women who had whole treasuries of material just seeping through their pores, looked at me and shook their heads. No, they had never heard of anything like that around there. Maybe it was over in the next county. Why didn't I try over there? I did, and got the self-same answer."

Boas did not mask his displeasure. After receiving a batch of material from Zora, he wrote to remind her of his previous instructions. "I find that what you obtained is very largely repetition of the kind of material that has been collected so much," he reprimanded.

Working with the nation's leading anthropologist required more than being a faithful transcriber of picturesque folk sayings. Like literature, anthropology exacted its own demands.

Hurston's initial failure to meet those demands had more to do with her vocational ambivalence than with her "Barnardese," which she quickly and judiciously dropped. In fact, after her Barnardese bombed in the field, Zora never again would put on airs. Whether on Lenox Avenue or Park Avenue, she always let the map of Dixie sprawl freely on her tongue—not in a way that mocked or mimicked the language of Eatonville, but in a way that honored it. By giving her primary language precedence in her speech, Zora presented herself as down-to-earth and unpretentious. From 1927 on, no matter where her work would take her, she was always unabashedly black and unapologetically southern.

These identities Zora balanced easily. Her trouble, however, was balancing her sometimes conflicting interests as anthropologist and writer. Although her research disappointed Boas, for instance, Zora was delighted with the folklore she'd collected for her own literary uses. "Getting some gorgeous material down here, verse and prose, <u>magnificent</u>," she wrote to Langston Hughes. Still thinking of the black folk opera on which they planned to collaborate, she promised him: "Shall save some juicy bits for you and me."

In addition to plotting her collaboration with Hughes, Hurston was working on a short story for the next issue of *Fire!!* (which never materialized). She also was beginning work on a novel—an adaptation of Annie Nathan Meyer's 1925 play *Black Souls*. "I do hope you will enjoy making it into a real novel," Meyer had coaxed a few weeks before Zora headed South. Meyer promised to fully and prominently acknowledge Hurston's work and to give her half of all royalties if the book was published or if a movie was made. Significantly, Zora had transformed herself—in less than two years— from Meyer's "faithful and obedient servant" to her artistic collaborator. As such, she assured Meyer that even with her demanding fieldwork, she was finding time to devote to the novel. "I take the mornings for writing and the afternoons and evenings for anthropology," Zora explained, "and get a great deal done for both."

She was not doing enough, however, where Boas was concerned. To be fair, Zora was a young anthropologist who had been given a

huge assignment—one that arguably stretched her beyond the training she'd received thus far. "No, I am <u>not</u> dead," she reported to
Meyer after a long silence, "but both Dr. Boas and Dr. Woodson are
rushing me like thunder along. I need at least a whole year to do
what I am doing in six months."

Personal complications—and complications of personality—also
compromised Zora's ability to meet Boas's expectations. For one
thing, she found herself feeling homesick for New York and its intellectual stimulation, even while she reveled in Florida's physical
beauty. "Nature has up-ended her horn-of-plenty here," she wrote to
one friend. "I really do think you'd go mad with pleasure if the ignorance and squalor that is 'smaddled' all over did not depress you too
much." To another, she confided, "I feel a little lonely cut off from all
of my friends."

While Zora was meeting new people every day, the tenets of
anthropology prevented her from actually befriending them. Her
charge, as a social scientist, was to study them, not to get to know
them—and certainly not to entertain them. This was a new and
unusual role for Zora: The woman who had been the life of every
party she'd attended in Harlem was now required to be a conscientious wallflower. If she went to a jook joint in Palatka, for instance,
she was not free to regale the crowd with her stories or to compete in
a black bottom contest. Instead, her job was to listen to other
people's stories, to watch other people dance, and to record their
mannerisms and movements scientifically and systematically. "I am
getting a certain amount of entertainment out of my work," she
noted, "but sometimes, I yearn to point the nose of my car due north
and throw her into high."

Though she did not abandon her fieldwork for the open road
back to New York, Zora did take at least two significant diversions
during her travels. The first was a detour to Memphis, where she visited her oldest brother, Bob. Zora and Bob had not seen each other
for more than a decade, not since she had run off with the Gilbert
and Sullivan troupe that deposited her in Baltimore. Now a successful physician, Bob apologized for not being of more help to Zora
in her struggle for an education. He also gave her details of their
father's last days in Memphis and of the train crash that killed him.
Zora was reunited, too, with younger brother Ben, who was now a

Memphis pharmacist, a husband, a dog lover, and "quite the witty, laughing person," his big sister was pleased to find. Bob and Ben updated Zora on their other siblings: Clifford Joel had become a high school principal in Alabama, Dick was a traveling chef on the East Coast, and Sarah was still a preacher's wife, and had recently become a mother. In turn, Zora reported that John Cornelius was doing well with his market in Jacksonville, and that Everett, "Mama's baby child," as Zora called him, was a postal employee in Brooklyn.

This impromptu family reunion, incomplete though it was, brought closure to the tenacious sense of loss and lonesomeness that had clung to Zora since 1904. "I felt the warm embrace of kin and kind for the first time since the night after my mother's funeral," she noted, "when we had huddled about the organ all sodden and bewildered, with the walls of our home suddenly blown down. . . .But now, that was all over. We could touch each other in the spirit if not in the flesh."

Zora's second diversion from her fieldwork was equally momentous: On May 19, 1927, she met Herbert Sheen in St. Augustine, Florida, and married him. Only a few weeks before, Zora had participated in a somewhat suggestive correspondence with another man, New Yorker Lawrence Jordan. ("Believe it or not, Larry, I want to see you tremendously," she'd flirted.) On May 19, though, Zora sought to put Jordan—and any other thoughts that challenged the wisdom of wedlock—out of her mind. Still, she would recall, "it was not my happiest day. I was assailed by doubts." Her love affair with Sheen had lasted through her time at Howard and Barnard and had survived almost five solid years of separation. On the eve of their wedding, however, Zora began to question her feelings: "For the first time since I met him, I asked myself if I really were in love, or if this had been a habit."

The distance Sheen had traveled from Chicago may have been what stopped Zora from voicing her misgivings, which were crowned by a disturbing dream she had the night before the Thursday courthouse ceremony. It was not an ordinary dream, she remembered, but a "vision-dream," like the ones she'd had as a child. In her prenuptial nightmare, she told Sheen decades later, "a dark barrier kept falling between us." One of Sheen's sisters called Zora's name harshly in the dream and commanded her to leave him alone or

guage of the rural black South in amazement, while Zora responded with laughing eyes that whispered, "I told you so." The two writers also did a lot of talking on their long road trip. They enthusiastically discussed ideas for their proposed folk opera, and Zora confided in Langston about her marriage—and her qualms. Hughes also divulged a secret: He told Zora about his patron, Charlotte Mason, a wealthy and generous New York widow; she would simply love Zora, Hughes promised. Intrigued, Zora gratefully accepted Langston's offer to put in a good word for her with Mrs. Mason once they were back in New York.

In Tuskegee—not far from Notasulga, the Alabama hamlet where both Zora's parents had grown up—Hughes and Hurston lectured the summer school students at Tuskegee Institute. While there, they ran into former *Crisis* literary editor Jessie Fauset, who'd been invited to participate in the school's Wednesday speakers series. Together, the three writers paid their respects at the grave of founder Booker T. Washington, the revered champion of black vocational training and industry who'd died in 1915. The Tuskegee stop, Hughes later boasted, "was our only contact with formal culture all the way from Mobile to New York."

Rummaging through the Georgia hinterlands, Zora and Langston visited the old Toomer plantation, where fellow Harlem Renaissance writer Jean Toomer had found inspiration for his masterpiece, *Cane*. In Fort Valley, they went to see a magician entertaining at a back-country church and barely suppressed their laughter when he closed his performance with a lively, harp-accompanied rendition of the Lord's Prayer: "Our Father who art in heaven, <u>Hollywood</u> be thy name!" he began. The next day, Hurston and Hughes drove north to Macon, where they'd gotten word that Bessie Smith would be singing in an intimate theater. The morning after the concert, they woke up to the sound of Smith's voice; she was staying in the same hotel, it turned out, and practiced every morning with gusto. The two writers met the Empress of the Blues and "got to know her pretty well," as Hughes reported. "The trouble with white folks singing the blues," Smith told them, "is that they can't get low down enough."

Both Hurston and Hughes were drawn to Smith: The lowdown blues aesthetic she represented was infinitely more appealing to them than the high-art philosophies espoused by W.E.B. Du Bois and some of the other midwives of the New Negro movement. Having chosen the open road over her husband's companionship, Zora must have found particular resonance in Smith's 1926 hit, "Young Woman's Blues," which she no doubt sang at her Macon concert. "See that long lonesome road/Lord, you know it's gotta end/I'm a good woman and I can get plenty men," Smith crooned. The song's heroine—like Smith herself—was black and southern, a complex blend of vivacity and vulnerability. This also was the kind of woman Zora was perhaps just now recognizing herself to be, and the kind she would later write about. "No time to marry, no time to settle down," Smith sang. "I'm a young woman and ain't done runnin' round."

Hurston and Hughes weren't done running around, either. Traveling east toward Savannah, they had supper with turpentine workers and stevedores, then went to see a Georgia conjurer deep in the backwoods. Hurston, who had visited many hoodoo doctors during her months in the field, was not impressed with this one's pomp and circumstance. She quickly dismissed him as powerless, and she and Hughes wondered at his popularity in that part of Georgia, where some medical doctors complained that he'd taken away their patients. On August 17, the two happy travelers sent a postcard digest to Van Vechten: "We are charging home in a wheezy car and hope to be home for Xmas. We are being fed on watermelon, chicken, and the company of good things. Wish you were with us. Lovely people not spoiled by soap-suds and talcum."

On the night of August 26, Hurston and Hughes rolled into Cheraw, in the northern part of South Carolina, after having a punctured tire repaired in Columbia. There was another mishap as well: "Somehow," Zora reported, "all the back of my skirt got torn away, so that my little panties were panting right out there in public. I suppose this accident will be classed as more tire trouble," she joked.

Near the first of September, the pair crossed the Mason-Dixon line and stopped briefly in Pennsylvania for lunch with one of Hughes's professors at Lincoln. Then they went on to New York, where Zora was soon resettled in her apartment on West Sixty-sixth Street, which she'd sublet to Dorothy West and Helene Johnson. Immediately, she got to work on her final report for Boas and finished up a couple of assignments for Woodson, whom she now regarded with contempt because he'd docked her two weeks' pay. "I hate that improperly born wretch," she grumbled to Hughes. Langston had no sympathy for the man, either. He'd once worked for "the father of Negro history" himself. Finding Woodson to be a strident taskmaster, Hughes had quit to become a busboy.

During her months in the field, Zora had been compelled to do some hack work for Woodson, investigating county court records that had nothing to do with her folklore-collecting mission. With his firm grip on her purse strings, Woodson also had prevailed upon Zora to transcribe historical records about Fort Moosa, a seventeenth-century black settlement in St. Augustine, the nation's oldest city. Again, Zora had little interest in this material, and she could not have been happy about the time she had to take away from her folklore research to transcribe the documents. Still, Woodson published the Fort Moosa transcriptions, under the title "Communication," in the October 1927 issue of his organization's *Journal of Negro History.* In the same issue, he published another Hurston article, "Cudjo's Own Story of the Last African Slaver."

This article was partly based on Hurston's interview with Cudjo Lewis in Mobile, but it was heavily supplemented by shamelessly plagiarized passages from Emma Langdon Roche's *Historic Sketches of the Old South*, which Zora evidently had picked up at the Mobile Historical Society. Hurston's sixteen-page essay made it clear that she did, in fact, interview Lewis; she had fresh quotes from him, as well as some new information and updated directions to his home, including references to roads that were built after Roche's 1914 study was published. Yet Hurston apparently had insufficient material to write the kind of essay that would satisfy Woodson. Consequently, she lifted whole pages from Roche's study—sometimes word for word—as would a freshman trying to finish a term paper in an all-night blitz. Of course, it's possible that Hurston turned in footnotes with the article that somehow got lost on the way to publication. Possible, but not likely. In the published story, only a short note on page one even hinted that Hurston had borrowed much of her material: "This story was secured by Miss Zora Neale Hurston, an investigator of the Association for the Study of Negro Life and History," the footnote stated. "She made a special trip to Mobile to interview Cudjo Lewis, the only survivor of this last cargo. She made some use, too, of the *Voyage of Clotilde* and other records of the Mobile Historical Society." Making "some use" of material from another writer is completely common and acceptable. But, as Zora knew, copying another's work, and passing it off as one's own, is not.

What would make Zora Neale Hurston—standing on the cusp of a promising career as an anthropologist—risk it all by committing such an atrocious academic crime? At this point, any answer is speculation. Perhaps the plagiarism was her way of getting back at Woodson for arbitrarily slicing her pay and cutting into her research time by having her do his dreck work. She was determined not to spend any more time than necessary working for Woodson, without pay, once she was back in New York. Copying from Roche's book, then, would have been an easy way to finish her report and let the last laugh be on Woodson. It's likely, too, that Hurston believed the report was only for Woodson's files; she did not expect it to be published any more than she thought her transcribed "Communication" was worthy of publication.

It's also possible that Hurston had resolved to save her most compelling material from Cudjo Lewis for her own work, as he was eagerly sought after by anthropologists and historians. Arthur Huff Fauset had collected a folktale from him and published it in *The New Negro* in 1925. White anthropologist Paul Radin was hot on Lewis's trail as well. Perhaps Hurston padded her report with passages from Roche's thirteen-year-old book to avoid revealing any new information about Lewis that would help her competitors. Or perhaps she did not get much new material from the old man at all. Reputed to be in his late eighties, Lewis was difficult to interview. He spoke with a heavy accent that was hard to decipher without prolonged acquaintance, and he was reluctant to talk about his native African religion and other matters that interested Hurston. Perhaps, too, the budding anthropologist simply had not asked the right questions.

No matter how Hurston justified the plagiarism to herself, the Cudjo Lewis story ultimately was a dramatic example of her initial failure at anthropology. It also may have been a subconscious attempt at academic suicide. Perhaps a part of Hurston *wanted* to get caught—so that she would no longer have to write sterile, uninventive scientific reports that bored her even as she wrote them. So that she would be free at last from her vocational ambivalence. So that she could be fully and unequivocally a creative writer.

Whether she wanted to or not, Hurston got away with her plagiarism like a master trickster. It was never discovered—by Boas, Woodson, or anyone else—during her lifetime.

Despite the Cudjo Lewis debacle, Hurston had matured, professionally and personally, during her southern sojourn. In October, she bowed out of her potentially lucrative collaboration with Meyer on a novelization of *Black Souls*. It was a question of integrity, in Zora's view: "The more I see of the South," she explained to Meyer, "the more am I convinced that it would strike a terribly false note."

In her six-month field trip, Hurston had come to know the South more intimately than her exceptional but limited Eatonville childhood had allowed. She also had acquired a respectable collection of conjure practices and enough honeyed expressions to draw from, if she wanted to, for dozens of short stories. Yet in her final report to Boas, a humbled Hurston admitted her disappointment at the formal fruits of her research. "Considering the mood of my going south, I went back to New York with my heart beneath my knees and my knees in some lonesome valley," she would recall.

"I stood before Papa Franz and cried salty tears. He gave me a good going over, but later I found that he was not as disappointed as he let me think. He knew I was green and feeling my oats, and that only bitter disappointment was going to purge me. It did."

Thoroughly purged of her anthropological hubris, Hurston soon would try her hand at fieldwork again. With the taste of humble pie fresh on her lips, she would walk softer upon her return to the South, and the overconfidence that had marred her first folklore-collecting trip would be gone, without a trace.

CHAPTER 17

I Want to Collect Like a New Broom

By the time she met Charlotte Mason in September 1927, Zora Hurston had come to believe in her own power to conjure good things in her life. Still, when Hurston walked into Mason's elegant penthouse at 399 Park Avenue, she must have been astonished. Not by the majestic view of Manhattan from the gleaming windows, nor by the old woman's excessive wealth, manifest in her impeccable dress and her beautifully furnished, art-filled home. What astounded Zora were the calla lilies.

In one of the prophetic dreams that recurred throughout her youth, Zora had seen herself entering a big house where two women waited for her. "I could not see their faces, but I knew one to be young and one to be old. One of them was arranging queer-shaped flowers such as I had never seen," Hurston remembered of the dream. "When I had come to these women, then I would be at the end of my pilgrimage, but not the end of my life. Then I would know peace and love and what goes with those things, and not before." As Mason's young assistant, Cornelia Chapin, orchestrated the calla lilies in their lovely vase, the white-haired lady of the house looked her visitor over with intense, shining eyes. Returning Mason's gaze, Zora realized that the last of her childhood prophecies had come true. In that surreal moment, she knew the fulfillment of her final vision could mean only one thing: "I had gotten command of my life."

Hurston's recent disappointing foray into fieldwork, however, had tempered her tendency toward cockiness. So when she wrote to Langston Hughes about her September 20 meeting with Mason, a sanguine Hurston downplayed the magical quality of the day: "I think that we got on famously," she ventured. "God, I hope so!"

In that first encounter—likely arranged by Alain Locke and certainly encouraged by Hughes—Zora spoke to Charlotte Mason about the black folk opera that she and Langston had been talking about for more than a year. "She likes the idea of the opera," Hurston reported to Hughes, "but says that we must do it with so much power that it will halt all these spurious efforts on the part of white writers."

Though wholly white herself, Mason—born Charlotte van der Veer Quick—often expressed disdain for white people elbowing in on black culture. A friend of presidents and bankers, Mason claimed to be "altogether in sympathy" with rank-and-file Negroes, according to Hurston, because she believed them to be "utterly sincere in living."

More than she liked the idea of the Hurston-Hughes folk opera, Mason liked Hurston. The septuagenarian was impressed by the young woman's effulgent intellect and absolute lack of pretension. Although she was thoroughly learned, Zora was unlike Locke and other carefully mannered Negroes of Mason's acquaintance in that her negritude seemed undiminished by her education. Zora's grammar was proper yet free from affectation. She did not pitch her voice in a way to mask the blackness of its timbre, nor did she shame-facedly chase the South out of her diction. Zora was, a delighted Mason observed, as *Negro* as she could be. And despite all the differences between them—in age, race, and wealth—Hurston and Mason had much to discuss.

The widow of prominent physician Rufus Osgood Mason, Charlotte Mason herself was an amateur anthropologist who had spent time, many years earlier, among the Indians of the Great Plains. Later, she'd financed the research that resulted in Natalie Curtis's *The Indians' Book*, a 1907 volume of songs and legends. Well into her seventies when Zora met her, Mason was a longtime champion of "primitivism." For her, this was a form of racial essentialism rooted in a conviction that black people—if they'd only be their "savage" selves—could save whites from the aridity of civilization. Mason believed in cosmic energies and intuitive powers, and she was sure that "primitive" people, particularly American Indians and Negroes, were innately more in tune with these supernatural forces than were whites, who, in Mason's view, were not only overly civilized but also spiritually barren.

As a daughter of the conjure-rich black South, Zora also believed in mystical forces, and often felt attuned to them, as her soothsaying dreams proved. Though Mason's money was generations old, Hurston saw in the blue-blooded woman someone who was, as she put it, "just as pagan as I." Convinced that Mason's interest in black culture was genuine, Zora immediately offered to take her to the Harlem church that she and Hughes liked to attend. The "primitivism" that Mason held in such high esteem flourished at this church, where worshipers sang God's praises in a raw, unrehearsed way—and welcomed possession by the Holy Ghost in keeping with an old-time religion that was more ancient than they themselves knew.

Mason did not need to go to church in Harlem, however, to get in the spirit. Months before, she had fully committed herself to supporting the New Negro movement, generously financing any black art that she deemed good and worthy. For several years, Mason had been mildly interested in Negro uplift and had donated money to black schools in the South. But her career as a Negrotarian began in earnest early in 1927 when she introduced herself to Alain Locke after hearing him lecture on African art. With all deliberate speed, Locke became Mason's trusted (and handsomely paid) adviser on Negro matters, introducing her to a series of talented artists. At Locke's urging, Mason became patron to painter Aaron Douglas, sculptor Richmond Barthe, musician and composer Hall Johnson, and writers Claude McKay and Langston Hughes. Viewing her patronage as a spiritual mission of sorts, the charismatic Mason required all those who benefited from her benevolence to call her "Godmother." She also insisted that they keep her identity a secret. Violation of this cardinal rule, she assured them, would result in immediate banishment from the queendom.

Godmother "possessed the power to control people's lives—pick them up and put them down when and where she wished," Hughes would observe. Yet, he wrote, she was "one of the most delightful women I had ever met, witty and charming, kind and sympathetic, very old and white-haired, but amazingly modern in her ideas, in her knowledge of books and the theater, of Harlem, and of everything then taking place in the world." Hughes added: "I was fascinated by her, and I loved her."

For Hughes and others, economic dependence on Godmother was not so much volunteer slavery as luxurious servitude. Mason not only doled out monthly allowances to her mostly male protégés, she also supplied them with hard-to-get theater tickets and, at least in Hughes's case, fine bond writing paper and even finer suits from the best shops on Fifth Avenue. Seeking to remove any drains on Hughes's creativity, Mason even footed the bill for Langston's recalcitrant stepbrother, Gwyn Clark, to attend a New England preparatory school. In return, Hughes's only obligation was to send a monthly itemized expense report to Godmother, who regarded the young poet as her "blessed child" and hailed him as "a golden star in the Firmament of Primitive Peoples."

According to one rough estimate, in the late 1920s and early 1930s, Mason gave between $50,000 and $75,000 to black writers and artists like Hughes. In today's money, that's close to $750,000.

Between 1928 and 1932, a significant chunk of this sum would go to Zora Neale Hurston. After her initial meeting with Mason, Hurston was invited back to 399 Park Avenue often enough to become accustomed to the muted bustle of the Swedish maids. Sculptor Cornelia Chapin and her sister, poet Katherine Biddle, were usually on hand during Zora's visits to anticipate Godmother's needs. And everyone seemed to speak in the hushed tones of vaulted money.

On December 8, 1927, Mason cracked open the door to the vault and summoned Hurston in. That Thursday, Zora went to Mason's vast penthouse to sign an employment contract that would enable her to spend all of 1928 collecting Negro folklore in the South. If things went well and more time was needed, Hurston and Mason tacitly agreed, the contract would be extended through 1929.

Hurston had no reason, on the surface, to feel wary about entering into such an arrangement with Mason. After all, from the moment they'd met, Hurston knew they were destined to have a relationship. And the "psychic bond" between them, as she called it, already was becoming apparent. Hurston also knew, on a more practical level, that Mason was Godmother to Hughes, Miguel Covarrubias, and other friends—and that the alliance had served these artists well. The crucial difference, however, between Godmother's contract with Hurston and her arrangement with her other "godchildren" was this: Mason hired Hurston as an "independent agent" to do research *on her behalf*. Unlike Hughes and others, Hurston was *not* funded to concentrate on her own work; instead, she was an employee—a hired hand.

Though choked with legalese, the contract made its origins clear: It had come about because Charlotte Mason was "desirous of obtaining and compiling certain data" but "unable . . . to undertake the collecting of this information in person." Simply put, Mason was an elderly woman who could not do much outside her own home. Yet she wanted certain research conducted "among the American negroes," as the contract stated. An able-bodied Zora Hurston, then, was hired to do the research for her. Specifically, Hurston was "to seek out, compile and collect all information possible, both written and oral, concerning the music, poetry, folk-lore, literature, hoodoo, conjure, manifestations of art and kindred subjects" among Negroes in the South. Further, she was to hand over all this information to Mason—"data, transcripts of music, etc."—and to refrain from sharing the material with anyone unless she had Mason's written approval to do so.

Because she was black, southern, a student of anthropology, and an already experienced folklore collector, Hurston was, of course, exponentially more suited for the research than Mason herself was, even if the widow had been well enough to undertake the project. In truth, Hurston was more qualified for the task than *anyone*. Knowing this, Mason agreed to compensate her with a decent wage—more money, in fact, than Zora had ever earned in her life. In exchange for Hurston's research services, the notarized contract stated, Mason would pay her $200 a month—equal to about $2,000 today—and furnish her with both a motion picture camera and an automobile. (Zora would have to pay for her own auto insurance, the fussy contract insisted.)

Despite its finickiness, the legal document contained nothing that was inherently oppressive, one might argue. It is not at all uncommon for writers (and others) to hire researchers with the understanding that the results of the research belong to the employer. The potential problem, however, was Zora's own literary and anthropological interest in the material—an interest that both women were aware of, but failed to address contractually. Since the contract gave Mason full control of any material Hurston collected, the old woman had no reason to bring up the matter. Seduced by Godmother's largesse, Hurston did not broach the subject, either.

On the afternoon of December 14, less than a week after signing the contract, Zora boarded the 3:40 train at Penn Station en route to Mobile. Just before leaving New York, she wrote to Langston Hughes at Lincoln University, inviting him to join her for another southern summer and promising that things would be different this time: "I will have a better car ALL PAID FOR, and a better salary. Also, you MUST promise to ask ME first when you get strapped," she admonished, all sister-love. Langston accepted Zora's gentle chiding—and her occasional offers of money—like a man who was born to be coddled by women. Hughes's troubled relationship with his mother (who often petitioned him for cash) had made him suspicious of all women yet especially susceptible to their kindness. Hence, he facilely accepted gifts from wealthy women like Mason and Amy Spingarn (who financed his Lincoln education), and even from friends like Zora. Yet Zora never felt exploited in this regard. She and Langston were close, and the trading of currency was part of their camaraderie. When she needed money, Zora knew, she could borrow from Langston and other friends; and when she had money, she lent it freely. Having just inked her deal with Mason, Zora felt flush and altruistic. Despite Hughes's $150 monthly stipend from Godmother, Zora vowed to send him money out of her first check. "I know that you NEEDS," she teased.

Zora was not as concerned, it seemed, about her husband's needs—and she certainly did not invite Herbert Sheen to join her again in the South. During the previous autumn in New York, while Zora organized her notes from her first collecting trip, she and Sheen had lived as husband and wife for a brief time at her West Sixty-sixth

Street apartment. Sheen had traveled to Manhattan to be with his wife soon after she and Hughes finished their southern excursion. In November 1927, Zora and Herbert joined all of Harlem in mourning singer-dancer Florence Mills, who'd died suddenly of appendicitis at the peak of her popularity. An ardent fan since 1921's *Shuffle Along*, Hughes also was among the 57,000 people who filed by Mills's casket; he skipped classes at Lincoln to attend the New York funeral, which ended with a flock of blackbirds flying over Mills's grave at Woodlawn Cemetery. A month before, Zora and Herbert had seen Langston under more cheerful circumstances: They joined him, Ethel Waters, Nella Larsen, Carl Van Vechten, and others for dinner at the home of Carlo's friend Eddie Wasserman.

Despite the couple's occasionally high-profile social appearances, the Hurston-Sheen relationship was largely "a Fannie Hurst marriage"—a term the media had coined, with some disdain, after the famous novelist's secret, five-year-old marriage (to Jacques Danielson) had come to light back in 1920. "LIVE APART, THEIR OWN WAY," *The New York Times* had blared on page one. The incredulous headline had gone on to tell the whole story: "Meet By Appointment—It's a New Method Which Rejects 'Antediluvian Custom.'"

Hurston had not set out to imitate her former boss, but her approach to marriage, like Hurst's, was remarkably advanced for the times. Zora seemed determined not to let marriage change the way she moved through the world—as a woman who was unencumbered, independent, and free. To that end, Zora kept her own name once she was married: She signed the contract with Mason as "Zora Hurston" and never appended the name "Sheen" to her own. Few of her friends in Harlem even knew she had acquired a husband. "Zora didn't seem to fit into a kitchen or a marriage," one acquaintance noted.

For the most part, the Hurston-Sheen relationship continued to be a long-distance one. Yet, even when they were together, the distance between them seemed to grow. Traveling again to the South—and encouraging Sheen to return to medical school in Chicago—appeared to be "a way out without saying anything very much," Zora would recall. "Let nature take its course." Apparently deciding nature needed some help, Zora abruptly severed her ties with Sheen in January 1928. The problem, again, was her career—or, perhaps more accurately, her fear that her career would stagnate in domestic bacteria if she remained with Sheen. "I am going to divorce Herbert as soon as this is over," she told Hughes, "this" meaning her second folklore-collecting trip. "He tries to hold me back and be generally obstructive, so I have broken off relations since early January and that's that."

Free from all obstructions, real or imagined, Zora began her second southern expedition in the Mobile Bay. She made Cudjo Lewis her first stop not just because, as she told Hughes, "he is old and may die before I get to him otherwise." Zora also had something to prove, if only to herself. She wanted to interview Lewis again to make up for the poor work that had spurred her to plagiarize, and she wanted to get material from him that no other researcher had successfully obtained. After a month or so, Hurston largely had accomplished both goals and eventually would write a book-length study of Cudjo Lewis. During a series of conversations at his home in Plateau, three miles from Mobile, Lewis recalled how his people, the Takkoi, had been captured by the warriors of neighboring Dahomey and sold to American slavers. Tears welled in his eyes as he described the trip across the ocean in the *Clotilde*. But what moved Hurston most about the old man—whom she always called by his African name, Kossola—was how much he continued to miss his people back in Nigeria. "I lonely for my folks," he told her. "After seventy-five years, he still had that tragic sense of loss. That yearning for blood and cultural ties. That sense of mutilation. It gave me something to feel about," Hurston wrote.

By January 31, Zora had finished her visit with Cudjo Lewis, bought a shiny gray Chevrolet (having sold off Sassy Susie), paid another visit to Eatonville, and moved into the living quarters of the Everglades Cypress Lumber Company in Loughman, Florida. About twelve miles below Kissimmee, Loughman was just across the line that divided Zora's home county, Orange, from Polk County—where the water tasted like cherry wine, according to a popular folk song. Zora had heard "Polk County Blues" so often, she could sing it from memory: "You don't know Polk County lak Ah do / Anybody been dere, tell you de same thing too." Hurston longed to know Polk County as well as the song's originator, and she was now free to get to know it on her own terms.

Liberated from the scientific dictates of Franz Boas and Carter G. Woodson, Hurston could utilize all that she'd learned from her field experience the previous year, but she no longer had to employ the techniques the two scholars required. Godmother only wanted results—as much folklore as Zora could collect—and didn't care so much about form or method. Zora was free to do it *her* way, and she was thrilled: "I want to collect like a new broom," she declared.

On February 29, 1928, when her long-sought bachelor's degree in English finally was conferred by the signing of a document in New York City, Hurston could not have been farther away from Barnard's consecrated corridors. The thirty-seven-year-old graduate was deep in the Florida woods answering the call of anthropology—and giving thanks, perhaps, that the leap year had afforded her an extra day for collecting.

In Loughman, Zora rented a room at a boardinghouse owned by the Everglades Cypress Lumber Company but run by a woman named Mrs. Allen. Her daughter, Babe Hill, had just gotten out of jail for shooting her husband to death. Because black men's lives were not deemed valuable in the South, however, she had been required to serve only a few months' time. "Negro women *are* punished in these parts for killing men, but only if they exceed the quota," Hurston noted wryly. "I don't remember what the quota is. Perhaps I did hear but I forgot."

Babe Hill was a member of Loughman's diverse black community, which included family men, Christian women, and itinerant preachers. She was among the work camp's sizable population of hard-loving, weapon-wielding women who did not mind fighting for what they wanted. "Fan-foot, what you doing with my man's hat cocked on *your* nappy head? I know you want to see your Jesus," Zora heard such women say. "Fool wid me and I'll cut all your holes into one." The camp also had its share of hard-driving, rough-talking men who, as Zora delicately put it, did not "say embrace when they meant they slept with a woman." Because of its transient nature, the sawmill camp was a place where love was quickly made and unmade: "Take you where I'm going, woman? Hell no!" men were heard to say. "Let every town furnish its own."

During Zora's first few nights at the boardinghouse, several men dropped by to check out the new addition to the quarters. But they said very little to her and bluffly fended off her efforts at friendliness. Zora's Barnardese was long gone, yet she still was getting a tepid reception among the people she needed to know. "This worried me," she admitted, "because I saw at once that this group of several hundred Negroes from all over the South was a rich field for folk-lore, but here was I figuratively starving to death in the midst of plenty."

The men came regularly to the women's boardinghouse for after-work socializing. Zora lent her guitar to a player who didn't have one, and men and women began chatting with her easily between songs and sips of cola. Yet she remained an outsider. At once, Zora recognized that these were the same "feather-bed tactics" that had stymied her previous folklore-collecting efforts. "The Negro, in spite of his open-faced laughter, his seeming acquiescence, is particularly evasive," she would write. "You see we are a polite people and we do not say to our questioner, 'Get out of here!' We smile and tell him or her something that satisfies the white person because, knowing so little about us, he doesn't know what he is missing. The Indian resists curiosity by a stony silence. The Negro offers a feather-bed resistance. That is, we let the probe enter, but it never comes out. It gets smothered under a lot of laughter and pleasantries."

Unlike the white questioner who might not know when his curiosity was being gently thwarted, Zora knew. She just didn't know why. Finally, a young man she'd managed to befriend told her: Her shiny Chevy had convinced everyone that she must be a revenue officer or a detective of some kind. And since the law was often lax in these southern work camps, several of the Loughman laborers were fugitives or had served some jail time. They certainly did not want to get too friendly with someone like her.

That night, in order to win the lumber camp's trust, Zora made up a plausible lie: She told everyone she was a bootlegger, on the run from the law in Jacksonville and Miami. It sounded reasonable enough; a bootlegger would need—and could afford—a car. Immediately, resistances began to melt.

The following Saturday night, Zora went to the bimonthly payday party, where soft drinks were served alongside "coon dick," a strong, homemade whiskey. The music of choice was guitar music, and the only dancing was square dancing. Zora, whose mother had been a huge fan of the square dance, was eager to participate. But she watched in frustration as all the other women—women with names like Big Sweet and East Coast Mary—got escorted onto the dance floor. At five feet four inches tall, and weighing about 130 pounds, Zora had generous hips that whispered for attention, while her full lips and candid eyes dared would-be suitors to keep silence. Yet no one asked her to dance.

Vexed, Zora went outside where several people stood talking in small collections near the fire; her presence brought conversation to a lull. After a few awkward moments, a wiry man came over and introduced himself as Pitts. Appreciative of Zora's laughing acceptance of his playful overtures, he let her in on a secret: A lot of men wanted to talk to her but were intimidated because they thought she was rich. Zora quickly scanned the crowd and saw that her $12.74 dress from Macy's stood out sorely among all the $1.98 Sears catalog outfits that populated the party. Mentally resolving to "fix all that no later than the next morning," Zora slipped into the handed-down language of Eatonville to assure Pitts that she was no better off—no different—than any of them. "Oh, Ah ain't got doodley squat," she said. "Mah man brought me dis dress de las' time he went to Jacksonville. We wuz sellin' plenty stuff den and makin' good money. Wisht Ah had dat money now."

Satisfied that she was one of them, Pitts treated Zora to some refreshments—her choice of roasted peanuts, fried rabbit, fish, chicken, or chitterlings—and asked her to dance. Soon, other men filled her dance card as well. Zora ended the evening standing on a table singing "John Henry" (a popular Negro work song) and inviting others to join in with the verses they knew. Vocally urged by all to "spread her jenk"—to have a good time—Zora did, and so did everyone else.

After that, Zora's car was everybody's car, and she was enjoined to sing "John Henry" at every party she attended—and she attended every one. In due time, she revealed to her new friends her real purpose for being there. They had trouble at first believing someone would want to document their tall tales and small-town lives. Zora convinced them of the value of their stories, however, by holding "a lying contest" and awarding prizes for the best-spun yarns. With this, the first of several such contests, Zora hit pay dirt. "I not only collected a great deal of material," she recalled, "but it started individuals coming to me privately to tell me stories they had no chance to tell during the contest."

The Loughman laborers felt comfortable going to Zora with their stories because she had become a part of their lives. Applying what anthropologists call the participant-observer technique, she immersed herself in the world of the sawmill camp. Writing to Langston Hughes about the folk opera they still planned to write, Zora confessed: "I have not written a line of anything since I have been down here. . . . I have several good ideas, but nothing worked out. I am truly dedicated to the work at hand and so I am not even writing, but living every moment with the people."

Zora's vocational ambivalence—which had first emerged in 1926 when she began studying anthropology—had temporarily resolved itself. For now at least, anthropology had won out over literature, simply because of the demands of her fieldwork. Hurston never *consciously* chose science over art, however; she always wanted to do both. In fact, her holistic, Eatonville-bred worldview would not have inclined her to regard it as an either/or question. Subconsciously, though, she had chosen anthropology over literature the moment she signed Charlotte Mason's contract, which effectively prevented her from taking any artistic license with the scientific material she collected. Yet Zora still saw limitless literary possibilities in the lore: "I can <u>really</u> write a village anthology now," she told Hughes, "but I am wary about mentioning it to Godmother for fear she will think I'm shirking, but <u>boy</u> I think I could lay 'em something now." In another letter, she wrote: "I am getting inside of Negro art and lore. I am beginning to <u>see</u> really. . . . Langston, Langston, this is going to be <u>big</u>. Most gorgeous possibilities are showing themselves constantly."

Hurston's frequent correspondence with Hughes was full of fun and complicity, a natural outgrowth of the closeness they'd cultivated the previous summer. Langston kept Zora abreast of the latest gossip in New York: Novice actors Bruce Nugent and Wallace Thurman had joined the massive cast of the stage version of *Porgy*, he informed her. ("More power to them," she responded.) Meanwhile, Zora had missed the biggest social event of the Harlem Renaissance: Countee Cullen's April 9 marriage to Yolande Du Bois, W.E.B.'s daughter. Many among the three thousand guests at the

extravagant ceremony believed it was the perfect marriage of intellect and beauty. Those who knew Cullen better—such as Hughes,
who'd rented tails to serve as an usher at Cullen's "parade," as he
called it—were not surprised when the homosexual poet announced
he was sailing to Paris, not with his bride but with his best man,
Harold Jackman. Cullen was going to Europe to study—armed with
a Guggenheim fellowship, Langston told Zora. "A Negro goes abroad
to whiteland to learn his trade! Ha!" Zora replied cynically. "That
was inevitable for Countee. It will fit him nicely too. Nice, safe,
middle-class."

Along with the chitchat, Hughes advised Zora on ways to stay in
Godmother's good graces: At his suggestion, she sent Mason some
fine carving wood from Mobile, for instance, and some succulent
melons from Florida. She also needed to write to Godmother more
regularly, Hughes counseled. Preoccupied with her work, Zora was
satisfied that her psychic connection with Godmother had ripened
and believed their telepathic communication was sufficient.
Sometimes, for instance, a letter from Godmother would find her in
the field, Zora noted, "and lay me by the heels for what I was *thinking*." But telepathy was not enough for the old lady, Hughes
cautioned; she needed more concrete and frequent reports on
Hurston's progress. In addition to this practical, watch-your-back
advice, Langston constantly plied Zora with suggestions for her
research—ideas that she found enormously helpful.

In turn, Hurston sent Hughes snippets of stories, an intercepted
love letter from one informant to another, and pages of Negro
verse—to use as he wished—straight from the mouths of the folk.
She also became something of a publicity agent for Hughes in the
South, reading regularly from his most recent collection of poetry,
Fine Clothes to the Jew. "An interpretation of the 'lower classes,' the
ones to whom life is least kind," as Hughes described it, the 1927
book overflowed with blues and sexuality and the unvarnished voices
of the black masses. Predictably, Negro critics panned it: One
reviewer at New York's *Amsterdam News* called *Fine Clothes* "about
100 pages of trash" and labeled Hughes a "sewer dweller." The
Chicago Whip was equally disgusted: "These poems are unsanitary,
insipid and repulsing." In Loughman, however, where Zora read from
the book to kick off a lying contest, "they got the point," she reported

excitedly, "and enjoyed it <u>immensely</u>." Seeing the reaction at the sawmill camp, Zora started reading Hughes's poetry wherever she went. She began each storytelling contest by telling people who Langston Hughes was, then reading a few poems from what soon became known as "De Party Book." "You are being quoted in R.R. camps, phosphate mines, turpentine stills, etc.," Zora assured her friend.

Obeying Godmother's command, Hurston was conducting her work in secret and in isolation. Her closeness with Hughes was helped along by the fact that he was one of the few friends who knew where she was or what she was doing. During this period, she was no longer in touch with Meyer, Hurst, Van Vechten, Lawrence Jordan, or any of her previous correspondents.

Hughes was not Hurston's only pen pal and would-be adviser, however. She also was receiving letters from Alain Locke offering suggestions for her work. He urged Zora to implore Cudjo Lewis to avoid talking with other folklore collectors—white ones, no doubt— who he and Godmother felt "should be kept entirely away not only from the project in hand but from this entire movement for the rediscovery of our folk material." He also advised Zora to pay particular attention to African survivals in the stories and games she collected and to look out for allusions to snakes and water. Such allusions, Locke advised, often showed up in the African literature he'd been reading recently.

Zora seemed to take Locke's suggestions with a box of salt; she most certainly did not receive them as gratefully as she did Hughes's advisories. Just the previous year, Hurston had envisioned herself, Hughes, and Locke as an intellectual triangle. She even sketched a figure to represent her vision, with herself and Hughes forming the triangle's base and Locke at its apex. Now, however, she clearly valued Hughes's thoughts far above those of her former Howard University professor. It was, perhaps, a case of the student exceeding the teacher. Of course, Zora was grateful to Locke for introducing her to Charlotte Mason—and, because he was Mason's closest adviser, she made sure her correspondence with him was cordial. Zora even invited Locke to join her for a week or two in her southern travels. Even so, she harbored an intuitive distrust for the fastidious professor and shared her findings with him sparingly. She confided to

Hughes: "I have come to 5 general laws, but I shall not mention them to Godmother or Locke until I have worked them out. Locke would hustle out a volume right away."

The "5 general laws"—actually six—that Hurston outlined for Hughes provided a glimpse of the richness of the material she was collecting. Touching on a range of ideas—from the Negro penchant for drama and mimicry to the "restrained ferocity" of black music and dance—Hurston's list of discoveries also illustrated just how much she had matured as an anthropologist.

Zora saved perhaps her most profound observation for the very end of her three-page epistle to Hughes. "Negro folk-lore is still in the making," she announced in an enthusiastic postscript. "A new kind is crowding out the old."

Hurston was eager to find an artistic outlet for this still-in-the-making folklore. And she was beginning to feel that writing it down was not enough. To be fully appreciated, this material needed to be performed—just as she had acted out Eatonville's stories at Harlem parties. Black folklore, Zora felt, demanded a stage: "Did I tell you before I left about the new, the _real_ Negro art theatre I plan?" she asked Hughes. "Well, I shall, or rather _we_ shall act out the folk tales, however short, with the abrupt angularity and naivete of the primitive 'bama nigger. Just that with naive settings. What do you think?" Inviting Hughes to be a fifty-fifty collaborator in the proposed theater ("in fact," she wrote, "I am perfectly willing to be 40 to your 60 since you are always so much more practical than I"), Zora barely could contain her zeal: "I _know_ it is going to be _glorious_! A really new departure in the drama." Hurston also offered Hughes a couple of street scenes to use in his own work, since she was contractually forbidden to use them. "Godmother asked me not to publish," she noted, "and as I am making money I hope you can use them."

Though Zora was beginning to chafe under Godmother's no-publication restriction, she was thankful for the opportunity to focus so one-pointedly on her collecting work. With her car, her camera, and no worries about money, she was able to move about freely and collect copiously. After fewer than three months in the field, she told Hughes, "I believe I have almost as many stories now as I got on my entire trip last year." With Loughman serving as her base, Zora took frequent jaunts to the phosphate mines in nearby Mulberry,

Lakeland, and Pierce, where she collected a bundle of children's tales and games, and met Mack Ford, a Pierce man who, in Zora's words, "proved to be a mighty story teller before the Lord."

Zora felt a warm familiarity with Ford, and others like him, because she'd spent a good deal of time in the company of such men. She'd grown up with six brothers, she'd routinely lingered among the mostly male storytellers on Joe Clarke's porch, and she'd inhaled the aftershave-scented air of the Washington barbershop where she once worked as a manicurist. Consequently, Zora had developed an appreciation for maleness that served her well in her fieldwork. At the male-dominated work camps in Polk County and elsewhere, she was able to establish a convivial connection, a kind of brotherly trust, with the men without having to compromise herself sexually. Zora rapidly "dug in with the male community," as she put it, and was even allowed to accompany a work gang to the cypress swamp, where Loughman's men told enough tales to keep her scribbling in her notebook all day.

Though some women were jealous of her easy rapport with the men—especially those they claimed as their own—most of them liked Zora, too. She was particularly fortunate to have developed a friendship with Big Sweet, the most powerful woman in the lumber camp.

Big Sweet's authority had become evident to Zora during her first week in Polk County, when Zora and three or four hundred other Loughman residents witnessed Big Sweet giving a public "reading" of an enemy. The word "reading" was borrowed from the fortune-tellers, and it was another way of describing the Negro tradition of playing the dozens, or signifying. No matter what she called it, Big Sweet was an expert at it: She swiftly silenced her opponent with a few well-selected phrases about his dubious ancestry. Later, Big Sweet—a heavyweight in size and influence but light on her feet—was chosen to judge the Loughman storytelling contests, primarily because no one would dare dispute her choice of a winner. As one resident advised Zora: "Tain't a man, woman nor child on this job going to tackle Big Sweet."

Big Sweet was the embodiment of the blues. She was Bessie Smith, Ma Rainey, and all the bad and brazen women they sang about rolled into one. Though she was rumored to have killed at least two men before arriving in Loughman, Big Sweet was not mean, folks said, she simply did not brook foolishness. Described by a male coworker as "uh whole woman and half uh man," Big Sweet even struck fear in the lumber camp's white boss. "Dat Cracker Quarters Boss wears two pistols round his waist and goes for bad," Zora's land-lady told her, "but he won't break a breath with Big Sweet lessen he got his pistol in his hand. Cause if he start anything with her, he won't never get a chance to draw it."

Wisely, Zora befriended Big Sweet, winning her over with her immense charm and ready wit—and frequent rides in the Chevy. In no time, Zora saw where the sweet part of her new friend's name originated. Calling Zora "Little-Bit," Big Sweet accompanied her well-traveled comrade on some of her collecting trips to nearby towns. "Big Sweet helped me to collect material in a big way," Zora recalled. "She had no idea what I wanted with it, but if I wanted it, she meant to see to it that I got it." Through the sheer force of her personality, Big Sweet prevailed upon balky informants to share their songs and stories. In gratitude—and in a girlish kind of bonding ritual—Zora gave Big Sweet one of her bracelets. Big Sweet, in turn, became Zora's protector. "I aims to look out for you, too. Do your fighting for you," she told Zora. "Nobody better not start nothing with you, do I'll get my switch-blade and go round de ham-bone looking for meat."

Big Sweet's vow soon was put to the test. A woman named Lucy began hurling slurs at Zora because of the inordinate amount of time she seemed to be spending with Slim, a man Lucy had once dated and still desired. Slim was a valuable source of material for Zora, so she frequently bought him drinks and let him ride in her car. Lucy, however, was convinced that Zora's interest in Slim was sexual rather than scientific. Though Lucy and Slim had gone their separate ways long before Zora's arrival in Loughman, the scorned woman blamed Zora for their breakup. Resenting the visitor's store-bought clothes, shiny car, and lighter skin, Lucy began threatening Zora in a way that made her especially glad she had befriended Big Sweet. Lucy had been to jail occasionally for small fights, but she didn't get the respect that was afforded Big Sweet because she had never killed anyone. Zora must have looked to Lucy like an easy target—and killing the nosy newcomer would not only eliminate a rival for Slim's attention, it also would hurt the indomitable Big Sweet, who was Lucy's arch-enemy.

At the next payday party, Lucy sought to make good on her threats by ambushing Zora. Long after midnight, when the soiree was in full swing, Lucy came in and immediately spotted Zora in a most incriminating position: leaning against the wall right next to Slim. Lucy "started walking hippily straight at me," Zora recalled, with an open knife in her hand. The jook only had one door and Zora was far from it. There was no place to run except into the knife. "I didn't move but I was running in my skin. I could hear the blade already crying in my flesh. I was sick and weak," Zora recollected. "But a flash from the corner about ten feet off and Lucy had something else to think about besides me. Big Sweet was flying at her with an open blade and now it was Lucy's time to try to make it to the door." Big Sweet tackled Lucy before she could get to the exit, then all hell broke loose. "It seemed that anybody who had any fighting to do decided to settle-up then and there. Switch-blades, ice-picks and old-fashioned razors were out," Zora observed in terror. One of Zora's allies yelled for her to run. Though Zora was loath to leave Big Sweet in such a predicament, she knew Big Sweet could take care of herself. And under the circumstances, running was about all Zora could do. "Curses, oaths, cries and the whole place was in motion," she noted. "Blood was on the floor." Zora fell out the door, ran to her room, flung her bags into her car, and promptly shoved the Chevy into high gear. "When the sun came up," she would remember, "I was a hundred miles up the road, headed for New Orleans."

CHAPTER 18

Hoodoo

When Zora finally brought the Chevrolet to a definitive stop, she had reached Alabama's Mobile Bay and had left Loughman five hundred miles behind her in a veil of dust. In the tiny town of Magazine, Alabama, about 150 miles east of New Orleans, Zora collected more stories, love letters, and "double words"—emphatic, redundant, and sometimes comic compounds in which the function of a noun was placed before it as an adjective. Among those in Zora's notebook: sitting-chair, suck-bottle, cook-pot and hair-comb. From her recent experience in Polk County, Zora might have added another word to her list: cutting-knife.

Zora's hasty, knifepoint departure from Loughman had left her vulnerable to an occasional wave of nostalgia for the place where she'd found firm footing as a folklorist. Though she had collected almost a full volume of material during her four and a half months in the Polk County area, Zora knew she would have gotten more if circumstances had allowed her to stay. She didn't even have a chance to say a proper good-bye to Big Sweet, Slim, and other friends. Yet, she wrote, "I shivered at the thought of dying with a knife in my back, or having my face mutilated." When she thought about it that way, the young anthropologist felt no regrets about moving on.

In Magazine, Hurston's work continued to please her: "I am getting much more material in a given area/space & time than before because I am learning better technique," she assessed. "I have about enough for a good volume of stories but I shall miss nothing." About two hundred miles upstate, on the Tombigbee River, Zora found "another one of the original Africans." This one, a woman, was older than Cudjo Lewis and easier to interview, Hurston told Langston Hughes. "But no one will ever know about her but us."

Zora's decision to keep her latest discovery a secret from Godmother was an indicator of the precariousness of their relationship—a precariousness that Zora was only just beginning to fully recognize and acknowledge.

In early May 1928, when her actual degree from Barnard arrived in the mail, Zora gazed at it proudly for a few days then sent it to Godmother for safekeeping. It was a bittersweet moment: Zora was grateful to have a maternal figure to dote on her degree. Yet, even when the seventy-something matron was being "as tender as mother love," Charlotte Mason was no Lucy Hurston. Nor did Zora want her to be. Zora had idealized (and idolized) her mother, and she was not looking for anyone to take her place. But Godmother certainly had a role to play: as the kind, generous—and wealthy—grandmother, perhaps, that Zora never had.

Before the end of May, however, Zora had seen another side of Godmother. "Her tongue was a knout," she learned, "cutting off your outer pretenses, and bleeding your vanity like a rusty nail." Godmother's fury seemed to come unbidden, though. The first time Zora experienced it, she felt waylaid. Godmother had sent her a copy of the recently published *Negro Workaday Songs* by Howard Odum and Guy Johnson and asked for her comments. Zora judged that the book "misses the point in numerous places"—and that its white authors, two of the most prominent collectors of the period, seemed to approach Negro folk songs the way an unschooled Nordic would dance the black bottom. In a letter to Godmother, Zora wrote a short criticism of the book in which she said "that white people could not be trusted to collect the lore of others, and that the Indians were right." At this, Mason became acerbic and angry. "I was quoting Godmother's words," Zora explained to Alain Locke later, "but somehow she felt that I included her in that category. . . . I was so sure we understood each other that I didn't say present company excepted. I am too sorry, but I can't see how I could have avoided it."

As soon as Godmother forgave her for that blunder, Zora committed another. When her essay "How It Feels to Be Colored Me" was published in the May 1928 issue of *The World Tomorrow*, Godmother was outraged. And again, Zora felt ambushed and unsure of what she'd done to provoke Mason's ire.

A memorable manifesto of individuality—of Zora's singular and affirmative sense of *me*-ness—the essay contained nothing that should have upset Godmother, as far as Zora could see. She began the two-page piece with disarming humor: "I am colored but I offer nothing in the way of extenuating circumstances except the fact that I am the only Negro in the United States whose grandfather on the mother's side was *not* an Indian chief," Hurston wrote with a personalized, unapologetic sense of race pride. "I am not tragically colored," she declared. "There is no great sorrow dammed up in my soul, nor lurking behind my eyes. I do not mind at all. I do not belong to the sobbing school of Negrohood who hold that nature has somehow given them a lowdown dirty deal and whose feelings are all hurt about it. . . . No, I do not weep at the world—I am too busy sharpening my oyster knife."

Godmother was not upset by anything Hurston wrote in the essay; rather, she was incensed that it had been published at all. In her view, its publication meant Zora had violated the terms of their agreement. But if either woman bothered to look at the contract again, they saw that it contained nothing explicitly forbidding Hurston from publishing her own creative work. The agreement simply prohibited her from publishing any material she collected on Godmother's behalf. Charlotte Mason, however, had effectively extended that clause to apply to *all* of Hurston's writing. She was not to publish *anything* without Godmother's approval.

As this realization set in, Zora had two choices: She could have confronted Mason about the bait-and-switch and refused to let the old widow dictate if and when she could publish her own work. This option was risky, however; it likely would have inflamed Godmother and caused her to snatch back her funding, leaving Zora in the lurch with her collecting work only partially finished. Zora's other option was to bite her tongue and bide her time.

Zora chose the latter, explaining to Godmother that "How It Feels to Be Colored Me" had been submitted to *The World Tomorrow*—the magazine where Wallace Thurman now worked—to help defray the printing debts for *Fire!!* Vouching for Zora, Locke assured

Godmother that she did not make any money from the essay and that it had gone to the magazine months before the two women even met. Given this explanation, Godmother's wrath soon subsided.

Exactly why Godmother wanted to prevent Hurston from publishing remains unclear. The fact is, Mason exercised considerable control over all her protégés and frequently interfered artistically. While painting a mural in Harlem, for instance, Aaron Douglas once was ordered down from his scaffolding to receive a tongue-lashing from Godmother for some perceived infraction. He also occasionally was required to withdraw from major commissions that affronted Godmother's sense of what was proper for a black artist.

With Zora a thousand miles away, however, and essentially free to do as she pleased because of that distance, Godmother's power over her was limited. Perhaps the old woman's publication ban was her attempt to rein in the young folklorist, whose reputation for independence was well known. Mason also distrusted Hurston's other primary white influence, Franz Boas; her prohibition ensured that Boas would not persuade Hurston to publish in any scientific journals, which had little value in Godmother's eyes.

Finally, in her egoistic conception of herself, Godmother genuinely believed she knew what was best for Zora and all her "godchildren." For Zora's own good, she did not wish for her to dissipate her powers "in things that have no real meaning"—that is, in writing or publishing anything that Godmother herself had not approved. Still, no matter how Mason justified the publishing ban to herself, it was ultimately a damning display of precisely the kind of racial arrogance she claimed to abhor in practically every other white person she met.

To be sure, Zora's financial relationship with Godmother both confined and liberated her. Hurston saw herself as a woman with a mission: She was going to show the world that "the greatest cultural wealth on the continent" was to be found in the "sayings and doings of the Negro farthest down." Godmother's publication ban—confining as it was—seemed to Zora a small price to pay for the freedom the dowager's money afforded her to fulfill this mission. Agreeing to abide by Godmother's rules for the present was Zora's compromise with her future. If this compromise effectively made her a prisoner, she could take some consolation in the knowledge that she was, at least, a captive of her own ambition, in a prison of her own design.

Zora spent all of June and July collecting material in Magazine, where her readings from Hughes's *Fine Clothes to the Jew* made the book so popular, folks began singing the poems at parties. On the July Fourth weekend, Zora reported, "two men came over with guitars and sang the whole book. Everybody joined in. It was the strangest and most <u>thrilling</u> thing." Delighted that people had made Hughes's literature "so much a part of themselves they go to improvising on it," Zora suggested that Langston send her some of his books to sell. The response to Hughes's poetry also fueled Hurston's own enthusiasm for writing books that celebrated common people so affectionately and portrayed them so authentically. To that end, she began planning a volume of work songs, with music for piano and guitar, and promised Godmother she would send her the first song to see if she liked it.

By the first week of August, Zora had moved into a three-room house at 7 Belville Court in Algiers, just across the Mississippi River from New Orleans. A short ferry ride to the French Quarter, the neighborhood was splendid for collecting, she'd been told, and the rent was only ten dollars a month, including electricity and running water. For sixteen dollars more, she furnished the entire place. In these comfortable lodgings, Hurston's plans for packaging her collected material mushroomed: She envisioned a compendium of folk stories; a collection of children's games; a volume on drama and the Negro; a collection of work songs with guitar arrangement, to be called "Mules & Men"; a volume on religion; one on words and their meanings; and a book of love letters.

Meanwhile, Hurston's work on conjure was still before her. On August 6, she wrote to Hughes: "I have landed here in the kingdom of Marie Leveau and expect to wear her crown someday."

Marie Leveau was a celebrated Creole conjurer who lived as a freedwoman during the 1800s in New Orleans's famous Vieux Carré. The self-proclaimed "Pope of Voodoo" also was a devout Catholic, reportedly attending Mass every day. Leveau died near the end of the nineteenth century, after at least one lifetime of extraordinary spiritual accomplishments. According to written and oral accounts, the original Marie Leveau had a daughter who also was a magisterial voodoo priestess. She bore a striking resemblance to her mother and did her work under the name Marie Leveau as well, causing some people to believe the conjure queen's power had given her an ageless beauty and an exceptionally long life. Whatever the facts, Leveau's legend was numinous and nothing short of awesome, Hurston discovered. Nearly fifty years after Marie Leveau's death (in 1881, according to most sources), her name alone still could cause believers and skeptics alike to quiver.

Hurston was a believer. And why not? "Belief in magic is older than writing," she once noted, implying that if she could believe in writing, she certainly could believe in magic. Hurston's Eatonville upbringing, along with her explorations of conjure in the summer of 1927, had convinced her that hoodoo was more than magic, however. It was a secret—and legitimate—religion. Now, she planned to devote the next six months to a serious study of it.

The terms "hoodoo," "voodoo," "obeah," and "conjure" are all used to describe a set of beliefs and practices centering on an abiding conviction that human beings—trained in certain rites—can reliably call upon spiritual forces to alter situations that seem rationally hopeless.

Conjure's roots are distinctly African. A fusion of beliefs from various parts of the continent, vodou—commonly called voodoo—is the name generally applied to an intricate, syncretic religion with several offshoots (such as Candomblé and Santería) that still hold sway in some parts of Africa, South America, and the Caribbean. The word "vodou" derives from *vodu*, which means "spirit" or "deity" in the Fon language of Dahomey (now Benin, in West Africa).

When Africans were brought to the Americas as slaves, they were forced to adopt Christianity. Purloined largely from the Yoruba peoples of West Africa, slaves in the United States—like those in Haiti, Brazil, and elsewhere—surreptitiously melded their traditional spiritual beliefs and practices with the white man's religion. In this way, on slave plantations throughout the South, vodoun's American cousin—hoodoo—was born.

At its most simplistic level, hoodoo is sympathetic magic. At its most complex, it is a sophisticated spirituality, as Hurston saw it, with "thousands of secret adherents." Her research in New Orleans—

"the hoodoo capital of America"—confirmed that the conjure tradition was "burning with a flame in America," as she wrote, "with all the intensity of a suppressed religion."

Hoodoo had taken such a tenacious hold in New Orleans for a variety of reasons: The French owned Louisiana throughout much of the eighteenth century, and they often imported slaves from Martinique, Haiti, and other French-speaking islands, where the captives had successfully grafted their traditional African spirituality onto Roman Catholicism, with its colorful pantheon of saints. Once imported, the slaves' blended religion flourished in New Orleans, even after the city became a U.S. property in the Louisiana Purchase of 1803. By the early 1900s, New Orleans was such a conjure stronghold, Hurston found, that many white Louisianans had become convinced of its effectiveness. But the vast majority of hoodoo's adherents in New Orleans, as elsewhere, were black.

Slyly counting herself as a believer by using the word "we," Hurston would write: "The way we tell it, hoodoo started way back before everything." According to many of the conjure experts Hurston met, God was the original hoodoo doctor, creating the world in "six days of magic spells and mighty words."

Hoodoo's practitioners are called hoodoo doctors, voodoo doctors, priests or priestesses, two-headed doctors (because they're said to have twice as much sense as regular people), conjure doctors, or, simply, conjurers. Many conjure doctors also are root workers, employing various medicinal herbs and roots for healing, as well as for supernatural effects. Some root doctors, however, have nothing to do with hoodoo; they are strictly healers.

Folks consulted root workers for a variety of reasons, Hurston found. Many black people in the rural South of the 1920s and thirties had little faith in conventional medicine and put their stock in the folk medicine of their ancestors instead. Consequently, they might visit a root doctor in search of a cure for anything from an upset stomach to blindness. Patients with rheumatism, for instance, were sometimes advised to steep five or six mullein leaves in a quart of water and drink three or four glasses a day. For excessive menstrual bleeding, some root doctors recommended cooking a grated nutmeg and a pinch of alum in a quart of water, then drinking a half glass of the mixture three times a day. And for the sores of syphilis, a salve of cigar ashes and blue ointment (purchased from the root doctor) was said to work wonders.

For matters of the heart, for tangled legal cases, for good luck, and for warding off enemies, many people turned to the arcane powers of hoodoo. If a man was murdered, for example, a hoodoo doctor might counsel his loved ones to bury him with his hat on, so the murderer would be brought to justice. To help someone get a job, a conjurer might take nine crumbs of bread, three slices of garlic, some steel dust, and lodestone and place it all in a small bag for the job seeker to clandestinely wear at his interview. With this amulet, it was said, one could not be refused a job. To compel a man to love her, a woman might wear a perfumed concoction called "Cleo-May." Or to keep her husband home, she might be advised to tie a sock in a knot and hide it under a rug.

Women often used hoodoo to gain power over men, Hurston observed, and black people sometimes used it to exact retribution for racial injustices that would never have their day in a southern court. Thus, hoodoo was an alternative form of power for people who might otherwise feel powerless. And when employed conscientiously, it was a restorative power, not a destructive one. Several practitioners Hurston met, for instance, adamantly refused to use conjure to kill, under any circumstances.

Some white scholars, Hurston knew, had horribly misrepresented hoodoo, as they had misconstrued much of black culture. In the 1926 book *Folk Beliefs of the Southern Negro*, for instance, white southerner Newbell Niles Puckett mocked the conjure remedies he learned about while masquerading as a hoodoo doctor himself. Puckett never seemed to consider it possible that the black conjurers who deigned to talk to him might have plied him with counterfeit information because of his whiteness and his charade. As a result, Puckett's "scholarship" portrayed hoodoo as a rather unsophisticated con game that could be exposed by any rational person. "It makes me sick to see how these cheap white folks are grabbing our stuff and ruining it," Hurston vented to Hughes. "My one consolation being that they never do it right and so there is still a chance for us."

As America's interest in psychic and paranormal phenomena grew—the nation's best-known psychic, Edgar Cayce, was frequently winning headlines—Hurston's research corroborated what she already knew: Hoodoo was not mere superstition, and its potency was not imagined; it was real. Of course, there were charlatans, as with any other religion. But hoodoo itself was an authentic spiritual path. That its huge body of followers protected it with such a guarded reticence was testament to its effectiveness: "It is not the accepted theology of the Nation and so believers conceal their faith," Hurston noted. "Brother from sister, husband from wife. Nobody can say where it begins or ends. Mouths don't empty themselves unless the ears are sympathetic and knowing."

With her sympathetic ears, Hurston studied hoodoo the same way she studied every aspect of black folk life: by immersing herself in it. To do this, she apprenticed herself to hoodoo's masters. For each doctor she studied with, however, she had to prove her sincerity and worthiness as a seeker by submitting to a rigorous process of initiation.

Hurston took these initiation rituals as seriously as a sannyasi would take the vows of monkhood. Some renunciation, in fact, was necessary. Most of Hurston's initiations required a period of celibacy and fasting. "The preparation period is akin to that of all mystics. Clean living, even to clean thoughts," she summed up. "A sort of going to the wilderness in spirit. The details do not matter."

The details do matter, however, in that they illustrate the purposefulness and dedication Hurston brought to her research. Some of her initiation ceremonies required intimate (though apparently not sexual) encounters with her teachers, several of whom were men. In one case, for example, Hurston had to allow her initiator, a middle-aged man, to come to her Belville Court home to give her a ritual bath in water embellished with various items she'd been instructed to collect, including parsley, a handful of salt, and three tablespoons of sugar. After her teacher had washed and dried her—paying particular attention to the "control" areas, the head, back, and chest—Zora put on new underwear bought for the occasion and was then given a specially prepared Bible. She was instructed to lie on her couch and read the third chapter of Job night and morning for nine days.

The mysterious rituals apparently paid off. By September, Hurston boasted: "I know 18 tasks, including how to crown the spirit of death, and kill."

Hurston left Algiers in October after a police crackdown routed out the best two-headed doctors. Crossing the muddy Mississippi, she moved to 2744 Amelia Street in New Orleans proper. Lush with cathedrals, speakeasies, and whorehouses, New Orleans was a mongrel metropolis—a place where the sacred and the profane seemed to meet on every street corner. Where hoodoo was concerned, Zora's move situated her exactly where she wanted to be: "in the lap of the activities."

There, she found that some teachers' initiation rituals demanded tremendous courage. In one terrifying rite of passage—the notorious "Black Cat Bone" ritual—Hurston was required to catch a black cat and throw it into a cauldron of boiling water, where it was ceremoniously cooked until its bones fell apart. This rite was for advanced practitioners whose work sometimes required them "to walk invisible," according to Father Joe Watson, Hurston's teacher at the time. "Some things must be done in deep secret," he explained, "so you have to walk out of the sight of man." For this, a conjurer needed the bone of a black cat to carry as a talisman. Hurston always recounted the Black Cat Bone experience with excessive and deliberate vagueness, saying only that she was impelled to pass several of the feline's bones through her mouth until one tasted bitter. Then some "unearthly terror" took hold. There were "indescribable noises, sights, feelings." Hurston concluded cryptically: "Before day I was home, with a small white bone for me to carry."

It's difficult to imagine the prissy Locke—or even the sometimes sickly Hughes—prowling the streets of New Orleans in the dead of night trying to catch a black cat, much less sampling its bones. (Merely locating and apprehending an appropriate cat was "hard work," Hurston reported, "unless one has been released for you to find.") To endure such rites, Hurston's interest in hoodoo had to be more than skin-deep and her belief in its power had to be genuine. Certainly, the conjure masters who accepted her as an apprentice possessed the innate intelligence to recognize a faker.

Father Watson, for instance, was an accomplished conjurer whose far-reaching reputation compelled Zora to seek him out. He was known throughout New Orleans and environs as "the Frizzly Rooster" because "he could remove curses, no matter who had laid them on whom," Hurston wrote. In that regard, he was like the frizzled chickens that many country folks kept in their yards to locate and scratch up any hoodoo that their enemies might have buried for them—hence his nickname.

The Frizzly Rooster, however, was not nearly as unkempt as his backyard counterparts. "Before my first interview with the Frizzly Rooster was fairly begun," Zora would recall, "I could understand his great following. He had the physique of Paul Robeson with the sex appeal and whatever-you-might-call-it of Rasputin. I could see that women would rise to flee from him but in mid-flight would whirl and end shivering at his feet. It was that way in fact." Watson's reckless sexual charisma caused his wife and assistant, Mary, to vow to leave him on numerous occasions. It also persuaded her to stay, Zora surmised.

As Watson's pupil, Zora was initiated as a "Boss of Candles" and empowered "to work with the spirits anywhere on earth." She was thus allowed to hold consultations on her own. On one occasion, for a five-dollar fee, she performed an intricate ritual to help a woman seeking justice for her husband's killer. On another, Zora and her teacher broke a glass at a woman's door to help her eject her bossy mother-in-law from her home. And, for a forty-dollar fee, Zora and Father Watson tied the hands of a doll behind its back—among other things—to abate a popular preacher's blind ambition.

"I am getting on in the conjure splendidly," Hurston reported to Hughes just before Thanksgiving. "I am knee deep in it with a long way to go." Thanking him for the New Orleans contacts he'd given her (from his visit the previous summer), Zora informed Langston that she had collected "lots of thrilling things," including "a marvelous dance ritual from the ceremony of death."

Zora learned the death dance—a ritual that was rarely performed—from her apprenticeship with Kitty Brown, whose specialty was bringing lovers together and spurring marriages. The well-paid conjure doctor also was a committed Catholic, as were many hoodoo practitioners Hurston met in New Orleans. Mother Kitty's Catholicism, however, did not prevent her from staging a death dance for a man who had occupied one woman's bed for three years, only to drain their joint savings and marry another. The wronged woman, Rachael, paid a hundred-dollar fee for her ex to be executed, by way of the dance. A good bit of the money was used to compensate the assembled dancers and to set the table with cake, wine, roast duck, and barbecued goat, which would feed the dancers as well as the spirit of Death.

A veritable who's who of New Orleans hoodoo doctors, the dancers were male and female, young and old. (Notably, the conjure world seemed remarkably egalitarian in terms of gender: Hurston met as many female hoodoo masters as male ones, and men and women often worked together.) After some discussion, Zora was allowed to dance as a delegate for Mother Kitty, whose neuritis impelled her to remain seated. Each of the six dancers had forty minutes alone on the floor, and the furious rhythm (created not by drums, which might have drawn police, but by heel-patting and hand-clapping) sustained Zora and the others for the full three-hour ceremony. Though all of the dancing served the same purpose—to beseech Death to cut down the womanizer—"there was no regular formula" to it, Hurston noted. "Some of the postures were obscene in the extreme. Some were grotesque, limping steps of old men and women. Some were mere agile leapings. But the faces! That is where the dedication lay." A person who had been danced upon was supposed to drop dead within nine days of the ritual. Five days after the dance, the philanderer—complaining of chest pains—deserted his bride and returned to Rachael, who then begged Mother Kitty to undo her death spell, which she did.

Using what she called "the vacuum method, grabbing everything I see," Hurston went for initiation to every conjure doctor she heard of. This method was costly—each doctor had to be paid—and naturally led to duplication. But Hurston felt this approach would yield the most thorough results, since many of the less famous doctors knew some details not known to the bigger ones.

Big or small, almost every hoodoo doctor in New Orleans professed some link with the great Marie Leveau. One of them, Luke Turner, claimed to possess the skin of the rattlesnake that had served Leveau's altar, and he always wrapped it around him when he had serious work to do. He also claimed to be Leveau's nephew. When all had been said and done, Zora would believe him.

When Hurston met Turner, she already had been initiated by five conjure doctors. Still, Turner brusquely refused to accept her as his pupil. "I could see he had no faith in my sincerity," Hurston would remember. "I could see him searching my face for whatever was behind what I said." After Zora's repeated visits and prodding, Turner eventually consented to at least consider her for an apprenticeship. In order to be sure, though, he made her sit before his altar for an hour. "We sat there silently facing each other across the candles and incense, for those sixty minutes," she recollected. Then Turner, who was in his seventies, stood behind Zora with his hands on her head. "After a while I forgot my fears, forgot myself, and things began to happen. Things for which I can find no words, since I had experienced nothing before that would furnish a simile," Hurston recalled. At one point, she could feel Turner's hands trembling atop her head. At another, she could hear him mumbling in an unrecognizable tongue. After that, Turner's body wrenched so violently, Zora thought he'd throw her from her chair. Instead, the man became completely still, as if he were listening to a voice. He soon answered: "Yeah, I goin' tell her. Yeah, I tell her all you say—yeah, unhunh, yeah."

Before Turner could tell Zora all she wished to know, however, she had to be initiated yet again. By this time, however, Turner had become so convinced of Zora's fitness as a hoodoo doctor that he wouldn't accept any money from her above what was needed for the actual cost of the ceremony. For nine nights, she was to sleep with her right stocking on and her left leg bare. "I must have clean thoughts," Hurston was told. "I must neither defile body nor spirit." At the end of the nine days, she went to Turner's aging pink stucco house in the Vieux Carré at nine o'clock in the morning carrying a bundle of necessary things. Among them were new underwear and three snakeskins, which the other hoodoo doctors who'd gathered for the occasion skillfully fashioned into garments for Zora to step into as soon as she was crowned.

Turner affixed the hide of a water moccasin to a green cloth and used it to cover the couch in his altar room. At 3:00 P.M., Zora, as naked as the day she came into the world, stretched out on the couch facedown, with her navel pressed to the snakeskin. For three days and three nights, she was to lie there, silent and fasting, while her spirit went in search of the Great Spirit, the Power-Giver, to accept her as Its own. Zora was not to have any food, but a pitcher of water was placed on a table at the head of the couch so that her soul would not wander off in search of water and risk being attacked by evil influences. "On the second day," Hurston would remember, "I began to dream strange exalted dreams. On the third night, I had dreams that seemed real for weeks. In one, I strode across the heavens with lightning flashing from under my feet, and grumbling thunder following in my wake." After sixty-nine hours and five psychic experiences, Hurston recalled, she awoke from her altered state "with no feeling of hunger, only one of exaltation."

Crowning Zora "the Rain-Bringer," Turner used two small brushes, dipped in yellow and red, to paint the lightning symbol on her back. Painted from her right shoulder to her left hip, it was to be Zora's sign forever. And the Great One was to speak to her through storms. "A pair of eyes was painted on my cheeks as a sign that I could see in more ways than one," Hurston remembered. "The sun was painted on my forehead."

Hurston remained in New Orleans through the 1928–29 winter, studying with Turner for several months. One day, he informed her that he had taught her all he knew and wanted her to become his partner. The Great Spirit had spoken, Turner said, and had notified him that Zora was the last conjure doctor he would make. In fact, the Spirit had told Turner, in one year and seventy-nine days, he would be dead. "He wanted me to stay with him to the end," Hurston would recall with emotion. "It has been a great sorrow to me that I could not say yes."

Though she was sufficiently trained in hoodoo to take over Turner's profitable business, as he wished, Zora had not forgotten her reason for embarking on the study of conjure in the first place. Her mission, she knew, was not to become a celebrated conjure doctor herself, but to chronicle the great hoodoo masters who thrived in the black South—and to legitimize their spiritual work by writing about it in a respectful fashion.

This did not mean she planned to expose all their secrets, however. As much as Hurston would reveal about her hoodoo studies in her subsequent writing, there was also much that she would conceal. A sacred silence shrouded hoodoo and protected it from religious intolerance, from those who would seek to stamp it out merely because they did not understand it. By the end of 1928, Hurston understood it more fully than any other scholar in America. "That is why these voodoo ritualistic orgies of Broadway and popular fiction are so laughable," she assessed. "The profound silence of the initiated remains what it is." And Hurston, herself an initiated practitioner, was bound to respect this silence, even while she pursued her scholarly ambitions and sought to set the public record straight. The balancing act required by this double consciousness—that of conjurer and that of chronicler—further sensitized Hurston's approach to hoodoo and to black folk culture in general. Her New Orleans experience also affirmed her conviction that the Negro farthest down, the so-called common man, was king: "That man in the gutter is the god-maker," she decided, "the creator of everything that lasts."

Hurston's immersion in New Orleans conjure completed her transition from an enthusiastic rookie folklorist to an adept and mature scholar. Recognizing this growth within herself, she wrote to Franz Boas to let him know that her unsuccessful 1927 fieldwork had not been in vain, after all. "The experience that I had under you was a splendid foundation, for whereas I got little for you, now, I know where to look and how," she told him. "Sometimes I have gotten in a week as much as I gathered for you through out. I regret it too, but I know that you understand, and will be pleased with me when I return."

By now, Hurston had joined the American Folk-Lore Society (and offered to nominate Hughes and Locke for membership), and soon would be invited to join the American Ethnological Society and the American Anthropological Society as well. In the fall of 1928, Margaret Mead's book _Coming of Age in Samoa_ (which devoted more than a quarter of its pages to a discussion of the Samoans' sexual liberalism) had become a surprise hit with lay readers—and had put the budding field of anthropology on the map. This surely alerted Hurston to the scientific and commercial possibilities of her own work. With this awareness, she felt it was appropriate to let the leading anthropologist in America know what she was doing. "This is confidential," Hurston wrote to Boas. "I accepted the money on the condition that I should write to no one." Yet, she added: "It is unthinkable, of course, that I go past the collecting stage without consulting you, however I came by the money."

Hurston's decision to consult Boas was not so much a rebellion against Godmother Mason as it was a further sign of her scholarly maturity. What serious anthropologist *wouldn't* want Boas's input on her work?

At the same time, Zora's deep dip into the well of New Orleans spirituality had matured her on another level that was beyond scholarship, beyond words. She had experienced a gradual ripening from within. And the depth of her mystical experience was lost even on Langston Hughes, whose regard for hoodoo was still superficial enough for him to jokingly ask Zora if she would conjure him. "Yes, I WILL conjure you too," she answered gently, "but only for good luck."

While she was in the hoodoo capital of America, however, Hurston did take the opportunity to conjure Godmother. Visiting a fortune-teller in Marrero, just across the river from New Orleans, Zora made a heartfelt wish, as she recalled, "that a certain influential white woman would help me." The seer put a light on the wish, then assured Zora that the woman in question would never lose interest in her as long as she lived. At 10:00 the next morning, Zora would remember, she received a telegram from Charlotte Mason "stating that she would stand by me as long as she lived." In the turbulent time ahead, this message would become Zora's anchor.

CHAPTER 19

Godmother's Rules

Godmother was kind enough to extend Hurston's employment contract through 1929, but not without a price: The "hazy dreams" of the Negro theater that Zora had spoken of with Langston Hughes and Alain Locke must be abandoned at once, Godmother demanded. "She trusts her three children to never let those words pass their lips again," a rebuked Hurston informed Locke, "until the gods decree that they shall materialize."

After a brief winter visit to New York to seal the extended deal with Godmother, Hurston returned to New Orleans to finish her conjure work. Her last night there, she gave a talk on poetry at the University of New Orleans and read six poems by *Fire!!* contributor Helene Johnson, a few from Hughes's *Weary Blues*, and *Fine Clothes to the Jew* from cover to cover. Though the frank language of *Fine Clothes* almost gave one old matron a heart attack, Zora told Langston, the students "et it up."

By the first week of April 1929, Zora had returned to her beloved Florida, where she stayed with her brother John and his wife, Blanche, on Evergreen Avenue in Jacksonville. "I am sitting down to sum up and I am getting on very well at it," Hurston apprised Hughes. "I am feeling full of my subjects," she added, but admitted she wasn't sure how established folklore scholars—the Odums and Johnsons and Pucketts of the world—would respond to her work. In fact, Hurston expected to hear "lots of hollering as various corns get stepped on."

After a couple of weeks in Jacksonville, Zora motored 170 miles downstate to Eau Gallie. Slap on the Indian River, this village near Melbourne was too tiny to warrant a pin on most maps, but it was just what Zora wanted: a beautiful and quiet place to sort through all the material she'd collected. She rented a small cabin there and hunkered down.

Some days, Zora felt swamped by the voluminosity of her material—and by the extraordinary task that lay ahead of her: to make sense of it all for the reading public. "I have more than 95,000 words of story material, a collection of children's games, conjure material, and religious material with a great number of photographs," she wrote to Franz Boas. Hurston then peppered her mentor with questions that would help to ensure her ethnographic accuracy: "Is it safe for me to say that baptism is an extension of water worship as a part of pantheism just as the sacrament is an extension of cannibalism? Isn't the use of candles in the Catholic church a relic of fire worship?" she wanted to know. "May I say that the decoration in clothing is an extension of the primitive application of paint (coloring) to the body?" Then—in direct defiance of her just-renewed contract with Godmother—Hurston promised Boas: "As soon as I can get the typing done, I shall send you the carbons."

Hurston knew the material she'd collected—and the conclusions she hoped to draw—could be academically contentious, as Boas suggested in his reply. That was exactly why she wanted his input. He could provide the anthropological perspective and expertise Hurston needed but could not get from Hughes, Locke, or Godmother, her trio of armchair collaborators.

Zora told none of the three—not even best friend Hughes—of her correspondence with Boas, but she was careful to keep them in the loop otherwise. Offering Hughes a stake in all that she did, Zora wrote: "Really I think our material is going to be grand, Langston." At the end of April, she surveyed her progress. "I am just beginning to hit my stride. At first I tried to do too much in a day. Now I am satisfied with a few pages if they say what I want. I have to rewrite a lot as you can understand," she told Hughes. "For I not only want to present the material with all the life and color of my people. I want to leave no loop-holes for the scientific crowd to rend and tear us."

Sensing that Godmother was getting anxious, Zora sent her some of the collected stories in raw form, with hopes of receiving the material back, along with Godmother's comments, by early June. Locke's place in the loop was a lesser concern for Hurston, who believed the professor merely "approves anything that has already been approved." Elaborating, she judged Locke severely, if soundly: "The trouble with Locke is that he is intellectually dishonest. He is too eager to be with the winner. . . . He wants to autograph all successes, but is afraid to risk an opinion first hand."

By the end of May, Zora had received a tentative thumbs-up from Godmother—parroted by Locke—on the material she'd sent to Park Avenue so far. She also was wrapping up first drafts of her volumes on lore and religion, the latter featuring an entire Baptist church service, rendered word for word and note for note. "I shall now set it aside to cool till it grows inside me," Hurston decided.

On a roll now, Zora spent part of the early summer working on the musical play she still hoped to cowrite with Hughes, despite Godmother's nixing of their plans for a Negro theater. Zora suggested they call their play "Jook." She already had worked out a filling-station skit, she reported, and had plenty of jook songs to include.

Hurston also suggested another collaboration of sorts with Hughes: She wanted to buy a tract of land on the Indian River, she told him, and build a Negro art colony—for "you, and Wallie, and Aaron Douglas and Bruce and me and all our crowd." The plat Zora had in mind, about three miles from Eau Gallie proper, would give the artists sufficient privacy while affording them a view of "the most beautiful river in the world," as well as the Atlantic. It would be "a lovely place to retire and write on occasion," she judged. At $4,000, she thought it was a good buy and felt it was "absolutely safe" from rednecks, though their group would be the first Negroes allowed to buy Indian River property. Zora didn't expect Hughes to contribute financially, she said; she just wanted his opinion. Did he think the wealthy A'Lelia Walker might like the idea enough to help with the $1,500 down payment? "We don't need too many. No big society stuff. Just a neat little colony of kindred souls," Zora fantasized. "I'm crazy to build me a house that looks something like an African king's menage. More elaborate, of course."

Zora's dream of becoming a homeowner, however, soon took a

backseat to more fundamental concerns. On a foray to St. Augustine in July, she was attacked by severe abdominal pains. Fearing she might need a stomach operation, Zora rushed to Flagler Hospital, a public facility occupying an elegant, new three-story building in the heart of the nation's oldest city. Her stomach was fine, doctors there said, but her liver was out of order—and had been dragging on her health for the past two years. Zora had to be hospitalized immediately. By July 23, though, she felt well enough to begin planning her drive down the coast to collect more lore and conjure in South Florida.

Zora spent all of August and early September in Miami, which she found pleasant and conducive to her work and her recovery. While waiting for her slowpoke stenographer to finish typing the work she'd given her, Zora collected more material and also started to develop new skit ideas for her folk opera with Hughes. By mid-August, she had seven skits completed and was beginning to try her hand at writing music. Her health and appetite were fully recovered: "I am getting on fine now," she reported, "and eating plenty." In early September, though, she hit a snag. Her collecting was "going at a rapid rate," she noted, but she felt a "little depressed spiritually."

Around the same time, in Miami's Liberty City, Zora heard some Bahamian music and saw a "jumping dance" that enthralled her. This spirit-elevating music struck her as "more original, dynamic and African" than the songs of American Negroes. Wanting to know more about Bahamian culture, Zora quickly convinced herself that a jaunt across the water to the island nation was just what she needed to permanently chase away her ennui. "Without giving Godmother a chance to object," Zora sailed for Nassau on September 12.

Hurston fell in love with the place before her feet even touched the ground. Her first night there, she stretched out in bed and listened to a rustling coconut palm whisper sweet nothings just outside her window. Then, she was delighted to hear a small chorus of male voices break into song. It was a lovely, melodious folk song about a rum-running boat called *Bellamina*. The next day, Zora met her serenaders, who gave her a hint at what prolific song makers they were. "You do anything, we put you in sing," they told her in lilting voices that hinted of Africa. Some Bahamians actually knew the African tribes from which they'd descended, Hurston soon discovered, and a

few even spoke the dialects of their ancestors. She immediately realized she needed to collect Bahamian folklore to contrast it with the
lore of black Americans—and to track its influence, since so many
Bahamians lived in South Florida. Before the end of September,
Hurston had collected twenty Bahamian songs and learned how to
"jump"—that is, how to dance in the way of the folk; she also had
recorded three reels of Bahamians performing their native folk
dances, including an impressive "Fire Dance." In addition, she had
acquired a Bahamian conga drum, called a gimbay, to take home
with her.

At one point, however, Zora thought she'd never make it home.
On September 28, Nassau was bashed by a devastating hurricane.
Traveling on the fierce wings of a 150-mph wind, the storm lingered
for five days. "It was horrible in its intensity and duration," recalled
Hurston, who was living with a Bahamian family. The second night,
as the tempest howled on, Zora had a premonition. Having learned
to trust the veracity of her visions—and having been told that the
Spirit would speak to her through storms—she leapt from her bed
and insisted that everyone in the house get out. Moments after they
heeded her warning, the building collapsed.

Zora temporarily joined the ranks of Bahamians who'd been rendered homeless by the storm, which blew down more than three
hundred houses in Nassau alone and also ripped through outlying
areas. In the days that followed, Zora found shelter, along with
dozens of Bahamians, at a local police station. Growing hungry, she
gave a man fifty cents to go out and bring back whatever food he
could find. He returned with a large bunch of bananas, about fifteen
rolls and a slab of bologna. Others at the shelter mobbed the man for
the food, despite the police presence, and Zora managed to get only
a couple of rolls and a banana. She was happy to have her life,
though. At least seven Bahamians lost theirs in the hurricane. "I saw
dead people washing around on the streets when it was over,"
Hurston remembered. "You could smell the stench from dead animals as well."

Despite the death and destruction, Zora stayed in Nassau for sev-
eral more days and collected some fragmented information on
Bahamian hoodoo, or obeah, as it was most commonly called there.
The day before she was scheduled to leave, she met a man who

she'd been told was the greatest of the island conjure doctors, but she didn't have sufficient time to spend with him. She did have time, though, to get the obeah man "favorably worked up" to her, as she put it. She then promised she'd return to study with him before the end of the year. "I had only my return ticket and 24 cents," she later explained, "so I had to come on."

When Zora returned to Miami and checked her post office box, Number 24, at the Lemon City Station, she found a pile of mail awaiting her. One piece in the stack was a wire from Hughes, responding to her early-September complaint of feeling down. So much had happened in the month since she'd sent that SOS, what with her trip to the Bahamas and all, but Hurston still was cheered by Hughes's encouraging, if tardy, reply. "Well, honey, your wire did me <u>so much</u> good," she wrote back. "Gee, I felt forlorn. Too tired. Been working two years without rest, & behind that all my school life with no rest. No peace of mind. But the Bahamas trip did me a world of good. I got rested while working hard."

Zora had been leaning heavily on Hughes during her exhausting two years of collecting. Langston's letters suggesting new angles of looking at her work—and ways to keep Godmother happy—were Zora's pillars during her time in the field. And she used her letters to him as sounding boards. "You know I depend on you so much," she often told him. Her reliance on Hughes was understandable: Hurston had not yet published a book; Hughes, on the other hand, had published two volumes of poetry that were well received among the proletariat, whose opinions mattered most to both writers. Hughes also had known Godmother longer than Hurston had, and he was geographically close to her—close enough, Zora figured, to gauge her moods. Now, Zora wanted to make sure Langston could read and edit the collection of stories—many from the Polk County lying contests—that she'd sent to Park Avenue. Godmother already had insisted that the stories' dirty words had to be toned down, Zora pointed out. "Can you not take them & edit them and indicate changes and generally touch up?" she asked her friend. "I want to close out all the volumes as soon as I can. When it is all in you and I can take plenty of time to edit it. Locke will be a great help too," she conceded, "but I am afraid he will not see it just as we do." Hurston suggested Hughes consult the original stories, in Godmother's safety deposit box, and make notes to send to her. Then she added a sisterly postscript: "Do you need some money?"

While Zora routinely offered to help Langston financially, she knew she could turn to him for something more valuable: emotional support. "You are my mainstay in all crises," she told him in October. "No matter what may happen, I feel you can fix it."

Another piece of mail awaiting Zora was from Locke, suggesting that she had not been specific enough about some of her religious material from New Orleans. She took his criticism constructively: As soon as she finished her collecting in Miami, around the end of October, she would simply go back to New Orleans to correct any oversights.

That settled, Zora slogged through the rest of her mail, then wrote a long-overdue letter to Franz Boas, responding to a job offer he'd extended her back in May. The anthropology department at Columbia University was embarking on a study of the "mental characteristics" of various ethnic groups, he told her. He and the study's director, Otto Klineberg, were particularly interested in "the special ability of the Negroes" in music. Boas wanted Hurston to join the Columbia investigation in New Orleans, and offered her a salary of $150 a month, plus reasonable expenses.

Hurston was enthusiastic about the idea, citing "a new birth of creative singing among Negroes" that she'd observed in New Orleans and elsewhere during her southern travels. "The old songs are not sung so much. New ones are flooding everywhere," Hurston advised Boas. She also updated him on her own work: She'd finished compiling her volume of folktales and was still wrestling with second drafts of the manuscripts on conjure and religion. "I have not quite located all that I want," she admitted. Even so, Hurston hoped soon to send Boas the volume of folktales for his scientific review. "I have tried to be as exact as possible. Keeping to the exact dialect as closely as I could, having the story teller to tell it to me word for word as I write it. This after it has been told to me off hand until I know it myself. But the writing down from the lips is to insure the correct dialect and wording so that I shall not let myself creep in unconsciously," she reported, detailing her fidelity to accuracy. Since she planned to return to New Orleans in November anyway, Hurston concluded, she would be happy to meet with Klineberg and offer her assistance with the Columbia study.

Hurston had not yet spoken with Charlotte Mason about Boas's promising job offer, but she knew her amended contract with Godmother was due to expire shortly, at the end of 1929. She assumed she'd be free then to take on other work, and believed Godmother might encourage her career independence—and welcome the chance to remove her from her payroll. Hurston was wrong. An aggravated Mason upbraided her young folklorist, letting her know she was not to take on any assignments for Boas or anyone else until she had completed the work at hand. She also reminded Hurston that she, Godmother, still had legal control over all the collected material.

Hurston's hands were tied—in a slipknot, it seemed, and Godmother was tightening the twine. Sensitive to rope burn, Hurston realized that if she ever wanted to see the fruits of her two years of labor published—under her name—she had to play by Godmother's rules. Embarrassed, Hurston wrote to Boas at once: "I find that I am restrained from leaving the employ of my present employers. . . . I cannot tell you how sorry I am, but I cannot say anything more. . . . I thought I could do it. I felt very sure," she apologized.

This news threw Boas and Klineberg into a tizzy. Although Hurston's apologetic dispatch included a list of potential contacts for Klineberg in New Orleans, America's leading anthropologist believed the project was doomed without Hurston's active participation. Boas immediately began making plans for Klineberg to launch a study of South Dakota Indians instead. Not warmed by the thought of a Dakota winter, Klineberg was relieved to receive a copy of Hurston's subsequent letter to Boas, explaining herself more fully.

"I am in a trying situation," she wrote from Miami. "If Dr. Klineberg will come on, I will give him all the assistance possible. Perhaps just as much as if I were entirely at liberty. But I wanted you to understand what I am up against." Without ever divulging her employer's identity, Hurston told Boas she had figured out a solution to her dilemma: She would tell Mason she was going to New Orleans to collect more conjure, which was true. Godmother never had to know she also was helping with the Columbia study. Hurston assured

Boas: "I shall see to it that Dr. K. has the proper openings, help, contacts and whatever else you want. . . . Really things will work out better than they sound. I pray that you trust me and send Dr. K. along."

Boas did, and in early November, Hurston and Klineberg met each other in the city of brass bands and beignets. The very next day, Hurston persuaded Klineberg to inaugurate his palate with some famous New Orleans oysters. The social scientist got a bad half dozen and was sick and shut in for the next week. When he finally recovered enough to write, Klineberg told Boas he was favorably impressed with Hurston, despite her dubious dining choice. "Miss Hurston strikes me as an extremely interesting and intelligent person," he wrote. "I think she will be a great help, and she seems to have a considerable amount of time for me." Relieved that all had turned out well, Boas wrote back to approve Klineberg's proposed new research direction: a study, "together with Miss Hurston," of the racial makeup, educational history, and mystical background of New Orleans Creoles. Boas was especially excited about the prospect of comparing the Creoles to the other Negroes of New Orleans. But he offered Klineberg a caveat: "Please be sure to check Miss Hurston in regard to accuracy. I have no reason to doubt her, but temperamently, she is so much more artistic rather than scientific that she has to be held down." No problem, Klineberg responded after another week in the field with Hurston. "She continues to be very active and very valuable," Klineberg assured Papa Franz.

Well into December, Hurston also was enjoying the collaboration: "Dr. Klineberg is <u>very</u> fine to work with," she told Boas. Her own work was proceeding smoothly, too, she added. She was now collecting conjure stories—"all the miraculous tales the people tell me about conjure and witchcraft"—to add to the actual ceremonies she'd recorded for her volume on hoodoo. "I want to make this conjure work very thorough and inclusive," she explained to Boas. "As soon as I have the latest material assembled in some order, I shall let you have it."

This promise would have been unremarkable had it not been a clear violation of Hurston's contract with Mason. Hurston flouted Godmother's ban against showing anyone her collected material because she believed, rightly, that exposing her work to Boas's scrutiny would make it better. And, she bargained, what Godmother didn't know couldn't possibly hurt her.

Deception, however, often takes a toll on the deceiver, Hurston found out. "I am simply wasting away with fear," she soon whispered to Hughes from New Orleans. Her fear, however, was not related to her dealings with Boas, which even Hughes knew nothing about. She was now fretting over the crucial matter of transportation. Because of all the miles she'd logged on the once-shiny Chevrolet, Zora had to have a new car. "Just HAD to," she told Hughes. When she mentioned her need to Godmother, the old woman exploded, insinuating that Zora was extravagant or "took her for a good thing." Neither accusation, Hurston noted, "was soothing to my self-respect." The next time the car gave her trouble, mechanics told Zora she would have to spend ninety-five dollars to get it back on the road. Instead, she took it upon herself to haggle for a new one, she wrote, "and keep my big mouth shut." But Godmother learned of the transaction when the car dealer checked Zora's references. Predictably, Godmother was livid. "She wrote me a letter that hurt me thru and thru," Zora told Langston. "Why couldn't Negroes be trusted?" Godmother demanded to know.

Rather than challenge the old woman on her bigoted view—indicting the whole race for one person's mistake—Zora dissembled to protect her cash flow and the research that it financed. But the episode left her feeling "half ill," she confided to Hughes. A cooled-down Godmother later sent the $400 to pay for the car. But now there was another problem. The used car that Zora had purchased—"as is"—started knocking before she had driven it a hundred miles. Without consulting Godmother, Zora immediately traded it in for a newer model—and, though she got some credit for the trade-in, she now had a balance of $300, which she planned to pay out of her monthly salary. "I am just praying that she won't find out what I have done," Zora worried. "I don't feel that I have done wrong for nobody knows what inconvenience I have suffered fooling with old cars. Always something to fix. Money I ought to spend on my work is spent on the old can and keeping me strapped," she grumbled. Then, more to the point, Hurston added: "I just feel that she ought not to exert herself to supervise every little detail. It destroys my self respect and utterly demoralizes me for weeks. I know you can appreciate what I mean. I do care for her deeply, don't forget that. That is why I can't endure to get at odds with her. I don't want anything but to get at my work with the least possible trouble."

Hughes certainly could appreciate Hurston's perspective, for he had begun to have his own run-ins with Godmother over what seemed to be her growing list of rules. Now that he had completed his studies at Lincoln University, for instance, Godmother did not want him living in Harlem because it harbored too many distractions, she said. Instead, she put him up in Westfield, New Jersey, an hour from Manhattan. Renting a room from a quiet, elderly black couple, Hughes was hard at work on his first novel, *Not Without Laughter*. Zora cheered his efforts from afar: "A poet should turn out marvelous prose," she nudged him. But Godmother—sometimes through Locke—was serving as Hughes's unwanted editor, admonishing him not to submerge the novel's beauty beneath a wave of propaganda.

Despite his own troubles with their shared patron, Hughes advised Hurston that the best thing to do was to be honest with Godmother about the car. She might explode again, he conceded, but explosions were part of the business. Besides, he assured Zora, Godmother loved her too much to cut her off completely.

Langston's words of advice, Zora told him, "comforted my soul like dreamless sleep." And he was right. Godmother's car conniption soon blew over. "Well, I tell you, Langston, I am nothing without you," Zora wrote. "That's no flattery either. We will talk a lot when I get there."

Zora spent much of December 1929 running about New Orleans, as she reported, "with my tongue hanging out to get everything I see." At Christmastime, she returned to the Bahamas for carnival season. After catching up with the noted conjure doctor with whom she'd promised to study, Hurston prepared to return to New York. She tarried a bit more in the Bahamas and Florida, however, before finally making her way North in early March.

When Zora returned to New York from more than two solid years in the South, she found the Big Apple (as the jazzmen had begun to call it) slightly bruised. The Wall Street crash of October 1929 had left some noticeable scars. "People were sleeping in subways or on newspapers in office doors, because they had no homes," Hughes would recall. "And in every block a beggar appeared." Hurston was disconcerted by this public poverty, as well as by the haggard faces of her friends in Harlem. "Some of my friends are all tired and worn out—looking like death eating crackers," she commented.

Still, Zora was heartened to be back among her old pals, who immediately informed her that she had a new dance to learn. The Lindy hop—named for Charles Lindbergh's famous transcontinental flight—had become all the rage at the Savoy Ballroom. No sooner had Zora learned the lively steps than Charlotte Mason summoned her to 399 Park Avenue to do a different dance.

When Zora arrived at the penthouse apartment, she found Godmother largely untouched by the Depression that was swelling all around her. Sitting at her dining room table in her high, throne-like chair, "over capon, caviar and gleaming silver," Mason exhorted Zora to tell the tales, sing the songs, and do the dances she'd picked up during her southern expedition. With the reels of film she'd shot as visual aids, Zora assented to the show-and-tell.

Hurston's footage showed deeply black children in Florida playing games and dancing like no one was watching. At one point, Hurston formed the children in a circle and slowly panned her camera around the ring, lingering lovingly on each child's face. Sometimes, she filmed them in extreme close-ups, as their wide eyes peered inquisitively into the lens. In another reel, a woman walked off her porch toward the camera; Zora zoomed in frankly on her face for a candid shot that showed both beauty and sorrow, curiosity and wariness. In the next scene, the woman and a friend, both wearing simple house-dresses, lounged comfortably on the porch. Zora also had footage of Cudjo Lewis, showing him to be handsome, active, and courtly. Another reel recorded Hurston's visit to the cypress swamp with the men at the Loughman sawmill camp. All of the footage—of the black men, women, and children—said as much about Hurston as it did about her subjects: Whoever recorded these images knew black people intimately, the footage insinuated, and loved them intensely.

The passion of Hurston's cinematic eye could not have been lost on Mason, and she did not wish to give the ardor a moment to cool. Ignoring Zora's obvious need for rest, and for some playtime, Godmother insisted she get to work immediately. And New York was no place to engage in the serious task of preparing her manuscripts. So Godmother set Zora up in villagelike Westfield, too, just a few doors from Langston Hughes's room at 514 Downer Street.

From the outset, the arrangement suited Zora well. She and Hughes were happy to be reunited, and neighbors, too. They talked constantly, and Langston, as promised, helped Zora to edit her stacks and stacks of collected material, which she was anxious to publish so she could return to a more creative groove. "I am stuffed with things I'd like to write now, and I shall get down hard at it as soon as I clear this work up," she vowed.

In their idyllic colony of two, Langston and Zora frequently had company: Louise Thompson, a bright and attractive young woman hired by Godmother the previous September to work as Hughes's secretary. Now that Zora was also in Westfield, Godmother decided, the two writers would share Thompson's services. Godmother had amply prepared Louise for Zora's arrival: "She used to talk about Zora, about this wonderful child of nature who was so unspoiled, and what a marvelous person she was," Thompson later recalled. "And Zora did not disappoint me. She was a grand storyteller."

Zora had not been similarly prepped to meet Louise, but she'd heard a little about her in a gossipy letter from Langston: Louise had been briefly, and disastrously, married to Wallace Thurman, who everyone knew was a homosexual—except, apparently, his bride. "Poor Wallie! I wish he might get a divorce," Zora had sympathized. Now, meeting Thompson, Hurston didn't think she was so bad after all. In fact, Hurston, Thompson, and Hughes got on famously. Zora entertained Langston and Louise with stories from her southern travels, and Louise's large apartment in the city, at 435 Convent Avenue, became a second home for the trio.

All the while, Hurston continued her efforts to organize her field notes. Now, the goal was to produce one comprehensive volume that would include folktales and conjure. "I am urged to do things as quickly as possible and so at present I am working furiously," Hurston reported to Boas in mid-April. On the 16th, she "received a word from headquarters" telling her to come over the following Friday at three o'clock, and to bring materials for discussion. Consequently, she told Boas, she would have to stop by his office to retrieve the essay he was secretly reading for her.

Several days after the penthouse appointment, Locke assured

Hurston that Godmother remained pleased with her. "I thought it would cheer you at this critical stage of your work that she really thinks you have done well and is eagerly looking forward to pushing the book," he wrote. Even so, Godmother thought the material might be too unwieldy. Her new idea—which Locke fully supported, of course—was to pare down the manuscript by selecting only the best material. "She thinks it would be a mistake even to have a scientific tone to the book, so soft pedal all notion of too specific documentation and let loose on the things that you are really best equipped to give—a vivid dramatizing of your material and the personalities back of it," Locke recommended. His implication that she was not "best equipped" to provide scientific documentation must have galled the anthropologist in Hurston. But Locke was not finished; he was to insult Hurston the writer as well: "You can do this in a feverish two or three days," he presumed, "and then it will be all over, but the shouting." Locke then would be happy to edit the manuscript, he offered. It would be grand to present Godmother with the finished document on her birthday, May 18. Didn't Zora agree? "I think we can whip it into shape by then," Locke asserted.

Hurston largely ignored Locke's ivory-towered advice. "It has been very hard to get the material in any shape at all," she complained; wrapping up the whole enterprise in a few days was impossible.

In lieu of a completed manuscript, then, Zora presented Godmother with a long, fawning letter for her birthday. "You are God's flower," Zora purred to Godmother, "and my flower and Miss Chapin's flower and Langston's flower and the world's blossom." This birthday epistle was both cloying and comic—though Godmother no doubt believed it utterly sincere. "Oh, my lovely just-born flower, if back there when you fluttered pink into this drab world—if they had but known how much joy and love you should bring! How much of the white light of God you would diffuse into soft radiance for the eyes of the primitives, the wise ones would have stood awed before your cradle and brought great gifts from afar." Hurston's references to Mason's pink skin and to "the white light of God" were almost certainly tongue-in-cheek, but she cleverly concealed her mocking words under a sugary sheen. And the joke, Hurston boldly wagered, was above Godmother's head. Or, perhaps more accurately, it was beneath her—just below the reach of her condescension.

Like Langston Hughes and Louise Thompson, Hurston sometimes felt uncomfortable with Godmother's obsession with the "primitive," but she knew how to play the wealthy widow like a guitar. This is not to say that Hurston did not care for Godmother. She did, genuinely. But in their remarkably complex relationship, Hurston certainly did not care for everything Godmother said or did—usually under the influence of her zealous devotion to "primitivism." Once, for example, Godmother sent an excessively exotic dress to Westfield for Zora to wear. On the phone to Park Avenue, Zora reported that the dress looked fabulous on her. Then she hung up and shared a laugh with Thompson about the gaudiness of the dress, which she would never dream of wearing. But what would have been the benefit of telling Godmother the dress was hideous? Perhaps it would have given Hurston a fleeting feeling of racial victory and, in the best possible scenario, it might have influenced Godmother to adopt a more realistic racial outlook. Yet that kind of bluntness was not what Godmother wanted—and certainly not something she would have continued to finance. True honesty, across racial lines, was possible and acceptable in relationships with some white people, Hurston found. With Carl Van Vechten, for instance, both Hurston and Hughes felt free to speak their minds. But he was their friend. Godmother was their patron. And Hurston understood the difference. So she usually told Godmother what she wanted to hear, which kept the checks coming—and enabled her to do the work she felt called to do.

In this regard, Zora's birthday missive was written for the express purpose of stroking Godmother's outsize ego, not to mention her Messianic complex: "I really should not extend my congratulations to you on this day, but to all those who have been fortunate enough to touch you," Zora wrote, the molasses practically dripping from her pen. "It is you who gives out life and light and we who receive."

Hurston's flattery got her nowhere, however, when she asked Godmother to consider funding her for graduate studies at Columbia. Boas had been impressed enough with the material Hurston had shared with him to write to Trevor Arnett, director of the General Education Board, recommending her for a graduate fellowship. "She is an unusually gifted person with a good deal of literary skill," Boas wrote, and "well fitted" for graduate work in anthropology. But the General Education Board, which had been founded by John D. Rockefeller in 1902, could not help; its policy was to assist scholars already teaching at one of the Negro colleges. Perhaps the Julius Rosenwald Fund might be of some use, Boas was advised.

Papa Franz suggested Zora ask her current employer to support her academic ambitions. "The 'Angel' is cold towards the degrees, but will put up more money for further research," Hurston reported back. Perhaps her patron might allow her to combine the degree program with her research, Boas offered, still unaware of the identity of Hurston's "angel." "Make it clear to her that your research work under the direction of a university would be much more profitable than without it and that she will further your own welfare considerably by making the combination," he counseled. The argument was useless, Hurston knew: "I have broached the subject from several angles," she told Boas, "but it got chill blains no matter how I put it."

Late that spring, the blains threatened to erupt, and both of Mason's godchildren in Westfield felt the pain. Without warning, Godmother's temper flared. Somehow, probably from Locke, she had gotten the impression that her Westfield pair was having too much fun—and not doing enough work. When Hurston and Hughes tried to calm Mason, she snubbed them both. Finally her hackles were smoothed by a letter of atonement from Langston, followed by a longer apology, for what he wasn't certain.

The most likely reason for Godmother's tantrum was her discovery of a secret that Hurston and Hughes had tried to keep from her. Back in March, the two had begun working on a play together, without Mason's consent. She was particularly upset with Zora over this, because she feared the play would pilfer time from her efforts to complete her folklore manuscript—the work Godmother was still paying her to do. Godmother's worry was unwarranted, though. The play, to be called *Mule Bone*, did not significantly slice into the time Hurston spent on her folklore work. *Mule Bone* would, however, have a sundering effect that no one could have anticipated—not even Godmother, the self-proclaimed clairvoyant. In the end, the play would rip the Hurston-Hughes friendship apart.

CHAPTER 20

A Bone to Pick

Mule Bone was the collaboration that Hurston and Hughes had long dreamed of. But it would not be a folk opera, they decided; instead, they would write a comedy—not a minstrel show, but a real Negro folk comedy. This change in direction was at least partly inspired by a casual comment from Theresa Helburn of the Theatre Guild, who complained that most of the scripts she saw painted too grim a portrait of black life. Why didn't someone write a comedy? Helburn asked Hughes at a party early in 1930. Hughes conveyed the suggestion to Hurston and, soon after she was settled in Westfield, the two writers got to work.

If Hurston was disappointed at the idea of collaborating with Hughes on a comedy rather than on their much-discussed folk opera—for which she already had written several scenes—she didn't say. She also never expressed, at least in print, how she felt when she learned that Hughes planned to write the folk opera without her. Though Hurston may not have been aware of it until later, Hughes had begun looking for another collaborator in early 1930; he'd decided he wanted to work with a musician on his "singing play"—and Godmother had given him $500 to travel to Cuba in late February in search of a composer. Still, Hughes wanted to collaborate with Hurston on *something*. *Mule Bone: A Comedy of Negro Life* seemed just the thing.

The play's basic plot came from Hurston's short story "The Bone of Contention." Set in Eatonville, it is a tale of two hunters who shoot at a wild turkey within seconds of each other, then argue over who actually killed the gobbler. In the heat of their dispute, one hunter knocks the other unconscious with the hock bone of a dead and discarded mule—an unlikely weapon found by happenstance during the tussle—and then runs off with the contested turkey. The assaulted hunter, Dave, demands that his assailant, Jim, be brought to trial. The mayor sets the trial for the next day at the Baptist church, the largest meeting place in town. Even before the proceedings begin, it's clear that the trial will be something of a holy war. "The assault and the gobbler were unimportant," Hurston wrote. "Dave was a Baptist, Jim a Methodist, only two churches in the town and the respective congregations had lined up solidly." Representing the defendant, Methodist minister Reverend Simms argues that a mule bone is not a weapon because it is not considered as such in the Bible nor in "the white folks' law." The Baptist leader, Elder Long, begs to differ, however, and reads the biblical account of Samson's slaying thousands with the jawbone of an ass. If a donkey's jawbone is so deadly—and mules are descendants of donkeys—then surely a mule bone is hazardous as well, he reasons. "Everybody knows dat de further back on a mule you goes, de mo' dangerous he gits. Now if de jawbone is as dangerous as it says heah, in de Bible, by de time you gits clear back tuh his hocks he's rank pizen [poison]," Long argues persuasively. Amid a roar of approval from most of the townsfolk (though some Methodists dissent), Jim is convicted of assaulting Dave with a deadly weapon. He is then run out of town and barred from returning for two years. The mayor invites those who wish to fight each other in protest of the verdict—more a triumph of language than of law—to go outside and scuffle as much as they want. "But don't use no guns, no razors nor no mule-bones," he advises.

This amusing story was based on a tale Hurston had absorbed as a child in Eatonville, where a man named Brazzle kept a mean old mule. When the mule died, its remains were hauled to the edge of the cypress swamp, on the outskirts of town, and left to the scavengers. "The elders neglected the bones," Hurston recalled, "but the mule remained with them in song and story as a simile, as a metaphor, to point a moral or adorn a tale." Naturally, then, "The Bone of Contention" was pure Eatonville, with familiar characters from Hurston's previous fiction and from the township's actual history—Mayor Joe Clarke, Hiram Lester, Elijah Moseley—speaking in the image-laden language that had become a hallmark of Hurston's portrayals of her hometown. Long before she *wrote* this story, in fact, Zora often *told* it at parties—using it as her "visiting card" when she first arrived in New York. "It was the regular thing for people to ask her for that story," Charlotte Mason would later note.

As Hurston and Hughes worked to develop the tale into a play, Louise Thompson put in long hours as their typist, recording dialogue and character flourishes almost as fast as the two writers invented and dictated. Hughes persuaded Hurston that they should place a woman, rather than a turkey, at the center of Jim and Dave's dispute, and he suggested that the last scene be set on a railroad track. Hughes later would claim that he structured "the plot, constructions and climaxes," while Hurston contributed "the little story" and spiced up the dialogue with southern flavor and wisecracks. Despite this attempt to minimize her input, it's obvious that "Hurston's contribution was almost certainly the greater" to a play set in Eatonville, as Hughes's biographer, Arnold Rampersad, has acknowledged. As Rampersad put it, Hurston supplied "whatever dramatic distinction the play would have," contributing "an abundance of tall tales, wicked quips and farcical styles of which she was absolute master and Langston not much more than a sometime student." Using the power of memory—and her natural gifts as a performer—Zora re-created the Eatonville milieu so authentically while working on *Mule Bone* that she sometimes reduced Langston and Louise to helpless, wet-eyed laughter, as she acted out all the parts, male and female, and changed her voice to suit each character.

Even with all the horseplay, the work on *Mule Bone* proceeded swiftly, and the trio continued to get along well. Sometimes Louise commuted from the city; other times, after long hours hunched over the typewriter, she spent the night at Zora's place in Westfield. Meanwhile, the friendship that Hurston and Hughes had nurtured since meeting in 1925 was stronger than ever and there was little one wouldn't do for the other. On May 4, for instance, Zora was short on cash and borrowed fifteen dollars from Langston, only to pay him back five days later after receiving her May stipend from Godmother.

These sorts of transactions were commonplace among the now-old friends, and Louise, too, became a part of their circle of generosity. On May 20, for instance, Zora—pleased with "the dandy job" Louise was doing—bought the younger woman dinner, as well as typing paper and a fresh ribbon for her typewriter.

By the end of May 1930, Hurston and Hughes had finished acts one and three of *Mule Bone*. Then suddenly the play seemed to stall. According to Hughes, Zora—"a very gay and lively girl"—felt uneasy in hemmed-in Westfield and became "restless and moody, working in a nervous manner." Meanwhile, Hughes acknowledged, both writers were "distressed at the growing depression—hearing of more and more friends and relatives losing jobs and becoming desperate for lack of work."

Indeed, the Great Depression was beginning to settle over New York like a cloak of smog, and Zora noticed its effects most acutely when she visited her old friends in Harlem. "All of them cried to me to come and put some life into the gang again," she reported to a friend living elsewhere. In contrast to her uptown buddies, Zora did not feel any older and not at all tired: "Perhaps the hectic life of Harlem wore them out faster while I was in the South getting my rest as well as getting some work done," she thought. So far, she had largely evaded the Depression's most deleterious effects, but she admitted to feeling nostalgic for her old apartment on West Sixty-sixth Street in New York, and for her friends' laughter. "Yes . . . I still yell with joy on the slightest provocation," she assured old friend Lawrence Jordan. "I have been away and kept down to business for almost three years and I am dying to spread my flannel with friends."

In Zora's letter to Jordan, the restlessness and moodiness that Hughes claimed to see in her were not apparent. But if Hurston did become moody during their collaboration on *Mule Bone*, Hughes certainly knew why. Sometime late that spring, the two friends had their first significant disagreement. As in the theatrical fight between Jim and Dave, at the root of the Hurston-Hughes dispute was a woman: Louise Thompson. Because the aspiring playwrights could not afford to pay Thompson for typing the script—which was above and beyond the secretarial work for which Godmother had hired her—Hughes proposed "a three-way split" of any profits. "Now Langston, nobody has in the history of the world given a typist an interest in a work for typing it," Zora countered. She then offered to pay Louise five dollars a day, but Louise declined. "No, I don't want a thing now," Zora remembered her saying, "but when it goes over, then you all can take care of me then." On the surface, this seems to be a generous offer, but Zora instantly became suspicious of Louise's motives. Further, she sensed that Langston had been privately discussing the matter with Louise—and, in his "magnificent gallantry," making promises that both writers would be expected to keep. As a result, she would recall, "I was just plain hurt." When she argued against the pay-Louise-later plan, Langston proposed that Louise be made business manager for the play. "That struck me as merely funny," Zora told Langston months later. "With all the experienced and capable agents on Broadway, I should put my business in the hands of some one who knows less about the subject than I."

At some point, Hurston and Hughes decided the only solution was to tell Godmother about the play and ask for her help. With this, the idea of paying Louise after *Mule Bone* was produced "lost its meaning," as Hughes put it, as did the suggestion that she be made business manager. This was because an annoyed Godmother picked up the typing tab for Louise—who, in her view, was "already overpaid . . . for doing next to no work." The old woman also admonished Zora and Langston to shelve *Mule Bone* until Zora had completed her folklore book. According to Hurston's account, the play was then dropped.

Apparently, however, Zora did not drop the feeling that she had been betrayed by Langston and Louise—and that they had colluded to "hi-jack" *Mule Bone*. She became deeply distrustful of Louise— unreasonably so—and believed that Langston was so enamored of their typist that talking with him about her concerns would be futile. "I felt that I was among strangers," she later said with some melodrama, "and the only thing to do was to go on away from there."

Rather than express the full extent of her distress over the situation, Zora simply walked away from it. Sometime in June, she left Westfield and moved to New York en route to the South for a bit more research to complete her folklore book. Yet she apparently left Hughes with the impression that she would finish act two of *Mule Bone* while she was down South and that all was well. In August, in fact, she mailed him a cheerful postcard from Magazine, Alabama:

"Off at last," she wrote. "Dreamed last night that you were working on the play."

Forwarded from Westfield, the postcard finally caught up with Hughes as he headed to Moylan, Pennsylvania, for a theatrical immersion of sorts. Hughes had been invited to the small valley town by Jasper Deeter, whom he'd met a few months before while visiting one of his former Lincoln University professors. Deeter ran an innovative theater company, the Hedgerow Players, from a converted mill in Moylan, about twenty miles from Philadelphia. Committed to producing provocative theater, Deeter had worked with Paul Robeson on *The Emperor Jones* in 1920, and had staged *In Abraham's Bosom*, the 1926 black-cast drama for which white playwright Paul Green was awarded a Pulitzer Prize. In the fall of 1930, Deeter planned to do a virtual Negro season, featuring several plays with black or integrated casts. He wanted Hughes to be the playwright in residence. In September, Hughes showed up at Hedgerow to assume those duties—and he came armed with acts one and three of *Mule Bone*, which he readily showed to Deeter. Offering a bit of advice on dialogue, Deeter "seemed to think it would be a grand play," as Hughes later recounted.

According to Hurston, Hughes contacted her, presumably by telephone, to share the good news from Hedgerow and to inquire about the progress of act two. At that point, Hurston later told Godmother, she expressed her true feelings to Hughes. She told him that she would not send him act two and that "the play was hers, that he had contributed no dialogue and that she had thrown out the one suggestion he had made of the railroad track and finished the play herself." Hughes then intimated, as Zora recalled, that "his friend Mr. Spingarn was a lawyer and a good one."

It's impossible to know what all was said in this conversation—or even if it took place, as Hurston claimed. Both Hurston and Hughes would freely revise history in their accounts of the *Mule Bone* episode and, before all was said and done, they would make shrill accusations and counteraccusations that dishonored and undermined their long and loving friendship. It is certain, though, that the Hurston-Hughes dispute was in no small measure spurred by both writers' precarious footing with Godmother Mason. In fact, Hughes's time at Hedgerow was partly an attempt to recover from one of the most devastating experiences of his life: Back in June, shortly after Hurston left Westfield, Hughes's relationship with Godmother had fallen apart.

Maybe Hurston experienced another premonition, similar to the one that had saved her from perishing in the hurricane in the Bahamas; in any case, she got out of Westfield, and New York, just in time. Perhaps finally feeling the pinch of the Depression, Godmother decided that several of her Negro godchildren were draining her resources and had to be cut off. She swung the ax first at Langston Hughes, whose relationship with her had begun unraveling in late May, when he took a trip to Washington in defiance of her mandate that he stay home and write. Soon after that disagreement, Hughes asked Godmother if they could dispense with the monthly account-ing system and go back to a happier time when money didn't come between them—a time when Godmother gave him *gifts*, not an allowance, and therefore possessed no authority to say "you must write now." In early June, an indignant Mason agreed to dispense with the accounting and sent Hughes a check for $250, along with her wish for his "success for whatever plan you make for revivifica-tion."

The finality of Godmother's tone unnerved Hughes, and when he was denied an audience with her a week or so later, he realized that she had washed her hands of him. In response, Hughes became psy-chosomatically ill, haunted variously by nausea, tonsillitis, and a chronic toothache. "I ask you to help the gods to make me good," he wailed to Godmother. "I am nothing now—no more than a body of dust without wisdom, having no sight to see." Hughes's desperate pleas had no effect on Godmother's now-hardened heart. "I love you, Godmother. I need you," begged Hughes, who was not consoled even by the July publication of his first novel, *Not Without Laughter*. "You can help me more than anyone on earth," he cried out, sending Godmother the first copy of his new book. "Forgive me for the things I do not know, the things I can not fight alone, the things I haven't understood."

Despite Hughes's despairing missives, the door to 399 Park Avenue appeared to be permanently closed to him, and it soon would be slammed in the face of Louise Thompson as well. On September 22, while Hughes nursed his wounds at Hedgerow, Mason summoned the literary stenographer to a downtown hotel. In what

Thompson recalled as "a short but excruciating" session, the old lady announced that their relationship, too, was over. Godmother had decided to rid herself of her Negro protégés, she told Louise, because they were all a lost cause.

Still in the South, Zora was spared such a cruel and abrupt severance. When she returned to New York in late September and heard about Godmother's casualties—and saw that the Depression was determined to linger—she decided there was only one way to survive, and to finish the important work she had started: By staying—or reestablishing herself—in Charlotte Mason's good graces. "Darling Godmother," Zora wired on September 24. "Safely home working while awaiting orders from you."

During her time away, Hurston had published, with Godmother's blessing, some of her research findings in the *Journal of American Folk-Lore*. Her article "Dance Songs and Tales From the Bahamas" appeared in the July–September 1930 issue and featured several folk-tales rendered by Bahamian children as well as adults. Godmother readily granted permission for this article to be published because Hurston's Bahamian research did not interest her as much as the material from the black South—and likely would not even warrant a place in the folklore volume Hurston was still working to complete.

Zora was consumed with this task in early November when Hughes, just back from Hedgerow, tried to interest her in resuming their collaborative work on *Mule Bone*. As Langston recalled, Zora studiously avoided him. They would set up an appointment for work, but when he arrived at her apartment—the old flat on West Sixty-sixth Street—she would not be there. Or if she was home, she would have to leave immediately. Else, she would claim to have no copies of the play on hand or protest that she was terribly busy and too nervous to work anyway. Hurston also told Hughes of some changes she planned to make to *Mule Bone*, namely, to take out the love interest and reinsert the turkey, in order to make the play more like the original tale from Eatonville. Hughes claimed to be completely bewildered: "I thought her behavior strange," he later acknowledged, "but since we have always been such good friends, and had had no disagreements about our work on the play together or anything else, I put down her actions to a rush of other work, and perhaps nerves."

If Hughes had spoken with Zora from Hedgerow, as she told

Godmother, then he was not as baffled by her behavior as he professed to be. Even if they didn't speak during his time in Pennsylvania, Hughes nevertheless was aware of their argument the previous spring over Louise Thompson. Thus, his assertion that he and Zora "had had no disagreements" was disingenuous. It is likely, though, that he sincerely could not believe the quarrel over Louise still stuck in Zora's craw. To him, it had been fairly insignificant, and it was certainly by now a thing of the past.

Hurston, however, had not let it go, and she had convinced herself that Louise meant her no good. Further, Zora understood that any association with Louise or Langston—both firmly out of favor with Godmother—would only jeopardize her own toehold in the queendom. In the hardscrabble of the Depression, Hurston could ill afford to do anything that would halt the flow of checks from Park Avenue. So she deliberately evaded Hughes throughout the autumn of 1930, inwardly rationalizing this unfriendly behavior by clinging to her now-stale anger over the Louise Thompson spat. What's more, she never fully discussed her feelings with Hughes—and never gave him an opportunity to apologize if he'd been wrong or to have his say if he believed he'd been right.

To be sure, Hurston's behavior was greatly influenced by the oppressive economic times. The Depression, writer Arna Bontemps recalled, hit Harlem and all of New York with "a very heavy blow that's so heavy it's hard to realize at this date how devastating it was." Speaking decades after the Depression's gradual demise, Bontemps asserted: "If it'd lasted a little longer the whole nation could have gone back to savagery. This was a terrible thing. The people on Wall Street were all jumping out of the windows, and in Harlem they were cracking up too."

Though Mason's support shielded Hurston from much of the Depression's desolation, she was not nearly as comfortably ensconced in Godmother's fold as she once had been. Charlotte Mason's infatuation with the Negro, it seemed, was over. "I am helping myself forget the discouraging things that have fallen on me from the Negroes," she told Alain Locke, "by talking about my Indian days." Determined to shake off all her black dependents, Godmother soon spoke with Zora about reducing her monthly salary. She also told her she needed to sell her car. In response, Hurston—still trying to finish her book—included a practical, passively worded addendum to her November 1930 expense report. "With the present economic situation in mind," she wrote, "it is suggested that I be given the usual allowance for Dec. to enable me to get a blanket, an oil stove to cut down fuel consumption, and a comfortable mattress. But that I be allowed only 100.00 after that." She then went on to explain her logic: "Oil is cheaper than either coal (as I need it) or gas. And it can be moved about so that it can heat the whole place with a minimum of both expense and effort. Keeping up the coal fire uses up a great deal of time, and time is so important now."

Time was vital to Hurston because it was precisely what she needed to complete her folklore book, which—in its incompleteness and its failure to pass muster with Godmother and Locke—was starting to weigh on her soul. "I am beginning to feel fagged," she admitted on November 11. "The weariness is beginning to break through my subconsciousness and call itself to my attention." To combat her fatigue, Hurston soon embarked on a working sabbatical in Asbury Park, New Jersey, where her sister, Sarah, now lived with her husband and her young daughter, Zora's namesake. There, Hurston threw herself into her work and, when not visiting with family, adopted a kind of monastic silence in an effort "to hold my spiritual forces together," as she put it, and "to find the gate to the future."

Although Zora had received a famed Louisiana fortune-teller's assurance that Godmother would stand by her as long as she lived, she knew it would be foolhardy to rely on her patron's kindness to last forever. "You see, Darling Godmother, I am trying to get some bone in my legs so that you can see me standing so that I shall cease to worry you," Zora assured Mason. "I don't need to call on your ebbing strength for every little thing. So I shall wrassle me up a future or die trying."

Just before Thanksgiving, Hurston spent four days rewriting and polishing the first act of *Mule Bone*, which she'd given to Godmother earlier in the month for feedback. In her notes on "Zora's play," as Godmother called it, she praised the introduction of the mule and judged "all the development of character and local color excellent." Zora's friend Carl Van Vechten also found the play delightful, even in its unfinished state. Zora had sent him a draft of *Mule Bone* on

November 14, along with a clarifying note: "Langston and I started out together on the idea of the story I used to tell you about Eatonville, but being so much apart from rush of business I started all over again while in Mobile & this is the result of my work alone."

Meanwhile, the Depression continued to truculently stalk the country, making it impossible for Zora to snag a buyer for her car, especially as the Christmas season began. Complicating matters, the Chevrolet Company had just unveiled its new model and, due to the economy, was selling it for less than Zora had paid for hers. The $500 Godmother hoped to get from the car's sale did not appear to be forthcoming, yet she continued to advise Zora to sell the Chevy—for whatever she could get. At the same time, Mason showed her compassionate side: Believing the $100 a month Zora had requested was too paltry for in-town living, Godmother decided instead on a monthly stipend of $150—to be paid, she told her young folklorist, "until your things begin to be published and you are free."

Zora relished this Yuletide news. Writing to her "Dear Darling Godmother" just after Christmas, Hurston cozied up to the old woman with gratitude: "You have given me the happiest Christmas season of all my life," she declared. Though her statement may have been exaggerated, her gratefulness was no doubt sincere as she watched people fall all around her from the ravages of the Depression. "For the first time ever," she told Godmother, "I was among friends <u>and</u> well fed and warm. I could give and receive. It was nothing expensive that I had to give, but I could give <u>something</u> as well as receive. I had love. I felt you warm and close and urging me on to happiness."

Inexplicably, Godmother took offense at Zora's thank-you letter, perhaps assuming her mention of having "nothing expensive" to give was an oblique way of complaining about her allowance. "That hurt. I can never tell you how much," Zora dared to inform Godmother early in 1931, perhaps emboldened by the arrival of her fortieth birthday that week. "I hope that my saying it doesn't hurt <u>you</u>," Zora hastened to add. "That is the last thing I'd like to do." As antici-pated, Zora's candor further vexed Godmother, who began to recite her own troubles. She was still in mourning with her beloved assis-tant and friend Katherine Biddle over the death of her young son just before Thanksgiving. Also, Godmother—like Zora and many others in the city—had been ill with the flu during the waning days of 1930 and had not been fit to go to the bank to make an additional withdrawal on Zora's behalf. Though Zora had asked for nothing of the kind, Godmother persisted in her defensive tirade, arguing that Zora had no business getting her feelings hurt simply because, in Godmother's words, "I said you had no right to dun me for the money." Then, Mason added a gratuitous and mean-spirited statement that must have hit Zora like a blow to the gut: This kind of behavior, she alleged, was "the reason the whole white world says 'You can't do anything with Negroes. They are unreliable.'"

As if to mitigate the sting of that hateful hurl of words, Godmother did manage a smidgen of kindness. She allowed that she was glad to hear of Zora's happy Christmas. Did she spend it with Langston, Godmother wondered. Had she heard from him at all?

Zora had not seen Langston Hughes since early December. But in mid-January, as she staggered from the slap of Godmother's insults, she received a letter from him that was almost as disturbing as her benefactor's bigotry. While visiting his mother in Cleveland, Hughes wrote, he had called on his old friends Rowena and Russell Jelliffe. The white couple ran the Karamu Theatre, a well-regarded community playhouse, and directed the Gilpin Players, a nonprofessional group of black actors in residence there. The Gilpins were planning to stage a new Negro comedy in February, the Jelliffes told Hughes: It was called *Mule Bone*, and it was written by one Zora Hurston. "Is there something about the very word theatre that turns people into thieves?" Hughes now wanted to know. What was going on?

Hurston did not have a clue. She had never heard of the agent, Barrett Clark, who'd brought the play to the attention of the Jelliffes, and she was genuinely surprised by the news—and by Hughes's accusatory tone. "I sense a good deal of emotion in your letter," she responded, "so I am answering it at once." Hurston then went on to write several pages explaining everything: She had been "cut to the quick" by several of Hughes's statements the previous spring regarding Louise Thompson's work on *Mule Bone*. While the play was based on Zora's story, she noted, she was happy to share it with Hughes—but then he seemed determined to give Louise an equal stake in it as well. Given this baffling bias toward their stenographer, Hurston said, she soon came "to feel that I hadn't much of a chance in that combination." She added: "I did not then, nor do I feel yet that you were trying to gyp me deliberately." But Hughes's proposals that they give Louise equal footing as a collaborator, Hurston argued, simply were not fair.

Although there had been no romance between Zora and Langston—and no desire for one—she reacted to his friendship with Louise almost like a spurned lover. But Zora assured Langston that her possessiveness was based on professional considerations, not personal ones, even if his feelings toward Louise *were* personal. "Now, get this straight, Langston. You are still dear to me," Hurston wrote emphatically. "I don't care who you love nor whom you marry, nor whom you bestow your worldly goods upon. I will never have any feeling about that part. I have always felt that if you had married anyone at all it would make no difference in our relationship. I <u>know</u> that no man on earth could change me towards you." But her hurt and anger over his proposals regarding *Mule Bone* had been too raw to discuss with him. Rather than "wrassle words with you," Hurston told Hughes, she had completed a new version of the play, "carefully not using what was yours."

Hurston apparently never mailed this letter to Hughes, however. A couple of days later, on January 18, she found it in a drawer and decided to send it to Godmother instead—writing a virtual duplicate of it to Hughes. In that typewritten version, Hurston again outlined her complaints against Louise Thompson and assured Hughes that she still cared for him: "I didn't intend to be evasive," she apologized. "With anyone else but you I could have said a plenty. Would have done so long ago but I have been thinking of you as my best friend for so long, and as I am not in love with anyone, that naturally made you the nearest person to me on earth, and the things I had in mind seemed too awful to say to you, I just couldn't say them. . . . So now, it is all said."

Before Hughes received this letter, however, he contacted Hurston by phone, and she told him, truthfully, that she knew nothing of how the play got to Cleveland. Hurston even wondered if Hughes had catalyzed the bidding for *Mule Bone* with his Karamu friends in an effort to make a claim on the play; he assured her that he had not. As for her evasive behavior the previous fall, she said, her forthcoming letter would explain everything.

While awaiting Hurston's letter, Hughes contacted Carl Van Vechten for advice. Carlo was able to help sort out the mystery of how *Mule Bone* had found its way to Cleveland. When Zora gave him the draft to read in November (explaining that it was a rewrite of the play she and Hughes had started together), Van Vechten liked it so much that he sent it to Barrett Clark, a reader for the Theatre Guild, with the understanding that it was an unfinished work. As such, *Mule Bone* was still fairly muddled: Hurston had rewritten act one, reinserting the turkey—but not taking out the love interest—and placing the fight offstage. The result was a "grand tangle" of a play, as Hughes saw it. Yet Clark thought it was nearly ready to be staged. Acting in his capacity as a representative for the Samuel French Agency, he gave the script to Rowena Jelliffe—"with no authority whatever," as Van Vechten complained—and did not bother to tell Van Vechten until the play was already in Cleveland. So it had all been a big misunderstanding—not a deliberate attempt on Hurston's part to have the play produced without Hughes's knowledge.

On the evening of January 19, Hurston conferred with Van Vechten herself and heard the same story of the play's odd route to Cleveland. She also expressed regret about the current confusion: "Zora came to see me and cried and carried on no end about how fond she was of you," Van Vechten told Hughes, "and how she wouldn't have had this misunderstanding for the world. And said she had written you six typewritten pages and talked to you over long distance and said she was going to write to you again." Still, Hurston was reluctant to authorize a Cleveland production, and Van Vechten agreed with her thinking. "A semi-amateur production of this play will kill it completely," he advised Hughes. "It needs the most careful and sympathetic production and casting," he warned; with these advantages, he believed, it could become a major Broadway hit.

When Hughes finally received Hurston's typewritten letter, dated January 18, he understood she had other reasons, as well, for not wanting to authorize the Cleveland production. While Hurston used much of her letter to detail her frustration over the favoritism she felt Hughes had shown Louise Thompson, she also made a clear statement regarding her feelings about the play's authorship: "I don't think that you can point out any situations or dialogue that are yours," she told Hughes. "You made some suggestions, but they are not incorporated in the play."

Infuriated by Hurston's claim, Hughes fired off an eleven-page letter to his lawyer, Arthur Spingarn, outlining his version of the *Mule Bone* events. Acknowledging Zora's feeling that she was more author of the play than he was, however, Hughes told Spingarn he would be willing to concede two-thirds of any royalties to Hurston, taking only one-third for himself "as a permanent agreement for all future productions of the play." He also wrote to Barrett Clark to assert his rights to *Mule Bone* and continued to seek advice from Van Vechten.

A friend to both Hughes and Hurston, Carlo sought to extricate himself from the matter altogether, assuring Hughes that he believed the "very amusing" story of the stenographer was at the root of the dispute. "I am convinced that this whole situation arises out of some feeling on Zora's part of which you are wholly unconscious," he ventured. Indeed, perhaps something more—something personal—had happened between the two women to account for Hurston's unremitting rancor toward Louise Thompson. If so, it was something neither woman revealed to Hughes nor to history.

As Hughes consulted his lawyer, Hurston turned to an even more formidable ally: Godmother. She kept her patron abreast of the situation by sending her copies of the letters that came from Cleveland, just as Hughes sent copies of the correspondence to Spingarn. Langston was attempting "to set up the claim that he is due something," Zora summarized, "because I didn't tell him to get out. You can't talk about a work with a person and then do it alone unless you pay them." Yet, she asserted, she had given him bits from her southern research that he freely used in his novel, *Not Without Laughter*. "Now I am not using one single solitary bit in dialogue, plot nor situation from him and yet he tries to muscle in," Zora complained to Godmother. "I wish it were possible for Locke to get him before you and then call me in and let him state his claims."

Hurston's insistence that *Mule Bone* was hers and hers alone may not have been literally true, but it did have some figurative validity: The play was an Eatonville story through and through and it celebrated the rural black folks who had been her parents, her teachers, her community. Chicago-born Louise Thompson, on the other hand, had grown up in predominantly white neighborhoods in Idaho and

Oregon before landing in the arms of a striving black community in Sacramento, California. The only time she'd spent in the South involved short and disappointing teaching stints in Pine Bluff, Arkansas, and Hampton, Virginia. From Hurston's perspective, Thompson knew absolutely nothing about the South of *Mule Bone*. And whatever the midwestern-bred Hughes knew, Hurston felt, he had largely learned from her in 1927 during their southern summer. In fact, Zora recalled, during the spring of 1930, when everything was going well back in Westfield, she had found herself arguing with Thompson, Locke, and even Hughes about the intrinsic value of the folk material. They "wrassled with me nearly all night long that folk sources were not important," she would remember, "but I stuck to my guns."

With all this in mind, Hurston would be damned if she was going to allow a folk-centered, Eatonville-set play to go onstage without *her* name on it—and certainly not with Louise Thompson getting credit for creative work. But this was not what Hughes wanted, either. He *was* fond of Louise, and, yes, he wished to be fair to her— feeling, correctly, that she was too intelligent to be merely a typist. Perhaps so, Hurston might have conceded, but typist was the only role she'd played in the making of *Mule Bone*, and that was the only credit she should get. For Hughes, that argument had been settled back in the spring, when Louise had been paid. Nearly a year later, he harbored no secret ambition to wrest the play from Hurston's hands and take all the credit for himself and Louise. Yet this was what Hurston feared—and this fear led to her series of overreactions. From her point of view, she was simply trying to protect what was hers. And she was hurt and angry that her best friend, Hughes, had effectively backed her into this corner.

Zora's emotions were tempered, however, when she received a conciliatory note from Langston. Explaining that the Gilpin Players were a nationally respected group of amateur actors—and that the production would open downtown under the publicity-assuring auspices of the Cleveland *Plain Dealer*, the leading newspaper in town—he urged Zora to authorize the performance. In his view, it would not "be a bad beginning for our first play, and for the first Negro folk-comedy ever written." While Hughes sensed the historical importance *Mule Bone* could have, he also needed the Gilpin production to boost his Godmother-less morale, as well as his income. "Let's not be niggers about the thing," he implored Hurston, "and fall out before we've even gotten started. Please wire me."

Moved by Langston's "pathetic letter," Zora wrote to Godmother at once and assured her that Hughes was sorry for the quarrel and appeared to have "at last gotten one eye open." She continued to blame the "vile" influence of Louise Thompson for his previous behavior and told Godmother they now had an opportunity to bring Hughes again "under noble influences." "Personally, I think that he has so much in him," Hurston wrote, "that it is worth my swallowing and forgetting if by extending a friendly hand I can bring him back into the fold." Zora cared less than Langston about the play's historic value, or even about the money it could make in the present; for her, it was a matter of principle. "Godmother, I am so happy that Langston has taken an honorable view of the thing, that I would give him part," she decided. "I shan't say that to him right now, but it takes all the sting out of things."

That same day, January 20, Hurston sent two telegrams to Rowena Jelliffe authorizing the Cleveland production: The first simply said "Okay." In the second wire, Hurston gave a more tentative nod, explaining that she needed to consult with her newly acquired literary agent, Elisabeth Marbury, before she could give final approval. Zora's second note also included a caveat: "not one word must be altered except by me." In response, Jelliffe invited Hurston to Cleveland for rehearsals, scheduled to begin February 1, and offered to pay half her train fare.

Meanwhile, Hurston sent Hughes a separate, appeasing telegram: "Just received your last letter. Awfully glad everything can be arranged. Sorry for misunderstanding. Letter follows." The letter that followed was even more amiable. "I suppose that both of us got worked up unnecessarily," Hurston admitted. "I am busy smoothing out my lovely brow at present and returning to normal. I am in fault in the end and you were in fault in the beginning," she judged. "I shall freely acknowledge my share at anytime and place. Somehow I don't mind reversing myself, especially when it moves me towards pleasanter relationships. Perhaps I am just a coward who loves to laugh at life better than I do to cry with it. But when I <u>do</u> get to crying, boy, I can roll a mean tear."

The next morning, after consulting with her agent, Hurston sent another wire to Jelliffe, as promised. "Proceed good luck," it said. Finally, the whole matter appeared settled—until Hurston received a letter from Hughes threatening litigation.

This was the terse letter Langston had written in response to Zora's claim of sole authorship—and it had crossed her conciliatory dispatches in the mail. Calling Zora's jealousy of Louise "absurd— because you know better than that," Hughes hinted at the possibility of a lawsuit—then, paradoxically, suggested they resume their collaboration to get the play in shape for a Cleveland premiere. Obviously rankled, he concluded dryly: "You're an awfully amusing person, Zora."

Within a day or so of receiving this letter—which no doubt caused her to furrow her brow once more—Hurston got a call from Hughes's attorney and friend, Arthur Spingarn. She met with him January 24 to explain her side of the story, and Spingarn summarized their meeting in a letter to Hughes, dictated in Hurston's presence: "Miss Hurston insists that the account you gave me of your collaboration in the play is grossly exaggerated and that virtually all of the play was written by her. She says that you should not have been surprised when the script arrived in Cleveland with her name thereon as the sole author, as she showed you this script last Fall with her name on it as sole author and that you made no comment at the time, except to say, couldn't there be two versions, so if we could not sell the one, perhaps we could sell the other." Further, Spingarn reprimanded Hughes for his litigation threats and said he agreed with Hurston that the matter of royalties should be addressed in a face-to-face conversation.

By then, Hurston had received another letter from Hughes, dated January 22, prodding her to make an agreement about the division of royalties so the play could proceed. In this letter, Hughes also attempted to bury the hatchet once and for all. "If you feel that the major part of MULE-BONE is yours," he told Zora, "I am quite willing that you have two-thirds of all incomes." Pleased that she planned a trip to Cleveland to work out a final version of the play, Langston assured Zora that he'd told the Jelliffes "what a grand person" she was. Having brought up the matter of reputation, he then wondered if his was still intact with Charlotte Mason: "I hope nothing will come out of this matter to worry Godmother," he fretted. "As you know, I had nothing to do with initiating this Cleveland production, so please get her straight on that point."

Meanwhile, Hughes wrote to the Library of Congress seeking a copyright for *Mule Bone* in his name, but listing both himself and Hurston as authors. Although Hurston had already gotten the play copyrighted—solely in her name—in October 1930, Hughes received a copyright confirmation January 27, 1931. This second copyright was granted without incident, apparently because Hurston had registered the play under a different name: *De Turkey and De Law*. Relieved to have the copyright notice in hand, Hughes told Hurston he was "glad things seem to be straight again now. I hate mixups. Everybody's happy—so O.K."

But the war of words was not over and numerous third parties now sought to jump into the fray. The same day Hughes received his copyright notice in the mail, Spingarn informed him that he'd spoken with Alain Locke, who "believed Miss Hurston was right and that you were wrong in the matter." When Hughes wired Locke to ask why he was backing Hurston, Locke responded with a note that Hughes found infinitely annoying: "Congratulations on the Harmon Award—but what more do you want?"

Hughes had just been awarded the prestigious Harmon Foundation literature prize, for which Locke had nominated him. Yet—not wanting to be anywhere near Godmother (or Locke, now)—Hughes declined to attend the New York awards ceremony, citing illness as an excuse. Determined to see *Mule Bone* through its Cleveland staging, which he hoped would open the door to Broadway and perhaps a movie, Hughes continued his efforts to make amends with Hurston, who was due in Ohio on the first of February, Langston's twenty-ninth birthday. *Mule Bone* needed extensive revisions, and he and Hurston would have to get to work as soon as she arrived. Any lingering animosity would only slow them down, Hughes reasoned.

"Zo darling," he cooed. "Whatever your personal feeling toward me may be, let's not break up what promises to be a good play." Teasingly alluding to Hurston's distaste for Louise Thompson, Hughes assured her that there were "typists aplenty" in Cleveland: "white, black, Jewish—and male, if you don't approve of women."

Finally, Langston managed a bit of an apology: "I'm not mad. Are you?" he queried Zora. "I'm perfectly willing to be friends again, and awfully sorry about anything I might have done to make you angry."

Around the same time, however, Hughes—still thinking litigiously—asked Louise Thompson to be prepared to serve as a witness for his case, if necessary. Louise's response indicated that Zora's dislike of her was reciprocated: "The only thing I can say is that Zora is crazy," she wrote, "but unfortunately maliciously so."

Zora did not strike Paul Banks, one of the Gilpin Players, as crazy or malicious. After meeting with her during a visit to New York and hearing her side of the story directly, Banks immediately wrote to tell Rowena Jelliffe that Hughes was in the wrong—and that he had been "stupidly untruthful" with the Gilpins about the play. In spite of this disturbing development, Hughes tried to remain hopeful that a face-to-face meeting would resolve the rumpus, he told his attorney, "as this strange and unpleasant business is beginning to get on my nerves."

The in-person conference was finally held on the afternoon of Monday, February 2, at the Karamu Theatre. The night before, however, the Gilpin Players had voted to discontinue the production because of uncertainty about Hurston's attitude. (She had not arrived in time for the February 1 rehearsal, as expected.) When Zora showed up in Cleveland on February 2, though, Mrs. Jelliffe thought the group might reconsider. First, Hurston and Hughes met alone, as he reported, "to straighten out our difficulties, so that we could then confer in unity with the representatives of the Gilpin Players." Again, Hurston's main complaint concerned Louise Thompson, whom she termed "a gold digger." Hurston also continued to maintain that Hughes's role in the creation of the play had been a small one, and that she should get first billing on any playbills and other notices. Hughes responded by clarifying "that I have never claimed the play as even half mine, and in talking about it, had always said that the wit and color were in the main hers—but that I did not see how one could make a mathematical division of construction and characterization as opposed to dialect and wisecracks, the latter being clothing for the former." The current version of *Mule Bone* was a "new play," Hurston retorted, and she had not used any of Hughes's ideas. Hughes again disputed this claim, but in the end, he and Hurston worked out their differences and agreed that the Gilpin production could go on—if the Players voted to do it. The group planned to meet the following evening to decide.

Before that final meeting was held, though, Hurston changed her mind. Overnight, she learned that Louise Thompson had been in Cleveland and had testified to the Jelliffes against her. In fact, Louise had visited Cleveland on January 17 for an unrelated matter. While there, however, she did go to Karamu to speak with the Jelliffes—and to back up Hughes's assertion of joint authorship. Hearing this news—and also learning that Louise, like Langston, was a friend of the Jelliffes—Hurston felt that she had been double-teamed and tricked. When she called Rowena Jelliffe the next morning to protest, Mrs. Jelliffe suggested they talk about the matter in person. Suffering now from full-blown tonsillitis, Hughes was under doctor's orders to remain in bed, so they all agreed to meet at his mother's home at 5:00 P.M. that same day, February 3.

It was a cold and snowy Tuesday and Hurston arrived for the meeting in what Hughes called "a most angry and emotional mood." She was accompanied by Paul Banks, the Gilpin Player who had contacted the Jelliffes from New York. He had driven to Cleveland with Hurston and was "strongly on her side," as Hughes put it. In "a noisy and most undignified scene," Hurston berated Mrs. Jelliffe as a dishonorable businessperson, implied that Hughes was trying to steal the play from her, and denounced Louise Thompson as a hussy, according to Hughes. Zora had not come all the way to Cleveland to be made a fool of, she said, and she would not allow the Gilpin production. In a most unflattering portrayal, Hughes reported to Van Vechten that Zora "pushed her hat back, bucked her eyes, ground her teeth and shook manuscripts in my face." Through the whole ordeal, an indisposed Hughes mostly sputtered and gasped. But as Hurston stormed out, Hughes's mother, Carrie Clark, suddenly dived into the fracas. "I had to get up out of bed to restrain my mother," Hughes recalled.

Meanwhile, Hurston—detonating with righteous indignation—claimed victory. Convinced that Hughes and Thompson had plotted to steal from her after all, she sent a triumphant telegram to Charlotte Mason immediately following the meeting, reporting that the play had been stopped and that she'd "smashed them all."

Though Hurston felt right (and wronged), her behavior toward Hughes was hardly admirable. Given her once-close friendship with him—and the fact that they'd reconciled the previous day— she might have granted him a chance to explain Louise's visit before leaping to the conclusion that she'd been bamboozled. Yet an overly suspicious Hurston reacted to this new hurt before it had been fully inflicted—and in so doing, she hastened the outcome that she had once dreaded: the loss of her deep friendship with Langston Hughes.

Hurston also lost the opportunity to see *Mule Bone* performed. The Gilpin Players, of course, gave up any hopes of ever staging the folk comedy, which Van Vechten had praised as "fresh and amusing and authentic." The actors themselves were divided over the controversy: Some held to the Hughes-Jelliffe point of view, while others—led by Paul Banks—supported Hurston. "The whole thing has developed into the most amazing mess I ever heard of," Hughes told Louise Thompson.

To make matters worse, on the Thursday after the brawl, Hurston "had the astounding nerve" (in Langston's words) to attend a Cleveland soiree in Hughes's honor given by his fraternity—and reportedly to bad-mouth him there. Hughes could not attend the Omega Psi Phi party because of his illness, but he heard from friends that Zora told everyone he was trying to steal her work. He also was told she said "some very unpleasant things" about Louise. Further, Godmother was now trying to actively insert herself into the melee: "I have received the most insulting note I have ever heard tell of from 399," Hughes sniffled to Louise. "How she thinks of such ungodly things to say, I don't know." Speculating that "Zora must be a little off," a weary Hughes offered Louise a bit of friendly advice: "Find yourself a mule-bone because the free-for-all is on."

Mostly, however, the skirmish was over. When Hurston got back to New York, she wrote to tell Hughes she'd stopped by his place in Westfield to pick up a couple of her books. She also was returning the check Rowena Jelliffe had sent to cover half her travel expenses to Cleveland. "In view of the fact that we did no business," she said, "I don't know whether I am due it." Zora signed off by wishing Hughes "lots of luck" with his tonsils and throat trouble.

Perhaps testing the waters to see if the friendship was irrevocably sunk, Hughes sent Hurston a note and a newspaper clipping in mid-March. Her reply was polite but curt. A week or so before, on March 5, Hurston had visited Hughes's lawyer to say "there was no possible chance" of her ever collaborating with Hughes on the play. She wanted to eliminate all parts in which he claimed collaboration and create a new play in which he would have no interest. When Hughes received this news from Spingarn, he thought it might be "just as well" to let Hurston have *Mule Bone*. "I've finished a play of my own," he proclaimed, apparently no longer caring so much about his stake in the contested comedy. As late as August, however, Hughes reiterated his rights to *Mule Bone* after learning that Hurston's agent, Elisabeth Marbury, had given it to Wallace Thurman to revise. Once he got wind of the controversy, Thurman returned the play to the Marbury agency untouched.

Mule Bone would remain largely untouched for the next sixty years, never to be produced in its authors' lifetimes. Both Hurston and Hughes later would express regret over the *Mule Bone* debacle—its denouement more a tragedy of Negro life than a comedy. Though he never publicly admitted any responsibility for the quarrel, Hughes—tellingly—would renounce all claims to the play in May 1932. "You know, I gave up to Zora all rights on *The Mule Bone*," he would tell Van Vechten in 1934. "Is she still mad at me?" And in 1939, Hurston would confide to a friend that she still woke up at night crying over her breakup with Hughes, which she described as "the cross of her life." This mutual remorse, however, would not find its voice for years—and by then, it would be too late.

In 1931, the two writers had run out of words for each other. Once able to talk about everything, they now had nothing to say. When they did try to talk, as their March correspondence suggested, their conversation was unbearably stilted. Soon, they gave up all efforts to communicate beyond the basic courtesies—and then usually through mutual friends. What, after all, was the use? *Mule Bone* was dead—and one of the most promising literary friendships of the twentieth century was finished.

CHAPTER 21

From Sun to Sun

Although their "art was broken," as Hughes put it, he and Hurston still occasionally "liked to laugh together," one friend recalled. But their infrequent contact and the worsening economic times afforded them few opportunities to do so. In fact, New York itself—and especially Harlem—seemed to be laughing less as the Great Depression continued to live up to its name.

By the spring of 1931, the black mecca was on its way to becoming a slum. Harlem continued to attract new residents, making it one of the most crowded areas of the country, but it offered its growing citizenry limited opportunity: unemployment in Harlem was five times that of the rest of the city. And while rents continued to rise, Harlem's median family income plummeted 43.6 percent during the Depression's first three years.

At the same time, the Harlem Renaissance was dancing on its last legs. Perhaps sensing the beginning of the end, the movement's midwives had started to push on. The forward-thinking Charles S. Johnson had stepped down as editor of *Opportunity* in 1928 and joined the faculty of Nashville's Fisk University. James Weldon Johnson followed him to Fisk in 1931. Meanwhile, Jessie Fauset, former literary editor of *The Crisis*, had gotten married in 1929 and become a housewife and a high school teacher. And Alain Locke— busy with his increasing activities at Howard University—was spending more time in the nation's capital and less in Harlem. "I hear almost no news from New York," he lamented in March 1931. "A younger crowd of 'Newer Negroes' are dancing in the candle flame. The older ones are nursing their singed wings."

Among the latter group were Hurston and Hughes. In early April, Hughes—flush with his $400 prize from the Harmon Foundation— boarded a boat to Havana, in search of sun. Still bitter about the *Mule Bone* tussle, Hurston greeted his departure cynically. "I know that Langston says he was going to Cuba," she wrote to Godmother, "but I suspect that he is really gone to hunt up Eatonville to pretend that he knew about it all along." With her folklore book still incomplete—and Godmother breathing impatiently down her neck—Hurston had no sunny vacation prospects. Instead, she retreated into her work.

The collapse of the Hurston-Hughes friendship in early 1931 was, in retrospect, the death rattle of the New Negro movement. "That spring for me (and, I guess, all of us) was the end of the Harlem Renaissance," Hughes confirmed. "We were no longer in vogue, anyway, we Negroes. Sophisticated New Yorkers turned to Noel Coward. Colored actors began to go hungry, publishers politely rejected new manuscripts, and patrons found other uses for their money."

Ever cynical, Wallace Thurman had forecast the decay of the movement some time before, soon after the 1929 publication of his first novel, *The Blacker the Berry*. Yet he believed the Renaissance's erosion would not be due to the economy but to a paucity of good work. In an erratically spelled rant to Hughes, Thurman bluntly evaluated many of his New Negro colleagues and offered droll solutions for everyone's inadequacies, including his own: "Claude [McKay] I believe has shot his bolt. Jessie Fauset should be taken to Philadelphia and creamated. . . . Countee [Cullen] should be castrated and taken to Paris as the Shah's enuch. Jean Toomer should be enshrined as a genius and immortal and he should also publish his new book about which gossipp is raving. Bud [Rudolph] Fisher should stick to short stories. Zora should learn craftsmanship and surprise the world and outstrip her contemporaries as well. Bruce [Nugent] should be spanked, put in a monastery and made to concentrate on writing. . . .I should commit suicide. Don't mind such ravings."

The most telling portent of the Renaissance's demise, however, was the sudden death that summer of A'Lelia Walker. By the middle of 1931, the Depression had forced the Harlem heiress to put Villa Lewaro, her Hudson River mansion, on the market. She had even rented out her Harlem townhouse and pawned much of her jewelry. Because most black women had reduced the amount of money they spent on cosmetic upkeep, Walker's once-thriving hair-care business now was only earning enough to meet its greatly reduced payroll. Still, Walker was living large. Paying no mind to her doctor's warnings about her high blood pressure and overeating—nor to her accountant's alarms about the company's finances—she motored to Long Branch, New Jersey, in mid-August for a friend's weekend-long birthday party. After a day at the beach and a lavish dinner of lobster, champagne, and chocolate cake, she woke up at 4:00 A.M. with a blinding headache. On August 17, Walker—only forty-six years old—was pronounced dead of a cerebral hemorrhage.

Her funeral, a final symbol of her opulence, was as grand as any of her parties had been. For one last look at Harlem's most famous hostess, more than 11,000 people filed past her open casket, decorated by two dozen orchids resting just above her head. The next morning, Hughes's poetic tribute, "To A'Lelia," was read at the invitation-only funeral, at which the Rev. Adam Clayton Powell officiated. In her deep and resonant voice, educator Mary McLeod Bethune delivered A'Lelia's eulogy. And the Bon Bons, a female nightclub quartet, sang Noël Coward's "I'll See You Again"—and "they swung it slightly," Hughes recalled, "as she might have liked it."

A'Lelia Walker's death alerted Harlem that no one, regardless of wealth, was immune to misfortune. The tightfisted Depression "brought everybody down a peg or two," Hughes remembered. And most Negroes "had but few pegs to fall."

Still, two things—at least so far—seemed Depression-proof: Harlem's nightclub scene and the Great White Way. Now more than ever, people craved their alcohol and their amusements, and Harlem was in a position to supply ample amounts of both. At many uptown speakeasies and dance halls, then, the good times rolled on. And on Broadway, producers and audiences alike appeared to be no less captivated by Negro subjects. As evidence, *The Green Pastures*—a retelling of the Old Testament from a black southern perspective—had begun a phenomenal run on Broadway in February 1930.

Written by white playwright Marc Connelly—based on a book of short stories by white writer Roark Bradford—the folk musical packed the Mansfield Theatre for 557 performances before beginning a national tour. Even tough-minded black critic Sterling Brown was enchanted by *The Green Pastures*, proclaiming it "a miracle."

Hurston was not nearly so entranced: She acknowledged Connelly's skills as a dramatist and thought Richard B. Harrison, who played "De Lawd," was "a great actor." But, in her view, the "swell spectacle" of a play reflected very little about black religion or folk life. "The Negro's idea of heaven," she protested, "is certainly not dusting out a plantation boss's office with aprons on their wings. Nothing like work and bossy white folks in our heavenly concept."

Watching *The Green Pastures* succeed so soundly, despite its patronizing images, Hurston began to sense possibilities for herself as a playwright, *Mule Bone* notwithstanding. In fact, *Mule Bone*—which Carl Van Vechten thought had the potential to "duplicate the success of *The Green Pastures*"—had rekindled Hurston's long-standing interest in the theater. And, whether *Mule Bone* ever made it to the stage or not, she had plenty more folk material on which to base several new scripts.

Hurston's enthusiasm for the theater soon would overtake her interest in shaping her collected folklore into a book. The folktales remained unwieldy and seemed to be going stale. Fatigued and frustrated, Hurston set aside her folklore project to write "Barracoon," a book-length manuscript on Cudjo Lewis. She also resumed work on a conjure volume—deciding, again, that her hoodoo experiences warranted their own book, separate from the folklore. But few publishers were accepting new manuscripts in the ugly face of the Depression (Boni and Viking both turned down "Barracoon," also called "The Life of Kossula"). And Knopf editor Harry Block, who'd befriended Hurston at one of Van Vechten's parties, believed her in-progress manuscripts needed more work. Though he thought her raw material "glorious," Block told Hurston frankly that she did not have a book yet—only notes for a book, or perhaps several volumes.

Hurston allayed her frustration over this news by taking a June jaunt with Fannie Hurst. The wildly successful novelist who'd been so helpful to Zora during her early days at Barnard asked her ex-amanuensis to join her for a road trip (with Zora as the driver) to visit their shared literary agent, Elisabeth Marbury, at her summer home in Maine. Annoyed by the workers who were noisily "tearing up 66th Street" just outside her door, Zora welcomed the chance to get away from the awful racket and the current unpleasantness of New York, which had "utterly disorganized" her thoughts.

Early on the morning of June 7, Zora showed up, as planned, at Fannie's "cathedral-like studio apartment" just around the corner from her own. An excited Fannie—"with her mouth all set like a Christmas present," as Zora recalled—joined her in the car. Reveling in the Sunday morning serenity, Zora expertly guided her just-serviced Chevrolet onto the open road.

An incident Hurst recounted years later most likely occurred during this trip. The way Hurst told the story, she and Zora stopped at a hotel in Westchester County for a bite to eat. The waiter glanced at Zora—decked out in "one of her bizarre frocks of many colors," as Fannie described it—and then looked "as if a window-shade had been drawn over his face." But a lightbulb flashed in Fannie's head. Before the waiter could dismiss the interracial duo by claiming all the empty tables were reserved, Fannie announced: "The Princess Zora and I wish a table." Confused by Zora's unusual, African-inspired attire—and reluctant to insult what might be visiting royalty—the waiter seated the women at the best table in the house. Zora played along with Fannie's game, but when they were back in the car, she lamented the need for such race-traversing tricks. "Who would think," she remarked, "that a good meal could be so bitter?"

During their nine-day junket, Zora and Fannie often encountered discrimination in hotels and restaurants in the rural and resort towns through which they traveled. Since this was all new to Fannie, she felt inclined to confront the discriminators—and to turn down accommodations herself when hotels refused to give Zora a room other than in the servants' quarters. Zora viewed this kind of protest as an insipid waste of time. "Zora's attitude was swift and adamant," recalled Fannie, who was startled by Zora's aloof lack of indignation. "If you are going to take that stand, it will be impossible for us to travel together," Fannie remembered Zora saying. "This is the way it is and I can take care of myself as I have all my life. I will find my own lodging and be around with the car in the morning."

With the ground rules laid, the travelers—accompanied by

Fannie's tiny Pekingese pooch—headed north to Albany, stopped briefly in Saratoga Springs, then motored east to Vermont to look at some farmland Fannie thought she might buy. Then, instead of heading toward Marbury's place in Maine, Fannie suggested they visit Niagara Falls. Zora had always wanted to see the natural wonder, she confessed, "so we pointed the nose of the Chevrolet due West with my foot in the gas tank splitting the wind for Buffalo." The two women arrived at Niagara Falls the next afternoon before sundown. Dashing to the rail to admire the "monstropolous" waterfalls, Zora was awestruck by what looked like "the Pacific Ocean rushing over the edge of the world." Fannie, who'd visited the falls before, thought Zora needed to glimpse the massive cascade from the Canadian side. So the pair crossed the international bridge and took in the view from Ontario. They then spent the next three days traveling through Hamilton, Kitchener, and other towns in that part of Canada.

Somewhere along the way, they met up with Arctic explorer Vilhjalmur Stefansson. Stef was Fannie's lover and he was the real point of the trip for her, whether she confided in Zora about the extramarital affair or not. Once Fannie had satisfied her craving for Stefansson, she lost all interest in Maine. No doubt aware of the tryst, but ever discreet, Zora pointed the car back toward New York as soon as Fannie signaled she was ready to go. The women spent the night of June 14 in Rochester, then took off at 6:30 the next morning for Manhattan. Driving through heavy rains, they stopped en route to rescue a Maltese kitten on the brink of drowning; the motley crew finally pulled into the city during the wee hours of June 16. Zora dropped Fannie off—along with the dog and the kitten—around two o'clock in the morning, then headed straight to her own bed to sleep the stormy night away.

As soon as she got rested, Zora busied herself with practical concerns. Accepting that she would not have a book on the shelves any time soon, she began casting about for another way to employ her talents and earn a living. By now, Godmother had loosened her grip on Zora's career, urging her to pursue writing opportunities that would hasten her departure from the Park Avenue payroll. Since Zora's return from her southern fieldwork the previous year, Godmother had gradually reduced her monthly stipend from a high of $200 to the current low of $100. "I don't see, really, how this month I can make the $100.00 do," Zora had negotiated just before hitting the road with Hurst. Vowing to find another source of income by July, she petitioned for more cash to tide her over. "I fully appreciate the present economic situation," Hurston assured her now-reluctant patron. "You have been most magnificent and generous to me in <u>every</u> way. . . . Even if you feel that you can do nothing for me anymore in a material way, I shall know that you are behind me, and taking me on your wings when you soar with the High Gods in space; that your love is sustaining me."

Charmed by Zora's words—and recognizing that her "sun-burnt child" could not live on love alone—Godmother sent her $200. Received June 23, it was supposed to last through the end of July, but fifty dollars of it was already spent by the end of the week. Zora used it to pay fifteen dollars in back rent, to buy groceries and writing paper, to take care of her scientific society dues, to visit the dentist, and to purchase agar-agar, the medicine she needed for her recurring bouts of intestinal illness.

For more than a year now, Zora had been suffering from a digestive disturbance that had followed her home from the Bahamas. The illness eventually forced her to seek out a specialist. At Godmother's behest, white writer Paul Chapin (another "godchild") arranged an appointment for Zora with a prominent and well-recommended white physician. Godmother was certain this doctor would provide the best of care. When Zora showed up at the specialist's swank office in Brooklyn, however, an "obviously embarrassed" receptionist ushered her into what the doctor called "a private examination room."

"Under any other circumstances," Hurston commented, "I would have sworn it was a closet where the soiled towels and uniforms were tossed until called for by the laundry. But I will say this for it, there was a chair in there wedged in between the wall and the pile of soiled linen." The doctor came in immediately and began a perfunctory examination. "It was evident he meant to get me off the premises as quickly as possible," Hurston observed. "Being the sort of objective person I am, I did not get up and sweep out angrily as I was first disposed to do. I stayed to see just what would happen, and further to torture him more." The great specialist hastily scrawled a prescription and asked for a twenty-dollar fee. "I got up," Hurston recalled, "set my hat at a reckless angle and walked out. . . ." She would later recount this as her "most humiliating Jim Crow experience" and marvel that it occurred not in the South but in supposedly sophisticated New York.

Despite this unsavory encounter—and the illness that prompted it—Hurston kept pace with her work. Within a month of receiving Godmother's $200 check, Zora had fulfilled her promise to find another source of income: She was writing several skits for a Negro revue called *Fast and Furious* and she'd been hired to write the book for another show, *Jungle Scandals*. On July 21, she secured copyrights for several theatrical sketches—"Poker," "Lawing and Jawing," "Woofing," and "Forty Yards"—that she wrote for the revues. Thoroughly bitten by the theater bug, Zora was working that summer, as well, to turn her 1925 short story "Spunk" into a play.

"I do not consider either of the revues as great work," she admitted to Godmother, "but they are making the public know me and come to me, and that is important. . . . Anyway, I like the idea of going from light and trivial to something better, rather than coming down from a 'Spunk' to 'Fast and Furious.' The public will see growth rather than decline, you see."

In addition to this welcome career bulletin, Zora shared with Godmother a bit of personal news. "I hear that my husband has divorced me," she wrote, "so that's that. Don't think I am upset," she added glibly, "for your lil Zora is playing on her harp like David. He was one of the obstacles that worried me."

Herbert Sheen had met another woman soon after he and Zora separated and he now wanted to marry her. In July 1931, Zora granted him an amicable divorce, without hesitation. In fact, Sheen would recall half a lifetime later, "she was a little too accommodating. I often wished that she had refused to get a divorce. I would have been a lot better off."

Hurston, too, might have been better off—at least financially—if she had stayed with Sheen, who was now a physician in St. Louis. Many of Zora's peers, including Sheen's new love interest, might have argued that being a doctor's wife wasn't bad work if you could get it, especially during the Depression. But Zora's motivation for marriage obviously was not financial; she had married Sheen for love and pleasure. When the marriage failed to deliver on these counts, it was no longer of use.

Actually, Zora had not lost her love for Sheen—"your own mother has never loved you to the depth that I have, Herbert," she would tell him years later—but she'd long ago abandoned her interest in matrimony. "Marriage and social laws were evolved primarily to protect children and the mothers of children," Hurston believed. Already forty at the time of her divorce, Zora in all likelihood had given up any hope of having children—dissuaded, no doubt, by the sacrificial example of her own mother. Refusing to see herself as a passive player in somebody else's story, Zora wanted to be her own woman, not someone else's wife or mother. And she felt certain that these domestic roles would conflict with her worldly ambitions. Consequently, Hurston chose to defect from the demands of marriage and motherhood, but she never once considered abstaining from passion and pleasure. "I look back upon my experience with you as a time of pleasure without regrets," she once told Sheen. Having thoroughly rebelled against the romantic plot that women of her generation were expected to act out, she added: "Love *should not* last beyond the point where it is pleasurable."

Godmother responded to the news of Zora's divorce—and her casual attitude toward it—with muted wonderment. Although the two women had grown closer since Zora's return to New York and the onslaught of the Depression, they rarely spoke about Zora's personal life. Mason was more vocal than ever, though, about her protégée's career choices. Hoping Zora's work on *Fast and Furious* and *Jungle Scandals* would provide her with a suitable outlet for her "natural creative impulse," Godmother encouraged her efforts. "God knows you are about the only person left among the Negroes who can translate that impulse into exact Negro language," she opined. Citing the need for "genuinely Negro" theater and admonishing Zora to "write something worthy of [her] own power," Godmother offered a simple but powerful directive: "Stick to your ideals for your people, Zora."

Hurston swiftly learned how difficult this was to do. *Fast and Furious* was plagued by financial problems and a producer, Forbes Randolph, whose approach Zora judged as "stupid and trite." When the show opened at the New Yorker Theatre on September 15, most critics agreed with Hurston's assessment. Billed as a revue in thirty-five scenes, *Fast and Furious* was "mediocre entertainment," the *New York Sun* blared. "It is fast, furious and rather tiresome in large doses," *The New York Times* concurred. But *The Times* singled out a court-room scene that Hurston wrote—in which a prisoner was sentenced to nine years in a watermelon patch with a muzzle—as one of the rare moments when the revue provided "a measure of genuine enter-tainment." Even talented actors like Etta Moten and Jackie Mabley (in her pre-"Moms" days) could not save the revue from its ama-teurish staging, one critic wrote, and its "doleful series of sketches which fall pathetically flat."

Hurston was not surprised by the terrible reviews. The producer "squeezed all Negro-ness out of everything and substituted what he thought <u>ought</u> to be Negro humor," she complained. Though at first Hurston tried to argue with Randolph about these matters, she finally became reconciled to take whatever money she could get from the show and wait for another opportunity to do something substantive. Within a week, however, *Fast and Furious* folded and the $525 Hurston had expected in royalties was reduced to a paltry $75.

In spite of its clear artistic shortcomings, Hurston had hoped *Fast and Furious* would last a few months, long enough for her to earn money to buy some much-needed clothes and move back to New Jersey, where rents were cheaper. "But that's out now," she brooded just ten days after opening night. Meanwhile, her other potential meal ticket, *Jungle Scandals*, had been canceled. No longer officially on Godmother's payroll—yet utterly dependent on the $100 gifts the old lady faithfully sent her each month—Hurston was desperate now for another source of income.

At the moment, she had only one appealing prospect: Steamship heiress Nancy Cunard contacted her that fall saying she planned to "publish a book of Negro-ness in Paris," as Hurston put it. French composer George Antheil, who was traveling in the States, met with Hurston on Cunard's behalf. Dazzled by Zora's knowledge and verve, Antheil returned to Paris with several Hurston folklore essays and the impression that she "would be the most stolen-from Negro in the world for the next ten years at least." Cunard's book, to be called *Negro*, would not appear until 1934, however, so Hurston's inclusion in the anthology had little immediate effect on her life, or her finances.

"I firmly believe that I shall succeed as a writer," Zora told Godmother, "but the time element is important." Therefore, she reasoned, she needed "a paying business" that would not distract her too much from writing. Her idea was to set up as "New York's Chicken Specialist"—selling chicken salad, chicken soup, chicken à la king, and hot fried chicken to the city's "finer hostesses." As it would be "an exclusive mouth to mouth service," she would not advertise and therefore would need little startup capital, just enough to buy jars, cartons, and other necessary supplies. For someone who enjoyed cooking, this idea of a niche catering business was not a bad one—and probably would have been more lucrative, in the short term, than Hurston's writing and folklore work. But Zora's heart wasn't in it, so the idea never took off.

Recognizing that her future was not in chicken, Hurston cooked up another idea—one about which she felt more passionate: She wanted to organize her own revue. "Outside of getting the story & conjure books ready for another try, I am planning a Negro concert of the most intensely black type," as she updated Godmother in late September. Several theater producers by now had expressed interest in Hurston's talent and in the treasury of folklore and music she'd collected in the South. Rather than allow this material to be plundered for another trifle like *Fast and Furious*, Hurston began creating a show that would be artistically true to the folk context, as well as to the folk themselves.

Meanwhile, she had finally found an outlet for her conjure studies: Hurston published a one-hundred-page article, "Hoodoo in America," in the October–December 1931 issue of *The Journal of American Folk-Lore* (edited by her former Barnard professor Ruth Benedict). But she was still struggling to shape her folktales into a semiscientific manuscript. At the same time, Hurston was starting to feel that "the flaming glory" of black life should not be buried in scientific journals. This material—particularly the music—belonged onstage, where it could be exposed to a wider audience and presented in the context of black folk life. "The Negro material is eminently suited to drama and music," Hurston believed. "In fact, it *is* drama and music and the world and America in particular needs what this folk material holds."

This idea of presenting black folk material onstage was not a new notion for Hurston, but something she'd dreamed of (at one time with Langston Hughes) for years. Ever since her return from the South, in fact, she'd been quietly looking for a stage—and an audience—for her huge collection of "Negro songs of all descriptions." Hurston had amassed this collection almost by happenstance while gathering folktales and conjure in the South. The music was easy to get, she commented, because black people "are not going to do but so much of anything before they sing something." Zora immediately saw the value of these songs and began to record them in her memory. "Sitting around in saw-mill quarters, turpentine camps, prison camps, railroad camps and jooks, I soaked them in as I went," she recalled. Upon returning to New York, Hurston gave this mass of music to her friend Hall Johnson, the most famous black choral director in the country, to do with as he wished. After sitting on the material for several months, Johnson—who'd been largely responsible for the success of *The Green Pastures*—returned it to Hurston, telling her "the world was not ready for Negro music unless it were highly arranged." He felt that these "barbaric melodies and harmonies" would not be well received, that audiences just wanted to hear spirituals—and then only if they were "highly flavored with Bach and Brahms," as Hurston put it. This attitude seemed to Zora "a determined effort to squeeze all of the rich black juice out of the songs and present a sort of musical octoroon to the public. Like some more 'passing for white.'"

Hurston wanted no part of this kind of diluted display—and she believed it was time to let the world hear "the real voice" of her people. In addition to presenting natural singing onstage—of ballads, work songs, and jook numbers—Hurston wanted her "concert in the raw" to showcase the authentic West Indian folk dancing she'd seen in the Bahamas. By October 1931, she'd drafted a script and assembled a group of sixteen Bahamian dancers for a performance that would celebrate (and contextualize) the mighty, unembellished voices of ordinary black folk—the kinds of voices that rang out with sweet authority in the churches and fields of Eatonville, Mulberry, Mobile, and Nassau.

Judging herself musically inadequate, however, Hurston went back to Hall Johnson and proposed they combine her dancers and his singers for the concert. (Hurston's own musical skills, in fact, were limited: She could hold a tune in the shower, peck out a few bars on the piano, and strum some decent chords on the guitar, but she was no maestro.) With a small nudge from the redoubtable Charlotte Mason, Johnson looked at Hurston's script and agreed to the collaboration. But after he kept her dancers "standing around his studio for three weeks without one rehearsal," as Hurston recalled, she started to wonder if she would have to produce her concert without the esteemed composer's help. An unfortunate incident in the studio transformed her wondering into certainty. While her dancers (mostly immigrants from the island of Bimini) idled around one day, eager for a chance to rehearse, Hurston heard two or three members of Johnson's choir (made up of black Americans) stage-whisper some derogatory comments about West Indians. Seeing the hurt on her dancers' faces, Hurston knew she could not let them believe she shared "the foolish prejudice" expressed by these singers. So she gathered her people, loudly voiced her vexation, and stalked out.

Determined to go it alone, Hurston began conducting rehearsals in her apartment for the performance, tentatively titled "In the Beginning: A Concert of Negro Secular Music." Within a few weeks, she had found singers of her own, including "a fine black girl as contralto soloist," as she reported to Godmother, "and a lovely black girl as soprano." The baritone was "a dark brown also," she added.

Against a backdrop where light skin was revered and dark skin reviled, Hurston's color-conscious casting was intended to make a statement. Zora did not have "any hang-ups about the color spectrum," according to her old friend Richard Bruce Nugent. To her, a Walter White—often described as a white man who *chose* to be black—was the same as a Wallace Thurman, who was so dark that the honey-hued Nugent initially found his color revolting. ("How dare he be so black," Nugent recalled thinking after their first meeting.) While newspaper ads in the 1930s routinely encouraged Negroes to bleach their skin—for "a complexion as charming as a movie star's," one broadside advised—Hurston aimed to represent her people onstage in all their dusky, down-home glory. And, though her own skin was a medium brown, she insisted on casting darker-skinned performers in the major roles. "No mulattoes at all," she vowed.

Pleased that "no diluted ones" would be "allowed on the plat-form," Godmother gave Zora access to the Fire Dance films she'd shot in the Bahamas, footage that was technically Mason's property, since she'd financed Hurston's expedition. With these films, Zora refreshed her memory on the details of the Fire Dance; she also set a definitive date for the performance: Sunday, January 10, 1932, at the John Golden Theatre.

Alain Locke, Godmother's chief adviser on all things Negro, was initially opposed to the concert. Having "never known the common run of Negroes," as Hurston phrased it, Locke "was not at all sym-pathetic to our expression." Eventually, though, he was won over (mostly by Godmother's interest in the production) and proceeded to serve as a theatrical spy of sorts. In this capacity, he occasionally dropped in on Zora's rehearsals and dispatched reports of her progress to Godmother.

Hurston did not need Locke's supervision; she was on fire about this project—now called *The Great Day*—and was absolutely com-mitted to it. Revising and typing her folklore manuscript in the mornings and rehearsing her performers in the afternoons, Zora was too busy "to even look out of the window, let alone make trips," as she told Fannie Hurst. The well-to-do novelist (who would soon take driving lessons) had tried to interest Zora in another auto excur-sion, this time to St. Louis and Cincinnati. But Zora politely declined. She had too much work to do to play the role of Fannie's "café-au-lait-learned-and-native-Georgia-cracker-Ph.D.-author-vagabond-friend-and-crack chauffeur," as Fannie once dubbed her.

Lacking money, however, Zora soon had to call upon Godmother's generosity once again. She needed $200 immediately for advertising and publicity photos, as well as another chunk for costumes. She'd already sold the Chevrolet to get funds for a deposit on the theater. She'd also sold another valued possession, her radio, for sixteen dol-lars, which she used to pay subway fares for her group—fifty-two people in all. "But now I have nothing more to sell," Hurston told Godmother on December 16. "I am on the brink of putting the thing over and it will break my heart to fall down now. Especially since no question of merit is involved, merely getting my advertising done on time." Zora asked Godmother for a loan, promising to turn over all box office receipts to her to guarantee it. "I have worked harder on this than I have anything else except collecting it," Hurston wrote persuasively, "and now . . . that I have gone thru the rigors of it, and worked so hard to get it into shape, I am willing to make <u>any</u> sacrifice, meet any terms, to give it a chance of success." She concluded: "If ever I needed you Godmother, I need you now."

Charlotte Mason came through once more, backing the performance for one night only—and hoping, along with Hurston, that a downtown producer would pick up the show and finance it for an extended run. A few days before Christmas, a buoyant Hurston thanked Godmother for her loan—amounting to $530—"with high hopes for our venture," as she signed her letter, "and glory bulging from my pores."

Emphasizing the authenticity of the material, the advertisement for *The Great Day* noted that the spirituals on the program were "fresh and without the artificial polish of rearrangement." Although the show featured musical arrangements by composer Porter Grainger and starred Leigh Whipper, an actor noted for his 1926 performance in the Pulitzer-winning *In Abraham's Bosom*, Hurston's publicity materials attempted to distinguish *The Great Day* from such Broadway successes, as well as from mediocre revues like *Fast and Furious*. "The dances have not been influenced by Harlem or Broadway," Hurston wrote in the advertisement, which promised "true Negro music" rather than "highly concertized spirituals." In addition to jook songs and work songs, the flyer vowed, the program was to include a sermon by an itinerant preacher, Negro lullabies and games, and a conjure ritual that had "never before been publicly performed."

At the last minute, however, Godmother insisted that the conjure ceremony be omitted from the concert. Zora had "given her word to the people down South she would not do this," Godmother argued; to violate that vow would be tantamount to breaking "a primitive law," and the cosmic consequences could be dire, she fretted. On a more practical level, Godmother also feared someone would try to steal the ritual and exploit it for commercial gain—with no respect for its spiritual origins. On the day of the show, as the seats in the West Fifty-eighth Street theater began to fill up, Hurston acquiesced to Godmother's wishes and took the conjure ceremony off the concert roster, announcing that it wasn't quite "finished" enough for the performance.

Even without the conjure ritual, the program was full and finished enough to satisfy its audience, "mostly white shirt fronts and ermine," as Hurston recalled. Godmother had purchased several tickets for her friends and godchildren, including Cornelia Chapin, Katherine Biddle, Paul Chapin, Miguel Covarrubias, and, of course, Alain Locke, who, dressed in flawless tails, went backstage before the performance to give Zora an encouraging pat on the back. Extremely nervous, Zora needed it. But the audience's enthusiastic response soon calmed her worries. "From the lifting of the curtain on the dawn scene where the shack rouser awakens the camp to the end of the first half," Hurston would remember, "it was evident that the audience was with us."

Rooted in Hurston's years of "intimate living among the common folk in the primitive privacy of their own Negro way of life" (as Locke phrased it in the program notes), *The Great Day* dramatized a day in the life of a Florida work camp. After opening with the shack rouser scene, the performance proceeded to show a group of men working to build a railroad, punctuating their labor with songs such as the everpopular "John Henry" and "Can't You Line It?" Singing in rhythm to the task at hand—driving a spike or swinging a pick—the men bellowed the lyrics Hurston had collected in the South. These songs, *The Great Day* revealed, were not just rhythmically appealing, but for the black folks who sang—and created—them, they often were assertions of power: "Cap'n got a pistol and he try to play bad, but I'm gonna take it if he make me mad," began one verse of "Can't You Line It?" The song continued playfully but purposefully: "Shove it over! Hey, hey, can't you line it? Ah, shack-a-lack-a-lack-a-lack-a-lack. Uh! Can't you move it? Hey, hey, can't you try?"

After a hard day in the fields, Hurston's workers then returned to the quarters, where their children played traditional Negro games popular throughout the South, such as "Chick-mah-chick" and "Mistah Frog." As night began to fall on Hurston's set—enhanced by a mossy backdrop from *Savage Rhythm*, playing at the same theater— an itinerant preacher (Leigh Whipper) entered the stage to deliver a bracing sermon in the quarters. The curtain for act one lowered to a roar of applause, as the preacher's makeshift congregation sang a piercing, unaffected "You Can't Hide."

The second part of the show began at "black dark" in the jook joint, where men and women reveled in secular songs such as "Halimufack," a blues tune Hurston had known for years: "You may leave and go to Halimufack/But my slow drag will bring you back," a confident lover croons. "Well, you may go/But this will bring you back." The jook scene was followed by the Fire Dance, then a group finale: Part of the cast sang "Deep River" on one side of the stage, while on the other side the rest of the performers belted out a blues song from the jook as a counterpoint. The audience thundered its approval, and Hurston—up to then "simply one of the crowd of Negro peasants on the stage," as one reviewer noted—was shoved out to take a bow and say a few words. She said "what should have been said in just the right way," according to the *New York Herald Tribune*, her "broad and ingratiating dialect" complementing the "natural and unpremeditated art" she and her cast had just presented.

The Great Day was a tremendous artistic success. Even Hall Johnson rushed backstage to congratulate Hurston: "I really came to see you do a flop," she remembered him saying, "but it was swell!" (If the old cliche is true—that imitation is the highest form of flattery—Hall Johnson soon would pay Zora the ultimate compliment: In March 1933, he would strike gold on Broadway with *Run, Little Chillun*, a folk musical containing several scenes clearly modeled on material from *The Great Day*.) The *Herald Tribune* critic was confident the warm reception for Hurston's show would guarantee a regular and extended run. "The evening was altogether successful," the reviewer wrote, "and carried off with a verve, a lack of self-consciousness, an obviously spontaneous enjoyment, as eloquent as it was refreshing."

Despite the critics' unstinting praise, *The Great Day* was not picked up by a deep-pocketed producer and Godmother was sorely disappointed by the box office receipts. Hurston, too, was displeased by the financial figures. Though she was showered with letters and phone calls, she had "no feeling of glory," she said, "because I am too keenly conscious of how far short I fell of the mark at which I aimed." Only $261 had been netted at the box office, not including the $88 in tickets Godmother had bought herself. When all was said and done, Hurston had not earned a dime; in fact, she *owed* money to her performers. Reluctantly, Godmother loaned Zora the $80.75 she needed to pay their salaries.

Conscientious of her running tab, Hurston now owed Godmother $610.75—the equivalent of about $7,700 today—and the only way she could ever hope to repay her was by staging another show. Technically, however, Godmother still owned the material that had thrilled the audience at the John Golden Theatre, and Hurston had to ask her permission to use it. "I know it is yours in every way," she appealed to Godmother, "and while I know it has great commercial value, I have no right to make a move except as you direct."

Godmother used this opportunity to rein in her young protégée— to reassert her sovereignty over Hurston's life. Although Zora was completely dependent on Godmother financially, she had approached *The Great Day* the way she conducted herself in the world—like a woman who was supremely independent and free. She'd never *asked* Godmother if she could present the concert, for instance; she'd simply *informed* her of her plans to do so. Now, Godmother reprimanded Zora for this creative and intellectual independence—for throwing herself at life and weighing the consequences later—and accused her of "trading on Godmother's big heart" to pull her out of the financial hole she'd dug for herself.

To ensure that this never happened again, Mason drafted a legally binding letter, listing the portions of the concert program she would allow Hurston to use for future performances. Anything not on the list—including the conjure material—"shall not be used for any purpose without further permission from me," Godmother declared. She also reminded Hurston that profits from any performances should be directed her way, to repay the $610.75 she was owed. The agreement, which Zora signed January 20, ended with Godmother's firm admonition: "In all that you do, Zora, remember that it is vital to your people that you should not rob your books, which must stand as a lasting monument, in order to further a commercial venture."

Godmother was right that Hurston's books would be "a lasting monument." But, as Hurston intuited, the timing was off: In the midst of the Depression—when theatrical producers appeared far more interested in Negro subjects than did publishers—Godmother expected Hurston to write books from the folklore she'd collected. Yet she barred her from presenting much of the same material onstage, where Hurston believed it belonged and where it had received a warm reception. If Zora was disturbed by Godmother's blind arrogance—and by her miserly hold on the material—she didn't say so. Momentarily putting on a face of contrition, she simply thanked Godmother for the liberated material and resolved to make the most of it.

Hurston immediately began plotting to present another version of the concert—renamed *From Sun to Sun*—at The New School for Social Research. "Your black gal has been stepping right along," she informed Godmother ten days before the March 29 performance. *Theatre Arts* magazine was publishing a photo of the cast in its April 1932 issue, and the Folk Dance Society had invited Hurston's dancers to perform at New York's chic Vanderbilt Hotel. There was even talk of a London engagement in the summer. With rehearsals every afternoon at four o'clock, Zora was whirling through her days, she reported, "rushing, writing notes, phoning and scratching my nappy head."

The New School performance of *From Sun to Sun* was similar to the program that had gone over so well at *The Great Day* premiere. To make up for the excised material, however, Hurston wrote a one-act play to round out the evening. Called *The Fiery Chariot*, the play dramatized a folktale about a slave who prays for death to deliver him from his life of servitude. Tired of hearing Ike's excessive prayers, Ole Massa shows up at his door one night in a white sheet, masquerading as God coming to carry him to heaven. Reconsidering his prayers, Ike then tries to outwit—or outrun—this fraudulent white being who claims to be God while clothed in the ridiculous costume of the Ku Klux Klan. Indeed, the apparel of intimidation and the master's arrogant attempt to make fun of his superstitious slave are comically exposed in Hurston's folk play, which was followed on the program by the Fire Dance—part of a finale that again brought the house down. "It was good it was the last thing," Hurston noted, "for nothing could have followed it."

This Tuesday night performance, like its predecessor, was a critical success. But Hurston failed to turn a profit—the country was facing economic disaster, after all—and Godmother and Locke quickly lost their patience with her. Judging the concert a "failure," Godmother confided to Locke that she felt Zora lacked leadership skills—and that other people, pretending to help her, were actually exploiting her to get ideas for their own work. Locke fomented the old lady's resentment and paranoia: He wondered aloud how Zora could afford the rent on her New York apartment and questioned why Godmother was continuing to give her a monthly allowance "with nothing to show for it."

Endeavoring to protect Godmother's interests (and his own), Locke took it upon himself to visit Hurston five days after her New School concert for a heart-to-heart talk. In their Sunday afternoon chat, Locke chided Hurston—who'd spoken to Barnard's alumnae the night before—as if they were back at Howard and he was her professor again. Her apartment was too expensive for her practically nonexistent income, he pointed out, and she should be writing to black colleges for employment. Locke also had a thing or two to say about Hurston's work: The latest version of her folklore book seemed to him the same as the first draft; further, she appeared to have lost interest in revising it. Zora countered by explaining that the new draft was vastly different from the first one—perhaps he just had not read it carefully—and that what he took as listlessness was actually poor health. Lately, she had not been able to afford the medicine for her persistent intestinal trouble; with illness draining her energy—and the concerts taking so much of her time—she'd had little stamina left for writing.

Ordinarily, Hurston would not have deigned to explain herself so thoroughly to the meddling Locke. But because he claimed to be speaking with her on Godmother's behalf, she felt compelled to give him the respect his position commanded. Hurston had always been "patronizingly fond" of Locke, according to her friend Bruce Nugent. Locke's exceptional intellect had won Zora's admiration, Nugent recalled, but the professor was "a man with rather effete gestures and a quiet way of speaking"—the kind of fellow that a "robust" Hurston "could have snapped in half." Rather than fight with Locke on this occasion, though, Hurston agreed with his suggestion that she seek a teaching job at one of the black colleges, and she conceded it was time for her to make some other changes, as well.

"I understand that both you and Alain feel that I have lost my grip on things," Zora wrote to Godmother immediately after her "long and intimate session" with Locke. Noting his suggestion that she move to a less expensive apartment, Hurston presented Godmother with a counterproposal: She wanted to go back home—to Eatonville. She would be hard-pressed to find cheaper living quarters—even a room—in New York, she argued. But the cost of living was much lower in the South. All she needed, really, was travel money to get there. "I'd love to go South if I could," Zora wrote. "There are several good reasons. 1. Atmosphere to work 2. Escape New York 3. Health 4. Chance of self-support."

After some initial reluctance, Godmother agreed to finance Hurston's return to Eatonville. "You do not seem to realize that I made a contract with you to hold for two years," she scolded Zora. "That was in 1927." Mason also agreed to settle up Hurston's bills, including $34.40 for telephone service and $18.40 for three months of unpaid heat; the old woman did not pay these debts in silence, however. "People do not run up bills for things," Godmother snarled, "with no prospect of paying for them." Hurston, of course, fully understood this, but she had used what little money she could scrape up to produce her concerts. And with no suitable, lucrative work to be found in New York, what could she do? "I know that my bills are huge," she shrugged, "but there they are."

Finally, there was one last item of expense: Zora needed a new pair of shoes. She'd been wearing the one pair she owned every day since December 1931. Now, as May 1932 approached, her big toe was threatening to burst out of the right shoe. Otherwise, Hurston informed Mason, she had plenty of clothes. Back in February, at Godmother's suggestion, sculptor Cornelia Chapin had given Zora several barely worn hand-me-downs—clothes that she accepted gratefully, but with characteristic immodesty. In an audacious and amusing thank-you letter, Hurston told Chapin: "I look very beautiful in the dresses and you will perhaps feel a tiny twinge of jealousy when you gaze upon me, but the artist in you will be so delighted at the sight of such a perfect union of clothes and woman that you will stifle your jealousy at once and rejoice with me."

Zora rejoiced alone, however, on April 28, when Godmother grudgingly gave her six dollars for a new pair of shoes, enough cash for a one-way ticket to Eatonville, and seventy-five dollars for the road. "Somehow a great weight seems lifted from me," Hurston noticed just before boarding a Florida-bound train. "I have been trying to analyze myself and see why I feel so happy. But I do." With a brand-new pair of shoes hugging her feet—and a small wad of fresh-start money lining her pocketbook—Zora Neale Hurston pointed her toes toward home.

CHAPTER 22

Home Again

Eatonville was Hurston's motherland. It was like a womb for her—and in its embrace, Zora felt the way she might have felt if she could have collapsed into Lucy Hurston's arms once more: nurtured and instantly renewed. "I am happy here, happier than I have been for years," she reported to Godmother after only a week back in Eatonville. "The air is sweet, yes literally sweet. Summer is in full swing. The days are hot but the nights are cool. The mocking birds sing off and on all night long and the honey suckle and magnolia are in bloom."

Having returned to Eatonville in search of "quiet, atmosphere, and economical existence," Hurston found all three there. She also found the town largely unchanged, despite its newly paved road. "Do you know that in more than fifty years of this town's existence that never has a white man's child been born here?" Zora informed Godmother. "There is no known case of a white-Negro affair around here. No white-Negro prostitution even."

In addition to its pure-Negro bloodline, Eatonville had maintained its hospitality and its humor. A few days after Zora's return, for instance, she was welcomed at a church supper by a man offering to buy her some baked chicken. Told that there was no more, the embarrassed man said to Zora: "There <u>was</u> some chicken, though, a little while ago." The woman serving the food retorted: "Oh, so you tryin' to offer her some chicken-<u>was</u>."

Despite the church's momentary shortage of victuals, Eatonville, which so far seemed immune to much of the Depression's unkindness, offered Zora bundles of fresh food, some raised by her own hand. "To keep in physical trim," as she put it, Zora planted a small garden that she happily tended every day before sunrise. Devoting her mornings to her crop of black-eyed peas, pole beans, lima beans, watermelons, okra, and tomatoes, she spent her afternoons and evenings polishing her folklore manuscript—even while eyeing a return to her first love: fiction.

Meanwhile, Hurston was conscious of her ongoing need to make a living. Godmother still sent her a monthly allowance (of only fifty dollars now), but the two women had agreed that Zora would be completely self-sufficient—ideally teaching at a black college—by fall. To that end, Hurston was pleased to receive an invitation to the fifty-seventh birthday celebration for Mary McLeod Bethune; she hoped the July 10 party would give her an opportunity to lobby for a job at Bethune-Cookman College, which Mrs. Bethune had founded in Daytona Beach, Florida, in 1918 as the Daytona Normal and Industrial Institute.

Hurston was not the only black writer looking for work in the summer of 1932. In New York, the deepening Depression had left many of her peers unemployed and desperate for something to do. On June 15, twenty-two young Negroes—mostly writers, artists, and students—sailed to Russia, with stenographer-turned-radical Louise Thompson as their leader. (Soon after she was booted out of Godmother's queendom, Thompson had dedicated herself to political work, helping to establish a Harlem branch of the Friends of the Soviet Union.) The twenty-two were traveling overseas to make a film about the history of American race relations. The Soviets were particularly interested in learning how their visitors felt about the Scottsboro Boys, the nine black youths in Alabama who'd been sentenced to death in April 1931 for allegedly raping two white prostitutes. Yet, according to one of the travelers, writer Dorothy West, several of the twenty-two learned the details of the Scottsboro case from their Russian hosts.

Arna Bontemps—who didn't go on the trip because he had a family to support—also noted a political apathy in some of the voyagers; they really went to Russia, he judged, "because it was sort of an adventure and because it was something to do at a time when it was very hard to find things to do." With only one acknowledged Communist Party member on board, the expedition absorbed "quite a bunch of the old Harlem group," as Bontemps recalled: Journalists Henry Moon and Ted Poston trudged up the gangplank of the *Europa*, as did singer Taylor Gordon and Bontemps's best friend, Langston Hughes. "Practically everybody that they could lay hands on, who didn't have a place to land . . . when the dispersal occurred, caught a ride on this trip to Russia," Bontemps observed.

Not invited by her nemesis, Louise Thompson, Zora ridiculed the whole idea: "Well, Langston, Louise and a crowd of white Negroes have sailed to Russia to make a Negro movie," she commented. This group of light-skinned elitists could never begin to authentically represent black America, Hurston felt. Although their movie, *Black and White*, was supposed to be set in Birmingham, Alabama, most of the twenty-two had never been south of the Mason-Dixon line, and "only two in the crowd look anything like Negroes," Zora complained. "So I'm still wondering where they will get the Negro movie out of that. Who will they use for actors? The world certainly will not know that the ones they have are colored, except by footnotes."

Though Hurston's criticism was rooted in her lingering bitterness toward trip organizer Louise Thompson—and an essentialized notion of blackness that was unfair to some of her Russian-bound friends— her concerns proved to be well founded. *Black and White* was never made. In fact, within a few days of setting sail, many of the twenty-two wayfarers were threatening mutiny against the seriously socialist Thompson (soon dubbed "Madame Moscow") and her right-hand man, Hughes. "Most of that crowd don't even know what Communism is," wagered political scientist Ralph Bunche, who happened to be sailing on the *Europa* (with Howard colleague Alain Locke) en route to Germany. What's more, most of the twenty-two could neither act nor sing. To make matters worse, some Soviet citizens complained that many of their visitors were not "genuine Negroes" (as Zora had forecast) because they were not dark enough. In mid-August, the whole production fell apart, the cast quickly disintegrated, "and most of them came back strongly anti-Communist as a result of it," Bontemps remembered.

Hurston did not need to go to Russia to know that communism was not for her. "My country, right or wrong," she'd said of America back in 1928. This statement notwithstanding, Hurston was not uncritical of the U.S. government, and she was fully aware of what she called "the pathos of Anglo-Saxon civilization" and its "false foundation." But she saw little logic in seeking refuge from racism in the "whiteland" of Europe. Black people could find their aesthetic, artistic, and emotional center only by turning within, she believed, and embracing their own culture. "As I see it," Hurston offered, "unless some of the young Negroes return to their gods, we are lost."

For Hurston, these gods were to be found in the folk culture—the music, the dance, the stories—of ordinary black people. As Zora well knew, though, many of her peers were embarrassed by these uneducated masses—people who, in some ways, still seemed bound by the rusty chains of slavery. Straining to prove themselves equal to whites, some Negro intellectuals sought to distance themselves from the ignorance and squalor, the broken English and country ways of those they claimed as their "skinfolk" but not their kinfolk. Hurston, however, perceived enormous beauty in the artful lives of these common, unheralded people. And she had long ago decided to become their champion.

In mid-June, as the *Europa* set sail with its cargo of New Negroes, Hurston—determined now more than ever to expose her collected folk material to broad audiences—began pitching the idea of staging *From Sun to Sun* in Florida. Since most of the material had been gathered in Orange and Polk counties, she thought it would be appropriate to present a series of concerts "in the native habitat of the songs and tales," as she wrote in an introductory letter to Edwin Osgood Grover. Grover was a creative arts professor at Rollins College in Winter Park, a quiet and wealthy town (boasting twenty-seven millionaires in winter) adjacent to Eatonville. Soliciting the college's support, Hurston cited her successes in New York and explained the genesis of *From Sun to Sun*: "Seeing the stuff that is being put forth by overwrought members of my own race, and well-meaning but uninformed white people, I conceived the idea of giving a series of concerts of untampered-with Negro folk material so that people may see what we are really like."

Grover and other Rollins faculty members—notably Robert Wunsch—liked the idea, as well as its originator, whom they immediately recognized as "a national authority on Negro ways." In early fall, with their support and Godmother's approval, Hurston began making plans for a concert at Rollins, which some of its students proudly called "the Harvard of the South."

Meanwhile, Eatonville's daughter—who'd "won an enviable place for herself in American dramatics," in Wunsch's view—was in demand elsewhere as well. Through Walter White of the NAACP, Hurston was invited to supply dancers for a musical based on Rene Maran's controversial *Batouala,* a 1922 novel portraying native life—and various sexual initiation rites—in an African village. Paul Robeson was cast in the lead, Maran penned the libretto, and Hurston agreed to supply the dancers. She also offered to perform in the musical; she could portray a conjure doctor, she suggested eagerly, or perhaps one of Robeson's polygamous partners. Because of the tough economic times, however, *Batouala* never made it past go. Godmother, for one, was hardly surprised: "The news here," she wrote to Zora from Manhattan, "seems to be that they are still putting Negro plays on the stage and they are still falling off!"

In mid-September, another dramatic possibility lured Hurston back to New York for a brief visit. Officials at Steinway Hall sent for her to discuss the possibility of booking several of her concerts for later that fall. Deciding she'd rather follow through with her plans to present *From Sun to Sun* at Rollins—which she saw as a chance to make a name for herself "without the Broadway drawbacks"—Hurston eventually declined the Steinway offer, noting that she felt "rather secure" in the South. On the other hand, she observed, "New York is painful to me now. I feel so out of place."

In Florida, Zora immersed herself in the slow-motion lives of ordinary country folk, and she became one of them herself. "She was just Zora," recalled a woman who met Hurston upon her return to Eatonville. "She never looked over none of her people because she had more education. She never looked over the lower class that was under her. She never did. She was always happy. She was always rejoiced." Agreeably ensconced in Eatonville, Hurston scribbled down the township's imaginative, ever-evolving language and learned "the chicken dance" from a local child. She contemplated buying three acres of lakefront property for $300 (less than a year's rent in New York); considered starting an adult school to teach cooking, sewing, and furniture making; and reveled in the state's natural beauty. "You'd love a Florida rain-storm," she told a friend in New York. "Raindrops huge and pelting. The sky ripped open by lightning, the heavens rocked by thunder. Then a sky so blue that there is no word to name its color, and birds bursting open with song."

As September scurried toward October, it was clear that Hurston would not be teaching that fall. Though Mary McLeod Bethune had graciously received her in Daytona Beach, the college president did not have money to hire a new faculty member. Hurston was disappointed, but she had another potential income source waiting in the wings: She expected to start earning a salary for her concert work, underwritten by Rollins, in mid-October. After that, "I shall be off of your financial hands forever," she promised Godmother. "I have not forgotten that you were only to help me until the beginning of the school year. But if you will see me thru October I shall be in a position to look out for myself henceforth."

Mason agreed to the one-month extension and both women felt relief as their fiscal relationship hastened toward closure. While Zora's financial dependence had not significantly injured Godmother's bank account, it certainly had tainted the women's bond, not to mention Zora's self-image. "I pray that when I no longer am a drain upon you financially," she told Godmother, "that you can see <u>me</u>, the Zora of the Eatonville gatepost, again."

Hurston already had begun to wean herself from Godmother psychically, no longer writing to her patron as frequently or as fawningly. For all intents and purposes, Godmother's financial and psychic hold over Hurston was released the moment she left New York. To be sure, the two forms of indenture were inextricably linked. Although her love for Godmother was genuine, the famously independent Hurston must have resented having to account to the white woman for every nickel she spent: ten cents for garters, fifteen cents for milk, twenty cents for carrots, forty-nine cents for Kotex, sixty cents for steak, seventy-five cents for cough syrup, a dollar for a book. As Zora was well aware, very few people in America had to subject their personal finances to such exacting scrutiny, not even in a relationship with a spouse. Thankfully, Zora's move back to Eatonville liberated her from this unreasonable and invasive requirement. And when the last check from Park Avenue arrived that October, officially severing her financial ties with Godmother, a part of Hurston cheered.

No longer under Mason's thumb—or Locke's watchful eye— Hurston was free to trust her own instincts, as a social scientist and an artist. As a result, her work flourished. Staying with her childhood friend Matilda Moseley, Zora, "humming little songs," would go off by herself and write. Though she was making good progress on editing and organizing her huge mass of folklore material, Hurston was still unsure how publishers would react to her manuscript—particularly because she had purposely avoided making it a treatise on "the Negro problem." Asking one of her newfound friends at Rollins for feedback on her book-in-progress, Hurston noted: "I know what is true, but I don't know how much truth the public wants. Of course I am not interested in Sociology and see no need for a mention of problems of the kind and I am wondering if the publishers will think I ought to appear slightly wrought up." In late fall, however, Hurston finished the manuscript to her satisfaction. Feeling she'd done all she could do with the compendium of folktales, which she called *Mules and Men*, she set it aside and turned her full attention to the Rollins concert.

Working with Bob Wunsch, the college's resident theater director, Hurston devoted herself to the task of training performers for the Florida premiere of *From Sun to Sun*, scheduled for January 20, 1933. She recruited most of her cast from friends and relatives in Eatonville—even convincing her uncle, the Rev. Isaiah Hurston, to play the role of the itinerant preacher. Hurston also plucked several talented vocalists from the choirs of Macedonia Baptist and St. Lawrence AME, instructing them in rehearsals "to just imagine that they were in Macedonia and go ahead."

Impressed with her knowledge and experience—and eager to introduce Rollins students "to the honest-to-the-soil material at their own doorsteps"—Wunsch invited Hurston to speak to his class in mid-November. His students were enthralled by the "young negress," according to an account in the college newspaper, the *Rollins Sandspur*. Hurston told stories, sang a few work songs, and even preached a portion of the sermon from her concert. "The whole thing," a student journalist reported, "was pure poetry, full of poetic figures, utterly lovely." The students' rapture over Hurston's visit may have been what caused the newspaper to misidentify her home-town, despite its proximity to Winter Park, as "Edenville." Riding the wave of this excellent advance publicity, Hurston and Wunsch worked together for the rest of 1932 to get *From Sun to Sun* ready for the stage; it took a lot of rehearsal, Hurston knew, to make her per-formers sound so natural.

While Hurston was soaring artistically, she was barely limping along financially. The shoestring budget Rollins had allotted for her concert was not sizable enough for her to be paid a salary. Instead, the whole amount had to be used for the production. Hurston some-how made do on fees earned from speaking to women's clubs in the area: ten dollars here, fifteen dollars there. The clubwomen—like the professors and students at all-white Rollins—were always kind, but Zora resisted asking them for any favors, she said, "because I real-ized that to do so would injure my prestige." Fortunately, Rollins sent a car to pick her up for rehearsals: the campus was three miles from Eatonville, so walking every day would not have been pleasant. Even so, the shoes Zora had bought before leaving New York were beginning to wear thin, and she did not own one pair of decent stockings. A hot, dry spell in Central Florida had killed Zora's garden long ago, but other gardeners who weren't as hurt by the drought fre-quently offered her okra, pole beans, and other crops from their vegetable patches. Always receptive to her neighbors' generosity, Zora also ate her fill of fruit from the area's fertile citrus groves. In this way, she never went hungry. But by the time Godmother's Christmas present arrived—the unexpected check "was the finest thing that could have happened to me," Zora exulted—she had run out of toothpaste and was washing her face with laundry soap.

With apostolic zeal, Hurston chose to make these very real sacri-fices (rather than find a paying job) because she saw her Rollins concert as a chance to do something great—"if I could forget the flesh pots of my own personal comfort long enough to get a foothold," as she put it. Hurston was consumed with the idea of building an authentic Negro theater—"not just the building but the heart, the reason for the building to be." For the moment, then, everything else—including the creature comforts—paled in com-parison with this grand ambition, which Zora hoped to launch with her sympathetic white colleagues at Rollins. "The small amount of personal comfort I have given up is so little to pay for what will come back to me," Hurston believed. "Perhaps I shall never roll in wealth. That is not the point. If we can give *real* creative urge a push forward here, the world will see a New Negro and justify our efforts. That is pay."

Hurston's only persistent problem was that she was frequently ill and unable to afford medicine for her worrisome colon. On January 5, just two weeks before the concert (and two days before her birthday), Zora began conducting rehearsals while perched on an automobile cushion—the excessive padding of which relieved her pain. She wanted to stay home in bed, she admitted, "but the 20th is too near and I am too eager for complete success."

The success Hurston sought would soon come, but not before she received a bitter reminder that Rollins, no matter how enlightened, was still in the South. The school's president, Hamilton Holt, cautiously approved the performance at Recreation Hall, a large on-campus theater, with one stipulation: none of the venue's 1,800 seats would be occupied by Negroes. "I see no reason why you should not put on in recreation hall the negro folk evening under the inspiration of Zora Hurston," Holt wrote to Wunsch, "but I assume that you will go over the thing enough to know that there will be nothing vulgar in it. Of course we cannot have negroes in the audience unless there is a separate place segregated for them and I think that would be unwise." This decision displeased Hurston and she attempted to fight it: "I tried to have a space set aside," she lamented to Godmother, "but find that there I come up against solid rock."

After arranging an early-February performance at the Hungerford School in Eatonville ("so that our own people may hear us"), Hurston and her cast made their bow to the local public January 20 in an invitation-only performance at a small experimental theater called The Museum. The next Friday, January 27, they staged a repeat performance for the general public—whites only—at Rollins's Recreation Hall. Again emphasizing the authenticity of her material, Hurston wrote detailed program notes for each of the secular songs. ("The spirituals," she noted, "are self-explanatory.") Zora performed in the Rollins productions as well: She played Dinah, Ike's wife, in her one-act, *The Fiery Chariot*; she sang "East Coast Blues"; and she led the Crow Dance. The Recreation Hall audience responded enthusiastically to the concert—with "thunderous applause and continuous demands for more," according to the *Rollins Sandspur*. "An unselfconscious spontaneity was successfully achieved," the newspaper observed. Even President Holt was impressed: "That was a great performance in Recreation Hall last night," he told Wunsch the next day.

Over the next few months, the group successfully performed in several Florida cities and Hurston developed a strong reputation for her folk concerts throughout the state. The people at Rollins thought so well of her that in March, when noted dancer Ruth St. Denis visited the campus, Hurston and her troupe were invited to do a special half-hour performance. St. Denis then approached Hurston with a proposition: The modern dance pioneer wanted to perform with Zora's group as soloist dancer. "I know it's novelty-publicity seeking," Hurston discerned, "but it will help us nevertheless."

Around the same time, though, Hurston was rocked by two devastating pieces of news from up North: In New Jersey, pneumonia had killed her sister, Sarah, who, at forty-three, was just a year older than Zora. And in New York, Godmother had been hospitalized indefinitely after taking a nasty, hip-breaking fall. Though Zora tried to keep her pain to herself—"I don't see why I should make others sad," she reasoned weakly—she admitted to being "hard hit" by the death of her only sister. "Then Godmother falls! It's as if the sun had lain down in the cradle of eternity," Zora grieved. Of course, there was nothing anyone could do for Sarah now and little to be done for Godmother, either, Alain Locke informed Zora. When Godmother had been sick before, Zora had "asked the powers invisible" to help her. Using the conjure skills she'd learned in New Orleans, Zora had burned candles for her benefactor and telepathically sent her love. Within a few days, Godmother had always reported feeling better. But now, Charlotte Mason was nearly eighty years old, and her doctors weren't sure if she'd ever be able to go back home. Too ill to write, Godmother stopped answering Zora's letters.

Seeking solace from her double despair, Hurston found it in her writing: "I am doing more and better work than ever," she observed, "somehow." Although her folk concerts were personally fulfilling and critically successful, they were rather sporadic and nearly as unprofitable in Florida as they'd been in New York. Hurston knew she needed more steady work, but the jobs available to black women in the South were limited, and almost always menial. With Godmother no longer able to serve as her safety net—or her hanging judge—Hurston turned again to fiction, which she had not written seriously since 1926. Despite her long sabbatical from the form, Hurston soon finished a short story she'd been toting around in her head for years. Next, she schemed, she would tackle "the novel that I have wanted to write since 1928."

Hoping to sell the short story—called "The Gilded Six-Bits"—to "one of the larger, better-paying magazines," Hurston gave it to Wunsch to read. The Rollins professor was so taken with it that he read it to his creative writing class, then sent it off to his friends Martha Foley and Whit Burnett, the editors of *Story* magazine. The husband-and-wife team immediately bought the short story for publication in their August 1933 issue. *Story* was a highly regarded magazine, but not a wealthy one. Zora only earned twenty dollars for her short story. Soon, though, it would pay off in other ways.

"The Gilded Six-Bits"—Hurston's first published fiction since 1926's "Sweat"—is a delightful story of love, infidelity, and redemption. Like the couple in "Sweat," Missie May and Joe Banks live in Eatonville, but their blissful marriage is the antithesis of the sinister union of Delia and Sykes. Reflecting Missie May's artistic sensibilities, the Banks home is decorated by glass bottles lining the walkway and "a mess of homey flowers . . . blooming cheerily from their helter-skelter places," as Hurston writes.

The story opens as Missie May prepares for her Saturday afternoon ritual with Joe: She has thoroughly cleaned her whitewashed house, cooked a special dinner, and is finishing up her bath when Joe comes back from the market. "Who dat chunkin' money in mah do'way?" she demands in mock anger, as Joe throws nine silver dollars into the open door for his wife to pile beside her plate at dinner—and then put away for their future together. As Joe darts from the shrubs to the chinaberry tree, Missie May chases him around the yard and into the house and finally thrusts her hands into his pockets, where she unearths candy kisses, a cake of sweet soap, and other gifts Joe has hidden for her to find. That evening, Joe takes his wife to the newly opened ice-cream parlor to show her off to its proprietor, Otis D. Slemmons, a man whose citified clothes, sizable gut, big talk, and mouthful of gold teeth have convinced all of Eatonville that he is wealthy. Further, Slemmons has excited the envy of every man in town, including Joe, by claiming that admiring white women in Chicago gave him the five-dollar gold piece he wears as a stickpin and the ten-dollar piece he wears on his watch chain. For Missie May, Slemmons's main appeal is his gold. "He'll do in case of a rush. But he sho is got uh heap uh gold on 'im. . . . It lookted good on him sho nuff, but it'd look a whole heap better on you," she tells her husband. Joe assures Missie May that as long as he has her, he doesn't need any gold watch charms.

After several Saturdays at the ice-cream parlor, Joe comes home from work early one night and finds his wife in bed with Slemmons. In his rush from Joe's fists, Slemmons loses his watch charm—the very piece he'd promised to give Missie May if she would give in to his persistent advances. The coin turns out to be a gilded half-dollar, though, rather than a ten-dollar gold piece, and Joe carries it in his pocket as a symbol of Missie May's infidelity and the tarnish of their marriage. "There were no more Saturday romps," Hurston writes. "No ringing silver dollars to stack beside her plate. No pockets to rifle." Aching with sorrow, Joe stays on his side of the bed, and Missie May on hers—until one evening Joe asks her to massage his ailing back. Before morning, Joe and Missie May find themselves making love for the first time in three months. Slowly and quietly, they then begin working together to recapture their love. In due time, Missie May gives birth to a baby boy, the spitting image of Joe. Finally, Joe's forgiveness is complete—and, to prove it, he uses the gilded coin to buy his wife some candy kisses. Completely ignorant of all the couple has been through, the white store clerk comments to another customer: "Wisht I could be like these darkies. Laughin' all the time. Nothin' worries 'em." The storekeeper articulates what Hurston viewed as an all-too-common reality: white blindness to the complexity of black people's lives. But Hurston's lean, economically written narrative focuses on the relationship between a black man and a black woman, rather than on interracial conflict. Consequently, she gives Missie May the last word: Hearing the familiar ring of metal on wood, the new mother creeps to the door, elated that Joe has revived their romantic ritual. "Joe Banks, Ah hear you chunkin' money in mah do'way," Missie May says playfully. "You wait till Ah got mah strength back and Ah'm gointer fix you for dat."

Hurston breaks ranks with other writers of her day by creating in Missie May a black female character who is sexually aggressive—and transgressive—but who is not a whore. Fitting into none of the predominant stereotypes of black women—mammy, tragic mulatto, or promiscuous Jezebel—Missie May is a sexually complex woman (with "stiff young breasts" that "thrust forward aggressively," Hurston points out) who simply makes a mistake. But Hurston refuses to doom Missie May to the bad-girls-have-to-pay narrative that had prevailed in American literature since at least 1850, when Nathaniel Hawthorne published "The Scarlet Letter." Unlike Kate Chopin's Edna Pontellier (*The Awakening*) or Hawthorne's Hester Prynne, Missie May doesn't have to pay for her adultery by losing her life or by living as a pariah. Instead, in Hurston's sympathetic and skillful hands, she becomes a mother—the ultimate ennobling act—even while reclaiming her sexuality. Love and happiness are at hand as well. In the end, Missie May seems to have it all.

Despite its protofeminist perspective, which some of Hurston's contemporaries might have found offensive, "The Gilded Six-Bits" is a subtly executed charmer—and that is the way *Story*'s readers responded to it. Soon after advance copies of the magazine were distributed, Hurston received four letters from publishers asking if she had any book-length fiction they might consider for publication. One of these inquiries was from Bertram Lippincott, of the J. B. Lippincott Company, whose "gentle-like letter" appealed to Hurston above all the others. She wrote Lippincott back to say that she was working on a novel. "Mind you, not the first word was on paper when I wrote him that letter," Hurston later admitted. "But the very next week I moved up to Sanford where I was not so much at home as at Eatonville, and could concentrate more and sat down to write *Jonah's Gourd Vine.*"

The idea for the novel had insinuated itself in Zora's brain in the late 1920s, while she was doing her fieldwork in the South. She'd put aside the thought, however, because "the idea of attempting a book seemed so big," as she recalled, "that I gazed at it in the quiet of the night, but hid it away from even myself in daylight." Another reason for Hurston's reticence was her concern that the novel she wanted to write would have trouble finding an audience—and a publisher: "What I wanted to tell was a story about a man, and from what I had read and heard, Negroes were supposed to write about the Race Problem," she explained. "I was and am thoroughly sick of the subject. My interest lies in what makes a man or a woman do such-and-so, regardless of his color."

Inspired by the opportunity Lippincott's letter promised, Hurston decided that fear was her only fetter. With clothes and card table in tow, she found a small house in Sanford, at 906 Locust Avenue, that she rented for a dollar fifty a week. There, during the first week of July 1933, Hurston began composing, in penciled longhand, a fictionalized account of her parents' marriage, even naming her main characters John and Lucy and making an appearance herself as their precocious daughter, Isis (the same name Hurston used for her child-self in her 1924 short story, "Drenched in Light"). After only two weeks of writing, though, Zora's money ran out. Tuning out her landlord's demands for dollars, she continued to write—living on only fifty cents a week, which her cousin gave her for groceries.

In her two-room house, furnished with only a bed and a stove, Hurston worked with monklike devotion to her craft and to her story. The novel taking shape on her wobbly card table was mostly the story of her father—a gifted orator, a man of God, and an individual who was deeply flawed. "Children begin by loving their parents; after a time they judge them," writer Oscar Wilde once observed. "Rarely, if ever, do they forgive them." In *Jonah's Gourd Vine*, Hurston endeavored to do all three. The novel was a daughter's attempt to reconstruct her father's life—and death—so she could understand him and ultimately forgive him. By the time Hurston finished writing *Jonah's Gourd Vine*, her former bitterness toward her father had been transformed into something else—something like compassion.

In early September, after only about three months of writing and revising, Hurston was ready to commit her manuscript to type, but she didn't have money to pay a stenographer. A secretary she'd met in Sanford took the manuscript home with her to read and then agreed to type it for a deferred fee. "It's going to be accepted all right," the typist declared. "Even if the first publisher does not take it, somebody will." Once the typing was complete, Hurston then had to borrow the dollar and eighty-three cents she needed to mail the manuscript to Lippincott's Philadelphia office. She finally sent it off on October 3, 1933.

On Monday, October 16, Hurston woke up in a good mood. She had been hired by the Seminole County Chamber of Commerce to entertain the city of Sanford with a mobile version of her concert. A sound truck had been rented to drive up and down the city's streets while her performers sang. And Hurston had been promised a day's salary of twenty-five dollars—her first earnings in three months and more than enough to pay the eighteen dollars she now owed in back rent. At eight o'clock that morning, though, her landlady came knocking: She wanted Zora to get out. Hurston assured the woman she'd be able to pay her back rent in full later that day, but her landlord didn't believe her; she just wanted her house back.

Evicted and dejected, Hurston hurriedly found a place to store her clothes and card table and then joined her cast on the sound truck for their 11:00 A.M. engagement. Sometime that afternoon, in the blur of the day, a messenger handed Zora a telegram, which she stuffed in her purse. At three o'clock, when the concert was finished, Zora received her twenty-five-dollar payment and a coupon to purchase whatever she wanted in a local store. While being fitted for a new pair of shoes, she remembered the telegram in her handbag and pulled it out for a once-over. When Zora saw that Lippincott had accepted *Jonah's Gourd Vine*—and was offering her a publisher's advance of $200—she responded as if she'd just received the keys to her very own queendom. "I tore out of that place with one old shoe and one new one on and ran to the Western Union office," Hurston recalled. "Lippincott had asked for an answer by wire and they got it! Terms accepted."

CHAPTER 23

The Will to Adorn

Hurston remained in Florida while she awaited the publication of *Jonah's Gourd Vine*, scheduled for May 1934. From her new quarters on East Ninth Street in Sanford, she wrote to Fannie Hurst, asking if she would pen an introduction, and to Carl Van Vechten, seeking an endorsement for the book jacket. She also made sure Lippincott sent advance copies to such important black intellectuals as Fisk University's James Weldon Johnson, who "*ought to have something to say*," Hurston felt, because he, too, had grown up in Florida. Johnson, Du Bois, and other black scholars were initially absent from Lippincott's list of people who would receive advance copies of Hurston's book: "No Negro names were on there," she complained mildly, "because they are not familiar with Negroes and did not know to whom they should send" the novel.

The Lippincott Company's ignorance about the Negro intelligentsia was not the only challenge Hurston faced as a black author. While her $200 advance stood her in good stead for a month or so (and covered the down payment for a used car), it was minuscule compared with the $5,000 advances that white authors such as Fannie Hurst routinely received. Hurst, in fact, had been making her living solely as a writer for two decades by the autumn of 1933. But Hurston, it seemed, was the only black woman in the country still trying to do so: Former *Crisis* literary editor Jessie Fauset published the last of her four novels in 1933, then retreated into a life of domesticity and full-time teaching. Gwendolyn Bennett, too, became primarily a teacher. Essayist and playwright Marita Bonner was still writing, but she'd married and moved to Chicago around 1930 and was now preoccupied with motherhood. A plagiarism scandal and a humiliating divorce in the early 1930s all but silenced Nella Larsen, who would spend her last two decades as a nurse. Helene Johnson married, had a child, and quietly withdrew from the writing community and from public life. And her talented young cousin, Dorothy West, had decided to extend her stay in Russia. "It was unheard of for a young black girl to aspire to be a writer," recalled Margaret Walker, a college student during the 1930s who would soon become a notable author herself. "Only one person had even tried," Walker believed, "and that was of course a woman from Florida, Zora Neale Hurston."

Try as she might, Hurston found it impossible to support herself solely from her writing, so she continued to seek out other sources of income as well as outlets for presenting black folklore, music, and dance onstage. In mid-November, the Dramatic Art Department at Rollins College invited her for a return engagement at Recreation Hall. After several weeks of rehearsals, Hurston and her reassembled and amended cast presented *All de Live Long Day* on January 5, 1934. Billed as a "unique and authentic representation of real negro folk life by talented native artists," the Friday night concert portrayed "black laborers in a typical Florida railroad camp at work, play, religion and love," the *Rollins Sandspur* reported. Similar to *From Sun to Sun* but featuring mostly new material, the production included a harmonica solo; *De Possum's Tail Hairs*, Hurston's one-act dramatization of a folktale she'd collected; and a series of work songs, jook songs, and spirituals. "But most unique were the dances," the *Sandspur* decided. "Colorful, primitive, intense—dark girls and men danced to the beat of an African drum, a chant and the pounding of naked heels." Marked by its "unselfconscious simplicity," the performance ended with the Fire Dance, which by now had become Zora's signature closing. *All de Live Long Day* was another stage triumph—"presented humbly," according to the *Sandspur*, "with all the spontaneous enthusiasm and brilliance of natural artists."

Hurston, meanwhile, sought to present herself as both a natural artist and a mature scholar in her application for a 1934 Guggenheim fellowship. Zora had initiated the application process for the coveted monetary awards the previous summer, around the same time she began writing *Jonah's Gourd Vine*. Established by U.S. Senator Simon Guggenheim as a memorial to a deceased son, the John Simon Guggenheim Memorial Foundation in 1925 began offering generous fellowships to scholars and artists "to engage in research in any field of knowledge and creation in any of the arts, under the freest possible conditions and irrespective of race, color, or creed." Hurston applied for a fellowship in order to explore the African roots of hoodoo and other black American cultural practices. Specifically, she proposed to take up residence in Nigeria or somewhere on the Gold Coast of West Africa—the region most plundered by the slave trade—to study indigenous religious practices, as well as African medicine and music. "I hope <u>eventually</u> to bring over a faculty from Africa and set up a school of Negro music in America," Hurston revealed in her application. "No Negro can remain a <u>Negro</u> composer long under white tutelage," she asserted. "The better he is taught, the less there is left of his nativity."

Emphasizing her successful studies of hoodoo practices in the South, Hurston proposed to conduct a similar investigation in West Africa. "I do not expect to ever finish collecting Negro folk-lore," Zora noted, "but I feel that I can finish the particular angle of the hoodoo phase upon which I am working at present in one or two years of intense labor." She planned to publish the results of her African research "both scientifically and in a moderated form for the general public." Hurston ended her application by reiterating her belief in the authenticity and worthiness of an autonomous black culture: "My ultimate purpose as a student is to increase the general knowledge concerning my people, to advance science and the musical arts among my people," she wrote, "<u>but</u> in the Negro way and away from the white man's way."

Asked for a list of references, Hurston chose five distinguished intellectuals familiar with her work: anthropologists Ruth Benedict and Franz Boas and writers Fannie Hurst, Carl Van Vechten, and Max Eastman. Given the still-striving status of most Negroes in the 1930s—and the dearth of publishing opportunities for black writers—Hurston's decision to list only white recommenders is understandable. A prestigious, mainstream organization such as the Guggenheim Foundation likely would have viewed even the most accomplished black scholars—W.E.B. Du Bois, James Weldon Johnson, Charles S. Johnson, Alain Locke, Carter G. Woodson—as marginal intellectual figures. Yet Hurston surely would have garnered better recommendations from these men (even those with whom she'd had disagreements) than she received from the references she listed. With the exception of Eastman, Hurston's white friends failed her—perhaps even betrayed her—in their reports to Henry Allen Moe, secretary of the Guggenheim Foundation. Because their letters were confidential, Hurston probably never saw them. If she had, she certainly would have been disturbed by her white mentors' frank—and sometimes racially clouded—assessments of her.

To be fair, Van Vechten had only positive things to say, but he said so little. "Among Negroes," his two-sentence statement began, "I think I know of no one so well fitted to do work with folk material as Zora Neale Hurston. She has already demonstrated her ability in this direction by a mass of collected material from which she has selected enough to make up several stage programs." That's all Van Vechten wrote. Fannie Hurst had considerably more to say, but she offered as much damnation as praise in a series of awkward, backhanded compliments. "She is an erratic worker," Hurst wrote of Zora, "but in my opinion, a talented and peculiarly capable young woman." With a hint of unconscious racism underscoring her words, Hurst added: "She is a rather curious example of a sophisticated negro mind that has retained many characteristics of the old-fashioned and humble type."

The anthropologists, Benedict and Boas, were clearer in their assessments, but not in Hurston's favor. "She has neither the temperament nor the training to present this material in an orderly manner," Benedict judged bluntly. Even Papa Franz failed to support his former student: "On the whole her methods are more journalistic than scientific," Boas disclosed in his confidential letter to Moe, "and I am not under the impression that she is just the right caliber for a Guggenheim Fellowship."

Only Max Eastman offered unadulterated praise: "Zora Hurston's qualifications in the field of anthropology will be attested by more competent authorities than I, I am sure," he assumed incorrectly, "but I can speak for her general intelligence, her social maturity and exquisite tact and good judgment. Moreover I think the program of work she outlines, the scope of her ambition captivating."

Given Hurston's other references, the Guggenheim board was not swayed by Eastman's enthusiastic report. On March 17, 1934, Henry Allen Moe wrote to tell Hurston her request for a fellowship had been denied.

Moe's letter caught up with Hurston at Bethune-Cookman College, where she'd begun teaching in January. Impressed by Hurston's work at Rollins and her folk concerts throughout the state, Mary McLeod Bethune—perhaps the most powerful and respected black woman in America—invited the young folklorist and dramatist to establish a school of dramatic arts at Bethune-Cookman, "based on pure Negro expression." When Hurston took the job in Daytona Beach, about forty miles east of Sanford, her hope was to "work out some good nigger themes," as she told a friend, "and show what can be done with our magnificent imagery." After only a few weeks at Bethune-Cookman, though, Hurston began to feel as if she'd been lured into a boondoggle. With a student body of only 226, the college needed the same pupils to perform in various dramatic groups, as well as for the choral ensembles and the major athletics. Hurston also was frustrated by what she saw as President Bethune's despotic but ineffective management style. Soon after Hurston joined the faculty, for instance, Bethune instructed her to direct a pageant celebrating the school's anniversary. Working from a script written by a faculty member "who had no more idea of drama than I have about relativity," Hurston was urged to make the performance grand. "Then the entire faculty was summoned to help me direct," she griped. "Not one besides myself had had any experience in the field. One day eight people were trying to direct one scene at the same time." As a result, Hurston lamented, "the performance was just some students stumbling around on the stage."

Near the end of March, Zora was still "plugging away in the dark," as she told Alain Locke. Apparently, she meant this literally: Hurston had trouble getting a lightbulb for her office, she claimed, much less the artistic autonomy she needed to breathe. In April, Hurston and Bethune had a showdown: The president was delighted when her enthusiastic new drama professor secured the previously segregated auditorium on the beach for a performance. But Bethune insisted that no new concert program was necessary. "The people always wanted to hear the same songs and recitations" that had been performed for years, she said. Defying the president's wisdom, Hurston began making plans to present a version of *From Sun to Sun* in the auditorium overlooking the Atlantic Ocean. With no authority from Bethune to call rehearsals, however, she had to rely on her personal popularity with the students to secure a cast and win their cooperation. "In the last two days of rehearsal," Hurston would remember, "they responded like heroes and put the thing over." Sitting in the middle of an appreciative audience of more than two thousand people, Bethune was proud of the end product, but Hurston "was a wreck from the exertions," as she recalled. "I could never go through that again."

Jonah's Gourd Vine was due to be published in little more than a month, and Lippincott had accepted *Mules and Men*—"the folktales done over and put back into their natural juices"—as Hurston's second book. "So I decided to abandon the farce of Bethune-Cookman's dramatic department," she noted, "and get on with my work." Seeking solitude, Zora moved into a small cottage in Longwood, just outside Sanford, in mid-April. To her friends, she announced that her days at Bethune-Cookman were over. "No, I shan't be with Mrs. Bethune next year," she informed Locke diplomatically. "She is a swell person, but the affair is too full of distraction. . . . Then there is no money."

In late April, Zora crammed four Bahamian dancers into her car and, using the extra funds she'd earned from her beachside concert to pay for gas, embarked on a thousand-mile trek to St. Louis. There, from April 29 to May 2, she and her group (others had driven their own cars) participated in the National Folk Festival, headed by respected playwright Paul Green. Though there was no money in it for her, Hurston believed an appearance at the folk festival would give her forthcoming books a push, especially *Mules and Men*, "in that it will increase my standing as a Negro folklorist," she reasoned, "outside of calling attention to me generally."

As Hurston began working to revise *Mules and Men*—Lippincott wanted a $3.50 book, which would require more than the 65,000 words she'd delivered—her standing as a folklorist was boosted further still by the spring publication of Nancy Cunard's anthology,

Negro. The rebellious daughter of a wealthy British family, Cunard published six of Hurston's essays in her hefty volume, which the heiress dedicated, with typical flamboyance, to her black lover, composer Henry Crowder.

In all of her *Negro* essays—"Characteristics of Negro Expression," "Conversions and Visions," "Shouting," "Mother Catherine," "Uncle Monday," and "Spirituals and Neo-Spirituals"—Hurston emphasized the originality and artfulness of black expression, from dancing to dialect, from lovemaking to prayer. (Hurston's seventh piece in *Negro*, not coincidentally, was a transcription of a sermon she'd heard at a church in Eau Gallie, Florida, in 1929.) Despite a talent and love for mimicry, "the Negro is a very original being," Hurston asserted in "Characteristics of Negro Expression," the most significant and analytical of her *Negro* essays. "While he lives and moves in the midst of white civilisation, everything that he touches is re-interpreted for his own use. He has modified the language, mode of food preparation, practice of medicine, and most certainly the religion of his new country," she wrote.

A summary of Hurston's observations from her fieldwork of the late 1920s, "Characteristics of Negro Expression" cogently identified several attributes of black artistry—including drama, angularity, asymmetry, originality and what Hurston called "the will to adorn." Feeling "that there can never be enough of beauty, let alone too much," black people tended to embellish whatever they undertook, Hurston observed. This held true in interior design—where "decorating a decoration" was not unheard of—as well as in musical and verbal expression. "Both prayers and sermons are tooled and polished until they are true works of art. . . . The beauty of the Old Testament does not exceed that of a Negro prayer," Hurston declared. In secular language, too, she argued, black people had made enormous contributions to the English language by introducing inventive metaphors and similes ("you sho is propaganda"), double-descriptive adjectives ("top-superior," "low-down"), and verbal nouns ("I wouldn't friend with her"). "The stark, trimmed phrases of the Occident seem too bare for the voluptuous child of the sun, hence the adornment," Hurston theorized. "It arises out of the same impulse as the wearing of jewelry and the making of sculpture." This impulse, she decided, was "the desire for beauty," "the will to adorn."

Hurston focused at length on how this will to adorn manifested in black language—and her conclusions stood in glaring opposition to those of folklorists Howard Odum and Guy Johnson, who'd complained in 1925 that black dialect was so difficult to record because "there is no regular usage for any word in the Negro's vocabulary." Newbell Niles Puckett, author of *Folk Beliefs of the Southern Negro*, viewed black speech even more condescendingly: "The Negro," he judged, "is constantly being lost in a labyrinth of jaw-breaking words full of sound and fury but signifying nothing."

Contrary to what these noted white folklorists seemed to believe, black vernacular speech was not just so much senseless gibberish, "full of 'ams' and 'Ises,'" as Hurston pointed out. "I know that I run the risk of being damned as an infidel for declaring that nowhere can be found the Negro who asks 'am it?' nor yet his brother who announces 'Ise uh gwinter.' He exists only for a certain type of writer and performer." Black dialect was semantically complex, Hurston asserted, and it abided by certain observable rules, some of which she outlined in "Characteristics of Negro Expression."

But Hurston's real answer to those who dismissed the validity and splendor of black vernacular speech was *Jonah's Gourd Vine*—a first novel that was, for its time, remarkable in its ambition and achievement. Even today, the novel holds up, in the words of Pulitzer Prize–winning poet Rita Dove, as "a glorious paean to the power of the word."

While the main characters in *Jonah's Gourd Vine* are clearly modeled on Zora's parents and the novel contains a number of important autobiographical elements, it is not an all-out family memoir. It is, in the final analysis, fiction. As Dove has noted, Hurston "did not make one of the major mistakes of first novelists—sticking too faithfully to the 'true story'—but knew how to fashion of her parents' lives a tale of compelling pathos and majesty."

Saturated in the folklore Hurston knew so well, *Jonah's Gourd Vine* tells the story of John Pearson, who rises from a spirit-crushing life as an Alabama laborer to become an admired and successful minister in Florida. While John is a powerful instrument of God on Sundays, he is just a "natchel man" during the week, succumbing again and again to the attentions of numerous women, despite the faithful love and steady support of his wife, Lucy. An inspired speaker in the pulpit and in worldly life, John has mastered the traditional metaphors of his culture and the expressive powers of the folk. With his magnificent verbal skills, he can lure women into his arms as facilely as he shepherds his congregation into the arms of Jesus. While he can help worshipers understand the most esoteric teachings of the Old Testament, though, John does not seem to understand himself as anything more than a confused amalgam of spirit and flesh—unable to control his senses or to simply say no to an enticing woman. In spite of his flesh's fallibility, Lucy is John's backbone—and it is she who gives him the strength to rise to a position of prominence in his community. After Lucy dies, however, the call of John's flesh outruns the call of the spirit, eventually prompting his congregation to reject him. Tragically, John dies—in an auto-train collision, as Hurston's father died—just as introspection dawns and he begins to look within for his own lost self.

In her early short stories, Hurston had self-consciously highlighted what she saw as the differences between black and white people. In 1925's "Black Death," for instance, after a white coroner discounted the possibility of hoodoo in a woman's demise, Hurston wrote bluntly: "White folks are very stupid about some things. They can think mightily but cannot *feel*." In *Jonah's Gourd Vine*, however, white people are largely irrelevant. Hurston presents black life as self-contained. "The characters in the story are seen in relation to themselves and not in relation to the whites as has been the rule," Hurston noted in a mock-review of *Jonah's Gourd Vine*. "To watch these people one would conclude that there were not white people in the world."

Initially called "Big Nigger"—the moniker Zora and her siblings used for their father behind his back—*Jonah's Gourd Vine* takes its name from a biblical story of a vine that grows up suddenly overnight, at God's command, to shade the prophet Jonah from a scorching sun. The next morning, to teach Jonah an essential lesson, God sends a worm to attack the plant and cut it down. "Great and sudden growth," Hurston summarized. "One act of malice and it is withered and gone." As a gifted image maker, John Pearson is certainly a rapidly growing vine; he becomes a spiritual and community leader almost in spite of himself. But, as in the Old Testament story, a single act of malice causes him to wither. Hurston leaves it to the reader to decide what—or who—the worm of malice is: Perhaps John incurs God's wrath through his own malicious act of striking Lucy on her deathbed after she confronts him about his philandering. Or perhaps the worm is Hattie Tyson—clearly fashioned after Hurston's stepmother, Mattie—who uses hoodoo to win John's passion and catalyze his downfall.

"I have tried to present a Negro preacher," Hurston explained to James Weldon Johnson, "who is neither funny nor an imitation Puritan ram-rod in pants. Just the human being and poet that he must be to succeed in a Negro pulpit." She then added a clarifying note, which accounts for her emphasis throughout the novel on the poetics of black language: "I do not speak of those among us who have been tampered with and consequently have gone Presbyterian or Episcopal. I mean the common run of us who love magnificence, beauty, poetry and color so much that there can never be too much of it."

A week before *Jonah's Gourd Vine* was published, Hurston confided to Carl Van Vechten that she was "scared to death of reviews." But she had little reason to worry; the advance buzz on the book was wholly positive. "Here is negro folk lore interpreted at its authentic best in fiction form of a high order," Fannie Hurst wrote in her introduction. Though Hurst employed some disastrous imagery in her preface—using words that contemporary readers would call racist ("a brilliantly facile spade has turned over rich new earth")—her praise of Zora's novel was unequivocal. "As a matter of fact," Hurst gushed, "not even excepting Langston Hughes, it is doubtful if there is any literary precedent for the particular type of accomplishment that characterizes *Jonah's Gourd Vine*."

Van Vechten was equally enthused. Zora "has just written a very swell novel," he told Hughes. "This is so good that I think you and Zora had better kiss and make up."

Bertram Lippincott himself was thrilled by the novel, a Book-of-the-Month Club "alternate" for May. He even thought *Jonah's Gourd Vine* would make a fine movie, with Paul Robeson starring as John Pearson. Although the film never happened, Lippincott remained deeply impressed by the book and its author. "Seldom have we had an author about whose work we have heard such good things prior to publishing her first novel, and who is so universally liked," Lippincott wrote to another Hurston admirer, Rollins Professor Edwin Osgood Grover. Though Zora was a late literary bloomer—she was forty-three when her first novel was published, compared with Langston Hughes, who was twenty-eight when he reached the same milestone—Lippincott was quick to recognize her extraordinary talent: "She is an excellent literary property and it would naturally be to our advantage as well as hers to see that she is as free as possible to pursue her writing," he observed. "I have never before read anything like JONAH'S GOURD VINE. It has a style and rhythm that a white writer simply could not do and I do not see how it can fail to make a big impression."

Lippincott's prediction, for the most part, proved to be dead-on. When *Jonah's Gourd Vine* was published during the first week of May, most white reviewers liked it—even if their calcified racial bias prevented them from fully comprehending what Hurston was trying to achieve. "*Jonah's Gourd Vine* can be called without fear of exaggeration the most vital and original novel about the American Negro that has yet been written by a member of the Negro race," Margaret Wallace declared in *The New York Times Book Review*. Meanwhile, *The New Republic*—despite the unfortunate title of its review, "Darktown Strutter"—praised Hurston for making her protagonist "a credible, human and almost appealing figure."

While black critics were free from racial bias, they sometimes seemed to be ruled by another kind of bias: a tendency to see every black character as a representative of "the Negro," rather than as an individual. *Opportunity* magazine, for example, reported that Hurston had set her story in "typical small southern towns in Alabama and Florida." Yet no town could have been more atypical than Eatonville, where much of the story unfolds. *Opportunity*'s critic further misconstrued Hurston's goals: "It seems as if Miss Hurston wished to depict certain phases of Negro life—life in a Negro home, a plantation, and the Negro preacher—and just thrust the characters in them regardless of any connection." Judging *Jonah's Gourd Vine* as "quite disappointing and a failure as a novel," a reviewer at *The Crisis* also misread Hurston's intent: "to write a novel about a backward Negro people, using their peculiar speech and manners to express their lives." In fact, Hurston wanted to write not about "*the* Negro preacher," as *Opportunity* assumed, but about *a* Negro preacher—an individual who was flawed but not "backward," a man who was a Negro but not a sociological type. "I do not attempt to solve any problems," Zora said of her novel. "I know I cannot straighten out with a few pen-strokes what God and men took centuries to mess up. So I tried to deal with life as we actually live it—not as the sociologists imagine it."

Despite their misreadings, critics universally praised Hurston's novel for its sonorous language. "She has captured the lusciousness and beauty of the Negro dialect as have few others," *The Crisis* conceded. Of all the novel's readers, only Virginia Gildersleeve—Zora's former dean at Barnard—was daunted by the dialect. Never a Hurston fan, Gildersleeve did not think as highly of *Jonah's Gourd Vine* as most reviewers, and she told Lippincott she found it difficult to get through, largely because of the dialect.

One critic, however, thought some of the novel's language was *too* eloquent to have come from the minds and mouths of ordinary, agrarian black folks. Writing for *The New York Times*, reviewer John Chamberlain particularly objected to the story's climactic moment, when John Pearson delivers a tour de force sermon just before renouncing his pulpit under mounting pressure from his congregation. Taking his text from the biblical account of the wounds Jesus received in the house of his friends, John calls upon all his allegorical powers to describe Christ's merciful descent from Heaven to Earth:

> I see Jesus
> Leaving heben with all of His grandeur
> Dis-robin' Hisself of His matchless honor
> Yielding up de scepter of revolvin' worlds
> Clothing Hisself in de garment of humanity
> Coming into de world to rescue His friends.
> Two thousand years have went by on their rusty ankles
> But with the eye of faith, I can see Him
> Look down from His high towers of elevation
> I can hear Him when He walks about the golden streets
> I can hear 'em ring under His footsteps . . .

Such language, Chamberlain asserted, was "too good, too

brilliantly splashed with poetic imagery to be the product of any one Negro preacher." In fact, the language was precisely that of one Negro preacher: the Rev. C. C. Lovelace of Eau Gallie, Florida. Hurston had recorded the sermon on May 3, 1929, and printed it verbatim from her field notes as an accompaniment to her essays in *Negro*. She simply lifted the virtuosic sermon from her notebook again when writing her novel and placed it in the mouth of John Pearson. In other words, the sermon had been "handed" to her, as she told James Weldon Johnson, who'd also captured the eloquence of black preachers in his 1927 book, *God's Trombones*.

"I suppose that you have seen the criticism of my book in The New York Times," Hurston wrote to Johnson. "He means well, I guess, but I never saw such a lack of information about us. It just seems that he is unwilling to believe that a Negro preacher could have so much poetry in him. When you and I (who seem to be the only ones even among Negroes who recognize the barbaric poetry in their sermons) know that there are hundreds of preachers who are equalling that sermon weekly." A successful black preacher, Hurston knew, must be "both a poet and an actor of a very high order," with a good voice and a striking countenance. John Pearson—like John Hurston—possessed all those gifts; he was, in short, a master of adornment. In her original dedication for *Jonah's Gourd Vine*, Zora unabashedly paid homage to the John Hurstons of the world, the men and women who served not only as God's trombones but as the booming, bardic voices of an often-silenced people: "To the first and only real Negro poets in America—the preachers, who bring barbaric splendor of word and song into the very camp of the mockers."

Certainly, *Jonah's Gourd Vine* is not without its flaws: among them, a disjointed structure and the imposition of folklore in a way that sometimes detracts from the narrative. But, as Dove has noted, "Hurston's language is superb, rich with wordplay and proverbs—not only compelling when it comes to rendering the dialect of the Southern rural black but also as an omniscient narrator who neither indulges nor condemns the actions of her characters but offers the complexity of life in a story that leaves judgment up to the reader." For a first novel, this was a fine achievement indeed.

Though Hurston traveled to New York in June to promote *Jonah's Gourd Vine*, she spent most of the summer focused on her next book,

Mules and Men. In her cottage in Longwood, Florida, Zora worked to turn her scientific manuscript into a narrative that would appeal to average, nonacademic readers, as Lippincott desired. In August, she asked Franz Boas if he would consider writing an introduction. "Full of tremors" that Boas would reject her work because it wasn't scientific enough, Hurston explained that she'd been required to make certain editorial changes to boost the book's marketability. "I have inserted the between-story conversation and business because when I offered it without it, every publisher said it was too monotonous," she told him. "So I hope that the unscientific matter that must be there for the sake of the average reader will not keep you from writing the introduction."

After reviewing the manuscript for accuracy, Boas agreed to write the introduction to *Mules and Men*, which Lippincott scheduled for publication in 1935. Meanwhile, Hurston immersed herself in the present moment: the autumn of 1934. In September, she published a short story, called "The Fire and the Cloud," in *Challenge*, a new literary magazine Dorothy West had founded in Boston. Zora enthusiastically encouraged the younger woman's efforts: "I'm too delighted at your nerve in running a magazine not to help all I can," she wrote to the twenty-six-year-old West. "I love your audacity. You have learned at last the glorious lesson of living dangerously. That's the stuff!"

"The Fire and the Cloud," which West published in her second issue, is a conversation between an inquisitive lizard and the biblical Moses—remade in Hurston's hands as a reluctant and underappreciated leader of a "horde of murmurers." With his head in the clouds but his heart fixed on strengthening his people for crossing the River Jordan, Hurston's Moses is part human and part divine. While "The Fire and the Cloud" is unremarkable in its execution, it is significant because it indicates Hurston was beginning to toy with the idea of appropriating Moses for her own fictional uses and resituating him in the context of black history and culture—an effort she would revisit later, in expanded form.

In early October, Hurston put her feet on the road to Chicago, where a group had invited her to present a version of her folk concert in November. On the drive north, she stopped in Nashville to visit Charles S. Johnson, Lorenzo Dow Turner, James Weldon

Johnson, and other old friends at Fisk University. James Weldon Johnson was out of town, so Zora had to be satisfied with a glimpse of his green-shuttered house. Still, she made some useful contacts on the Fisk campus—not the least of whom was the college's president, Thomas Jones. Impressed by Hurston's knowledge of Negro folklore and by her multistate efforts to present this material onstage, Jones proposed that she apply for a faculty position at Fisk. Specifically, he wished to sponsor Hurston for a year of study in the noted drama program at Yale University, then hire her to establish an experimental theater at Fisk, using her vast knowledge of black folklore as a dramatic base—"the idea being to create the Negro drama out of the Negro himself." Excited about the prospect, Zora drove the five-hundred-mile stretch from Nashville to Chicago in a day, then immediately sat down to write President Jones a formal letter of application outlining her background and achievements. "I would love to work out some of my visions at Fisk University," she offered.

Hurston's first few weeks in Chicago sped by in a lively blur: On October 11, the young author spoke at the formal dinner of the Delta Sigma Theta sorority; a few days later, she addressed the Women's Civic Glee Club of Chicago, then another women's club on the sixteenth. On October 25, the *Daily News* of Chicago reported on her upcoming activities: "The fascinating Zora Neale Hurston," the paper noted, was scheduled to speak at a local bookstore on the twenty-sixth, and she would be the guest of honor and speaker November 4 at the Uptown Players' November Tea. "Anyone who has heard Miss Hurston speak once will be there," the newspaper advised. "She's too good to miss."

Anthropologist Melville Herskovits (who'd directed Hurston's first Barnard fieldwork, measuring heads in Harlem) invited Zora to his home for a spirited Sunday afternoon tea party. Hurston saw Herskovits again several days later at a party given in her honor by Katherine Dunham, a young black dancer, choreographer, and budding anthropologist who'd come to Herskovits's attention while a student at the University of Chicago. Dunham was preparing for fieldwork in the Caribbean by studying with Herskovits, now a Northwestern University professor who'd published several works on African and Haitian culture—and who was among the first scholars in the United States to recognize that black Americans were a people with a rich African past.

Dunham's party for Hurston was not as successful as Herskovits's tea had been. Six decades later, Dunham—who would become an esteemed anthropologist and world-renowned choreographer— admitted the real problem with the evening was her own jealousy of Hurston. "I don't know who gave me the idea that I was going to be the only little black girl in anthropology," Dunham said, laughing at her own brief flirtation with pettiness. Hoping her soiree for Hurston would prove she was bigger than her insecurities, Dunham was dismayed when she realized Zora had not come to the party to win her friendship or curry her favor: "First, she came late. I held that against her," Dunham recollected. Second, Zora was more attractive than Dunham expected. "I guess I hadn't seen a good photo of her; I didn't think she was very pretty. I thought at least I had that on her." Finally, Dunham remembered, Zora "didn't care a thing about me. She knew the other anthropologists [at the party] better than I did." As Hurston mingled easily with Herskovits and others in Dunham's second-floor flat, her hostess "wondered if I'd be safe in Herskovits's hands," as she put it, "or if he'd always keep her [Hurston] on a pedestal."

Zora "had more experience at these sorts of things than me," Dunham realized, as she observed Hurston's seemingly effortless rapport with her white anthropological colleagues. "I was touched by the way she handled her relationships with them," Dunham admitted. "She was a woman who'd made up her mind to do what she'd decided was her work. And frankly, she knew none of them could do it." Dunham also thought Hurston's unself-conscious ease had to do with the fact that she was older than her hostess—though "not a lot older," she hastened to add. (The then-twenty-five-year-old Dunham had no way of knowing that Hurston, in fact, was nearly twenty years her senior.) In the end, Dunham summarized, Hurston was polite and "gave us a good evening." But she didn't linger: "She came late," Dunham noted, "and left early."

None of this prevented Dunham from helping Hurston get a foothold in Chicago: "Katherine Dunham loaned us her studio for rehearsal twice," Hurston acknowledged, "which was very kind of her." Living at the South Parkway branch of the YWCA, Hurston cast her Chicago folk concert from people she met in drama classes at the Y and then rehearsed them in Dunham's studio and other loaned spaces. After only a few weeks of preparation, Hurston and her novice cast performed the show—a version of *The Great Day* and *From Sun to Sun*, but renamed *Singing Steel*—on the evenings of November 23 and 24, with a Saturday matinee on the twenty-fourth as well.

Like Hurston's previous folk concerts, *Singing Steel* earned enthusiastic reviews. "The vehicle, packed with folklore, drama and dancing, brings to the public not only the song and drama of a working day, but all the pathos, joy and innate feeling of freedom so characteristic of and inherent to the worker," wrote one Chicago critic, obviously impressed by *Singing Steel*'s insightful portrayal of the proletariat. "From the chant of the shack-rouser just before the break of day until the end of the fire dance at midnight," the reviewer continued, "it is a remarkable revelation of the laborer's heart and mind."

Just days before *Singing Steel* successfully hit the boards, Zora had been buoyed by an evening out with Carl Van Vechten, who was in town with Paris-based writer Gertrude Stein. (Author of the 1932 bestseller *The Autobiography of Alice B. Toklas*, Stein was visiting the States for the first time in thirty years, on a national lecture tour.) While in Chicago, Carlo persuaded Zora to sit for a few photographs. By now the fifty-something Van Vechten had practically given up writing and had begun to devote his creative energies largely to photography. More than mildly obsessed with documenting the times, Van Vechten set about photographing nearly every celebrated black artist or intellectual in America—and most of the white ones as well. "Frankly I feel flattered that you wanted to photograph me," Hurston told him as she anxiously watched for the pictures in the mail. "I am conscious of the honor you do me."

Zora also was waiting to hear back from her old friend Ethel Waters about a song she'd written; she hoped to sell the tune to Waters for $200, to help pay for a trip to China with nightclub singer and music critic Nora Holt. But Waters, performing on Broadway in the musical revue *As Thousands Cheer*, apparently was too busy to think about acquiring new songs. Consequently, Holt—dubbed by New York gossip columnists as "The Mamma Who Can't Behave"—

went to China alone, and Hurston spent the next several weeks at the Chicago Y, where she was treated like a minor celebrity and even given the use of a secretary. On Thanksgiving, Zora had so many dinner invitations she couldn't get around to them all, though she tried her best: "I buried many turkey bosoms that day," she allowed, "to say nothing of turkey hammers."

When Van Vechten's package finally arrived December 10, Zora was elated with the results of the photo shoot. "The pictures are swell!" she told him. "I love myself when I am laughing. And then again when I am looking mean and impressive."

Evidently, Hurston had looked plenty impressive (if not mean) during her staging of *Singing Steel*. Representatives of the Julius Rosenwald Fund had been in the audience that November weekend and subsequently invited Zora to apply for a Rosenwald fellowship. Founded by Jewish humanitarian Julius Rosenwald, the fund in 1929 began offering fellowships for black creative workers—money that was conscientiously dispensed by fund president Edwin Embree. Initially, there was talk of subsidizing Hurston for a chair in the drama department at Fisk. But when the university's president, Thomas Jones, began to back away from the idea of appointing her to his faculty—apparently he was disturbed by Hurston's reputation for flamboyance and her notoriously strong will—her conversations with the Rosenwald Fund turned to "something bigger," as she saw it. In mid-December, Hurston was awarded a Rosenwald fellowship to study at Columbia University for a doctorate in anthropology. As she prepared to head to New York for Christmas, Zora was thrilled by this unexpected gift of fate: "Life has picked me up bodaciously," she judged merrily, "and throwed me over the fence."

CHAPTER 24

Parachute Jump

In her rush to get to New York so she could enroll in Columbia in January, Hurston missed Christmas. On December 19, the Rosenwald Fund sent her a $100 check to facilitate her move from Chicago. Within a few days, she was at the wheel of her car (she nicknamed this one "High Yaller") and traveling due east through Indiana, Ohio, and Pennsylvania. Once she arrived in New York, Zora realized she'd taken time for "no holiday pleasures at all," as she lamented from Harold Jackman's bachelor quarters in Harlem—where she was bunking temporarily and recovering from her eight-hundred-mile drive. In early January, Zora was still waiting to see if she'd received any Christmas cards or presents in the mail, which was being forwarded from Chicago.

Christmas presents or not, Zora had much to be grateful for this Yuletide season. The $100 moving allowance from the Rosenwald Fund was gravy, served on top of the $100 per month she'd been promised for two years of graduate work, in addition to the $500 stipend the fund offered for fieldwork and international travel. In all, Hurston had been granted a two-year, $3,000 fellowship—close to $38,000 in today's money. But, as Hurston's award letter stressed, it was all contingent upon her "continuance of work satisfactory to the professors" who would be directing her studies.

To her delight, Hurston's supervising professor at Columbia would be none other than Franz Boas himself. And Papa Franz was pleased that Zora would be able to devote herself to graduate studies in anthropology—a course of action he'd recommended for her back in 1930, but which Charlotte Mason had refused to support. Hurston now assured her longtime mentor that she was up to the task: "Now I realize that this is going to call for rigorous routine and discipline, which every body seems to feel that I need. So be it. I want to do it. I have always wanted to do it and nobody will have any trouble about my applying myself," she told Boas, somewhat defensively. "I wonder if it ought not to be taken into consideration that I have been on my own since fourteen years old and went to high school, college and everything progressive that I have done because I wanted to, and not because I was being pushed? All of these things have been done under most trying circumstances and I stuck. . . . I have had two or three people to say to me, why don't you go and take a master's or a doctor's degree in Anthropology since you love it so much? They never seem to realize that it takes money to do that."

Hurston finally had the money she needed for graduate school, and the fellowship she'd secured was a plum, the Rosenwald Fund wanted her to know. "We are glad to cooperate in your further studies in an amount far beyond our normal fellowship awards," Edwin Embree informed her, "because we believe you will greatly benefit by a full two years of study and supervised field work, and because we have such great confidence in the contributions which ultimately you may make to anthropology and to an understanding of the special cultural gifts of the Negroes."

The "special cultural gifts of the Negroes" had become Hurston's field of expertise and she never seemed to tire of talking about the intrinsic value of these gifts. In an article published during the final days of 1934—in *The Washington Tribune*, a black D.C. newspaper— Hurston stressed the significance and worth of black folk expression. And she urged her people to go the way of Chaucer, the *Canterbury Tales* author "who saw the beauty of his own language in spite of the scorn in which it was held" by England's French-speaking Norman conquerors. In stern words, Hurston decried "the intellectual lynching" that black people perpetrated upon themselves whenever they sought to emulate whites, in art or in life. "Fawn as you will. Spend an eternity standing awe-struck," she concluded her essay forcefully. "Roll your eyes in ecstasy and ape his every move, but until we have placed something upon his street corner that is our own, we are right back where we were when they filed our iron collar off."

For Hurston's friends in Harlem—particularly those artists and intellectuals who'd devoted their young lives to placing something of their own on the white man's cultural street corner—1934 had been a brutal year. From Jackman's apartment at 442 Manhattan Avenue, Hurston could survey the toll the Depression had taken on Harlem and on what used to be known as the New Negro Renaissance. Many of the movement's most vital participants were dead or gone. Jackman's intimate friend Countee Cullen, one of the most promising poets of the Renaissance, had returned to his old high school to teach French, a job he would cling to for the rest of his life. His chief poetic rival, Langston Hughes, was in Mexico seeking to settle the estate of his recently deceased father; though Hughes was still writing prolifically, he was collecting a pile of rejection slips for his latest batch of short stories. Others suffered more grave denouements. Novelist and physician Rudolph Fisher died of cancer December 26—the same week that Wallace Thurman, one of the movement's brightest fireflies, burned out unceremoniously in a charity hospital on New York's Welfare Island. Fisher was only thirty-seven years old. Not to be outdone, Thurman was only thirty-two. Tuberculosis—aided by chronic unhappiness—killed Thurman, whose death devastated his peers. "He was our leader," Dorothy West proclaimed, "and when he died, it all died with him." Following Thurman's funeral—on Christmas Eve 1934—everyone in the old circle seemed to realize, as Bontemps put it, that "the golden days were gone."

In January 1935—as if to confirm Bontemps's dolorous assessment—the biggest sensation in Harlem was not a book by a black author or a play by a black dramatist. It was *Imitation of Life*, a Hollywood film that was drawing crowds at all the uptown movie houses. Starring black actors Louise Beavers and Fredi Washington (and white starlet Claudette Colbert), *Imitation of Life* was based on the 1933 novel by Hurston's erstwhile traveling companion, Fannie Hurst. After their 1931 jaunt to Canada, Zora and Fannie had traveled together again, accompanied by Fannie's friend Helen Worden, a columnist at *The New York World-Telegram*. The trio had driven from Palm Beach, Florida, to Winter Park, where Fannie gave a talk at Rollins College. En route to Fannie's speaking engagement, Zora had taken the two white women to visit Eatonville, where Worden snapped pictures for an article she planned to write about the quaint Negro town. This was in February 1934, when Zora was teaching at Bethune-Cookman. At that time, Hurst's *Imitation of Life* had been in bookstores for just a few months. If Zora had not yet read the novel, she'd surely heard some of the stories behind it: Harper & Brothers had offered Hurst a $5,000 advance for *Imitation of Life* before she'd even drafted half its pages. More astonishingly, *Pictorial Review*, a popular women's magazine, had paid Hurst a whopping $45,000 to serialize the novel, under the title "Sugar House."

By any name, *Imitation of Life*—at least the film version—was a controversial hit. It is the story of Bea Pullman, a white widow who begins selling maple syrup to support herself and her daughter, Jessie. After a short time as a working woman, Bea hires Delilah—whom Hurst described as "an enormously buxom" black maid—to take care of her house. Delilah and her light-skinned daughter, Peola, move in with the white family (which includes Bea's disabled father), and Delilah soon concocts a delicious recipe for waffles to go along with Bea's maple syrup. In short order, Bea figures out a way to capitalize on Delilah's fabulous waffles and maple candy hearts. With Bea's business sense and Delilah's kitchen expertise, the women eventually open a chain of coffee shops and become millionaires. But the selfless black maid doesn't use her share of the money (only 20 percent) to strike out on her own. Instead, Delilah—at least partly modeled on "Aunt Jemima," the ubiquitous icon for what was already America's favorite pancake mix—wants only to maintain her role as Bea's domestic servant. In the end, both women's daughters grow up to break their mothers' hearts: Jessie by falling in love with the same man her mother loves; Peola by denying her mother and trying to pass for white.

Though this racial subplot was not a selling point for the magazine series, or for the novel, it galvanized black audiences, particularly when the film version of *Imitation of Life* was widely screened in early 1935. Some black viewers and readers responded with admiration, others with outrage. E. Washington Rhodes, editor of the *Philadelphia Tribune*, could not praise *Imitation* enough; the black journalist called the film "the greatest condemnation of American racial prejudice ever screened." Sterling Brown, on the other hand, angrily dismissed the film—and Hurst's novel—for trading in stereotypes: "the contented Mammy, and the tragic mulatto; and the ancient ideas about the mixture of races."

Preoccupied with her own work, Hurston stayed out of the fray, at least overtly. While she didn't say anything to Hurst about the novel or the movie in their correspondence of the period, she may have voiced her views in person. And in a 1934 article she wrote for *The American Mercury*, Hurston took a covert (if thinly veiled) swipe at *Imitation of Life*: "Whenever I pick up one of the popular magazines and read one of these mammy cut tales," she vented, "I often wonder whether the author actually believes that his tale is probable or whether he knows it is flapdoodle and is merely concerned about the check." (Zora's use of the word "flapdoodle," so close to flapjacks, and her mention of popular magazines—of which Fannie Hurst was the top-dollar queen—read like daggers expertly aimed at her former boss.) Hurston went on to name several white writers—Dubose Heyward, Julia Peterkin, Paul Green—who seemed to look beyond convenient stereotypes in their portrayals of black characters. But even these writers did not fully escape Hurston's criticism. For instance, Peterkin—author of the black-themed, Pulitzer-winning *Scarlet Sister Mary*—had made "a collection of Negro sayings and folk ways," Hurston acknowledged, but "she does not assemble her material in a pattern to give a true picture." Still, Zora conceded, "all these whom I have mentioned are earnest seekers, halted only by the barrier that exists somewhere in every Negro mind for the white man." Conspicuously absent from Hurston's list of true seekers was Fannie Hurst.

The American Mercury, a magazine edited by journalist H. L. Mencken and theater critic George Jean Nathan, never published Hurston's scathing essay, called "You Don't Know Us Negroes." The editors' decision to kill the article may have saved Zora some friendships, but the piece never should have been consigned to the slush pile. It is one of the most persuasive and engaging essays Hurston wrote in the 1930s, and it is fierce in its critique of what she called "the oleomargarine era in Negro writing." For the past decade, Hurston argued, many of the novels and plays that claimed "they were holding a looking-glass to the Negro had everything in them except Negroness"—the real butter, so to speak, of black literature.

Hundreds of years of slavery had induced most whites to think of black people "as creatures of tasks alone," Hurston theorized. "When in fact the conflict between what we wanted to do and what we were forced to do intensified our inner life instead of destroying it." Hasty generalizations and a mistakenly simplistic view on the part of whites had resulted in "near-Negro literature" that portrayed black people as "obvious and simple." And these portrayals, Hurston pointed out, were all the more exaggerated onstage, where "all Negro characters must have pop eyes" and speak in a jumble of misplaced prepositions. "Most white people have seen our shows but not our lives," Hurston declared bluntly. "If they have not seen a Negro show they have seen a minstrel or at least a black-face comedian and that is considered enough. They know all about us. We say, 'Am it?' And go into a dance. By way of catching breath we laugh and say, 'Is you is, or is you ain't' and grab our banjo and work ourselves into a sound sleep. First thing on waking we laugh or skeer ourselves into another buck and wing, and so life goes. All of which may be very good vaudeville, but I'm sorry to be such an image-breaker and say we just don't live like that."

After providing more such mordant examples—and asserting that "this attitude on the part of editors and producers is deforming the Negro writers themselves"—Hurston challenged her artistic peers, both black and white, to "go buy a cow and treat the public to some butter": "Negro reality," she concluded, "is a hundred times more imaginative and entertaining than anything that has ever been hatched up over a typewriter."

As this bitingly insightful essay hinted, Hurston's "golden days"— to use Bontemps's phrase—were still ahead. At the moment, her biggest problem was deciding whether she would study for her Ph.D. at Columbia, as planned, or return to the Chicago area to attend Northwestern, where she could work under the supervision of Melville Herskovits. Boas suggested Hurston consider the university in Evanston, Illinois, because of her interest in doing fieldwork in Haiti—on which Herskovits was a world authority. Hurston was willing to go to Northwestern if Boas believed it in her best interest, but she let him know she preferred to stay in New York and attend Columbia. Embree, of the Rosenwald Fund, preferred Columbia, too—but for different reasons, as he confided to Boas. At Columbia, he hoped, Boas would be able to provide the "certainly brilliant" Hurston with "the rather detailed direction" he felt she needed to be "transformed into a sound student."

Once everyone had agreed on Columbia, Hurston sat down with Boas to work out her degree plan. She resisted the normal graduate coursework, largely because of her previous field experience and because many of the courses Columbia offered were unrelated to her specific interests in documenting black culture. Finally, she and Boas agreed that she would study general ethnology in the spring 1935 semester and then, beginning the following fall, for the whole 1935–36 school year. After that, she would embark on a field trip to Haiti, where she planned to explore the origins of hoodoo.

In mid-January, Zora said good-bye to Jackman—the gallant Harlem schoolteacher who'd shared his flat with her for several weeks—and moved into her own place a few blocks away in the Graham Court apartments, at 116th Street and Seventh Avenue. Haggling with the Rosenwald Fund over its methods of doling out money (the $100 monthly disbursements would not allow her to pay her tuition all at once), she nevertheless enrolled in Columbia in early 1935. Within a matter of days, however, Embree effectively snatched back Hurston's fellowship.

Ostensibly distressed that she would spend only three semesters in graduate classes before going into the field, Embree claimed Hurston's coursework did "not indicate a permanent plan on the basis of which we feel justified in awarding a longtime fellowship." This despite the fact that Hurston had met what the Rosenwald Fund had put forth as its primary criterion—that her work be satisfactory to her professors. Franz Boas, the leading anthropologist in the country, had personally approved Hurston's degree plan. But this was not enough for Embree: He arbitrarily cut Hurston's fellowship from $3,000 to $700, limiting it to a seven-month period ending in June 1935. Rather than covering Hurston's graduate school expenses for two years, the Rosenwald Fund was only committing to one semester. After this initial time—if her professors judged that she'd done "thorough and careful work"—Hurston would be free to apply for another fellowship, Embree noted, but "we are not now inclined to contribute further."

Hurston was mortified by the Rosenwald Fund's dishonorable

maneuver, and after several weeks of brooding and seething, she turned to Boas for succor. The embarrassed professor immediately wrote to Embree for an explanation: "Naturally the uncertainty in which she finds herself now is not favorable for her work," Boas argued on Zora's behalf. In a few days, he received a reply revealing the real reasons Embree had decided to so drastically reduce Hurston's fellowship. "The young woman, while unquestionably brilliant, has a capacity for keeping her plans—and her friends and sponsors—in tumult," Embree complained to Boas. Essentially, Embree's objection to Hurston as a Rosenwald fellow was a matter of personality: He did not approve of her maverick style, nor her knack at self-promotion, which he thought crippled her potential as a student.

Specifically, Embree might have been reacting to an article on Hurston that appeared in *The New York World-Telegram* in early February, under the headline "Author Plans to Upbraid Own Race." Prominently mentioning Hurston's headfirst dive into Harlem nightlife and the recent teas that had been held in her honor—at Barnard and on Park Avenue—the article also revealed a bit of information that must have dropped Embree's jaw: "Miss Hurston said that she had just about decided to pass the proffered Julius Rosenwald scholarship in anthropology at Columbia and start in writing a book that would give her own people 'an awful going over,' particularly the ones who talk about the tragedy of being Negroes." Several weeks after the article appeared—and the original fellowship offer had been rescinded—Embree confessed to Boas: "We have been distressed at the over-zealousness in her own behalf of this young woman, and at her lack of tendency to serious quiet scholarship."

Hurston probably never saw Embree's letter to Boas, but she could have guessed its contents. Her response to the Rosenwald Fund's parsimonious policy change was a trickster move, or what Zora might have regarded as a devious deal with the Devil: She accepted the reduced fellowship money and remained enrolled in Columbia—but stopped attending classes.

In his eagerness to develop her into a "serious" student, Embree was trying to treat Hurston like someone fresh out of college, and demanding that she remain "quiet" in the process. Yet she was a member of the American Folk-Lore Society, the American Ethnological Society, and the American Anthropological Association. She also was the author of a published novel (*Jonah's Gourd Vine* had just been released in England as well) and a soon-to-be-published book of folklore; as such, self-promotion was part of her job. Wholeheartedly rejecting Embree's paternalism, Zora used the Rosenwald money to finance her life as a writer. At the beginning stages of a new novel, she was "working like a slave and liking it," she told a friend. "But I have lost all my zest for a doctorate. I have definitely decided that I never want to teach, so what is the use of the degree? It seems that I am wasting two good years out of my life when I should be working." For Hurston, working meant writing, and that's what she set about doing. By April, Boas was inquiring of her whereabouts—as was Fannie Hurst and "a perfect hotbed" of Zora's friends, all "eager and greedy for news" about her. "Where did you disappear," Fannie wanted to know, "and why haven't I heard?"

Hurston's friends would have had better luck locating her at their local newsstands. On April 6, New York's *Amsterdam News*, a popular black newspaper, ran a huge profile of her. In it, Zora bragged about her Rosenwald fellowship—as if the original terms were still intact—and revealed that renowned artist Miguel Covarrubias was illustrating her forthcoming *Mules and Men*. Noting that she'd only taken one class in creative writing—"an absolute waste of time, for writing is a gift"—Hurston said she liked to write in bed at night. "Since I don't compose well at the typewriter, I prepare my manuscript in long hand, revise and revise, and then type it. 'Hunt and peck' is my system on a portable machine." Hurston's favorite American author, she disclosed, was Robert Nathan (who wrote several books of fantasy fiction, including *The Bishop's Wife* in 1928 and, interestingly, a 1934 novel called *Jonah or the Withering Vine*). But, she added, 1921 Nobel Prize winner Anatole France was her "author of authors."

As this exuberant piece of personal publicity suggested, Hurston had not disappeared into some cosmic void of depression. Her scarceness among her friends had another root: Zora had fallen, it seems, into that mysterious black hole called love. Or, as she put it: "I did not just fall in love. I made a parachute jump."

Soon after her return to Manhattan, Zora started dating "the man who was really to lay me by the heels," as she would recall. A graduate student at Columbia, his name was Percival McGuire Punter. Zora had met him four years before, when he was an undergraduate at the City College of New York. A member of his college orchestra, Punter had enough musical talent to land a singing part in Hurston's original production of *The Great Day*, at the John Golden Theatre in January 1932. Zora had noticed Punter then: "He was tall, dark brown, magnificently built, with a beautifully modeled back head. His profile was strong and good," she observed. "But his looks only drew my eyes in the beginning. I did not fall in love with him just for that. He had a fine mind and that intrigued me. When a man keeps beating me to the draw mentally, he begins to get glamorous."

Still, Zora—so recently divorced from Sheen—did not express her interest in Punter at the time. When they met again in 1935, though, their mutual attraction soon became obvious. "He began to make shy overtures to me," Zora would remember. "I pretended not to notice for a while so that I could be sure and not be hurt. Then he gave me the extreme pleasure of telling me right out loud about it. It seems that he had been in love with me just as long as I had been with him, but he was afraid that I didn't mean him any good, as the saying goes."

The reasons for Punter's initial reticence toward Zora are fairly obvious. With her gingerbread-colored skin, her intrepid eyes sparkling like polished pennies, and her one-of-a-kind wardrobe, Zora had a funky elegance that many men found attractive. Would-be wooers occasionally approached her on short acquaintance, panting something like this in her ear: "You passionate thing! I can see you are just *burning* up! . . . Ahhh! I know that you will just wreck me! Your eyes and your lips tell me a lot. You are a walking furnace!" Such breathless proclamations usually amazed Zora, and tickled her, too. "I may be thinking of turnip greens with dumplings, or more royalty checks, and here is a man who visualizes me on a divan sending the world up in smoke," she once said. "It has happened so often that I have come to expect it. There must be something about me that looks sort of couchy."

Beyond her sex appeal, Zora also had a certain amount of notoriety that Punter at first may have found intimidating. She'd been the subject of feature articles in the New York press, she'd been toasted on Park Avenue, and she'd traveled the country. Punter, on the other hand, was just a poor graduate student whose father, an immigrant from the Caribbean island of Antigua, was "a maintenance engineer" at a big building downtown. Punter had no money, Zora knew, and "nothing to offer but what it takes—a bright soul, a fine mind in a fine body, and courage."

Another inhibiting factor for Punter—and for Hurston—may have been the age difference between them. Born in 1912, Punter was twenty-three years old in 1935. Zora was forty-four. Punter surely knew his love interest was older than he, but because of Zora's persistent mendacity about her age, he probably had no idea she was more than twenty years his senior. Zora knew, though. And—despite her clear ability to maintain what she called her "mental youth"—she must have questioned the long-haul wisdom of getting involved with a man so much younger than herself.

She did not question it for long, however. Punter's forthright gaze, refulgent smile, and licorice skin—not to mention his "fine mind"—became too tempting for Zora to resist. "People waste too much time worrying about whether an affair will *last*," she rationalized. "Enjoy it while it does last and then suffer no regrets later."

In no time, Hurston and Punter were immersed in an intensely passionate, mutually satisfying romance. It was, Zora would recall, "the real love affair of my life." Before Punter (and after Sheen), Zora's courtships had been rather casual. Valuing her freedom above all else, she could find ardor in a given moment, but those moments tended to pass fairly quickly: "Under the spell of moonlight, music, flowers or the cut and smell of good tweeds, I sometimes feel the divine urge for an hour, a day or maybe a week," she once said. "Then it is gone and my interest returns to corn pone and mustard greens, or rubbing a paragraph with a soft cloth. Then my ex-sharer of a mood calls up in a fevered voice and reminds me of every silly thing I said, and eggs me on to say them all over again. . . . It is asking me to be a seven-sided liar. . . . I was sincere for the moment in which I said the things. . . . It was true for the moment, but the next day or the next week, is not that moment."

With Punter, however, the moment appeared to be never ending, and Zora began to make room in her life for a committed relationship. She enjoyed cooking for her sweetheart when she could; her

Zora Neale Hurston's father, the Rev. John Hurston. Zora and her siblings were awed by "his well-cut broadcloth, Stetson hats, hand-made alligator-skin shoes and walking stick," she recalled. (Florida State Archives)

John Hurston in 1906 with Zora's stepmother, the young Mattie Moge. (Courtesy of Robert E. Hemenway)

At age 21, Zora lived in Nashville, Tennessee, with her oldest brother, Hezekiah Robert (Bob), while he finished his studies at Meharry Medical College. She is pictured with Bob, his wife, Wilhemina, and their third child, newborn Hezekiah Robert, Jr. This is the earliest known photograph of Hurston, who moved with Bob and his family to Memphis after he finished medical school in 1913. (Courtesy of Winifred Hurston Clark)

When the 26-year-old Hurston arrived in Baltimore in 1917, she still looked young enough to pass for 16, which she did—in order to qualify for free public schooling. "I got tired of trying to get the money to go," she would recall. "My clothes were practically gone. Nickeling and dimering along was not getting me anywhere." (ZNH Collection, University of Florida)

Hurston moved to Washington, D.C., in 1918 with hopes of attending Howard University. After working as a waitress all summer, she enrolled in the high school division, Howard Academy, in December. (ZNH Collection, University of Florida)

Hurston came into her own during her years at Howard, which she called "the capstone of Negro education in the world." While attending classes full-time, she worked as a manicurist at a black-owned barbershop that served a white clientele. Averaging $12 to $15 a week in tips, she began to dress stylishly, favoring chic hats, long dresses, and dramatic colors. (ZNH Collection, University of Florida)

Alain Locke, pictured in 1926, was one of Hurston's mentors at Howard and a key figure in the Harlem Renaissance. (Yale Collection of American Literature, Beinecke Rare Book and Manuscript Library, Yale University)

Carl Van Vechten (*left*) and Fannie Hurst (*above*), both wealthy writers and well-known "friends of the Negro," befriended Hurston shortly after her arrival in New York in 1925. (Photographs by Carl Van Vechten/Library of Congress, Prints & Photographs Division, Carl Van Vechten Collection)

Hurston, shown displaying a variety of ethnic dolls, became interested in anthropology while studying with Franz Boas at Barnard College. Still, she felt certain that she wanted to be a writer. "I have had some small success as a writer and wish above all to succeed at it," she wrote on an occupational interest form. "Either teaching or social work will be interesting but consolation prizes." (ZNH Collection, University of Florida)

Carrying a pistol for protection, Hurston traveled through the South collecting folklore in 1927 in a car she called Sassy Susie. (Beinecke Rare Book and Manuscript Library, Yale University)

Hurston ran into Langston Hughes during her tour of the South and they decided to travel back to New York together. The identities of the other men in the photo are unknown. (Beinecke Rare Book and Manuscript Library, Yale University)

Jessie Fauset, Langston Hughes, and Zora Neale Hurston in front of the statue of Booker T. Washington at Alabama's Tuskegee Institute, 1927. (Photograph by P. H. Polk/Beinecke Rare Book and Manuscript Library, Yale University)

H. A. SHEEN

In May 1927, Hurston married her Howard University sweetheart, Herbert A. Sheen, who was then a medical student in Chicago. "He could stomp a piano out of this world, sing a fair baritone and dance beautifully," she said of him. Though they'd been dating for years, Zora was "assailed by doubts" on their wedding day. (Rush-Presbyterian–St. Luke's Medical Archives)

Charlotte Osgood Mason—patron to Hurston, Hughes, and several other artists of the Harlem Renaissance—required everyone who benefited from her largesse to call her "Godmother." (Yale Collection of American Literature, Beinecke Rare Book and Manuscript Library, Yale University)

Hurston returned to the South in 1928 to collect Negro folklore for Charlotte Mason (*above*), who furnished her with a motion-picture camera and a shiny Chevrolet. (Dorothy West Collection, Boston University Library)

Langston Hughes and Louise Thompson en route to Russia in 1932, a year after their dispute with Hurston over the play *Mule Bone*. (Beinecke Rare Book and Manuscript Library, Yale University)

Hurston (*far right*) rehearsing a group of performers for *From Sun to Sun*, a folk concert she presented under a variety of names in New York, Florida, and elsewhere. This photograph was originally published in the April 1932 issue of *Theatre Arts* magazine. (ZNH Collection, University of Florida)

Zora Neale Hurston as pictured in Nancy Cunard's massive 1934 anthology, *Negro,* to which Zora contributed six essays and a transcribed sermon. (ZNH Collection, University of Florida)

A portrait of the writer, photographed in Chicago by Carl Van Vechten, 1934. (Library of Congress, Prints & Photographs Division, Carl Van Vechten Collection)

Percival Punter, the man with whom Hurston had what she called "the real love affair of my life." When they began dating, in 1935, Punter was 23 years old; Hurston was 44. (Reproduced from the 1934 yearbook of the City College of New York)

The woman pictured at left has often been misidentified as Zora Neale Hurston. Her identity is unknown, according to Alan Lomax—who snapped the photo during the summer of 1935, when he, Hurston, and Mary Elizabeth Barnicle traveled through the South collecting folk songs for the Library of Congress. (Library of Congress, Prints & Photographs Division, Lomax Collection)

At right is a 1935 photo of Hurston by painter and lithographer Prentiss Taylor. Note that Hurston's grin is not as toothy as her doppelganger's, her eyes do not disappear into her smile, and she appears to be of a stockier build. (Beinecke Rare Book and Manuscript Library, Yale University)

Hurston, at home in New York,
demonstrating the Crow Dance.
(Photographs by Prentiss
Taylor/Beinecke Rare Book and Manuscript
Library, Yale University)

Detail of a page from Hurston's manuscript of *Their Eyes Were Watching God*, which she wrote in Haiti in 1936. (Hurston Collection, Beinecke Rare Book and Manuscript Library, Yale University)

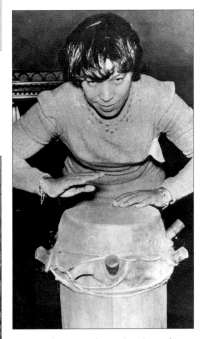

Hurston has some fun with a drum she brought back from her 1936–37 trip to Haiti. The photo above was published in *Voodoo Gods: An Enquiry into Native Myths and Magic in Jamaica and Haiti*, the U.K. version of *Tell My Horse*. (*New York World-Telegram & Sun* Collection, Library of Congress)

At the New York Book Fair in November 1937, shortly after *Their Eyes Were Watching God* was published. A newspaper photographer snapped Hurston inspecting *American Stuff,* an anthology that included two of her most persistent critics, Sterling Brown and Richard Wright. (Library of Congress, Prints & Photographs Division, WPA Collection)

Hurston (*fourth from right*) onstage in Jacksonville, Florida, at a 1938 performance inspired by *Their Eyes Were Watching God.* (Courtesy of the Skip Mason Archives)

At a football game in Durham in 1939, during her brief teaching stint at the North Carolina College for Negroes. (Photograph by Alex M. Rivera, Rivera Pictures)

On a folklore-collecting trip in 1940, on the coast of South Carolina. (Library of Congress, Prints & Photographs Division, Margaret Mead Collection)

Portrait of the author in the 1940s. (Courtesy of the Archives of *The Atlanta Journal-Constitution*)

In 1943, Hurston received a Howard University Alumni Award for "distinguished service" in literature. Also honored at the charter day ceremonies were Dr. Orville L. Ballard (*left*) and Lt. Col. Campbell C. Johnson. (Reprinted from the March 3, 1943, issue of the Washington *Evening Star*)

In 1948, shortly before the publication of *Seraph on the Suwanee*. (ZNH Collection, University of Florida)

In 1951, Hurston returned to Eau Gallie, Florida, where, for $5 a week, she rented the same one-room house where she'd written *Mules and Men*. (Courtesy of *The Saturday Evening Post*)

At age 65, Hurston was a special podium guest at the 1956 commencement exercises at Bethune-Cookman College in Daytona Beach, Florida. Two weeks later, she began a job as a librarian for $1.88 an hour. She spent her final years laboring on a book about the life of King Herod. She was working, she said, "under the spell of a great obsession." (ZNH Collection, University of Florida)

cool, crystallized grapefruit peel was a particular favorite as warmer temperatures began to descend on the city. The lovers stayed up late talking about religion (he was considering the ministry), art, and literature. Punter was impressed by Zora's instinct for art; she intuitively knew what was good and lasting, he observed, and seemed to quietly recognize the enduring value of her own writing. (She once told him she knew she was a better writer than Fannie Hurst, despite Hurst's fame and money.) To keep up with her work, Zora sometimes got up in the middle of the night to write. Even this adjustment did not curb the couple's calenture. Punter called his beloved "Skookums"—because she reminded him of the Indian on the Skookum brand apples label—and every day, Zora found new angles for her adoration. "No matter which way I probed him," she allowed, "I found something more to admire. We fitted each other like a glove."

Zora emerged from the love nest on the afternoon of Friday, May 10, to attend a tea in her honor at the Women's University Club on East Fifty-second Street. Annie Nathan Meyer, who'd sponsored Zora's education at Barnard, helped to plan the tea. "Celebs too numerous to mention were there," Zora boasted. Among them, publisher Bertram Lippincott, who traveled from Philadelphia for the occasion, and novelists Robert Nathan, Pearl S. Buck, and, of course, Fannie Hurst, who said a few congratulatory words. Zora wore "a flaming white dress, a terrific-looking kind of thing," as Lippincott recalled, "and all kind of big wraps all around her like a movie actress." Comfortable being the center of attention—and "really amazing to look at"—she made a brief speech that thrilled the mostly white crowd. Or, as Hurst cooed proudly to Meyer: "And didn't our Zora cover herself with glory?"

Punter did not attend the tea with Hurston. Her increasing celebrity—and the apparent delight she took in it—was beginning to rattle him. Perhaps because of the age difference, and because of Zora's worldliness, Punter was starting to wonder how long he could hold her attention. "I was hog-tied and branded," she admitted, "but he didn't realize it. He could make me fetch and carry, but he wouldn't believe it." So when Zora attended literary parties or met people on business, Punter often sulked and then Zora became unhappy, too. One evening, for instance, the two were at Zora's apartment, "soaked in ecstasy," when her telephone rang. A literary celebrity was in town and wanted to meet her. Zora was eager to go but Punter asked her not to; she invited him to join her. He refused and walked out. Zora went to the gathering, as she recalled, but was distracted and downcast all evening.

Another time, looking at the very serious Van Vechten photo of Zora in which she looked "mean and impressive," Punter said he wanted her to look that way all the time unless she was with him. Zora almost laughed out loud—not because she found the statement absurd, but because she felt the same way about Percy, as she called him. "He was so extraordinary that I lived in terrible fear lest women camp on his doorstep in droves and take him away from me," she confessed. "I hated to think of him smiling unless he was smiling at me."

Punter's jealousy, though, soon was exacerbated by his machismo. At first, Zora thought his resolute sense of "manliness" was chivalrous and sweet, but she quickly discovered that it could get out of hand. One time, for example, Punter became angry when Zora offered him a quarter. He'd used his last nickel to travel uptown (from his place on Sixty-fourth Street) to visit her. As he and Zora lingered in an embrace at the door, he asked her to let him go so he could begin the long walk home. Concerned that he would have to hoof it for more than fifty blocks, Zora got a quarter out of her purse to loan him until his payday. Punter was insulted: He'd known he didn't have the return fare when he left home, he protested, but he'd come because he wanted to see her; now he must bear the consequences of his choice like a man. "No woman on earth could either lend him or give him a cent," Zora remembered him saying. "If a man could not do for a woman, what good was he on earth?"

Eventually, Punter asked Zora to give up her career, marry him, and leave New York. The marrying and leaving New York parts were fine. Zora preferred to write in Florida anyway. ("New York is not a good place to think in," she once complained. "I can do hack work here, but I need quiet to really work.") The idea of giving up her career, however, was chilling. "I really wanted to do anything he wanted me to do," she would recall, "but that one thing I could not do."

Punter did not seem to understand that Hurston's work was her

sustenance. "I
wouldn't want my parachute jump
looking like Skookum.   you work so hard," he told her. "I
more with her life than lo   hing but look after me. Be home
he might be. "I had things ch   here." But Zora needed to do
she tried to explain. "I could not n, no matter how wonderful
difference in marriage. He was all of me that must be said,"
that. One did not conflict with the othe work should make any
ferent with him. He felt that he did not m   thing else to me but
was the master kind. All, or nothing, for him."   ind. But it was dif-
                                                              me enough. He

Hurston and Punter continued to see each other,
damental conflict, and their mutual jealousies escalate this fun-
smiled too broadly at a woman on Seventh Avenue, Zora   if Punter
she accepted a kiss on the cheek from a male acquaintance, Punter
smoldered. Their love became blissful misery. "We were alternately
the happiest people in the world," Zora recognized, "and the most
miserable."

One night, an argument turned particularly ugly, Hurston
recalled. "Something primitive inside me tore past the barriers and
before I realized it, I had slapped his face. This was a mistake." Angry
over some week-old hurt, Punter struck back. To Zora's horror, she
and Punter were soon trading slaps and shoves. "No broken bones,
you understand, and no black eyes," but combat nonetheless.
Stunned by the wrong turn their passion had taken, the two ended
up on the floor together, apologizing to each other profusely. He
went out and bought a pie while she made a pot of hot chocolate,
over which they made up fervently. The next day, he built her a
bookcase and the couple became more affectionate than ever.

But something had changed for Zora. "Then I knew I was too
deeply in love to be my old self," she admitted. "For always a blow to
my body had infuriated me beyond measure. Even with my parents,
that was true. But somehow, I didn't hate him at all." Hurston—
"delirious with joy and pain"—had lost hold of herself. And this
frightened her. "I suddenly decided to go away and see if I could live
without him. I did not even tell him that I was going. But I wired him
from some town in Virginia."

The second week of June, Hurston left Manhattan with New
York University Professor Mary Elizabeth Barnicle for fieldwork in

the South. On June 15, af..ed
Barnicle met collector ..gro
Brunswick, Georgia. Lo.. Congress. Hurston—whom Lomax
and orders to collect ..rmed person today on Western Negro
Music Division of th.. e the locales for their research and contact
recognized as "the
folk-lore"—was ..
the subjects. ..urston's influence," the young Lomax noted,
"Through..ving, in an isolated community on St. Simon's island,
"we were s..lly terms with the Negroes as I had never experienced
on such f..
before ..t. Simon's, a tiny black community on the Georgia coast,
had ..en largely untouched by progress because of its isolation; it
would be a rich source of folk songs, Hurston assured her coworkers.
The interracial trio rented a little shanty and sent out a call for
folksingers. "The first evening our front yard was crowded," Lomax
reported. And the crowds never let up. "They have thronged our
house by day and night ever since we have been here," he wrote to
his folklorist father, John Lomax. "They have been perfectly natural
and easy from the first on account of Zora who talks their language
and can out-nigger any of them. She swaps jokes, slaps backs, honies
up to the men a little when necessary and manages them so that they
ask us for no money, but on the other hand cooperate in the friend-
liest sort of spirit." In a week's time, the researchers had made about
forty records. They recorded children's game songs, work chants,
ring shouts, jook songs, spirituals, and ballads. "We felt when we
left St. Simon's island that we had turned back time forty or fifty
years and heard and recorded some genuine Afro-American folk-
music of the middle of the nineteenth century," Lomax informed
Oliver Strunk of the Library of Congress.

From St. Simon's, the researchers went to Eatonville, where
Hurston acquainted her white colleagues with "the finest Negro guitarist" Lomax had ever heard, "better even than Lead Belly, although
of a slightly different breed," as the folklorist put it. (Leadbelly, a.k.a.
Huddie Ledbetter, was an ex-convict whom Lomax and his father
had met at Louisiana's Angola Prison Farm. Floored by his talent as
a folksinger and guitarist, they convinced the governor to parole
him into their custody, then brought him to New York and arranged

a record deal for him. By 1935, he was a star.) After recording Eatonville's answer to Leadbelly, as well as a small collection of spirituals and work songs, the trio moved on to Belle Glade, where folk songs were "as thick as marsh mosquitoes." For the first three or four days, the researchers recorded songs from the thousands of black workers who populated the Everglades, where the soil was rich, black muck. Then Hurston introduced her colleagues to a small community of Bahamians. Lomax and Barnicle witnessed the Fire Dance and heard songs that were as close to Africa as they ever hoped to find in America. Satisfied with their work so far, the three social scientists moved on to Miami for a bit of rest.

From there, Hurston sent a tart dispatch to Edwin Embree, of the long-forgotten Rosenwald Fund, in response to a form letter requesting a report on her activities. With genuine excitement, she apprised him of her fieldwork with Lomax and Barnicle, but she did not attempt to hide the sarcasm in her tone when she told of her other recent work. She also did not try to hide the fact that she'd pulled a little bait-and-switch of her own: "I am a little tardy with this letter but life has been rushing," she began. "I want to express my appreciation for all that I was able to do under your grant. You would understand that I would not be able to do anything important towards a doctorate with a single semester of work. So I did what could amount to something. I wrote two plays, both of which have a more than even chance of being produced in the fall. I wrote the first draft of my next novel which has already been accepted by my publishers. It was six months of most intensive labor, because I considered it <u>simply must</u> count constructively."

At Hurston's suggestion, Lomax and Barnicle went on to the Bahamas for further research, but she opted not to join them. Hurston and Barnicle did not get along so well, as Lomax recalled, and their quarreling had come to a head in Eatonville, where Barnicle wanted to photograph a child eating watermelon, a ridiculously stereotypical image that Hurston simply could not abide. Of course, Zora could enjoy a good slice of watermelon as well as anyone, and she sometimes reveled in the sweet, wet taste of it, the juice running down her arms. Once, at a ritzy interracial party in New York, Zora had angered some of her fellow New Negroes by going straight for the watermelon. They viewed its inclusion on the buffet as a test of sorts, almost an insult, and had collectively vowed to abstain from the forbidden fruit. "And leave all this good watermelon for the white folks?!" Zora dissented. But her objection to Barnicle's photograph was different; there was something in the New York professor's motive that she distrusted. Though Lomax felt a deep kinship with Hurston—"we were interested in exactly the same things," he noted—he took Barnicle's side when the women argued. Barnicle was like a second mother to him, he explained, and perhaps Zora was overreacting. After all, Hurston had "a temperament as big as a house," as Lomax remembered fondly, and was "a macaw of brilliant plumage." Hurston also was "almost entirely responsible for the success" of their expedition, Lomax acknowledged.

For Hurston, though, the excursion was over. In mid-August, she returned to New York—and to Percy Punter's arms, "just as much his slave as ever," as she put it. To her dismay, the same old jealousies soon resurfaced and she and Punter again were locked in a vise of divine nights and devilish days. "Our bitterest enemies could not have contrived more exquisite torture for us," she commented.

Meanwhile, Hurston spent her first few weeks back in New York looking for work, her feet getting more tired and her spirits lower with each rejection. For a celebrated young author whose second book was about to be published, this was a difficult time; dramatically, Hurston called it "the hour of my dumb agony." In early September, though, she could sense a turnaround: "I have lived thru a horrible period of grim stagnation but I see my way out of the woods at last," she confided to Carl Van Vechten. "My mental state was such that I could neither think nor plan. . . . A love affair was going wrong too at the time. I think it is O.K. now. You know about it already." A weekend trip to the country had helped to clear her head, she said. "Honest, Carlo, I had got to the place I was talking to myself."

The Great Depression was still wreaking economic and emotional havoc on the country. Writers and other artists, particularly black ones, found it practically impossible to secure suitable work in the private sector. Fortunately, the federal government had stepped in to offer some relief. Back in 1932, Franklin D. Roosevelt had won the presidency with his promise of a "New Deal" for America. Significantly, he'd garnered an overwhelming majority of the black vote, marking the first time in the nation's history that Negro voters favored the Democratic candidate over the Republican. Black voters had maintained their loyalty to the Republican Party for decades, largely because it was the party of Lincoln, whose signing of the Emancipation Proclamation had ended slavery. "Go home and turn Lincoln's picture to the wall," the *Pittsburgh Courier* had urged before the election of '32. "The debt has been paid in full." Following the newspaper's advice, many New Negroes had helped to catapult Roosevelt into office, but they'd been disappointed by the Democrat's behavior once he'd moved into the White House. Hurston and her contemporaries found the president's refusal to sign antilynching legislation particularly disturbing.

To his credit, though, FDR had launched several relief programs that benefited many black professionals. Among them was the Works Progress Administration (later named the Work Projects Administration), whose various programs offered artists employment and the chance to earn a respectable wage. On October 1, 1935, Hurston joined the newly formed "Negro Unit" of the WPA's Federal Theatre Project in New York. As a "dramatic coach," she was paid $23.66 a week, less than the $100 a month she'd received, briefly, for her work on the Lomax-Barnicle expedition, and far less than the $200 a month she'd collected from Godmother starting in 1928.

On this small salary, however, Hurston supported herself and, for a short time, her niece and namesake. The little girl was sent to live with various relatives, including her Uncle Everett in Brooklyn, following the 1933 death of her mother, Sarah, and up until her father's remarriage around 1937. For a few months, she lived with her Aunt Zora, who—having faced the same predicament thirty years before—kindly empathized with her niece's muddled emotions. "She was very nice to me," Zora Mack recalled. Hurston cooked often for the ten-year-old and managed to buy her "the most gorgeous clothes" and lots of "beautiful things," even on her slim WPA earnings.

At work, Hurston kept company with many talented black theater people, as well as some white ones, including a youthful Orson Welles and John Houseman, who directed the Federal Theatre Project's Negro Unit in Harlem. Hurston participated in the Harlem unit's staging of its first production, *Walk Together Chillun!*, and *The New York Times* reported that her newly penned, still untitled play would be among the troupe's upcoming productions. Zora had written it, she confessed to a friend, in a week. Years later, John Houseman would remember Hurston's play as a racy adaptation of *Lysistrata*, the Aristophanes comedy in which the women of Greece pledge to withhold sex from their men until they agree to end the war. Hurston's bawdy, all-black version—which was never produced—was set in a Florida fishing village, as Houseman recalled, and it "scandalized both the Left and the Right in its saltiness."

Hurston held on to her employment with the Federal Theatre Project through the publication of *Mules and Men* that fall, but she only stayed on the job for a total of six months, despite her March 1936 promotion to "senior research worker." By April, when the Harlem unit staged its most famous production, *Macbeth*—set in nineteenth-century Haiti, with an all-black cast—Zora was not among the thousands who rushed the Lafayette Theatre to applaud the performance. Nor was she among the hundred-plus players trying to help director Orson Welles impose imaginary voodoo sensibilities onto the thickets of Shakespearean verse. Instead, Hurston was en route to the Caribbean. There—in real twentieth-century Jamaica and Haiti—she would experience things that Welles and company could scarcely fathom.

CHAPTER 25

Mules, Men, and Maroons

When *Mules and Men* was published to critical acclaim in October 1935, Zora Neale Hurston must have felt as if she could write her own ticket—to Jamaica, Haiti, or wherever else she wished to go.

With a preface by Franz Boas, and a dust jacket endorsement by Melville Herskovits, Hurston's second book inspired a plethora of praise. "A bold and beautiful book, many a page priceless and unforgettable," Carl Sandburg cheered. "To read *Mules and Men* is a rich experience," Lewis Gannett concurred in his *New York Herald Tribune* review.

Hurston's lively recounting of her fieldwork in the South in the late 1920s, *Mules and Men* is part folklore, part hoodoo chronicle, and part immersion journalism. That these disparate elements come together so seamlessly, and successfully, is a testament to the author's narrative skill.

Hurston devotes the second half of her book to describing her apprenticeships with the hoodoo masters of New Orleans, material that continues to compel even though it had been published before, in her 1931 "Hoodoo in America" article. At the core of *Mules and Men*, however, are seventy Negro folktales, gathered on Eatonville porches, in Loughman work camps, and in Polk County lying contests. But Hurston "did more than record these tales," as the black critic Henry Lee Moon noted in his *New Republic* review. "Alert and keenly observant, she studied the *mores*, folkways, and superstitions, the social and economic life of these people as an essential background for her book." As a result, *Mules and Men* was, in Boas's words, "an unusual contribution to our knowledge of the true inner life of the Negro."

Inserting herself into the narrative as a semifictional and self-effacing Zora, Hurston effects as much intimacy with the reader as she achieved with Big Sweet, Mack Ford, Luke Turner, and all the men and women who vividly populate her book. Or, as Moon put it, "the intimacy she established with her subjects, she reproduces on the printed page, enabling the reader to feel himself a part of that circle."

Like *Jonah's Gourd Vine*, *Mules and Men* offered a glimpse of what black southern life was like when white people weren't watching. "She has plunged into the social pleasures of the black community," *The New York Times* summarized, "and made a record of what is said and done when Negroes are having a good gregarious time, dancing, singing, fishing, and above all, and incessantly, talking."

It's fair to say that no book—certainly not the "Uncle Remus" tales, to which it was sometimes compared—had ever given such precedence, such loving regard, to black speech; to what black people had to say, and *how* they said it. As with *Jonah's Gourd Vine*, Hurston's skill at recording black dialect in *Mules and Men* is extraordinary. As *Times* reviewer H. I. Brock noted, "a very tricky dialect has been rendered with rare simplicity and fidelity into symbols so little adequate to convey its true value that the achievement is remarkable."

Even captious critic Sterling Brown praised Hurston's "sensitive ear." But Brown, a Washington, D.C., native who'd collected folklore in the South himself, found much to criticize in Hurston's "richly diversified" collection. Her rendition of black southern folk life was charming and authentic, as far as it went—but it did not paint a total picture, argued Brown, author of *Southern Road*, a 1932 book of poetry inspired by folk sources. Though he had not spent as much time in the field as Hurston had, Brown had noticed much "misery and exploitation," much resentment and animosity, in the black South. Yet these bitter elements were largely missing from Hurston's narrative. "There are one or two grousing references to mean cracker bosses and the chain gang," he conceded, "but little else." Hurston's informants are portrayed as "naïve, quaint, complaisant, bad enough to kill each other in jooks, but meek otherwise, socially unconscious," Brown complained. "Their life is made to appear easy-going and carefree. This . . . makes *Mules and Men* singularly *incomplete*. These people live in a land shadowed by squalor, poverty, disease, violence, enforced ignorance and exploitation. Even if browbeaten, they do know a smouldering resentment." He concluded: "*Mules and Men* should be more bitter; it would be nearer the total truth."

Although Hurston never responded directly to Brown's criticism, she might have argued that portraying black southern bitterness was not—and should not have been—part of her intent for *Mules and Men*. Of course, she was aware of racism in the South and of the kaleidoscope of black responses to it. But, in her view, the most remarkable response—the one most worth writing about—was the creative response: That is, black people's striking propensity to go on living their lives—even enjoying themselves—largely unconsumed by thoughts of some imaginary white man's foot on their neck. "We talk about the race problem a great deal," Hurston acknowledged, "but go on living and laughing and striving like everybody else." Therefore, any literature that attempted "to point out to the world fourteen million frustrated Negroes," she felt, was "insincere."

Then, too, Hurston knew there were some things white publishers would not print. She'd certainly absorbed this lesson during her protracted struggle to get *Mules and Men* published. The manuscript had been finished long before she found a publisher for *Jonah's Gourd Vine*, but Lippincott agreed to publish *Mules* only after *Jonah* was accepted; even then, the editor required Hurston to make extensive revisions to her folklore book. The kind of bitterness Brown wanted to see in *Mules and Men* would be hard-pressed to make it into print, Hurston thought, at least coming from the pen of a black author. Besides, she believed, racial bitterness was the stuff of sociology, not of folklore or of literature.

Similar criticism from Harold Preece, writing in *The Crisis*, must have struck Eatonville's daughter as particularly ignorant. The radical white critic wondered why Hurston was "devoting her literary abilities to recording the legendary amours of terrapins" while black men were being condemned to unfair prison sentences in the South. If Hurston had responded, she might have told him that she believed it was just as important to celebrate the marvels of nature and the verbal agility of her people as it was to rail against white racism and southern injustice. And she certainly would not tolerate anyone—particularly a white man—telling her what she should and should not write about.

In an otherwise insightful essay that questioned the responsibility of "professional folklorists" to the people who supplied their material, Preece, a folklorist himself, made the crucial mistake of lumping Hurston in with "a cult of sophisticates whose patronizing interest in folklore obscures the basic creative instincts of the masses." Among this "snobbish" school of folklorists, he included Roark Bradford and Julia Peterkin—white writers whom Hurston herself had criticized on similar grounds. These writers—and Hurston, too—were "more concerned with their pocketbooks than with the authentic life of the race," Preece accused, pointing out that "those who profit from Negro primitivism have an obvious interest in preserving that primitivism." Hurston was interested in preserving black folk culture—what Preece pejoratively called "primitivism"—not because it was primitive, but because it was poetic and ingenious and worthy of serious study. Chronicling and celebrating the intrinsic beauty of this culture was Hurston's main concern—not her pocketbook, which had scarcely benefited from her efforts.

In what almost became a screed against capitalism, Preece lamented the Negro's lack of economic and political power, and he urged Hurston to "cast [her] lot with the folk," as if her two years of living in southern work camps and studying with hoodoo doctors counted for nothing. Preece failed to see that Hurston—with her Eatonville background and her working-class bank account—had long ago cast her lot with the folk; in fact, she *was* the folk. And whatever educational, economic, or political gains she'd made over the years had not fundamentally changed that.

Hurston wrote about black folk life from the inside out—as a person who'd been born "in the crib of negroism." But Preece had no trouble grouping her with white collectors who mined black traditions for their own gain. "For when a Negro author describes her race with such a servile term as 'Mules and Men,'" he sniped, "critical members of the race must necessarily evaluate the author as a literary climber."

Of course, Hurston wanted literary success. What author didn't? But a "climber"? Preece's arrogant, wrongheaded criticism missed the irony of Hurston's title. A phrase like "mules and men" subtly mocked white America's determination to keep Negroes "in their place," as the saying goes. (Perhaps Preece was subconsciously engaging in this racist tradition himself, in his attempt to dictate Hurston's "place" as an author.) Black people, Hurston's title said, were *not* the ignorant beasts of burden that some whites still seemed to think they were. To the contrary, her book showed them to be imaginative storytellers, clever songwriters, gifted healers, and inventive thinkers. At the same time, though, Hurston knew that black men and women historically had embraced the mule as a brother, so to speak, because of its singular stubbornness, strength and unpredictability—attributes that an oppressed people naturally would find admirable. Titling her book *Mules and Men* was Hurston's surface way of acknowledging this affinity and of honoring the animal folktales that were so much a part of black southern lore. It also was a black writer's lyrical way of celebrating the resilience of her people—and a humorist's way of "signifying," to use the vernacular, of "putting her foot up" on notions of white cultural supremacy.

But Preece obviously didn't get it. His comments—along with Brown's insistence that *Mules and Men* should have had sharper edges—were clear examples of what Hurston saw as northerners' simplistic tendency to view black southern life as nothing more than a vale of tears. On his visit to the South in 1927, for example, Langston Hughes had been amazed at how thoroughly black folks below the Mason-Dixon line enjoyed themselves. "It seemed rather shameless to be colored and poor and happy down there at the same time," he remarked soon after his southern ramble with Hurston. "But most of the Negroes seemed to be having a grand time."

The novels and newspaper accounts of the day—especially those that emphasized the lynchings, the courtroom railroadings, and the other very real horrors of racism—offered no hint of the black joy, just as real, that existed alongside these atrocities. "There is certainly more outspoken racial prejudice in the South than elsewhere," Hurston allowed, "but it is also the place of the strongest inter-racial attachment. The situation is so contradictory, paradoxical and what not, that only a Southerner could ever understand it. And Northern

Negroes, unless they have spent years in residence and study, know no more about Negro life in the South than Northern white folks do," she asserted. "Thus a great deal of literary postures and distortion [have] come from Negro pens."

Brown and Preece might have argued that *Mules and Men* contributed to the distortion, but Hurston believed her book was a valuable, and veridical, foray into the inner lives of ordinary black folks. "While the white writers have been putting it in the street that we laugh and laugh and hold no malice," she'd written in 1934, "the Negro writers have set out to prove that we can pout." *Mules and Men*—full of laughter but deep thought, too—sought to offer a more complex view.

In any case, by the time the Brown and Preece articles were published, in February and December 1936, Hurston probably felt impervious to their criticism. She had become—with the publication of her second book and its attendant publicity—a nationally recognized authority on Negro folkways and a widely respected author to boot. In November 1935, after *Mules and Men* had been out for about a month, Fannie Hurst asked Zora for an autographed photo. And in December, when Hurston applied again for a Guggenheim fellowship, Hurst's recommendation—like all the others—was wholly enthusiastic.

Hurston's two published books "speak eloquently for themselves," Fannie Hurst wrote in her recommendation letter. "I think that the security, the leisure and the confidence that a Guggenheim Foundation scholarship would mean to Zora Hurston would immeasurably accelerate her realization of certain qualities which, I feel sure, she has not even begun to realize." Carl Van Vechten's short note was even more affirmative. "Zora Hurston is one of the most important, some might consider her the most important, of the young Negro writers," he judged. "She has an amazing talent, perhaps even genius, for the collection, selection, and creative application of folk material." Rollins College Professor Edwin Osgood Grover also sang Zora's praises. "Miss Hurston is a thorough and scientific investigator and reliable in every way," he wrote. "I know of no one of her race who is more likely to do more original or valuable research and creative work in the next ten or fifteen years."

Hurston applied for a Guggenheim to complete the fieldwork she would have done for her doctoral studies if her Rosenwald fellowship had not been revoked. But a Guggenheim grant would allow her to skip the classrooms and go straight into the field. As Hurston explained in her application, she wanted to study obeah practices in the Caribbean, but without the scientific constraints she would have faced as a Ph.D. candidate in anthropology. In fact, she did not wish to undertake her Caribbean studies as a scientific project, but "as a basis for fictional work." Specifically, she planned to "search for the Moses legends" in the Caribbean—mainly to inform a novel she was writing on the biblical figure recast as a black folk hero. Hurston had written a draft of this novel during her Rosenwald-funded semester, but she and her publisher agreed that the book, provisionally called "Moses," needed more work. In addition to polishing this novel, Hurston wanted to write a nonfiction book about Caribbean conjure practices—but for general readers, à la *Mules and Men*, not as an anthropological tome.

Given these goals—and in the aftermath of the Rosenwald fiasco—Hurston did not ask Franz Boas to write a recommendation for her. The only anthropologist among her Guggenheim references was Caribbean expert Melville Herskovits, who wrote: "I think it is not saying too much to state that Miss Hurston probably has a more intimate knowledge of Negro folk life than anyone in this country." Hurston, however, was not interested in following too closely in Herskovits's or Boas's footsteps. She wanted to use her expanding knowledge of black folk life in a literary way, rather than in a strictly scientific fashion. The combined success of *Jonah's Gourd Vine* and *Mules and Men* had led Hurston to this definitive decision, which may have disappointed Papa Franz. Nonetheless, Hurston was a writer, bona fide, and she was now turning her attention more fully to building her career as an author rather than as an anthropologist. Writing, she'd finally decided, was her first and most enduring love. From now on, she would employ her secondary career interest, anthropology, to serve what she had decided was her primary purpose: telling stories that reflected the truth, as she knew it, of black people's lives.

Further, the success of her two books had taught Hurston that these stories need not be written in drab, scientific language—even when they were classified as anthropology. She could, and would, tell her stories—fiction and nonfiction—through engaging narratives written for public consumption. "My ultimate purpose as a student," she asserted in her Guggenheim application, "is to collect for scientific scrutiny all phases of Negro folk-life and to personally produce or create fiction . . . that shall give a true picture of Negro life . . . at the same time that it entertains." Scientific scrutiny of black folk life was good and necessary, and Hurston hoped to deposit her collected material, presumably for others to access, in the libraries of the American Folk-Lore and American Ethnological Societies, she noted. But what Hurston "personally" planned to do was the work of an artist rather than a scientist.

And now, more than ever, Zora wanted to do her artist's work on the page rather than on the stage. Godmother had been right about one thing: A book was a more reliable chronicler—more of "a lasting monument" to black people, as she put it—than a theatrical production could ever be. Despite publishers' demands, writing a book also was far less collaborative than producing a play. Hurston certainly had more control over what was finally printed under her name in her two books than she had, for example, over what was staged—with her name attached—in a *Fast and Furious*. Besides, less money was required to sit down and write a *Jonah's Gourd Vine* than to organize and stage a show like *From Sun to Sun*.

Through her concerts, Hurston had been instrumental in bringing authentic black folk expression—jook songs, West Indian dances, sermons—to the public's attention. Now, other black artists (including Hall Johnson and, soon, Katherine Dunham) were also celebrating these folk sources onstage, with considerably more financial success than Hurston had achieved. "I made no real money out of my concert work," she admitted. "I might have done so if I had taken it up as a life work. But I am satisfied in knowing that I established a trend and pointed Negro expression back towards the saner ground of our own unbelievable originality."

While Hurston would never give up her interests in theater and anthropology completely, she had decided that her "life work" was literature. On the Guggenheim application form, the first question asks: "In what field of learning, or of art, does your project lie?" In her application for a 1934 fellowship, Hurston's answer was anthropology. In 1936, her answer had changed tellingly: "literary science," she wrote.

On March 16, 1936, Guggenheim Foundation secretary Henry Allen Moe informed Hurston that she had been awarded a $2,000 grant for "a study of magic practices among Negroes in the West Indies." The fellowship—almost double Hurston's WPA salary—would last for twelve months, beginning immediately. On March 18, Hurston wrote Moe a formal letter of acceptance; two days later, she resigned her job with the Federal Theatre Project and began to spread the news among her friends. "Hurrah! Zora got her Guggenheim Fellowship," Fannie Hurst gabbed to Carl Van Vechten. "Can't you see the Caribbean heaving with anticipation?" On March 30, when the fellowships were reported in the press, Zora jubilated in her "great good fortune": "I received the official announcement a few minutes ago and saw my name thru a mist," she wrote to Moe with typical ebullience. "I go to perform my vows unto God."

Hurston told Guggenheim officials she would be ready to board a steamer to Jamaica any time after April 1. She'd turned in her health certificate (all was well) and settled her business affairs in New York. Personal affairs did not wrap up so easily, however. Although Percy Punter still wanted to marry Zora, her career continued to balk "the completeness of his ideal," as she phrased it. "To me there was no conflict. My work was one thing, and he was all of the rest. But, I could not make him see that. Nothing must be in my life but himself."

Given this ongoing and elemental conflict, Zora had quietly concluded that marrying Punter was not an option. When she said good-bye to him and headed off to the Caribbean for a year of study, though, she claimed to be acting in *his* best interests. "As soon as he took his second degree, he was in line for bigger and better jobs," she observed, but Punter seemed rather disinterested in his own career. "I began to feel that our love was slowing down his efforts. . . . I grew terribly afraid that later on he would feel that I had thwarted him in a way and come to resent me. That was a scorching thought. Even if I married him, what about five years from now, the way we were going?" Hurston also knew (but never said) that in five years, she would be almost fifty years old, while Punter still would be under thirty. This knowledge, quiet as she kept it, surely impacted her decision as well.

The Guggenheim fellowship, as Hurston saw it, was "my chance to release him, and fight myself free from my obsession. He would get over me in a few months and go on to be a very big man." With this justification, Zora said a hasty farewell to her beloved and sailed off to the Caribbean. "But I freely admit that everywhere I set my feet down, there were tracks of blood. Blood from the very middle of my heart," she declared. "I did not write because if I had written and he answered my letter, everything would have broken down."

Punter told a different story. Hurston was possessed of an "almost priestly" devotion to her work, he believed, and she fully understood what her career demanded. Her work was her master, and she followed its commands obediently, as would any faithful disciple. As a mere man, Punter simply could not compete. Zora may have "cried on the inside" when she left him, he said, but he never saw any tears.

On Monday, April 13, Hurston touched land in Haiti, where she introduced herself to government officials and made plans for returning to the small island nation in September. From her Port-au-Prince pit stop, she mailed a postcard to Carl Van Vechten seeming to confirm Punter's perception that she had little trouble walking away from their love and turning her mind to other matters: Promising to write Carlo at length from Jamaica, Zora noted, "Weather fine, men plentiful."

Hurston arrived in Jamaica, about 160 miles southwest of Haiti, on April 14. Perhaps feeling a bit distrustful because of her Rosenwald experience, she immediately went to the Barclays Bank in Kingston to make sure Guggenheim officials had wired her funds for the trip. Once she found everything in order, she relaxed and set about the task of gathering material—"with the eye to a good book, not necessarily a scientific one." Within a few days, Hurston made headlines. "U.S. Woman on Hoodoo Hunt in Jamaica," the Kingston *Daily Gleaner* reported on April 24. The story featured a photo of Hurston outfitted—in jodhpurs and riding boots—for a sally into the backwoods, or "the bush," as Jamaicans called it. By the first week of May, Hurston had begun "to gather material wholesale," she reported to Moe. It wasn't difficult to do, she'd found: "Just squat down awhile and after that things begin to happen."

Hurston's initial impressions of Jamaica—still a British colony—were mixed. After a short time in Kingston, she left the capital city for St. Andrew's parish and later for St. Mary's, where she delighted in the lush greenery, the majestic mountains, and the luminous sea. At the same time, though, Hurston was disturbed by the intraracial color prejudices she witnessed in Jamaica, especially among the "coloured people"—the light-skinned elite who "feel like suing you if you call them Negroes," as she put it. "I have corrected several who called me a <u>coloured</u> person," she noted after less than a month on the island. "They wonder why we insist on being Negroes."

Recognizing that "it takes many generations for the slave derivatives to get over their awe for the master-kind," Hurston was nevertheless dismayed by what she saw as the "frantic stampede white-ward" on the part of Jamaican "mixed bloods." What they most wanted, it seemed to her, was "to escape from Jamaica's black mass"—even to the point of identifying themselves as white on census records, despite all outward appearances.

Equally disturbing to Hurston was the way women were widely viewed as nothing more than instruments for men's pleasure. One man Zora met in St. Mary's did not hesitate to expound upon this perspective. Women who pursued careers "were just so much wasted material," and American women "were destroyed by their brains," he contended. "Oh, these wisdom-wise Western women, afraid of their function in life, are so tiresomely useless! We men do not need your puny brains to settle the affairs of the world," he told Zora. "The truth is, it is yet to be proved that you have any."

Hurston argued with the man for much of an afternoon but, being a woman, never came close to changing his mind. She did, however, manage to extract from him some intriguing information for her research. There were "specialists" in Jamaica, he told her, who prepared young brides for their wedding nights—and for what was considered their true purpose in life: pleasing their men. These specialists were always women and were usually elderly widows. Hurston arranged to observe the work of one of these hush-hush practitioners for two weeks. During this time, she witnessed young virgins undergoing *Kama Sutra*–type training in the art of sexual pleasure. "The wish is to bring complete innocence and complete competence together in the same girl," Hurston summarized. "She is being educated for her life work under the experts."

For days, Hurston observed as the specialist instructed her

teenage trainee on bedroom posture and muscular control "inside her body and out," as Zora put it. "This also was rehearsed again and again, until it was certain that the young candidate had grasped all that was meant." On the trainee's wedding day—the final day of her studies—Hurston watched the specialist give her student a hot herbal bath, a homoerotic ritual designed to prime the young woman for receiving her husband with utmost eagerness. The old woman massaged the girl from head to toe with a fragrant oil—"the very odor of seduction," Hurston decided—then manipulated her body until the girl swooned. Finally, the preceptor reminded the bride of all she'd learned, then sent her to her groom with these words: "You are made for love and comfort. Think of yourself in that way and no other. . . . That is all that men ever want women for, love and softness and peace, and you must not fail him."

While Hurston may have learned a few sensual tips from the old instructor, she was not persuaded to adopt what seemed to be the island's prevailing attitude toward women. "It is a curious thing to be a woman in the Caribbean after you have been a woman in these United States," she remarked. "You meet a lot of darkish men who make vociferous love to you, but otherwise pay you no mind." Given the country's color politics, dark-skinned women bore the heaviest load of oppression, Hurston observed. If a woman was poor and black, "she had better pray to the Lord to turn her into a donkey and be done with the thing," Zora commented sarcastically. "It is assumed that God made poor black females for beasts of burden, and nobody is going to interfere with providence."

Because of her status as a visiting American, though, Hurston was treated a bit differently from her Jamaican counterparts. In St. Mary's parish, for example, a goat was cooked in her honor for a curry goat feed—an elaborate moonlight feast that had never before been offered for a woman. At the same time, a respected Jamaican medicine man welcomed Hurston as a student, and people began to seek her out to tell her things. Twice, she participated in "Nine Night" ceremonies, designed to keep the dead in their graves lest they do harm to the living. At these rituals, usually held on the ninth night after death, men and women warmly welcomed the spirit of the dead—"the duppy"—and sang to it, danced for it, then bade it farewell forever. At one ceremony, the dancing was so rapturous,

Hurston noted, that it felt as if the drums had become people and the people had become drums. By mid-May, she reported to the Guggenheim Foundation that Jamaican chauvinism had not prevented her from collecting "a gracious plenty."

Hurston got a bitter taste of what it was like to be a poor black woman in Jamaica, however, when she lost her letter of credit and all her cash on May 19. Zora had met and befriended a group of Maroons, descendants of warriors who fought their way out of slavery and successfully resisted all attempts to reenslave them. They still governed themselves in an isolated community—just the kind of find that any anthropologist would want. Having secured permission to live among the Maroons in Accompong, Hurston rushed back to Kingston to get enough money for her stay in the "Maroontown" settlement. She withdrew $100 from the Barclays Bank, then placed the money and her identification papers in a large wallet. Before leaving, though, she attempted to deposit her letter of credit at the bank for safekeeping, but the managers refused to accept responsibility for it.

Annoyed, Zora placed the credit letter in her wallet, along with her other valuables, and went to a Kingston beauty shop for a haircut, clutching her belongings closely all the while. From the hair salon, she walked half a block to a restaurant for a bowl of soup, resting her wallet on the table while she dined alone. She then paid her tab and went out to hail a taxi. As soon as she took her seat, though, she realized the wallet was gone. Hurston stopped the car, went back to the restaurant, and summoned her waiter and the restaurant manager; no one had seen the wallet. Immediately, she went to the police as well as to the bank. Although bank personnel could identify her on sight, they refused to give her any more money from her Guggenheim account until she could produce the letter of credit. Borrowing money from a friend on May 21, Hurston cabled the Guggenheim office in New York: "CREDIT LETTER LOST PENNILESS BANKS WARNED."

Henry Allen Moe, the foundation's director, was out of town when Hurston's desperate dispatch arrived, so it took him two days to respond. On May 23, he wired Hurston twenty-five dollars to tide her over until other arrangements could be made, but her days of destitute waiting had been tormenting. While dealing with the dismissive response of bank officials, Zora worried that her bad luck might mean the end of her fellowship. "I am the most unhappy person in the world because I fear your organization may feel that I am too much trouble to bother with," she wrote to Moe after her cable had gone unanswered for more than a day. Offering a reward for the return of her valuables, she even convinced the *Daily Gleaner* to print a story about her misfortune: "Visiting Lady Writer Loses Letter of Credit and £19 in Cash," the newspaper announced.

By the first of June, Moe had sent Hurston a check for $100 and arranged for a new letter of credit. Because she'd vowed to never set foot in the Barclays Bank again, the Guggenheim Foundation agreed to send her paperwork to a more accommodating financial institution. Though Hurston was convinced her wallet had been stolen, she gave up hope that police would ever find the thief. She also continued to apologize to Moe for being "so much trouble" to the Guggenheim Foundation. "I feel that I have no talents whatsoever in money and business matters," she allowed. "I get too thoroughly immersed in my dreams. But somehow life is so organized that I find myself tied to money matters like a grazing horse to a stake."

Moe responded kindly, urging Hurston to move forward with her work. "Don't feel so sad and don't be so apologetic!" he advised. "The first day I ever had a letter of credit I lost it; but I was lucky and I got it back again. So I don't myself feel at all superior to anyone who had such a document stolen." Then he added: "Your material, at this distance, looks grand. Go to it."

Hurston's next letter to Moe, written a week later, indicated she'd taken his advice. Her collecting work in the bush was going so well, she reported, that she was already thinking of how she might organize her material. "It has occurred to me to make a collection of all the subtle poisons that Negroes know how to locate among the bush and the use of which they are so expert. No one outside of the hoodoo or bush doctors know these things. But as I am learning day by day more and more I think that I will be doing medical science a great service to identify these weeds so that antidotes can be prepared. The greatest power of voodoo rests upon this knowledge." Confessing her own fascination with this powerful information, she added: "Some of these 'bushes' are quite marvelous. One of them I <u>know</u> will kill by being placed so that the wind will blow from it to the victim. Another can be rubbed on the clothing and enters thru the pores as soon as the victim sweats."

Hurston spent three more months in Jamaica, passing much of this time with the Maroons in Accompong, where, she discovered, "so many weird and wonderful things still happen." The Maroons lived high up in the mountains of St. Catherine and their leader sent a mule to transport Zora up to the highest peaks. But the mule—as stubborn as those Hurston had met in the American South—refused to cooperate. "The only thing that kept her from throwing me was the fact that I fell off first. And the only thing that kept her from kicking me, biting me and trampling me under foot after I fell off was the speed with which I got away after the fall," Zora recalled. With the help of an attendant, she finally made it onto the mule's back, but not for long. "I was the one who felt we might be sisters under the skin," Hurston mused. "She corrected all of that about a half mile down the trail and so I had to climb that mountain into Accompong on my own two legs."

After the arduous struggle to get there, Hurston was disheartened to learn that Melville Herskovits had recently sent another of his protégés, Katherine Dunham, to live among the Maroons in Accompong. "She had been there for a month," Hurston learned, "but had done nothing that anyone could take account of." Deciding that Dunham's lack of experience nullified her as a real competitor, Hurston went on with her collecting, which, at first, meant simply living among the people. The Maroons offered to stage various rituals for her, but she declined. "If I do not see a dance or a ceremony in its natural setting and sequence, I do not bother," she explained. "Self-experience has taught me that those staged affairs are never the same as the real thing."

Hurston saw plenty of the real thing when she began studying with the Maroons' chief conjure doctor, whom she identified only as Medicine Man. One night, he astonished her by commanding the thousands of croaking frogs in the bush to hush. The frogs "ceased chirping as suddenly as a lightning flash," Hurston would remember. As if nothing unusual had occurred, Medicine Man continued instructing Hurston about the powers and perils of this and that plant until she stopped him. "I had to listen to this sudden silence for a while."

Another time, Hurston instigated a hunt for a wild boar. She joined Medicine Man and other Maroons in search of a hog to kill for the fabulous jerk pork she'd heard so much about and had begun to crave. With dogs in tow, food for several days, cooking utensils, and weapons, the hunting party left before dawn. Carrying their own guns and blades, the lean hunters walked for hours without rest. "I stumbled along with my camera and note book," Hurston reported, "and a few little womanish things like comb and tooth brush and a towel." As the countryside became more rocky and full of jagged edges, she began to wonder why she'd insisted on coming along. Though Zora had flunked physical education at Howard in 1923, she was now fit enough, at age forty-five, to keep up. But by the time the hunters stopped for food, her boots were chafing her heels and her whole body was sore. Yet she dared not reveal her tiredness to the men, who marched on vigorously, refreshed by their brief break.

On the night of the third day, the hunters found their hog, and Hurston came face-to-face with it. "I had never pictured anything so huge, so fierce nor so fast," she recalled. After a bit of struggle, the men subdued the beast and began to make a fire. As the pig cooked all night, the men told stories and sang songs. Near morning, the group feasted on jerk pork then packed up what was left to share with friends and family. As they began the long trek back to Accompong, with the men singing songs of victory, Hurston's "blistered feet told me time and time again that we would never get there," she recollected, "but we finally did." Once her feet were healed, she looked back on the hog hunt and judged it "one of the most exciting things in the Western world."

As Hurston prepared to leave Jamaica on September 22 for the second half of her trip—six months in Haiti—she felt pleased with all the material she'd collected. Convinced that the Maroons were "worth a year's study in themselves," she nevertheless felt that her time in Jamaica had been most productive. She'd lived in every parish and had become acquainted with a wide range of people. "I have seen things!" she assured Moe. Noting that barely a week passed in Kingston when someone wasn't prosecuted for witchcraft, Hurston decided that Jamaica was "a seething Africa under its British exterior."

As thrilling as her Jamaican studies were, Hurston found the complex voodoo beliefs of Haiti almost overwhelming. Within three weeks of her September 23 arrival in the capital city of Port-au-Prince, she wrote to Moe asking if she might apply for a second Guggenheim fellowship to continue her studies there. "I know that thousands of other people want a chance, but I want another one too. There is so much to write about in these waters," she explained. "If I cease gathering material now and write, I will miss a great deal that I came for. If I continue to collect until March, I shall have no time to write. I have considered this dilemma a great deal recently. Nobody realizes more than I what a wonderful thing has happened to me. I have grown in every direction in these six months."

After a short time at the Hotel Bellevue, Hurston rented a house in the suburbs of Port-au-Prince, where she was aided and protected by her kind and trustworthy maid, Lucille. Within a few months, the unflagging researcher had honed her Creole, acquired a working knowledge of the major voodoo gods of Haiti, met several priests of the path, and found eight "authentic cases" to prove that zombies were real.

Remarkably, Hurston wrote during this period as well. In Jamaica, she'd thrown herself into her research so fiercely because she wished to "smother" her feelings for Percy Punter—and her remorse over the abrupt way she'd ended their relationship. In Haiti, though, she realized that her emotions had not been smothered at all; they'd simply been "dammed up" inside her. On the shores of the celestial blue sea, Zora's flimsy emotional embankments gave way, releasing a flood of feelings that forced her to sit down and write—sometimes late at night after a strenuous day of collecting. Under "internal pressure," she started writing a novel, working urgently for days on end. All the while, her love for Punter stayed on her mind. "The plot was far from the circumstances," she noted, "but I tried to embalm all the tenderness of my passion for him" in the writing. In seven weeks, Hurston finished her second novel. She called it *Their Eyes Were Watching God*.

CHAPTER 26

A Glance from God

Hurston completed *Their Eyes Were Watching God* on December 19, 1936, mailed the manuscript to her publisher, and immediately sailed to La Gonave—an enchanted Haitian island lying in a horseshoe bay to the west of Port-au-Prince. According to local legend, La Gonave was really a whale who lingered so long in the sea that he became an island. The way the Haitians told the story, their ancestors prayed to Damballah—the Great Source—for peace and prosperity. Moved by their prayers, Damballah sent one of his wives, the goddess Cilla, with a message for the Haitian people. She rode to her destination on the back of a whale, who carried her so gently that she fell asleep, never realizing she'd arrived at Haiti's shore. From certain vistas in Port-au-Prince, some people said, you could still see Madame Cilla sleeping on the whale-shaped island, the formula for peace resting in her folded hands.

Zora found La Gonave to be every bit as serene as the legend held. Its dramatic scenery and cultural isolation delighted her, making her feel as if she were "in the heart of Africa for all outward signs." At night, the Caribbean Sea "glowed like one vast jewel," she observed, and "the moonlight tasted like wine." On La Gonave, Zora would recall, she experienced "a peace I have never known anywhere else on earth."

Hurston spent the holidays in the remote lushness of La Gonave, sharing stewed goat with the chief of police on Christmas Day. She-found the island's policemen friendly and entertaining and she spent her days chatting with them, as well as with the Haitian peasants, who taught her some traditional folk games and told stories about Ti Malice, the country's famous trickster.

By the first week of January, Hurston knew she would have to spend many more months in Haiti before she could ever hope to understand the vast complexities of voodoo, which she respectfully defined as "the old, old mysticism of the world in African terms." Even writing a letter about her voodoo studies proved daunting: "It is like explaining the planetary theory on a postage stamp," she decided.

Despite the challenge, Hurston sweated out a three-page report on her activities and a formal appeal to the Guggenheim Foundation for a renewal of her fellowship. "I am not starved with a paucity of material as is usual," she explained, "but flooded with so much that I realize the task is huge, so huge and complicated that it flings out into space more fragments than would form the whole of any other area except Africa." Hurston was only just beginning to grasp all that voodoo was—and wasn't. "It is more than the sympathetic magic that is practised by the hoodoo doctors in the United States," she judged. "It is as formal as the Catholic church anywhere."

Hurston also revealed that her voodoo studies had begun to test her own beliefs. "No I have not been converted locally," she assured her Guggenheim backers, "tho I am not a christian either." This was a bold admission for Hurston to make in a letter asking for a continuation of her funding, but she had been deeply affected by her experiences in Haiti. "Voodoo is a religion of creation and life," she'd come to understand. "It is the worship of the sun, the water and other natural forces, but the symbolism is no better understood than that of other religions and consequently is taken too literally."

Hurston did not pretend to understand voodoo well enough to explain it to anyone just yet. But she was confident she could get a handle on it with intensive study—even though she recognized the job ahead of her was "a hundred times bigger" than she'd ever imagined. Still, the task was crying out for her to do it, she told Henry Allen Moe. "I beg the opportunity to finish what I have begun."

From La Gonave, Hurston went to Archahaie, which she described as "the greatest place known in Haiti for Voodoo." There, she studied with Dieu Donnez St. Leger, one of the area's greatest voodoo priests, or *houngans*. He instructed his chief priestess, or *mambo*, to take Hurston step-by-step through various rituals and to teach her the songs and dances of every ceremony. In this way, Hurston spent a good deal of time with Mambo Etienne, who was in charge of the daily operations of the hundred-member compound.

Dieu Donnez had inherited the priesthood from his father; as a hereditary *houngan*, he was widely respected throughout Haiti, and rituals were held in his compound almost every day. Hurston participated in the ceremonies fully and was allowed to watch the *houngan* heal the sick and, one time, raise the dead. On that occasion, another *houngan*—recently deceased—was brought to Dieu Donnez for a ceremony in which he would pass his power on to his successor. After a sacrifice of pigeons and chickens, and after Dieu Donnez had whispered the proper incantations, the dead man sat up, Hurston reported, opened his eyes, and nodded his head. The ceremony was a success: the deity, or *loa*, that lived inside the dead man had been separated from him, so the deceased *houngan* could rest in peace and the *loa* could be employed by someone else.

Dieu Donnez was an educated and literate man. All of his lectures were written and he instructed Zora in a gentle, businesslike manner, drawing the signatures of the *loa* on the ground and demanding that she copy them until he was satisfied with her progress as a pupil. Witnessing a gamut of ceremonies, possessions, and sacrifices, Hurston studied with Dieu Donnez until her Guggenheim money— and thus her time in Haiti—ran out. "Haiti is so thrillingly real and unreal that I have wished that the whole twelve months had been spent there," she said, looking back on her year in the Caribbean. "But still I would not have missed what I saw in Jamaica for anything."

When Hurston returned to New York in March, she learned that Lippincott planned to publish *Their Eyes Were Watching God* in the fall. As with *Jonah's Gourd Vine*, her editor had found little need for revisions. Hurston's words and sentences seemed to flow "with no effort," Bertram Lippincott recalled. "She was a natural writer."

From Hurston's perspective, however, she expended a great deal of effort on her writing—and was rarely satisfied with the results. Invariably, an "ideal of achievement" seemed just beyond her grasp. "Always there is the hope that I shall confine it in the written word," she commented while reading the final proofs of *Their Eyes Were Watching God*. "So far my fingers have not touched its garments. But when one has a burning bush inside, one keeps on trying, whether or not."

The Guggenheim Foundation renewed Hurston's fellowship in March 1937, but a passport delay prevented her from returning to Haiti until May. Traveling on the Panama steamship line, she enjoyed good food, a large cabin, and a pleasant voyage. When the steamer deposited her in Port-au-Prince on May 23, however, she found Haiti drowning in seasonal rains. The downpour hindered Hurston only slightly; as soon as the roads were deemed safe, she resumed her voodoo quest with great enthusiasm. By the first week of July, her research had succeeded beyond her own expectations, she reported to Moe. But, she added ominously, "there have been repercussions."

By now, Zora had spent several months in Haiti seeing and feeling things. During both her trips, she'd found the Haitian people to be "drenched in kindliness and beaming out with charm." She'd consumed sizable quantities of the native dish of jean-jean and rice and she'd witnessed a ritual where people cooked food without fire— using prayers and songs and a family secret that they dared not divulge. She'd spent hours sprawled upon the porch swings of Dr. Reser, a white American who'd become a respected *houngan* after finding "his soul and his peace," as Hurston put it, "in the African rituals of Haiti." She'd attended numerous ceremonies in which *houngans* invoked Jesus, Mary, Joseph, and a long list of Christian saints right alongside the *loa* of the voodoo pantheon. She'd joined the people of Haiti, high and low, for an annual pilgrimage to a sacred waterfall, where she'd been moved by their worship of God in Nature. She'd slept under the trees and the stars and she'd been awakened by the crowing of roosters and the delicate dawn wind. Regarding voodoo as "a religion no more venal, no more impractical than any other," Hurston had even become an initiate herself. After being claimed by a certain *loa*—a spirit she declined to name—Hurston went through the necessary ceremonies and was consecrated as a *hounci*, the first step toward priesthood. She was preparing to "go Canzo"—to undergo the second degree of initiation—when friends began to caution her in hushed but insistent tones.

As a foreign woman traveling alone, Hurston needed to be careful about picking acquaintances among the *houngans*, one friend had advised early on. "You are liable to get involved in something that is not good. You must have someone to guide you." Hurston laughed off this initial warning, but others followed. One night, her live-in maid, Lucille, actually stood guard in the doorway to prevent her inquisitive employer from seeking out the source of a certain drum. Because Lucille had been supportive of her previous efforts to study voodoo, Hurston pressed the housekeeper for an explanation. "Some things are very dangerous to see, Mademoiselle," Lucille told Hurston. "There are many good things for you to learn. I am well content if you do not run to every drum you hear."

There were two kinds of voodoo gods, Hurston had learned. The Rada gods—under the command of Damballah, the Almighty— were high and pure and did only good things for people; all they required of their devotees in the way of sacrifice were chickens and pigeons. The Petro gods, on the other hand, were wicked, but also powerful and quick. They could be made to do good as well as evil, so people often solicited them for health, wealth, and other things that seemed impossible to achieve solely by human striving. The Petro gods granted big favors but demanded huge sacrifices: dogs, hogs, cows, and, some said, human beings. Just as there were different classes of gods, there were different kinds of priests. A real and true priest of voodoo, a *houngan*, only did good work, some people believed. But there were also *bocors*, priests who did great harm. Some priests "worked with two hands," Hurston's friends cautioned, so it was not always easy to tell who was a *houngan* and who was a *bocor*. "Often," Hurston came to know, "the two offices occupy the same man at different times."

Perhaps the most terrifying work of the *bocor* was the business of turning people into zombies. Hurston had come face-to-face with a zombie at a Haitian hospital. She had even been allowed to photograph the dreadful-looking woman, the first picture ever taken of one of "the living dead," as zombies were called. The woman Hurston photographed had been brought to the hospital after wandering onto a farm that she claimed once belonged to her father. After some commotion, the farm boss identified the woman—despite her blank face and lifeless eyes—as his sister, who had died and been buried nearly thirty years before. The doctors believed a *bocor* had given the woman a drug to simulate death, then summoned her out of her grave with an antidote. Both the drug and the antidote were known to only a few, probably a secret brought from Africa and handed down from generation to generation, the physicians speculated. The drug destroyed parts of the brain that governed speech and willpower, so that when the apparently dead person was "resurrected," he usually could not speak or form independent thoughts. But the zombie could work tirelessly in the fields of his owner and be put to use as a thief.

The doctors longed to know the secret of the drug, they said, because the revelation would render a great service to Haiti—where zombies were not uncommon—and to medical science generally. Ever fearless, Hurston volunteered to do everything she could to unearth the secret of the drug. At this, she received her sternest admonition yet—and from one of Haiti's leading physicians: "Perhaps it will cost you more than you are willing to pay, perhaps things will be required of you that you cannot stand," he cautioned. "Suppose you were forced to—could you endure to see a human being killed? . . . Perhaps one's humanity and decency might prevent one from penetrating very far. Many Haitian intellectuals have curiosity but they know if they go to dabble in such matters, they may disappear permanently. But leaving possible danger aside, they have scruples."

Heeding the doctor's warning, Hurston backed off from investigating the mysteries of how zombies were made, but she otherwise persisted with her research. In late June, though, she suddenly took ill. "It seems that some of my destinations and some of my accessions have been whispered into ears that heard," she reported to New York. "In consequence, just as mysteriously as the information travelled, I HAVE HAD A VIOLENT GASTRIC DISTURBANCE." For two weeks, Hurston was unable to leave her bed under her own power. "For a whole day and a night, I thought I'd never make it," she admitted. Deeply shaken, she arranged to be carried into Port-au-Prince and taken to the bank, where she withdrew enough money to pay her way back to the States when, and if, she became well enough to travel. She took the money to the American consul for safekeeping; shocked by her condition, he insisted she convalesce at his home. "I am sleeping and eating at his house now," she told Henry Allen Moe in early July.

Hurston was convinced that her illness and her research were directly related. She had noticed long ago that many Haitians seemed to regard unsolicited food with great suspicion. They seemed ever alert to the possibility of poisoning. Yet Hurston had not been very careful about where she ate—even after she learned that hair from the tail of a horse, when chopped fine and put in someone's food, could fill that person's stomach and intestines with sores. This effect resulted not so much from some supernatural power, but simply from ingesting all the germs of the horse's hair. Similarly, *houngans* and *mambos* knew which plants, spiders, and worms were poisonous, and they knew how to slip these ingredients undetected into the food of those they wished to harm or scare—including foreigners who might go off and say bad things about Haiti.

With this in mind—and while lying on her sickbed—Hurston decided to retreat from her rigorous investigation of voodoo; she'd learned enough. "I am <u>extremely pleased</u> with the progress of the work so far," she assured Moe. "But I know that I could not survive a repetition of alimentary infection and so . . . with your permission, I shall do my polishing on American soil." Moe responded at once: "You have complete liberty to return to the United States whenever you wish and I should urge you, if your health is in question, to take no chances at all."

By mid-August, though, Hurston had recovered her health and resumed some of the less perilous aspects of her research. Now, she was in the central plains of Haiti—"in a hot-bed of what I want," as she put it. Mostly, she was reviewing and verifying the material she'd gathered already and tying up loose ends. But she was still active on the voodoo trail: An event was taking place there on September 18, for example, that she "would not miss for anything," not even the publication of *Their Eyes Were Watching God* on the sixteenth. Her plan was to sail back to the States on September 22, stop off in New York, then head to Florida to write. The material she'd gathered in Haiti was engulfing her, she said, and she was anxious to get it down on paper: "It is swelling up in me like a jeenie in a bottle, or like southern Negroes would put it, like a barrel of molasses in the summertime."

When Hurston returned to New York the fourth week of September, she found her name on an assortment of tongues. Lippincott had just published *Their Eyes Were Watching God* and the critics were lapping it up. On Zora's first Sunday back in the city, the *New York Herald Tribune* ran a dreamy review. *Their Eyes Were Watching God* was "a lovely book" by "an author who writes with her head as well as with her heart," critic Sheila Hibben opined.

The same day, *The New York Times* ran an equally complimentary review. "This is Zora Hurston's third novel, again about her own people—and it is beautiful," Lucille Tomkins declared. Calling the book—actually, Hurston's *second* novel—a "well nigh perfect story," the reviewer added (for skeptical white readers): "It is about Negroes, and a good deal of it is written in dialect, but really it is about everyone, at least every one who isn't so civilized that he has lost the capacity for glory."

Their Eyes Were Watching God is the story of Janie Crawford, a deep-thinking, deep-feeling black woman who embarks on a quest for her own self. Janie is raised by her grandmother, Nanny, an ex-slave who hopes to fulfill through Janie her own broken dreams "of whut a woman oughta be and to do." She tells Janie: "Ah wanted to preach a great sermon about colored women sittin' on high, but they wasn't no pulpit for me. Freedom found me wid a baby daughter in mah arms, so Ah said Ah'd take a broom and a cook-pot and throw up a highway through de wilderness for her. She would expound what Ah felt. But somehow she got lost offa de highway and next thing Ah knowed here you was in de world. So whilst Ah was tendin' you of nights Ah said Ah'd save de text for you. Ah been waitin' a long time, Janie, but nothin' Ah been through ain't too much if you just take a stand on high ground lak Ah dreamed."

Nanny works for a family of "quality white folks" and raises Janie along with the white children she is paid to care for. Janie spends so much time with these children that she doesn't even know she's black until she sees a picture of herself, when she's about six years old. Hurston does not portray Janie's discovery as devastating; it is simply a metaphor for her lack of self-awareness. It illustrates, as well, how unrealistic Nanny's attempts are to shield her grand-daughter from the real world.

To Nanny's dismay, Janie's womanhood comes on quickly. When

she catches the sixteen-year-old kissing a boy she deems "shiftless" and "trashy," Nanny sits Janie down to educate her on the facts of life: "Honey, de white man is de ruler of everything as fur as Ah been able tuh find out. . . . So de white man throw down de load and tell de nigger man tuh pick it up. He pick it up because he have to, but he don't tote it. He hand it to his womenfolks. De nigger woman is de mule uh de world so fur as Ah can see." From Nanny's perspective, the only way Janie can hope to escape her fate as a beast of burden is to have the protection of good white folks or a good man. Soon before she dies, then, Nanny marries her granddaughter off to Logan Killicks, a man with sixty acres, a mule, and a pone of fatback on his neck that Janie despises. "She knew now that marriage did not make love," Hurston writes. "Janie's first dream was dead, so she became a woman."

When Logan begins to speak harshly to Janie and threatens to buy a second mule so she can help with his farm work, Nanny's metaphor is almost made literal. But Janie rebels and runs off with Joe Starks, a citified fellow with big dreams and a big voice. Joe takes Janie to Eatonville, where he soon becomes mayor, postmaster, and primary landowner. The kind of man who has "uh throne in de seat of his pants," Joe does not represent "sun-up and pollen and blooming trees," but he buys Janie the best of everything and gives her a comfortable, if unromantic, existence.

Working in Joe's store, Janie is fascinated by the lively stories the townsfolk tell on the store porch. She even thinks of some stories herself, but Joe forbids her to indulge in the "picture talk," reminding her of her station in life: "You'se Mrs. Mayor Starks, Janie. I god, Ah can't see what uh woman uh yo' sability would want tuh be treasurin' all dat gum-grease from folks dat don't even own de house dey sleep in."

Joe's gloating self-importance cows the town and his supercilious chauvinism cows Janie. "No matter what Jody did, she said nothing," Hurston writes. "She had learned how to talk some and leave some. She was a rut in the road. Plenty of life beneath the surface but it was kept beaten down by the wheels." The years take the fight out of Janie's face, but not out of her spirit; she finally reacts to Joe's constant derision with a public, verbal revolt. A short time later, Joe dies, bitterly, leaving Janie an attractive widow with property and money in the bank.

Soon, the forty-year-old Janie meets and falls in love with Tea Cake, a free-spirited laborer and gambler much younger than herself. For Janie, Tea Cake is sweet talk, strawberries, and laughter; he is "a glance from God." Tea Cake matches Janie's love; in his view, she holds "de keys to de kingdom." Even after they marry, Tea Cake treats Janie as his equal: he urges her to play checkers with him, teaches her to drive, and dares her to "have de nerve to say whut you mean." With Tea Cake, Janie is free to become herself.

Leaving Eatonville's wagging tongues behind, Janie follows her young husband from job to job. Eventually, they move to the Everglades, where they join other seasonal workers picking beans from the rich black soil of "the muck." Working side by side, Janie and Tea Cake romp and play behind the white boss's back, then come home and make supper together in their perfectly organic union. Meanwhile, their house becomes a gathering spot for the community, a place where all their working-class friends come in the evenings to play cards, to sing, and to tell stories. And Janie is an integral, vocal member of this community.

Janie and Tea Cake's almost-ideal life comes to an abrupt end, however, after they barely escape a horrible hurricane. Trying to protect Janie, Tea Cake is bitten by a rabid dog, but he is largely unaware of his illness until it devolves into madness. In this state, he tries to kill Janie. In self-defense, she kills Tea Cake instead. After being acquitted of murder, Janie returns to Eatonville and tells her story to her friend Phoeby. Despite her tragic loss, Janie's tale is ultimately triumphant: She has been to the horizon and back, and she has acquired the verbal power to tell all about her journey. In fact, Janie sitting on her own porch, telling her own story, is the narrative frame on which Hurston hangs her novel.

No matter how detailed, a plot summary fails to do justice to *Their Eyes Were Watching God*. It is a book that has to be read, and felt, to be fully appreciated. Or, as Janie tells Phoeby: "you got tuh *go* there tuh *know* there."

In *Their Eyes Were Watching God*, Zora Neale Hurston ransacked the language—the King's English as well as Eatonville's Ebonics—to achieve a precision of expression that was stunning. For more than fifteen years, Hurston had been working to capture in words the beauty, the wisdom, and the complexity of her people and of her

Eatonville experience. In *Their Eyes Were Watching God*, she nailed it. Significantly, she did so by making a crucial revision to her memories of the village: In all her previous attempts to depict Eatonville in fiction, the porch sitters—the storytellers—had been mostly men. In this novel, however, Hurston put her story in the mouth and the mind of a woman—and the result is a book of transcendent appeal.

At heart, *Their Eyes Were Watching God* is a love story, inspired by Hurston's relationship with Percy Punter. But Tea Cake is not Punter and Janie is not Zora Neale Hurston. To be sure, Hurston imbued Janie with some of the questing quality that characterized her own life. But Janie is more conventional than Hurston ever was; consequently, she seeks her identity, her selfhood, in the eyes and arms of men. Hurston, on the other hand, sought her identity in her own self, in her work, in writing and speaking her mind. Not coincidentally, the capacity to know her own mind—and to speak it—is a large part of what Janie seeks in the novel, and eventually finds.

Because Hurston placed Janie on the road to self-realization, autonomy, and independence, *Their Eyes Were Watching God* has been hailed as a feminist novel. Whether Hurston saw it that way or not, she certainly used its pages to convey what to her was a given: that women are the equals of men in every way—and that their inner lives are infinitely rich and worthy of exploration. She also wrote about some of the resistances to this point of view: namely, men's sexism and women's collaboration with that sexism.

All the men in Hurston's novel, including Tea Cake, are sexist to varying degrees. And Janie is constantly called upon to assert her autonomy in the face of their ideas about the kind of woman she ought to be. The most problematic and complex of these confrontations occurs in her relationship with Tea Cake. In a plot twist that some readers have found incongruous, Tea Cake slaps Janie around a bit to show her—and everyone on the muck—who's boss. Hurston appears to let this disturbing incident go, without critical comment. When read closely, though, this is the point where Hurston hints that Janie and Tea Cake's marriage is doomed. In fact, the hurricane that demolishes their paradise occurs in the very next chapter. A parallel can be drawn from Hurston's own life: When the man she loved hit her, she did not immediately order him to get out. Instead, by her own account, she tried to take responsibility for the fight. Yet a part of her knew, in that very moment, that the relationship could not last. In the same way, a careful reader gets the subtle sense that Hurston will not let Tea Cake get away with "whipping" Janie, even if Janie will. Thus, the awful moment when Janie is forced to kill Tea Cake—in defense of her own life—is inevitable.

Marriage, Hurston seems to say, is a deadly proposition: someone has to give up his or her life. In most cases, it would be a figurative giving up, with the woman subordinating her life to the man's, or giving up her life in the world, as Punter asked Hurston to do. In dramatizing this struggle, though, Hurston made the choices literal. Although Tea Cake is the polar opposite of Sykes, the baneful husband in 1926's "Sweat," each man forces his wife to choose her life or his. In both cases, the woman chooses to live. In both cases, too, Hurston gives the impression that the woman will not die of grief or remorse for her actions. In *Their Eyes*, particularly, she makes it easy for readers to envision Janie—still young and attractive, with "firm buttocks like she had grape fruits in her hip pockets"—living a fulfilling life and loving whomever she chooses.

Author and critic June Jordan has called *Their Eyes Were Watching God* the "most successful, convincing and exemplary novel of blacklove that we have. Period." Jordan was speaking of Janie's dawning awareness of the possibility of an equitable love between black men and black women. But Hurston's novel is ultimately about self-love, about Janie's hard-willed choice to love nobody—not even the love of her life—more than she does herself.

As much as it is a love story, *Their Eyes Were Watching God*—in its critique of black male-female relationships—is also protest literature. Hurston was not wailing *White Man, Listen!* (as the young author Richard Wright soon would), but she was sounding a wakeup call, just as urgent, for her own people. In *Their Eyes Were Watching God*, Hurston raised crucial feminist questions concerning the intimidation and oppression inherent in too many relationships—and she challenged black men (and everyone else) to listen and then to "act and do things accordingly."

Their Eyes Were Watching God is a protest novel in other regards as well. The smoldering resentment of the black South that Sterling Brown had longed to see in *Mules and Men* is evident in *Their Eyes*, a fact Brown acknowledged in his fairly positive review of the novel in *The Nation*. "The author does not dwell upon the 'people ugly from ignorance and broken from being poor' who swarm upon the 'muck' for short-time jobs," Brown wrote. "But here is bitterness, sometimes oblique, in the enforced folk manner, and sometimes forthright." After the hurricane, for example, Tea Cake and a small army of other men are conscripted, at gunpoint, to bury the dead. Although the hurricane has killed black and white people with equal disregard—sometimes making their races undetectable—the white guards force the gravediggers to examine the corpses' hair to determine their race. The white people are to be buried in coffins; the black ones are to be dumped into a common hole. Hurston borrowed this brutal scene from actual events following the 1928 Lake Okeechobee hurricane, which killed nearly two thousand people in the Florida Everglades. Her reconstruction of the mass burial is a devastating yet subtle indictment of the racism that formed the backdrop for her characters' lives: "They's mighty particular how dese dead folks goes tuh judgment," Tea Cake observes. "Look lak dey think God don't know nothin' 'bout de Jim Crow law."

Such incidents, while powerfully rendered, remain in the background. Hurston's subject is not white oppression; it is Janie's journey of self-discovery. And while racism affects Janie's development, it does not define her quest nor dominate her thoughts. In this sense, Hurston believed Janie was typical of black people everywhere. "Only a few self-conscious Negroes feel tragic about their race, and make a cage for themselves," Hurston assessed. "The great majority of us live our own lives and spread our jenk in our own way, unconcerned about other people. Sufficient unto ourselves."

In this self-sufficient spirit, Janie and Tea Cake and the other people in Hurston's novel go on with their living and their loving, largely oblivious to white approval or disapproval. Significantly, Hurston opens her story at sundown, when Eatonville's citizens are gathering on their porches to talk among themselves. "These sitters had been tongueless, earless, eyeless conveniences all day long," she writes. "Mules and other brutes had occupied their skins. But now, the sun and the bossman were gone, so the skins felt powerful and human." Hurston wrote about life *within* a particular black community—not about that community's reactions to white oppression. She was interested in what black people felt and said and did after they'd banished the white man from their minds and turned their thoughts to more interesting things. In this way, *Their Eyes Were Watching God* becomes protest literature on yet another level: It protests white oppression by stripping it of its potency, by denying its all-powerfulness in black people's lives. Hurston's literary method was not confrontation but affirmation. Yet, as June Jordan has pointed out, "affirmation of black values and lifestyle within the American context is, indeed, an act of protest."

Richard Wright—soon to become the king of the protest novel— did not read *Their Eyes Were Watching God* that way. In fact, he had trouble taking it seriously. "Miss Hurston seems to have no desire whatever to move in the direction of serious fiction," the twenty-nine-year-old upstart carped in his *New Masses* review. "Miss Hurston can write," he admitted, but he believed she was perpetuating a minstrel image for the benefit of white readers. "Her characters eat and laugh and cry and work and kill; they swing like a pendulum eternally in that safe and narrow orbit in which America likes to see the Negro live: between laughter and tears." A member of the Communist Party at the time, Wright deplored the lack of overt protest in Hurston's novel. That she was writing about a black woman's internal life did not help matters. Not known for his progressive views on women, Wright must have seen Hurston's novel as so much female frivolity. In the end, he dismissed it as such: "The sensory sweep of her novel carries no theme, no message, no thought."

Over the years, of course, most critics have emphatically disagreed with Wright's dim assessment of Hurston's book. Even Sterling Brown has called it "a very fine American novel." Today, in fact, *Their Eyes Were Watching God* is widely regarded as a masterpiece. In 1937, though, the jury was still out, but certainly leaning in Hurston's favor. That fall, her name was being bandied about so positively that the prestigious *Saturday Review of Literature* invited her to write a piece on Fannie Hurst. This was a valuable opportunity for Zora to showcase her writing for white readers, while giving Fannie a much-needed boost for her new book, *We Are Ten*, which *The New York Times* had assailed the same day it applauded Hurston's novel. Understanding the mutual benefits at stake, Hurston wrote a playful profile of Hurst for the *Saturday Review*'s October 9 issue. Fannie loved it, as did Carl Van Vechten, though Zora soothed his ego a bit by claiming she would have preferred to write about him. Carlo, in turn, informed Zora that she was featured in the new edition of *Who's Who in America*. "I must look to see as soon as I have time to get around to it," the busy author responded. Meanwhile, Pulitzer Prize–winning poet Edna St. Vincent Millay sent Hurston a telegram congratulating her on her new novel. And journalist Helen Worden interviewed the suddenly popular black writer for a forthcoming profile in *The New York World-Telegram*. "God <u>does</u> love black people, doesn't He?" Zora joked with a friend. "Or am <u>I</u> just out on parole?"

Living comfortably off her remaining Guggenheim funds, Hurston rented an apartment in the relative quiet of Jamaica, Long Island, where she would stay through the end of the year. She'd intended to stop off in New York only long enough to get her furniture out of storage and ship it to Florida. But Bertram Lippincott urged her to remain up North a while to push her new book. From her Long Island outpost, she helped to promote *Their Eyes Were Watching God*, started writing her book on Jamaica and Haiti, and stoically refused to pick up the telephone to call Percy Punter. He'd left his number at her publisher's office, but Zora decided not to use it. "Not because I didn't want to," she said, "but because the moment when I should hear his voice something would be in wait for me." Whether that something was "warm and eager" or "cool and impersonal," Zora was not ready to hear it. She had too many other things to do.

Hurston attended the Boston Book Fair on November 8 and the New York Book Fair on November 15. There, at Rockefeller Center, a newspaper photographer snapped a picture of her inspecting *American Stuff*, a just-published anthology of WPA writers including Claude McKay, Sterling Brown, and her newest critic, Richard Wright. Scheduled to speak at the book fair that day, Zora looked elegant and coolly above it all in leather gloves, a shimmering dress, and a brimless hat with veil.

Between such high-profile appearances, she was quietly working on a folk concert she planned to stage at the Ambassador Theatre on December 12. With new material from Jamaica and Haiti, it was going to feature "good singing and plenty hip-wringing," Zora promised. Around the first of December, though, she decided to cancel the show: "My publishers insist that I finish my book on Haiti immediately," she explained to friends. "Consequently, I do not find the time to work on the concert at the moment."

Hurston turned her full attention to her in-progress manuscript, but before she could get anywhere close to the eighty thousand words her contract required, she was distracted by a voice from her past. It was the high-pitched, often-caviling voice of Alain Locke.

Writing in the January 1938 issue of *Opportunity*, Locke included *Their Eyes Were Watching God* in his annual survey of the previous year's black literature. The professor praised Hurston's "gift for poetic phrase, for rare dialect, and folk humor." But these very elements, he complained, kept her "flashing on the surface of her community and her characters." Rather than focus on folklore as her "main point," Hurston needed to dive deeper into "the inner psychology" of her characters or to a "sharp analysis of the social background." *Their Eyes Were Watching God* was "folklore fiction at its best," Locke conceded, but when was Hurston going to "come to grips with motive fiction and social document fiction?" It was time, he concluded, to move beyond "condescension" and "oversimplification."

Locke's disparaging review cut Hurston like a buzz saw. And its noise drowned out all the praise songs she'd heard from other critics. Like many creative artists, Hurston harbored doubts about the merit of her own work. Of *Their Eyes Were Watching God*, she once said: "I wish that I could write it again. In fact, I regret all of my books." Locke's criticism touched that place where Hurston usually kept these nagging self-doubts safely hidden. Although Richard Wright's review of *Their Eyes Were Watching God* was far more negative than Locke's, the erudite little professor knew how to push Hurston's buttons—and push them he did.

Zora responded to Locke's criticism with a venomous counterattack. Dropping everything, she reeled off a one-and-a-half-page rant against Locke and sent it to *Opportunity*. Called "The Chick with One Hen," the essay was an all-out assault on a man who'd helped Hurston often, but with whom she'd always had a rickety relationship. Nearly twenty years before, when she was his student at Howard, Zora had noticed Locke's active disinterest in women. But for some reason, he'd treated her differently. Still, in the late 1920s, Zora confided her distrust of Locke to Langston Hughes, who shared some of her concerns. But after her break with Hughes—when

Hurston and Locke became the last black survivors in Godmother's crumbling queendom—Zora suppressed her suspicions of Locke and embraced him as an ally. Soon after Godmother became ill, however, Hurston and Locke peacefully went their separate ways. Now, five years later, Hurston was ready to rumble.

Locke knew nothing about literary criticism, she accused, but "in his eagerness to attract attention he rushes at any chance to see his name in print, however foolish his offering." She called his review of *Their Eyes Were Watching God* "an example of rank dishonesty" and "a conscious fraud." Locke's main, unstated objection to Hurston's book, she believed, was twofold: that she did not consult him before writing it, and that she did not write like Sterling Brown, the one "chick" who still conferred with Locke as a mentor, as a mother "hen." Hurston claimed she had no quarrel with Brown. He was "free to write volumes and volumes" about his political philosophy, she commented, "but not between the covers of my books." At least Brown had a political viewpoint that was his own. Locke, on the other hand, "has not produced one single idea, or suggestion of an idea, that he can call his own." Locke knew "less about Negro life than anyone in America," Hurston wrote hyperbolically. "I will send my toe-nails to debate him on what he knows about Negroes and Negro life, and I will come personally to debate him on what he knows about literature on the subject. This one who lives by quotations trying to criticize people who live by life!!"

Wisely, *Opportunity* declined to print Hurston's harangue. But her distaste for Locke persisted. "I get tired of the envious picking on me," she wrote privately to James Weldon Johnson at Fisk. "And if you will admit the truth you know that Alain Leroy Locke is a malicious, spiteful little snot that thinks he ought to be the leading Negro because of his degrees. Foiled in that, he spends his time trying to cut the ground from under everybody else."

Hurston's appraisal of Locke was severe, but she was not the first writer to express such views. Claude McKay once called Locke "a dyed-in-the-wool, pussyfooting professor." And Jessie Fauset judged that Locke's "failure as a writer" had turned him into a literary critic who wrote "with utmost arrogance and obsequiousness to whites." Further, Hurston believed Locke was an intellectual thief: "So far as the young writers are concerned, he runs a mental pawnshop. He lends out his patronage and takes in ideas which he soon passes off as his own," she complained to Johnson.

By this time, Hurston was back in Eatonville. And if Locke had taken her up on her dare, she would have been obliged to send her toenails to debate him, as she'd threatened, because the rest of her was otherwise engaged—working to finish her book on Haiti and Jamaica. Hurston had packed up her life and transported it to Florida in February, attempting to escape the New York winter. "I dislike cold weather and all of its kinfolk," she once said; "that takes in bare trees and a birdless morning." Hurston also wanted to escape New York's distractions. Believing she always had been "too hurried before," she hoped to find in her home state the peace and quiet she needed to write at the peak of her powers. Or, as she put it, "I want . . . to sit down and try to learn how to write in truth."

CHAPTER 27

Deep South

For all its bluster, "The Chick with One Hen" did not address the fundamental question Locke raised in his review of *Their Eyes Were Watching God*: "When will the Negro novelist of maturity, who knows how to tell a story convincingly—which is Miss Hurston's cradle gift, come to grips with motive fiction and social document fiction?" Hurston did not answer Locke's question until she was back in Eatonville—and when she did, she answered it with another question: "Can the black poet sing a song to the morning?"

The "social document fiction" that Locke wanted Hurston to write was exactly what she'd spent her whole career trying to avoid. That is, using literature as a platform for writing about "the race problem," or for overtly advancing a particular political viewpoint. In the 1930s, however, social document fiction—influenced by the widespread social realism movement—was all the rage. And for Hurston, that's what this kind of writing was all about: rage and resentment.

In his "Blueprint for Negro Writing"—published around the same time as his critical review of *Their Eyes*—Richard Wright urged black writers to embrace a social realism informed by Marxist theory, which he believed offered "the maximum degree of freedom in thought and feeling . . . for the Negro writer." Wright condemned the work of the Harlem Renaissance school of writers as "parasitic and mannered"—and, worst of all, contrived to please their patrons, who were nothing but "burnt-out white Bohemians with money." Up to this point, he asserted, black literature had been "the voice of the educated Negro pleading with white America for justice." From now on, black writers needed to write for and about "the common people."

Apparently, Wright had not read Hurston closely. Along with Langston Hughes and a few of the other folk-inspired Harlem Renaissance writers, she had spent her entire career writing about the common people. But the folks Hurston knew in the rural South were not the same common people Wright would have met in his role as Harlem correspondent for the *Daily Worker*, the Communist Party newspaper. And they were not the anger-doused, violence-prone black men who populated Wright's stories.

Hurston knew black people to "love and hate and fight and play and strive and travel and have a thousand and one interests in life like other humans," as she wrote in her 1938 essay, "Art and Such." The average black man she knew might be angry about racial injustice, Hurston acknowledged, but he thought about other things too. "When his baby cuts a new tooth he brags as shamelessly as anyone else without once weeping over the prospect of some Klansman knocking it out when and if the child ever gets grown."

In a stout defense of her own literary philosophy, written soon after her return to Eatonville, Hurston responded to Locke's lingering question and to criticism from Richard Wright and Sterling Brown as well. Obviously referring to Locke, she condemned the self-proclaimed "Race Leaders" who—upon hearing of white people's "curiosity about some activity among Negroes"—rushed forward to offer themselves "as an authority on the subject whether they have ever heard of it before or not." The day of the race leader was done, she proclaimed, even if the race man did not realize it himself. "Though he is . . . paid scant attention, the race man is still with us," she complained. "His job today is to rush around seeking for something he can 'resent.'"

Then, Hurston got to her real point: Black writers should have the same freedom as white writers, she declared. They should not feel obligated to write about "the race problem" or other social ills, but should claim the same liberty that white writers enjoyed. Namely, the right—and the responsibility—to write about anything at all. "Can the black poet sing a song to the morning?" she implored. "Up springs the song to his lips but it is fought back. He says to himself, 'Ah, this is a beautiful song inside me. I feel the morning star in my throat. I will sing of the star and the morning.'" But then Hurston's imaginary black writer realizes that other things are expected of him: "Ought I not to be singing of our sorrows?" he asks himself. "If I do not some will even call me a coward. The one subject for a Negro is the Race and its sufferings and so the song of the morning must be choked back. I will write of a lynching instead."

Because of pressure from within the racial ranks, black writers continually rehashed "the same old theme" and "the same old phrases"—and they did so "to the detriment of art," Hurston assessed. "The writer thinks that he has been brave in following the groove of the Race Champions, when the truth is, it is the line of least resistance and least originality."

Determined to write with originality, Hurston rented a barnlike house—a former jook joint—on the edge of Eatonville, where she pushed herself to finish her manuscript on her Caribbean travels. Just outside her door, the orange trees were in bloom and Zora could hear the mockingbirds crooning all night in the moonshine. In this picturesque setting, she wrote briskly, but found it challenging "to give a true picture" of the time she'd spent in Jamaica and Haiti. "Perhaps I have chosen too big a canvas for my work," she worried. But then she corrected herself: "The picture is infinitely too huge for the canvas."

During her nearly two years in the Caribbean, Hurston had gathered enough material for several volumes: one on Jamaica alone, she believed, and at least a couple of tomes on Haiti. "I have so much material now, that I can do about three books without stopping to search for more," she told a friend. But her publisher only wanted one book. "It was to be half and half Jamaica-Haiti," Hurston decided. "Not strictly a scientific work, but burning spots from the ensemble." By March 26, she had finished her manuscript and placed it in the hands of a typist. Lippincott decided on a publication date of October 13.

Just as Hurston finished her manuscript, the *Saturday Review* contracted her to critique *Uncle Tom's Children*, a collection of short stories by Richard Wright. The book had won a nationwide competition sponsored by *Story* magazine; the grand prize was $500 and publication by Harper & Brothers. Perhaps negatively swayed by Wright's slam of *Their Eyes Were Watching God*, Hurston was not as impressed with *Uncle Tom's Children* as the contest judges had been. (Interestingly, the most prestigious of the judges, Sinclair Lewis—the first American writer to win the Nobel Prize for literature, in 1930— voted against Wright's book.)

"This is a book about hatreds," Hurston began her review. Acknowledging that "some bright new lines to remember come flash- ing from the author's pen," Hurston did not deny Wright's obvious talent as a writer. "Some of his sentences have the shocking power of a forty-four," she declared. But Hurston thought Wright's use of dialect was laughable: "One wonders how he arrived at it. Certainly he does not write by ear unless he is tone-deaf." Aside from this, she conceded, "the book contains some beautiful writing." Still, Hurston objected to Wright's Communist-influenced portrayal of the South as "a dismal, hopeless section ruled by brutish hatred and nothing else." More than anything, she deplored the violence in the book; in one story alone, there was "lavish killing," she complained—"perhaps enough to satisfy all male black readers." Every character in the book was "elemental and brutish," Hurston concluded. "Not one act of understanding and sympathy comes to pass in the entire work."

Although the violence in *Uncle Tom's Children* was admittedly disturbing—"so vivid that I had a most unhappy time reading it," First Lady Eleanor Roosevelt said—most critics disagreed with Hurston's generally unfavorable review. In a statement that rudely discounted the work of Langston Hughes, Jean Toomer, and Zora Neale Hurston, among other contenders, *Time* magazine lauded Wright as the great black hope in literature. "The U.S. has never had a first-rate Negro novelist," the magazine asserted. "Last week, the promise of one appeared."

Even if *Time* did not recognize Hurston's talent, officials of the Federal Writers' Project did—to a certain extent. When they found out Hurston was in Eatonville, they approached her about working as a consultant for *The Florida Negro*, a proposed chronicle of black life in the state. Citing a heavy work schedule—she was completing her Caribbean manuscript at the time—Hurston declined. By April, though, her money from the Guggenheim Foundation was running low, so she began to reconsider the job offer.

Another program of President Roosevelt's WPA, the Federal Writers' Project was inaugurated in 1935 to provide jobs to hundreds of writers unable to find employment during the Depression. Under the direction of Henry Alsberg, the FWP embarked upon an ambitious plan to produce an "American Guide" series that would "hold up a mirror to America," as FWP documents phrased it. The proposed guidebook series would consist of fifty volumes, devoted to each of America's forty-eight states and two territories. In Florida, Louisiana, and Virginia, separate "Negro Units" were established for black writers with the intention of producing volumes specifically devoted to black life in those southern states. Many writers, black and white, found work with the FWP: Among its participants over the years were Richard Wright, Arna Bontemps, Ralph Ellison, Margaret Walker, Saul Bellow, Studs Terkel, John Cheever, and Sterling Brown, who was hired in Washington as the national editor of Negro affairs.

To be eligible for a job with the FWP, writers had to certify that they were in need of "relief"—which, during those New Deal days, was the equivalent of welfare. The economy made it easy to qualify, recalled Stetson Kennedy, a white writer who worked for several years with the Florida FWP. "Most of the entire population, including former millionaires, were eligible," Kennedy judged, pointing out that as many as sixteen million Americans were unemployed during the Depression era.

Most of the editorial staff on the Florida FWP had journalistic backgrounds; many came from defunct Florida weeklies. But according to Kennedy, the majority of the project's fieldworkers—those who actually went knocking on doors to interview people for the Florida guides—were "housewives with a high school education and a penchant for writing." This being the case, national director Alsberg believed "one person of writing and editorial ability" was "worth fifty people without writing experience." Thus, FWP administrators set aside a few perks—including job security and higher wages—to attract people with literary and editorial skills. Evidently, though, these set-asides—at least in the South—were reserved for white professionals. Despite that she was an experienced writer with impressive credentials, including two Guggenheim fellowships and three published books, Hurston was not officially given a slot on the editorial staff of the Florida Writers' Project, and she was certainly not paid an editor's salary. In fact, she was paid less than her white counterparts on the "junior interviewer" level. Stetson Kennedy recalled being hired as a junior interviewer, at age twenty, for $37.50 every two weeks. On April 25, the Florida FWP hired Hurston at a salary of $63 per month.

For this lowly wage, Zora joined a revolving staff of about two hundred people who worked for the Writers' Project in Florida. Assigned to collect material throughout the state, the fieldworkers, black and white, mostly operated out of their own homes. At state headquarters in Jacksonville, where the supervisory team was based, black writers never were invited to participate in editorial conferences, recalled Kennedy, who was quickly named the Florida project's director of folklore, life history, and social-ethnic studies. Black employees deposited their timesheets at an office in "colored town," the black section of Jacksonville. "Manuscripts from the Negro Unit came to us by mail or messenger," Kennedy remembered, "and every two weeks they sent someone for their paychecks." In this way, the white editors rarely saw a black face in their downtown office.

In May 1938, however, state FWP director Carita Dogget Corse called a meeting of her editorial staff and announced that Zora Neale Hurston was coming onboard. Though she would primarily work from her home in Eatonville, the celebrated black author soon would be paying a visit to the Jacksonville office. "Unaccustomed as we were to receiving blacks of any description," Kennedy recalled, "Corse cautioned us that Zora had been lionized by New York literary circles and was consequently given to 'putting on airs,' including the smoking of cigarettes in the presence of white folks, and we would therefore have to make allowances. And so Zora came, and Zora smoked, and we made allowances." Hurston's white FWP colleagues didn't know what to make of her, Kennedy remembered. "We were sort of bemused by the fact that we had a novelist, a published novelist, on staff in need of $37 every two weeks," he would recall (still assuming Hurston was paid as much as he and his white colleagues received).

Corse—who'd earned a master's degree from Columbia and was well aware of Hurston's work—viewed her newest employee as a woman of "great verve." Zora "didn't have to put it on," Corse judged. "She just had it in her. Every inch of her was alive and graceful."

Soon after Hurston's initial visit to the Jacksonville office, she invited Corse to join her at a storefront church in the city's black community. When they arrived around 10:00 P.M., the church was packed and the preacher was in full blast, as Corse recalled, but the congregation seemed rather lackluster. "We sat in the back and Zora whispered to me, 'Watch me get them on their feet.' . . . And she got up and began clapping. Well it didn't seem to matter to the congregation at all; they started clapping, too. And she had them rolling on the floor in ten minutes." Corse became uncomfortable with this "uncontrolled activity," she admitted, so she whispered to Zora that she wanted to leave. Zora assented to her boss's wish, of course, but not before she'd given Corse a glimpse of the black sanctified church. Hurston wanted the state's FWP director to have this experience not because the church was a quaint little curiosity, but because it was a gold mine of black folk expression—a place where religious music was "dance-possible," as she put it, and where Negroes called "old gods by a new name."

The church visit made a "deep impression" on Corse, she said, but the deeper impression was made by Hurston herself. Corse viewed Hurston as "a very dynamic, a very attractive person." She soon learned that Zora also was "very hard to control." Often, Corse complained, "she would go off and you wouldn't know where she was, and she was supposed to be working by the week."

During one of her early absences, soon after she took the FWP job, Hurston went to Washington. Still interested in presenting black folk material onstage whenever she could, Zora organized a group of dancers and singers—"Chanters," she called them—to perform at the National Folk Festival. Just before the Chanters were to leave for the drive north, they presented a folk concert at the Winter Park Women's Club, under the auspices of the Rollins College Folk Lore Group. Using her connections at the college, Hurston conceived the concert as sort of a dress rehearsal and fund-raiser for the performance at the National Folk Festival. Charging a modest admission fee, she raised enough money in Winter Park to put her Chanters on the road a couple of days later. Hurston's group, the only one from Florida, performed twice at the three-day National Folk Festival. They were among some five hundred participants—including American Indians, cowboys, lumberjacks, and coal miners—representing twenty-nine states.

While in Washington, Hurston inadvertently created a bit of trouble for Corse. Visiting FWP headquarters, she met national director Henry Alsberg and impressed him so much that he wrote to Corse suggesting she place Hurston in charge of Florida's Negro Unit. He also proposed that Hurston be given primary responsibility for editing *The Florida Negro* and that her monthly salary be boosted to $150.

As much as Corse claimed to have liked Hurston, she was not willing to offer her a supervisory position or a salary that was equal to—or perhaps greater than—what some white editors earned. Florida was still in the South, after all, and Jim Crow was still king. Consequently, Corse did not follow Alsberg's liberal recommendation, but she did not directly defy him, either. Instead, she decided to give Hurston an additional travel allowance of seventy-five dollars. She also began to refer to her as the "Negro editor," but offered her none of the benefits that should have gone along with the position. She did not give Hurston any real editorial power, either. Kennedy was the de facto editor for *The Florida Negro* and, despite Hurston's title, he remained in charge. Meanwhile, Corse let the national office think Hurston had more say-so than she actually did. The Jacksonville office, still lily-white, did not even give Hurston a place to work. "Although Zora was frequently referred to, particularly in correspondence to and from the Washington office, as our 'Negro Editor,' or 'Supervisor of the Negro Unit,' to the best of my knowledge she never had a FWP desk in Jacksonville, or anywhere else for that matter," Kennedy recalled.

Hurston continued to work out of her home in Eatonville, an arrangement that suited her just fine. She knew she was not getting what she deserved from the FWP, but she was getting what she desired: a steady paycheck and the freedom to write. Using her self-supervised time to work on her "Moses" novel, Hurston sometimes moved a card table and chair outdoors and wrote in her backyard.

Under the imposing oak trees, draped with shawls of Spanish moss, she wrote all day. On other days, she would read or travel to neighboring towns to do a bit of FWP research. Occasionally, Hurston would decide to go to New York for a brief spell.

One of these visits, in June 1938, was not a pleasure trip. It was for the funeral of James Weldon Johnson, the venerable "Lord Jim," as Zora called him. The Fisk University literature professor—sixty-seven years old but in good health—had been driving through a Maine rainstorm with his wife, Grace Nail Johnson, when a train plowed into their car at a railroad crossing, killing Johnson and critically injuring his wife. An author and former NAACP official, Johnson was one of the most widely respected and admired black intellectuals in America. Zora was especially fond of him because of their shared interest in the artfulness of black preachers' sermons; Johnson also was a fellow Floridian. That he died in an auto-train collision—precisely as her father had died—must have unnerved Zora. On June 30, she joined Langston Hughes, Carl Van Vechten, and more than 2,500 other mourners at Salem Methodist Episcopal Church in New York to pay her final respects. In an essay she'd written the previous summer in Haiti—called "My People, My People!"—Hurston had joked about Johnson's regality. He didn't parade down the street like some black people, she wrote, he *proceeded*. And he never grinned, he *smiled*. "The man is just full of that old monarch material," she wrote. "If some day I looked out of my window on Seventh Avenue and saw him in an ermine robe and a great procession going to the Cathedral of St. John the Divine to be crowned I wouldn't be a bit surprised. Maybe he'd make a mighty fine king at that."

Soon after Zora got back to Eatonville, her niece Winifred came to live with her. Winifred was the daughter of Zora's oldest brother, Bob, who'd died recently in Memphis. Winifred was eighteen years old and just out of high school; she was following her big sister, Wilhemina, to Eatonville. The twenty-year-old Wilhemina had moved in with her Aunt Zora several months before and she was constantly writing to Winifred about what a good time she was having in Eatonville. By the time Winifred got there, in the fall of 1938, Wilhemina had married a local orange picker and moved into a place of her own. Still, Winifred enjoyed her time in Eatonville with her aunt. Just embarking on her life as an adult, she found in Zora a curious and enthralling example of what a woman could be.

Zora stayed home most evenings, cooking often—and well—for Winifred, who got a job at a local nursing home. Despite the regularity of the meals, Zora also showed her niece her impulsive side, as Winifred Hurston Clark would recall. Once, Zora asked her if she wanted to visit her Uncle John in Jacksonville, 135 miles away. Winifred agreed to the jaunt, thinking they'd leave in a couple of days. But Zora said, "Get ready, let's go." To the teenager's embarrassment, her Aunt Zora wore overalls on their whirlwind day-trip. Like Janie in *Their Eyes Were Watching God*, Zora often wore overalls when she was working at home—but she cleaned up nicely too, Winifred admitted: "When she wanted to dress, you talk about dress!"

Confirming Winifred's fashion sense, one photograph from 1938 shows Hurston draped down in a light-colored, two-piece number that was stylish yet unconventional. The picture was taken at a Jacksonville performance—inspired by *Their Eyes Were Watching God*—that Hurston and her Chanters staged sometime that year. This little-reported event was among several enterprising projects Hurston was able to pursue while working for the FWP.

Checking in only occasionally with the state office in Jacksonville, Zora enjoyed the freedom of her job and wanted to keep her good thing going. Sometimes, after long silences, she would write Corse a "much-felt letter." Addressing her as "Boss," Hurston once confided in Corse (who also was an author) about her occasional bouts of writer's block. "Every now and then I get a sort of phobia for paper and all its works," she wrote. "I cannot bring myself to touch it. I cannot write, read or do anything at all for a period. . . . But when I do come out of it, I am as if I had just been born again."

Perhaps because of these blocks—or, more likely, because of Hurston's other activities—the Jacksonville office sometimes did not hear from her for several weeks. Periodically, Corse would ask: "Anybody heard from Zora?" When everyone in the room looked back at their boss blankly, she would turn to Kennedy and say, "Better write her a letter and jog her up!"

"In response to my letters," Kennedy remembered, "we would receive a thick packet of fabulous folksongs, tales, and legends, possibly representing gleanings from days long gone by. We did not care how, where, or when Zora had come by them—each and every one was priceless, and we hastened to sprinkle them through the *Florida Guide* manuscript for flavoring."

One Hurston essay that gave her editors pause was "The Ocoee Riot." In a reportorial tone, Hurston described the mob violence that broke out on election day in 1920 in Ocoee, a small town not far from Eatonville. Hurston told the story from the perspective of Ocoee's black residents, who recounted a marauding mob of white men burning down whole rows of Negro houses, attacking black people in the streets, and eventually dragging one man to death and leaving his body swinging from a telephone pole beside the highway. Not surprisingly, this essay never made it into the Florida guidebook. "The white/black relationship was generally regarded as a fixed one," Kennedy explained, "and therefore not a fit subject for commentary. The specifics of racial discrimination, on the other hand, could sometimes be pointed to in passing, provided this was done without rancor." In the end, only a few lines of Hurston's Ocoee story were included in the *Florida Guide*.

Hurston wrote several pieces specifically for *The Florida Negro*, a volume that national Negro affairs editor Sterling Brown hoped would be a comprehensive account of black Floridians past and present. For the book's chapter on religion, she wrote an essay called "The Sanctified Church," in which she discussed various aspects of black religious expression and expounded upon themes she'd asserted in *Jonah's Gourd Vine*. Unimpressed by the "businesslike" prayers and songs of the white man, black worshipers at sanctified churches were unknowingly "influencing American music," Hurston wrote, "and enjoying themselves hugely while doing so, in spite of the derision from the outside." Asked to write a chapter on art and literature for *The Florida Negro*, Hurston penned an impassioned essay, called "Art and Such," that defended her own literary views. Judging it to be nothing more than "a nine-page diatribe" against Sterling Brown and her other detractors, Kennedy shelved Hurston's essay as being "inappropriate" for *The Florida Negro*.

In her chapter on Florida folklore and music—an essay called "Go Gator and Muddy the Water"—Hurston presented a compendium of black folktales and folk songs and offered a creative analysis of why folklore was necessary and valuable. "Folklore," she summed up, "is the boiled-down juice of human living." In other pieces written for *The Florida Negro*, Hurston compared Floridian and Bahamian music and dance and pointed out the importance of rhythm in black children's games. In another, she offered an amusing list of Negro mythical places. Among them were "Diddy-Wah-Diddy," a kind of Negro heaven where there is no work, no worry, and plenty of good food; and "Beluthahatchie," where "all unpleasant doings and sayings are forgotten." Portions of these writings were strewn throughout the Florida guidebook, but never incorporated as a whole into *The Florida Negro* nor in the mainstream guide. In the end, white editors in the state FWP office cut all of Hurston's pieces down to a few lines or excised them altogether.

Hurston, it seems, was not following the unwritten rules of the Florida Writers' Project. She essentially wrote whatever she wanted, while most of the other writers adhered to a different code, as Kennedy recalled. "Jim Crow kept watch over the shoulders of white and black writers alike, giving rise to varying degrees of pejorative and paternalism on pages produced by the former and sometimes deference and ingratiation in the pages of the latter," he observed. "It was a form of job insurance for both parties."

While Hurston's FWP writings do not exhibit this ingratiating tendency, she was not above ingratiating herself with her boss in person. Sometimes, Carita Corse recalled, after Hurston had been away for several weeks, "she'd come back and stick her head around the corner of my office and say, 'Now you know that I'm your favorite darkey.'" In at least one letter, too, Hurston referred to herself as Corse's "pet darkey," a phrase of self-degradation that contemporary readers might find repugnant. For Hurston, though, it was another form of "job insurance," and an emotionally complex way of negotiating the rocky racial terrain of the 1930s South. Uttered with a kind of crafty humor, this phrase was a tool Hurston used to charm and shame Corse simultaneously—in the same way that a twenty-first-century African American might ironically refer to herself as "the token black" in her office or in a pool of white friends. By calling herself a "pet darkey," Hurston—obviously a woman of remarkable achievement, verbal skill, and personal effervescence—played up to whatever feelings of racial superiority Corse held, while also slyly accusing the white woman of participating in a system where such tokenism ruled.

"The South has no interest, and pretends none, in the mass of Negroes but is very much concerned about the individual," Hurston once wrote. Thus, the South had long ago developed a "pet Negro" system, whereby a white person of prestige and power would choose a particular Negro as a "pet," so to speak, as someone who could have and do "all the things forbidden to other Negroes." After all, this one was "different," the white person assured himself. Hurston did not condone this system, but she believed it was "too deep-rooted to be budged." Knowing how to play by its rules was a good skill to have, she felt, "if you have any plans for racial manipulations in Dixie." She added pointedly: "You cannot batter in doors down there, and you can save time and trouble, and I do mean trouble, by hunting up the community keys."

In October, Hurston took a break from the racial intricacies of the South and traveled to New York for the publication of her book on the Caribbean. Initially, she'd planned to call it "Bush." But during her first trip to Haiti, another title had come to her: *Tell My Horse*.

This phrase—"Parlay cheval ou" in Creole—was one Hurston heard daily in Haiti. These were the words that the powerful and boisterous god Guede (pronounced geeday) said when he began to speak—always bluntly and always through a person he'd "mounted." Guede, Hurston explained, was never visible; this *loa* manifested himself by mounting someone, as a rider mounts a horse, then speaking and acting through his mount, or horse. A spirit "with social consciousness, plus a touch of burlesque and slapstick," as Hurston described him, Guede always began his caustic commentary with these words: "Tell my horse." Often, too, Haitian peasants used this phrase as a disclaimer—feigning possession by Guede in order to express resentment of the upper class, to make devastating revelations about their enemies, or to otherwise say things they lacked the courage to say in their ordinary, unmounted state. Hurston chose to use Guede's introductory phrase as the title of her book because she identified with this *loa* as "the deification of the common people of Haiti."

Hurston's use of this title signaled her intent to speak bluntly in her book, to reveal things about Haiti and Jamaica that required courage to say. In some ways, she did this. Her chapter on "Women in the Caribbean," for example, candidly critiques the chauvinism she witnessed there, particularly in Jamaica. And her chapter on Haitian zombies is particularly vivid and informative. For the most part, though, Hurston pulled her punches with this book. No doubt, the violent gastric disturbance she suffered in Haiti influenced her decision to do so.

Hurston's material on Jamaica is exhilarating but truncated; she seems to rush through it to get to Haiti. Once she gets there, Hurston consistently writes about voodoo with great respect, reminiscent of her treatment of hoodoo in *Mules and Men*. Nowhere in *Tell My Horse* does she attempt to make Haitian spiritual beliefs sound lurid or ridiculous. Presenting it as a sophisticated and legitimate religion, she attempts to rescue voodoo from the sensationalistic images perpetuated by many white writers and moviemakers. Sometimes, however, Hurston hampers her own good intentions by bogging down her narrative in a jumble of gods and ceremonies—while offering little explanation of the ultimate spiritual goals of the religion. While she sees "deep meanings in Voodoo practices," Hurston does not always convey those meanings so clearly to the reader. Maybe this was intentional: As a *hounci*, a first-level initiate in the religion, Zora was bound by a code of secrecy. Perhaps there were some things she could not say in her book without fear of repercussions—if not from the gods, then from the *bocors* (or whoever was responsible for the illness that gripped her intestines in Haiti).

Written in a hurry to satisfy Lippincott, *Tell My Horse* also suffers from poor organization. Rather than presenting a sustained narrative—organized chronologically, for instance—Hurston produced what amounts to a series of tenuously connected essays exploring various topics. As such, *Tell My Horse* is often redundant and occasionally contradictory. In the final analysis, it is an ambitious, flawed mix of reportage, folklore, political commentary, and travelogue. And the voodoo material is simply overwhelming—to the reader and, apparently, to the author as well. In a disclaimer about the scope of the book—one that also acknowledged the religion's complexity—Hurston wrote: "This work does not pretend to give a full account of either Voodoo or Voodoo gods. It would require several

volumes to attempt to cover completely the gods and Voodoo practices of one vicinity alone. Voodoo in Haiti has gathered about itself
more detail of gods and rites than the Catholic church has in Rome."

Tell My Horse received mixed reviews. Several publications praised
the book but seemed put off by its arcane subject and its hybrid
style. *The New Yorker*, for instance, thought it "disorganized but
interesting." *The New York Times Book Review* called it "an unusual
and intensely interesting book richly packed with strange information." And the *Saturday Review of Literature* found it "full of fine
things." That reviewer's conclusion, however, was more ambivalent:
"That Miss Hurston loves Haiti is obvious, but there is a general feeling that the material was not completely digested."

On the other hand, Carl Carmer, writing in the *New York Herald
Tribune*, could not praise Hurston and her book enough: "Seldom has
there been a happier combination than that of the vivid, fantastic
folklore of the West Indies and interpreter Zora Neale Hurston," he
enthused. "Miss Hurston is a trained scholar. She is also one of the
most delightfully alive personalities of our day. She knows what she
is talking about and she talks with a zest and a humor and a gen-
uineness that make her work the best that I know in the field of
contemporary folklore." The critic concluded his review with a statement that Zora must have saved for her scrapbook. "The judges who
select the recipients of Guggenheim fellowships honored themselves
and the purpose of the foundation they serve when they subsidized
Zora Hurston's visit to Haiti. I hope the American reading public will
encourage her further wanderings. She ought not to be allowed to
rest. I am for putting her to work at once on the Virgin Islands,
Cuba, Puerto Rico, the coastal islands off the Carolinas and each of
our Southern states. I know she does not need vacations for every
sentence she writes proves her work gives her a grand time."

Despite such effusions, *Tell My Horse* did not sell well in the
States—presumably because its subject matter was a bit far-flung for
the average American during the Depression. But when the book
was published in England—as *Voodoo Gods: An Inquiry Into Native
Myths and Magic in Jamaica and Haiti*—sales were so brisk that the
publisher earned back Hurston's $500 advance after only a week.

Around the first of December, Zora returned to Florida and
resumed her work with the state Writers' Project, which now needed

her skills as a dramatist. Roosevelt's New Deal was facing a backlash in Congress, where some anti-WPA members had begun to object loudly to federal funding for the arts. In an effort to fight back, the WPA's arts programs started staging national and state exhibitions to win the public's support. Knowing Hurston's background in theater—and viewing her as a "pure showoff"—Corse asked her to stage a demonstration of Florida folklore. Hurston organized a group of black teenagers, mostly from Eatonville and Orlando, and trained them to perform the Fire Dance, the hit finale from *The Great Day*, *From Sun to Sun*, and other versions of her well-traveled folk concert. The Hurston-scripted performance was presented twice at the WPA's National Exhibition of Skills in Orlando, from January 16 to February 6, and the white, middle-class audiences responded favorably. On the teenagers' slim, young hips, the undulations of the Fire Dance were not as suggestive or shocking as they might have been if performed by adult dancers. In Corse's view, "they were the most exquisite things you ever looked at."

The Federal Writers' Project then called upon Hurston's diverse skills in another arena. Aware of her previous collecting work in the South, Corse and Ben Botkin, newly appointed national director of the FWP's folklore program, asked Hurston to participate in a statewide recording expedition. Botkin planned to send an audio recording machine—similar to the one Hurston had used while working with Alan Lomax and Mary Elizabeth Barnicle—for FWP workers to record the songs and stories of Florida. Mere written transcriptions did not provide enough detail and ambience, he'd decided. With its melting-pot ethnic population—including Bahamians, Haitians, Latinos, and Greeks—Florida was certainly fertile with songs and lore. Asked to formulate a plan for recording all this folkloric diversity, Hurston wrote an impressive report—called "Proposed Recording Expedition Into the Floridas"—that divided the state into four major areas and outlined recording possibilities in every corner.

As they waited for the "infernally heavy" recording machine to arrive, Stetson Kennedy recalled, no one in the Florida office ever considered sending an interracial team into the field. "Those were the days when so innocent a gesture as a white man lighting a black woman's cigarette could get them both lynched," he remembered.

"The solution, handed down from above, was to send Zora ahead as a sort of 'talent scout' to identify informants."

In this new assignment, Hurston finally got a raise. On May 8, 1939, the WPA increased her salary to $79.80 per month. Hurston earned every dime of it—and then some. She was sent to Cross City, a tiny town in Suwanee County, in northwestern Florida. Though it was only 125 miles from Jacksonville, Cross City seemed like another universe. There, the Aycock and Lindsay Company—ruled by the comely, gun-toting Catherine Lindsay, a.k.a. "Miss Catherine"— employed more than three hundred turpentine workers and held them and their families in virtual slavery. In addition to scouting out informants for the soon-to-arrive recording crew, Hurston was to interview the turpentine workers for the WPA's newly instituted life-history program. She quickly won the trust of the laborers, who supplied her with ample amounts of song and lore, as well as an earful of horror stories: The white camp bosses regularly beat the workers, the turpentiners said, and they forced themselves on any woman they wanted. If the woman's husband dared protest, his surliness would earn him a beating—or even murder. Black bodies were often weighted down with cement, the laborers told Hurston, and dumped into the Gulf of Mexico.

To the turpentine workers, Hurston represented hope. She was a black woman working for the federal government who seemed genuinely concerned about their lives. Disturbed by what she heard, Hurston tried to help, but there seemed to be no one to turn to. Apprehensive about writing a full report of the atrocities, she wrote cryptic notes to the white FWP staffers who followed her into the turpentine camps to do the actual recording: "There is a grave not far from here of a hand they beat to death," one note said. "A woman told me she cooks, cleans, washes and irons all for $2.25 a week," said another. Following up on Hurston's leads, Kennedy and other white FWP researchers heard about the abuses as well. But they were folklorists, not government agents, so there was little they could do. When Hurston left Cross City, she reportedly wrote to Miss Catherine about the irregularities, but her disclosures could not have been news to the head of the company. In any case, nothing was ever done—and Hurston might have counted herself lucky to get out of town unharmed. As Kennedy put it, "The terrorism was real, not fancied, and a constant in the recording of folk material in those days, at least in the South."

Kennedy told a story that illustrated the depth of the racial prejudice Hurston had to negotiate in a place like Cross City. When Kennedy and his recording crew were leaving the turpentine camp, a white "woods rider"—one of the same overseers who demanded sexual submission from any black woman he fancied—stopped them: "Who was that colored gal who came in here ahead of y'all?" the camp boss wanted to know. "She was right smart for a colored girl. Of course, I figured she was about three-fifths white."

Despite her ultimate powerlessness to change the turpentine workers' lives, Hurston was deeply moved by her experience at the camp. She wrote twenty-six pages of field notes, as well as a brief essay called "Turpentine." The Federal Writers' Project never published these pieces, but Hurston would revisit her Cross City material later, in her own work.

In mid-June, she returned to Jacksonville for another assignment. As part of a seven-state WPA tour, Herbert Halpert, a young white folklorist, was coming to town to record songs and personal interviews, and Hurston was needed to help organize the recording session. Working with other black FWP staffers, Hurston gathered a group of railroad workers, musicians, and church ladies at the Clara White Mission on Ashley Street, a landmark institution in Jacksonville's black community. There, Halpert used his cumbersome recording machine to capture the voices of various informants singing, telling stories, and occasionally hamming it up for posterity.

The dominant voice on the recordings, though, is Hurston's; she can be heard calling out instructions to the musicians and urging them on. She also selected and sang a wide range of songs herself, including blues, work chants, and a couple of risqué jook numbers. Corse and Kennedy were present at the session "to prod Zora along," as Kennedy recalled, but she seemed to need little prodding. Hurston sang more than a dozen songs in a high-pitched but forceful voice, explained the context and significance of each song, and answered questions between tunes. Some of the questions came from Corse, but most were from the twenty-something Halpert. Speaking matter-of-factly in her affable southern accent, Hurston ignored Halpert's condescending tone and answered his questions thoughtfully and forthrightly, though sometimes impatiently. She giggled at a joke here or there, but her seriousness and commitment as a researcher were evident throughout the session, particularly when she explained her method for learning songs: "I just get in a crowd with the people if they are singing and I listen as best I can. And then I start to joining in with a phrase or two and then finally I get so I can sing a verse, and then I keep on till I learn all the sounds and all the verses. And then I sing them back to the people until they tell me that I can sing 'em just like them. And then I take part and try it out on different people who already know the song, until they are quite satisfied that I know it. Then I carry it in my memory."

As an aside, the recording session illustrated how effortlessly Hurston lied about her age. Asked to state her particulars for the record, Zora didn't miss a beat. "My name is Zora Neale Hurston," she said, "and I'm thirty-five years old." In actuality, Hurston was forty-eight.

On June 27, 1939, Hurston shaved yet another six years off her life. That Tuesday, at the Nassau County Courthouse in Fernandina, Zora married Albert Price III, a twenty-three-year-old employee with the WPA's education department. On the marriage license, Hurston gave her birth year as 1910, passing herself off as a twenty-nine-year-old marrying a man who was only slightly younger than herself.

Price—described by one woman as "a smooth brown with handsome features"—hailed from a prominent Jacksonville family. Zora may have met him on one of her trips to check in at the state FWP office or she may have met him at a church service at Bethel Baptist. Price was a member of the popular Jacksonville church that Zora had joined way back in 1914—and that she still occasionally attended with her brother John when she was in town for a visit. No matter how they met, Albert and Zora must have felt an instant and intense attraction; after a brief courtship, they became husband and wife.

As with her previous attempt at matrimony, however, marriage dampened Zora's passion like a cold shower. Immediately, she realized she'd made a mistake. Her niece Winifred was not surprised. Months before, she'd reported back to family members in Memphis: "Aunt Zora doesn't have any business with a husband. She doesn't have time for that. 'Cause she likes to go when she gets ready. She didn't want anyone to tell her 'don't go, don't do,' or something like that. She was a career woman."

Price was "an average-size, nice-looking Afro-American man, kind of pretty brown," as one woman who knew him recalled. But aside from his looks, he did not have much to recommend him as a husband, Zora soon discovered. Still a college student, Price expected his wife to take care of him while he finished his education. He later claimed that this was their premarital agreement—that Zora urged him to quit his job because her salary was greater than his, and WPA rules prevented husband and wife from both being on the federal payroll. Price said Zora assured him that he did not need any money because "all that she wanted was his SWEET SELF."

If Zora muttered these words in the heat of passion, she swiftly repudiated them in the cold light of day. Her list of complaints was long: Price expected her to live at his mother's home, he refused to work, he sometimes took her car and stayed away for long stretches, and he was often verbally abusive. During this period, Zora rented a small house in Jacksonville, while Price shuttled back and forth between his mother's house and Zora's. The young husband did not help his wife with any household expenses. As she'd done all her adult life, Zora said, "I was compelled to support myself."

Hurston and Price never lived together as husband and wife for more than a few days at a time. Fed up with his "obscene language" and his threats to "beat hell out of her," Hurston abandoned her boy-husband after only six weeks of marriage. On August 11, she left her job with the now-floundering Federal Writers' Project, packed up her car, and got out of town.

CHAPTER 28

Road to the Promised Land

At the North Carolina College for Negroes in Durham, Zora Neale Hurston filled out her faculty record card in red ink. One of the first questions on the card quizzed her about her marital status. "Married (getting divorced)," she scrawled. Leaving the age question blank, she was more forthcoming on other matters: Morgan College (where she'd attended high school and reinvented herself) had awarded her an honorary doctor of letters degree in June, she offered. And *Their Eyes Were Watching God* had been published recently in Italy, as well as England. Marking through several headings on the preprinted card, such as "Graduate Study" and "Teaching Experience," Hurston wrote in her own categories: "Fellowships." "Writing." "Books." Her bold, slanted cursive transgressed the margins of the five-by-seven, two-sided index card, as if she were straining to fit her lifework onto it, and into its confining categories.

Hurston joined the faculty of the North Carolina college in the fall of 1939 at the invitation of the school's president, Dr. James E. Shepard. Like Mary McLeod Bethune of Bethune-Cookman College, Shepard had built his institution from "a one-horse religious school," as Hurston once called it, into the leading college in the state for black students. With several new buildings situated on a beautiful, well-manicured campus, NCCN also had a fine national reputation that attracted students from several neighboring states. What the school lacked, however, was a drama department. And

Shepard hired Hurston to initiate one. "We are going to try to make Negro plays out of Negro life in the Negro manner," she promised her students. But she warned them: "We are going to have to struggle against people who think if we don't do something highbrow we haven't accomplished anything."

A month after settling in Durham, in the north-central part of the state, Hurston gave a lecture at the University of North Carolina in nearby Chapel Hill. The Carolina Playmakers, a respected drama group associated with the university, invited her to the all-white campus to outline her plans for creating "a Negro folk theater" at NCCN. Speaking at the annual fall meeting of the Carolina Dramatic Association, Hurston beguiled the crowd with her disarming humor. She opened her talk with a story: As she was driving onto the campus in her convertible, she said, a Tarheel student tried to insult her, but she ended up getting the last word. "Hi, nigger!" he called out. "Hi, freshman!" she replied.

During her talk, as elsewhere, Hurston "made a point of her race, in both dress and manner," as one audience member recalled, but she did so in a way that delighted her listeners. Just as the Carolina Playmakers had staged several plays about the state's mountain culture, Hurston wanted to create a production company at the Negro college that was committed to dramatizing black folklife. "We want to follow in your footsteps," she flattered her white hosts. In a wide-ranging and animated talk, Hurston ridiculed the white man's idea of good food, discussed the Negro's love of drama, and contrasted black and white attitudes toward religion. "You have a mistaken idea that we're more religious than you," she said. "We're more ceremonial than you. We're not half as scared of God as you. . . ." All these comments were by way of discussing the differences in black and white cultural patterns and the importance of creating drama that reflected black life as it was really lived. "She had serious points to make," attendee Don Pope observed, "but was wonderfully unpedantic about making them."

Among those in the audience that evening was Paul Green, who'd won the 1927 Pulitzer Prize for *In Abraham's Bosom*, a play about a black man whose dreams of founding a school for Negro children are thwarted by a violent mob. An esteemed professor of drama at the University of North Carolina, Green was conscientious and thoughtful about racial issues. As a little boy growing up in rural North Carolina, he recalled, he had many Negro playmates. But inevitably the time came when "we had to separate," as he put it. "As a child I couldn't see why that had to be, and some of that inability to see has always been with me." Immediately after Hurston's talk, Green invited her to join his playwriting seminar, which met weekly at his home in Chapel Hill. Zora was delighted: "I think that is one of the most pleasant things that has ever happened to me, and I think I'll benefit by it," she told a friend. "I think it is the door to a new phase of my career."

The University of North Carolina had no black students and Chapel Hill was a segregated town, not accustomed to Negroes who weren't servants. Most of the students in the playwriting seminar shared Green's liberal racial views, however, so they welcomed Hurston to the group, of which she quickly became "the star," according to class member Pope. But an Alabama woman—"the clod of the group"—objected strenuously to Hurston's presence. She just did not think it was right that a "nigra" should be included, she argued. "Green, with his Carolina country drawl, was all sympathy," Pope recollected. "He understood exactly how she felt, he could see it was painful for her, he certainly wouldn't ask her to put up with such an indignity." So Green told the woman, "We're certainly going to miss you." The daughter of the Confederacy left and Eatonville's daughter stayed.

At the Sunday night meetings of the group, Hurston read from a folk opera she was writing, as Pope recalled. It was "very funny, ironic, drawing on her anthropology among backwoods blacks in Florida." In typical Hurston style, the play did not take itself too seriously, Pope remembered, "but Green steered her toward significance, and I had the impression that this was against the grain of her gift for wry humor and not for the good."

Hurston's wry humor was on full display in her new novel, *Moses, Man of the Mountain*, which she'd quietly finished in Eatonville while working for the Federal Writers' Project. Scheduled for publication on November 2, the book was already eliciting praise in New York literary circles. Carl Van Vechten—who wrote an effusive blurb for the dust jacket—thought it was the best thing Zora had done. But the author had her doubts: "It still doesn't say all that I want it to say," she brooded. Even so, Hurston's publisher, Bertram Lippincott, was delighted with the novel, which he believed was "a remarkable book, possibly a great book."

Just before *Moses* was published, Hurston traveled up North to promote it a bit. She spoke to a women's club in Milwaukee on October 24, then at the Boston Book Fair on the twenty-sixth. At these appearances, she was as upbeat and engaging as usual. While passing through New York, though, Zora stopped to see Van Vechten and confided in him about her disappointment in *Moses*: "I fell far short of my ideal in the writing," she said.

If Hurston fell short of her goal in writing *Moses*, it is testament only to the extraordinarily high standard she set for herself. Brimming with multiple meanings, *Moses, Man of the Mountain* was Hurston's second masterpiece. As in her first one, *Their Eyes Were Watching God*, she wrote at the peak of her powers throughout much of the novel. And for Hurston, that was a towering peak indeed.

At its most basic level, *Moses, Man of the Mountain* is a retelling of the Old Testament story of Moses leading the enslaved Hebrews out of Egypt. As allegory, *Moses* is many, many things: Written in the Negro idiom that Hurston had mastered by 1939, it is a story of black America and its continuous yearning to be free. At the same time, it is a satire on the whole notion of race and racial purity, and it is a deeply philosophical exploration of the very nature of freedom and self-empowerment.

For many generations—before Hurston wrote her novel and after—black people in America have identified with the Hebrew children in Egypt. Oppressed by a Pharaonic system in a strange land, many of Hurston's ancestors survived slavery by resolutely identifying themselves as a "chosen people"—chosen to suffer multitudinous indignities and years of wandering in the wilderness, yes, but also chosen to eventually occupy a Promised Land. As a consequence, Moses—the great liberator, the law-giver—became a figure of unparalleled splendor in black folklore. Negro spirituals are full of references to him, to his courage, and to his magical powers: "Go Down, Moses," God tells him in one famous spiritual, and tell ol' Pharaoh to "let my people go."

Hurston worked on *Moses, Man of the Mountain* for several years, longer than she had on any of her previous books. She actually began the novel back in 1934, when she wrote its precursor, her short story "The Fire and the Cloud." She continued her exploration of the subject in 1936 when she went to the Caribbean, partly in search of Moses legends. In Haiti—where Moses was associated with the supreme deity, Damballah—Hurston's research confirmed her commitment to the novel and broadened her understanding of the monumental task she was taking on. In the legends of black America, in Africa, in the Caribbean, and in Asia, Hurston discovered, Moses was worshiped as a god—and as the greatest conjure man who ever lived. "Wherever the children of Africa have been scattered by slavery, there is the acceptance of Moses as the fountain of mystic powers," she wrote in her introduction to the novel. "Some even maintain that the stories of the miracles of Jesus are but Mosaic legends told again."

In all the legends Hurston had studied, Moses was remade into the image of the people who told the tales. Following in this tradition, Hurston re-created Moses in her own image, so to speak, as a man who is black, self-possessed, a lover of Nature, a masterful hoodoo man, a contemplative thinker, and a great leader—though never a ruler. Hurston's Moses is the product of the mass mythmaking and improvisation that had made him special to people of color the world over—and he is also the product of her own singular, lyrical vision.

Though *Moses* abounds with humor, it is not, as one critic has suggested, merely a good joke. In fact, the beginning of the novel is not very funny at all. It poignantly evokes the horrors of slavery: men are forced to do backbreaking work under threat of the lash, women are denied the right to scream out in childbirth, and whole families become "hunted beasts," cowed by the unseen but all-seeing eyes of the secret police. Because the Egyptian Pharaoh has declared that Hebrews can have no more boy babies, women have to endure labor silently—with their husbands' hands stifling their screams—lest the police seek them out to slay each newborn boy.

In the opening pages of the novel, a Hebrew couple, Amram and Jochebed, give birth to a boy. With help from their older children, Aaron and Miriam, they hide the unnamed baby in a hole for three months, then decide to place him in a basket and float him down the Nile. Maybe some people in a far-off land will find him and take him in, they pray. Miriam is instructed to stay on the riverbank and watch what happens, but she falls asleep at her post. When she wakes up, "with a guilty start," the little ark on the river that contained her baby brother is gone. To avoid punishment for her negligence, Miriam tells her parents that the Pharaoh's daughter—taking a bath in the Nile that very morning—picked up the basket containing the baby and adopted him as her very own. A child's fantasy, created to avoid a spanking, quickly takes on the aura of legend in a Hebrew community famished for some semblance of power. A Hebrew is in the Pharaoh's house, the people of Goshen gloat. "Ho, ho! Pharaoh hates Hebrews, does he? He passes a law to destroy all our sons and he gets a Hebrew child for a grandson. Ain't that rich?" The people do not question Miriam's story too closely because they desperately want to believe it. Yet when Jochebed goes to the palace to see if the Princess's newly adopted baby needs her services as a nursemaid, she is turned away: "There was no new baby to be nursed, they told her. The Princess had been summoned home from Assyria on the death of her husband and had brought her infant son with her several months ago. But what is that to you, Hebrew woman?" Even with this other, more plausible explanation for the baby in the palace, the Hebrews never give up their belief that one of their own has infiltrated the Pharaoh's family. And the child Miriam comes to believe every detail of her story the more she tells it.

With this setup, Hurston calls into question Moses's racial identity. By rooting the biblical legend of the baby's rescue in a child's alibi, she seems to make Moses black—the son of an Egyptian princess and an Assyrian prince. By uniting these two peoples—African and Asian—in Moses's blood, Hurston gives herself license to employ various Mosaic legends from these continents throughout her novel. In this way, too, she removes Moses from the strictures of Scripture and relocates him in the black tradition.

Then, in an amazing literary sleight of hand, Hurston makes race irrelevant by muddling its markers. The Hebrews are Israelites, presumably Jewish people with white skin. But in her retelling of the story, Hurston turns the Hebrews into black Americans—primarily by assigning them the language and lore of the folk. Meanwhile, her allegory transforms the Egyptians into oppressive white Americans, determined to keep Negroes down at any cost. By shifting the racial dynamics this way, Hurston throws the reader off and mocks the whole notion of racial purity; a hundred pages into the novel, you're no longer sure if Moses is black or white, Egyptian or Hebrew. But you realize that it doesn't matter—and that perhaps race itself doesn't matter, at least not based on skin color. Perhaps, Hurston suggests, identification, culture, and "inside feelings" are the only things that count.

Growing up as royalty, Moses learns from the Egyptian priests, from books, and from the folk—embodied in the stableman Mentu, who teaches him to appreciate Nature as a divine source of empowerment. As a young man, Moses becomes a great Egyptian military leader and an egalitarian who is pained by the oppression of the Hebrews. He does not identify as one of them, but he is sympathetic and practical: "It was a weak spot in any nation to have a large body of disaffected people within its confines," he reasons. "And then again, civilization and decency demanded less harsh treatment for human beings." Like the liberal American politicians of the 1920s and 1930s, Moses proposes gradual empowerment for the people of Goshen, but his ideas are resisted by the Pharaoh and his successor, Ta-Phar, who is Moses's uncle. As in the biblical story, Moses kills an Egyptian overseer who senselessly beats a Hebrew slave, thus gaining a reputation as a friend of the Hebrews—just as Carl Van Vechten and other whites were considered "friends of the Negro."

Around the same time, Miriam wanders up to the palace and asks to see Moses, claiming he is her brother. When the story spreads that Moses might be a Hebrew, the power-hungry Ta-Phar questions his nephew's birthright, and Moses's wife accuses him of rape because he kissed her, just once, to seal their marriage of convenience two years before. Hurston's gentle satire turns slightly fierce as she calls to mind the Scottsboro Boys and all the other black men in America who'd been rashly accused of defiling white womanhood. "It is rape for you to even look at me," Moses's wife declares. "Get out of my bedroom. This is no place for Hebrew slaves. Get back to your place in Goshen."

Moses does not know who or what he is. Is he Egyptian royalty? Or is he the son of a Hebrew slave? Choosing to leave the palace before he is confronted and possibly killed, Moses crosses the Red Sea at a secret point where the ebb of the tide leaves a dry path. On the other side, Moses's racial identity, slippery as it is, means nothing. He is not black, not white, not Hebrew, not Egyptian; he is only himself. In the repetitive cadence of a black preacher, Hurston evokes a host of images—about race, about "passing," about spiritual crossings—in one magnificent paragraph:

> *Moses had crossed over. He was not in Egypt. He had crossed over and now he was not an Egyptian. He had crossed over. The short sword at his thigh had a jewelled hilt but he had crossed over and so it was no longer the sign of high birth and power. He had crossed over, so he sat down on a rock near the seashore to rest himself. He had crossed over so he was not of the house of Pharaoh. He did not own a palace because he had crossed over. He did not have an Ethiopian Princess for a wife. He had crossed over. He did not have friends to sustain him. He had crossed over. He did not have enemies to strain against his strength and power. He had crossed over. He was subject to no law except the laws of tooth and talon. He had crossed over. The sun who was his friend and ancestor in Egypt was arrogant and bitter in Asia. He had crossed over. He felt as empty as a post hole for he was none of the things he once had been. He was a man sitting on a rock. He had crossed over.*

In crossing over into his new life, Moses is, for now, a nobody. He has no language, no culture, no people, no weapons, no past, no plan, no keys. He only has himself and the freedom to be whatever he wants to be. Moses decides to live humbly as a student of Nature, hoping to return to Egypt someday far into the future to read the Book of Toth, where, he has been told, "the secrets of the deep" are written. He soon settles down in Midian to live with a wise priest, Jethro—another representative of the folk. Jethro becomes a father to Moses and teaches him everything he knows, just as the old stableman Mentu had done during Moses's youth. Moses also falls in love with Jethro's daughter, Zipporah, a beautiful woman with "night-black eyes," crinkly hair, and "warm, brown arms." As Zipporah's husband and Jethro's son-in-law and student, Moses lives for twenty years in his own private heaven. He embraces Jethro's monotheistic God of the mountain, learns to speak in the vernacular of the common people of Midian, and becomes a better hoodoo man than Jethro himself. Eventually, Moses travels back on a dangerous mission to Egypt to consult the secret Book of Toth, increasing his supernatural power beyond those of any man. "He was able to command the heavens and the earth, the abyss and the mountain, and the sea," Hurston writes. "He saw the sun and the moon and the stars of the sky as no man had ever seen them before, for a divine power was with him."

In Hurston's conception, Moses is largely a self-made man. Nothing has been given to him; he has attained divine power from his own efforts, from his own questioning, from his own inner urge to seek and to know. When Moses returns to Midian with the newly acquired powers from his journey, his friend Jethro suggests he is ready to fulfill his divine destiny: "How about them Israelites?" he challenges Moses. "They're down there in Egypt without no god of their own and no more protection than a bareheaded mule. How come you can't go down there and lead them out?" A lover of silence and quiet places, Moses protests: "I just want to sit on the mountain and ask God some questions about life." Eventually, though, Moses sees the burning bush, hears the Voice, and makes a promise to God to go down to Egypt and tell Pharaoh—his uncle and old rival, Ta-Phar—to let the Israelites go.

Reluctantly, Moses does as he is commanded and ends up engaging in a long battle with Ta-Phar and his priests. At first, the Pharaoh believes it is merely a contest of hoodoo one-upmanship, and he thinks his priests know all of Moses's tricks. Soon, though, after Moses rains down plague upon plague on the Egyptian people, Pharaoh realizes that his nemesis holds the secrets of the universe in his mighty right hand. Under mounting political pressure, Pharaoh agrees to emancipate the slaves. As the Exodus begins, however, he reneges. When he and his soldiers go after the escaping Hebrews to reenslave them, Pharaoh's army is drowned in the Red Sea. After this encouraging victory, though, the Hebrews—crippled by their slave mentality—wander in the wilderness for forty years, constantly questioning Moses's leadership. Over time—and generations—they lose faith, regain it, receive the commandments, and finally find themselves poised to cross the River Jordan and enter the Promised Land.

Along the way, Hurston gently pokes fun at Negroes who want freedom without responsibility; skewers white Americans who wonder why black folks would want freedom anyway and why they always seem to be complaining; attacks intraracial color prejudice; caricatures self-important "race leaders" more interested in regalia than real change; and sets forth her own provocative views on the elusive and individual nature of freedom. While Hurston packs a lot of serious, soul-searching issues into her narrative, she peppers it with a resonant humor, deriving largely from the novel's language. Her use of the black idiom hilariously deflates the highfalutin seriousness of the Judeo-Christian Bible. Acknowledging Moses's special ability to talk directly with God, for instance, one man says to another: "God don't talk to everybody that comes slew-footing down the road." In an amusing evocation of the slave mentality, a committee is formed to confront Moses with their complaints: "I wish to God we had of died whilst we was back in Egypt," they say. "There we was sitting down every day to a big pot of meat and bread. If this God you done got us mixed with just had to kill us, we sure wish He had of killed us down in Egypt on a full stomach." Moses retorts: "I had the idea all along that you came here hunting freedom. I didn't know you were hunting a barbecue."

Hurston endows Moses with the verbal agility to speak many languages, according to the occasion and the audience. Whether he is speaking to Egyptians, Hebrews, or Midians, his language throughout the novel is marvelous and full of meaning. In dethroning Aaron, an officer who is more concerned about his appearance than his people, Moses tells him: "You didn't think about service half as much as you did about getting served, Aaron. Your tiny horizon never did get no bigger, so you mistook a spotlight for the sun." Talking to his loyal left-hand man, Moses instructs: "Joshua, when you find a man who has lost the way, you don't make fun of him and scorn him and leave him there. You show him the way. If you don't do that you just prove that you're sort of lost yourself."

Hurston's novel is full of such language—at the heart of which is an ongoing, passionate debate about the very nature of freedom. Moses gives up his personal freedom to lead the Israelites out of bondage. Because he is human, as well as divine, it is not a choice he makes easily. "I had to quit being a person a long time ago, and I had to become a thing, a tool, an instrument for a cause," Moses laments after the death of his beloved father-in-law and friend. "Jethro is dead and I might have spent several more happy years with him instead of out in the wilderness leading a people and being reviled for doing what was best instead of what was popular."

In the end, Moses decides that he has done all he can. "He had meant to make a perfect people, free and just, noble and strong, that should be a light for all the world and for time and eternity. And he wasn't sure he had succeeded," Hurston writes. "He had found out that no man may make another free. Freedom was something internal." With this powerful statement, Hurston lays out her own views: There is no such thing as a perfect people or an earthly utopia. And freedom is an elusive thing—won, day by day, from within.

Moses, Man of the Mountain is a tour de force of language, humor, insight, protest, and prophecy. It is not a flawless book, but its flaws are relatively minor, which makes them all the more maddening. They set the mind to wondering what the novel could have been if Bertram Lippincott had not been so convinced (in an almost patronizing, anti-intellectual way) that Hurston was a "natural writer." Any of the novel's shortcomings could have been addressed with a little more time and with the input of a good editor, a Jethro-like figure to push Hurston even beyond her considerable capacity to push herself. What could *Moses* have been, for example, if fate had put the manuscript into the hands of a masterful editor like Scribner's Maxwell Perkins, who'd cajoled superb novels out of F. Scott Fitzgerald, Ernest Hemingway, and Thomas Wolfe? Would Perkins have prodded Hurston to more fully delineate Moses's relationship with God, to smooth out some of the racial confusion, to write just one more draft? Despite these unanswered questions, *Moses, Man of the Mountain* remains, as Lippincott discerned, "a great book," its flaws only slightly distracting from its sweeping brilliance.

Critics, past and present, have paid the novel little attention, however. A week after it was published, the *Saturday Review of Literature* responded with qualified praise: "It is not a logically projected work, but it has a racial vitality, a dramatic intensity worthy of its gifted author." *The New York Times* was more enthusiastic, but also a bit condescending. Praising the narrative as "one of great power," the reviewer went on to say: "It is warm with friendly personality and pulsating with homely and profound eloquence and religious fervor.

The author has done an exceptionally fine piece of work far off the beaten tracks of literature. Her homespun book is literature in every best sense of the word." Similarly, the *New York Herald Tribune* called *Moses* "a fine Negro novel" and praised Hurston's "uncommon gifts as a novelist."

On the other hand, Hurston's growing gang of black male critics—if they bothered to read the novel at all—had few good words to say about it. Alain Locke thought it was "caricature instead of portraiture." The young writer Ralph Ellison was even harsher: "For Negro fiction," he wrote, "it did nothing." Locke and Richard Wright both had publicly dared Hurston to move beyond folklore—to step off the porches of Eatonville and into an examination of contemporary racial issues. In *Moses*, Hurston did just that. But because she cast her social concerns in terms of antiquity and cloaked her protest in humor, many critics failed to recognize the novel's depth. To Hurston's belittlers, *Moses* was another example of her insistence on writing what Locke called "folklore fiction," and it was more evidence of her alleged refusal to deal with racial issues or contemporary political concerns—precisely what *Moses* was all about.

Hurston's writing and her worldview would always be informed by her Eatonville experience, but *Moses* was not an Eatonville story. Although many of her characters speak in the black idiom, and the novel relies heavily on various folk legends about Moses, Hurston used no dialect spellings and included few (if any) directly rendered folktales. In this way, she made a shift in style, as well as in subject. With *Moses*, Hurston strode off the porches of Eatonville and into an ancient history and an infinite future, even while traveling to these far horizons on the vernacular language of the folk—a language that she believed could carry her, and her people, anywhere.

Moses, Man of the Mountain was Hurston's most ambitious book; it was her Promised Land—an opportunity to fully realize her artistic and intellectual powers. But when she read dismissive reviews by the likes of Locke and Ellison, she felt confirmed in her fear that the Promised Land remained ahead. Stranded on the banks of the River Jordan, Zora did not rush to defend *Moses* against its detractors, as she'd done for *Their Eyes Were Watching God*. In some ways, she rather agreed with her critics. "I have the feeling of disappointment about it. I don't think that I achieved all that I set out to do," she told a friend. "I thought that in this book I would achieve my ideal, but it seems that I have not reached it yet."

Back in Durham, Hurston retreated into a small log cabin in the woods, a few miles from the campus of the North Carolina College for Negroes. President James E. Shepard—by all accounts a strict disciplinarian—was displeased with her decision to live off-campus; on-campus housing was available for unmarried female faculty members and he expected them to take advantage of it. When Hurston explained that she needed the solitude for her writing, Shepard relented. As an acclaimed author, Hurston had brought some national publicity to the small black college, publicity that Shepard undoubtedly appreciated. Hurston also was working to bring a few New York celebrities to campus over the next few months. She'd already issued open invitations to Ethel Waters, Carl Van Vechten, and Fannie Hurst; any of them would be happy to visit the campus as soon as their schedules permitted, she assured Shepard. Perhaps not wanting to upset any impending negotiations with these prestigious potential visitors, Shepard did not haggle with Hurston over her housing choice.

Hurston's old friend Arna Bontemps thought something else was at play, too. The hard-nosed Shepard had simply fallen under Zora's spell, Bontemps concluded after visiting the Durham campus in mid-November. "She had the president hypnotized," Bontemps would recall, just as she'd once hypnotized partygoers in Harlem. "I remember she took me and introduced me to him. When she came in he started laughing and just settled back, you know, and dropped his cares to listen to Zora as usual."

In town from Chicago to promote his new novel, *Drums at Dusk*, Bontemps was wowed by Zora, too. "She gave me a wonderful time," he reported to ace buddy Langston Hughes. "Zora is really a changed woman, still her old humorous self, but more level and poised," he assured "Lang." Bontemps then brought up the eight-year-old *Mule Bone* dispute: "She told me that the cross of her life is the fact that there has been a gulf between you and her. She said she wakes up at night crying about it even yet. I told her not to be ridiculous, that you have never ceased to insist that she is wonderful. After that she could not do too much for me."

Hughes was receiving reports on Zora from other quarters as well. "Have you heard that Zora is married again," Van Vechten asked. Not two weeks later, the men were gossiping about her again: "Just in your last letter I learn that Zora is married. And in this week's paper I see that she is getting a divorce," Langston tittered to Carlo. "What goes on here? Huh?"

Zora officially filed for divorce from Albert Price a couple of months after the news hit New York. Price denied her allegations that he'd been guilty of "habitual drunkenness" and "extreme cruelty." He also disputed Zora's far-fetched claim that she was "the meek and humble type, easy to be imposed upon." To the contrary, Price retorted, Zora had enticed him to marry her "in total disregard of [his] youth." Further, he asserted, she had an "uncontrollable temper," and she had even infected him with a venereal disease during the short time he "co-habited" with her. Though the court records are chock-full of ugly charges and countercharges, one accusation, at least, offers a sense of the resources Hurston might have called upon in a domestic duel: Price claimed he was in constant fear for his life because Hurston once threatened him with the powers of "black magic or voodooism" that she'd acquired in Haiti. According to the court documents, she professed to have "power both in spirits and in the uses of certain preparations to place individuals under certain spells and that if the Defendant would not perform her wishes she possessed the power to 'FIX HIM.'" Black magic or no, the court eventually sided with Hurston and granted her petition for a divorce.

Zora's brief run to the altar with Price must have confounded Van Vechten and other friends. It may even have baffled Zora herself. Surely, she did not marry Price for money, since he obviously had none. Though he was the son of a minister, it's unlikely that Price had any qualms about premarital sex; Zora, also a preacher's kid, certainly did not. So why marriage? Of course, there's the possibility that Zora really loved Price. But she was not the kind of woman who necessarily equated love and marriage. She'd loved before, after all, but it had not sent her barreling down the aisle. A more likely explanation is that Hurston was pining for Percy Punter—"the perfect man," as she would call him years later. On the rebound perhaps, she sought a man who was similar to Punter—in age, attractiveness, and potential—but who might be a bit more tractable. This is not to say

Zora wanted a henpecked husband, but she did want a partner who was not so hellbent on being "a man" that he impinged on her determination to be her own woman. Whatever faults Price may have had, he certainly did not begrudge Hurston her career, particularly since she was the primary breadwinner in their brief marriage. But Price simply was not the man Hurston wanted him to be; she'd left that man in New York.

With Punter and Price both in her past, Hurston had begun to exhibit a definite penchant for younger men. Just as she chased youth by lying about her age, she pursued it, too, by loving youthful men. In some ways, this inclination was understandable, given Zora's own mental and physical vitality. But her propensity for younger men also seemed related to a need to retain a certain amount of control over her life—a life she did not feel she had "gotten command of" until well into her adulthood. Whether Zora was domineering in the daily doings of love or not, the life experience she had over these men certainly gave her a subtle upper hand.

According to the Durham grapevine, Hurston was soon involved with yet another younger man. This one, the rumor mill said, was one of her students.

Zora admitted privately that her move to Durham had brought a new man into her life, but she said nothing of his age or educational status: "Well, to tell you the truth, I am a little 'tetched' with love myself, though it has not gone beyond the palpitating stage. No commitments as yet," she confided to a friend. "He has a magnificent bass voice. I am trying to find out if that is what I am stuck on or if it is the man himself. I do like strong, big wrassly men and he seems to fit the bill in many ways. I wish he had some money, but then I have never been wealthy, so—"

Zora's telephone-free log cabin, isolated as it was on the outskirts of town, afforded her a good deal of privacy. But she must have known that in a place like Durham, no secrets were kept for long. Motoring to campus frequently—"she was as cute as she could be when she would dress up and put on that little hat," one man recalled wistfully—Zora must have been the oddest thing the eyes of the town had ever seen. As such, she captured the people's attention and galvanized their tongues.

The heart and soul of its community, the North Carolina College for Negroes was located on Fayetteville Street, a long stretch of elegant, middle-class homes, neighborhood stores, churches and one or two funeral parlors. Perhaps because of the college's presence, the community had a palpable dignity and optimism. It was the kind of black neighborhood where Zora would have felt comfortable, though the neighborhood might not have felt so comfortable with her.

Throughout this small, proud community, President Shepard was well loved—even among those who found him "staid and tyrannical," to use the words of Alex Rivera, a 1941 NCCN graduate. Parents sent their daughters and sons to the North Carolina College for Negroes because they knew "certain things would not take place under Dr. Shepard's leadership," said Brooklyn T. McMillon, another NCCN graduate. Men and women lived in separate dorms, of course, and Shepard instituted limited "social hours," half-hour windows when male and female students could openly converse. After dinner, students were expected to retreat into their separate dorms. On weekends, women could receive male visitors during designated hours, and a dance was occasionally held on campus in the gym. "But some parents didn't believe in dancing at all," Rivera remembered, so the dances often were called "socials." "There were a lot of marching-type dances," he chuckled, "to keep men and women from embracing." Chapel was compulsory, and Shepard regularly raised his office window to shout wayward students off the campus, as Rivera recalled. The president's authority was rarely challenged.

Dr. Shepard may have been enchanted with Hurston when Arna Bontemps visited the campus in November, but the spell did not last. As the months went by, Hurston's unorthodox behavior increasingly rankled the president. Not only did she live in a cabin in the woods, she invited students there—male and female. This despite the fact that college policies clearly forbade "social intercourse" between faculty and students. Hurston drove a flashy convertible, dressed immodestly—she once wore a red dress to campus—and seemed to be spending an inordinate amount of time hobnobbing with Paul Green and the other white folks in Chapel Hill.

"She was a bit advanced for Durham and the college community," acknowledged Adelle Ferguson Lafayette, a 1941 NCCN graduate who admired the new drama professor from afar during the fall of 1939. Hurston "carried herself in a very confident manner," Rivera concurred, noting that she appeared to be in her late thirties at the time. He went to her one-bedroom log house once—to take photos of some drama students—and he had several conversations with Hurston. She saw no need to comply with Shepard's rules and regulations, Rivera surmised, and she did not seem at all "fearful of losing her job." Added Lafayette: "Her colorful clothing, extreme styles and bold use of cosmetics would be commonplace today." But in 1939, Shepard and others in the conservative college community were "aghast" at Hurston's audacity.

When the redoubtable Dr. Shepard heard the rumor that Hurston was dating a student, he was "visibly shaken," Rivera recalled. And by the way, he corrected, it was not merely a rumor. Hurston *was* dating a student, Rivera asserted, offering up a name and pointing out a dark, handsome Percy Punter look-alike in the 1939 yearbook. McMillon, too, believed the rumor was true, but he disagreed with his classmate on the identity of Hurston's young paramour. In any case, Rivera summed up, "she upset things while she was here," and Dr. Shepard became determined to "get rid of her."

If Shepard had problems with the way Hurston ran her personal life, she had problems with the way he ran his school. In mid-December, she complained that the administration had not yet organized any plans for her work. The one course that the registrar's office had scheduled for her was English 261, which students had no way of knowing was a drama class. Plus, she protested, it was at an inconvenient hour for most of the students interested in drama. Hurston then went on to suggest an ambitious curriculum for the emerging drama department. It should include classes in playwriting, directing, and production, which would cover lighting, scene design, construction, and costume design. "These courses are not only basic and necessary," she told the president bluntly, "they are irreducible minimum if anything at all is to be accomplished, and I assume that you do want something accomplished or you would not have invited me to join the faculty in the first place."

Scheduled to present a play on campus in a few days, Hurston begged off. "I find with the little time that we have had to prepare a presentation that it will not be what I wish to have represented as my work." She suggested they postpone the play until January, then present it at the Playmakers Theater at UNC in Chapel Hill. While a Chapel Hill staging may have given NCCN drama students more exposure, the idea of his students performing at the segregated college—rather than on his own campus—could not have charmed President Shepard.

By the end of January, Hurston no longer cared what Shepard thought. She'd become distracted from her NCCN responsibilities by an opportunity to collaborate with Paul Green on her in-progress play, *John de Conqueror*. A collaboration with an experienced and acclaimed playwright like Green promised to give Hurston the theatrical breakthrough she'd long coveted, so this became her top priority. "If you have decided to work on JOHN DE CONQUEROR, you do not need to concern yourself with the situation here at the school," she told Green, apparently responding to some conflict-of-interest questions he'd raised. "I won't care what happens here or if nothing happens here so long as I do the bigger thing with you. My mind is hitting on sixteen cylinders on the play now." The comedic play Hurston envisioned would feature a protagonist who was a blend of Marcus Garvey, Father Divine, and the folk figure John Henry. If the play succeeded, she hoped for other collaborations with Green. "I see no reason why the firm of Green and Hurston should not take charge of the Negro playwriting business in America," she said, "and I can see many reasons why we should."

It's unclear whether President Shepard ever responded to Hurston's reasonable, if extensive, requests for instituting a drama curriculum and putting her skills to use. Perhaps he decided not to give her anything to do because he wanted her to become so frustrated that she would leave, taking her unconventional behavior with her. At any rate, the head of the theater program did not stage any plays during her six months at NCCN, though she did create a lot of drama in Durham. "When those two personalities clashed in a small town like this, you had a lot to talk about," Rivera recalled. "I got a kick out of all the confusion," he admitted, believing other people did, too. By early February, Hurston had all but given up on Shepard and his college. She told a friend she hoped to be back in New York soon. "Then I will tell you all about this mess around here that they call education." A whirlwind among breezes, Hurston tendered her resignation on March 1.

CHAPTER 29

A Straight Lick with a Crooked Stick

Hurston was not unemployed for long. At the end of March 1940, she put her furniture in storage and crossed the border to South Carolina to begin a new job. This one was not in the academy, but in the field—where Zora seemed far more comfortable and far less confined.

Anthropologists Jane Belo and Margaret Mead had recently begun a study of religious trances in various cultures, including Bali and Haiti. For comparative purposes, they wanted to study religious ecstasy behavior in a sanctified church. At a salary of $150 a month, Belo hired Hurston for a two-month research expedition in Beaufort, on the coast of South Carolina. Beaufort's rich black cultural heritage dated back hundreds of years, when people from various West African countries were first transported across the Atlantic Ocean and forced to work as slaves on the prosperous rice and indigo plantations in the South Carolina Low Country. To communicate with each other, the slaves developed their own language, a kind of English-based patois rooted in the tongues of their various homelands. They called this new language—and the culture that sprang up around it—"Gullah." (This name, some scholars believe, is a derivation of Angola, the West African country from which many slaves were taken.) Because of isolation from the mainland and the sheer number of slaves in the area, the coastal islands of South Carolina and Georgia soon became a stronghold for this new-sprung culture in which the language, the foods, the crafts, the stories, and the songs were more African than American. When Hurston arrived in Beaufort in the spring of 1940, she found the Gullah culture still thriving. And she saw that Africa still had its say in the way people worshiped.

In early April, Belo traveled from New York and met Hurston in Beaufort. Soon, the two women became regulars at the Rev. George Washington's Commandment Keeper Seventh Day Church of God, which Hurston described as "a revolt against the white man's view of religion." Here, she observed, the keynote was rhythm. "In this church they have two guitars, three cymbals, two tambourines, one pair of rattle goers, and two washboards." In this church, too, worshipers often experienced religious trances—exactly the kind of material Belo wished to study. The white social scientist was delighted: "We got some perfectly grand stuff in a very short time," she soon reported to New York, "thanks to Zora's high-spirited and accomplished cooperation."

After visiting several other churches in the area, Belo went back to New York for her wedding, leaving Hurston in Beaufort to carry on the research. Hurston interviewed the communicants of the Seventh Day Church, who told her all about their visions and conversion experiences. She recorded their stories in a semiscientific essay, which she titled "Ritualistic Expression From the Lips of the Communicants of the Seventh Day Church of God." Hurston also was well aware of the dramatic potential of these people's stories— for either the page or the stage. Speaking of the miracles of God, for example, Reverend Washington told her: "On the Fourth of July I went nine miles from Beaufort to pick huckleberries which were plentiful. I heard a great something under my feet. It was a great big rattlesnake. He hit me in the arm. I turned to run and the snake hit me in the hip. The snake tooth hung in my overalls and I run one hundred and fifty feet with the cold snake whipping against my leg. As I was running the spirit spoke to me and said: 'Read Mark 16:17. Where is your faith?' I rode the bicycle the ten miles home. I got well without going to the doctor." Speaking of more worldly matters, a widow named Sister Mary said: "I didn't know that you could get yourself another man and just keep on having children. Sure I would have had more children if I had known that. I would have had forty or fifty—raise up a nation of your own."

In addition to the stories, Hurston was thrilled by the music at the Seventh Day Church and at other churches in the area. Some local singers were even creating new spirituals that commented on current events. Although Belo already had gotten from Beaufort what she came for—evidence of religious trances—she agreed with Hurston that the music of these churches needed to be recorded. ("God knows current events these days need spirituals sung for them," she quipped.) Shortly after her return to New York, Belo wrote Hurston with good news: She was sending down some equipment for making a sound film. The only problem was that the recording equipment would be accompanied, as Zora put it, "by two very enthusiastic Jews who want to take the spirituals for <u>commercial purposes</u>."

Hurston already had other plans for the songs: she wanted to record them for use in the play that she and Paul Green were still thinking of doing together. She immediately wrote to him for help. "We can't let all that swell music get away from us like that," she warned, urging him to send a recording machine (and someone to operate it) from the University of North Carolina as soon as possible. That way, she could do her own recording first, before the New York "sharks" arrived. "I hope that we can exhaust all the fat juicy places before them two get here," she explained, "and then I will show them some nice places. There will be plenty still, but I don't want them to get ahold of certain tunes which I have earmarked" for the Hurston-Green play. Green responded by wire right away. He'd arranged for an audio recording machine and a man to operate it, he told Hurston. All she had to do was come and get them. "Good going," he added, "and so glad to hear from you."

Meanwhile, Hurston donned a mask that seemed to work particularly well with her white female supporters, writing to "Jane, the Incomparable" with a different message: "<u>Please</u> send the men with the equipment and let me go on finding out things," she said, all sweetness and cooperation. "I am having great luck at that, and leave the instruments alone." When they arrived in mid-May, the New York filmmakers—Norman Chalfin, Lou Brandt, and Bob Lawrence—were not the "sharks" Hurston feared they'd be. The men drove into Beaufort around midnight, recalled Chalfin—"a nice little Jewish boy with a good deal of charm," as Belo described him. The next morning, Zora took them to the Seventh Day Church so they could set up their bulky equipment. Because the church had no electricity, they had to drag their web of wires six hundred yards to the nearest farmhouse, while Zora helped Reverend Washington and his congregation adjust to the white men's presence.

Hurston participated fully in the church services and ended up in much of the recorded footage. In one scene, she enthusiastically played the maracas, while others played cymbals, guitars, and tambourines. Each of the dozen or so church members seemed to have an instrument and no one was a spectator. After some words from the preacher and some prophesying by a woman in a trance, the congregants took up their instruments again. This time, with equal confidence and concentration, Zora picked up sticks and played a drum. At the next day's service, outdoors on the banks of the Beaufort River, the filmmakers recorded the church members singing, praying, and responding to their minister's animated sermon. Hurston was as much a part of the ritual as anyone. Wearing a chic, low-cut dress with an overjacket, large beads, and a scarf to protect her coiffure from the breezy winds, she placed a conga drum between her legs and played it with enthusiasm and abandon. This was Zora: Three months after leaving the assurances and encumbrances of academia, here she was sitting on the edge of the river, making music with her people, living in the moment. With the drum between her legs and her torso swaying with each beat, Zora was doing what she loved most: documenting black culture—and reveling in it.

The "saints" of the church, as they called themselves, seemed at ease with the camera and the microphones, and certainly with Zora's presence among them. The crew recorded a Friday evening service, a Saturday morning baptism in the river, a Saturday evening service, and Sunday ceremonies as well. "Without Zora," Chalfin reported to Belo, "most of it would have been impossible."

Despite her initial resistance, Hurston enjoyed collaborating with the filmmakers, who returned to New York and used their recordings for various projects, including several radio broadcasts on the "Adventures in Music" program on WNYC. Zora stayed in Beaufort through the summer, doing more recordings of her own. In early

August, she read a review copy of Langston Hughes's new book, *The Big Sea*, an autobiography that was "a blend of disingenuousness and complexity," as Hughes's biographer has put it. Writing about his life up to 1931, Hughes discussed his relationship with Hurston and recounted their *Mule Bone* quarrel comically—and a bit condescendingly. ("Girls are funny creatures!" he'd decided.) Nevertheless, Hurston judged the book "very good," and planned to write a favorable review to send to Hughes's publisher, Blanche Knopf.

Although *Newsweek* thought Hughes's autobiography the most readable book of the year, *The Big Sea* was eclipsed by another offering from a black writer. Published in March 1940, Richard Wright's *Native Son* sold 215,000 copies in three weeks—more books than either Hurston or Hughes had sold in nearly two decades of publishing. The first best-selling black author in America, Wright bought some new suits, some new ties, and a house in Chicago for his mother. Then he sailed off to Mexico with his white wife and her family.

As soon as he returned to the States, Wright eclipsed Hurston in a more direct way. That summer, while Zora was still in Beaufort, Paul Green invited Wright to Chapel Hill and began collaborating with the young novelist on a stage adaptation of *Native Son*, the controversial story of Bigger Thomas, a black man who murders a white woman. For the past six months, meanwhile, Green had been evasive and noncommittal about his interest in Hurston's play, finally prompting her to offer him an out: "I have the uncomfortable feeling that I have pestered you too much about this HIGH JOHN DE CONQUEROR," she told him. "You have tried to feel it and you can't. So I will take High John out of your lap and go off and sit with him awhile. As I said, I will write through the thing and let you see what I have done. If you then feel like bothering with the thing again I will be very happy. If not, well then, you just don't feel that way."

Over and again, Hurston's experience had taught her that she had only herself to rely on when it came to making art. Although she gradually accepted this notion, she did so reluctantly, and it invariably disappointed her. The one thing she always sought—but never found—was a collaborator, an artistic soul mate, a partner. She'd been looking for a perfect collaborator all her life, it seemed—ever since she'd begged her schoolmate, Carrie Roberts, to walk out to the horizon with her to see what the end of the world was like. Forty years later, she was still looking for someone to take that journey with her; someone who would be the other half of her equation; someone she could learn from but also teach; someone who would, like Jethro in *Moses*, push her to find the very best in herself. Langston Hughes had fulfilled that role for her in the late 1920s, but *Mule Bone* had ended that. And while Hughes had found a replacement for Hurston in his tight bond with Arna Bontemps, Hurston had never quite found anyone to take Hughes's place. Carl Van Vechten was "God's image of a friend," in Zora's words, but because of the nature of his work, he was not a suitable collaborator, and neither was novelist Fannie Hurst. For a moment, it looked like Paul Green might be the one. But then along came Richard Wright.

Perhaps it was just as well: In terms of artistic collaboration, race would have been a huge barrier to an equal partnership with Hurst or Green, if not Van Vechten. Carlo, who often referred to himself as a "cullud" man, never let any of his black friends call him "Mr. Van Vechten" beyond the second or third letter. But in a thirty-five-year association, Hurst never told Zora to call her Fannie. It was always "Miss Hurst"—or, in less formal letters, "Dear Fannie Hurst" or "Dear Friend." Green, too, failed to extend the first-name prerogative to Hurston; in the southern tradition, he called her "Zora Neale" and she called him "Mr. Green"—or, on brazen days, "Paul Green." Even in his close collaboration with Richard Wright, Green maintained the mister, while calling Wright by his first name or reducing it to "Dick." Thirty years later, Green regretted the way lingering racial prejudices limited his relationships with both Wright and Hurston. "I was so conditioned," he apologized. "Some of the Old South kept hanging on me so that I wasn't able to do what I should."

Stonily resolving to finish her play by herself, Hurston made plans to return to New York by Labor Day. Beaufort was "a nice quiet place to work, but insufferably dull," she judged. "I want to see and to feel."

In Manhattan, Zora contemplated what she would write next, renewed old friendships, and called her old flame, Percy Punter. When they met to talk, she found him the same "shy, warm man I had left." And in "a triumph that only a woman could understand," Zora was pleased to see that Punter "had not turned into a tramp" in her absence, that he'd let his waistline go a bit, and that he'd resigned himself to a plodding desk job. In other words, he wasn't better off without her. "That made me happy no end," she admitted. "No woman wants a man all finished and perfect. You have to have something to work on and prod." Before long, Zora and Percy were an item again. "That waistline went down in a jiffy," she bragged, "and he began to discuss work-plans with enthusiasm. He could see something ahead of him besides time. I was happy. If he had been crippled in both legs, it would have suited me even better."

Hurston spent the winter of 1940–41 in New York, enjoying Punter's company, battling a lingering strain of malaria—apparently picked up during her last days in Haiti—and taking a short hiatus from her writing. After two well-received, Eatonville-inspired novels, two nonfiction books on her anthropological adventures, and an underappreciated attempt to fictionalize biblical history, she pondered her next literary move. Bertram Lippincott—no doubt aware of the hosannas Hughes was hearing for *The Big Sea*—suggested she write an autobiography. Hurston objected, feeling that a look back on her life, and her career, was premature. But Lippincott urged her to think of it as volume one; she could write another volume many years down the road.

Reluctantly, Zora agreed. In the spring of 1941 she said a temporary good-bye to Punter and, with their relationship still intact, left New York so she could focus on writing her autobiography. At the invitation of a wealthy white friend, anthropologist Katharine Edson Mershon, Zora moved to California. A former modern dancer and instructor at Ruth St. Denis's famous Denishawn school, Mershon had conducted a clinic in Bali for years, along with her husband, Jack. But the couple had recently moved back to the States at the first rumblings of a second world war. Anxious for intellectual stimulation, Katharine Mershon invited Hurston to be her houseguest for as many months as it might take her to finish her book. "She fed me well," Hurston recalled, "called in the doctors and cleared the malaria out of my marrow, took me to I. Magnin's and dressed me up." Living at the Mershons' comfortable home in Altadena, just outside of Pasadena, Hurston again took pencil to paper; by mid-July, she'd finished a first draft of her autobiography, which she called *Dust Tracks on a Road.*

It had been a busy period of writing for Zora. The same month, she published a short story, called "Cock Robin Beale Street," in the *Southern Literary Messenger.* Told in the form of an animal tale, the story gently mocked the concept of racial purity. Bull Sparrow shoots Cock Robin on Beale Street because Mrs. Sparrow is no longer producing "plain white eggs." In fact, ever since Cock Robin has been hanging around, Bull Sparrow complains, "every time I go off on a worm hunt, when I get back, I find another blue egg in my nest." Sparrow's brother birds complain of the same paternal puzzle and agree that Cock Robin got what he deserved. After some arguing about who will bury him, they decide to form "one big amalgamated, contaminated parade" down to Sister Speckled-Hen's fish fry and barbecue—and to leave Cock Robin's burial to "de white folks" since "dey always loves to take charge." Never had a story of American miscegenation—written in dialect and camouflaged as an animal tale—been so charmingly told.

As Hurston awaited her editor's comments on her autobiography, she relaxed with other erstwhile New Yorkers now on the West Coast, including Ethel Waters and another popular black singer-actress, Etta Moten. She also spent a good deal of time with Mershon, who made it her business to show Zora all of California. Traveling in Mershon's Buick from San Diego up, Hurston saw deserts, poppies, Joshua trees, orange groves, and "beaches full of people in dark sun glasses." The travelers then went to northern California, where Zora took in redwood forests, cable cars, giant sequoias, wharves, and plenty of mountains. California was "*buen* nice," she decided, although the mountains didn't sit too well with a flat-footed "Florida Fiend" like herself. "To my notion, land is supposed to lie down and be walked on—not rearing up, staring you in the face. It is too biggity and imposing," Zora joshed. "But on the whole, California will do for a lovely state until God can make something better."

During her stay in southern California, Hurston also saw Hollywood, up close and personal. On October 29, 1941, Paramount Studios hired her as "a writer and technical adviser" for an impressive $100 a week. Equivalent to $1,200 today, it was the highest weekly salary she had ever earned. Still, Zora was not seduced by Hollywood's shine. "This job here at the studio is not the end of things for me," she decided. "It is a means." Commuting eighteen miles one way from Altadena to the Paramount office on L.A.'s Marathon Street, Hurston had little success interesting the studio in making movies from her novels. But her generous salary enabled her to save a bit of money as she awaited the publication of her new book.

For Zora and many other Americans, December 7, 1941, was an ordinary Sunday, that bittersweet day of the week that always seems to inspire reflection—and that always ends with a deep intake of breath to prepare for the five days ahead. On that Sunday, though, no one in America was prepared for what was to come. That day, the United States actively entered World War II after Japanese aerial forces battered Pearl Harbor. The sneak attack on the U.S. naval base near Honolulu destroyed over two hundred American aircraft and killed more than two thousand servicemen. More Americans certainly would have lost their lives but for the courageous work of Dorie Miller, a black mess attendant on one of the U.S. Navy battleships. Normally confined to menial kitchen labor in the segregated navy, Miller seized a machine gun during the attack and shot down four enemy planes. Because he had never been trained nor treated like a sailor, Miller surprised everybody by acting like one. The next day—as news of the attack reached the mainland and black Americans proudly applauded Miller's bravery—the United States officially declared war on Japan.

U.S. involvement in the war greatly influenced Bertram Lippincott's reading of Hurston's manuscript. Her critical comments about the U.S. government and its foreign policies would have to be excised from the autobiography, he soon told her. In wartime, she would find no audience for a book challenging America's assertions that it was a beacon of justice: "I see that the high principles enunciated so throatedly are like the flowers in spring—they have nothing to do with the case," Hurston had written in a chapter called "Seeing the World As It Is." Before the book could be published, Lippincott warned, these sorts of statements would have to go, as would Hurston's blunt criticism of the president: "President Roosevelt could extend his four freedoms to some people right here in America before he takes it all abroad, and, no doubt, he would do it too, if it would bring in the same amount of glory," she'd written. "I am not bitter, but I see what I see. He can call names across an ocean, but he evidently has not the courage to speak even softly at home."

As Hurston revised her manuscript, per Lippincott's instructions, she began to think about returning East, particularly as war activity mounted on the Pacific Coast. The Mershons decided to take no chances; while in Saginaw, Michigan, for the Christmas holidays, they vowed to stay away from the coastline upon their return to California.

Zora, meanwhile, spent Christmas Day with Ethel Waters at her house on Hobart Street in Los Angeles. Joined by other intimates, including former Dunham dancer Archie Savage (the new man in Waters's life), Zora and Ethel played bridge and "exchanged confidences that really mean something to both of us," as Hurston recalled. Waters had recently completed a successful Broadway run in the musical *Cabin in the Sky*, which she felt paled in comparison to her role as Hagar in *Mamba's Daughters*, the 1938–39 Broadway smash in which she made her triumphant debut as a dramatic actress. Also in 1939, Waters had appeared on that still-experimental medium called television. Her performance—in a scene from *Mamba's Daughters*—was "the best presented by television thus far," the *Pittsburgh Courier* declared.

Hurston undoubtedly viewed her chumminess with Waters as a marker of her own success. But the most published black woman writer in America also genuinely found in Waters someone to admire. Spending time with Ethel was "just like watching an open fire," Zora observed in barefaced adoration; "the color and shape of her personality is never the same twice." Despite her sometimes-lusty stage persona, Waters was "deeply religious," Zora noted. A practicing Catholic, the entertainer did not allow any card-playing or dancing in her house on Sundays. But she definitely had a ribald side: "You know I can give a guy a tongue-lashing in a split second," Waters once boasted. "And I never hesitate to do it." Though she could cuss like a pimp, Waters shared with Zora a distaste for liquor and the behavior it sometimes elicited. Waters didn't smoke, either, and she usually exiled Zora onto the balcony or into a distant corner of the room whenever she lit up a Pall Mall.

Among other things, the two women shared a firm determination to avoid racial bitterness. "I don't lament the prejudice," Waters once told a reporter. "You can read *Native Son* and there is one statement of the Negro's case, and you can then read *Grapes of Wrath* and realize that white holds down white. It's all a struggle for supremacy." In 1941, Waters reigned supreme in the entertainment world; according to one report, she pocketed $2,000 a week—more than $24,000 in today's money. But Waters had grown up in the slums of Philadelphia, she'd never made it past the third grade, and she'd once worked as a chambermaid for $4.75 a week. As a result, she believed with Zora that one of life's keys was the ability to play the hand you were dealt, with the understanding that the hand could change, for better or worse, at any time. Or, as Waters herself put it: "Don't care how good the music is, Zora, you can't dance on every set."

On New Year's Eve, Zora resigned from her job at Paramount; she collected her last check on January 3, 1942, then made plans for her coast-to-coast trek back to Florida. Traveling leisurely, she stopped along the way to lecture on the black college circuit, speaking with "dynamic informality" at Tuskegee and other schools. Finally arriving in St. Augustine in the spring, Zora immediately took ill with pneumonia, tonsillitis, and sinus problems, which kept her down for several weeks. Once she reclaimed her health, though, Zora resumed her efforts to polish her autobiography and got to work on several theatrical ideas.

In order to "keep on eating," Hurston secured a summer job teaching literature at Florida Normal and Industrial College. There, in early July, she met novelist Marjorie Kinnan Rawlings, winner of the 1939 Pulitzer Prize (for *The Yearling*) and a frequent speaker at the small Negro college. Deciding that Hurston was "the most wonderful woman," Rawlings invited her to tea the next day. As soon as Zora accepted, the white writer panicked. "Oh, my God, I've done something terrible," she told her husband, Norton Baskin. Explaining that she'd invited a Negro to tea at their apartment—on the top floor of her husband's segregated Castle Warden Hotel—Rawlings worried about what Baskin's customers would say. "We can get around that," he assured her. Baskin instructed his "colored bell boy" to escort his wife's visitor to their apartment; she was expected at 5:00 P.M. the next day, he explained. The appointed hour came and went, however, without Baskin or his bellhop seeing any sign of Zora. Around 5:20, Baskin phoned his wife from his downstairs office to tell her she'd been stood up. "Are you crazy? She's up here," Rawlings replied. "And if you know what's good for you, you better come on up; I've never had so much fun." When Baskin joined his wife and her visitor in the apartment, he found out what had happened. When Zora arrived at the whites-only hotel, she immediately realized her presence might cause trouble. "I didn't want to upset anybody," Baskin remembered her saying, "so I came through the kitchen and walked up."

Hurston's uncomplaining compliance with Jim Crow was not what impressed the Baskins most, however. "She really was just sensational," Norton Baskin would recall. "She was the funniest thing you've ever seen, smart as could be too." Yet Zora's visit stirred more complex emotions in Baskin's wife. Writing to a friend the next day, Marjorie Kinnan Rawlings described Hurston as "a lush, fine-looking café au lait woman with a most ingratiating personality, a brilliant mind, and a fundamental wisdom that shames most whites." Speaking of herself in third-person, Rawlings added: "The Missus has had quite a jolt and feels rather small. By all her principles, she should accept this woman as a human being and a friend—certainly an attractive member of society acceptable anywhere—and she is a coward. If she were on her own, she would do it. She feels that she cannot hurt her husband in a business way. But her pioneer blood is itching—"

To understand how much Hurston's dazzling presence upset the racial order of things in Rawlings's segregated little world, one only has to read an offhand, off-color remark the author made in the same letter, about another black woman. While her maid Idella was on vacation, "a tie-tongued darky" was substituting, Rawlings reported. "She asked, 'Ih ah ohhing oo oot ou c e i?' which meant, apropos of some rat poison in the bathroom, 'Is that something you put out for the mice?'"

While Rawlings contemplated whether she would be a racial coward or a pioneer, whether she would continue to look down upon black people generally while accepting one person as exceptional, Hurston went on about her business at Florida Normal. Hortense

Williams taught children's literature that same summer in St. Augustine. In an on-campus building designated for single female faculty members, Hurston and Williams lived on separate ends of the corridor in identical rooms that Williams remembered as "comfortable, clean and orderly." A recent Fisk graduate, Williams was twenty-two years old and recognized Hurston as "an older woman—probably in her 30s." (The "attractive, reddish" Hurston, as Williams described her, was actually fifty-one, though she was passing for about forty.) One day, Williams recalled, she noticed some red roses in Zora's room. When she commented on their beauty, Hurston shocked the younger woman with her earthiness: "Flowers from the king," Zora exclaimed, "for shaking that thing!"

Williams was probably shocked even further if she read Hurston's "Story in Harlem Slang," which appeared in the July 1942 issue of *The American Mercury*. Written in the coded, sexually charged "slanguage" of Lenox Avenue, it is the story of two uptown hipsters who while away a day playing the dozens as they stalk out their next meal. Jelly and Sweet Back are both unemployed men whose sexual skills are for sale to any woman who will support him, either with a free meal or a no-commitments, live-in arrangement. After signifying colorfully about who is the best at his game, the men get a chance to compete head to head when a young woman comes walking down the avenue. It is Wednesday, which means all the domestics are off for the afternoon with their pay in their pockets. "Some of them bound to be hungry for love," both men think. "That meant a dinner, a shot of scrap-iron, maybe room rent and a reefer or two. Both went into the pose and put on the look," Hurston writes. The woman, though, proves to be too much for the men. After some pleasantries and passes, she peeps their game: "You skillets is trying to promote a meal on me," she says. "But it'll never happen, brother. You barking up the wrong tree. I wouldn't give you air if you was stopped up in a jug. I'm not putting out a thing. I'm just like the cemetery—I'm not putting out, I'm taking in! Dig?" Sweet Back, who has "not dirtied a plate since the day before," tries to snatch the woman's purse. Instead, she grabs the coattail of his zoot suit and threatens to split it up the middle: "If your feets don't hurry up and take you 'way from here, you'll *ride* away," she threatens. "I'll spread my lungs all over New York and call the law. Go ahead. Bedbug!

Touch me! And I'll holler like a pretty white woman!" She then walks away haughtily, leaving the men to their bloated language and empty stomachs.

Hurston's published story was accompanied by a "Glossary of Harlem Slang" that included definitions for such terms as "scooter-pooker" ("a professional at sex"), "8-rock" ("very black person"), "Aunt Hagar" ("Negro race"), and "dusty butt" ("cheap whore"). Before publishing the piece, *The American Mercury* eliminated several of the more explicitly sexual definitions from Hurston's glossary, originally called "Harlem Slanguage." Similarly, the magazine editors cut some interesting sections from the story itself, which was initially called "Now You Cookin' with Gas."

In the unedited version, much of Hurston's dialogue has racial undertones, comparable to the hilarious holler-like-a-white-woman bit. At one point in the courting competition, for instance, Sweet Back suggests that he and the woman, who's from Georgia, go back there and settle down. Jelly snorts, "You crazy in the head? Christ walked de water to go *around* Georgy. What you want to go in it for?" Along these same lines, Jelly explains that he left Alabama to get away from white oppression: "Mister Charlie down there plays too rough to suit me. . . . Them peckerwoods down there liable to make me hurt some of 'em." Later in the conversation, Sweet Back claims that he once killed a white policeman in the South: "A cracker cop down in Georgy got in my face one time and I shot him lightly and he died politely." After the woman spurns both men, Jelly loses his cocky pose for a moment and wonders if his hungry new life in New York is any better than the full meals he left behind in Alabama. "He was thinking corroding thoughts about the white folks in this man's town—so cold and finicky about jobs," Hurston writes. "They would call you 'Mister' all right, just like he had been told that they would. . . . [But] you better not never ask them about a loan before pay-day." All these references to racial strife, South and North, were excised from Hurston's story when it was published, turning it into a harmless little tale about a couple of shiftless Harlem gigolos.

In a more straightforward, journalistic mode, Hurston published a piece in the September 5 edition of *The Saturday Evening Post*. Called "Lawrence of the River," it was a profile of black cattleman Lawrence Silas of Central Florida. Under her byline, Hurston was identified as "a distinguished Negro novelist." And—as the world remained at war—the *Post* sought to present Silas's story as "a symbol of the strength of our nation."

This kind of censorship on the one hand and enforced patriotism on the other were both at work when Hurston's autobiography, *Dust Tracks on a Road*, was published in November. "She has lived in primitive simplicity in remote communities where folklore is a part of daily life," the flap copy said of Hurston; "she has lived in the inner circles of literary New York, has known the glamor of Hollywood. All this comes to life in her story. . . . It breathes a spirit which should give every reader courage for the future of America."

Zora Neale Hurston's life story, as presented in *Dust Tracks on a Road*, is the enchanting tale of how one extraordinary black woman rose from Eatonville dreamer to Gotham achiever. The cover of the first Lippincott edition traced Hurston's remarkable trajectory with an amusingly literal illustration. In the cover's top left-hand corner is a scene of bucolic security: a little girl and a woman (representing Zora's mother, perhaps, or maybe her own woman-self) are depicted on a country porch, gazing out to some unseen future. From this image, a diagonal dusty road extends to the scene in the front right-hand corner of the cover: It is the true picture of success—the triumphant New York City skyline.

Hurston was not nearly so literal in recounting the events of her life. First off, she had a logistical problem. Zora had been lying about her age for the past twenty-five years. When she started the fib in 1917, it was arguably for a good enough reason: She needed to present herself as a teenager so she'd be eligible for free schooling. Over the years, though, Zora kept the lie going because it had become convenient, it was simpler in some ways than telling the truth, and it was certainly easy on her ego. Besides, if she could get away with it, why not? As Phoeby says of Janie in *Their Eyes Were Watching God*, "The worst thing Ah ever knowed her to do was taking a few years offa her age and dat ain't never harmed nobody." Now that Hurston was trying to write about her life in some kind of chronological order, however, she was faced with a challenge. How could she track the progress of her life without giving away her true age? How could she make all those dates jibe?

Hurston's solution was to adopt an evasive attitude about her own birth. In the chapter called "I Get Born," she studiously avoids giving a birth year, and she presents her birth as folklore, as a handed-down story of questionable veracity. "This is all hear-say," she begins with a charming wink and a smile. "Maybe, some of the details of my birth as told me might be a little inaccurate," she writes, "but it is pretty well established that I really did get born." Hurston then describes herself as a bright, imaginative child whose curiosity and self-esteem were nurtured by the small, all-black town of Eatonville and whose personal dreams were nourished by her mother but squashed by her father. After her mother died, the girl-child had a difficult time in the world. But through perseverance and pluck, she survived the hardships to become a celebrated author and folk-lorist whose Eatonville sensibilities have remained intact. The first eleven chapters of *Dust Tracks* are devoted to an exuberant descrip-tion of this uphill climb. In the last quarter of the book, Hurston veers from the autobiographical form—and the more-or-less chrono-logical narrative—and offers her views on a variety of topics, such as love, religion, and "My People, My People!"

Beyond the falsehoods she invents to support the deception about her birth year (placing her birth in Eatonville, for instance, rather than in Notasulga, where all the older Hurston children were born), Zora does not tell many (if any) out-and-out lies about her life. Through omission, however, she presents a questionable and care-fully constructed version of the truth. For example, she reports having "no lurid tales to tell of race discrimination at Barnard," con-veniently forgetting the taunting laughs of her classmates in French class. Similarly, she relegates her discussion of the Harlem Renaissance to one paragraph; she leaves out her friendship and feud with Langston Hughes; and she fails to mention her second marriage (to Albert Price). As narrator of *Dust Tracks on a Road*, Hurston fully embraces and embodies the words she wrote on the first page of *Their Eyes Were Watching God*: "Now, women forget all those things they don't want to remember, and remember every-thing they don't want to forget. The dream is the truth. Then they act and do things accordingly."

The "truth" that Hurston presents in *Dust Tracks*, then, is insep-arable from the "dream." That is to say, the vision—the selective remembrance—of what her life *should* have been, even if that remembrance is occasionally contrary to what *was*. In that regard, *Dust Tracks on a Road* is what readers today might view more as memoir than autobiography. Acknowledging the unreliability of memory, writer William Zinsser has asserted that the two essential elements of memoir are "integrity of intention" and "carpentry." "Memoir writers must manufacture a text, imposing narrative order on a jumble of half-remembered events. With that feat of manipulation they arrive at a truth that is theirs alone, not quite like that of anybody else who was present at the same events." The memoirist's job, in other words, is to capture not the letter of the life, but the spirit of it. And *Dust Tracks* does that exceedingly well.

The story of a self-invented woman, *Dust Tracks on a Road* offers a reliable account of a writer's *inner* life. Unfortunately, Hurston's omissions of some external realities have caused many contemporary critics to dismiss *Dust Tracks* as nothing more than a pack of lies. It is one of Hurston's best pieces of fiction, they chortle. To jettison the book so glibly, however, is a mistake. Zora played fast and loose with the facts, to be sure. But readers cannot dismiss *Dust Tracks* unless they also are willing to dismiss Langston Hughes's *The Big Sea* and Richard Wright's *Black Boy*—two other autobiographies published in the 1940s in which black writers engaged in mythmaking about their lives. Often, the critical tendency has been to excuse or ignore this "will to adorn" when the perpetrator is a black man, but to vehemently attack Hurston—one of the few black female autobiographers of the first half of the twentieth century—for doing the very same thing. Truth be told, *Dust Tracks on a Road* is an "imaginative autobiography," a term Wright applied to *Black Boy*. And every so-called lie in Hurston's book is an avenue to the truth.

Intriguingly, Hurston fills *Dust Tracks* with factual clues, as if playfully daring her readers (and future biographers) to see between the lines. For instance, although she says she was nine years old at the time of her mother's death in 1904, she voluntarily ticks off the names of several childhood friends. A check of the 1900 census reveals that these schoolmates would have been thirteen years old in 1904, a piece of information that helps confirm Hurston's 1891 birth date. If she had *really* wanted to maintain her age facade, it seems that she would have chosen some younger girls and listed them as her playmates, rather than name her real childhood friends, who were her own (true) age. Similarly, Hurston doesn't readily identify the school she attended in Jacksonville, but she discloses the name of its president. A search for a President Collier in Jacksonville eventually leads to Florida Baptist Academy, the same school that Hurston freely tells us her oldest brother attended. In the same vein, Hurston identifies the most significant man in her life only by his initials, "P.M.P.," but she also reveals that he's of West Indian parentage, a member of the Alpha Phi Alpha fraternity, and a graduate of City College of New York and Columbia University. With these clues, all roads eventually lead to Percival McGuire Punter. In this way, Hurston disguised many truths of her life in a confounding but crackable code.

Why the coding at all, though? The answer to that question begins with Hurston's reluctance to write an autobiography in the first place. "I did not want to write it all," she admitted, "because it is too hard to reveal one's inner self, and there is no use in writing that kind of book unless you do." Hurston's solution to this dilemma was to expose limited aspects of her inner and outer self in masterful, figurative language behind which she could shrewdly hide. Sometimes, Hurston lets the reader know outright that she is not telling all: "What will be the end? That is not for me to know," she writes at one point in *Dust Tracks*. "And even if I did know all, I am supposed to have some private business to myself. What I do know, I have no intention of putting but so much in the public ears." More often, though, Hurston uses the "feather-bed resistance" that she'd described in *Mules and Men* years before. Black people, she'd asserted, were often evasive about revealing "that which the soul lives by." But that evasion was usually subtle and hidden under a surface sheen of "laughter and pleasantries." She went on to explain "the theory behind our tactics": "The white man is always trying to know into somebody else's business. All right, I'll set something outside the door of my mind for him to play with and handle. He can read my writing but he sho' can't read my mind," Hurston wrote tellingly.

Hurston practiced this kind of featherbed subterfuge in her autobiography not only because she wanted to keep her private self private; she also wanted to get her book published—and she'd been duly informed that there were some things Lippincott would not print, especially in wartime.

Autobiography, like memoir, is an assertion of identity. The mere act of writing an autobiography was an audacious step for Hurston to take, despite her reluctance. It was a way of saying: "This life, black and female, matters. And if this life matters, then all the other black and female lives matter as well." In 1942, this was an almost-revolutionary statement, and Hurston and her publisher needed to work hard to make sure it did not offend the book's potential readers, most of whom, in the 1940s, were not black and female.

To frame Hurston's life as "a great American success story"—as radio personality Mary Margaret McBride called it—Hurston and Lippincott had to work a bit of literary magic. Hurston's magic took the form of several rhetorical strategies she employed in *Dust Tracks;* namely, indirection, opacity, and humor—all aspects of the Negro folklore that she'd mastered. Thus, she either avoided sensitive topics, such as race and racism, or she masked her views in humor or other forms of subtle, indirect expression. Near the end of the book, for instance, Hurston writes: "What do I want, then? I will tell you in a parable. A Negro deacon was down on his knees praying at a wake held for a sister who had died that day. He had his eyes closed and was going great guns, when he noticed that he was not getting anymore 'amens' from the rest. He opened his eyes and saw that everybody else was gone except himself and the dead woman. Then he saw the reason. The supposedly dead woman was trying to sit up. He bolted for the door himself, but it slammed shut so quickly that it caught his flying coat-tails and held him sort-of static. 'Oh, no, Gabriel!' the deacon shouted, 'dat ain't no way for you to do. I can do my own running, but you got to 'low me the same chance as the rest.'"

In this way, Hurston told her white readers—through a humorous, nonthreatening parable—that what she wanted was equal opportunity, "the same chance as the rest." But *Dust Tracks*, as published in 1942, did not go any further in challenging white injustice. This is not because Hurston did not have stronger feelings, but her more stoutly worded views were excised from the final book.

Bertram Lippincott took the slash-and-burn approach to editing Hurston's manuscript, cutting out whole chunks of it. The most notable losses were the chapters "The Inside Light—Being a Salute to Friendship" and "Seeing the World As It Is." In the first of these eradicated chapters, Hurston paid homage to all those people who had helped her over the years. Though this chapter was little more than an extended acknowledgments section, it was important because it countered the portrayal throughout most of the book that Hurston was a completely self-made woman. "I wrote a chapter in my new book dedicated to friendship," she told Carl Van Vechten, "but the publishers deleted it. In it, I tried to show my inside feelings for certain people, because I am not sure that I have ever made it clear how I feel. . . I regretted the loss of that chapter." To another friend, she voiced her regret more vividly: "Now, I look like a hog under an acorn tree guzzling without ever looking up to see where the acorns came from."

In another significant lost chapter, "Seeing the World As It Is," Hurston expressed her opinions on various social and political issues with a let-the-chips-fall-where-they-may honesty that Lippincott apparently could not abide. Zora did not mince words in this chapter and nothing seemed to escape her critical eye. Speaking of Christian hypocrisy, for example, she wrote: "Popes and Prelates, Bishops and Elders have halted sermons on peace at the sound of battle and rushed out of their pulpits brandishing swords and screaming for blood in Jesus' name. The pews followed the pulpit in glee. So it is obvious that the Prince of Peace is nothing more than a symbol." In the same chapter, Hurston attacked American injustice in all its forms and criticized U.S. military intervention in other countries, where machine gun bullets were thought to be "good laxatives for heathens who get constipated with toxic ideas about a country of their own." In a cogent critique of communism, Hurston admitted that she saw "many good points" in the Communist Party. "Anyone would be a liar and a fool to claim that there was no good in it. But I am so put together that I do not have much of a herd instinct. Or if I must be connected with the flock, let *me* be the shepherd my ownself." She added: "You cannot arouse any enthusiasm in me to join in a protest for the boss to provide me with a better hoe to chop his cotton with. Why must I chop cotton at all? Why fix a class of cotton-choppers?"

In this chapter, too, Hurston delineated her own political philosophy, which valued individualism over "race pride," a social construct that she believed divided people into separate camps in a manner that was potentially explosive. "And how can Race Solidarity be possible in a nation made up of as many elements as these United States? It could result in nothing short of chaos. The fate of each and every group is bound up with the others," she argued. Hurston saw America in more complex terms than limited racial thinking allowed, and she saw black America as more complex than most "race leaders" acknowledged. "Anybody who goes before a body and purports to plead for what 'The Negro' wants, is a liar and knows it. Negroes want a variety of things and many of them diametrically opposed," she stated candidly. "There is no single Negro nor no single organization which can carry the thirteen million in any direction."

Hurston was equally candid about her impatience with what she viewed as white people's widespread, unfounded notions of supremacy: "I just think it would be a good thing for the Anglo-Saxon to get the idea out of his head that everybody else owes him something just for being blonde," she wrote. "I am forced to come to the conclusion that two-thirds of them do hold that view. The idea of human slavery is so deeply ground in that the pink-toes can't get it out of their system." If white people were really superior, she suggested, they would feel no need to "rig the game so that they cannot lose." Racism, she felt, was just an attempt at "limiting competition." But why stack the deck? Addressing her white readers directly, Hurston dared: "If you are better than I, you can tell me about it if you want to, but then again, show me so I can know. . . . And then again, if you can't *show* me your superiority, don't bother to bring the mess up, lest I merely rate you as a bully."

None of these courageous, potentially incendiary comments made it into Hurston's book, prompting some black critics to chide her, once again, for refusing to confront racial or political issues. In a review of *Dust Tracks* in the *New York Herald Tribune*, Arna Bontemps noted dryly: "Miss Hurston deals very simply with the more serious aspects of Negro life in America—she ignores them."

Given all that was edited from Hurston's manuscript, Bontemps was only partially right. Hurston was not deaf, dumb, and blind to the facts of American racism. But she'd long ago made a decision that was reflected in her autobiography: She would not *allow* white oppression to define or distort her life.

Bertram Lippincott told a story that illustrated this point. When

Hurston visited his office in Philadelphia, he and other editors would take her out to lunch to discuss business or to simply celebrate her latest publishing success. In Philadelphia and other northern cities, unlike in the segregated South, the law required restaurants to admit and serve any paying customer, regardless of race. But some restaurants, Lippincott recalled, "weren't very agreeable now and then." Consequently, at these lunches with Hurston, Lippincott and his staff sometimes fretted about a potential scene. But Hurston always seemed unconcerned, he observed. On one occasion Lippincott phoned ahead to a restaurant where he frequently dined and asked if it would be all right to bring in a black client. "There were book buyers and a dozen more of us with her and we got a table right in the middle of the dining room," he remembered. "And Zora was there chattering away and everybody was listening—that's the way it always was, you know. And yet I would glance around here and there, and the people around us looked glum; they didn't like any part of it." Hurston seemed oblivious to the stares and rude treatment, Lippincott marveled. "I noticed it again and again. We'd all be mad at the headwaiter and want to knock him down and all that, and Zora . . . didn't care at all about all the goings-on."

Hurston surely noticed these slights, but her racial approach—her survival strategy—was to act as if they didn't matter. And in the larger scheme of things, they didn't. Other customers' sullenness would not prevent Hurston from enjoying her free meal, unless she *allowed* it to have that effect. And the headwaiter's impertinence would not prevent her from doing business with her publisher. His whiteness notwithstanding, he was only a waiter, after all; *she* was the published author.

"I know that there is race prejudice, not only in America, but also wherever two races meet together in numbers," Hurston acknowledged in a passage that was cut from *Dust Tracks*. "I have met it in the flesh," she said. But "I do not give it heart room because it seems to me to be the last refuge of the weak."

This willful position certainly grew out of Hurston's childhood experience in Eatonville, where she'd been part of a community that maintained a vigorous sense of racial health. In Eatonville, racism was largely an outside force that affected the citizenry in few ways discernible to Hurston as a child. In other words, it existed, but it hardly mattered. With this background, Hurston seemed to conduct her life as an elaborate "what if" experiment: What if black people acted as if racism did not affect them? As if it were the discriminator's problem, rather than the problem of those who were discriminated against? If black people collectively acted this way, would racism cease to affect them? Would it eventually cease to exist? And perhaps more important, would this attitude help them to escape bitterness, anger, and resentment—killers just as sure as the Ku Klux Klan? In *Dust Tracks*, Hurston essentially reported that her lifelong experiment with these questions had been a success.

In the last paragraph of the book, as published in 1942, Hurston declared: "I have no race prejudice of any kind." But she then went on to express a special love for black people: "My kinfolks and my 'skinfolks' are dearly loved. My own circumference of everyday life is there. But I see their same virtues and vices everywhere I look," she wrote. Then, in a sly shift of tone, Hurston turned "race prejudice" on its head, assuring her white readers that she did not view them as inferior because of their whiteness: "In my eyesight," she offered, "you lose nothing by not looking just like me."

Hurston's insistence that she had "no race prejudice of any kind" did not prevent her from making such ambiguous, ironic statements. Nor did it preclude her from speaking out against injustice or bigotry wherever she perceived it. Put another way, her claim to racial high-mindedness was not a gag order. In *Dust Tracks on a Road*, however, her publisher provided the muzzle.

Following Lippincott's bridling editorial direction, Hurston eliminated—or allowed her editor to eliminate—all overt statements in *Dust Tracks* that might have been viewed as inflammatory. She did not, however, eradicate the sentiments behind those statements. Instead, she tried to hit a straight lick with a crooked stick, as the folk would say. That is, she subtly masked her feelings in the kind of wit, irony, and indirection at play in the last paragraph of her book and indeed throughout the narrative. Ultimately, the price Hurston paid for this choice was that the Zora of *Dust Tracks* was not as politically astute, outspoken, irreverent, or complex as the real Zora was.

Yet Hurston was amply rewarded for publicly presenting this muted portrait of herself. White critics loved *Dust Tracks on a Road*. Admiring Hurston's "charming practicality" and "reckless heroism," the *Saturday Review of Literature* judged it "a fine, rich autobiography, and heartening to anyone, white, black, or tan." Similarly, *The New York Times Book Review* called Hurston's story "an encouraging and enjoyable one for any member of the human race." Noting that her book was "full of the graphic metaphors and similes that color Negro speech at its richest," the reviewer added: "Any race might well be proud to have more members of the caliber and stamina of Zora Neale Hurston."

Buoyed by such reviews, *Dust Tracks* sold well and elevated Hurston's status as a literary celebrity. In this regard, Hurston hit a straight lick with a crooked stick yet again—achieving perhaps her greatest fame and acclaim for a book she never wanted to write, a book that was heavily censored by her editors, a book that deliberately disguised as much as it disclosed. Despite its duplicity, white readers praised *Dust Tracks on a Road* for its honesty. Calling Hurston's book "a masterpiece of understanding," one white supporter proclaimed: "You have told a perfectly splendid story that makes for glorious reading, and that should be of great service to your race and to mine. We need to know each other better."

CHAPTER 30

Solitude

Near the end of 1942, Hurston happily noted that she was "working harder and more consistently now than ever in my life." With the success of *Dust Tracks on a Road*, Zora Neale Hurston became something just short of the "race leaders" she'd always scorned: She was a recognized black spokesperson whose opinions were hotly sought by the white reading public. Just after *Dust Tracks* was published, Hurston was profiled in *Twentieth Century American Authors*, *Current Biography*, and again in *Who's Who*. Having moved from St. Augustine to Daytona Beach, about fifty-five miles south, she juggled several magazine assignments in the final months of the year, hoping to wrap them all up before Christmas. The *Saturday Evening Post* had commissioned two more articles from her, she'd been asked to contribute to *The American Mercury* and *Reader's Digest*, and she'd set her sights on cracking that segregated bastion of journalistic hoity-toityness, *The New Yorker*. "Do you think it can come off?" she asked Carl Van Vechten.

Just before Thanksgiving, more than two hundred of Van Vechten's friends met at the Port Arthur Restaurant in New York's Chinatown to honor Carlo and to help support his latest passion: the James Weldon Johnson Memorial Collection of Negro Arts and Letters. Van Vechten had been among those most devastated by Johnson's death in 1938; he had known Johnson since 1924, and the men had always celebrated their shared birthday together. About a year after Johnson's death, Van Vechten approached the head librarian at Yale University about establishing an archival collection in his friend's name. Carlo would spend the next two decades of his life asking his black friends to donate their work to this important collection. At the November 20 dinner, "a galaxy of socialites" attended, including Johnson's widow, Grace Nail Johnson, Alain Locke, actor Canada Lee, and the NAACP's Walter White, who was master of ceremonies. Several of the musicians present, including Marian Anderson and W. C. Handy, performed. Although the society columns reported otherwise, Zora was not there. Having spoken at Kentucky State College in Frankfort the night before, she could not get transportation to New York in time to make the celebration. "I ached in my heart over missing that dinner," she apologized. Before the end of the month, though, she made it up to Carlo. For the collection he was building at Yale, she sent Van Vechten the handwritten manuscripts of four of her books. Telling a mutual friend about the acquisition, Carlo exclaimed: "Isn't it grand!"

Meanwhile, an executive at Lippincott wrote to another of Hurston's most enthusiastic white supporters, Rollins College Professor Edwin Osgood Grover, asking if he might make suggestions for enlarging Hurston's readership. "Zora Neale Hurston's books do not get the distribution they deserve," he noted, "and it is up to us who are friends of hers, or who think that she really has a message to convey, to do everything possible to spread the good word."

Grover had just read *Dust Tracks*, which he judged "in many ways . . . the best book that Zora Hurston has written." Praising its "artistry and reader appeal," he sent a gushy blurb for the publisher to use in promoting the book. He also sent a list of suggestions for augmenting Hurston's audience. One of his ideas was particularly intriguing: Why not get the author to personally inscribe a copy to Eleanor Roosevelt—known for her interest in Negro progress—and airmail it to England, where the first lady was currently visiting Queen Mary?

Whether Mrs. Roosevelt ever received a signed copy of *Dust Tracks* or not, many Americans were reading it and responding favorably. Grover thought the autobiography so grand that he urged Zora to forget about her journalistic pursuits and get to work on her next book. "Don't serve any more time on what you once called 'reporting' or working for someone else," he advised. "Your creative genius is your divinest gift and the world is waiting for what you have to give it."

Praise for *Dust Tracks* came from a variety of quarters. Borrowing the book from Grover, Rollins College President Hamilton Holt read it in one night and wrote a breathless letter to Hurston the next day. "I cannot forbear to write and tell you what a good job I think you have done. It has the three attributes of good autobiography writing, namely, candor, courage, and literary ability, and gives a picture of your experiences and your environment from the inside, that ought to interest everybody. What an interesting and worth-while life you must have had."

One person Hurston did not hear a laudatory word from that winter was Franz Boas, whose theories on racial and cultural equality had certainly influenced Zora's own views. But Boas likely never read Hurston's book; at age eighty-four, Papa Franz died in December, about a month after *Dust Tracks* was published.

Other voices from Hurston's past did emerge, however. In January 1943, as Zora marked her fifty-second birthday, Alain Locke, of all people, dispatched his kudos. He had spoken with Charlotte Mason recently, he told Zora. Still in the prolonged-care unit at the New York Hospital, where her room afforded her a view of the East River, Godmother had read *Dust Tracks* and liked it, too. Hurston had not heard from Godmother in almost a decade. The woman who had once exercised imperious authority over her life was now just a specter from her past. Looking back, Zora felt that their relationship had been an inevitable matter of karma. "Born so widely apart in every way, the key to certain phases of my life had been placed in her hand," she wrote in *Dust Tracks*. "I had been sent to her to get it." Zora thanked Locke for passing on Godmother's blessings, but clearly she no longer needed them: "I am extremely happy if Godmother is pleased," she told Locke politely but rather dispassionately. "She is so sure and right in her judgments."

Somehow Zora seemed more gratified at having won Locke's approbation than Godmother's. "You will never know how happy your letter made me. Really, I want your approval," she purred. The last time Hurston had mentioned Locke's name on paper, in 1938, she'd spit it out. Thus, her sweet-tempered response to his congratulatory letter was surprising, to say the least. She complimented him on his recent article in the *Survey Graphic* and gently teased him about a current photo she'd seen in the papers: "Very dignified and impressive, old thing." Now that they'd both met with some success, and were both getting older, perhaps they should put their quarrels behind them and make a lasting peace, her letter hinted. Telling Locke she would be visiting Washington soon, Zora suggested they tool around town together in a taxi (if the war effort left enough gas for such a luxury). "Really, Alain, I am through being a smart-aleck," she assured him. "You must forget that I ever was one and let us have some fun while I am there."

Before her trip to D.C., however, Zora stopped in Manhattan for radio and newspaper interviews and other promotional efforts. Staying at Harlem's famous Hotel Theresa, she had dinner at Van Vechten's Central Park West apartment the night of January 24. The next day, she talked up her book on Mary Margaret McBride's popular radio show. From 1:00 to 1:45 that Monday afternoon, Hurston recounted for McBride her life story, as told in *Dust Tracks on a Road*. She talked about the visions she'd had as a child, her time at Barnard, the writing of her first novel, her experience of photographing a zombie, and her relationships with two of the most famous women of the day, Ethel Waters and Fannie Hurst. About fifteen Red Cross volunteers were in the WEAF studio that day, and they served as a responsive audience for Zora's live, and lively, interview. For instance, when McBride interrupted the conversation to hawk her advertisers' products—including La Rosa macaroni and Fannie Farmer candy—Zora chimed in that she was hungry. "I wanted macaroni when you were talking about macaroni. . . . Now I want candy." The Red Cross volunteers joined McBride in laughing at Hurston's hearty, down-home humor. Yet when the author became serious and reflective—"nobody's been able to make me as unhappy as I've been able to make myself," she said at one point—the studio audience could almost be heard holding its breath.

At the end of the week, Hurston sat down with a reporter for *The New York World-Telegram*. In an article published February 1, 1943, Hurston was quoted as saying: "The lot of the Negro is much better in the South than in the North. . . . There is, of course, segregation, no social intermingling. I can't go into certain white nightclubs or dine in first-class white hotels. But for everything put up in the South for white people there is the equivalent for the Negro. In other words, the Jim Crow system works."

Understandably, these comments upset black politicians who sought to link the fighting abroad with the ongoing struggle for justice at home. These leaders believed the global conflict could exert tremendous pressure to end discrimination in America. After being threatened with a massive March on Washington, President Roosevelt already had signed Executive Order 8802 outlawing employment discrimination in government and defense industries. Yet the War Department continued to maintain a higher minimum intelligence score for black recruits than for whites, and various forms of sanctioned segregation persisted in all branches of the U.S. military. This discrimination had to end, many black leaders warned, if the United States and its Allies had any hope of winning the war against Adolf Hitler and his Axis forces. They also believed an Allied victory over Hitler's vision of Aryan world supremacy would be a powerful strike against the Jim Crow system. This was no time for Zora Neale Hurston to come along claiming Jim Crow worked.

Responding on behalf of the NAACP, Roy Wilkins took Hurston to task in his "Watchtower" column in New York's *Amsterdam News*. "Miss Hurston is a bright person with a flair for actions and sayings that yield rich publicity dividends," he allowed. "She gets talked about. She gets cussed and praised. All that helps the Hurston book sales." But if "the brother" was going to "get any benefit from this world upheaval," people like Hurston needed to refrain from spouting "arrant and even vicious nonsense." No one ever denied that Jim Crow worked, Wilkins said, but it only worked for white people. "The point is, it does not work for Negroes—except to their disadvantage." Stopping just short of calling Hurston a traitor to the race, Wilkins concluded: "Now is no time for tongue-wagging by Negroes for the sake of publicity. The race is fighting a battle that may determine its status for fifty years. Those who are not for us, are against us."

Hurston was in Washington when Wilkins's column appeared at the end of February. On the twenty-third, she'd addressed a national gathering of her sorority, Zeta Phi Beta, during its "Finer

Womanhood Week." The woman Hurston wanted to join her on the dais was Edna St. Vincent Millay, the famous white poet and notorious bisexual seductress. No doubt, many of Hurston's sorority sisters, not being as liberated as their speaker, would have found Millay an odd choice to represent "finer womanhood." But "the genius Millay" was someone Hurston admired "immensely as a poet and a woman," she said. Unable to get in touch with Millay in time for the event— the two had never met, except through telegrams—Zora addressed the sisters of Zeta Phi Beta alone.

Remaining in Washington for several days, she stayed at the Lucy Diggs Slowe Hall—the capital city's "most distinctive hotel for women"—at Third and U streets. On March 2, Howard University presented her with a distinguished alumna award. With painted nails and hoop earrings, Zora showed up at the morning ceremony wearing a wide, radiant smile to go along with her cap and gown. Following a banquet that evening, she made plans to return to Daytona Beach, but not before addressing Wilkins's *Amsterdam News* comments.

To the NAACP's gratification—and almost everyone's surprise— Hurston repudiated the statements attributed to her in the *World-Telegram*. "The article is untrue and twisted," she said in a story that ran in the *Atlanta Daily World* and other black newspapers. "I categorically deny that I ever said that Negroes are better off in the South. Neither did I approve of segregation in the South or anywhere else." Though Hurston claimed "only high regard" for white reporter Douglas Gilbert, who wrote the *World-Telegram* article, she suggested that in his effort to fit all her comments into a brief space, he "left out the essentials or perhaps permitted his own views to gain ascendency."

What Hurston said was this, she clarified: "I do not see the business of race prejudice as a sectional one; there is plenty of race prejudice both North and South, but the South has worked out a system." In the North, however, many whites claimed to be distressed about the awful conditions down South, yet they continued to exhibit a "cold hardness" toward the average Negro. "In some instances, the South was kinder than the North," Hurston felt, because southerners were more honest about their racism, wrong as it was. "Perhaps my saying the North was prejudiced too was far off the norm, and too distressing after all the fine phrases which have been poured over us up there," she added. "But I look behind the phrases and see that Harlem is a segregated neighborhood just like any in the South."

Zora disavowed the *World-Telegram* article again in a letter to her old friend Countee Cullen. The poet and high school teacher had written to congratulate her on *Dust Tracks*. In response, Zora wrote him a warm, five-page letter that indicated how much her political ideologies had evolved since the 1920s, when she'd scoffed at his going to the "whiteland" of Europe to study. Now, she praised him for following his own mind.

Hurston's personal politics had moved well beyond the simplicities of black and white, and far afield of the Eatonville model of Baptists versus Methodists. Though she would express bits and pieces of her self-styled political philosophy throughout her journalism of the 1940s, nowhere did she voice her views more clearly, completely, or candidly than in her correspondence with Cullen. For this reason, the letter bears quoting at length.

"Now, as to segregation, I have no viewpoint on the subject particularly, other than a fierce desire for human justice. The rest of it is up to the individual," she wrote to Cullen. "Personally, I have no desire for white association except where I am sought and the pleasure is mutual. That feeling grows out of my own self-respect. However blue the eye or yellow the hair, I see no glory to myself in the contact unless there is something more than the accident of race. Any other viewpoint would be giving too much value to a mere white hide. I have offended several 'liberals' among the whites by saying this bluntly."

Although Hurston had several white "liberal" friends, including Carl Van Vechten and Fannie Hurst, she found the label itself problematic and limiting. In some ways, Hurston viewed "liberalism"—as practiced by most white people she'd met—as just another form of condescension toward black people. "I have been infuriated by having them ask me outright, or by strong implication, if I am not happy over the white left-wing association with Negroes," she told Cullen. "I always say no. Then I invariably ask why the association should give a Negro so much pleasure? Why any more pleasure than association with a black 'liberal'? They never fail to flare up at that . . . which proves that they feel the same superiority of race that they claim to deny. Otherwise, why assume that they have done a noble deed by having contact with Negroes?"

Hurston then went on to describe the extent to which some white liberals seemed to believe that all black people *really* wanted was to get as close to whites and whiteness as possible. "Countee, I have actually had some of them to get real confidential and point out that I can be provided with a white husband by seeing things right!" Zora had no trouble attracting white men. ("I only wish that I could get everything else as easily as I can get white men," she asserted.) But it was an absolutely useless skill, since she had no interest in interracial romance. "If a white man or woman marries a Negro for love that is all right with me," she told Cullen, "but a Negro who considers himself or herself paid off and honored by it is a bit too much for me to take. So I shall probably *never* become a 'liberal.'"

Because Hurston so soundly rejected liberalism, as practiced by the whites she knew, some observers have been quick to label her a "conservative." Others—thinking her views more progressive and actually prophetic—have called her a black cultural "nationalist." Hurston likely would have rejected each of these labels with equal disdain because they both—like the term "liberal"—reek of limitation and oversimplification. Calling it a "slippery word," Hurston once argued that the "liberal" label could not be adequately applied to black people because "naturally, the relaxing of racial lines is something that must come from the other side of the race line." It's arguable, too, that all of these labels, especially "conservative," are now highly charged with meanings they hadn't yet acquired in Hurston's day. The truth is, we don't know how she would have responded to a Malcolm X *or* a Clarence Thomas. The only thing we can know for sure is this: She would have evaluated them as *individuals*.

Hurston's political thinking was her own and it defied easy categorization. Indeed, if a label *must* be applied to Hurston's politics, the only one that comes close to describing her self-reliant disposition is "individualist." Or, as she told Cullen, "I mean to live and die by my own mind."

Hurston's individualist stance, however, did not nullify her identity as one of the folk. Nor did it render her insensitive or indifferent to the welfare of black people collectively. In fact, as her letter to Cullen revealed, her desire for racial justice was so acute that she advocated its appropriation by "any means necessary," as Malcolm X would put it some twenty years later. "I <u>know</u> that the Anglo-Saxon mentality is one of violence," Hurston commented. "Violence is his religion. He has gained everything he has by it, and respects nothing else. When I suggest to our 'leaders' that the white man is not going to surrender for mere words what he has fought and died for, and that if we want anything substantial we must speak with the <u>same</u> weapons, immediately they object that I am not practical. . . . Why don't I put something about lynchings in my books? As if all the world did not know about Negroes being lynched!"

Speaking in no uncertain terms, Hurston went on to outline a revolutionary solution that would have made many white fans of *Dust Tracks* choke with disbelief. "My stand is this: either we must <u>do</u> something about it that the white man will understand and respect, or shut up. No whiner ever got any respect or relief. If some of us must die for human justice, then <u>let us die</u>. . . . A hundred Negroes killed in the streets of Washington right now could wipe out Jim Crow in the nation so far as the law is concerned, and abate it at least 60% in actuality. If any of our leaders start something like <u>that</u> then I will be in it body and soul. But I shall never join the cry-babies. . . . I have the nerve to walk my own way, however hard."

This was how Zora Neale Hurston felt about the pressing racial and political issues of her time. But her dissembling performance in *Dust Tracks on a Road* offered no clue as to how radical her thinking was. Short of massive bloodshed in the streets, Hurston already had articulated her solution for "the race problem" in her most recent novel, *Moses, Man of the Mountain*: "No man may make another free," she wrote. "Freedom was something internal."

This freedom, Hurston believed, was not a commodity that one race could give another—nor take away—because it had little to do with political or even economic gains. For her, it was deeper than that. It was a "self-respect," as she called it, that was born of cultural and spiritual attainment. In *Moses*, after all, the people had to wander in the wilderness until "they had songs and singers," until they had a "god of their own," until they could "grow men and women in place of slaves." Once a critical mass of black people had attained this internal freedom, Hurston felt, more pragmatic freedoms would be inevitable. Or, as one scholar has put it, Hurston's "revolutionary message" was this: "Liberate the self, and all else follows. Never succumb."

Unaware of the superb complexity of Hurston's views (as they were never publicly articulated in full), the *Saturday Review of Literature* bestowed yet another accolade for *Dust Tracks*. Along with the Anisfield-Wolf Foundation, the magazine presented Hurston with the John Anisfield Award in Racial Relations—for writing "an admirable autobiography revealing the flexibility, the sensitiveness, and the emotional color of the Negro race in America." Hurston was featured on the cover of the February 20 issue of the *Saturday Review*, where the prize was announced. And the prestigious national award carried a $1,000 purse.

With this boon, Hurston returned to Florida to fulfill a long-held dream: "The minute I have real money," she'd told a Florida friend the previous month, "I plan to own me a home out in the woods somewhere around there. I love Orange County!" And, to *Twentieth Century American Authors*, she'd disclosed: "I want my residence to be Orange County, Fla., but my career keeps me living in my Chevrolet." In Daytona Beach—just northeast of Orange County— Hurston found a way to settle down even while maintaining her mobility. In early May, she used a chunk of her Anisfield money to buy what amounted to a waterborne Chevrolet: a thirty-two-foot-long, forty-four-horsepower houseboat. Called the *Wanago*—as in "want to go"—the boat needed a little paint on the inside and a bit of carpentry work, Zora assessed, but it was certainly livable.

Because of the gas shortage brought on by the war, Zora berthed the *Wanago* at Howard Boat Works in Daytona Beach and stayed put for several months. "All the other boat-owners are very nice to me," she observed. "Not a word about race." By the end of summer, she'd completed most of the needed work on the boat, including having the hull scraped and painted and getting the motor fine-tuned. The work kept her "as broke as a he-hant in torment," she complained, but on the other hand, this was as close to homeownership as Zora had ever come, and she felt lucky to have the money to invest in the project. Though the boat was a little cramped with all her books and papers, Zora found it a wonderfully pleasant existence. "I have that solitude that I love," she exulted.

Zora used this solitude to develop what her years of rootless though fruitful roaming had denied her: a simple and meaningful routine. She cooked abundant meals almost every day—hushpuppies and shell turtle were among her favorites, though she hadn't yet perfected her hollandaise sauce. She also began to wonder if knowing her way around a kitchen was an altogether good thing. "Literary secret: I am getting fat just where a cow does—under the tail," she confided to Marjorie Kinnan Rawlings.

Zora spent most evenings reading and her literary tastes were wide and broad. She had become especially interested in the Chinese philosophy of Taoism and in the work of seventeenth-century Dutch philosopher Benedict de Spinoza. She also enjoyed the work of such contemporary writers as Willa Cather, Sinclair Lewis, and Anne Morrow Lindbergh. And she read everything written by or about Negroes. Bucklin Moon's *The Darker Brother*, for instance, gave "a falsely morbid picture of Negro life," in Zora's view. Yet she loved Rawlings's *Cross Creek*. "You have written the best thing on Negroes of any white writer who has ever lived," Hurston flattered her. "Maybe you have bettered me, but I hope not, for my own salvation, so I won't compare too closely to keep up my self love."

Hurston devoted her days to writing. Focusing more at the moment on journalism than fiction or drama, she produced a flurry of pieces for *The American Mercury*. Her essay about the complexities of race relations in the South—"The 'Pet Negro' System"—was published in the May 1943 issue. A short piece praising the Florida Negro Defense Committee, called "Negroes Without Self-Pity," appeared in the November number. In between these pieces, in the October issue, Hurston published a fascinating essay called "High John de Conquer," based on some of the same folk stories she'd hoped to dramatize in her ill-fated collaboration with Paul Green.

"High John de Conquer" was an essay that praised the subtle power of love and laughter to overcome oppression. For generations of black people in America, Hurston explained, High John had served as "our hope-bringer." Though he was a mythical figure, High John could not have been more real in the hearts of his believers. For them, he could beat the unbeatable. "He was top-superior to the whole mess of sorrow. He could beat it all, and what made it so cool, finish it off with a laugh," Hurston wrote. With a trickster's ability to make "a way out of no way," High John for years had been "winning his war from within," she asserted. In fact, High John was the embodiment of that quintessentially black ability to use laughter as a shield and a weapon. "Way over there, where the sun rises a day ahead of time, they say that Heaven arms with love and laughter those it does not wish to see destroyed," Hurston wrote poignantly. "Moreover, John knew that it is written where it cannot be erased, that nothing shall live on human flesh and prosper. Old Maker said that before He made any more sayings."

Movingly written, this essay was essentially about the redeeming power—the saving grace—of black folklore. But the message of the piece was altered slightly by opening and closing paragraphs that Hurston wrote to appease her *American Mercury* editor, who "had to have it sugared up to flatter the war effort," as Zora put it. "That certainly was not my idea," she explained to a friend, "but sometimes you have to give something to get something."

During World War II, Hurston, Langston Hughes, and other prominent black writers were routinely asked to offer words of encouragement for a nation at war. Former radical socialist Hughes, for instance, had published a pro-U.S.A. essay—"My America"—in February 1943, and the next month, he'd penned a rah-rah prose poem called "Freedom's Plow." The American people, black and white, needed to hold fast to their common dream, he exhorted: "Keep your hand on the plow! Hold on!"

In her effort to sugar up—or water down—the "High John" essay, Zora addressed white readers directly: Black people, she pointed out, "have put our labor and our blood into the common causes for a long time. . . . Maybe now, in this terrible struggle, we can give something else—the source and soul of our laughter and song." The hope-bringer was not just for Negroes anymore, she assured her white audience. "You will know, then, that no matter how bad things look now, it will be worse for those who seek to oppress us. Even if your hair comes yellow, and your eyes are blue, John de Conquer will be working for you just the same," she wrote, a bit unconvincingly.

Pitching another story idea, Hurston offended her *American Mercury* editor by talking about northerners' racial prejudice.

Because of well-meaning but misguided abolitionist-era books like *Uncle Tom's Cabin*, she believed, white northerners had long ago developed "a fixed idea that we should all be sweet, long-suffering Uncle Toms, or funny Topsys. When the real us shows up, there is disillusionment." Hurston blamed this white disillusionment—and black southerners' false impression "that Northerners love Negroes"—for the recent unrest in several northern cities. In June 1943, Detroit police killed at least seventeen black people—but no whites—after the races battled in the worst riot of the World War II period. And in August, six people were killed and 185 injured in a Harlem race riot, spurred by a white policeman's treatment of a black woman in the company of a black soldier. When Hurston suggested a story about northern racism to *American Mercury* editor Eugene Lyons, however, "he did not like it one bit," she reported to Alain Locke. Many white northerners "have so long thought of themselves as holy angels as regards the Negro," Hurston theorized, "that they object to being shown up as no better than the people whom they have denounced so long."

The editor's irritation with Hurston did not last, however. For his March 1944 issue, he asked her for another article. Hurston went to her Cudjo Lewis files and pulled out a piece that Lyons published under the title "The Last Slave Ship." The editor apparently wanted a black perspective in his magazine—to assure his readers that all of America was united behind the war effort—and he needed someone to interpret black subjects for a white readership. Soon, *The American Mercury* would develop a stridently right-wing tone, but in the early 1940s, there was still room for a greater diversity of opinions, if "sugared up" enough.

Living off her Anisfield funds and her freelance fees, Hurston remained in Florida through the end of 1943. Her home base was Daytona Beach, but she traveled up and down the St. Johns and the Halifax rivers whenever she could, visiting with friends in Eatonville, Sanford, and Winter Park. In November, she became involved with a community-based effort to develop a recreation center in Eatonville. "I was glad to see some feeling of making Eatonville a better place for young folks to be—especially for girls," she noted. "When I was a child, the Hungerford School was the social center. What went on at the school concerned Eatonville and vice versa."

Now, she lamented, the school had become "sort of a reformatory" for "unmanageable children" from all over the state. And there was little in the once-proud town for young people to do "besides hang around the shop (and fornicate)." The number of unwed pregnancies was "awful," Hurston wrote to Rollins Professor Edwin Osgood Grover, asking for his advice on securing a community center. "It is both my school and my town," she reminded him, "so I feel things deeply."

Hurston also became involved in a program called Recreation in War, sponsored by Mary Holland, wife of Florida Governor Spessard Holland. The purpose of the program was to entertain the many soldiers, black and white, who were stationed (in segregated quarters) throughout the state. Mrs. Holland was immediately drawn to Zora, who wore a leather vest and "good-looking pants" to a Recreation in War meeting. "In those days, not many women wore pants, you know." But Zora "was an individualist," Mrs. Holland recalled, and "she looked so attractive" that Florida's first lady made a point of talking with her and inviting her to meet her husband the next day at the governor's mansion. Governor Holland commented on Hurston's vernacular way of speaking, his wife recalled. "Did you learn to speak that way at Barnard?" he jokingly asked Zora. "No, Your Excellency, that am Florida talk," she replied.

In February 1944, Zora's personal life made headlines in New York: "Z. Hurston to Wed," the *Amsterdam News* announced. Zora's relationship with Percy Punter had survived her months in California and evidently was still thriving when *Dust Tracks* went to press. (She mentions it in the book as a current affair.) By early 1944, though, the relationship was over, and Zora had moved on. According to the *Amsterdam News*, she was engaged to marry Cleveland businessman James Howell Pitts. The only time Hurston had been in Ohio in the past few years was in February 1939, to do a series of radio broadcasts promoting her work as a novelist and folklorist—but she'd been in Cincinnati, in southwest Ohio. Cleveland, perched at the top of the state along Lake Erie, is more than 250 miles away. So there's no telling where Hurston met Pitts, an Aiken, South Carolina, native with a degree in pharmacy from Meharry Medical College. In any case, the *Amsterdam News* was a little late in its announcement. By the time the short article appeared in the newspaper, Hurston's third marriage was old news. On January 18, 1944, she married Pitts in Volusia County, Florida. In the documents that facilitated their union, Pitts gave his address as Brunswick, Georgia, which was about 160 miles from Daytona Beach, where Zora was living on the *Wanago*. Pitts was forty-five, according to the paperwork, and Zora gave her age as forty—though she had just turned fifty-three. While there was only an eight-year age gap between Zora and her latest younger man, this marriage, too, was extraordinarily short-lived. Just eight months after they took their vows, the couple would get a divorce, on October 31, 1944.

Their breakup, no doubt, was helped along by Zora's continued ambivalence about marriage and her unflagging commitment to her work. Within a few weeks of the wedding, she took off for an extended visit to New York. Lodging at Harlem's Hotel Theresa, she spent several weeks there working with Dorothy Waring, a white woman, on a musical play to be called "Polk County." The comedy—with Zora's old pal Big Sweet as its central character—was to incorporate elements of "High John de Conquer," *Mules and Men*, and *Mule Bone*. Since all of this was Zora's material, it's unclear why she felt the need to collaborate on the project with Waring, author of a minor book from 1935, *American Defender*. Or, as Carl Van Vechten put it in a note to Harold Jackman: "Who is Dorothy Waring paired with Zora?" The only reason Hurston seems to have worked with Waring at all was that her husband, Stephen Kelend-d'Oxylion, was a theatrical producer who thought he could mount the musical on Broadway by the fall. One version of the play, dated March 25, 1944, listed only Hurston as author. A later version added Waring's name—but the play itself seemed to be virtually all Zora.

During their brief collaboration, Hurston and Waring had several differences of artistic opinion, the white writer recalled. At one point, she urged Zora to keep "a sort of Gershwinesque feeling" about the musical, subtitled "a comedy of Negro life on a sawmill camp." Hurston—who'd actually lived at a sawmill camp and knew its music had little to do with Gershwin—flatly told Waring, "You don't know what the hell you're talking about."

As soon as Zora finished plodding through "Polk County" with Waring, she headed back south. Traveling down the Atlantic Coast en route to Daytona Beach, she stopped off in Hampton, Virginia, to lecture at Hampton Institute. Her talk at the respected black college was part of a two-day program, on July 6 and 7, focusing on cultural relations between the United States and Latin America. After leaving Hampton, Zora spent the rest of the summer on her houseboat in Daytona Beach, never mentioning to any of her correspondents that she'd gotten married—or that she was soon to be divorced. Instead, she spoke of how much she cherished her solitude and commented on the enjoyment she found in "the various natural expressions of the day." Away from the glare of public attention, quietly floating along the Halifax River, she was supremely content, as she told a friend—"happier than I have ever been before in my life."

CHAPTER 31

Adrift

Hurston was about two-thirds through writing a new novel, tentatively titled "Road in the Wilderness," when she met Reginald Brett, a mining engineer who'd recently returned to the States after several years of gold mining in Honduras. Having read *Tell My Horse*, Brett sought Hurston out to encourage her to take a research trip to the Central American country. Honduras was brimming with "plentiful and virgin" folklore, Brett assured her, and he had seen the ruins of an ancient Mayan city that no other white person had ever gazed upon. As a Negro—and an anthropologist who'd written sensitively about other cultures—Hurston would be more acceptable to the people of Honduras than any other American writer, Brett told her. There were all kinds of anthropological treasures in Honduras, he testified, just waiting to be discovered.

Hearing all this, Hurston decided she would go—"even if I have to toe-nail it all the way down there, and take my chances on eating and sleeping . . . after I get there," she said. "But go I will and <u>must</u>." In September, a determined Hurston wrote to Henry Allen Moe of the Guggenheim Foundation seeking funds for the trip. Her plan was to collect folklore among the Paya Indians, as well as among the Caribs and Mayans living on the country's coastlines. She also planned to spend a good deal of time among the Zambu Indians of southeastern Honduras, whose knowledge of astronomy was legendary. Further, Hurston hoped to list and describe the country's extensive medicinal plants; visit the geometrically intriguing cemetery of the ancient Mayans; and explore the lost city that Reginald Brett had glimpsed in the jungles.

Moe was happy to hear from Hurston, but he responded to her letter cautiously. The Guggenheim Foundation limited its support to two years, he reminded her, and she already had received two fellowships extending over a period of about a year and a half. It was unlikely she would receive yet another fellowship, no matter how deserving her work.

Hurston pitched ahead with the idea anyway, writing to anthropologist Jane Belo about the proposed expedition and inviting her to come along. Hurston did not want to put too much on paper about her plans, she told Belo, because "some one else may beat us to it." That was the reason she was trying to undertake the expedition on her own, rather than proposing it to the Department of Anthropology at Columbia, for instance. "Have you a motion picture camera now?" she asked Belo. "We will need it badly. I am trying to get a recording machine for the records," she wrote, explaining that she planned to spend at least two years in Central America.

By the first of October, Hurston had found a way to get there, at least. Miami adventurer Fred Irvine had agreed to let her charter his boat, the *Maridome*, for unlimited research in the tropics. Irvine was not an anthropologist, but he was "a wonderful seaman," Zora judged. The Englishman would do the sailing for free, but Hurston consented to pay for a new paint job for his twenty-seven-ton schooner, new sails, and a few minor repairs. She also agreed to stock the *Maridome* with provisions, as the explorers planned to use the "comfortable and stout craft" as a movable habitat to cut down on lodging costs. Hurston estimated she needed to spend about $800 on the boat and supplies before they headed out to sea. "I have sold my car and everything to finance the thing," she confided to Belo. "So you know how I feel. . . . I am going no matter how I get there because I know that it is going to be epoch-making."

Belo and her husband, Frank Tannenbaum, wrote back with enthusiasm. Perhaps they would join Zora in Central America once she'd established camp, they said. Meanwhile, Hurston wrote to Ben Botkin of the Library of Congress asking if she might borrow a recording machine to take with her. She might even be able to pay for one, if he could suggest where she might find a good secondhand machine for a reasonable price. "Naturally," she explained, "I must hoard every penny I can rake and scrape, beg and borrow. From what I have been told, it is worth it. I may even murder up a couple of old guys suspected of having research money in their pants and not donating." All of Botkin's recording machines were tied up in war work, he responded, but he suggested she contact the Inter-American Indian Institute for support.

By the end of October 1944, Hurston had survived a tonsillectomy and a tropical hurricane ("this boat is rearing and pitching like a mule in a tin stable," she said of the *Wanago* during the storm), but her eyes were still fixed on Honduras. She'd even secured commitments from magazine publishers for material she would write from Central America. The only things she didn't yet have were a recording machine and enough money to pull the trip off.

Because she was working day and night on her novel—hoping to finish it and see it published before setting sail—Zora slacked up on her journalistic efforts. Other than the Cudjo Lewis article in *The American Mercury*, the only piece she published in 1944 was an essay for *Negro Digest's* continuing series, "My Most Humiliating Jim Crow Experience." Published in the June issue, Hurston's article recounted her 1931 visit to the Brooklyn doctor who examined her in a laundry closet. "I went away feeling the pathos of Anglo-Saxon civilization," she concluded. "And I still mean pathos, for I know that anything with such a false foundation cannot last. Whom the gods would destroy, they first make mad."

This madness, Hurston believed, was now stalking the country as a kind of reckless hatred. "These do be times that take all you have to scrape up a decent laugh or so," she fretted privately that fall. "I do not refer to the battlefields, but to this enormous pest of hate that is rotting men's souls. When will people learn that you cannot quarantine hate? Once it gets loose in the world, it rides over all barriers and seeps under the doors and in the cracks of every house. I see it all around me every day. I am not talking of race hatred. Just hate. Everybody is at it. . . . Once it was just Germany and Japan and Italy. Now, it is our allies as well. The people in the next county or state. The other political party. The world smells like an abattoir. It makes me very unhappy. I am all wrong in this vengeful world. I will to love."

Hurston's will was tested when she returned to New York in November to try to secure further backing for *Polk County*, which was now looking like it might not make it to Broadway. After her solitary, 1,500-mile sea voyage on the *Wanago*, Zora found New York unbearably crowded and unpleasant. She soon made her way back to Florida without a production of *Polk County* in sight.

Back in Daytona Beach, Hurston replaced the weathered *Wanago* with a new boat, the *Sun Tan*, and continued to enjoy her floating homestead. "I love sunshine the way it is done in Florida," she'd decided. "Rain the same way—in great slews or not at all." Even the hurricane weather suited her. "I like violent aspects of nature (if I am safe)," she allowed.

Soon after she got back to Florida, Zora received official word from the Guggenheim Foundation that her application for a fellowship had been denied. Cold in hand, she would spend most of 1945 looking for funding for her dream trip and working to finish her novel. Both these efforts were stymied, however, when her "guts started to raising Cain." After months of silence, she wrote to Carl Van Vechten in July 1945: "I have been sick with my colon and general guts for a long, long time. And really for a while, I thought that I would kick the bucket." Now, however, Hurston was feeling fine and her new book was nearly finished. "The sun is shining in my door," she told Van Vechten, inviting him to bring along his camera and join her in Honduras. Still in search of the perfect collaborator, she added: "I believe that you and I could do something remarkable together."

Hurston told Carlo all about Fred Irvine—born in England, raised in New York, and not "hard-up for spending change." Describing Irvine as "a staunch and loyal friend," Zora assured Van Vechten that her relationship with the thirty-one-year-old seafarer was strictly platonic. "No, I have not tried any of it, but it must be good, because he has mobs of girls running after him all the time. And I know Fred well enough to know that he loses no time with women unless he is getting some," the fifty-four-year-old Zora wrote unblushingly. "I have not bothered to try it, because I am going off with him, and it could cause a lot of trouble in the end." Besides, she added, "there will be lots of men down there too, and I am liable to run up on something that suits."

Given the human and anthropological finds that awaited her in Central America, Hurston was eager to get away from the United States, where the waning war continued to cast a pall. It was hard to even publish a decent magazine story, she griped, "because the publishers seem frightened, and cut every thing out that seems strong. I have come to the conclusion that for the most part, there is an agreement among them to clamp on the lid."

The only magazine piece Hurston had published so far in 1945 was an essay in the March issue of *The American Mercury*. Called "The Rise of the Begging Joints," the tough-talking article took aim at certain black colleges. Hurston exempted "Class A seats of learning" such as Howard, Fisk, Morgan, Tuskegee, Morehouse, Hampton, Florida A&M, and Atlanta University from her criticism, as well as several state schools. But she railed against the inferior education that some lesser-known black colleges offered their students. Though she did not name the schools where she'd taught, she implicated them by defining a "Begging Joint" as a "puny place without a single gifted person on its meager faculty, with only token laboratories or none, and very little else besides its FOUNDER." These institutions would have been "a miracle in 1875," Hurston acknowledged, but in the mid-1940s, they were outdated and only gave Negroes a chance "to get hamstrung for life." They preyed upon uneducated black people, she asserted, janitors and washerwomen who sent their children to these schools because they didn't know any better, and because they wanted to say they'd sent their young ones off to college. Yet these schools turned out graduates who "may have learned a smattering of some trade," as Hurston put it, but who were hardly qualified for skilled labor.

White donors to these begging joints needed their heads examined, Hurston continued bluntly. "Instead of being a help, many donors have been giving aid and assistance to the defeat of those who need a chance more than anyone else in America." Rather than give money to "Chitterling Switch" College in backwoods Mississippi, Hurston asked, why not contribute to a school that already had something to build on? Rather than assume that all black schools were created equal, she suggested, white donors should do some investigating to see how the colleges compared with one another, and with their white counterparts. Addressing her white readers directly, Hurston wrote: "I wouldn't put it past some of you to tell me that it is your own money, and you can do with it as you please. You are free, white and twenty-one. But you see, I'm free, black and twenty-one; and if you tell me that, I will know and understand that you have no genuine interest in Negro education."

On September 2, 1945, World War II officially ended with the formal Japanese surrender aboard the U.S.S. *Missouri* in Tokyo Bay. More than a million Negro servicemen—mostly assigned to all-black units, often under white leadership—had helped to win the war abroad. For them and other black Americans, however, the battle at home was only beginning. Roosevelt was dead, Harry Truman was the new president, and black Americans began stepping up their protests against segregationist policies in all walks of life, from lunch counters to major league baseball. While it was an exciting time to be a black American, it also was a difficult time, as white resistance mounted in direct proportion to black demands.

Timidity still reigned in New York publishing houses, Hurston noted, and black writers still had to contend with "publishers who think of the Negro as picturesque," as she'd told a black reporter the previous year. "There is over-simplification of the Negro. He is either pictured by the conservatives as happy, picking his banjo, or by the so-called liberals as low, miserable and crying," Hurston said. "The Negro's life is neither of these. Rather, it is in-between and above and below these pictures. That's what I intend to put in my new book."

By September, though, Hurston's new book—"a serious one on the upper strata of Negro life"—had been canned. She was about two-thirds finished with the novel, called "Mrs. Doctor," when "Lippincott (timid soul) decided that the American public was not ready for it yet." So she'd started in on yet another new manuscript. This one, set in Eatonville and using some material from *Mule Bone*, was "a story about a village youth expelled from town by village politics," as she described it. The novel followed him "going places, including Hell and Heaven and having adventures, and returning after seven years to achieve his childhood ambition of being a fireman on the railroad, and the town hero."

Hurston's editors at Lippincott did not like this novel, either. She thought it was because they didn't like what she had to say, but her editors argued that the problem was in the way she said it. "Zora was a natural writing genius at first," Bertram Lippincott would recall, but her new manuscripts seemed a bit sloppy and needed more editing, making him wonder if she had just gotten lazy. But perhaps the editors were the ones who were lazy. Holding Hurston to certain expectations, they seemed unwilling to do their job—to edit—to help make her books better. As she'd demonstrated with *Moses, Man of the Mountain*, her last Lippincott novel, Hurston was attempting to write about big, complex subjects. But what Lippincott wanted from her was another *Jonah's Gourd Vine*. Hurston's first novel was "a loner," Lippincott maintained four decades after its publication. "That there *Gourd Vine* . . . it's a work of genius. There ain't no question of it."

Hamstrung by the high standard she'd set for herself with her early novels, Hurston faced the end of 1945 with no book prospects in sight and not enough money to embark on her journey to Honduras. She stayed afloat by pursuing freelance magazine articles and writing a couple of encyclopedia entries, including one on "the Negro" for Funk & Wagnall's 1946 edition of *The New International Year Book*.

In December 1945, Hurston published "Crazy for This Democracy," her most politically honest piece of journalism of the 1940s. Not surprisingly, the essay ran in a black publication, *Negro Digest*, which, after condensing most of her *American Mercury* articles, eventually made Hurston a contributing editor. The war was officially over now and Zora felt liberated to express some of the more hard-hitting political views that had been edited out of *Dust Tracks*. In "Crazy for This Democracy," she wrote with biting humor, wondering if she had misheard the late President Roosevelt when he boasted that America was "the Arsenal of Democracy." Maybe he'd really said the "arse-and-all," which would help explain the United States' chauvinistic foreign policy. In all the fighting, she wondered, "Have we not noted that not one word has been uttered about the freedom of the Africans? . . . The Ass-and-All of Democracy has shouldered the load of subjugating the dark world completely."

Turning her attention to American shores, Hurston wrote, "I am crazy about the idea of this Democracy. I want to see how it feels." The only thing preventing her from giving it a try, she said, "is the presence of numerous Jim Crow laws on the statute books of the nation." But Jim Crow was a global problem, not just a peculiarity of the American South, she wrote, pointing out instances of Jim Crow–type discrimination in South Africa, British-held India, and colonial Asia as well. Jim Crow was "a social smallpox" and it could not be cured by picking at particular bumps or blisters, she asserted. "The symptoms cannot disappear until the cause is cured."

The root of the problem, as she saw it, was psychological. The purpose of relegating black people to the backseats of trains or excluding them from certain places was to instill in the smallest white child a feeling of superiority. "Talent, capabilities, nothing has anything to do with the case. Just FIRST BY BIRTH," she protested. For the dark child, the daily humiliations had a converse purpose: to convince that child of his inferiority, so that "competition is out of the question, and against all nature and God." It was, she noted, "the unnatural exaltation of one ego, and the equally unnatural grinding down of another." Hurston concluded her essay on a strong, uncompromising note: "I am for complete repeal of All Jim Crow Laws in the United States once and for all, and right now. For the benefit of this nation and as a precedent to the world. . . . Not in some future generation, but repeal *now* and forever!"

With its righteously indignant, take-no-prisoners tone, Hurston's article did not betray that she was actually "depressed and distressed by the state of the world." She'd been hearing reports about "the unlovely social conditions" in New York that made her skittish about returning. Crime was rampant in Harlem, she'd heard, and there was so much "robbing and cut-throating and such awful carryings on" that her brother Everett was thinking of abandoning Brooklyn for Florida.

Hurston, meanwhile, welcomed 1946 aboard the *Sun Tan*, still berthed in Daytona Beach. In February, as part of her research for yet another new novel, she went out to sea on a shrimping boat. "It was tough and rough," she admitted, "but highly informative. The men, white and black, who put shrimp on the table of the nation are made of the stuff of pioneers."

Still laboring to put shrimp on her own table, Zora planned an ambitious year of work: she was pursuing an opportunity to write an article for *The New York Times Sunday Magazine*; she wanted to pen a play for Ethel Waters; and she thought her novel-in-progress had both play and movie possibilities. Beyond all that, she was still determined to go to Honduras.

But the early part of the year brought sad news. Back in 1943, Hurston had told Countee Cullen he was her "favorite poet." A year later, she'd invited Cullen and his longtime companion Harold Jackman to visit her in Daytona Beach on her houseboat, warning them that the galley was small and the toilet tiny. Cullen and Jackman never got around to seeing the boat, though. In early 1946, Zora learned that Cullen was dead. The forty-two-year-old poet and teacher had passed away, on January 9, of high blood pressure and uremic poisoning.

Zora had first met Cullen in 1925, when they'd both won prizes in the first *Opportunity* literary contest. In 1926, they'd worked together on *Fire!!* In the twenty years that had sped by since then, the two writers had gone their separate ways artistically, but they'd always maintained a warm affection built on their shared past. Cullen's death reminded Hurston that those Harlem yesterdays—of being young, gifted, and brash—were long gone.

Three months later, another piece of Hurston's past fell away. On April 15, Charlotte Mason—known to her protégés as Godmother— died at the New York Hospital in Manhattan, where she'd been living for thirteen years. At the time of her death, she was just a month shy of her ninety-second birthday. Her body was disposed of at the New York & New Jersey Crematory on April 17, 1946, according to her death certificate. Under "trade, profession, or particular kind of work done," Charlotte Mason—the woman who'd nurtured and neutralized so many artistic careers during the 1920s and early 1930s—was described as a "housewife."

More anxious than ever to leave the States, Hurston secured her passport in June, having indicated on her application that she intended to sail to Honduras on the twenty-fourth of the month. Once the passport was in hand, however, she still did not have enough money for the trip. With cash from the sale of the *Sun Tan*— and with a royalty check from *Story* magazine, which planned to anthologize "The Gilded Six-Bits"—Hurston went instead to New York, to hunt up some freelance work.

Soon after her arrival, she became involved in the Harlem congressional campaign of Grant Reynolds, the Republican candidate running against Adam Clayton Powell Jr. In 1946, the term "black Republican" was not considered an oxymoron nor an invective. In fact, in the 1944 presidential election, black voters were split an even 40 to 40 percent between Democratic and Republican in terms of party identification. Illustrating the influence of the Communist Party and the American Labor Party, the other 20 percent identified themselves as "independent/other." Many voters also regularly crossed party lines when a particular candidate suited them. Hurston, for example, was a registered Republican, having never joined the passel of black voters who abandoned the party of Lincoln for the New Deal of Roosevelt. But Hurston thought Democrat Harry Truman "a solid kind of a man" for the White House. (On the other hand, Powell would outrage his fellow Democrats in 1956 by endorsing Republican President Dwight D. Eisenhower for reelection.)

Hurston was not alone among black voters who wagered that Republican Reynolds could represent Harlem better than Powell did. Among Reynolds's prominent supporters were singer-actress Etta Moten, the great pianist Mary Lou Williams, and the wildly popular heavyweight boxing champion Joe Louis. Hurston backed Reynolds in his congressional bid, she told a reporter, not because he was a Florida-born, Howard-educated Negro, but because she believed he was "the finest man we could have chosen." Criticizing Powell's "part-time performance in Washington," Hurston felt that he was "too engrossed in his private affairs to be a good Congressman," citing the time he spent "promoting speaking engagements for himself" and concert appearances for his wife, pianist and popular nightclub performer Hazel Scott.

Working out of Reynolds's "little cubby hole" of an office in Harlem, Hurston "would be out on the streets at night listening to the campaign speeches, passing out literature in the crowd and that sort of thing," recalled Reynolds, an army officer who'd just returned from the war when he launched his campaign. Hurston also wrote press releases occasionally, but her main role was "trying to encourage the participation of people involved in the arts and the theater and the sciences," as Reynolds remembered. "She was very good at it," he added, noting that she seemed to know everyone in Harlem.

Reynolds needed all the help he could get. The incumbent Powell "was so high and mighty . . . it was hard to distinguish between him and the Almighty himself," as Reynolds put it. "He didn't even want to come out and campaign against me; he was going to ignore me." Noting his opponent's growing popularity, however, Powell did eventually come out fighting. And in the end, the god was not deposed. But, Reynolds noted proudly, "it was the closest race he ever had."

After Reynolds's November 1946 defeat, Hurston remained in Harlem, renting a room on West 124th Street. From there, she organized an innovative "Block Mothers" plan, whereby one mother would take care of all the children on the block on a given day. In this way, Harlem's many working mothers were not forced to leave their children on the streets or home alone for long hours every day. The program incorporated trips to parks, beaches, and play centers. And Hurston got several "interested citizens" to donate funds for children who could not afford the picnic lunch or carfare for the program's activities. Children too young for the outings were cared for in the homes of young mothers or elderly women who'd retired from the workforce. "It's the old idea, trite but true, of helping people to help themselves that will be the only salvation of the Negro in this country," Hurston told a reporter from Barnard's alumnae magazine. "No one from the outside can do it for him."

The political arena had become increasingly important to Hurston, the article pointed out. Demonstrating what one male contemporary would later call "something of a women's lib attitude," Hurston believed it was important to fight against the apathy of women, "whether Negro or white, who vote as their husbands do without questioning the issues involved," the magazine reported.

Hurston stayed in Harlem through the new year, writing several book reviews for the *New York Herald Tribune*. Among them were critiques of books by anthropological colleagues Katherine Dunham (*Journey to Accompong*) and Melville and Frances Herskovits (*Trinidad Village*). Zora also worked on some bigger stories—including an attempt to explore gang life and drug use among teenagers in Harlem—for *The New York World-Telegram*. Her contact there was Helen Worden Erskine, whom she'd met years before through Fannie Hurst. During this same period, Hurston submitted two intriguing essays to Erskine: a satirical piece on the role of women in modern society, called "The Lost Keys of Glory," and a denunciation of communism, titled "Back to the Middle Ages, Or How to Become a Peasant in the United States." Neither essay was published, although they both were certainly of publishable quality. While Zora was finding plenty to do—she pitched some ideas to *Reader's Digest* as well—the 1946–47 winter was hard on her financially, and she had to borrow money from Erskine to make ends meet.

Depressed about her own situation and the current conditions in New York, Hurston stayed close to her homefront in Harlem. She did not even visit Carl Van Vechten, explaining to him later: New York "was too much of a basement to Hell to suit me. Everybody busy hating and speaking in either brazen lies or using just enough truth to season a lie up to make their viewpoint sound valid. Not hating anyone, I felt entirely out of place. I'm afraid that I got a little unbalanced. I got so that it was torture for me to go meet people, fearing the impact of all the national, class and race hate that I would have to listen to."

That spring, though, Zora felt cause for optimism again. With a nudge and an introduction from Marjorie Kinnan Rawlings, Hurston met with Maxwell Perkins, Rawlings's editor at Charles Scribner's Sons. Perkins was the literary world's "brightest editorial light," in Zora's view; many writers who'd worked with him, including Rawlings, Fitzgerald, and Hemingway, agreed. After two meetings at the esteemed editor's Fifth Avenue office in early April, Hurston walked away with a book deal for her next novel, a $500 advance, and a new publisher.

Hurston had spent her entire career as a published author with the J. B. Lippincott Company; after a dozen years, though, the relationship had gone flat. Hoping to benefit from Perkins's "editorial genius"—and a fresh start at Scribner's—Hurston took her advance money and did what she had longed to do for more than two years: On May 4, 1947, she set sail for Honduras.

Despite the cash Zora had sunk into Fred Irvine's boat, the *Maridome* did not carry her to Central America. Irvine had moved on to other matters and Hurston sailed alone aboard a commercial liner. "Except for the waters of the Gulf being almost godly blue," she reported, "the voyage was uneventful." Zora moved about at first, visiting the capital city of Tegucigalpa and other areas, then decided to settle on the North Coast, taking a room at the Hotel Cosenza in the Caribbean port of Puerto Cortés. She was alarmed to find that the inflation in Honduras was almost as bad as in the States. "I feel half stranded already," she told Perkins just two weeks after her arrival. Still, she was grateful to Honduras, she said, "because it has given me back myself."

In about a month, Hurston sent a stack of draft pages from her in-progress novel to her new literary agent, Ann Watkins. On June 20, Watkins wrote to tell Hurston that everyone at the agency thought she'd done "a grand job" so far. But she would not be sending the manuscript to Scribner's right away. Max Perkins was dead, Watkins informed Zora, and his sudden passing, at age sixty-two, had left the company in a tailspin. Hurston was saddened profoundly by Perkins's death; she had been "revering him for years," she said, and felt "tremendous exaltation" at the thought of working with him. "It is useless to repeat that Maxwell Perkins was easily the greatest force in the literature of our times," she grieved.

Hurston soon received official notice of Perkins's death from Burroughs Mitchell at Scribner's; he would be her new editor and she should let him know if she needed anything. Zora wasted no time responding. She had not been paid yet for some "pot-boilers" she'd written for *Holiday* magazine and therefore was in dire need of money. "A drab terror has settled upon me by reason of my situation," she said, "though possibly you can never know the feeling, never having been in a foreign country and finding yourself without." As soon as Mitchell received Hurston's letter, he contacted her agent and asked to see the first half of her novel. After reading it, he sent her a check for $500 as an additional advance, writing: "I hope that tells you what we mean it to—that we have great confidence in this new book of yours."

Postponing her expedition into the interior of Honduras, Hurston spent long hours holed up in the Hotel Cosenza. The lost city could wait; the novel could not. In early September, she sent the second half of the book to New York, asking for editorial comments as quickly as possible. "No use in having SCRIBNER'S for a publisher and not be helped by that justly celebrated editorial brain," she reasoned. "I do want to grow along as a writer."

After a few weeks of editing Hurston's novel—about a family of white southerners—Mitchell sent her a detailed critique. She received his editorial suggestions happily and set about applying them at once. She also thanked Mitchell for his keen eye and his editorial honesty. "Please remember that I am neither Moses nor any of the writing apostles," she encouraged him. "Nothing that I set down is sacred. Any word or sentence can be changed or even cut out. What we want is success, not my deification."

Hurston finished her revisions in late fall and sent her editor yet another version of the book-in-progress, tentatively titled "So Said the Sea." She then went out into the Honduran field at last, heading for the rain forests of the Mosquitia region. "Being what they call here a Mestizo (mixed blood) I am getting hold of some signs and symbols through the advantage of blood," she soon reported. The onset of the rainy season cut Hurston's expedition short, however. "Another month of this weather," she told Mitchell in early December, "and I will be waving you a greeting with a fin."

Zora's Honduran Christmas was rather ho-hum, as she was prevented by "the endless rains" and the "affectionate" mud from going back into the interior for more research. Eighteen inches of rain in three days left her with nothing to do but "gnaw finger-nails" and think about writing a couple of personal essays—or, as she put it, "some articles from the inside of me." Zora also continued to think of title ideas for her new book: "Good Morning, Sun" was her latest offering.

Near the end of January 1948, Mitchell summoned Hurston back to the States. He wanted to make a few small but essential revisions to her novel, and her presence in New York would speed the process greatly. He sent a $250 check to cover the expenses of her return trip, certain that her finished novel would be "a fine and unusual book."

After some difficulty securing her exit papers from Honduran officials, Hurston finally booked passage for the five-day boat ride to New York. On February 20, she would be heading home—after nearly ten months in Central America. "Having been down here in the bush so many months, you might have to run me down and catch me and sort of tie me up in the shed until I get house-broke again," she warned Mitchell. "No telling what I might do when I see all them houses. When I get tame I might have some interesting things to tell you."

Working intensely with her editor for several weeks in New York, Hurston saw her novel—now called "The Sign of the Sun"—scheduled for publication on October 11. She then headed upstate to Rhinebeck, where she spent the summer months relaxing with Constance Seabrook, wife of author and adventurer William Seabrook.

On September 9, Mitchell wrote Zora in Rhinebeck, urging her to return to Manhattan as soon as she could. Scribner's publicity people had big plans for *Seraph on the Suwanee*, as the novel was finally called, and they needed to make certain arrangements with her. The editor also let Hurston know that she had a future at his publishing house. "Have you been working on a new book or books?" he asked. "We ought to talk over what you are going to do next."

CHAPTER 32

West Hell

The charges came out of nowhere, like a puff of poisonous gas. Or like a sudden, savage thunderstorm on a cloudless day.

Anticipating the publication of *Seraph on the Suwanee*, Hurston was back in the city, renting a room on West 112th Street in Harlem. On September 13, 1948, not long after she'd settled into her new lodgings, she heard a sharp knock on her door. Nothing in Zora's fifty-seven years of living could have prepared her for what was on the other side: a New York City police detective bearing a warrant for her arrest.

That Monday afternoon, Zora Neale Hurston was hauled into the police station, fingerprinted, and booked on charges of sodomizing three schoolboys. At Manhattan's Twenty-fourth Precinct, Detective Howard Clancy questioned Hurston for a long time, as did Alexander Miller, an officer of the New York Society for the Prevention of Cruelty to Children, the organization bringing the charges against her. Zora soon learned that her former landlady from 124th Street had instigated her arrest. The Harlem chambermaid—who'd rented Zora a room in her home from October 1946 to May 1947—told the Children's Society that Hurston had been molesting her ten-year-old son for more than a year. Two other neighborhood boys made similar accusations.

The charges were groundless and Hurston categorically denied them, urging the Children's Society and the police to conduct a full investigation. Her passport proved she'd been in Honduras for nearly a year, from May 1947 to February 1948, when she'd returned to finish revisions on her book. After that, she'd spent much of the summer upstate in Rhinebeck. When would she have had time to run around Harlem sodomizing these children? Appalled by the heinous allegations, Zora offered to take a lie-detector test on the spot. Her offer was ignored and she spent the better part of the evening in police lockup. Finally, Scribner's editor Burroughs Mitchell—accompanied by attorney Louis Waldman—arrived and secured her release. Zora stayed the night at Mitchell's home, comforted, if only slightly, by his and his wife's kindness.

The next day, Hurston appeared before a magistrate, who advised her of her right to a preliminary hearing and set her bail at $1,500. Hurston also faced her accusers—her former landlady and the woman's ten-year-old son, Billy, and two other boys Zora barely remembered from 124th Street: Bobby and Jerry, both eleven years old.

Hurston was distressed when she discovered that the Children's Society "had fixed the date, the ONLY positive one as August 15th" of 1948. This fixed date had come about only after she told Alexander Miller that she'd been out of the country for much of the time on which his charges were based. Now, it seemed that the statement Zora had given at the police station was being used against her. "Then the horror took me," she told friends, "for I saw that he was not seeking the truth, but to make his charges stick. . . . I could not believe that a thing like this could be happening in the United States and least of all to me. It just could not be true! I must be having a nightmare."

Hurston was fortunate to have the counsel of Louis Waldman, an attorney she would not have been able to afford on her own. Scribner's hired Waldman on her behalf, placing a $1,000 cap on his fees and charging all payments against Hurston's open account. For his part, Waldman was amazed that the Children's Society would press these charges so doggedly "without any investigation at all," as he saw it. He believed Hurston completely and thought her passport and other evidence would prove she could not have committed the crimes of which she was accused. Waldman, who also represented the American Writers Association, soon found out that his client was highly thought of by her fellow writers, capable of objectivity (even under such extreme circumstances), and, as he put it, "absolutely fearless."

As an outward expression of her fearlessness—and as if to remind herself of her own inner flame—Zora wore a red scarf to her preliminary hearing on September 21. In Haiti, believers wore red kerchiefs as a sign that Ogoun—the warrior god, the deity of fire—was protecting them. This thought surely crossed Zora's mind as she tied the scarf around her neck that Tuesday morning, a week and a day after police had barged into her home and capsized her life. Then, too, red was one of her favorite colors (along with white), and it would certainly send a message to those who wished to see her defeated: Here was a woman who comported herself like a bright fire, even in this cold, cold time.

At the preliminary hearing, Francis X. Giaccone, the presiding magistrate, was responsible for deciding if sufficient evidence existed to justify a trial. By design, a preliminary examination is largely one-sided, with the prosecutor attempting to offer enough evidence to convince the judge that there is "probable cause" to continue. The accused, through her attorney, is entitled to challenge the prosecution's evidence and introduce evidence on her own behalf. In the matter of The People of the State of New York Against Zora Hurston, "the people's" case was presented by District Attorney Frank Hogan and Assistant D.A. Edward Dunleavy. The prosecutors offered the only evidence they had: the testimony of three little boys.

Billy—Zora's main accuser—pointed out the woman in the red scarf as "Mrs. Hurston," and testified that she'd lived with him and his mother in their six-room Harlem apartment two years earlier. He then went on to tell a bizarre story of meeting Hurston at 4:30 every Saturday afternoon for almost two years in the basement of a building on 124th Street. At these meetings, the boy claimed, Hurston placed his "private parts" in her mouth, then did the same to his friends, Bobby and Jerry, and always gave them each fifty cents. Further, the boy claimed that two other adults were present at these weekly coal-bin gatherings and that they participated as well. Hurston had never met or even heard of the other two adults the boy named: "Rufus," a World War I vet who was a janitor in the building where the crimes allegedly took place, and "Sally," a Puerto Rican mother of four who owned a candy store in the neighborhood. The janitor had been arrested in the case; the mother had not as yet.

Searching her mind for some reason behind all this, Zora remembered Billy as a likable boy who had a reputation in the neighborhood for being "bad." Once when she was still a renter at his 124th Street apartment, Zora had urged Billy's mother, a single parent, to take her son to Bellevue for observation and treatment, which he was now receiving. Although she knew the boy was emotionally disturbed, Zora could not fathom the root of this "vile charge," and she was astonished by Billy's graphic testimony. As the boy painted an unthinkable picture of "Mrs. Hurston" down on her knees in front of him, while the fifty-five-year-old janitor and the other boys watched, Zora was struck by the preposterousness of it all. At that point, she emitted a small sound that the judge interpreted as a laugh. He stopped the proceedings to ask her about it. "I am not laughing," Zora responded stonily. "It may be a matter of nervousness," the judge offered. "Yes," Zora replied.

Hurston did not bother to tell the judge that black laughter "has a hundred meanings," as she'd put it in *Mules and Men*. On the lips of black folks—who'd spent generations laughing to keep from crying—a laugh "may mean amusement, anger, grief, bewilderment, chagrin, curiosity, simple pleasure or any other of the known or undefined emotions." Zora may have laughed in court that day, but she was not tickled. Although she did not explain all this to the judge, she didn't need to; her face said enough. The judge called for a short recess.

After the pause, near the end of Waldman's cross-examination of Billy, the boy made a crucial admission: He, Jerry, and Bobby often went down to the basement alone, usually on Saturday afternoons, and "practiced" oral and anal sex with one another. No one forced them to do it, the boy said. They just did it because they wanted to. "Jerry said it was nature," Billy allowed. Based on this testimony, Waldman moved that the charges against Hurston be dismissed. The judge admitted that the situation was "absurd," but not enough "to discredit the whole thing," he said. The case would have to go before the grand jury.

To strengthen their chances of securing indictments, prosecutors presented their cases against Hurston and the janitor together, since the boys claimed the two had been in cahoots. On September 30, the grand jury heard from all three boys, as well as from Alexander Miller of the Children's Society and from a doctor who'd examined the boys and found medical evidence of anal injury in two of them. This damage could have been caused by the janitor's alleged abuse of the boys—as the prosecutor asserted—or by the admitted activities of the boys themselves. Although the janitor testified that he did not know Hurston, the grand jury on October 1 issued indictments against both defendants.

On October 11, in the General Sessions Court of Judge Saul Streit, Hurston was arraigned on three counts of sodomy, one count of assault in the second degree, and one count of "placing a child in such a situation as likely to impair morals." Provided with a written copy of the indictment, Hurston was asked to enter a plea. "Not guilty," she declared in a strong, sure voice.

The same day, Scribner's published Hurston's new novel, *Seraph on the Suwanee*. Waldman was confident that the indictment against Hurston would be dismissed, so he did not advise Scribner's to halt its plans to publish her book. Even if the charges were not dropped, the case would not come up for trial for some time, he counseled, so Zora should attempt to put her pain aside and go on with her life as usual. Proceedings in children's cases were private; there was no call for anyone beyond the involved parties to know about it. Thus, Hurston's arrest and indictment should have no effect on her career, nor on her ability to promote her book.

Waldman's recommendation seemed sound enough, and Scribner's appeared undaunted by Hurston's legal trouble. A few days after the grand jury indicted her, the publisher offered her a $500 advance on an option for her next novel. She received $100 upfront and the rest was paid in weekly installments of $40. The money was a great help. In all that Zora was going through, at least she didn't have to worry about paying her rent.

Initial reviews of *Seraph on the Suwanee* confirmed Scribner's decision to stand by its author. The *New York Herald Tribune* praised "Miss Hurston's astonishing, bewildering talent." The author's new novel defied description, the critic raved. "Emotional, expository; meandering, unified; naïve, sophisticated; sympathetic, caustic;

comic, tragic; lewd, chaste—one could go on indefinitely reiterating this novel's contradictions and still end helplessly with the adjective unique."

Such intriguing descriptions of Hurston's book delighted her publisher and boosted sales. Within a few days of publication, three thousand copies of *Seraph on the Suwanee* had been sold, prompting Scribner's to order a second printing of two thousand. The company also scheduled national advertising in *The New York Times*, the *New York Herald Tribune*, and the *Chicago Tribune*.

If Hurston's previous novel, *Moses, Man of the Mountain*, was about independence and liberation, then *Seraph on the Suwanee* was about dependence and frustration. It is the story of Arvay Henson Meserve, a humorless Florida cracker whose life is defined by her marriage to Jim Meserve—strong, handsome, fun-loving, upwardly mobile, and shamelessly chauvinistic. "I have to stay with you and stand by you and give my good protection to keep you from hurting your ownself too much," he tells Arvay early in their courtship. "Didn't take me long to learn just how you're made . . . and now I know how to handle you. You and me are going to have a mighty high old time together," he decides. After that, Jim rapes Arvay and then marries her, triumphantly promising that she was "going to keep on getting raped" for the rest of their life together. Mocking Arvay's ambition to become a Christian missionary, Jim whoops: "No more missionarying around for you. You done caught your heathen, baby."

Seraph on the Suwanee is full of the rich language that readers had come to expect of Hurston, though she renders the white rural idiom slightly differently from the black idiom of her previous books. She does not use dialect spellings, for instance, except when the black supporting characters speak. And the metaphors generally are not as rich or elaborate as those of the black wordsmiths in *Jonah's Gourd Vine* or *Their Eyes Were Watching God*. Still, it is rather odd to hear a Tea Cake–like boast coming out of Jim Meserve's mouth: "You don't have to worry about a thing," he tells Arvay. "You got a man who can bring it when he come."

The decision to put such words in the mouths of southern white folks did not come easily for Hurston, but her research had led her to believe the language of Joe Clarke's porch had a close counterpart in poor white southern communities. As an anthropologist, she felt duty-bound to show the cross-cultural borrowings of language that she'd discovered—or at least not to hide them. Certainly, an unschooled Florida cracker would talk more like a Tea Cake than he would like a Carl Van Vechten. "About the idiom of the book, I too thought that when I went out to dwell among the poor white in Dixie County that they were copying us," Hurston explained to a friend. "But I found their colorful speech so general that I began to see that it belonged to them. After my fit of jealousy was cooled off, I realized that Negroes introduced into N. America spoke <u>no</u> English at all, and learned from the whites. Our sense of rhythm points it up a bit, but the expressions for the most part are English held over from the Colonial period."

Throughout the novel, Arvay struggles to find language to express her feelings, but her deep sense of inferiority prevents her from protesting Jim's confident navigation of their future. She is also hopelessly in love with Jim, despite his blatant sexism and his obvious disregard for her intelligence. All Arvay needs to do, Jim tells her, is "love and marry me and sleep with me. That's all I need you for." Arvay takes this as a good sign: "He had just as good as excused the woman he married from all worry and bother," she thinks. "Her whole duty as a wife was to just love him good, be nice and kind around the house and have children for him. She could do that and be more than happy and satisfied, but it looked too simple. There must be a catch in it somewhere."

In no time, Arvay and Jim find themselves trapped in a marriage that is full of love, but a trap nevertheless. They are both captives of the confining gender boxes they've built for themselves, and they are mutually dependent on each other to validate their limited and limiting roles. Motivated by his determination to take care of Arvay and prove himself a big man in her eyes, Jim steadily climbs the rungs of success, becoming a turpentiner, a citrus farmer, a moonshiner, and, ultimately, a shrimp boat captain. Oblivious to almost everything but the frantic goings-on in her own head, Arvay is unaware of Jim's efforts to make her happy. Instead, she spends all her time worrying about whether she'll be able to hold "this miracle of a man"; about whether he blames her for their first child being mentally disabled; and about anything else she can think to worry over. Meanwhile, Jim resents Arvay for not noticing his sacrifices, he believes she is dumb (since "women folks were not given to thinking nohow"), and he uses his considerable charm to abuse his power over her.

Hurston follows this unhappy but binding love through more than twenty years, the birth of three children, the death of one, and many days and nights of loving, fighting, and very little communicating. When the story ends, Arvay and Jim are in middle age, trying to negotiate a peaceful and loving denouement for the final chapter of their marriage. Ultimately, Arvay realizes that "just like she had not known Jim, she had known her own self even less."

In *Seraph on the Suwanee*, Hurston makes a statement about marriage—similar to the statement she'd made in *Their Eyes Were Watching God* and, even earlier, in her short story "Sweat." Again, she presents marriage as a deadly proposition. And though neither Arvay nor Jim literally dies, they both lose their own lives, in a way, as they become prisoners of the gender roles their marriage forces them to play.

In her simple-minded acceptance of the circumscribed life her husband imagines for her, Arvay is the exact opposite of Zora Neale Hurston. At least three times over the past twenty-five years, Hurston had rejected marriage as a suitable option for her own life. *Seraph* hints at some of her reasons.

Significantly, Hurston based Arvay's extreme inferiority complex on the sense of inadequacy she'd observed in some of the men she'd loved in the past. "Have you ever been tied in close contact with a person who had a strong sense of inferiority?" Zora asked her editor. "I have, and it is hell. They carry it like a raw sore on the end of the index finger. You go along thinking well of them and doing what you can to make them happy and suddenly you are brought up short with an accusation of looking down on them, taking them for a fool, etc. . . . It colors <u>everything</u>," she said, giving an example from her own life with a man she once dated. "It is a very common ailment," Zora concluded. "That is why I decided to write about it. The sufferers do not seem to realize that all that is needed is a change of point of view from fear into self-confidence and then there is no problem."

The problem with Hurston's novel, though, is that Arvay never convincingly moves "from fear into self-confidence." Accordingly, she is difficult to like, hard to sympathize with, and a dubious protagonist at best. "I get sick of her at times myself," Zora admitted.

Hurston's decision to place a white woman at the center of her story was a curious choice, but one that can be traced to at least a couple of sources. First, she had endured a good deal of criticism and misunderstanding for her portrayals of black people; one way to take a break from this kind of scrutiny was to write about whites. Few of Hurston's black male critics were interested in the author's concentration on complex questions of female sexuality even when the protagonist was a sympathetic, vividly drawn black woman, as in *Their Eyes Were Watching God*. In *Seraph on the Suwanee*, a novel that relegated black people far into the background, black critics found little reason to read the book, much less to review it.

Second, Hurston was interested in writing for the movies, but her 1941 job at Paramount had taught her that Hollywood was hardly interested in telling black stories. Her solution, then, was to write a white story. Whites wrote about black characters all the time, often with great commercial success. (Witness: Carl Van Vechten, Fannie Hurst, and Marjorie Kinnan Rawlings.) Hurston—and other black writers of the 1940s and 1950s, including Richard Wright and Ann Petry—thought the reverse should be true as well. Aiming to gain access to a mass-market audience, Hurston once told Van Vechten: "I have hopes of breaking that silly old rule about Negroes not writing about white people."

In some ways, *Seraph on the Suwanee* was more ambitious and experimental than any of Hurston's previous novels, except *Moses*, perhaps. Like all of her books, *Seraph* has moments of breathtaking brilliance. Describing Arvay's loneliness, for instance, Hurston writes: "Her days had nothing in them now but hours. . . . Like raw, bony, homeless dogs, they took to hanging around her doorway. They were there when she got up in the morning, and still whimpering and whining of their emptiness when she went to bed at night." But just as Arvay and Jim do not consistently and completely engage the reader, they don't seem to fully engage the author, either. Hurston gives off the subtle sense that she does not care about Arvay and Jim as much as she did about Janie and Tea Cake, for example, or about John and Lucy Pearson. Mostly, this becomes evident through her narrative voice. While still colloquial, the narrator's tone is slightly different from the authorial voice Hurston used in her previous novels. It is more reserved, coolly observant, and almost tongue-in-cheek, as a reviewer for *The New York Times* pointed out.

"The author knows her people, the Florida cracker of the swamps and turpentine camps intimately, and she knows the locale," the *Times* critic wrote. "One gets the impression that she took a textbook on Freudian psychology and adapted it to her needs, perhaps with her tongue in her cheek while so doing. The result is a curious mixture of excellent background drawing against which move a group of half-human puppets."

The *Herald Tribune* critic found Hurston's characters more true to life, however. She'd captured the "mores and language" of poor white southerners so accurately that it was hard to believe the novel had been written by "one not born to the breed," the reviewer declared. "Reading this astonishing novel, you wish that Miss Hurston had used the scissors and smoothed the seams," he concluded. "Having read it, you would like to be able to remember every extraneous incident and every picturesque metaphor."

If the positive reviews and brisk sales of Hurston's novel gave her cause for celebration, the next week's headlines brought fresh reasons to weep. Tipped off by a black court employee, a reporter for *The New York Age* caught up with Hurston soon after the initial hubbub of good reviews and asked her about the felony charges pending against her. With tears in her voice if not in her eyes, "a hysterical and almost prostrate" Hurston denied the "impossible accusation." She also questioned how the judicial system could take the word of an emotionally unstable child over her own word as "a writer of note and a person of integrity," as the newspaper phrased it. "It smacks of an anti-Negro violation of one's civil rights," Hurston complained, pointing out that "if such injustice can happen to one who has prestige and contacts, then there can be absolutely no justice for 'the little people' of this community." Zora was "visibly upset" as she talked with the reporter, he noted. Undoubtedly she was worried that her name soon would be all over the paper's front page—and, then, all over New York. But at least her voice would be included in the story, she reasoned, to balance out whatever the court employee had peddled to the newspaper. And, thankfully, the reporter had the decency to come to her before printing his story.

The Afro-American, a Baltimore-based newspaper, extended

Hurston no such courtesy. In its October 23 national edition, *The Afro* spread Zora's troubles across its front page in four separate, scurrilous headlines: "Boys, 10, Accuse Zora," the main headline blared in huge type. Below that, in smaller letters: "Novelist Arrested in Morals Charge." Then, under that: "Reviewer of Author's Latest Book Notes Character Is 'Hungry for Love.'" Linked with that third headline was one even more odious. Above the main head, the paper ran a kicker: "Did She Want 'Knowing and Doing' Kind of Love?" These last two headlines referred to dialogue from *Seraph on the Suwanee*. At one point, Jim says to Arvay: "I feel and believe that you do love me, Arvay, but I don't want that stand-still, haphazard kind of love. I'm just as hungry as a dog for a knowing and a doing love. You love like a coward. Don't take no steps at all. Just stand around and hope for things to happen out right."

The newspaper took these words out of their fictional context and viciously used them against Hurston, apparently never even reading her book, but lifting the lines from the *Herald Tribune*'s review, which had run almost two weeks before. Further, *The Afro*'s story quoted sentences from the favorable review in a way that seemed to incriminate Hurston: "The reviewer noted that Miss Hurston revealed intimate physical details about her central character 'to the point of absurdity,' but said the author had to 'construct a visible Freudian fretwork to give us understanding of herself.'" In the review, the "herself" that the critic referred to is Arvay. In *The Afro*'s bastardized quote, it sounds like the "Freudian fretwork" is about Hurston herself. Tossing a box of salt into the wound, *The Afro-American* printed an old photo of Hurston in which she happened to be grinning mischievously and wearing a low-cut, cleavage-revealing dress. Directly below her photo was a headline for another lurid story that had nothing to do with her: "7 Men Held in Sex Orgy Cases Probe." The subhead was equally racy: "Teen-Age White Girls Illicitly Involved."

The Afro-American's sensationalized, openly libelous report thoroughly upstaged *The New York Age*'s tamer, more balanced story, published the same day. "Noted Novelist Denies She 'Abused' 10-Year-Old Boy," the *Age*'s front-page headline announced sensibly. "Zora Neale Hurston Released on Bail," the subhead clarified. *The New York Age* story, which did not include a photo, explained the charges calmly and offered several fresh quotes from Hurston. "I intend to fight this horrible thing to the finish," she declared, "and clear my reputation."

Yet the story that newspapers around the country decided to pick up was *The Afro*'s "sluice of filth," as Zora called it. Distributed by the National Negro Press Association, the article was reprinted—though with less damaging headlines—in newspapers as far away as Iowa. Hurston was humiliated by the whole ordeal; the fact that a black court employee leaked the story was almost too much for her to bear. "That is the blow that knocked me loose from all that I have ever looked to and cherished," she cried.

Immediately after the story hit the press, Zora halted all her promotional activities for *Seraph on the Suwanee* and fled Harlem. The law required her to remain in New York to await her trial, so she quietly moved to the Bronx, where she could be relatively anonymous.

Fearing that the lies were everywhere and that everyone was talking about her, Zora sank into a deep depression. Several friends risked invading her privacy to track her down and offer their support. Among those who reached out to her were Fannie Hurst, Mary Margaret McBride, Marjorie Kinnan Rawlings, and Carl Van Vechten and his wife, Fania Marinoff. Several women from her old neighborhood in Harlem also hunted her up to express their indignation over the ridiculous charges. Zora had organized the Block Mothers initiative during the months she lived on 124th Street with Billy and his mother. As a result, she had become well known and liked in the community: "124th St. is in a state of horror over the thing because they know that it is not true," she soon learned. "I find that various simple people have been running around trying to make themselves heard by officialdom, but they have no force, being ordinary colored people."

While some of Hurston's enemies may have wanted to believe the story, most people simply dismissed it, Arna Bontemps recalled. By then a librarian at Fisk University, Bontemps said he never saw the article in *The Afro-American* "and actually I don't know anybody who took it seriously," he added. "I think the people who had known her during the Renaissance pretty well assumed that she was telling the truth about that." Nevertheless, Bontemps snickered with Langston Hughes about Zora's predicament. Their gentlemanliness prevented them from mentioning her name, however. "Have you heard," Hughes gossiped, "the awful story going around about one of [our] leading lady writers of color (not a poet, thank the Lord) getting in jail, to stand trial next week, on a charge that should hardly be written down?"

Waldman assured Zora that the charges against her were "so patently false" that she would have a good chance of suing both the Children's Society and *The Afro-American* once the case was resolved. But none of that mattered now: "I care nothing for anything anymore," Zora told Carl and Fania. "My country has failed me utterly. My race has seen fit to destroy me without reason, and with the vilest tools conceived of by man so far." More than she blamed the children or their parents, Hurston blamed the Children's Society for veering so far from its "announced purpose to <u>protect</u> children." Instead, the Children's Society had opted "to exploit the gruesome fancies of a pathological case," she charged, and ruin the lives of decent people. "For leaving the havoc that they have wrought upon me as a public figure, think of what happens to . . . that poor building Supt. who is lying in jail because he cannot make bail and his job gone and his name ruined. What real estate agent will hire this poor man after this?"

The Children's Society—and the judicial system—seemed indifferent to the fact that neither Zora nor the janitor had ever been arrested before, that they were upstanding American citizens. "Please do not forget that this thing was not done in the South, but in the so-called liberal North. Where shall I look in this country for justice?" Zora wanted to know.

In Florida and other states where Negro folklore flourished, black people collectively had invented several mythical places, some of which were good—like "Beluthahatchie," a land of forgiveness—and some of which were exceedingly, unbearably bad. The worst place of all was "West Hell." As Hurston described it in a piece she wrote in 1938: "West Hell is the hottest and toughest part of that warm territory."

Zora had suddenly been flung into West Hell—and she saw no way out of its howling despair. "All that I have ever tried to do has proved useless. All that I have believed in has failed me," she decided. "I have resolved to die. It will take a few days for me to set my affairs in order, and then I will go. . . . No acquittal will persuade

some people that I am innocent. I feel hurled down a filthy privy
hole."

As Zora contemplated suicide, all the bitter moments from her life
must have surged to the forefront of her mind. But then the sweet
moments crowded in for consideration, too. As much as she may
have wanted to, Zora knew she could not just lie down and die.
Through all the hardships of her life, she had never allowed anything—not her mother's death, not her father's neglect, not her
years of poverty—to break her spirit. "I love courage in every form.
I worship strength," she'd told a reporter a few years earlier. And way
back in 1926, when she was stumbling through Barnard, she'd written these words: "To be brave costs something. . . . It is so much
easier to die out of one's troubles than it is to live with them. It is
much less painful to die for a principle than to live for it."

Remembering all this, Zora chose to live. Some days were harder
than others, to be sure. Take November 6, for instance. On that
day, *The Afro-American* scandalized Hurston's name again.
Responding to a reader's complaint about the paper's front-page
treatment of Hurston's case, *Afro* editors haughtily defended their
indefensible coverage and demonized Hurston once more by care-
lessly tossing around such words as "perversion" and "the facts." The
newspaper's statement read in part: "It is the AFRO's belief that a
hush-hush attitude about perversion has permitted this menace to
increase. One method of combatting it is to give publicity to it, particularly when it is found among persons·of education and social
advantage who should be setting a good example by obeying the
social laws. . . . Here is a disease which must be stamped out and we
believe that we would be derelict in our duty to close our eyes to the
facts, unpleasant as they may be."

Zora must have felt like storming into *The Afro*'s newsroom with
a machete. Instead, she stayed in the Bronx and kept the lowest of
profiles, only occasionally venturing into Manhattan to pick up her
mail from the Scribner's office. She went on living this way, in virtual
isolation and silence, through the end of the year and into 1949.

In January, another "inconceivable horror" swept over her.
Richard Rochester, a white man she'd met in Los Angeles, suddenly
launched a slander campaign against Hurston. Described in one
newspaper account as a Park Avenue public opinion analyst,

Rochester made numerous phone calls to Scribner's, to several black newspapers, and to *New York World-Telegram* columnist Helen Worden Erskine. In all these conversations, he claimed that Zora owed him money and that she was guilty of smoking marijuana and indecent exposure. The third week of January, he hauled Zora into Municipal Court, charging that she'd refused to pay two debts amounting to $270.15. As far as Zora could tell, Rochester's motive had something to do with a car transaction that had taken place between him and another man, a friend of hers. Rochester had tried to sue the other man, and to persuade Zora to be a witness on his behalf, though she knew nothing of the case. When she refused to perjure herself, Rochester "threatened me with a nation-wide bath of filthy publicity," as Zora put it.

Hurston and her attorney told *The New York Age* that Rochester's "spiteful and untruthful charges" were designed to smear her name before her court date in the sodomy trial. Hurston and Waldman also began to wonder if Rochester had somehow been responsible for those earlier charges as well. In some ways, Waldman later admitted, it all seemed like "a professional frame." In any case, his job was to clear Hurston of *all* the charges against her, big and small. "This man Rochester is a pain in the neck," the lawyer decided, "and will have to be treated accordingly." On February 9, Waldman and Hurston defeated Rochester in his civil suit, and the former Gallup Poll employee found himself unable to get a hearing for his other charges.

The day after the small-claims victory, Zora wrote to Fannie Hurst asking for a loan—"enough to keep me alive for two weeks," she said. "After that I can go to work. I owe room rent now and other things. I have used up every available resource before appealing to you— even to the pawning of my typewriter. I have counted up and find that I just must get hold of 76.00 at once." Zora's $40-a-week payments from Scribner's had ended after ten weeks, as agreed. And any profits from the sales of *Seraph on the Suwanee* would have to go toward attorney's fees, she explained. Meanwhile, Zora had been unable to work because the bad publicity had driven her underground. She actually had considered "taking a job as a domestic" because of its anonymity, she told Hurst, but her numerous court appearances had made even that option impractical. "I am now strapped and most desperate in mind," she confessed. Fannie Hurst came through with a check immediately and Zora thanked her for her "magnificence of spirit."

Although Zora did not find out about it until March, November 18, 1948, had been a good day for her. On that Thursday, Alexander Miller of the Children's Society—along with two deputy assistant district attorneys—had again questioned each of the three boys who'd accused Hurston of molesting them. By then, the boys had implicated several other adults in their wild finger-pointing spree. As a result of their accusations, three other Harlemites—two men and a woman—had been arrested.

As for Hurston's case, Louis Waldman had privately approached District Attorney Frank Hogan and laid the facts before him. He gave Hogan a copy of Hurston's passport proving she'd been out of the country when most of the alleged crimes took place, and he told the D.A. about the kind of character witnesses he could bring forth to testify on his client's behalf. He implored Hogan to conduct a full and thorough investigation of the case before proceeding with the trial. In response, Hogan—whom Waldman judged "a good man"—appointed two of his deputy assistant district attorneys to look into the matter. In their efforts to do so, the two men—Jack Cotton and Aloysius Melia—called on the boys again to repeat their charges.

On November 18, each of the boys admitted—to Cotton, Melia, and Children's Society officer Alexander Miller—that Hurston and all four of the other defendants were completely innocent of the charges against them. Billy confessed that he invented the story because he did not want to admit to his mother that he and his friends had been having sex with one another. The other two boys confirmed this statement. Less than a week later, all three repudiated it. Unconvinced, however, the grand jury refused to indict the other three adults who'd been arrested.

As for the two defendants already indicted—Hurston and the janitor, Rufus—the district attorney's office submitted a recommendation for discharge. The seven-page report cited the boys' conflicting and everchanging testimony. It also pointed out that the charges had all emerged on August 15, 1948, after Billy's mother beat him until he explained why he'd been behaving strangely and why he suddenly seemed to always have change in his pockets. (He'd been skipping school and saving his lunch money, he confessed November 18, and he'd recently robbed his piggy bank.) Poor Billy had simply manufactured the abuse charges to hide his own misbehavior, the district attorney's office concluded. In her dislike of Hurston (because of the Bellevue suggestion, perhaps), the mother was quick to believe Billy's story. Seeing this, the boy began to hurl accusations at practically every adult he didn't like. And he convinced the other two boys to support his desperate lies.

In light of the prosecutor's report and recommendation for discharge, Judge Saul Streit saw no need for a trial. On March 14, 1949, he dismissed all charges against Zora Neale Hurston and ordered her record expunged. The other defendant was cleared as well.

With respectful exuberance, Zora's editor, Burroughs Mitchell, wrote to her the following week: "We have had official notification from Louis Waldman that the whole terrible mess is finished. I know how happy about it you must be, so are we; you must forget all about it now and devote yourself to 'Barney Turk.' Stop in when you can."

"Barney Turk" was the new novel Hurston was supposed to be working on, but no one at Scribner's had heard from her in weeks.

She published a book review in the *New York Herald Tribune* on March 20, an effort to earn some money and to bravely get back into the public eye, no doubt. Apparently, though, the effort took its toll and Zora soon retreated again into the sheltering silence of her Bronx apartment. "I haven't heard from her in a long time," her editor wrote to her agent near the end of April. "Have you?"

Finally, in May, Zora contacted a couple of friends to thank them for their support. By summer, she'd begun writing again, selling a short story—called "The Conscience of the Court"—to the *Saturday Evening Post*. She planned to leave New York, she told her agent, as soon as she had enough money to go. Hearing this, Mitchell wrote her another gentle note, asking her to drop by his office before heading South. "I haven't anything important to say," the editor allowed, "and I'm not going to hound you about the book."

Zora stayed in the Bronx through the summer, but embarked on a healing hegira to Miami in early September. She and her friend Fred Irvine had resumed their plans to travel to Central America together, this time on his newly acquired cargo boat, *The Challenger*, which was berthed in Biscayne Bay. Zora moved onto the large ship with the Englishman (still just a platonic friend), and the two adventurers soon took a calming cruise to the Bahamas. Once back in Miami, they began to prepare the motor vessel for the longer trip to Honduras. Both were short on money, though, so their plans moved along at a languid pace. Meanwhile, Zora settled down to work on "The Lives of Barney Turk." "I am feeling fine," she reported to Burroughs Mitchell, "and in a working mood."

Nurtured by the sunshine and the comforting drone of traffic pouring to and from Miami Beach, Zora worked hard on her novel during the autumn of 1949. But she worked harder to forget her six-month nightmare. "I feel that I have come to myself at last," she observed that fall. "I can even endure the sight of a Negro, which I thought once I could never do again." Ironically, Zora had to "insist on remaining colored" in Miami. Because of her long conversations in Spanish with Argentinians on two neighboring vessels, "everybody along the waterfront tries to make me out Cuban or Mexican," she chuckled to Mitchell.

Moored along the MacArthur Causeway—near the Thirteenth Street bridge and directly across from Miami's stunning skyline—*The Challenger* provided the perfect setting for Hurston's recovery. Most mornings, she strolled a few steps ashore to a little park, where she picked ripe sapodillas and coconuts knocked loose by high winds. On the waterfront, Zora met a cross-section of colorful characters, all fish in the writer's net, she assured her editor. "And God keeps His appointment with Miami every sundown," she marveled, sounding like herself again. "Berthed on the east side of Biscayne Bay, I can look to the western side, which I never fail to come top-side and do around sunset. Thus I get the benefit of His slashing paint brush all the way. . . . The show is changed every day," Zora noted, "but every performance is superb."

CHAPTER 33

Up from the Muck

Each time Zora glanced in the mirror, she recognized herself more than she had the day before. Slowly, during her months in Miami, she reclaimed her soul. "I have regained my peace of mind and cheerfulness," she assured Carl Van Vechten at Christmastime. And a month later, she offered a particularly refreshing report: "Day by day in every way I'm getting human again. I caught myself laughing fit to kill yesterday."

Hurston's period of exile in the Bronx had placed a veil between her and the world that was difficult to lift. This is the way she described what happened to Miriam in *Moses, Man of the Mountain* after her seven days as a leper. In Miriam's case, the veil of silence and brooding finally led to an acute wish to die. Unlike Miriam, however, Zora was an optimist. So she quietly tore away at the veil until it disintegrated, becoming so thin and so subtle, in fact, that it was virtually invisible. Most days, Zora couldn't even see it herself.

By the third week of January 1950, she was close to completing a draft of her new novel and she'd ventured into public speaking again. Following a talk before a group of Dade County librarians, Zora received a warm response as usual. One woman even wrote to Scribner's wondering why all of Hurston's books, other than *Seraph on the Suwanee*, were out of print. "Hurston writes well and we have a demand for her books which we are not able to fill," the librarian commented. "Would you please let us know why her books are not being printed?" Because Scribner's had only published Hurston's most recent novel, the Miami library would have to take that question up with the J. B. Lippincott Company, Mitchell's secretary replied.

Meanwhile, Zora had been forced to scrap her plans for returning to Honduras. Plagued by love troubles and (some said) a weakness for the racetracks, Fred Irvine never secured a paying cargo for *The Challenger*, so he sold off the freighter. Though Zora found Fred "a fascinating study," she was relieved to get away from him and his complicated life. Renting a small house in the northwest section of Miami, she considered returning to New York but changed her mind, she told Burroughs Mitchell, when she remembered how chilly the city could get—literally and figuratively. "To misquote a popular song," she wrote, "'Baby, it's cold up there.'"

In early February, Hurston mailed her editor a draft of "The Lives of Barney Turk," her in-progress novel about a southern cracker who travels through Honduras, the military, and a range of other experiences on his journey toward "openness of feeling." Mitchell replied in mid-March with a long letter outlining the strengths and weaknesses of Hurston's manuscript. The weaknesses were extensive, in his view, and he suggested drastic changes in plot and setting. "It means work," the editor told Zora, "but that has never frightened you."

Hurston took the news well and agreed to the rewrite, but no acceptance meant no money. As one of the few black authors in the country still attempting to survive solely on her writing, Zora had no other source of income. Six of her seven books were out of print, so she was not receiving any royalties to speak of. *Seraph on the Suwanee* was still selling well, but any royalties she might have earned from that book went directly into Scribner's coffers, to pay off the $1,000 she had cost the company in legal fees. And her months of intense work on the new novel had prevented her from taking on any quick (and quick-paying) magazine assignments.

"Nagged by the necessity of living," Zora, at age fifty-nine, decided to look for a job. She wanted work that would not occupy her mind too much, so that she might continue thinking about her book. Something a bit physical would be good, too, to help her lose the weight she'd picked up recently. With these criteria in mind, she found a job rather quickly—using the talents the South seemed to value most in black women: cooking and cleaning.

For $30 a week, plus room and board, Zora accepted a job as a maid for a couple in the swank Miami suburb of Rivo Alto Island. To Mr. and Mrs. Kenneth Burritt, she was just another pleasant, middle-aged black woman who seemed to have the skills to make their lives more comfortable. Few white employers bothered to ask their domestic help much about their lives, assuming their stories would be most uninteresting. The Alabama-born Mrs. Burritt was no exception in this regard. "I have been amazed by the Anglo-Saxon's lack of curiosity about the internal lives and emotions of the Negroes," Hurston wrote around the same time she began working for the Burritts.

One afternoon, however, Mrs. Burritt came upon something that compelled her curiosity about her maid. Thumbing through the latest issue of the *Saturday Evening Post*, the southern matron was shocked to find a story by her "girl" Zora, who was contentedly (or so it seemed) dusting off bookshelves in the next room. "It was a difficult few hours we spent after that," the white woman would recall. "Servants are servants and must act accordingly unless the whole traditional relationship of employer and employee is to be endangered. But adjustments certainly were called for in this case. I must say without reservation that Zora is one of the most cultured women I have ever met and surely one of the finest. You just have to like her."

Mrs. Burritt was so impressed with Zora that she couldn't keep the story to herself. ("For the first time in my life," she enthused, "I found myself going into my kitchen to hear my maid talk.") Soon, *Miami Herald* reporter James Lyons was ringing the doorbell in search of the writer-turned-maid. On March 27, Lyons's story appeared under the headline: "Famous Negro Author Working As Maid Here Just 'To Live A Little.'" With stiff-necked pride, Zora denied that she'd taken the job for financial reasons. "You can only use your mind so long," she told the reporter. "Then you have to use your hands. A change of pace is good for everyone." Lyons described Zora as "a plumpish woman with laughing sloe eyes," and noted that her "infectious good spirits and disarming modesty belie her attainments." The reporter also seemed to believe Zora when she told him she planned to use her experiences on the job to start a national magazine for and by domestics.

Hurston did concede, however, that she was temporarily "written out" and needed to "shift gears" for the moment. "I was born with a skillet in my hands," she declared. "I like to cook and clean and keep house. Why shouldn't I do it for somebody else a while? A writer has to stop writing every now and then and just live a little."

The story was picked up by the national wire services and printed in newspapers all over the country. The *St. Louis Post-Dispatch* commissioned Lyons to write a longer version for its Sunday magazine, and New York's black-owned *Amsterdam News* printed the story under a red-inked, incredulous headline: "Famous Author Working As Maid For White Folks Down In Dixie!" This article speculated beyond the others as to why Zora might have accepted her "lowly domestic position," even bringing up the "unfavorable headlines" of recent years. It also included an insightful editor's note: "Although Miss Hurston is one of our best known writers, she never did make a reasonable pile of money." Interestingly, all these articles gave Hurston's age as forty-two, although the unfortunate stories from two years before had reported her age as forty-five. If Zora (who was fifty-nine) was embarrassed by the nationwide stir she'd provoked in her simple effort to earn a living, she perhaps could take some comfort in being the only woman in the history of the world to reverse the aging process, at least as far as the inattentive press was concerned.

Actually, Zora didn't seem particularly embarrassed about the "tremendous sensation" she'd caused. "I tried to avoid the publicity but the paper <u>insisted</u>," she informed Mitchell. "I am being lectured about at poetry & other literary clubs and there seems to be nothing I can do about it." There were even some advantages to the thing. "Miami is certainly Hurston-conscious," she observed, asking her editor to send twenty copies of *Seraph on the Suwanee* right away, as Miami's demand for autographed copies of the book had suddenly surged. "All I wanted was a little spending change when I took this job," Zora summed up, "but it certainly has turned out to be one slam of a publicity do-dad."

Sending the twenty books along, Mitchell joked: "What I want to know is are you getting any cooking done with all this hullabaloo, or are those poor people living off sandwiches?"

Soon, what the Burritts ate for dinner was no longer Zora's concern. Almost immediately after the article appeared in the *Miami Herald*, she gave her employers her two weeks' notice. She didn't need the job anymore because the unexpected publicity led to several ghostwriting offers. Zora was finding outlets again for her own writing as well.

The piece in the *Saturday Evening Post* that set off all the commotion was "The Conscience of the Court," a curious short story that must have confirmed Mrs. Burritt's favorable view of Zora, who demonstrated, in her employer's words, "a humility the likes of which I have never encountered in an intelligent person." In "The Conscience of the Court," a lifelong and loyal family servant, Laura Lee, stands trial on assault charges after physically stopping a white man from illegally collecting a debt against her beloved employer, "Miz' Celestine." Considering that Zora wrote the piece while she was waiting for a white judge to decide her fate, and that she subsequently worked as a maid, the story is rife with ironies.

Hurston presents Laura Lee as almost a stereotype of the dutiful black maid, and she makes the white judge almost heroic in his sympathy for the unlettered defendant. Yet there is often something ironic in Hurston's tone, as when Laura Lee describes her sound pummeling of the white bill collector. And the story's ending is particularly odd. Cleared of the charges against her, Laura Lee comes home hungry. She is also remorseful about ever doubting Miss Celestine's love for her and the ultimate rightness of the world. Thus, before she will eat, Laura Lee pulls out the silver platter to polish, making "a ritual of atonement by serving." Hurston's attitude toward Laura Lee seems intentionally ambiguous—but on one level, she certainly appears to mock the servant who is so blindly loyal to her mistress that, even in her absence, she pushes her own hunger aside to serve. For many readers of the *Saturday Evening Post*, however, this ambiguity and irony would not have been evident.

Consequently, Mrs. Burritt may have been surprised when Zora exhibited no Laura Lee–like loyalty to her job, hanging up her skillet the moment she could afford writing paper again. If the white woman had stumbled across Hurston's next published article, "What White Publishers Won't Print," she might have been further surprised by her former maid's forthrightness.

In that story—published in the April 1950 issue of *Negro Digest*, a magazine unlikely to find its way onto the affluent island of Rivo Alto—Hurston bluntly attacked publishing policies that only gave ink to "exceptional" or "quaint" aspects of black life. "For various reasons," she wrote, "the average, struggling, non-morbid Negro is the best-kept secret in America." Hurston argued for a literature revealing "that Negroes are no better nor no worse, and at times just as boring as everybody else." This revelation would help dispel the white assumption "that all non-Anglo-Saxons are uncomplicated stereotypes," she asserted, and it would help "to do away with that feeling of difference which inspires fear, and which ever expresses itself in dislike."

As she began rewriting her novel, Hurston took a temporary job working for the campaign of George Smathers, who was running against liberal incumbent Claude Pepper in the Florida Democratic Senate primary. Soon after the May vote (which Smathers won), Hurston wrote an article that was published in the November issue of the *American Legion Magazine*. In this essay, she angrily denounced the buying and selling of black votes that she witnessed during the primary. Although the magazine was anti-Pepper—and welcomed the chance to run the story as a slam against him—Hurston's piece was more about the importance of the ballot than about a particular campaign. "Under our Constitution, there is no royal ruler," she pointed out. "Every American is part of the king that rules over this nation. To sell your vote is to abdicate your part of the throne, and that is that."

Aiming her words primarily at black voters, Hurston challenged them to take seriously their hard-earned, blood-soaked ballot. "It is positively astounding that any adult Negro could look upon the right to vote as a small thing, let alone regard this highest right in civilization in such a way as to put a price upon it," she wrote passionately. (The following year, the black-owned *Negro Digest* would reprint the article so that a sizable number of black voters might actually read it.)

Hurston charged that certain so-called friends of the Negro had bought black votes in the Democratic primary for two dollars apiece in Miami—a city full of educated black people who should know better than to be taken advantage of so easily, and so cheaply. "There has to be an overload of self-pity and insufficient self-confidence and respect" to cause a Negro to sell his vote, she asserted, "then look for some 'friend of the Negro' to look out for his advancement."

True to her political stance as an individualist, Hurston was offended that anyone could think of the black vote as one "dark, amorphous lump," as she put it. "It is time for us to cease to allow ourselves to be delivered as a mob by persuasive 'friends' and become individual citizens."

Zora's brief work on the Smathers campaign led to another unusual job—ghostwriting a book for Smathers's father, retired Judge Frank Smathers. After only a couple of months, though, Zora "escaped" from the employ of the irascible old judge. "I wanted the money, but never did I think I was taking on such a task," she told her editor. With his Old South background and beliefs, Smathers "could not accept the reality that a descendant of slaves could do something in an intellectual way that he could not," Zora soon discovered. Because of his wealth and his chronic illness, the judge had a habit of beating down everybody under his power. "I do not beat down easily," Zora pointed out, "and we fought like tigers from day to day, and I came to see that he loved it. He had met at last a foeman worthy of his steel. I saw his wife and his two sons backing off him with bowed heads, but not your Topsy gal. I let him have it with both barrels time and time again."

Once, when the old man stuffed his fingers into his ears to occlude Zora's words, she jerked his fingers out and kept on talking— to the astonishment of the judge's wife and adult sons. "The way I saw it, all he could do was to fire me, and I wouldn't mind that at all." Despite his wife's outrage over Zora's "temerity," the judge refused to fire her. Soon, though, Zora quit. "All I wanted was <u>out</u> from there."

Stirred by "the extravaganza of summer," Zora tried to loaf, but her work would not let her. She spent most of the summer rewriting her novel, sending a new version to New York in early September. Zora soon headed North, too, where she spent the autumn catching up with her old crowd. "Zora in person is in town!" Carl Van Vechten announced to a mutual friend in late October, a few days before giving the keynote address at a dinner honoring Ethel Waters. Zora likely attended the October 29 dinner for Waters—then starring on Broadway in *The Member of the Wedding*—and she saw Carlo again at a cocktail party at his place in late November. By early December, though, Zora was ready to return to sunny Florida. "I hate snow! You could make a song out of that by just repeating it two thousand times, and that might give you an idea of how bare trees, cold winds, dirty snow under foot, no birds, no blooms, etc. get me down," she told a friend.

The biggest downer of the season, however, was the news from Burroughs Mitchell that Scribner's would not publish "Barney Turk." Zora was disconcerted by the rejection: Her editor had seemed to think the novel had so much promise. And *Seraph on the Suwanee* was proof that readers would respond to a black writer's take on poor white southerners. But Mitchell simply didn't think "Barney Turk" worked. There was not enough Zora Neale Hurston in it, he said.

Part of the challenge Zora faced was something she'd hinted at when asked why she was working as a maid. Simply put, she was "written out." Exploring the inner lives of ordinary, rural black folk had given Hurston a whole shelf of great books. But, as an artist, she'd already said everything she felt compelled to say about "the Negro farthest down." When she'd attempted a novel about "the upper strata of Negro life"—"Mrs. Doctor"—her publisher rejected it before it was even finished, saying the world wasn't ready yet for "literature about the higher emotions and love life of upper-class Negroes," as Zora phrased it in "What White Publishers Won't Print." She had then turned her attention to writing about the South's "poor white trash"—and she'd found some success in this arena with *Seraph on the Suwanee*. But the problem was, Zora simply did not have the same depth of feeling for an Arvay Meserve or a Barney Turk as she did for a Janie Crawford or a John Pearson. In other words, she just didn't seem to *love* these new characters enough. And the absence of love was palpable on the page. "Somehow, the reader is not made to feel that what happens to Barney or what he does is important; the reader isn't taken right into the story, persuaded by it," Mitchell complained. "There are of course wonderful flashes of writing—as there always are in anything you do. But they are not enough to make this a good piece of your work. It is a hard thing to have to say," the editor wrote to Hurston, "but I must tell you that we think the publication of this book would be a disservice to you. We would not do well with it, we are sure of that, and your reputation would suffer." Mitchell urged Zora to put the manuscript aside and move on to something else. Perhaps she should turn away from fiction for the moment and consider writing the second volume of her autobiography, he suggested.

Given the recent unhappy events of her life, Hurston did not feel moved to write another autobiography. Stunned by the rejection, and "with a year's work gone for nothing," a penniless Zora reluctantly moved in with friends on the muck in Belle Glade. There, she worked on a novelette and a few short stories, desperately hoping to sell a piece of writing soon so she could afford her own place, at the very least. "Being under my own roof, and my personality not invaded by others makes a lot of difference in my outlook on life and everything," she told literary agent Jean Parker Waterbury, who'd taken over her account at the Watkins Agency. "Oh, to be once more alone in a house!"

In January 1951, the *American Legion Magazine* asked Waterbury if Hurston might be interested in writing an article "telling how the Communists cynically exploit the Negro." Zora was delighted to tackle the story—as she had been arguing with her Communist friends about the pros and cons of the party for years. Aside from Miguel Covarrubias's wife, Rose Rolando, "always haggling me to go Communist, and me being stubbornly unconverted, we are very fond of each other," Hurston once said. "I keep telling her and others that if I ever meet a Communist with a sense of humor, and a sentence he or she thought up him or herself, I will take the matter under serious consideration. Pooling material things is not so bad, but if I have to quote and repeat the same identical phrases, down to the last stress on a syllable as everybody else, they can count me out of the Party. I don't see what Old Maker went to the trouble of making me a head for if He didn't expect me to use it once in a while the way I want to use it."

Hurston expressed similar anti-Communist sentiments—in an equally salty tone—in her article "Why the Negro Won't Buy Communism." She argued that most Negroes resented and rejected the Communist Party because of its "insulting patronage" toward "pitiable" black people. The party had underrated black Americans' "intelligence and self-esteem," she said, and what it had to offer "as a way of life is as morbid and ugly as the devil's doll-baby, when we are on the hunt, like everybody else, for something pretty." Despite an all-out recruitment effort, black membership in the Communist

Party remained "slack and scanty," partly because "the Negro is the most class-conscious individual in the United States," Hurston asserted. "The dear peasant in the Soviet Union in his shapeless felt boots and slurping his cabbage soup, meant exactly nothing to us. Just the thing we are striving to get away from. For us to long for that would call for much more persuasion than the party has been able to deliver." Hurston finished the article within a couple of weeks, and the *American Legion Magazine* bought it—for a fee of $600—for publication in the June issue.

While she awaited payment for the story, Zora remained in Belle Glade, struggled to pay her car note, and worried about her brown-and-white terrier, Spot, who was missing for the two weeks she worked on the *American Legion* piece. When Spot was safely returned—"a frightened, heart-broken dog whom I am nursing back to mental health again"—Zora wrote a short story about her beloved pet, called "Miss Spot," and worked further on the novelette she'd begun. She sent both pieces to Waterbury in late February.

The short story did not compel, the agent judged, but the novelette, which Zora eventually hoped to turn into a play, was another matter. Called "The Golden Bench of God," it was based on the life of black hair-care empress Madam C. J. Walker and that of her daughter, A'Lelia, whom Zora had known during the heyday of the Harlem Renaissance. Zora was hopeful about the story: "I would pray that it get serialized in one of the big women's mags, but since I have paid no church dues in quite some time, Old Maker is under no obligation to me whatsoever." Zora's agent saw even bigger things for the novelette. Sending Zora a couple of pages of commentary, Waterbury said she thought it was "novel material." Zora appreciated the sentiment. "But the very mention of 'novel' gives me a shudder," she said. Citing her financial difficulties of the past six months, Hurston resisted the idea of devoting so much time to writing something that might not find a publisher. She could not bear a repeat of the "Barney Turk" episode. On the other hand, she agreed that the story could use some expansion. "I had just tried not to write a novel. Some of the economic kicks I have suffered in the last half year have reached my vitals." Ultimately, Zora assented to expanding the piece into a full-blown novel, "as soon as I get some permanent place to live," she said.

To that end, she urged Waterbury to prod the *American Legion Magazine* about her freelance payment, "because I am all too weary of going to the Post Office and turning away cold in hand and having to avoid folks who have made me loans so that I could eat and sleep," she explained. "The humiliation is getting to be too much for my self respect."

A week later, with the *American Legion* check still lost in the mail, Waterbury sent Hurston a loan of $100 as an advance against the $600 payment. Zora—who'd just moved into her own house on the muck—could not have been more grateful. "I had exactly four pennies when it arrived, and my landlord was growing restless," she said. With the roof over her head secured for the moment, Zora reported that she'd "caught fire on the novel, and I am back at work on it already." She added: "I feel more confident about this story than anything I have done since THEIR EYES WERE WATCHING GOD."

Her confidence was soon rattled, though, by an intense bout with the flu. When a friend found her "only half conscious" on March 24, she rushed her to the hospital, where Zora remained for almost two weeks. "Never have I been so ill since I have been grown," reported Zora, who'd recently turned sixty.

With the *American Legion Magazine* check finally arriving—and immediately going to pay off her car note, income tax, and other debts—Zora was "feeling grand" as the month of May began on a bright and clear day. She was beginning work on an article she'd pitched to the *Saturday Evening Post* about Ohio Senator Robert Taft, a leading candidate for the 1952 Republican presidential nomination. Meanwhile, her work on the novel was proceeding at a fast clip. She aimed to make this book the first "truly indigenous Negro novel," she said. No such book had been written, she believed, because "punches have been pulled to 'keep things from the white folks' or angled politically, well to show our sufferings, rather than to tell a story as is." She told her agent: "I have decided that the time has come to write truthfully from the inside. Imagine that no white audience is present to hear what is said."

By the end of May, Hurston had finished the Taft article, as well as the novel. In June, she received word that the *Saturday Evening Post* was buying the Taft story. Hurston's profile of the Ohio

Republican was a favorable one, which helped her case with the magazine, where Taft was well liked. Her initial intent was just "to take a good look at the man who might easily be our next prexy," as she put it. "You know, I did not start out to be enthusiastic about Senator Taft, but the more research I did on the man, the better I liked him," Zora told Waterbury. Her article, called "A Negro Voter Sizes Up Taft," was scheduled for publication in December.

Zora was financially strapped again, but this time, she had no debts. Hoping to save some of the money from her forthcoming *Post* payment, she packed up Spot and all her worldly belongings and moved to the tiny town of Eau Gallie, where she could rent a house for five dollars a week—half the cost of her rent in Belle Glade. Eau Gallie also was cleaner than the muck, she judged, and cooler because of the coastal breezes from the Atlantic. Zora was elated to find that the house where she wrote *Mules and Men* was vacant. Owned by Eau Gallie's mayor, the one-room house was in what had become a white neighborhood since Zora lived there nearly twenty years earlier. But the mayor agreed to rent to her if she was willing to do the work necessary to make the place livable. The huge yard— covering two blocks of grounds—was grown over with weeds and full of old tin cans, bottles, and other junk when Zora moved in. "It looked like a jungle three weeks ago," she reported in early July, "and it took a strong heart and an eye on the future for me to move in when I arrived."

Getting up every morning at five o'clock, Zora spent her days chopping down weeds, clearing land, and planting flowers—going to bed around nine most nights, "happily tired." After several days of this, her neighbors began stopping by to compliment her on the improvements. Admiring her efforts, the manager of the local dairy surprised her one Saturday with a load of compost as a gift. Within a few weeks, the place was not only comfortable but moving toward beautiful. "I have to do some pioneering," Zora told Waterbury, "but I find that I like it." She found another benefit in the hard work, too: "From all that hoeing and what not, I am losing weight, God be praised!"

Zora put so much work into the place because she hoped to buy it one day: "Somehow, this one spot on earth feels like home to me. I have always intended to come back here. That is why I am doing so much to make a go of it. No house in a block of me four ways. No loud radios and record-playing to irritate me, and great oaks and palms around the place."

In addition to spending a good deal of money on the home improvements, Zora paid up her health and accident insurance for a year—at a cost of $67.70—and bought an icebox and furniture. She'd asked Waterbury to put away some of her freelance earnings for her, but now she had to draw on those savings for gas, groceries, and a nice pair of black slacks to wear when she went downtown, so she wouldn't have to waste time laundering a dress. Feeding the numerous cardinals and bluejays on the property and enjoying the antics of Spot and "her daughter," Shag, Zora finally had found her own little slice of heaven, she told friends. "Living the kind of life for which I was made, strenuous and close to the soil, I am happier than I have been for at least ten years."

On the second Sunday in July 1951, Zora had a vivid dream of her mother. It was only the third dream she'd had of the beloved Lucy Potts Hurston since her death almost a lifetime ago, in 1904. In this dream, Lucy was in her teens, younger than Zora had ever known her. "A serene and happy aura was about her," Zora recalled. "She said nothing, just smiled and beamed on me, handed me a note written on the lined paper of a cheap tablet, and somehow was gone. I unfolded the note, written in lead pencil, and read, 'The hidden enmity will come out into the open now, but do not be afraid. Thank them for the insincere advice given with cheerfulness. Make the new arrangements suggested to you, and see your self go to greater heights.'"

The next day, Burroughs Mitchell wrote Zora a letter. Scribner's was not interested in publishing her new novel, "The Golden Bench of God." The story's protagonist was "a fine, warm, attractive character," Mitchell wrote, "but we can't feel that this novel—the book as a whole—comes close to success. And the damn trouble is that we don't know what to suggest in the way of revision." Thinking more highly of the manuscript, Jean Parker Waterbury was surprised by the rejection. So the agent immediately sent the novel to Tay Hohoff, one of Hurston's former editors at Lippincott, for a second opinion. She also wrote to Zora to try to cushion the blow.

"Let not your heart be troubled, honey," Zora wrote to Waterbury in response. The dream of her mother had prepared her for the rejection. A week later, a mellow and magnanimous Zora wrote Mitchell a warm note: "Digging in my garden, painting my house, planting seeds, and things like that, makes me lazy about getting to the Post Office, and so I did not get your letter until Friday P.M. So belatedly I thank you for your editorial comments, and the time you spent reading the book."

Zora went on to talk not about the rejected novel but about her happy surroundings. "There is a flowing artesian well about fifty feet of the house, and already I have arranged a bit of ornamental water. I am planting butterfly ginger around it," she told Mitchell, who shared her enthusiasm for nature. She'd also planted pink verbena and bright-colored poppies that she intended to let grow wild. Next, she was planting papayas.

Zora's yard, which was "beginning to have a park-like sweep to it," had the benefit of being situated only two blocks from the Indian River, which was not really a river, "but a long arm of the sea cut off by sand-bars," as Zora saw it. "The tropical water is so loaded with phosphorus, that standing on the bridge at night, every fish, crab, shrimp, etc., glows as it moves about in the water. When the surface is disturbed, it scintillates like every brilliant jewel you can mention."

Mitchell responded to Hurston's pleasant letter with a brief report on his own new digs. He also encouraged her to think again about writing another autobiographical book. By September, she was seriously considering it. "I am bunching my muscles for the leap," she said.

While she summoned her courage to take on another book-length manuscript, Zora proposed several magazine pieces to her agent, including "a tongue-in-cheek exhortation to career women to return to the home lest we lose our ascendancy over men." She also wanted to write an article called "Do Negroes Like Negroes?" This piece, she said, would go "behind the curtain of the lack of concerted action" among black Americans—"the eternal pacing," as she put it, "of an invisible cage." Waterbury liked the ideas and encouraged Zora to move forward with them.

Meanwhile, Zora's "farm," as she called it, was "coming along splendidly," despite some recent bad news: The property was involved in an estate dispute, so there could be no sale any time soon, maybe not for years. Since she didn't have the funds to buy at present anyway, Zora took the news in stride, particularly after her landlord assured her that she could continue to live there as long as she liked.

Zora handled a second piece of bad news with equal dispassion. Tay Hohoff at Lippincott was no more interested in publishing "The Golden Bench of God" than Scribner's was. The editor would be happy to look at a revised version of the novel, but then Zora had to decide if she was willing to invest the time, with no guarantee of successful results. Responding to Waterbury's overly solicitous letter, Zora told her: "You and Tay Hohoff do not need to handle me with kid gloves so. I feel all right about the refusal of the book. I know that you mean me all the good in the world."

Goodwill notwithstanding, Zora needed to do something to make money, and quickly. In early October, her financial situation became so crucial that she ran out of groceries and had to hock her typewriter to buy staples for her pantry. But her nerves were "in fine shape now," she assured her friends. "Keeping outdoors and raising a fine garden, both flowers and vegetables, has done me a world of good. As soon as I can get hold of money to get my machine out of hock, I will be in high spirits."

Growing her own crops, Zora made it through the end of 1951 somehow, but health problems assailed her at the beginning of the new year. She'd picked up a tropical virus from impure drinking water in Honduras, and it periodically racked her system, leaving her so weak she could hardly lift a hand. It also caused severe headaches and swelling in her groin area and under her arms. Doctors could do little to ease the pain of the mysterious illness, leaving Zora to lie in bed and wait out its attacks. A severe siege in early 1952 confined her to bed for several days. Then, just as suddenly as the illness attacked, it dissipated.

Feeling better by the end of January, Zora organized a group of performers and staged a series of five folk concerts in the Eau Gallie area, one for a black audience and four for whites. In this way, she was able to pick up some much-needed money. But she found the concerts took too much time from her writing: "Too much work for too little money," she decided.

In early March, Hurston was asked to speak at a Taft versus Eisenhower debate in Boston (the two men were vying for the Republican presidential nomination), but she demurred because she didn't have a winter coat. Of course, she didn't need one in Eau Gallie; her two sweaters and one short jacket were sufficient for Florida's mild winters. Yet Boston, even in March, was a different story. Several weeks later, Zora was invited to New York to work on the Citizens for Taft Committee; again, she wanted to go, but she didn't have enough money for the trip.

Kicking around various story ideas with her agent, Zora wrote constantly, but most of her pieces didn't sell. "She could write like an angel and be absolutely sloppy when she was desperate for money," Waterbury would recall. Sloppiness was not the only issue, though. "It seemed to me that she was writing about less and less valid things. She'd pick any little incident and try and build it up," the agent observed. "And just as long as there were words on a page she felt that she could get some cash for it."

The need for cash was a major problem for Zora in 1952. And that need prevented her from having what writers require most to create well: unhurried, unworried time. "I try to get down to work," she told Waterbury in June, "but it is hard now when I worry about money."

With Burroughs Mitchell urging her on, Zora finally started a second volume of her autobiography that summer. Around the same time, she was invited to write a column for a small black newspaper, *The Weekly Review*, in Augusta, Georgia. The pay was small but regular and it would bring attention to Hurston's books, so she decided to accept. In early fall, though, she got a better offer: the *Pittsburgh Courier*, a nationally circulated black newspaper with thirty-five thousand readers in Florida, asked Zora to cover one of the most notorious criminal trials in the state's history.

In the small town of Live Oak, about 255 miles northwest of Eau Gallie, a black woman named Ruby McCollum was facing trial for the murder of one of the area's most prominent white citizens, Dr. C. Leroy Adams. In October, Zora began shuttling back and forth between Live Oak and Eau Gallie to write about the drama as it unfolded in the Suwannee County Courthouse.

The thirty-seven-year-old Ruby McCollum was the wife of the

county's wealthiest black man, Sam McCollum, who ran the area's numbers racket—known in Florida as *bolita*. Ruby also was the mistress of the town's best-loved white man, C. Leroy Adams, a popular young physician and newly elected state senator. The affair had gone on for several years, with all of Live Oak knowing about it but not daring to speak of it above a whisper. After August 3, 1952, though, it became the only thing Live Oak talked about. That day, Ruby allegedly shot the doctor to death, flung the gun into some bushes, and went home to make dinner for her three youngest children. (Her fourth child was away in college.) When police arrived to arrest Ruby, they had to hustle her out of town under heavy guard while a white mob clawed at her. Her husband fled town with the children, but when he arrived at the home of Ruby's mother in another part of the state, he suffered a heart attack and died. Within forty-eight hours, Ruby McCollum had lost her lover, her husband, and her freedom. She was now standing trial for first-degree murder, and Adams's widow had filed a $100,000 civil suit against her. Prosecutors were pushing for the electric chair.

Ruby McCollum proved an engaging character for Hurston as both a reporter and a novelist. Given her own run-in with the law, Hurston expressed a kind of sensitivity to McCollum's plight that few other reporters could have brought to the coverage. And as a novelist, she attempted to look deeply into McCollum's character. The result was journalism of the most compelling order—and arguably Hurston's most effective writing of the 1950s.

Her first report on the case ran in the October 11 issue of the *Courier*. It essentially consisted of Zora's courtroom observations. "I watched her for an hour and a half this morning and she did not utter a single word, except in a short whispered conference with her lawyer," Hurston wrote of McCollum. At one point in the article, Zora commented on all the courtroom spectators who'd turned out to hear Ruby McCollum's story, "forgetting their own worries," feeling "lucky for not being in her shoes."

Among those feeling most lucky, no doubt, was Zora Neale Hurston, whose money problems seemed almost petty when measured against the troubles Ruby McCollum faced. Zora had been educated by books and travel; she'd published four novels, two books of folklore, an autobiography, and numerous short stories, essays, and plays. She had no children, but most days she counted that as a blessing. "At times I have wished that I might have one of those from Japan where the mothers were unwed by American fathers," she once said. "Then again, I am glad that I have none to tie me down." What she did have were two delightful dogs, a new cat, a comfortable roof over her head, and a yard so beautiful that tourists often stopped to take pictures of it. And now she had a regular income too, thanks to the *Pittsburgh Courier*—and to Ruby McCollum. Watching Ruby's life devolve before the unsympathetic eyes of twelve white men—supposedly a jury of her peers—Zora decided she had no worries to speak of.

Despite a tendency to litter its stories with exclamation points, the *Pittsburgh Courier* was interested in covering the Ruby McCollum trial thoroughly and well. And the editors were wise to realize what a seasoned—and, in many ways, unparalleled—writer like Hurston could bring to their team coverage. Under her byline, the editors identified her as "Noted Novelist, Lecturer and Newspaperwoman." Or, once, in an unedited fit of redundancy: "Famous Author, Novelist, Writer." The editors also seemed to encourage Hurston's focus on the human-interest angle of McCollum's story. Zora wrote a few straightforward news reports about the case—"Ruby Is Sane; Trial Date Set" and "Ruby's Lawyer Disqualified; Plot Reported"—but most of her articles focused on Ruby as a woman, rather than as a defendant. Over the course of her coverage of the case—from October 11, 1952, to May 2, 1953—Hurston's empathy for McCollum gradually mounted as she dug to the bottom of the younger woman's story.

Although evidence strongly supported Ruby McCollum's contention that she shot her lover in self-defense and in a tussle over his gun, prosecutors portrayed her as a cold-blooded killer who murdered Adams over an outstanding doctor's bill—a bill that the wealthiest black woman in Live Oak would have had no trouble paying. At one point during her trial, Ruby (who'd had one child by Adams and was pregnant again at the time of the shooting) said famously: "I was not his enemy. I loved him." In denial about the well-known affair, however, the jury bought the prosecution's story and convicted Ruby McCollum of first-degree murder. A few days before Christmas, the mother of four was sentenced to die in Florida's electric chair.

In the weeks following the trial, Hurston wrote a powerful ten-part series for the *Courier*, interviewing friends, relatives, neighbors, and apparently Ruby herself. "The Life Story of Mrs. Ruby J. McCollum!" was a sensitive but unsentimental account of a black woman's complicated and sometimes sordid life, from her childhood to her death sentence.

The series gave Hurston an opportunity to display not only her skills as a journalist, but her talents as a literary stylist. She called back images of Janie Crawford, for example, when she described Ruby's romantic longings as a teenager: "She wanted beauty and poetry mingled in her life, something to make her everyday side-meat taste more like ham." Explaining Ruby's strong sense of independence, not so different from her own, Zora wrote: "By nature, Ruby did not walk in footprints."

Hurston ended her weekly series in May 1953 by giving Ruby McCollum a sister's embrace: "As she said, she does not know whether she did right or wrong," Zora wrote, "and neither does anyone else, including the sovereign State of Florida, in spite of the verdict."

Several months after Hurston's series ended, readers were still writing letters to the *Courier* about the stories and about Ruby McCollum herself. Because of the volume of mail, the paper started a separate section of letters to the editor, called "Ruby! Good or Bad?" Many readers condemned Ruby McCollum not so much for killing the white doctor as for sleeping with him and claiming to love him. "Ruby is disgraceful to the colored race," one reader wrote in a typical letter. Another defended her: "Don't blame the colored woman. She just beat Dr. Adams to the draw. She wanted her life like Dr. Adams wanted his." And a high school girl from Pinehurst, Georgia, wrote touchingly: "I think we should be more careful about our attitude toward Ruby. Just think how much misery she is in. . . . So why don't we be for Ruby instead of against her?"

Realizing that there were certain angles to the story she could not reach as a black woman in a white-run town like Live Oak, Hurston interested white Alabama journalist William Bradford Huie in the case, which was appealed to the Florida Supreme Court. Both writers became active in the effort to save Ruby McCollum from the electric chair. Ultimately, she was declared insane and committed to a mental institution, where she remained for twenty years. In 1956, Huie would publish a book about the case, called *Ruby McCollum: Woman in the Suwannee Jail*. It included a long and passionate section by Hurston, based on the series she wrote for the *Courier*.

If Zora helped to save Ruby McCollum's life, Ruby helped to save Zora's as well. Writing about Ruby McCollum, Hurston found not only a responsive black audience for her work, she also found her voice again.

CHAPTER 34

Every Hour a Stranger

After her long immersion in the life of Ruby McCollum, Zora returned to her own life in Eau Gallie with a renewed sense of appreciation for its relative simplicity.

In the spring of 1953, she tried unsuccessfully to buy a tract of land behind her house, borrowing $300 from her ex-husband, physician Herbert Sheen, to help make the $1,100 down payment. The land was in a white area, close to the Indian River, and highly desirable. When it began to look like a big corporation was going to squeeze her out of the land deal, Hurston wrote to her ex, who was now a good friend: "Mumble a prayer for me, honey. I wish that you were here to help me out with the thinking and planning. I know that I have literary ability, but that does not mean reasoning power. Talent and intelligence are not the same thing at all, you know. . . . A person may be a genius in some way, and have no real intelligence at all."

Hurston was no genius in money matters, as she implied, but neither was she the improvident imbecile that some people seemed to think she was. She was generous to a fault, some of her friends remembered, and she couldn't seem to keep a dollar from slipping through her fingers. But Hurston's almost perpetual lack of money did not stem from any particular wastefulness. The fact is, most writers of her generation, especially black ones, simply did not earn enough money from their craft alone to support themselves, much less to plan for retirement.

Accordingly, Zora's story was not some tragic rags-to-riches-to-rags tale. In truth, Hurston never acquired any riches, despite her illustrious career. The largest royalty payment she ever earned from any of her books was $943.75. Her $100-a-week salary at Paramount in 1941 was the highest wage she was ever paid. And the $1,000 she received with her Anisfield Award was among the largest lump sums she ever handled.

Hurston had arrived in New York City in 1925 with a dollar and fifty cents in her purse. When she left for good, almost twenty-five years later, she did not have much more than she'd started out with. That is, unless you count her seven outstanding books as the treasures that they were. But a shelf full of books, no matter how great, would not pay the rent.

At age sixty-two, Hurston should have been in a financial position to be semiretired, writing at her leisure rather than in a scuffle to make a living. Leisure, however, was costly. And as a younger woman, Zora had not possessed the patience or the prudence to align herself for the long haul with a black college, for example, as Arna Bontemps had done at Fisk, or Sterling Brown at Howard. Hurston always had been too busy contending with the present to give much thought to the future. "I don't know any more about the future than you do," she'd written in *Dust Tracks on a Road*. "I hope that it will be full of work, because I have come to know by experience that work is the nearest thing to happiness that I can find. No matter what else I have among the things that humans want, I go to pieces in a short while if I do not work. What all my work shall be, I do not know that either, every hour being a stranger to you until you live it."

Despite her lack of vocational foresight, a richly endowed faculty position at one of the nation's universities would have been a fitting denouement to Hurston's exceptional career. Of course, Jim Crow prevented black intellectuals from teaching at most white universities, where the biggest endowments were. Still, there were several black colleges where Hurston might have taught in the 1950s, such as Florida A&M, Morgan State, or Howard University. The latter two both had honored Hurston as an alumna during the peak of her career. Now, however, given the bad publicity of 1948, none of these institutions was beating Hurston's door down to offer her a job. And she had become, for good reason, too proud to beg.

Consequently, Hurston continued to write for a living, although her powers appeared to be declining with age—a predicament no more unusual for a writer than for a boxer or a basketball player. In some ways, in fact, a writer is very much like an athlete. The demands of the work are physically and mentally exhausting, and one cannot be expected to perform at his or her peak forever.

Hurston's peak had been extraordinarily productive, however. She wrote and published six of her seven books between 1933 and 1942—a span of less than ten years. All three of the novels she wrote during this time—*Jonah's Gourd Vine*, *Their Eyes Were Watching God*, and *Moses, Man of the Mountain*—were remarkable. If Hurston had done nothing except publish these three novels over the course of her life—let alone in one decade—she would have earned bragging rights for a distinguished career. But Zora had done so much more and still felt she had even more to do. Yet, as any athlete or writer would attest, a human being can only run so fast, jump so high, or put pen to paper for so many hours a day. And these feats all somehow seem to become more difficult with age.

If Hurston was past her peak as a writer by 1953, she was in good company. The forty-five-year-old Richard Wright, American literature's favorite black boy of the early 1940s, had become an expatriate in Paris. And his 1953 novel, *The Outsider*, was published to decidedly mixed reviews. None of his books of the 1950s would achieve the critical or commercial success of his first novel, *Native Son*.

Meanwhile, Langston Hughes, a decade younger than Hurston, had ended 1952 with nine dollars in his bank account. And he spent much of 1953 struggling to avoid being upstaged by several younger black male writers: When Ralph Ellison received the National Book Award in January 1953 for his novel *Invisible Man*, Hughes attended the ceremony, but reported that it was rather dull. Later that year, a young New Yorker named James Baldwin was proclaimed the hottest new sensation in black literature upon the publication of his first novel, *Go Tell It on the Mountain*. Hughes found the book rather lacking—and found himself paying a compliment to an old friend. If Zora Hurston, "with her feeling for the folk idiom," had written *Go Tell It on the Mountain*, Hughes declared, "it would probably be a *quite* wonderful book."

Hughes needn't have been so worried about his literary successors.

Eventually, Ellison and Baldwin, too, would peak out. Every writer did, it seemed. Unfortunately, it was the nature of the game. After *Invisible Man*, for example, Ellison would never publish another novel in his lifetime. James Baldwin, on the other hand, would have a distinguished career as a novelist, essayist, and playwright. But he published his last novel when he was just fifty-five years old, teaching and taking on less strenuous projects as he aged. Similarly, Hurston's friend Marjorie Kinnan Rawlings published her last novel in 1953, when she was in her midfifties. Another great writer of Hurston's generation, William Faulkner, continued to write—and publish—past the age of fifty-five. But he wrote *The Sound and the Fury* and *Absalom, Absalom!*—regarded as his greatest masterpieces—when he was in his thirties. Ernest Hemingway wrote *The Sun Also Rises* when he was in his twenties, won the Pulitzer Prize for *The Old Man and the Sea* when he was in his midfifties, and then— unable to write—killed himself at age sixty-two.

Though not usually as dramatic as Hemingway's example, this kind of burnout happened to the best of writers. Sometimes it was a case of the author simply being unable to write as compellingly as he or she wanted to, or with as much concentration and discipline. As Hurston once told her editor, "The spirit is willing but the flesh is lazy as hell." In other cases, the writer might be producing tomes of beautiful material, but the times and the tastes might have changed so much over her lifetime as to make her words seem obsolete the moment they take shape on the page.

Because the manuscripts for "The Lives of Barney Turk" and "The Golden Bench of God" do not survive, it's impossible to know for sure if Hurston's powers as a writer had declined significantly by the 1950s or if publishers were passing on her novels for other reasons. Her editor's comments certainly indicate Hurston was not writing at the level of her previous novels. But it's possible that editors held her to an extraordinarily high standard. On any publicity tour, the bad headlines of 1948 would inevitably resurface; to justify that risk, a publisher would need to be dazzled by Hurston's writing. And from all evidence, Hurston wasn't writing dazzling manuscripts anymore, at least not on first draft.

If Zora had not been dependent on her writing to put food on her table, she might not have minded so much if her manuscripts didn't sell. She already had prepared herself for this sundown time emotionally if not financially. "When I get old, and my joints and bones tell me about it," she once said, "I can write for myself, if for nobody else, and read slowly and carefully the mysticism of the East, and reread Spinoza with love and care. All the while my days can be a succession of coffee cups."

Hurston might have been in a better position to "get mellow and think kindly of the world," as she put it, if she and Herbert Sheen had stayed together. Sheen was a well-off physician and community activist in Los Angeles who could have provided Zora with a comfortable life. If she'd had this comfort, however, she might not have had a writing career at all. Or perhaps she would have written seven great books and kept them in a trunk at the foot of her bed, to be discovered by some fresh-faced Ph.D. candidate in 2042. In any case, Zora had long before chosen career over comfort—and, even in her last decade, she harbored no regrets about that choice. "It is interesting to see how far we both have come since we did our dreaming together in Washington, D.C.," she wrote to Sheen in 1953. "We struggled so hard to make our big dreams come true, didn't we? The world has gotten some benefits from us, though we had a swell time too. We lived!"

Hurston and Sheen had become close again, exchanging letters and confidences often. Sheen's complicated personal life prevented them from considering a reconciliation at this late date, but they shared a special kind of bond, to be sure. Hurston ended one letter to Sheen by assuring him that he was "the most loved man on earth." She clarified: "That does not mean that I hope or expect to thrust myself into your life except as a friend. I am with you to the end. Just something you can think about on a cloudy day when you might feel depressed."

Like clandestine pen pals, Zora and Herbert once decided to trade photographs. "I have one to send you so you can see how your battle-axe looks at present," Zora wrote, thanking him for the picture he'd recently sent. "I should be as gray as you by all rights, but somehow I do not seem to grow gray easily."

Indeed, a 1953 photograph reveals no gray hairs on Hurston's head. Looking relaxed, healthy, and completely self-assured, Zora wears a black-and-white dress, belted at the waist to show off her slimmed-down figure. One hand rests sassily on her hip and she beams with a smile that is all confidence and kindness. The photo ran in the August 1953 issue of *All-Florida Magazine*, along with a brief profile of the author, who looked no older than the fifty years she acknowledged for the reporter. She'd recently laid off from her writing to treat an ulcer, she confided. "You wouldn't think I'd ever have an ulcer, would you?" Zora joked with the reporter. "No, and then again, yes," he answered in his story. "For behind that infectious laughter is a brilliant mind keenly alert to the fast moving events of today's world."

The reporter was right about Hurston's interest in current events, but her present passion was ancient. She was working on a play about the biblical figure King Herod. By October, she'd decided to turn it into a book, and she wrote a breathless letter about it to Burroughs Mitchell at Scribner's. She'd been wanting to write King Herod's story for years. She'd devoted many months to research and written several chapters already, she told Mitchell. "If I can only carve him out as I have conceived him, it cannot help from being a good book. The story, his actual life, has EVERYTHING. He is set forth by all writers of his time as a man of the greatest courage, of high intelligence, one of the handsomest men of his time." King Herod was a misunderstood figure, Hurston believed, and her research showed that he was not the butcher who'd murdered innocent babies in Bethlehem "in the hope of catching the infant Jesus in the dragnet." Her revisionist, fictionalized biography would reveal the full strength of his character, she promised Mitchell. "Not only a swell book is inherent in the theme, but a most magnificent movie."

Mitchell responded to the idea enthusiastically. "I remember your sitting in our living room, several years ago now, and talking about Herod. Now you are doing something about it," he wrote to Hurston. "By all means, send along those chapters; I want very much to see them."

Encouraged by Mitchell's interest, Hurston labored on the book for a long time before she felt it was ready to send to Scribner's. For the rest of 1953 and all of 1954, she worked on the Herod manuscript as if "under the spell of a great obsession." To support herself over this period, she contributed to the Ruby McCollum book, ghostwrote an autobiography for a local white man, and secured a few speaking engagements here and there. As Christmas 1954 approached, Zora was "deep in creative mood," as she phrased it, "and did not emerge until I realized that the day was here."

On January 7, 1955—her sixty-fourth birthday—Zora told Sheen that she was still working on the King Herod book in "a very hard and continuous grind." By May, she'd finished two-thirds of a new version of the manuscript, which she'd decided to retool after conducting extensive additional research. "It is a hard, tough assignment," she said, "but I think that it should be done." She thought the story so momentous that she asked British Prime Minister Winston Churchill to write the book's introduction and a running commentary on the political implications of each chapter. To Hurston's surprise, Sir Winston actually responded to her letter. Citing poor health, he graciously declined.

On June 3, Zora finally sent her manuscript to Burroughs Mitchell, via express mail. All told, she had put five years of active work into the project, three years on research alone. Nonetheless, on July 21, Burroughs Mitchell wrote her another rejection letter. "In spite of your knowledge of your subject and your clearly deep feeling about it, the book does not seem to us to accomplish its intention. I mean to say that it does not vividly recreate the man and his time," the editor told Hurston. "There is a wealth of fine material here but somehow it has failed to flow in a clear narrative stream. We think the book would prove difficult reading for the layman."

Zora responded to the rebuff with startling calm. "Please, please do not think I feel badly about the rejection," she wrote to Mitchell. "I was astonished myself how easily I felt. Perhaps it is because I have such faith in the material and now my conviction that I can handle it. All is well." Shrugging off the rejection, Hurston would continue to work on the King Herod book for the rest of her life.

In August 1955, though, she took a break from antiquity to weigh in on one of the pressing issues of the day. On August 11, the *Orlando Sentinel* printed a letter to the editor from Hurston that shoved her back into the national spotlight. Under the headline "Court Order Can't Make Races Mix," Hurston criticized the 1954 Supreme Court decision in *Brown v. Board of Education*, which ruled segregated schools unconstitutional. Hurston was not opposed to desegregation, she said in her letter, but she objected to "forcible association," as she put it.

"If there are not adequate Negro schools in Florida, and there is some residual, some inherent and unchangeable quality in white schools, impossible to duplicate anywhere else, then I am the first to insist that Negro children of Florida be allowed to share this boon," she wrote. "But if there are adequate Negro schools and prepared instructors and instructions, then there is nothing different except the presence of white people. For this reason, I regard the ruling of the U.S. Supreme Court as insulting rather than honoring my race."

In Hurston's view, Florida's black schools were "in very good shape and on the improve." She felt that time and money would be better spent developing Negro schools and enforcing compulsory education for black children in the South, rather than legislating schoolroom integration. Although Hurston's position was out of step with most black leaders at the time, it was a completely consistent opinion for the daughter of Eatonville to have. She had attained an excellent primary education in an all-black school; sitting next to white children could not have enhanced her experience, she believed. "I can see no tragedy in being too dark to be invited to a white school affair," she wrote in the *Sentinel*. "It is a contradiction in terms to scream race pride and equality while at the same time spurning Negro teachers and self-association."

Hurston's letter was widely reprinted in southern newspapers and elicited fervid commentary on both sides of the issue. Rabid segregationists began to write Zora fan mail, and some civil rights leaders denounced her, as she'd predicted, "as one of those 'handkerchief-head niggers' who bow low before the white man and sell out my own people out of cowardice."

Hurston was about as far from cowardice as a person could get. But her position, brave as it was, seemed out of touch with the truth of most black people's lives. Hurston's view of segregation, of course, was informed by her exceptional Eatonville experience. Yet she seemed to never really acknowledge that there were few Eatonvilles. And she did not take into account the reality that most black schools in the South were far from equal to white schools—not because of the absence of white people, but because of the absence of resources.

Astonished by the nationwide debate her letter incited, Hurston stuck by her sentiments: "Physical contact means nothing unless the spirit is there," she explained further to a white acquaintance in

December. "I actually do feel insulted when a certain type of white person hastens to effuse to me how noble they are to grant me their presence. But unfortunately, many who call themselves 'leaders' of Negroes in America actually are unaware of the insulting patronage and rejoice in it."

From a certain contemporary perspective, Hurston's views don't seem so shocking. Many twenty-first-century African Americans would readily acknowledge that integration was not the great panacea that some civil rights leaders seemed to hope it would be. Black people gained the right to eat at any restaurant, choose any seat on the bus, and drink from any water fountain. And certainly, it now seems ludicrous that such basic human freedoms were ever denied to any group of American citizens. But integration was costly. Black communities lost a great deal—particularly in terms of self-respect and self-sufficiency—in the process. In fact, some contemporary black intellectuals go so far as to say that integration was one of the biggest tactical mistakes in African-American history.

Thus, Hurston's opinions on "forcible association" may have been prescient. But in 1955, they just seemed reactionary. Desegregation was inevitable—and Hurston did not oppose it, actually. She simply objected to the idea of achieving it by court order. "As a Negro, you know that I cannot be in favor of segregation," she told a friend early in 1956, "but I do deplore the way they go about ending it."

All around her, the world was changing fast. When Zora first left home to attend school in Jacksonville in the early 1900s, her brother had taken her to the train station on a buckboard—a horse and buggy. Now, in Eau Gallie, she lived near a "jet plane base." Every few days, Zora had the pleasure of seeing "something that looks like a silver barracuda tearing across the sky ahead of its own sound. As many as I have seen now, the thrill is still strong." Similarly, black people across America, intent on seizing their civil rights, were no longer moving at buckboard pace. In 1950, a poet named Gwendolyn Brooks had become the first black writer to win a Pulitzer Prize. And in 1953, Roy Campanella was named the Most Valuable Player of the year in National League baseball, a sport that had been strictly segregated until 1947, when Jackie Robinson broke the color barrier. And the early headlines of 1956 announced that a young preacher by the name of Martin Luther King Jr. was leading a bus boycott in Montgomery.

Hurston's personal world was changing, too. In March, she reluctantly began looking for a new place to live. Her house in Eau Gallie, where she'd been happily ensconced for five years, had been sold, leaving Zora "terribly distressed at the thought and necessity of stopping everything to pack up my numerous papers and books to find another location."

Because of her lack of output over the past few years, Zora no longer had a literary agent and was handling her own business affairs. She engaged "a book-hunting agency" to find copies of her out-of-print books to send to Dutch writer and translator Margrit Sabloniere, who was eager to translate Hurston's work. Though the amount of mail she received sometimes seemed overwhelming, Zora was gratified by the news many of these letters brought: Though all her books were out of print, she was not forgotten. Magazine editor Hoyt Fuller wanted to include her in a story on black women authors. A North Carolina professor wrote for advice on his paper about "the foremost Negroes in American History," of which Zora was one. She frequently received letters asking for permission to excerpt and anthologize her work. And several people wrote wondering what they might do to help get her books back in print.

Meanwhile, Zora was invited to be a special podium guest at the commencement exercises at Bethune-Cookman College. On May 28, she attended the ceremony in Daytona Beach and proudly accepted an award from the college for "education and human relations."

Two weeks later, on June 18, Zora reported to the Patrick Air Force Base in Cocoa at 7:15 A.M. She was there to begin her job as a librarian, at a salary of $1.88 per hour. Though Zora was not thrilled with her job duties—she was hired to keep track of technical literature for Pan American World Airways—she did not object to having a regular salary for the first time in years. The $300-plus per month kept her from worrying about money as she continued to work with devotion on her King Herod book. "If I can set it down as I see it," she believed, "it bears upon the state of the entire world at present— ideological, racial & political—without sounding didactic and 'smelling of the lamp' (labored)."

Zora rented a small house in Cocoa, just twenty miles north of Eau Gallie. She took Spot, her hybrid terrier, with her, but found other homes for the cat and for Spot's daughter, Shag. Within a few months, though, Zora and Spot moved again—into a house-trailer on Merritt Island, just across the river from Cocoa. The island was conducive to privacy and good for her writing, Zora assessed. Motoring about town in an old station wagon, she considered returning to New York in the spring, but not to live permanently. "That is suicide for a creative artist," she proclaimed.

Zora remained a librarian at Patrick Air Force Base for almost a year, bored by her job and at odds with several of her coworkers. On May 10, 1957, she was fired; her supervisor, a white man with only a high school education, told her she was "too well educated for the job." Zora was sorry to lose her income, but happy to leave the air force base, where the constant "low-rating of Southerners" had infuriated her. "I don't mean Negroes. <u>All</u> Southerners," she told a friend. "Ignorant Northerners not only expect us to eat missionaries, but eat them raw."

To combat what she perceived as a national prejudice against southerners, Zora outlined an article called "Take For Instance Spessard Holland." In it, she wanted to profile the Florida senator and former governor to show that southern lawmakers were not "mere bigotted jumping-jacks." The South had changed, she felt. "This is not the South of say, 1900," she wrote, and most southern congressmen "see the problems, economic and sociological, and ponder them seriously and intelligently, seeking the answers infinitely more earnestly than the on-lookers from above the Mason-Dixon line."

Hurston never completed the article. Instead, she collected her unemployment benefits, took on a few speaking engagements now and then, and continued to work on her Herod book with enthusiastic purpose. Informing Herbert Sheen that she'd pledged all her papers and correspondence to the University of Florida in Gainesville, Zora found herself in a reflective mood. "I have no sentimental involvements. I have no talent for business nor finance, but I do not mind that. . . . I am not materialistic," she told Sheen. "I do take a certain satisfaction in knowing that my writings are used in many of the great universities both here and abroad, both literary and anthropological." Then she added: "If I happen to die without money, somebody will bury me, though I do not wish it to be that way."

In *Moses, Man of the Mountain*, one of Hurston's characters says: "I wanted a long life, but I didn't mean to get old." At sixty-six, Zora was beginning to feel this way herself. After decades of lying about her age—she was still passing for at least ten years younger—her body was beginning to betray her. She'd developed ruffles around her hips, a touch of arthritis, and high blood pressure. Her agile mind took her places where her body could no longer keep up, and her age was beginning to feel tiresome.

In recent years, Zora had started to keep a writer's journal of sorts, in a green, hardcover sketchbook. Mostly, she used it for notes on her book, which she was calling "The Life of Herod the Great." Occasionally, though, she wrote personal notes to herself. One day, when she was beginning to wonder if she'd ever finish the book—and if she'd ever be published again—Zora wrote herself a note of stern upliftment: "You are alive, aren't you? Well, so long as you have no grave you are covered by the sky. No limit to your possibilities. The distance to heaven is the same everywhere."

Near the end of 1957, C. E. Bolen, owner of a black weekly in Fort Pierce, about eighty miles south of Merritt Island, paid Zora a visit. He offered her a part-time job writing for his paper, the *Fort Pierce Chronicle*. Having applied unsuccessfully for a job with General Electric a few months before, Zora gladly accepted Bolen's offer, packed up her few belongings, and moved to Fort Pierce. Borrowing from her earlier research, she wrote a column for the *Chronicle* called "Hoodoo and Black Magic." She also wrote "some very good articles about the Indian River area," as Bolen recalled. With her still-voracious intellectual appetite, Hurston read everything "from the funny books to Caesar's works," he remembered in amazement. Awed by her command of the English language, Bolen added: "A lot of times Zora said things to me with words that I had never heard. She kept me running to the dictionary all the time."

In February 1958, the assistant principal at Lincoln Park Academy—the black public high school in Fort Pierce—asked Hurston if she would be interested in filling a vacancy in the English department. Bragging that she knew her subject "both by college courses, and practical application as an author," Zora accepted the job and soon took over homeroom 10-C, rumored to be the worst class on campus. She was shocked by the lack of discipline in the school; many students toted knives and some boys brought their dice to class, she complained. Teaching six hours a day, Zora got along fine with her students, but she felt estranged from most of her coworkers. "My name as an author is too big to be tolerated, lest it gather to itself the 'glory' of the school here. I have met that before. But perhaps it is natural," she surmised. "The mediocre have no importance except through appointment. They feel invaded and defeated by the presence of creative folk among them."

Acknowledging that Hurston was "criticized by some teachers," Leroy C. Floyd, principal of the school at the time, said the real problem with Zora's employment was her lack of a Florida teaching certificate. After a delay in getting her transcript from Barnard—necessary for state certification—Zora left the job. "I can live without teaching," she declared.

For ten dollars a week, Zora had been renting a pea green, concrete-block house, at 1734 School Court. Her landlord, Dr. C. C. Benton, had grown up not far from Eatonville, and he remembered Zora's father and some of her brothers. The popular general practitioner was happy to have Zora as a tenant and to be back in touch with a Hurston after all these years. When he learned that Zora was living off unemployment checks and part-time work at the *Fort Pierce Chronicle*, Dr. Benton gladly waived her rent. He also made it a point to visit her often. "She was an incredible woman," the physician would remember. "Sometimes when I closed my office, I'd go by her house and just talk to her for an hour or two. She was a well read, well traveled woman and always had her own ideas about what was going on."

Marjorie Silver, a local white journalist who befriended Zora, had a similar impression of her. Silver had lived in New York during the 1920s and was well aware of Hurston's work. Or, as she put it: "I was a great fan of hers." Once she discovered Zora was living in Fort Pierce, she invited her for a visit—an invitation that Zora apparently accepted with some wariness. "The first afternoon Zora came over, it was like she was digging in an archaeological site for something.

After that, she blossomed out and was Zora," Silver recalled. The two women immersed themselves in long, wide-ranging conversations in the months to follow, and Zora became a regular at Silver's frequent dinner parties. She was always the only black guest, recalled newspaperwoman Anne Wilder, who also befriended Zora. Some of Silver's other guests balked at sharing a meal with a black woman, but neither Silver nor Hurston paid these party poopers any attention. "Zora was very secure. She knew her talents, her worth as a writer," Wilder assessed. "She was just herself. If people accepted her, fine. If not, tough."

Along with Dr. Benton, Silver and Wilder were among the few people in Fort Pierce who knew Zora's literary reputation. Most of the black people in her community just knew her as "Miss Hurston," a quiet, well-thought-of lady who did some writing for the *Chronicle* and who used to teach at the high school. But there was at least one thing about Zora that stood out: During a time when black people in the South entered white people's houses by the back door, if at all, one man remembered his astonishment at seeing Zora walk right up to Silver's front door any time she pleased. Other than this anomaly, she seemed just like every other black person in the community. Unable to afford to do otherwise, Zora dressed modestly—"plainly and comfortably," as one neighbor put it. "She didn't carry any air of importance," recalled Zanobia Jefferson, who taught art at Lincoln Park Academy. "If you saw her walking down the street, you'd think she was someone's mother or a housewife."

Immersed in her efforts to finish "The Life of Herod the Great," Zora kept to herself for the most part, venturing out only to fish the Indian River occasionally or to visit Marjorie Silver or Dr. Benton. Every Sunday at three o'clock, Dr. Benton came by to pick Zora up to take her to his house, where she joined him and his daughters, Arlena and Margaret, for dinner. After dessert, Zora and Dr. Benton would sit and talk for hours, Margaret Benton recalled, while she and her sister retired to their own pursuits.

With his dark beige skin, his concerned eyes, and his healing hands, Dr. Benton was many things for Zora: doctor, brother, friend. Though she spoke occasionally with Clifford Joel and Everett, Zora was rarely in contact with her other brothers or with any of her old friends from New York. She hadn't corresponded with Carl Van

Vechten, Fannie Hurst, Harold Jackman, Ethel Waters, or any of her old gang since her last trip North eight years earlier, in 1950. Thus, she valued the friendships she'd found in Fort Pierce, particularly with Dr. Benton. The country doctor was a careful reader of her work, well informed on current events, and an excellent conversationalist. One evening, after a lively debate about some issue, Dr. Benton said to Zora: "I wish I had as much sense as you have." She replied: "You got more sense. I'm a genius; I can do only one thing. You're smart. You can make a living."

Dr. Benton and his older daughter, Arlena, took turns dropping in on Zora, frequently taking her a plate for dinner. "She was a typical artist," Arlena Benton remembered. When she was caught up in her work, "she didn't seem to think to cook."

Zora had a small kerosene oil stove on which to prepare her meals, as Dr. Benton recalled. She also had a lamp, a table, a throw rug, bookshelves made out of fruit boxes, and other simple furnishings. "The things that were precious to her were her typewriter, her trunkful of letters and her reference books," Marjorie Silver observed. "She spent her time at that typewriter."

When Zora wasn't at the typewriter, she was usually working in her yard, where she planted a small, year-round vegetable garden and a slew of azaleas, morning glories, and gardenias. As always, Zora was an energetic gardener. She loved climbing into her dungarees, burying her hands in the soil, and then watching to see what sprung up from her efforts. "I am very fond of growing things; I shall end my days as a farmer if I have my way," she'd said some years before.

The gardening usually had another benefit that Zora enjoyed: the physicality of the work helped her to stay trim. Now, though, the extra pounds seemed to cling to her hips without mercy. She was tipping the scales at over two hundred pounds, and Dr. Benton warned her that the extra weight—not to mention her smoking—exacerbated her high blood pressure.

In the summer of 1958, Marjorie Silver and her husband, Doug, put Zora in touch with *Miami Herald* editor George Beebe. Zora proposed to do a series of stories on migrant labor camps in Florida. When the editor received the first installment, though, he decided to cancel the series. Zora's story didn't "jell," he said. He'd read her articles in several national magazines and was familiar with her books. "I have always had great admiration for Miss Hurston," he told Doug Silver. "She evidently needs a ghost writer, however."

Unfazed by the *Miami Herald* rejection, Zora continued to work intensely on the Herod manuscript. By September, she felt it was ready to send to publishers. She'd lost touch with Burroughs Mitchell at Scribner's, however, so she decided now was a good time to shop around for a new publisher. About a year before, Zora had received a letter from a small, emerging outfit called the David McKay Company. On September 4, she wrote to ask if the publisher might be interested in seeing her new book. In the middle of the month, she received a letter from the managing editor expressing "strong interest" in reading her manuscript.

Before Zora could get it in the mail, however, she became ill. Admitted to Fort Pierce Memorial Hospital on September 19, she was suffering from "hypertensive heart disease," caused by exposure of her heart to prolonged high blood pressure.

Hypertensive heart disease resulted in a progressive thickening of the heart muscle. This thickening made it more difficult for the heart to become full, which in turn forced the lungs to work harder to push blood into the vital organ. All this typically led to shortness of breath, fatigue, and chest pains. In severe cases, Zora was told, patients were unable to do basic household tasks or care for themselves without becoming severely short of breath or experiencing chest discomfort. The disease was treatable, but it could also be fatal, leading to heart failure or stroke.

Zora had been lucky this time; she was soon sent home with a prescription and a reprimand to take better care of herself. Losing weight and giving up cigarettes vaulted to the top of her to-do list. By mid-October, though, Zora had returned to her typewriter.

In January 1959, a week after her sixty-eighth birthday, Zora wrote a letter to the "editorial department" of a New York publishing house: "This is to query you if you would have any interest in the book I am laboring upon at present—a life of Herod the Great." The letter was short, vague, and written by hand—Zora's small, neat penmanship sloping slightly to the right. Though she was loath to admit it, her illness was getting worse, and she was finding it hard to "manage herself," as Dr. Benton put it.

Growing increasingly concerned about Zora's health, the

physician tried to persuade her to contact her family; perhaps she should go live with one of her brothers, he suggested. Belligerently independent, Zora refused. She insisted that she could take care of herself as she'd always done, with a little help now and then from her friends. "Sometimes she would run out of groceries—after she got sick—and she'd call me," Dr. Benton recalled. "'Come over here and see 'bout me,' she'd say. And I'd take her shopping and buy her groceries."

In May 1959, Zora applied for welfare aid to purchase prescription drugs, and then in June for food. On October 12, she was again admitted to Fort Pierce Memorial. This time, she'd suffered a stroke.

Zora was transferred October 29 to the segregated Lincoln Park Nursing Home, operated by the St. Lucie County Welfare Agency. She didn't want to go, Dr. Benton recalled, "but she had to, because she couldn't do a thing for herself." He frequently visited Zora at the nursing home, as did Silver and Wilder. "She couldn't really write much near the end," Dr. Benton remembered with regret. "She had the stroke and it left her weak; her mind was affected. She couldn't think about anything for long."

Still, Zora was no different, no more or less tragic, than any of the nursing home's other residents who'd also led abundant lives. Even as illness lingered at her doorstep, Zora refused to style herself as a victim and she exhibited no traces of self-pity, Wilder recalled. "She didn't focus on that."

Remaining in good spirits, Zora was as committed to self-sovereignty as ever. Her brother Clifford Joel visited her at the nursing home, along with his wife, Mabel, and their nineteen-year-old daughter, Vivian. Zora told her relatives "she was fine; this is where she wanted to be," Vivian Hurston Bowden would recall. "Dad offered her some money and we went out and bought some things for her. She gave everything we bought to all the patients in the place. She didn't want them. She didn't want anything from anybody." Clifford asked Zora if she had everything in order. "Well, when I die, the state is going to bury me," Vivian remembered her aunt saying. "She said she came in the world with nothing and that's the way she wanted to leave."

If Zora was prepared to die, it was because she had lived such a full—and fulfilling—life. "I have known the joy and pain of deep friendship," she once wrote. "I have served and been served. I have made some good enemies for which I am not a bit sorry. I have loved unselfishly, and I have fondled hatred with the red-hot tongs of Hell. That's living."

Believing, as she did, that people do not die—that they simply extend into new fields, into subtle realms—Zora faced death with the same courage and independence with which she had confronted life. "Why fear?" she asked. "The stuff of my being is matter, ever changing, ever moving, but never lost."

On Thursday, January 28, 1960, Zora had another stroke. She was pronounced dead on arrival at Fort Pierce Memorial Hospital. Like Moses, Zora Neale Hurston had crossed over. The time was 7:00 P.M., an hour past sundown.

The next day, Marjorie Silver received a call from the Percy S. Peek Funeral Home. "They said they had Zora's body and didn't have enough to bury her and what should they do?" Silver wrote an article about Zora's death for the *Miami Herald*. The story was soon picked up by wire services, and publications around the country, including *The New York Times* and *Time* magazine, began running their own obituaries. The news reports quarreled over Zora's age. Most—following what was listed on her death certificate—gave her age as fifty-seven. Some reported she was as young as fifty-two. In truth, Zora was sixty-nine years old, having lived three years longer than the average black American woman was expected to in 1960.

Despite their inconsistencies, all the stories agreed on one crucial point: Hurston had died "in poverty." As a result of this concerted report, donations began to trickle into Fort Pierce over the next week. Both Lippincott and Scribner's mailed $100 to Percy Peek's small office on Avenue D. Fannie Hurst also sent a check, as did Carl Van Vechten. Schoolteachers from Lincoln Park Academy canvassed the small community seeking donations. And a group of Hurston's former students contributed $2.50 in small change. All told, $661.87 was raised. A bit short of the $900 necessary for what was considered "a nice funeral" in 1960, the undertaker donated the burial plot.

On Sunday, February 7, 1960, Zora Neale Hurston was given an "impressive" funeral, according to the *Fort Pierce Chronicle*. Clifford and Mabel Hurston were there to represent Zora's family. More than a hundred people—including at least sixteen whites—attended the three o'clock service at the mortuary's tiny chapel. "There were so many folks here," funeral director Curtis E. Johnson recalled, "we had to set chairs out to the sidewalk."

From New York and elsewhere, so many people sent floral arrangements that "you could hardly see the casket for the flowers," C. E. Bolen commented. The sturdy steel coffin was pink and white, chosen by Percy Peek's wife, Helen. Zora's body was dressed in "a pale pink, fluffy something," Marjorie Silver remembered. "She would have been holding her sides laughing."

Fittingly, the Baptists and the Methodists came together for Zora's funeral. The Rev. R. J. Cliffin of Mount Olive Baptist read a scripture and the Rev. Wayman A. Jennings, pastor of St. Paul AME, delivered the eulogy. A choir from Lincoln Park Academy sang "Just a Closer Walk with Thee," and they sang it like the country folks they were, just as Zora would have preferred it. "They said she couldn't become a writer recognized by the world," the Reverend Jennings said in his remarks. "But she did it. The Miami paper said she died poor. But she died rich. She did something."

After the service at the chapel, many of the black residents of Fort Pierce proceeded to Genesee Memorial Gardens, the segregated cemetery, to witness the final ritual. One of the whites in attendance, Florida writer Theodore Pratt, later commented: "The local Negro population did not need a white Florida writer to be there . . . to tell them who Zora Neale Hurston was. She was someone they may not have understood too well but they knew she had pulled herself up by her bootstraps and done something not many white people ever do." Pratt added: "The wonderful understanding of Negroes for the human race, born perhaps of their necessity to tolerate it, was never better expressed than at Zora's funeral when these people, among whom she had lived so briefly, nevertheless stood by one of their own."

The community collection had not yielded enough for a headstone, but Zora "*didn't* have a pauper's funeral," as Dr. Benton would recall emphatically. "Everybody around here *loved* Zora." The preachers expressed the community's sentiments in the incantations they uttered at the graveside that sun-drenched afternoon. Then, as a northwesterly wind whispered a private tribute, Zora's body was slowly lowered, covered with Florida topsoil, and patted to rest in the earth.

Given her spiritual beliefs—born in Macedonia Baptist, warmed by the fire of hoodoo and voodoo, then finding a resting place in Eastern philosophy—death was not the end for Zora Neale Hurston. Instead, it was a new beginning—of her life as an ancestor, as a spirit. "I know that nothing is destructible; things merely change forms," she once said. "When the consciousness we know as life ceases, I know that I shall still be part and parcel of the world."

The Resurrection of
Zora Neale Hurston

A few weeks after the funeral, Fannie Hurst composed a tribute to Hurston for Yale University's *Library Gazette*. The publication's editor had invited Carl Van Vechten to write the appreciation, but Carlo deferred to Fannie, fearing that his eighty-year-old memory would not sustain him through the task. In "Zora Neale Hurston: A Personality Sketch," Hurst called Zora "a gift to both her race and the human race." Her shortcomings were among her most endearing qualities, Fannie declared. "Zora late, Zora sleeping through an appointment, Zora failing to meet an obligation, were actually part of a charm you dared not douse," she wrote.

"To life, to her people, she left a bequest of good writing and the memory of an iridescent personality of many colors. Her short shelf of writings deserves to endure. Undoubtedly, her memory will in the minds and hearts of her friends. We rejoice that she passed this way so brightly but alas, too briefly."

Fannie's tribute to Zora made Van Vechten weep. "You make all the girl's faults seem to be her virtues," he told Fannie. "As a matter of fact, they were NOT faults, they were characteristics and there's quite a difference. What it comes down to is the fact that Zora was put together entirely differently from the rest of mankind. Her reactions were always original because they were always her OWN."

To another friend, he wrote: "I LOVED Zora and want her

memory kept green." For a time, however, it looked as if Van Vechten's last wish for Zora would not be granted. Immediately following her death, Fate itself seemed determined to efface her memory.

In what Marjorie Silver called "a weird postlude," Zora's manuscripts and papers almost went up in smoke a few days after her funeral. One evening in February 1960, "around dusk-dark," Patrick Duval, a black deputy with the St. Lucie County Sheriff's Department, was driving past Zora's old home at 1734 School Court when he noticed smoke rising from the backyard. Hurrying to a stop, he soon discovered that people hired to clean out the place were burning Hurston's old storage trunk. Knowing who Zora was, Duval thought the contents of the trunk might be valuable. So he grabbed a garden hose and put out the fire, saving many of Hurston's papers, including an incomplete manuscript of "The Life of Herod the Great."

The rescued papers—many of them badly charred—were donated, as Zora intended, to the Department of Rare Books and Manuscripts at the University of Florida in Gainesville. The documents languished at the university for years, however, until scholar Robert E. Hemenway visited the library in the early 1970s to peruse them for a biography he was researching.

Meanwhile, a young writer named Alice Walker had become enamored of Hurston's work. She soon wrote: "Condemned to a deserted island for life, with an allotment of ten books to see me through, I would choose, unhesitatingly, two of Zora's: *Mules and Men*, because I would need to be able to pass on to younger generations the life of American blacks as legend and myth, and *Their Eyes Were Watching God*, because I would want to enjoy myself while identifying with the black heroine, Janie Crawford, as she acted out many roles in a variety of settings, and functioned (with spectacular results!) in romantic and sensual love. *There is no book more important to me than this one*."

In August 1973, Walker traveled to Fort Pierce to place a marker on the grave of the novelist and anthropologist who had so inspired her own writing. Genesee Memorial Gardens, at the dead end of North Seventeenth Street, had become the Garden of Heavenly Rest. The segregated graveyard was now abandoned and overgrown by yellow-flowered weeds.

Back in 1945, Zora had foreseen the possibility of dying without money, and she'd proposed a solution that would have benefited her and countless others. Writing to W.E.B. Du Bois, "Dean of American Negro Artists," she suggested "a cemetery for the illustrious Negro dead" on a hundred acres of land in Florida. Citing practical complications, Du Bois (or "Dr. Dubious," as Zora called him privately) wrote a curt reply discounting her persuasive argument. "Let no Negro celebrity, no matter what financial condition they might be in at death, lie in inconspicuous forgetfulness," she'd urged. "We must assume the responsibility of their graves being known and honored."

As if impelled by Hurston's nearly thirty-year-old words, Walker bravely entered the weed-choked, snake-infested cemetery where Zora's remains had been laid to rest. The intrepid young author soon stumbled upon a sunken rectangular patch of ground that she determined to be Zora's grave. Unable to afford the marker she wanted—a tall, majestic black stone called "Ebony Mist"—Walker chose a plain gray headstone instead. Borrowing from a Jean Toomer poem, she dressed the marker up with a fitting epitaph: "Zora Neale Hurston: A Genius of the South."

Walker wrote a moving essay about her Fort Pierce pilgrimage in *Ms.* magazine in 1975, and her act of reclamation spurred a renewed interest in Hurston and her work. Then, in 1977, Hemenway published *Zora Neale Hurston: A Literary Biography*, which further propelled the Zora revival. In time, all of Hurston's out-of-print books were reissued and *Their Eyes Were Watching God*—once hastily Xeroxed in college English departments and passed from hand to hand—secured a permanent place on university syllabi across the country. At last count, it was required reading for eighteen courses at Yale.

As enthusiasm for Hurston swelled during the 1980s, one particular photograph became especially popular. It is an image of a young black woman wearing a loose dress, a wide-brimmed hat, and a big smile that has transformed her eyes into slits of merriment. Printed on T-shirts, postcards, and even on the covers of some books, this image, ironically, is *not* Zora Neale Hurston. The photograph was taken by Alan Lomax during the summer of 1935, when he, Hurston, and Mary Elizabeth Barnicle traveled the South together collecting folk songs for the Library of Congress. The picture apparently became mixed up with the library's collection of Hurston photographs, causing archivists to assume it was a shot of Zora. Once it was published as such, scholars continued to perpetuate the error—despite Lomax's notifying the Library of Congress, in 1993, that the photo was not of Hurston.

In some realm of the cosmos, wherever the most bodacious spirits dwell, Zora is no doubt smiling mischievously at the mix-up. In fact, it seems a fitting tribute to a writer who dedicated much of her career to honoring ordinary black folk—people just like the peasant woman with the toothy grin who has been misidentified so often as the acclaimed author. Because of Zora, this unknown, uncelebrated woman's face has become famous.

Meanwhile, Hurston's books continue to sell well in the United States: more than a million copies of *Their Eyes Were Watching God* were in print as the twenty-first century dawned. Her titles also do a lively foreign business, with books in print in Spain, Italy, Brazil, Germany, France, Japan, the Netherlands, and the United Kingdom.

In Eatonville, the Preserve Eatonville Community hosts an annual festival each January in Zora's honor that combines an academic conference with a rollicking street fair. Started in 1989, the Zora Neale Hurston Festival of the Arts and Humanities has received national media coverage on such popular television shows as *Good Morning America* and *CBS Sunday Morning*. Many of the people who travel to Eatonville for the festival also make it a point to drive the hour and a half to Fort Pierce to visit Zora's now-well-tended grave.

In addition to being triply canonized—in the black, the American, and the feminist literary traditions—Hurston is on the verge of becoming a pop-culture icon. Magazines like *Interview* and *Vibe* have introduced her to younger readers as an interminably hip blast from the past. Further, *Mule Bone*, the folk comedy Hurston cowrote with Langston Hughes, was given a full-blown Broadway production in 1991. And her play *Polk County* was staged, to favorable reviews, in 2002 at Washington's Arena Stage. Her life has been the subject of numerous stage plays, and at least two popular novelists—both Connie May Fowler in *Before Women Had Wings* and Terry McMillan in *Disappearing Acts*—have named characters after Zora.

As these examples attest, Hurston has deeply influenced at least two generations of writers and readers of all colors and cultures. For these people—Zora's literary children and grandchildren—her legacy is not tragic. It is, to the contrary, one of fierce independence and literary excellence. For black women writers, specifically, Hurston has bequeathed a priceless gift. Through her tenacious efforts, and her very real sacrifices, she made it possible for black women to write about their interior lives and to have such work taken seriously. Her success—in her lifetime and posthumously—legitimized the kinds of intimate narratives that are now taken for granted in African-American literature. Yet if Hurston had not created a Janie and a Phoeby, for example, it might not have been possible for Toni Morrison to produce a Sula and a Nel, or for Alice Walker to create a Celie and a Shug. In other words, because Hurston wrote what she wrote, and published the books she published, American literature was altered for the good.

In this regard, Hurston's death hardly matters. Everyone, after all, has to die. But because of the way she *lived*, Zora Neale Hurston irrevocably changed the world. And now, at last, she is getting the acclaim she has long deserved. Remarkably, Hurston never seemed to doubt she would one day receive the recognition she was due. As she put it: "God balances the sheet in time."

Notes

Author's Note: In an effort to make Zora Neale Hurston's voice manifest throughout this biography, I quote from many of her writings—including numerous candid letters to friends and associates, which I culled from various archives as cited in the notes below. The comprehensive collection of Hurston's available correspondence has now been compiled. Readers interested in the full text of her letters may wish to consult Carla Kaplan, ed., *Zora Neale Hurston: A Life in Letters* (New York: Doubleday, 2002).

CHAPTER 1

5 "whether it was sort of tucked": Zora Neale Hurston, *Dust Tracks on a Road* (New York: HarperPerennial, 1996), p. 27.

6 "I did not give up the idea": ZNH, *Dust Tracks*, p. 28.

6 "So for weeks I saw myself": Ibid.

6 *"I want a fine black riding horse"*: ZNH, *Dust Tracks*, p. 29.

7 "No one around me knew": Ibid.

7 "over the creek": ZNH, *Dust Tracks*, p. 7. Also, 1880 Census, Lee County, Alabama.

8 By 1880: 1880 Census, Lee County, Alabama. Also, Family Record Page, Hurston Family Bible. Courtesy of Lois Hurston Gaston.

8 "bee-stung yaller": ZNH, *Dust Tracks*, pp. 8–9.

8 Lucy's parents: 1880 Census, Lee County, Alabama.

8 "great come-down in the world": ZNH, *Dust Tracks*, p. 8.

8 Lucy and John were married: Marriage License Record, Lee County, Alabama, p. 242.

8 The bride had just turned sixteen: Family Record Page, Hurston Family Bible. Lucy Hurston's birthday was December 31, 1865; John Hurston was born January 1, 1861. Also, Hurston comments on her parents' unusually close birth dates in *Jonah's Gourd Vine* (New York: HarperPerennial, 1990), p. 51.

9 *When [Lucy] rode off beside John*: ZNH, *Jonah's Gourd Vine*, p. 79.

9 "dat yaller bastard": ZNH, *Dust Tracks*, p. 9.

9 In November 1882: 1900 Census, Orange County, Florida. Also, Family Record Page, Hurston Family Bible.

9 "What was it": ZNH, *Dust Tracks*, p. 74.

10 "It seems that one daughter": ZNH, *Dust Tracks*, p. 19.

10 January 7, 1891: 1900 Census, Orange County, Florida. Also, Family Record Page, Hurston Family Bible. Although Hurston often cited her birth year as 1901 or later, the 1900 census lists her as nine years old and gives 1891 as her birth year. The Family Record Page of the Hurston Family Bible also gives 1891 as the year of Hurston's birth, though it cites January 15 as the date. However, Hurston consistently gave January 7 as the date of her birth—no matter how many variations she gave of the year. Also, as Hurston scholar Cheryl A. Wall has pointed out, all the entries on the Family Record Page of the Hurston Bible appear to be recorded in the same handwriting, which suggests one person may have made all the entries retrospectively, perhaps based on family research and memory, rather than various family members recording events as they occurred. For this reason, I have only cited the Family Bible when I could corroborate its information with at least one other primary source. No such corroboration exists for the January 15 birth date. Therefore, the best available evidence indicates Zora Neale Hurston was born on January 7, 1891. Finally, this date is further supported by a letter, dated November 15, 1974, that ZNH's brother, Everett Hurston, wrote to Fort Pierce attorney Elsie O'Laughlin in an attempt to probate Hurston's estate. Letter courtesy of Ms. O'Laughlin and attorney Ron Jayson.

10 hog-killing time: Author interview with Roger Boyd, a former Alabama tenant farmer, May 24, 1999.

10 "this is all hear-say": ZNH, *Dust Tracks*, p. 19. This account of Hurston's birth is largely taken from her description of it in her autobiography. Yet one significant deviation is made in this account: Hurston always identified Eatonville, Florida, as the place of her birth. In fact, she was born in Notasulga, Alabama, according to the 1900 Census, Orange County, Florida, and the Family Record Page, Hurston Family Bible.

11 "he took out his Barlow knife": ZNH, *Dust Tracks*, p. 21.

11 "She complained that the cord": Ibid.

11 Zora Neal Lee Hurston: No other corroboration for the name "Lee" has been found, and Hurston never used this name in any public records or private correspondence. The 1900 Census, Orange County, Florida, lists nine-year-old Zora as "Zora L." The "L" could have been for "Lee" or it could have been the mistake of a census taker who misheard "Neal(e)" as "L."

11 "Perhaps she had read it somewhere": ZNH, *Dust Tracks*, p. 21.

12 "I don't think he ever got over": ZNH, *Dust Tracks*, p. 19.

CHAPTER 2

13 "crushing to his ambition": ZNH, *Dust Tracks*, p. 7.

13 "the black back-side": ZNH, *Dust Tracks*, p. 1.

14 "You mean uh whole town": ZNH, *Jonah's Gourd Vine*, p. 107.

14 voted to incorporate Eatonville: Frank M. Otey, *Eatonville, Florida: A Brief History* (Winter Park, FL: Four-G Publishers, 1989).

14 "The terrain was as flat": ZNH, *Dust Tracks*, p. 4.

15 "No more backbending": ZNH, *Dust Tracks*, p. 5.

15 Joe Clarke: Otey, p. 2.

16 At Eatonville's incorporation meeting: Otey, Chapters 1 and 2.

16 a second church: Otey, p. 10.

17 "Negroes are made to feel": Booker T. Washington, *The Negro in Business* (Wichita, KS: Devore and Sons, 1907; 1992 reprint), p. 53.

17 "the city of five lakes": ZNH, *Mules and Men* (New York: Harper & Row, 1990), p. 4.

17 "He wouldn't let her walk": ZNH, *Jonah's Gourd Vine*, p. 108.

18 "Lucy sniffed sweet air": ZNH, *Jonah's Gourd Vine*, p. 109.

CHAPTER 3

19 the Hungerford School: Otey, p. 11. The Robert Hungerford Normal and Industrial School, named for the deceased son of its benefactors, Edward and Anna Hungerford, was founded in Eatonville in 1889 by Russell and Mary Calhoun.

20 "But I was not taking this thing": ZNH, *Dust Tracks*, p. 22.

20 "The strangest thing about it was": ZNH, *Dust Tracks*, p. 23.

20 "Wherever you go": For a recent, artful evocation of this abiding folk principle, listen to vocalist Cassandra Wilson's "Run the Voodoo Down" on the CD *Traveling Miles* (Blue Note, 1999).

20 Notasulga, Alabama: Interestingly, Zora's older brothers, who'd spent more of their childhood time in Alabama than Zora had, also would claim Florida as their state of birth in some public records.

21 "Races have never done": ZNH, *Dust Tracks*, pp. 248–49.

21 a talented seamstress: ZNH interview, *Twentieth Century Authors,* ed. by Stanley Kunitz and Howard Haycraft (New York: H. W. Wilson, 1942).

21 "He could put his potentialities to sleep": ZNH, *Dust Tracks*, p. 68.

21 the "empty house threw back": ZNH, *Jonah's Gourd Vine*, p. 52.

21 "His trial sermon had": ZNH, *Jonah's Gourd Vine*, p. 111.

22 "God's Battle-Axe": *Sanford Herald*, November 25, 1910.

22 Lucy gave birth to another child: 1900 Census, Orange County, Florida. Also, Family Record Page, Hurston Family Bible.

22 "It was a common thing": ZNH, *Dust Tracks*, p. 12.

23 "Jump at de sun": ZNH, *Dust Tracks*, p. 13.

23 "It did not do": Ibid.

23 "The white folks": Ibid.

23 "Zora is my young'un": ZNH, *Dust Tracks*, p. 14.

23 "If the rest of us": ZNH, *Dust Tracks*, p. 75.

24 "We black folks don't love": ZNH, *Jonah's Gourd Vine*, p. 5.

24 If Lucy spanked John's favorite child: ZNH, *Dust Tracks*, p. 74.

24 "I was the one girl": ZNH, *Dust Tracks*, pp. 29–30.

25 "Dolls caught the devil": ZNH, *Dust Tracks*, p. 30.

25 "I was driven inward": Ibid.

25 "It did not matter": ZNH, *Dust Tracks*, p. 75.

25 "Behind Mama's rocking chair": ZNH, *Dust Tracks*, p. 14.

26 Booker T. Washington's National Negro Business League: Paula Giddings, *When and Where I Enter: The Impact of Black Women on Race and Sex in America* (New York: William Morrow and Company, 1984), p. 75.

26 "What's de use": ZNH, *Dust Tracks*, p. 14.

26 "On two occasions": ZNH, *Dust Tracks*, p. 10.

26 "She definitely understood": Ibid.

27 "with the muzzle of his Winchester rifle": Ibid.

27 "She was glad to see him": ZNH, *Jonah's Gourd Vine*, p. 114.

27 "There came other times": ZNH, *Jonah's Gourd Vine*, p. 115.

27 "Every time Mama cornered him": ZNH, *Dust Tracks*, p. 16.

28 "I looked more like him": ZNH, *Dust Tracks*, p. 19.

28 "a wife-made man": ZNH, *Jonah's Gourd Vine*, p. 113.

28 "My mother took her": ZNH, *Dust Tracks*, p. 69.

28 "Maybe he was just born": ZNH, *Dust Tracks*, p. 11.

29 "I know that I did love him": ZNH, *Dust Tracks*, p. 68.

29 "All that part": Ibid.

CHAPTER 4

30 "I know that my mother": ZNH, *Dust Tracks*, pp. 10, 11.

30 "For a long time I gloated": ZNH, *Dust Tracks*, p. 26.

31 "That was my earliest conscious hint": ZNH, *Dust Tracks*, p. 27.

31 "the most interesting thing": Ibid.

31 "The movement made me glad": ZNH, *Dust Tracks*, p. 33.

31 "I know now": ZNH, *Dust Tracks*, p. 34.

32 Zora's maternal grandmother: Family Record Page, Hurston Family Bible.

32 "Git down offa": ZNH, *Dust Tracks*, p. 34.

32 "The Southern whites": ZNH, *Twentieth Century Authors*, 1942.

32 Washington himself: Otey, p. 11.
33 "Mrs. Calhoun always": ZNH, *Dust Tracks*, p. 34.
33 *We stood up in the usual line:* ZNH, *Dust Tracks*, pp. 35–36.
33 "They asked me": ZNH, *Dust Tracks*, p. 37.
34 "My sandy hair": Ibid.
34 "Perhaps I shall never": ZNH, *Dust Tracks*, p. 38.
35 "The clothes were not new": ZNH, *Dust Tracks*, p. 39.
35 "In that way I found out": ZNH, *Dust Tracks*, p. 40.
35 "thin books about this and that": ZNH, *Dust Tracks*, p. 39.
35 "Of the Greeks": Ibid.
36 "Stew beef, fried fatback": ZNH, *Dust Tracks*, p. 41.
36 "the heart and spring": ZNH, *Dust Tracks*, p. 45.
36 "There were no discreet nuances": ZNH, *Dust Tracks*, p. 46.
36 "God, Devil, Brer Rabbit": ZNH, *Dust Tracks*, p. 48.
37 Eatonville's second mayor: Otey, p. 16.
37 "while Mama waited on me": ZNH, *Dust Tracks*, p. 48.
37 her father became pastor: Otey, p. 10.
37 moderator of the South Florida Baptist Association: ZNH, *Dust Tracks*, p. 51.
38 "Life took on a bigger perimeter": ZNH, *Dust Tracks*, p. 52.
38 "You hear dat young'un": ZNH, *Dust Tracks*, pp. 53–54.
38 "my mother was always": ZNH, *Dust Tracks*, p. 13.
38 "She'd listen sometimes": ZNH, *Dust Tracks*, pp. 53–54.
38 "How was she going to tell what": ZNH, *Dust Tracks*, p. 54.
39 visions of events to come: ZNH, *Dust Tracks*, pp. 41–42.
39 *I had knowledge before its time:* ZNH, *Dust Tracks*, p. 42.
40 "I consider that my real childhood": ZNH, *Dust Tracks*, pp. 43–44.

CHAPTER 5

41 "I named it": ZNH, *Dust Tracks*, p. 52.
41 September 18, 1904: The Hurston Family Bible lists September 19, 1904, as the date of Lucy's death, but in her autobiography, Hurston gave the date as September 18—a date that she likely found impossible to forget.
41 "I noted a number of women": ZNH, *Dust Tracks*, p. 65.
41 "Death stirred": Ibid.
41 "She kept getting thinner": ZNH, *Dust Tracks*, pp. 63–64.
42 Lucy only had one sister: 1880 Census, Lee County, Alabama.
42 "Aunt Dinky had": ZNH, *Dust Tracks*, p. 63.
42 "He went to a party": ZNH, *Dust Tracks*, p. 64.
42 "There was never any move": Ibid.

43 "Mama could just go on back": ZNH, *Dust Tracks*, p. 63.

43 "I could not conceive": ZNH, *Dust Tracks*, p. 64.

43 several superstitions about death: ZNH, *Mules and Men* (New York: Perennial, 1990), pp. 228–29. Also, Margaret M. Coffin, *Death in Early America* (Nashville, TN: Thomas Nelson, 1976), pp. 97–98.

44 "I was not to let them": ZNH, *Dust Tracks*, p. 64.

44 "Papa was standing": ZNH, *Dust Tracks*, p. 65.

44 *Somebody reached for the clock*: ZNH, *Dust Tracks*, pp. 65–66.

45 "In the midst of play": ZNH, *Dust Tracks*, p. 66.

45 "That moment was the end": ZNH, *Dust Tracks*, pp. 66–67.

45 The warm climate: Coffin, pp. 79, 102. Also, Eugene D. Genovese, *Roll, Jordan, Roll: The World the Slaves Made* (New York: Vintage Books, 1976), p. 198.

45 "Bob's grief was awful": ZNH, *Dust Tracks*, p. 67.

46 "from the kitchen to the front porch": ZNH, *Dust Tracks*, p. 68.

46 "I have often wished": ZNH, *Dust Tracks*, pp. 67–68.

46 "Pull up your socks": Toni Morrison, *Song of Solomon* (New York: Signet, 1978), pp. 310–11.

47 "That hour began my wanderings": ZNH, *Dust Tracks*, p. 67.

CHAPTER 6

48 "The village came behind": ZNH, *Jonah's Gourd Vine*, p. 135.

48 "the finality of the thing": ZNH, *Dust Tracks*, p. 69.

49 "That night, all of Mama's children": Ibid.

49 "Mama died at sundown": Ibid.

49 "The loss of a parent": Hope Edelman, *Motherless Daughters: The Legacy of Loss* (New York: Delta Trade Paperbacks, 1994), p. xxiii.

49 "Researchers have found": Edelman, p. 8.

49 "a love-*hurt* relationship": Deborah G. Plant, *Every Tub Must Sit On Its Own Bottom: The Philosophy and Politics of Zora Neale Hurston* (Urbana and Chicago: University of Illinois Press, 1995), p. 160.

50 "choose goals realistically": J. Irving & E. Scott, *The Education of Black People in Florida* (Philadelphia: Dorrance & Company, 1974), p. 53.

50 "I had seen myself": ZNH, *Dust Tracks*, p. 70.

51 "Jacksonville," she wrote cryptically: Ibid.

51 "School in Jacksonville": ZNH, *Dust Tracks*, p. 71.

52 "Lessons had never worried me": ZNH, *Dust Tracks*, p. 79.

52 "My underskirt was hanging": ZNH, *Dust Tracks*, p. 70.

52 "In a week or two after": ZNH, *Dust Tracks*, p. 73.

52 John Hurston's second wedding: Orange County Marriage License Record, Book 2: 1889–1909, p. 262.

53 Mattie Moge: The 1910 Census gives Mattie Moge's birth year as 1885.

53 "My father certainly": ZNH, *Dust Tracks*, p. 97.

53 "Ah got dese li'l chillun": ZNH, *Jonah's Gourd Vine*, p. 138.

53 "Sarah just married": ZNH, *Dust Tracks*, p. 73. Hurston's youngest brother, as an adult, spelled his name Everette, with an "e" on the end; ZNH always spelled it without the "e." I have chosen to use ZNH's spelling of her brother's name throughout.

53 John Robert Mack: Author interview with Zora Mack Goins, daughter of Sarah Hurston Mack, June 30, 2000.

54 "I had gotten used to": ZNH, *Dust Tracks*, p. 79.

54 "After a while": Ibid.

54 "I received an atlas": Ibid.

54 "He acted like he was satisfied": ZNH, *Dust Tracks*, pp. 79–80.

55 "I made up my mind": ZNH, *Dust Tracks*, pp. 80–81.

55 "A child who loses a parent": Edelman, p. 42.

55 "Maybe it *was* Mama": ZNH, *Dust Tracks*, p. 71.

56 "I kept looking out of the window": ZNH, *Dust Tracks*, p. 81.

56 "she seemed to speak a little softer": Ibid.

57 "The very walls were gummy": ZNH, *Dust Tracks*, p. 84.

57 "To see this interloper": ZNH, *Dust Tracks*, p. 85.

57 "His well-cut broadcloth": Ibid.

CHAPTER 7

59 "So my second vision picture": ZNH, *Dust Tracks*, p. 85.

60 "bare and bony": ZNH, *Dust Tracks*, p. 119.

61 "I was miserable": ZNH, *Dust Tracks*, p. 87.

61 64 percent of black schools in the South: Darlene Clark Hine, Kathleen Thompson, *A Shining Thread of Hope: The History of Black Women in America* (New York: Broadway Books, 1998), pp. 206–7.

61 "people who had no parents": ZNH, *Dust Tracks*, p. 88.

61 "A child in my place": Ibid.

62 more than 40 percent of all black: James D. Anderson, *The Education of Blacks in the South, 1860–1935* (Chapel Hill: University of North Carolina Press, 1988), p. 150.

62 "Housewives would open the door": ZNH, *Dust Tracks*, p. 88.

62 an average wage: ZNH, *Dust Tracks*, p. 93. Also, Economic History Resources, "How Much Is That?" Conversion Calculator.

62 She also was drawn to Jacksonville: 1910 Census, Duval County, Florida.

63 "It did sound grand": ZNH, *Dust Tracks*, p. 95.

63 No white man: Hine, Thompson, p. 215.

63 "Right then": ZNH, *Dust Tracks*, p. 95.

64 "He went on down the steps": ZNH, *Dust Tracks*, p. 96.

64 "There is something about poverty": ZNH, *Dust Tracks*, p. 87.

64 "I wanted family love": ZNH, *Dust Tracks*, p. 97.

65 "like a stepped-on worm": ZNH, *Dust Tracks*, p. 98.

65 "The bottle came sailing slowly": ZNH, *Dust Tracks*, p. 76.

66 "I was so mad": ZNH, *Dust Tracks*, p. 77.

67 "I could not bear the air": ZNH, *Dust Tracks*, p. 98.

CHAPTER 8

69 Zora "luxuriated in Milton's syllables": ZNH, *Dust Tracks*, p. 98.

69 By 1912, only two remained open: Hine, Thompson, p. 222.

69 "When I got on the train": ZNH, *Dust Tracks*, p. 99.

70 While Bob finished medical school: Author interview with Lois Hurston Gaston, Bob's granddaughter. October 4, 2000. Also, Kristy Anderson, "The Tangled Southern Roots of Zora Neale Hurston," 1995, an unpublished paper by filmmaker working on a biographical documentary on Hurston.

70 The soon-to-be-famous dance: ZNH, "Characteristics of Negro Expression," in Nancy Cunard, ed., *Negro: An Anthology* (New York: Continuum, 1996). Originally published by Hours Press, 1934. Also, Marshall and Jean Stearns, *Jazz Dance: The Story of American Vernacular Dance* (New York: Da Capo Press, 1994).

70 A studio portrait: Family photo in the possession of Winifred Hurston Clark, Bob's youngest daughter. First published in Pamela Bordelon, "New Tracks on Dust Tracks," *African American Review*, vol. 31, no. 1, 1997.

70 "That did not make me happy": ZNH, *Dust Tracks*, p. 100.

71 After graduating from Meharry in 1913: Bob Hurston's year of graduation was verified in a phone interview with Quinton Jones, archivist at Meharry Medical School.

71 The two-story house: Winifred Hurston Clark, in Bordelon, "New Tracks on Dust Tracks."

71 "My brother was acting": ZNH, *Dust Tracks*, p. 100. Also, interview with Bob Hurston's daughter, Winifred Hurston Clark, in Pamela Bordelon's *Go Gator and Muddy the Water* (New York: W. W. Norton, 1999).

71 directory of Bethel Baptist Institutional Church: This church directory is the only known record of Hurston from this period of her life. And she is not listed in subsequent church directories, nor in city directories in Jacksonville or Memphis.

72 "a house, a shot-gun built house": ZNH, *Dust Tracks*, p. 42.

72 "the house that needed paint": ZNH, *Dust Tracks*, p. 119.

73 "Don't you love nobody": ZNH, *Jonah's Gourd Vine*, p. 130.

73 Though Hurston virtually hid this fact: Hurston scholars previously had assumed that Bob Hurston's home in Memphis was the house Zora Hurston fled to join the Gilbert and Sullivan tour. But a careful study of her language reveals otherwise. See ZNH, *Dust Tracks*, pp. 100–101; p. 119. Also, the church record places her in Jacksonville in 1914, *after* her time in Memphis, casting further doubt on the notion that she fled Bob's home to join the troupe.

73 "to my own self": ZNH, *Dust Tracks*, p. 101.

73 The singer offered to pay ten dollars: Economic History Resources, "How Much Is That?" Conversion Calculator.

73 "It wouldn't take long for me": ZNH, *Dust Tracks*, p. 103.

73 "Everything was pleasing": Ibid.

74 men and women migrated: Hine, Thompson, pp. 214–19.

74 "I was the only Negro": ZNH, *Dust Tracks*, p. 104.

75 "burnt-ettes": ZNH, *Dust Tracks*, p. 118.

75 "I was a Southerner": ZNH, *Dust Tracks*, pp. 104–5.

75 "I just happened to be there": ZNH, *Dust Tracks*, p. 117.

76 "That was the way we parted": ZNH, *Dust Tracks*, p. 116.

76 "Working with these people": ZNH, *Dust Tracks*, p. 119.

CHAPTER 9

77 Baltimore had suffered: Maryland Historical Chronology, 1900–1999. Maryland State Archives.

77 "But theatrical salaries being so uncertain": ZNH, *Dust Tracks*, p. 121.

77 "those presumptuous cut-eye looks": ZNH, *Dust Tracks*, pp. 121–22.

78 "I bet God that": ZNH, *Dust Tracks*, p. 122.

78 listed in the 1917 Baltimore City Directory: Baltimore City Directory, 1917 and 1918.

78 "struggling along": ZNH, *Dust Tracks*, p. 142.

78 Sarah would name her daughter after Zora: Author interview with Zora Mack Goins, daughter of Sarah Hurston Mack, June 30, 2000.

79 "I was only jumping up and down": ZNH, *Dust Tracks*, p. 122.

79 "I got tired of trying": ZNH, *Dust Tracks*, pp. 122–23.

79 The Maryland Code: The Maryland Code, 1903. Volume II, Chapter 18, Article 125.

79 she shaved ten years off: Cheryl A. Wall and other Hurston scholars have cited Hurston's return to school as the moment she began her deception about her age. See Wall's chronology in *Zora Neale Hurston: Folklore, Memoirs, And Other Writings* (New York: Library of America, 1995).

80 a matter of necessity: The General Educational Development (GED) Diploma—a high school equivalency certificate awarded upon successful completion of a test—would not become available until decades later, in 1942.

80 "So I went to the night high school": ZNH, *Dust Tracks*, pp. 123–24.

80 "This was my world": ZNH, *Dust Tracks*, p. 123.

81 she was given credit: Morgan College Entrance Record. From the Office of the Registrar, Morgan State University.

81 "good-looking, well-dressed girls": ZNH, *Dust Tracks*, pp. 125–26.

81 "Sometimes somebody would ask me": ZNH, *Dust Tracks*, p. 127.

82 "Once I had the history classes": Ibid.

82 Predictably, Zora did well: Morgan College Record, Morgan State University.

82 "I did not do well": ZNH, *Dust Tracks*, p. 129.

82 "The atmosphere made me feel right": Ibid.

82 Her father recently had moved: Bordelon, "New Tracks on Dust Tracks." Also, ZNH, *Dust Tracks*, pp. 141–42.

82 John Hurston had been elected mayor: Otey, p. 17.

82 he had become pastor of Friendship Baptist Church in Jacksonville: 1916 and 1917 Jacksonville City Directory.

82 not listed as married: According to Hurston's account, John and Mattie Hurston separated a few months after the Zora-Mattie fight. See *Dust Tracks*, p. 78. Bordelon, in "New Tracks on Dust Tracks" and *Go Gator*, argues that Mattie was living with John in Memphis, based on the testimony of Bob Hurston's youngest daughter, Winifred Hurston Clark. But Mrs. Clark was not born until 1920, two years after John Hurston's death, and no corroborative evidence has been found to prove that John and Mattie were still living as husband and wife at the time of his death.

83 "the engine struck": ZNH, *Jonah's Gourd Vine*, p. 200.

83 John Hurston was fifty-seven years old: The date of John Hurston's death is not clear. The Hurston Family Bible is difficult to read; Bordelon has reported John Hurston's death date as May 1918; Wall lists it in her chronology as August 10. His youngest son, Everett Edwin Hurston, also remembered it as August 10 in a letter to attorney Elsie O'Laughlin.

CHAPTER 10

84 "the capstone of Negro education": ZNH, *Dust Tracks*, p. 129.

84 higher education for Negroes: David Levering Lewis, *When Harlem Was in Vogue* (New York: Vintage Books, 1979), pp. 157–58.

84 "Zora, you are Howard material": ZNH, *Dust Tracks*, p. 129.

84 Howard had been founded in 1867: William M. Banks, *Black Intellectuals: Race and Responsibility in American Life* (New York: W. W. Norton, 1996), p. 45.

85 Zora withdrew from Morgan: Morgan College Record, Morgan State University. The record indicates that Hurston did not graduate from Morgan, as previously reported, but withdrew.

85 On December 2, 1918: Student's Record, Academy Division. Office of the Registrar, Howard University. On the record from the Academy Division, 1919 has been noticeably erased, with 1920 written over it, indicating that Hurston may not have actually received the diploma until May 1920. But that would have been a mere technicality: her university records clearly indicate she entered the college division in autumn 1919.

86 "You have taken me in": ZNH, *Dust Tracks*, p. 130.

86 Zora's first quarter: Howard University Scholastic Record. Office of the Registrar, Howard University.

86 "My soul stood on tiptoe": ZNH, *Dust Tracks*, p. 131.

87 "I know that my discretion": Ibid.

87 "I know a place": "Home." Unpublished poem from the Hurston Collection at the Schomburg Center for Research in Black Culture, New York City.

88 "Who has not felt the fire": Untitled poem, dated April 21, 1919. Hurston Collection, Schomburg Center for Research in Black Culture, New York City.

88 Herbert Arnold Sheen: Unpublished bio of Herbert A. Sheen, M.D., from Robert E. Hemenway Files.

88 "She wasn't narrow-minded": REH Interview with Herbert A. Sheen, M.D. REH Files.

89 "He noticed me, too": ZNH, *Dust Tracks*, p. 204.

89 Alpha Kappa Alpha: 1920, 1923 Howard University yearbooks. Howard Dodson, Christopher Moore, Roberta Yancy, *The Black New Yorkers: The Schomburg Illustrated Chronology* (New York: John Wiley & Sons, 2000), p. 129.

89 "There were these three sororities": Eleanor Des Vessey Stinette, "An Oral Memoir of Mrs. Ophelia Settle Egypt," 1981–82. Manuscripts Division, Moorland-Springarn Research Center, Howard University.

90 "stimulating and producing authors": ENOPRON, 1920–21, Howard University, Moorland-Springarn Research Center.

90 a popular literary salon: Lewis, *When Harlem Was in Vogue*, p. 127.

90 "Listening to him": ZNH, *Dust Tracks*, pp. 136–37.

91 set in an unnamed Florida village: ZNH, "John Redding Goes to Sea," in *The Complete Stories* (New York: HarperCollins, 1995).

92 "Hurston's fully developed use": John Lowe, "Hurston, Humor, and the

Harlem Renaissance" in Victor Kramer's *The Harlem Renaissance Re-Examined* (New York: AMS Press, 1987), p. 292.

93 "did a lot for the family": REH Interview with Herbert Sheen. Unpublished bio of Herbert A. Sheen, M.D. REH Files.

93 she published three poems: Hurston published "Night," "Journey's End," and "Passion" in *Negro World*, the official newspaper of Marcus Garvey's Universal Negro Improvement Association. See chronology in Cheryl Wall's *Zora Neale Hurston: Folklore, Memoirs, And Other Writings* (New York: Library of America, 1995).

93 "soulful poet": ZNH to Georgia Douglas Johnson, July 18, 1925, The Georgia Douglas Johnson Papers, Howard University, Moorland-Springarn Research Center. For the full text of Hurston's correspondence, see Carla Kaplan, ed., *Zora Neale Hurston: A Life in Letters* (New York: Doubleday, 2002).

93 "I have a heart": *The Bison*, 1923. Howard University, MSRC.

CHAPTER 11

94 her grades were faltering: Howard University Scholastic Record. Office of the Registrar, Howard University.

94 "I was out on account of illness": ZNH, *Dust Tracks*, p. 138.

94 "to lay bare Negro life": Nathan Irvin Huggins, *Harlem Renaissance* (New York: Oxford University Press, 1971), p. 28.

95 "When the magazine would report": Ibid.

95 "The Negro Speaks of Rivers": Arnold Rampersad, *The Life of Langston Hughes, Volume I: 1902–1941, I, Too, Sing America* (Oxford, New York, Toronto: Oxford University Press, 1986), p. 48.

95 "He was primarily responsible": George Hutchison, *The Harlem Renaissance in Black and White* (Cambridge, MA: Belknap Press of Harvard University Press, 1995), p. 173.

96 Langston Hughes was in Paris: Lewis, p. 90. Also Rampersad, p. 107.

96 "What American literature decidedly needs": Lewis, pp. 94–95.

96 "the progressive spirit": Steven Watson, *The Harlem Renaissance: Hub of African-American Culture, 1920–1930* (New York: Pantheon Books, 1995), p. 28.

97 "did more to encourage": Langston Hughes quoted in Lewis, p. 125.

97 "so-called Negro Renaissance": ZNH, *Dust Tracks*, p. 138.

97 "press agent": Lewis, p. 149. Watson, pp. 23–24.

97 "Although Locke rarely saw promise in": Watson, pp. 70–71.

98 exuberant sense of humor: For further discussion of Hurston's humor, see "Hurston, Humor, and the Harlem Renaissance," by John Lowe, in Victor Kramer's *The Harlem Renaissance Re-Examined*, op. cit.

98 "in an ecstasy of joy for a minute": ZNH, "Drenched in Light," available in *The Complete Stories*.

99 Isis was considered: This is a gross oversimplification of the Egyptian mythology surrounding Isis. For a more refined discussion, see George Hart's *A Dictionary of Egyptian Gods and Goddesses* (New York: Routledge Kegan & Paul, 1986).

99 "Drenched in Light": For this analysis, I am indebted to the work of Robert E. Hemenway in *Zora Neale Hurston: A Literary Biography* (Urbana and Chicago: University of Illinois Press, 1977), pp. 10–11.

100 "no job, no friends": ZNH, *Dust Tracks*, p. 138.

100 In this trio's relatively plush Harlem flat: Lewis, pp. 126–129; Watson, p. 26.

100 "a terrifically warm person": Richard Bruce Nugent, 1971 interview with Robert E. Hemenway. REH Files.

100 she was two years older: Johnson was born in 1893. Banks, *Black Intellectuals*, p. 275.

100 During Zora's early days: ZNH, *Dust Tracks*, p. 139.

101 "fun to be a Negro": Arna Bontemps, quoted in Lewis, p. 103.

101 "When I set my hat": ZNH, "How It Feels to Be Colored Me," May 1928, *The World Tomorrow*.

101 "At one time or another": Lewis, pp. 210–11.

102 Harlem's rents: Watson, p. 130.

102 thirty dollars was a significant chunk: Economic History Resources, "How Much Is That?" Conversion Calculator.

102 1924 Urban League study: Winthrop D. Lane, "Ambushed in the City: The Grim Side of Harlem," *Survey Graphic*, March 1925.

102 40 percent of his or her income: Lewis, pp. 107–11.

102 "flop-wallies": Frank Byrd, "Rent Parties," August 23, 1938. Reprinted in *A Renaissance in Harlem: Lost Voices of an American Community*, edited by Lionel C. Bascom (New York: Avon Books, 1999), pp. 59–67. Also, Lewis, pp. 107–11; Watson, pp. 130–31.

102 "You would see all kinds": Willie "the Lion" Smith, quoted in Lewis, pp. 107–8.

103 "When Zora was there": Arna Bontemps and Sterling Brown, quoted in Hemenway, p. 61.

103 "where all of the members are saints": ZNH to Annie Nathan Meyer, undated letter from 1926. Annie Nathan Meyer Papers, American Jewish Archives, Cincinnati, OH.

103 The March 1925 *Survey Graphic*: Watson, p. 28.

104 "In Harlem": *Survey Graphic*, March 1925.

104 "a certified misogynist": Lewis, p. 96.

104 more than seven hundred submissions: "Contest Awards," *Opportunity*, vol. 3, no. 29, May 1925, p. 142.

105 "a novel sight": Watson, p. 66.

105 the May 1 awards dinner: Lewis, pp. 113–14.

105 The winner of the most prizes: "Contest Awards," *Opportunity*, vol. 3, no. 29, May 1925, pp. 142–43.

105 John Matheus won: "Prizes to Negro Writers," *The New York Times*, May 2, 1925. Also "Contest Awards," *Opportunity*, vol. 3, no. 29, May 1925.

105 cool temperature: Weather Report, May 2, 1925, *The New York Times*. High temperature for May 1 was 56, low was 41.

106 "*Coloooooooor Struuckkkk!*": May Miller interview notes, April 29, 1971. REH Files.

CHAPTER 12

107 "Zora Neale Hurston is a clever girl": Hughes to Carl Van Vechten, June 4, 1925. Emily Bernard, *Remember Me to Harlem: The Letters of Langston Hughes and Carl Van Vechten, 1925–1964* (New York: Alfred A. Knopf, 2001), p. 19.

107 "less and less the more I see of her": Eslanda Robeson, quoted in Martin Duberman, *Paul Robeson: A Biography* (New York: New Press, 1989), p. 82.

107 "In appearance, Zora": Arna Bontemps interview, November 1970. REH Files.

108 "one of the most amusing people": Carl Van Vechten, in letter to his wife, Fania Marinoff, June 3, 1925, quoted in Watson, p. 71.

108 "the gift": Fannie Hurst, "Zora Neale Hurston: A Personality Sketch," *Library Gazette*, Yale University, 1961.

108 Meyer had played a critical role in: Unpublished biographical sketch, part of the Inventory to the Annie Nathan Meyer Papers at the American Jewish Archives, Cincinnati, OH.

109 "Being of use to the Negro": Lewis, pp. 100–101.

109 of the thirteen thousand or so black people: Lewis, p. 158.

109 "I am tremendously encouraged": ZNH to Annie Nathan Meyer, May 12, 1925. Annie Nathan Meyer Papers, American Jewish Archives.

109 "It is mighty cold comfort": Ibid.

110 "Do you think you could get": Virginia C. Gildersleeve to Annie Nathan Meyer, June 9, 1925. Annie Nathan Meyer Papers, American Jewish Archives.

110 who had secured a publishing contract: Rampersad, pp. 109–10.

110 Annie Pope Malone: ZNH to Meyer, July 18, 1925. Annie Nathan Meyer Papers, American Jewish Archives. Also, Hine and Thompson, p. 204.

110 "your humble and obedient servant": ZNH to Meyer, July 18, 1925, September 15, 1925. Annie Nathan Meyer Papers, American Jewish Archives.

111 "I see white people do things": ZNH to Meyer, June 23, 1925. Annie Nathan Meyer Papers, American Jewish Archives.

111 "if she showed certain scars": Author interview with John Henrik Clarke, May 28, 1997.

111 "We wear the mask": Excerpt from Paul Laurence Dunbar, "We Wear the Mask," 1895. The full poem has been reprinted in various anthologies, including Henry Louis Gates, Jr., and Nellie McKay, general editors, *The Norton Anthology of African American Literature* (New York: W. W. Norton, 1997), p. 896.

112 "I have had some small success": Record of Freshman Interest, Barnard College.

112 "The Hue and Cry About Howard University": ZNH, "The Hue and Cry About Howard University," *The Messenger*, September 1925.

113 "If spirits kin fight": ZNH, "Spunk," *The Complete Stories*.

113 Fannie Hurst wrote to Carl Van Vechten: Brooke Kroeger, *Fannie: The Talent for Success of Writer Fannie Hurst* (New York: Times Books, 1999), pp. 122–23.

114 "I am sure she would help": ZNH to Meyer, October 17, 1925. Annie Nathan Meyer Papers, American Jewish Archives.

114 She owed $117: Gildersleeve to Meyer, October 2, 1925. Annie Nathan Meyer Papers, American Jewish Archives.

114 "I still must get": ZNH to Meyer, October 12, 1925. Annie Nathan Meyer Papers, American Jewish Archives.

114 "I need money worse": Langston Hughes, *The Big Sea* (New York: Hill and Wang, 1993), p. 240. Originally published by Alfred A. Knopf, 1940. Also, Arna Bontemps interview, November 1970. REH Files.

114 "I have been my own sole support": ZNH to Meyer, October 17, 1925. Annie Nathan Meyer Papers, American Jewish Archives.

115 Zora had moved into Fannie Hurst's apartment: Kroeger, p. 123. Also, ZNH to Meyer, November 10, 1925. Annie Nathan Meyer Papers, American Jewish Archives.

115 She told Meyer of a student loan fund: Gildersleeve to Meyer, November 5, 1925. Annie Nathan Meyer Papers, American Jewish Archives.

115 "I knew getting mad": ZNH to Meyer, November 10, 1925. Annie Nathan Meyer Papers, American Jewish Archives.

115 With a load of seven classes: Barnard College transcript, Barnard Archives.

116 "You see": ZNH to Meyer, November 10, 1925. Annie Nathan Meyer Papers, American Jewish Archives.

116 "Perhaps Zora bartered": Kroeger, p. 123.

116 Hurst had become: Kroeger, pp. 104, 121–27, 187–90.

116 "blazing zest for life": Fannie Hurst, "Zora Hurston: A Personality Sketch," *Library Gazette*, Yale University, no. 35, 1961.

116 Hurst was only five years older than Hurston: Kroeger, p. 126. Fannie Hurst was born in 1885.

116 "a great artist and globe famous": ZNH, *Dust Tracks*, p. 197.

117 "She knows exactly what goes": Ibid.

117 "a stunning wench": ZNH, "Fannie Hurst by Her Ex-Amanuensis," *Saturday Review of Literature*, October 3, 1937.

117 "I doubt if any woman on earth": ZNH, *Dust Tracks*, p. 197.

117 "Her shorthand was short": Fannie Hurst, "Zora Hurston: A Personality Sketch."

117 "My idea of Hell": Undated letter to Tracy L'Engle, Tracy L'Engle Angas Papers, University of Florida.

117 "Though the myth holds otherwise": Kroeger, p. 124.

117 "The girls at Barnard": ZNH to Meyer, December 13, 1925. Annie Nathan Meyer Papers, American Jewish Archives.

118 "But even if things were different": ZNH to Meyer, December 17, 1925. Annie Nathan Meyer Papers, American Jewish Archives.

118 "I feel most colored": ZNH, "How It Feels to Be Colored Me," *The World Tomorrow*, May 1928.

118 "I suppose you want to know": ZNH to Constance Sheen, January 5, 1926. ZNH Collection, University of Florida.

118 "Barnard's sacred black cow": ZNH, *Dust Tracks*, p. 139.

118 "Partly because you took me under your shelter": ZNH to Fannie Hurst, March 18, 1926. Fannie Hurst Papers. Harry Ransom Humanities Research Center, University of Texas at Austin.

119 "I do not wish to become Hurstized": ZNH to Meyer, December 13, 1925. Annie Nathan Meyer Papers, American Jewish Archives.

119 At a December 19 party at Fannie's home: ZNH to Constance Sheen, January 5, 1926. ZNH Collection, University of Florida.

119 "They are OFTEN insincere": ZNH to Constance Sheen, February 2, 1926. ZNH Collection, University of Florida.

119 working part-time as a waitress: ZNH to Meyer, December 13, 1925. Also, ZNH to Fannie Hurst, March 18, 1926.

119 "That was how he": ZNH, "The Emperor Effaces Himself," typescript. ZNH Papers, Yale.

119 Her play *Color Struck* was scheduled: ZNH to Meyer, November 10, 1925. Annie Nathan Meyer Papers, American Jewish Archives.

120 "Youth speaks": Alain Locke, "Negro Youth Speaks," *The New Negro* (New York: Atheneum, 1974). Originally published in 1925.

120 all routinely lied about their ages: Cheryl A. Wall, *Women of the Harlem Renaissance* (Bloomington and Indianapolis: Indiana University Press, 1995), p. 12.

120 Meyer, in turn, sent Zora a copy: ZNH to Meyer, January 15, 1926. Annie Nathan Meyer Papers, American Jewish Archives.

120 "I got the scholarship!!!": ZNH to Meyer, postmarked February 5, 1926. Annie Nathan Meyer Papers, American Jewish Archives.

120 "I wonder whether": Virginia Gildersleeve to Annie Nathan Meyer, February 9, 1926. Annie Nathan Meyer Papers, American Jewish Archives.

121 "I felt that I was highly privileged": ZNH, *Dust Tracks*, p. 140.

121 "just running wild": ZNH to Constance Sheen, February 2, 1926. ZNH Collection, University of Florida.

121 "Your rebuke is just": ZNH to Meyer, undated [January 1926]. Annie Nathan Meyer Papers, American Jewish Archives.

CHAPTER 13

123 "All this is a reason": ZNH to Meyer, undated [January 1926]. Annie Nathan Meyer Papers, American Jewish Archives.

123 "like a foretaste of paradise": Arna Bontemps, quoted in Watson, p. 66.

123 "It was not a spasm": Charles S. Johnson, quoted in Lewis, p. 115.

123 Soon after the *Opportunity* triumph: Lewis, pp. 178–80; Watson, p. 205.

124 "a song I and most southerners": ZNH to Cullen, March 11, 1926. Amistad Research Center, Tulane University, New Orleans.

124 "I want to start on it": ZNH to Meyer, February 22, 1926. Annie Nathan Meyer Papers, American Jewish Archives.

124 "the best novel": Lewis, p. 179.

124 "It is the Mecca": Charles T. Crowell, "The World's Largest Negro City," *Saturday Evening Post*, August 8, 1925.

125 the first anthropology department: "Rethinking Anthropology," *Columbia Magazine*, Fall 1999, Columbia University.

125 "full of youth and fun": ZNH, *Dust Tracks*, p. 140.

126 "Almost nobody else": Hughes, *The Big Sea*, p. 239.

126 anthropometry: The most infamous use of anthropometry was by the Nazis, who classified Aryans and non-Aryans based on measurements of the skull and other physical characteristics. Now, anthropometry has many practical, and benign, uses. For example, it is used to assess nutritional status, to monitor children's growth, and to assist in the design of office furniture. Source: "The Skeptic's Dictionary" by Robert Todd Carroll. Online copyright 1998.

126 "learn as quickly as possible": ZNH to Annie Nathan Meyer, undated letter from 1926.

126 "Of course, Zora": ZNH, *Dust Tracks*, p. 140.

126 "the King of Kings": Ibid.

127 "like a tight chemise": ZNH, *Mules and Men*, p. 1.

127 "make people work": ZNH, *Dust Tracks*, p. 140.

127 "The regular grind": ZNH to Countee Cullen, March 11, 1926. Tulane University.

128 "the Niggerati": Hughes, *The Big Sea*, p. 235. Also, Lewis, pp. 193–95.

128 "our business of": ZNH to Alain Locke, June 5, 1925. Alain Locke Papers, Howard University Library.

128 "Zora would have been Zora": Bruce Nugent interview, May 1971. REH Files.

128 "the perfumed orchid": Watson, p. 90.

129 "She was not the gentle person": Bruce Nugent interview, May 1971. REH Files.

129 "with nothing but his nerve": Theophilus Lewis, quoted in Watson, p. 85.

129 the Krigwa Players: Dodson, Moore, Yancy, *The Black New Yorkers*, p. 192.

130 "chief mid-wife": ZNH to Alain Locke, Alain Locke Papers, Howard University, Washington, D.C.

130 "I rather think": Du Bois to ZNH, March 19, 1926. Tulane.

130 "in a Negro neighborhood": Huggins, p. 292.

130 "Could you": ZNH to Du Bois, July 3, 1926. Tulane.

130 "We want Negro writers": Du Bois, *The Crisis* 31 (January 1926).

130 "I do not care a damn": Du Bois, "Criteria of Negro Art," *The Crisis* 32 (October 1926).

131 "that crowd": Lewis, p. 193.

131 "We younger Negro artists": "The Negro Artist and the Racial Mountain," *The Nation* 122 (June 23, 1926), pp. 692–94.

CHAPTER 14

132 "This year has been": ZNH to Fannie Hurst, March 16, 1926. Fannie Hurst Papers. Harry Ransom Humanities Research Center, University of Texas at Austin.

132 Despite her flagging stamina: Barnard College transcript, Barnard Archives.

132 a "furniture" party: Author interview with John Henrik Clarke. Also, Hughes, *The Big Sea*, p. 239.

133 "I have been going through": ZNH to W.E.B. Du Bois, July 3, 1926. Tulane.

133 "She was always prepared": Nugent interview, May 1971. REH Files.

133 "It fills 'em up quick": ZNH in radio interview with Mary Margaret McBride, January 25, 1943. 7. Recorded Sound Reference Center, Library of Congress.

133 Perhaps because of the hunger: Nugent interview, May 1971. REH Files.

133 "I wrote at Zora's": Ibid.

133 "all greased curls": Fannie Hurst's description of ZNH in letter to Carl Van Vechten, April 1926. Carl Van Vechten Papers, Yale University.

133 if she had an appointment: Carolyne Rich Williams, quoted in Hemenway, pp. 60–61.

134 "Those were the days": Theophilus Lewis, quoted in Watson, p. 89.

134 *Meet the Mamma*: Typescript for this previously unknown work is available in the Music Division of the Library of Congress.

135 "He suggested": Nugent, quoted in Rampersad, p. 134.

135 "The way I look at it": ZNH to Alain Locke, October 11, 1927. Locke Collection, Howard University Library.

135 "would burn up": Hughes, *The Big Sea*, p. 235.

135 "were going to do something": Nugent interview. REH Files.

135 "I believe we can": ZNH to Langston Hughes, March 17, 1927. James Weldon Johnson Collection, Yale University.

135 "the fullest embodiment": Lewis, p. 193.

135 "a strangely brilliant": Hughes, *The Big Sea*, p. 234.

135 "welling up": West, quoted in Mae Gwendolyn Henderson, "Portrait of Wallace Thurman," Arna Bontemps, *The Harlem Renaissance Remembered* (New York: Dodd, Mead, 1972), p. 149.

135 "Thurman fitted": West, quoted in Watson, p. 89.

136 "sexualized the narrative": Ann Douglas, *Terrible Honesty: Mongrel Manhattan in the 1920s* (New York: Noonday Press, 1995), p. 47.

136 "If it gets its yearning": Quoted in Lillian Faderman, *Odd Girls and Twilight Lovers: A History of Lesbian Life in Twentieth-Century America* (New York: Penguin Books, 1992), p. 62.

136 "This generation was the first": Douglas, p. 53.

137 Zora saw: ZNH to Van Vechten, 1926 postcard. Van Vechten Papers, Yale University.

137 "BE COOL AND LOOK HOT": Douglas, pp. 16 and 48.

137 "mere sightseers": Hughes, *The Big Sea*, pp. 246–49.

138 "The Negro": Watson, p. 105.

138 "the Coon Age": Mencken in October 1927 issue of *The American Mercury*, quoted in Douglas, p. 77.

138 "Negro stock is going up": Fisher, quoted in Watson, p. 66. Originally in Fisher, "The Caucasian Storms Harlem," *The American Mercury*, May 1927.

138 "Sullen-mouthed": Quoted in Watson, p. 99.

138 "*so* Negro": Hughes, *The Big Sea*, p. 251.

139 "taboo-tea": Kroeger, p. 187.

139 "Harlem is an all-white picnic ground": Both McKay and Fisher quoted in Watson, p. 126 and p. 105.

139 "I dance wildly": ZNH, "How It Feels to Be Colored Me," *The World Tomorrow*, May 1928.

139 "a sincere friend": Nugent interview, May 1971. REH Files.

140 "If Carl was a people": ZNH as quoted in Fannie Hurst, "Zora Neale Hurston: A Personality Sketch," *Library Gazette*, Yale University, 1961.

140 "Anyone who would call": Watson, p. 103.

140 "We could find a counterpart": Lewis, p. 181.

140 "Colored people": Hughes, quoted in Rampersad, p. 134.

140 "a copyrighted racial slur": Lewis, p. 181.

141 "go inspectin'": Lewis, p. 182.

141 "family secrets": Johnson, quoted in Lewis, p. 186.

141 "They had shows": Ruby Walker Smith, quoted in Faderman, p. 74.

141 "Jungle Alley": Watson, p. 128.

142 Homosexual nightclubs: Watson, pp. 128–29.

142 "Miss Bentley was": Hughes, *The Big Sea*, p. 226.

142 Less is known: Faderman, p. 232. See also Gloria Hull, "Under the Days: The Buried Life and Poetry of Angelina Weld Grimke," *Conditions: Five, The Black Women's Issue*, Autumn 1979.

142 In 1925, Rainey: Faderman, pp. 74–75.

142 Harlem housewives: For an excellent discussion of lesbianism in the 1920s, see Faderman, pp. 62–92.

143 "Nobody was in the closet": Nugent, quoted in Watson, p. 134.

143 Harlem's "joy-goddess": Hughes, *The Big Sea*, pp. 244–45.

143 She'd inherited a fortune: For an excellent study of Madam Walker, see A'Lelia Bundles, *On Her Own Ground: The Life and Times of Madam C. J. Walker* (New York: Scribner, 2001).

143 "funny parties": Mabel Hampton interview by Joan Nestle. Lesbian Herstory Archives.

144 "Zora would go": Bontemps interview. REH Files.

144 Zora was on her way: Story recollected by Hurston family member. Hemenway, p. 30.

144 "Will you walk": Nugent interview. REH Files.

145 "He was fond of her": ZNH, *Dust Tracks*, p. 198.

145 "She is shy": ZNH, *Dust Tracks*, p. 200.

145 Waters's bisexuality: Alberta Hunter, Ethel Waters's peer and sometimes rival, made pointed references to Waters's bisexuality in Frank C. Taylor

with Gerald Cook, *Alberta Hunter: A Celebration in Blues* (New York: McGraw-Hill, 1987).

145 "I am her friend": ZNH, *Dust Tracks*, p. 199.

145 "There was nothing in her": Bontemps interview. REH Files.

146 "At the time": Herbert Sheen interview. REH Files.

146 "Whatever I 'knew' about Zora": Nugent interview. REH Files.

CHAPTER 15

147 "For artists and writers": Hughes, *The Big Sea*, p. 236.

147 "It was really a": Nugent interview. REH Files.

147 "worthy of the drawings": Hughes, *The Big Sea*, p. 236.

148 "We are all under thirty": Unsigned, handwritten letter of introduction to *Fire!!* Aaron Douglas Papers, Schomburg Center for Research in Black Culture.

148 "She never made": Nugent interview. REH Files.

148 "for his pseudo-sophisticated": Thurman, "Fire Burns," *Fire!!*, vol. 1, no. 1, November 1926, p. 47.

148 "a flawed, folk-centered masterpiece": Lewis, p. 195.

148 "We have no": Unsigned, handwritten letter of introduction to *Fire!!* Aaron Douglas Papers, Schomburg Center.

149 "his usual ability": Rean Graves, quoted in Hughes, *The Big Sea*, p. 237.

149 "I have just tossed": Watson, p. 92. Hughes, *The Big Sea*, p. 237.

149 "original in all its aspects": Robert Kerlin, writing in *Southern Workman*, quoted in Lewis, p. 194.

149 At Craig's restaurant: Lewis, p. 194.

149 "none of the older Negro intellectuals": Hughes, *The Big Sea*, p. 237.

149 A friend told Cullen: Lewis, p. 194.

149 "If Uncle Sam": Brawley, quoted in Lewis, p. 194.

150 "We had no way": Hughes, *The Big Sea*, p. 237.

150 close to $10,000: Economic History Resources, "How Much Is That?" Conversion Calculator.

150 An optimistic Zora: ZNH to Hughes, March 17, 1927. Langston Hughes Papers, Yale University.

150 "*Fire!!* is certainly": Thurman, quoted in Mae Gwendolyn Henderson, "Portrait of Wallace Thurman," Arna Bontemps, *The Harlem Renaissance Remembered* (New York: Dodd, Mead, 1972), p. 154.

150 "I suppose that *Fire!!*": ZNH to Alain Locke, October 11, 1927. Alain Locke Papers, Howard University.

150 "I think that only two": Nugent Interview. REH Files.

151 "so despises her own skin": ZNH, *Color Struck, Fire!!*, November 1926.

151 "an idea of searing": Lewis, p. 195.

151 "Ah done tole you": ZNH, "Sweat," *Fire!!*, Vol. 1, No. 1, November 1926. Reprinted in ZNH, *The Complete Stories*.

154 "Under the Bridge": ZNH, "Under the Bridge." The story was lost for years, but rediscovered by collector Wyatt Houston Day in 1996. It was published in *American Visions*, December/January 1997.

154 "Muttsy": ZNH, "Muttsy," *The Complete Stories*, pp. 41–56.

155 "The Eatonville Anthology": ZNH, "The Eatonville Anthology." *The Messenger*, September, October, November 1926. Reprinted in ZNH, *The Complete Stories*, pp. 59–72.

156 "Only to reach": Hughes, *The Big Sea*, p. 239.

156 "Zora had shone": Nugent, "Smoke, Lilies and Jade," *Fire!!*, p. 36.

156 Sweetie May Carr: Wallace Thurman, *Infants of the Spring* (Boston: Northeastern University Press, 1992), p. 229. First published in 1932 by the Macaulay Company.

156 "Zora showed at *any* party": Nugent interview. REH Files.

CHAPTER 16

158 "the affairs of the world": ZNH, *Dust Tracks*, p. 271.

158 With this sum: Franz Boas to Carter G. Woodson, November 6 and December 7, 1926. Also, Boas to Elsie Clews Parsons, December 7, 1926, and Woodson to Boas, February 17, 1927. American Philosophical Society.

159 "So I knew": ZNH, *Mules and Men*, p. 1.

159 "formalized curiosity": ZNH, *Dust Tracks*, p. 143.

159 "too much impressed": Franz Boas to Elsie Clews Parsons, December 7, 1926. American Philosophical Society.

159 "penetrate through": Franz Boas in preface to ZNH, *Mules and Men*, p. xiii.

159 "gorgeous sunlight": ZNH to Lawrence Jordan, May 3, 1927. Schomburg Center for Research in Black Culture.

159 "dirty upholstery": ZNH, *Dust Tracks*, p. 237.

159 "My brother plays": ZNH to Lawrence Jordan, undated, postmarked February 18, 1927. Schomburg Center.

160 Her brother's logic prevailed: ZNH to Franz Boas, March 29, 1927. Franz Boas Papers, American Philosophical Society.

160 "because I knew": ZNH, *Mules and Men*, p. 2.

160 "I was delighted": ZNH, *Mules and Men*, p. 7.

160 "like a four-walled room": Russ Rymer, *American Beach* (New York: HarperCollins, 1998), p. 296.

161 "Folklore is not as easy": ZNH, *Mules and Men*, p. 2.

161 "habitual movements": Franz Boas to ZNH, May 3, 1927. Franz Boas Papers, American Philosophical Society. Copies also at the Library of Congress.

161 "Oh, I got a few little items": ZNH, *Dust Tracks*, p. 144.

161 After about ten days: ZNH to Carter G. Woodson, undated letter. Expense report shows Hurston was in Eatonville from June 20 to June 30. Carter G. Woodson Papers, Library of Congress.

161 For this, Zora packed: REH interview with Everett Hurston Jr., 1976. Cited in Hemenway, p. 112.

161 In 1926: These figures, which are widely believed to be conservative, are from the Archives at Tuskegee Institute. Also see "The Negro Holocaust: Lynching and Race Riots in the United States, 1890–1950," by Robert A. Gibson. Published online by the Yale–New Haven Teachers Institute.

162 Zora heard a firsthand account: ZNH to Meyer, May 22, 1927. Annie Nathan Meyer Papers, American Jewish Archives.

162 "forsaking the creature comforts": ZNH to Lawrence Jordan, postmarked February 18, 1927. Schomburg Center.

162 "Sometimes, I feel": ZNH, "How It Feels to Be Colored Me," *The World Tomorrow*, May 1928.

163 "The poor whites": ZNH to Meyer, March 7, 1927. Annie Nathan Meyer Papers, American Jewish Archives.

163 "Flowers are gorgeous now": ZNH to Lawrence Jordan, March 24, 1927. Schomburg Center.

163 "A man arrested": ZNH to Lawrence Jordan, May 3, 1927. Schomburg Center.

163 "The glamor of Barnard College": ZNH, *Dust Tracks*, p. 144.

163 "I find that what you obtained": Boas to ZNH, May 3, 1927. Franz Boas Papers, American Philosophical Society. Copy also at the Library of Congress.

164 "Getting some gorgeous material": ZNH to Hughes, March 17, 1927. Langston Hughes Papers, Yale.

164 "I do hope": Meyer to ZNH, January 21, 1927. Annie Nathan Meyer Papers, American Jewish Archives.

164 "I take the mornings": ZNH to Meyer, March 7, 1927. Annie Nathan Meyer Papers, American Jewish Archives.

165 "No, I am not dead": ZNH to Meyer, May 22, 1927. Annie Nathan Meyer Papers, American Jewish Archives.

165 "Nature has up-ended": ZNH to Meyer, March 7, 1927.

165 "I feel a little lonely": ZNH to Lawrence Jordan, March 24, 1927. Schomburg Center.

165 "I am getting a certain amount": ZNH to Lawrence Jordan, May 3, 1927. Schomburg Center.

166 "I felt the warm embrace": ZNH, *Dust Tracks*, p. 142.

166 Zora's second diversion: Marriage license, Herbert Sheen and ZNH, May 19, 1927. Marriage Book 5, p. 17. Court records, St. Johns County, Florida.

166 "Believe it or not": ZNH to Lawrence Jordan, May 3, 1927. Schomburg Center.

166 "For the first time": ZNH, *Dust Tracks*, p. 204.

166 "a dark barrier": ZNH to Herbert Sheen, January 7, 1955. REH Files.

167 "Somebody had turned a hose": ZNH, *Dust Tracks*, p. 204.

167 "interested in tramping around": Herbert Sheen interview with Robert Hemenway. REH Files.

168 One male admirer: Countee Cullen, quoted in Rampersad, p. 81.

168 "I knew it would be fun": Hughes, *The Big Sea*, p. 296.

169 "our only contact": Hughes, *The Big Sea*, p. 296.

169 "Our father who art": Hughes to Carl Van Vechten, August 15, 1927. Van Vechten Papers, Yale University.

169 "The trouble with white folks": Hughes, *The Big Sea*, p. 296

170 "Young Woman's Blues": Lyrics by Bessie Smith. Recorded October 26, 1926. Columbia Records, 14179-D. For an excellent analysis of this song, see Wall, *Women of the Harlem Renaissance*, p. 20.

170 "We are charging home": Hughes and Hurston to Van Vechten, August 17, 1927. Note is in Hurston's handwriting and signed by both. In Hughes–Van Vechten correspondence at Yale University.

170 "Somehow," Zora reported: ZNH to Van Vechten, August 26, 1927. Van Vechten Papers, Yale University.

170 "I hate that": ZNH to Hughes, undated. Langston Hughes Papers, Yale University.

171 "This story was secured": *Journal of Negro History* XII (October 1927), p. 648.

173 Whether she wanted to or not: The discovery was made in 1972—a full twelve years after Hurston's death—by linguist William Stewart. It was first exposed in Robert E. Hemenway's 1977 book, *Zora Neale Hurston: A Literary Biography*. I relied heavily upon Hemenway's report for my discussion of Hurston's plagiarism.

173 "The more I see of the South": ZNH to Meyer, October 7, 1927. Annie Nathan Meyer Papers, American Jewish Archives.

173 "Considering the mood of my going south": ZNH, *Dust Tracks*, p. 144.

CHAPTER 17

174 "I could not see": ZNH, *Dust Tracks*, p. 42.

175 "I had gotten command": ZNH in audiotaped radio interview with Mary Margaret McBride, January 25, 1943. Library of Congress.

175 "I think": ZNH to Hughes, September 21, 1927. Langston Hughes Papers, Yale University. Also September 20, 1928, letter from ZNH to Hughes, in which Hurston mentions that it is the anniversary of her meeting Mason.

175 "She likes the idea": ZNH to Hughes, September 21, 1927. Langston Hughes Papers, Yale University.

175 "altogether in sympathy": ZNH, *Dust Tracks*, p. 145.

176 "just as pagan as I": ZNH, *Dust Tracks*, p. 144.

176 Godmother "possessed the power": Hughes, *The Big Sea*, p. 324 and pp. 312–15.

177 Seeking to remove any drains: Rampersad, pp. 156–59.

177 According to one rough estimate: Hemenway, p. 105. Also Economic History Resources "How Much Is That?" Conversion Calculator.

178 "desirous of obtaining and compiling": Contractual agreement between Hurston and Mason, signed December 8, 1927. Alain Locke Papers, Howard University.

179 "I will have a better car": ZNH to Hughes, December 9, 1927. Langston Hughes Papers, Yale University.

180 In November 1927: Mills died on November 1, 1927. U. S. Thompson, "Florence Mills," in Cunard, *Negro: An Anthology*. Also, Watson, p. 117.

180 A month before: Rampersad, p. 154.

180 "a Fannie Hurst marriage": *The New York Times*, May 4, 1920. Quoted in Brooke Kroeger, *Fannie*, pp. 63–64.

180 "Zora didn't seem to fit": Author interview with John Henrik Clarke, May 28, 1997.

180 "a way out": ZNH, *Dust Tracks*, p. 205.

181 "I am going to divorce Herbert": ZNH to Hughes, March 8, 1928. Langston Hughes Papers, Yale University.

181 "he is old": ZNH to Hughes, December 9, 1927. Langston Hughes Papers, Yale University.

181 "I lonely for my folks": ZNH, *Dust Tracks*, p. 168.

181 "Polk County Blues": ZNH, *Mules and Men*, p. 60.

182 "I want to collect": ZNH to Hughes, April 12, 1928. Langston Hughes Papers, Yale University.

182 On February 29, 1928: Barnard College transcript, Barnard Archives.

182 "Negro women *are* punished": ZNH, *Mules and Men*, p. 60.

182 "Fan-foot, what you doing": ZNH, *Dust Tracks*, pp. 149–50.

183 "This worried me": ZNH, *Mules and Men*, p. 60.

183 "The Negro": ZNH, *Mules and Men*, p. 2.

184 At five feet four inches tall: Height and weight information taken from Hurston's driver's license. ZNH Collection, University of Florida.

184 "Oh, Ah ain't got": ZNH, *Mules and Men*, pp. 63–64.

184 "I not only collected": ZNH, *Mules and Men*, p. 65.

185 "I have not written a line": ZNH to Hughes, March 8, 1928. Langston Hughes Papers, Yale.

185 "I can really write": ZNH to Hughes, April 12, 1928. Langston Hughes Papers, Yale.

185 "I am getting inside": ZNH to Hughes, March 8, 1928. Langston Hughes Papers, Yale.

186 "A Negro goes abroad": ZNH to Hughes, April 12, 1928. Langston Hughes Papers, Yale.

186 "and lay me by the heels": ZNH, *Dust Tracks*, p. 144.

186 "An interpretation of": Rampersad, p. 140.

186 "they got the point": ZNH to Hughes, March 8, 1928. Langston Hughes Papers, Yale.

187 "You are being quoted": ZNH to Hughes, July 10, 1928. Langston Hughes Papers, Yale.

187 He urged Zora: Locke to ZNH, February 24, 1928. Alain Locke Papers, Howard University.

188 "I have come to 5 general laws": ZNH to Hughes, April 12, 1928. Langston Hughes Papers, Yale.

188 "Did I tell you": Ibid.

188 "I know it is going": ZNH to Hughes, May 6, 1928. Langston Hughes Papers, Yale.

188 "Godmother asked me": ZNH to Hughes, March 8, 1928. Langston Hughes Papers, Yale.

188 "I believe I have": Ibid.

189 "proved to be": ZNH, *Mules and Men*, p. 157.

189 Zora rapidly "dug in": ZNH, *Dust Tracks*, p. 152.

189 "Tain't a man": ZNH, *Dust Tracks*, p. 154.

190 "uh whole woman": ZNH, *Mules and Men*, p. 152.

190 "Dat Cracker Quarters Boss": ZNH, *Dust Tracks*, p. 154.

190 "Big Sweet helped me": Ibid.

190 "I aims to look out": Ibid.

191 "I didn't move": ZNH, *Mules and Men*, p. 179.

191 "It seemed that anybody": ZNH, *Dust Tracks*, p. 156.

191 "Curses, oaths, cries": ZNH, *Mules and Men*, p. 179.

191 "When the sun came up": ZNH, *Dust Tracks*, p. 156.

CHAPTER 18

192 though she had collected: In a recently discovered, previously unpublished manuscript called "Negro Folk-tales from the Gulf States," Hurston recorded her time spent in Polk County and nearby places (including Eatonville) as January 15 to June 2, 1928. See ZNH, *Every Tongue Got to Confess: Negro Folk-tales from the Gulf States* (New York: HarperCollins, 2001), pp. 257–58.

192 "I shivered at the thought": ZNH, *Mules and Men*, p. 154.

192 "I am getting much more": ZNH to Hughes, July 10, 1928. Langston Hughes Papers, Yale University.

193 "as tender as": ZNH, *Dust Tracks*, p. 145.

193 "Her tongue was a knout": Ibid.

193 Zora judged: ZNH to Alain Locke, May 10, 1928. Alain Locke Papers, Howard University.

193 "white people could not be trusted": ZNH to Alain Locke, June 14, 1928. Alain Locke Papers, Howard University.

194 "I am colored": ZNH, "How It Feels to Be Colored Me," *The World Tomorrow*, May 1928.

195 While painting a mural in Harlem: Lewis, p. 152.

195 "in things that have": Charlotte Mason, as quoted by ZNH in *Dust Tracks*, p. 144.

195 "the greatest cultural wealth": ZNH to Thomas E. Jones, October 12, 1934, Fisk Archives. Also ZNH, *Dust Tracks*, p. 145.

196 "two men came over": ZNH to Hughes, July 10, 1928. Langston Hughes Papers, Yale University.

196 "I have landed here": ZNH to Hughes, August 6, 1928. Langston Hughes Papers, Yale University.

196 Marie Leveau was: The conjure queen's last name is sometimes spelled Laveau. For a fascinating fictionalized account of Leveau's life, see Jewell Parker Rhodes's novel, *Voodoo Dreams* (New York: Picador USA, 1995).

197 Conjure's roots are distinctly African: This is an enormously simplified summary of a tremendously complex subject. For further reading, a suggested beginning is Robert Farris Thompson's *Flash of the Spirit: African and Afro-American Art and Philosophy* (New York: Random House, 1984). Also, in New Orleans, conjure's U.S. stronghold, most contemporary practitioners refer to their spirituality as Vodou, to link it with its African roots. In Hurston's time, however, the conjure tradition in the black South was most often called hoodoo, so that is the term most frequently used in this discussion.

197 "thousands of secret adherents": ZNH, *Mules and Men*, p. 183.

198 "The way we tell it": Ibid.

198 Folks consulted root workers: All of the prescriptions listed are taken from Hurston's *Mules and Men* and "Hoodoo in America," *Journal of American Folk-Lore*, vol. 44, no. 174, October–December 1931.

199 "It makes me sick": ZNH to Hughes, September 20, 1928. Langston Hughes Papers, Yale University.

200 "It is not the accepted theology": ZNH, *Mules and Men*, p. 185.

200 "The preparation period": ZNH, *Mules and Men*, p. 198.

200 "I know 18 tasks": ZNH to Hughes, September 20, 1928. Langston Hughes Papers, Yale University.

201 "in the lap of": ZNH to Hughes, October 15, 1928. Langston Hughes Papers, Yale University.

201 "Some things must be done": ZNH, *Mules and Men*, p. 220.

201 "unearthly terror": ZNH, *Mules and Men*, p. 221.

201 "hard work": ZNH, *Mules and Men*, p. 220.

201 "the Frizzly Rooster": ZNH, *Mules and Men*, p. 213. Hurston identified the Frizzly Rooster as Father George Simms in "Hoodoo in America," an article she published in the *Journal of American Folk-Lore* (vol. 44, no. 174, October–December 1931). In fact, she used different names for each of the hoodoo doctors she studied with in the "Hoodoo in America" article, probably to conceal their identities from other folklore collectors until she could publish her research in book form. In an attempt to determine which set of names is authentic, I found that the 1928 New Orleans city directory had listings for each of the names Hurston used in her *Mules and Men* account, but not for all the names used in the "Hoodoo in America" article. Therefore, I have chosen to consistently use the names given in *Mules and Men*.

202 "Before my first interview": ZNH, *Mules and Men*, p. 214.

202 "Boss of Candles": ZNH, *Mules and Men*, p. 216.

202 "I am getting on": ZNH to Hughes, November 22, 1928. Langston Hughes Papers, Yale University.

202 "lots of thrilling": ZNH to Hughes, October 15, 1928. Langston Hughes Papers, Yale University.

202 Kitty Brown: Kitty Brown is called Ruth Mason in ZNH, "Hoodoo in America," *Journal of American Folk-Lore*, vol. 44, no. 174, October–December 1931.

203 "Some of the postures": ZNH, *Mules and Men*, p. 242.

203 "the vacuum method": ZNH to Alain Locke, October 15, 1928. Alain Locke Papers, Howard University.

203 Luke Turner: Hurston called this particular hoodoo doctor Luke Turner in *Mules and Men*. But in "Hoodoo in America," she called him Samuel

Thompson. It's probable that Turner was his real name, but that Hurston used Thompson in the 1931 article to conceal his identity until she could publish her research in book form.

203 "I could see": ZNH, *Mules and Men*, p. 192.

204 "We sat there silently": ZNH, "Hoodoo in America," *Journal of American Folk-Lore*, vol. 44, no. 174, October–December 1931, p. 358.

204 "I must have clean thoughts": Ibid.

205 "On the second day": ZNH, *Dust Tracks*, p. 156.

205 "with no feeling of hunger": ZNH, *Mules and Men*, p. 199.

205 "A pair of eyes": ZNH, *Mules and Men*, p. 200.

205 "He wanted me to stay": ZNH, *Mules and Men*, p. 205.

205 "That is why": ZNH, *Mules and Men*, p. 185.

206 "That man in the gutter": ZNH to Hughes, November 22, 1928. Langston Hughes Papers, Yale University.

206 "The experience that I had": ZNH to Boas, December 27, 1928. Franz Boas Papers, American Philosophical Society. Copies also in Manuscript Division, Library of Congress.

206 Margaret Mead's book: Douglas, p. 50.

206 "This is confidential": ZNH to Boas, December 27, 1928. Franz Boas Papers, American Philosophical Society.

207 "Yes, I WILL conjure": ZNH to Hughes, November 22, 1928. Langston Hughes Papers, Yale University.

207 "stating that she would stand by me": ZNH, *Mules and Men*, p. 226.

CHAPTER 19

208 "She trusts her three children": ZNH to Locke, December 16, 1928. Alain Locke Papers, Howard University.

208 "I am sitting down to sum up": ZNH to Hughes, April 3, 1929. Langston Hughes Papers, Yale University.

209 "I have more than 95,000 words": ZNH to Boas, April 21, 1929. Franz Boas Papers, American Philosophical Society.

209 "Really I think our material": ZNH to Hughes, April 30, 1929. Langston Hughes Papers, Yale University.

210 "The trouble with Locke": ZNH to Hughes, undated 1929 letter. Langston Hughes Papers, Yale University.

210 "I shall now set it aside": ZNH to Hughes, May 31, 1929. Langston Hughes Papers, Yale University.

210 She wanted to buy: Ibid.

211 "I am getting on fine now": ZNH to Hughes, August 17, 1929. Langston Hughes Papers, Yale University.

211 "little depressed spiritually": ZNH postcard to Hughes, postmarked September 9, 1929. Langston Hughes Papers, Yale University.

211 "Without giving Godmother": ZNH, *Dust Tracks*, p. 157. Also, ZNH to Hughes, October 15, 1929. Langston Hughes Papers, Yale University.

211 "You do anything": ZNH, *Dust Tracks*, p. 158.

212 "It was horrible": ZNH, *Dust Tracks*, p. 159.

212 Growing hungry: "The Seventh Child: Zora Neale Hurston Success as Author and Scientist," *New York Amsterdam News*, April 6, 1935.

212 "I saw dead people": ZNH, *Dust Tracks*, p. 159.

213 "I had only my return ticket": ZNH to Hughes, October 15, 1929. Langston Hughes Papers, Yale University.

213 "Well, honey": Ibid.

213 "You know I depend": ZNH to Hughes, May 31, 1929. Langston Hughes Papers, Yale University.

213 "Can you not take them": ZNH to Hughes, October 15, 1929. Also, ZNH to Hughes, undated letter. Langston Hughes Papers, Yale University.

214 "You are my mainstay": Ibid.

214 "mental characteristics": Boas to ZNH, May 17, 1929. Franz Boas Papers, American Philosophical Society.

214 "The old songs are": ZNH to Boas, October 20, 1929. Franz Boas Papers, American Philosophical Society.

215 "I find that I am restrained": ZNH to Boas, October 22, 1929. Franz Boas Papers, American Philosophical Society.

215 "I am in a trying situation": ZNH to Boas, undated, but clearly from October 1929. Franz Boas Papers, American Philosophical Society.

216 "Miss Hurston strikes me": Otto Klineberg to Franz Boas, November 18, 1929. Franz Boas Papers, American Philosophical Society.

216 "Please be sure": Boas to Klineberg, November 25, 1929. Franz Boas Papers, American Philosophical Society.

216 "She continues to be": Klineberg to Boas, November 29, 1929. Franz Boas Papers, American Philosophical Society.

216 "Dr. Klineberg is very fine": ZNH to Boas, December 10, 1929. Franz Boas Papers, American Philosophical Society.

216 "all the miraculous tales": ZNH to Hughes, undated 1929 letter. Langston Hughes Papers, Yale University.

216 "I want to make this conjure work": ZNH to Boas, December 10, 1929. Franz Boas Papers, American Philosophical Society.

217 "I am simply wasting away": ZNH to Hughes, undated letter from late 1929. Langston Hughes Papers, Yale University.

218 "A poet should turn out": Ibid.

218 Despite his own troubles: Hughes's handwritten note on back of Hurston's

undated 1929 letter about the car. Langston Hughes Papers, Yale University.

218 "Well, I tell you, Langston": ZNH to Hughes, December 10, 1929. Langston Hughes Papers, Yale University.

218 "with my tongue hanging out": Ibid.

218 "People were sleeping in subways": Hughes, *The Big Sea*, p. 319.

219 "Some of my friends": ZNH to Lawrence Jordan, May 31, 1930. Schomburg Center.

219 "over capon": Hurston, *Dust Tracks*, p. 145.

219 Hurston's footage: Author's notes from ZNH's footage, which is housed in the Margaret Mead Collection at the Library of Congress.

220 "I am stuffed": ZNH to Hughes, undated letter from late 1929. Langston Hughes Papers, Yale University.

220 "She used to talk about Zora": Thompson, quoted in Rampersad, p. 182.

220 "Poor Wallie!": ZNH to Hughes, undated 1929 letter, Langston Hughes Papers, Yale University.

220 "I am urged": ZNH to Boas, April 16, 1930. Franz Boas Papers, American Philosophical Society.

221 "I thought it would cheer you": Locke to ZNH, April 28, 1930. Alain Locke Papers, Howard University.

221 "It has been very hard": ZNH to Franz Boas, June 8, 1930. Franz Boas Papers, American Philosophical Society.

221 "You are God's flower": ZNH to Godmother, May 18, 1930. Alain Locke Papers, Howard University.

222 Godmother sent an excessively exotic dress: Louise Thompson recalled this story in Hemenway, p. 139.

222 "I really should not extend": ZNH to Godmother, May 18, 1930. Alain Locke Papers, Howard University.

223 "Make it clear to her": Boas to Hurston, June 13, 1930. Franz Boas Papers, American Philosophical Society.

223 "I have broached the subject": ZNH to Boas, June 8, 1930. Franz Boas Papers, American Philosophical Society.

CHAPTER 20

224 Why didn't someone: Hughes to Carl Van Vechten, January 16, 1931. Carl Van Vechten Papers, Yale. Also Hughes to Arthur Spingarn, January 21, 1931. Alain Locke Papers, Howard University.

224 Hughes had begun looking: Rampersad, pp. 175–76.

225 "The assault and the gobbler": ZNH, "The Bone of Contention," undated. Alain Locke Papers, Howard University. This story was not published until 1991 in *Mule Bone: A Comedy of Negro Life*, edited with introductions by

George Houston Bass and Henry Louis Gates Jr. (New York: HarperPerennial).

225 "The elders neglected": ZNH, "The Bone of Contention." Alain Locke Papers, Howard University.

226 "It was the regular thing": Charlotte Mason's notes, headed "Zora-L.H." January 29, 1931. Alain Locke Papers, Howard University.

226 Hughes later would claim: Hughes to Van Vechten, January 16, 1931. Carl Van Vechten Papers, Yale. Also Hughes, *The Big Sea*, p. 320.

226 "Hurston's contribution was": Rampersad, p. 184.

227 "the dandy job": ZNH to Lawrence Jordan, May 31, 1930, Schomburg Center. Also, "Zora's Account for May, 1930," Alain Locke Papers, Howard University.

227 "a very gay and lively girl": Hughes, *The Big Sea*, p. 320.

227 "All of them cried to me": ZNH to Lawrence Jordan, May 31, 1930, Schomburg Center.

227 "Now Langston, nobody": ZNH to Hughes, January 18, 1931. Alain Locke Papers, Howard University.

228 "lost its meaning": Hughes to ZNH, January 20, 1931. Alain Locke Papers, Howard University.

228 "already overpaid": Charlotte Mason's handwritten notes, headed "Zora-L.H." January 29, 1931. Alain Locke Papers, Howard University. Hughes wrote two conflicting accounts of the *Mule Bone* dispute—one to his lawyer at the time, another nine years later in his autobiography, *The Big Sea*. Hurston apparently never wrote a comprehensive account of the *Mule Bone* episode, but her letters to Hughes at the time outline her perspective. She also told her side of the story to Mason in early 1931, and Godmother recorded Hurston's account—cited here—for her personal files.

228 "I felt that I was among strangers": ZNH to Hughes, January 18, 1931. Alain Locke Papers, Howard University.

229 "Off at last": ZNH to Hughes, postmarked August 11, 1930. Langston Hughes Papers, Yale.

229 "it would be a grand play": Hughes to Van Vechten, January 16, 1931. Hurston Papers, Yale.

229 "the play was hers": Charlotte Mason's handwritten notes, headed "Zora-L.H." January 29, 1931. Alain Locke Papers, Howard University.

230 In early June, an indignant Mason: Mason to Hughes, June 6, 1930, Langston Hughes Papers, Yale. Quoted in Rampersad, p. 186.

230 "I ask you to help": Hughes to Mason, draft, August 15, 1930. Langston Hughes Papers, Yale. Also quoted in Rampersad, p. 188.

230 "You can help me": Hughes to Mason, draft, undated. Langston Hughes Papers, Yale. Quoted in Rampersad, p. 187.

231 "a short but excruciating" session: Louise Thompson, quoted in Rampersad, p. 192.

231 "Darling Godmother": ZNH to Mason, September 24, 1930. Alain Locke Papers, Howard University.

231 "Dance Songs and Tales from the Bahamas": ZNH, in *Journal of American Folk-Lore*, vol. 43, July–September 1930.

231 "I thought her behavior strange": Hughes to Arthur Spingarn, January 21, 1931. Alain Locke Papers, Howard University.

232 "a very heavy blow": Arna Bontemps interview, December 18, 1970. REH Files.

232 "I am helping myself forget": Charlotte Mason to Alain Locke, August 8, 1930. Alain Locke Papers, Howard University.

233 "With the present economic situation": Hurston's November 1930 expense sheets, Alain Locke Papers, Howard University.

233 "I am beginning to feel": ZNH to Mason, November 11, 1930. Alain Locke Papers, Howard University.

233 "to hold my spiritual forces together": ZNH to Mason, November 25, 1930. Alain Locke Papers, Howard University.

233 "You see, Darling Godmother": Ibid.

233 In her notes on "Zora's play": Charlotte Mason's notes, "Zora's Play," November 8, 1930. Alain Locke Papers, Howard University.

234 "Langston and I started out": ZNH, as quoted by Van Vechten in a January 19, 1931, letter to Hughes. Langston Hughes Papers, Yale.

234 a monthly stipend of $150: Mason's notes headed "Zora," December 21, 1930. Alain Locke Papers, Howard University.

234 "You have given me": ZNH to Mason, undated. Alain Locke Papers, Howard University.

234 "That hurt": ZNH to Mason, January 12, 1931. Alain Locke Papers, Howard University.

235 "I said you had no right": Mason's notes, draft of letter to ZNH, headed "Zora," January 15, 1931. Alain Locke Papers, Howard University.

235 "Is there something": Hughes to Van Vechten, January 16, 1931. Hurston Papers, Yale.

235 "I sense a good deal": ZNH to Hughes, undated. Alain Locke Papers, Howard University.

236 "Now, get this straight": ZNH to Hughes, undated. Alain Locke Papers, Howard University.

236 "I didn't intend to be evasive": ZNH to Hughes, January 18, 1931. Alain Locke Papers, Howard University.

237 "grand tangle": Hughes to Van Vechten, January 18, 1931. Hurston Papers, Yale.

237 Acting in his capacity: Van Vechten to Hughes, January 21, 1931. Langston Hughes Papers, Yale.

237 "Zora came to see me": Van Vechten to Hughes, January 20, 1931. Langston Hughes Papers, Yale.

237 "I don't think": ZNH to Hughes, January 18, 1931. Alain Locke Papers, Howard University.

238 Infuriated by Hurston's claim: Arthur Spingarn was the brother of longtime NAACP officer Joel Spingarn, whose wife, Amy, had financed Hughes's education at Lincoln University.

238 "as a permanent agreement": Hughes to Arthur Spingarn, January 21, 1931. Alain Locke Papers, Howard University.

238 "I am convinced that": Van Vechten to Hughes, January 21, 1931. Langston Hughes Papers, Yale.

238 "to set up the claim": ZNH to Godmother, January 20, 1931. Alain Locke Papers, Howard University.

239 "wrassled with me": ZNH to Eslanda Robeson, April 18, 1934, quoted in Duberman, p. 170.

240 "Let's not be niggers": Hughes to ZNH, January 19, 1931. Alain Locke Papers, Howard University.

240 "pathetic letter": ZNH to Mason, January 20, 1931. Alain Locke Papers, Howard University.

240 "not one word": Telegrams, as typed by Hughes and sent to Spingarn. Alain Locke Papers, Howard University.

240 "I suppose that both of us": ZNH to Hughes, January 20, 1931. Alain Locke Papers, Howard University.

241 Calling Zora's jealousy: Hughes to ZNH, January 20, 1931. Alain Locke Papers, Howard University.

241 "Miss Hurston insists": Spingarn to Hughes, January 24, 1931. Alain Locke Papers, Howard University.

241 "If you feel": Hughes to ZNH, January 22, 1931. Alain Locke Papers, Howard University.

242 This second copyright: Hurston had secured a copyright for a revised version of *Mule Bone* on October 29, 1930, under the name *De Turkey and De Law*, according to the records of the Copyright Office of the Library of Congress. At the same time, she secured a copyright for *Cold Keener, A Revue*, which incorporated the filling station skit and other bits she'd written for the proposed folk opera with Hughes. In addition, see ZNH to Mason, August 14, 1931, and Spingarn to Hughes, January 28, 1931. Both in Alain Locke Papers, Howard University.

242 "glad things seem": Hughes to ZNH, January 22, 1931. Alain Locke Papers, Howard University.

242 The same day: Spingarn to Hughes, January 27, 1931. Alain Locke Papers, Howard University.

242 "Congratulations": Locke as quoted by Hughes to Spingarn, January 30, 1931, Alain Locke Papers, Howard University.

242 "Zo darling": Hughes to ZNH, January 27, 1931. Alain Locke Papers, Howard University.

243 "The only thing": Thompson to Hughes, January 28, 1931. Alain Locke Papers, Howard University.

243 "stupidly untruthful": Hughes to Spingarn, January 30, 1931. Alain Locke Papers, Howard University.

243 "to straighten out": Hughes to Spingarn, February 3, 1931. Alain Locke Papers, Howard University.

244 In a most unflattering portrayal: Hughes to Van Vechten, February 4, 1931. Hurston Papers, Yale.

244 "I had to get up": Hughes, *The Big Sea*, p. 333.

244 "smashed them all": ZNH to Mason, February 3, 1931. Alain Locke Papers, Howard University.

245 "fresh and amusing": Van Vechten to Hughes, January 19, 1931. Langston Hughes Papers, Yale.

245 "The whole thing": Hughes to Thompson, February 7, 1931. Alain Locke Papers, Howard University.

245 "had the astounding nerve": Ibid.

245 "In view of the fact": ZNH to Hughes, February 14, 1931. Alain Locke Papers, Howard University.

246 "there was no possible chance": Spingarn to Hughes, March 5, 1931. Alain Locke Papers, Howard University.

246 "just as well": Hughes to Spingarn, March 6, 1931, and March 15, 1931. Alain Locke Papers, Howard University.

246 *Mule Bone* would remain: *Mule Bone* was finally produced in 1991 at New York's Lincoln Center.

246 Though he never publicly admitted: ZNH to Mason, May 17, 1932. Alain Locke Papers, Howard University. Hurston wrote: "I have a most ungracious letter from Langston in which he renounces his claim upon the play."

246 "I gave up to Zora": Hughes to Van Vechten, March 5, 1934, quoted in Bernard, p. 121.

246 "the cross of her life": Bontemps to Hughes, November 24, 1939. *Arna Bontemps–Langston Hughes Letters, 1925–1967*, edited by Charles H. Nichols (New York: Paragon House, 1990), p. 44.

CHAPTER 21

247 their "art was broken": Hughes, *The Big Sea*, p. 334.

247 "liked to laugh together": John Henrik Clarke, in an interview with the author, May 28, 1997. Clarke's assessment is confirmed by several letters from 1931 and 1932 in which Hurston tells Mason she has heard from Hughes. On January 21, 1932, for instance, she mentioned that Hughes had written her from Jacksonville, FL, where he'd been hosted "magnificently" by Hurston's brother and sister-in-law. This letter, and others mentioning Hurston's post-*Mule Bone* contact with Hughes, are in the Alain Locke Papers, Howard University.

247 unemployment in Harlem: Lewis, p. 240.

247 "I hear almost no news": Locke to Mason, March 29, 1931. Alain Locke Papers, Howard University.

248 "I know that Langston says": ZNH to Mason, April 18, 1931. Alain Locke Papers, Howard University.

248 "That spring for me": Hughes, *The Big Sea*, p. 334.

248 In an erratically spelled rant: Wallace Thurman to Langston Hughes, undated, Langston Hughes Papers, Yale University.

249 Paying no mind: Bundles, pp. 290–91.

249 "they swung it slightly": Hughes, *The Big Sea*, p. 246.

249 "brought everybody down": Hughes, *The Big Sea*, p. 247.

250 Even tough-minded black critic: Sterling Brown, quoted in Lewis, p. 246.

250 "The Negro's idea of heaven": ZNH, "You Don't Know Us Negroes," an unpublished article written in 1934. Manuscript Division, Library of Congress.

250 "duplicate the success": Van Vechten to Hughes, January 20, 1931. Langston Hughes Papers, Yale.

250 Knopf editor Harry Block: ZNH to Mason, March 10, 1931, April 18, 1931. Alain Locke Papers, Howard University.

251 "tearing up 66th Street": ZNH to Mason, June 4, 1931. Alain Locke Papers, Howard University.

251 Early on the morning of: ZNH, "Fannie Hurst By Her Ex-Amanuensis," *Saturday Review*, October 9, 1937.

251 "one of her bizarre frocks": Fannie Hurst, "Zora Hurston: A Personality Sketch," *Library Gazette*, Yale University, no. 35, 1961.

251 "Zora's attitude": Ibid.

252 "so we pointed the nose": ZNH, "Fannie Hurst By Her Ex-Amanuensis," *Saturday Review*, October 9, 1937. Also, Kroeger, p. 167.

252 Zora dropped Fannie off: For further details of the Zora-Fannie trip, see Kroeger, pp. 166–69.

252 "I don't see": ZNH to Mason, June 4, 1931. Alain Locke Papers, Howard University.

253 "sun-burnt child": Hurston used this term to describe herself, in ZNH to Mason, November 25, 1930. Alain Locke Papers, Howard University.

253 Received June 23: ZNH expense sheets, June 1931 and July 1931. Alain Locke Papers, Howard University.

253 "Under any other circumstances": ZNH, "My Most Humiliating Jim Crow Experience," *Negro Digest*, June 1944.

254 she secured copyrights: Library of Congress Copyright Deposit Collections. Plays are registered as unpublished dramas in the Manuscript Division.

254 "I do not consider": ZNH to Mason, July 23, 1931. Alain Locke Papers, Howard University.

254 "I hear that my husband": Ibid. The divorce decree was issued July 7, 1931, County Court Records, St. Louis County, MO.

254 "she was a little too accommodating": Herbert Sheen interview, REH Files.

255 "Marriage and social laws": ZNH to Herbert Sheen, March 13, 1953, May 7, 1953. REH Files.

255 "God knows you are": Mason to ZNH, July 28, 1931. Alain Locke Papers, Howard University.

255 "stupid and trite": ZNH to Mason, September 25, 1931. Alain Locke Papers, Howard University.

256 "mediocre entertainment": Richard Lockridge, "Negro Revue Offered," *New York Sun*, September 16, 1931.

256 "It is fast, furious and rather tiresome": J. Brooks Atkinson, "Harlem Fandango," *The New York Times*, September 16, 1931.

256 Even talented actors: John Mason Brown, "'Fast and Furious,' a Colored Review in Thirty-seven Scenes, Is Put On at the New Yorker," *New York Evening Post*, September 16, 1931.

256 "squeezed all the Negro-ness": ZNH to Mason, September 25, 1931. Alain Locke Papers, Howard University.

256 "the most stolen-from Negro": ZNH to Mason, September 25, 1931, and October 15, 1931. Alain Locke Papers, Howard University.

257 "I firmly believe": ZNH to Mason, September 25, 1931. Alain Locke Papers, Howard University.

257 "Outside of getting": Ibid.

257 "The Negro material": ZNH to Thomas Jones, October 12, 1934. Fisk University; copy in Hurston Papers at Tulane. Also ZNH in application for Julius Rosenwald Foundation fellowship, December 14, 1934. Rosenwald Fund Papers, Fisk University.

258 "Sitting around": ZNH, *Dust Tracks*, p. 280.

258 "the world was not ready": ZNH to Thomas Jones, October 12, 1934. Fisk University; copy in Hurston Papers at Tulane.

258 "a determined effort": ZNH, *Dust Tracks*, p. 280.

259 An unfortunate incident in the studio: ZNH to Thomas Jones, October 12, 1934. Fisk University; copy in Hurston Papers at Tulane. Also, ZNH, *Dust Tracks*, p. 282.

259 "a fine black girl": ZNH to Mason, October 15, 1931. Alain Locke Papers, Howard University.

259 Zora did not have "any hang-ups": Richard Bruce Nugent interview, May 1971. REH Files. Also Nugent quoted in Watson, p. 88.

259 "a complexion as charming": 1930s-era newspaper ad from the *Baltimore Afro-American*, reproduced in Avonie Brown and Laura Lieberson, "Black or White," an article available online at www.afro.com.

259 "No mulattoes at all": ZNH to Mason, October 15, 1931. Alain Locke Papers, Howard University.

260 "no diluted ones": Mason to ZNH, draft, October 18, 1931. Alain Locke Papers, Howard University.

260 "never known the common run": ZNH, *Dust Tracks*, p. 282.

260 Zora was too busy: ZNH to Mason, September 25, 1931. Alain Locke Papers, Howard University.

260 "café au lait-learned": Kroeger, p. 212.

260 "I am on the brink": ZNH to Mason, December 16, 1931. Alain Locke Papers, Howard University.

261 "with high hopes": ZNH to Mason, December 21, 1931. Alain Locke Papers, Howard University.

261 "The dances have not been influenced": Advertisement for *The Great Day*, Hurston Papers, Yale University.

261 Zora had "given her word": Mason to Locke, notes for conversation, January 10, 1932. Alain Locke Papers, Howard University. Also theater critic Arthur Ruhl, reporting on the show and the last-minute removal of the conjure ritual in "Second Nights," *New York Herald Tribune*, January 17, 1932.

262 "From the lifting of the curtain": ZNH, *Dust Tracks*, p. 283.

262 "intimate living": *The Great Day*, program notes by Alain Locke, reprinted in Lynda Marion Hill, *Social Rituals and the Verbal Art of Zora Neale Hurston* (Washington, D.C.: Howard University Press, 1996).

262 "Cap'n got a pistol": *The Great Day*, program notes. Hurston sings this song, which is also sometimes called "Shove It Over," in a WPA recording session in Jacksonville, FL, in June 1939. Recording available at the Library of Congress, Archive of Folk Song. Transcription by author.

263 "You may leave": Hurston also had a character sing some of the lyrics of

this song in her 1926 short story "Muttsy." Also, Hurston sings it on WPA recording, June 1939. Library of Congress, Archive of Folk Song. This song, as recorded by Hurston, has been reproduced on the accompanying CD for *The Norton Anthology of African American Literature*.

263 Part of the cast sang "Deep River": Hemenway, p. 180, based on interviews with performers and audience members.

263 "simply one of the crowd": Arthur Ruhl, "Second Nights," *New York Herald Tribune*, January 17, 1932.

263 "I really came": ZNH, *Dust Tracks*, p. 284.

263 In March 1933: Comparison of Hurston's program notes with a program from *Run, Little Chillun*, staged at the Lyric Theatre. Also, see ZNH, *Dust Tracks*, p. 284.

263 "The evening was altogether successful": Arthur Ruhl, "Second Nights," *New York Herald Tribune*, January 17, 1932.

263 "no feeling of glory": ZNH to Mason, January 14, 1932. Alain Locke Papers, Howard University.

264 Hurston now owed Godmother: "Box Office Statement," John Golden Theatre, January 10, 1932. Also, Economic History Resources "How Much Is That?" Online Calculator.

264 "I know it is yours": ZNH to Mason, January 14, 1932. Alain Locke Papers, Howard University.

264 "trading on Godmother's big heart": Mason to ZNH, notes, January 17, 1932. Alain Locke Papers, Howard University.

264 Mason drafted a legally binding letter: Mason to ZNH, January 20, 1932, typed legal agreement. Alain Locke Papers, Howard University.

265 Hurston immediately began plotting: Hurston likely changed the production's name to avoid confusion with *Great Day*, an unsuccessful blackface musical from 1929.

265 "Your black gal": ZNH to Mason, March 19, 1932. Alain Locke Papers, Howard University.

265 *The Fiery Chariot*: The program notes for *From Sun to Sun* make it clear that *The Fiery Chariot* premiered at the New School concert—not in a later concert at Rollins College, as reported in previous accounts of Hurston's theatrical career.

265 "It was good": ZNH, *Dust Tracks*, p. 284.

266 Locke fomented the old lady's resentment: Mason to ZNH, draft, April 8, 1932. Alain Locke Papers, Howard University.

266 "patronizingly fond": Richard Bruce Nugent interview, May 1971. REH Files.

266 "I understand that both you and Alain": ZNH to Mason, April 4, 1932. Alain Locke Papers, Howard University.

267 "You do not seem to realize": Mason to ZNH, draft, April 8, 1932. Alain Locke Papers, Howard University.

267 "I know that my bills": ZNH to Mason, April 27, 1932. Alain Locke Papers, Howard University.

267 "I look very beautiful": ZNH to Cornelia Chapin, February 29, 1932. Alain Locke Papers, Howard University.

267 "Somehow a great weight": ZNH to Mason, April 27, 1932. Alain Locke Papers, Howard University.

CHAPTER 22

269 "I am happy here": ZNH to Mason, May 8, 1932. Alain Locke Papers, Howard University.

269 "quiet, atmosphere, and economical existence": ZNH to Thomas Jones, October 12, 1934. Fisk University; copy in Hurston Papers at Tulane.

269 "Do you know": ZNH to Mason, May 17, 1932. Alain Locke Papers, Howard University.

269 "There was some chicken": Ibid.

270 Bethune-Cookman College: Darlene Clark Hine, Elsa Barkley Brown, Rosalyn Terborg-Penn, editors, *Black Women in America: An Historical Encyclopedia*, vol. I (Bloomington, Indianapolis: Indiana University Press, 1994).

270 several of the twenty-two: Lewis, pp. 288–91.

270 "it was sort of an adventure": Arna Bontemps interview, December 18, 1970. REH Files.

271 "a crowd of white Negroes": ZNH to Mason, July 6, 1932. Alain Locke Papers, Howard University.

271 "Most of that crowd": Bunche, quoted in Lewis, pp. 288–92.

271 "most of them came back strongly": Arna Bontemps interview, December 18, 1970. REH Files.

271 "My country, right or wrong": ZNH, "How It Feels to Be Colored Me," *The World Tomorrow*, May 1928.

272 "the pathos": ZNH, "My Most Humiliating Jim Crow Experience," *Negro Digest*, June 1944.

272 "As I see it": ZNH to Mason, October 15, 1931. Alain Locke Papers, Howard University.

272 "skinfolk": As Hurston reported in *Dust Tracks on a Road* and elsewhere, this phrase was commonly used in her day by African Americans seeking to distance themselves from other black people with whom they did not wish to be associated.

272 "Seeing the stuff": ZNH to Edwin Osgood Grover, June 8, 1932. ZNH Collection, University of Florida.

273 "won an enviable place": Robert Wunsch to Rollins College President Hamilton Holt, October 29, 1932. Hurston Papers, Rollins College Archives.

273 "The news here": Mason to ZNH, draft, May 22, 1932. Alain Locke Papers, Howard University.

273 "New York is painful": ZNH to Mason, September 16, 1932. Alain Locke Papers, Howard University.

273 "She was just Zora": Annie Davis, in Anna Lillios, "Excursions Into Zora Neale Hurston's Eatonville," *Zora in Florida*, edited by Steve Glassman and Kathryn Lee Seidel (Orlando: University of Central Florida, 1991), p. 23.

274 "You'd love a Florida rain-storm": ZNH to Mason, July 29, 1932. Alain Locke Papers, Howard University.

274 "I shall be off": ZNH to Mason, September 16, 1932 and September 28, 1932. Alain Locke Papers, Howard University.

274 "I pray that": ZNH to Mason, September 28, 1932. Alain Locke Papers, Howard University.

274 every nickel she spent: Figures taken from Hurston's expense reports, June and July 1931. Alain Locke Papers, Howard University.

275 "humming little songs": Annie Davis, who met Hurston when she visited Eatonville, discussed what she saw of Hurston's writing process in Anna Lillios, "Excursions Into Zora Neale Hurston's Eatonville," *Zora in Florida*, p. 24.

275 "I know what is true": ZNH to Edwin Osgood Grover, June 15, 1932. ZNH Collection, University of Florida.

275 "to just imagine": ZNH, *Dust Tracks*, p. 172.

275 Impressed with her knowledge: Robert Wunsch to Hamilton Holt, president of Rollins College, October 29, 1932. Rollins College Archives.

275 "The whole thing": "Wunsch's Class Hears Hurston," *Rollins Sandspur*, November 16, 1932.

276 "because I realized": ZNH to Mason, January 6, 1933. Alain Locke Papers, Howard University.

276 "if I could forget the flesh pots": ZNH to Alain Locke, March 20, 1933. Alain Locke Papers, Howard University.

276 "The small amount of personal comfort": ZNH to Mason, January 6, 1933. Alain Locke Papers, Howard University.

277 "but the 20th is too near": Ibid.

277 "I see no reason": Hamilton Holt to Robert Wunsch, copy, November 1, 1933, misdated; was actually written in 1932, in response to Wunsch's October 29, 1932, memo. Rollins College Archives.

277 "I tried to have a space": ZNH to Mason, January 6, 1933. Alain Locke Papers, Howard University.

277   "so that our own people": Ibid.

277   "The spirituals": Program notes, *From Sun to Sun: A Program of Negro Folklore*, Rollins College.

278   "An unselfconscious spontaneity": "Enthusiastic Response Is Given 'From Sun to Sun'," *Rollins Sandspur*, February 8, 1933.

278   "That was a great performance": Hamilton Holt to Robert Wunsch, January 28, 1933. Rollins College Archives.

278   "I know it's novelty-publicity seeking": ZNH to Locke, March 20, 1933. Alain Locke Papers, Howard University.

278   pneumonia had killed her sister Sarah: Sarah Hurston Mack died on January 28, 1933, according to a letter that her youngest brother sent to the attorneys representing the Hurston Estate in the 1970s. Everette Edwin Hurston Sr. to Elsie O'Laughlin, November 15, 1974. Letter courtesy of Ms. O'Laughlin and attorney Ron Jayson.

278   "Then Godmother falls!": ZNH to Locke, March 20, 1933. Alain Locke Papers, Howard University.

278   "asked the powers invisible": ZNH to Mason, October 10, 1931. Alain Locke Papers, Howard University.

278   "I am doing more": ZNH to Locke, March 20, 1933. Alain Locke Papers, Howard University.

279   "the novel that I have wanted to write": ZNH to Mason, May 8, 1932 and May 17, 1932. Alain Locke Papers, Howard University.

279   "one of the larger": ZNH to Mason, May 26, 1932. Alain Locke Papers, Howard University.

280   "Joe Banks, Ah hear you": ZNH, "The Gilded Six-Bits," August 1933 issue of *Story* magazine. Reprinted in *The Complete Stories*.

281   In the end: This "bad-girls-have-to-pay" narrative continues to hold sway in American popular culture, particularly in films—even those that claim to present a feminist perspective: *She's Gotta Have It, Body of Evidence,* and *Thelma and Louise* are just a few examples.

281   "Mind you, not the first word": ZNH, *Dust Tracks*, p. 173.

281   "the idea of attempting a book": ZNH, *Dust Tracks*, p. 171.

282   "What I wanted to tell": Ibid.

282   "Children begin": Oscar Wilde, quoted in Barbara Belford, *Oscar Wilde: A Certain Genius* (New York: Random House, 2000), p. 15.

282   "It's going to be accepted": ZNH, *Dust Tracks*, p. 174.

283   "I tore out of that place": ZNH, *Dust Tracks*, p. 175.

CHAPTER 23

284   "No Negro names": ZNH to James Weldon Johnson, January 22, 1934. JWJ Correspondence, Yale.

284 the $5,000 advances: Kroeger, p. 126.

285 "It was unheard of": H. Kamau, "Interview with Dr. Margaret Walker Alexander," 1986, Amistad Research Center, Tulane University.

285 "unique and authentic representation": Program notes, *All De Live Long Day*. Rollins College Archives.

285 "black laborers in a typical Florida railroad camp": "Zora Hurston Gives Program," *Rollins Sandspur*, January 10, 1934.

285 "with all the spontaneous enthusiasm": Ibid.

286 "to engage in research": Guggenheim Fellowships General Information Page, online at www.gf.org.

286 "I hope <u>eventually</u>": ZNH, in Guggenheim application, dated July 25, 1933. From the Archives of the J. S. Guggenheim Foundation.

287 "Among Negroes": Carl Van Vechten, "Confidential Report on Candidate for Fellowship," stamped as received January 1934. Archives of the J. S. Guggenheim Foundation.

287 "She is an erratic worker": Fannie Hurst, "Confidential Report on Candidate for Fellowship," November 29, 1933. Archives of the J. S. Guggenheim Foundation.

287 "She has neither the temperament": Ruth Benedict, "Confidential Report on Candidate for Fellowship," November 15, 1933. Archives of the J. S. Guggenheim Foundation.

287 "On the whole": Franz Boas, "Confidential Report on Candidate for Fellowship," November 29, 1933. Archives of the J. S. Guggenheim Foundation.

287 "Zora Hurston's qualifications": Max Eastman, "Confidential Report on Candidate for Fellowship," December 22, 1933. Archives of the J. S. Guggenheim Foundation.

288 "work out some good": ZNH to Van Vechten, January 22, 1934. Van Vechten Papers, Yale University.

288 "Then the entire faculty": ZNH to Thomas Jones, October 12, 1934. Tulane.

289 "plugging away in the dark": ZNH to Locke, March 24, 1934. Alain Locke Papers, Howard University.

289 "In the last two days": ZNH to Thomas Jones, October 12, 1934. Tulane.

289 "the folktales done over": ZNH to Van Vechten, January 22, 1934. Van Vechten Papers, Yale University.

289 "So I decided to abandon": ZNH to Thomas Jones, October 12, 1934. Tulane.

289 "No, I shan't be": ZNH to Locke, May 21, 1934. Alain Locke Papers, Howard University.

289 "it will increase my standing": ZNH to Van Vechten, March 24, 1934. Van Vechten Papers, Yale University.

289 Lippincott wanted a $3.50 book: Ibid.

290 "there can never be enough beauty": ZNH, "Characteristics of Negro Expression," *Negro: An Anthology*, Nancy Cunard.

290 "there is no regular usage": See Odum and Johnson, *The Negro and His Songs*, 1925. And Puckett, *Folk Beliefs of the Southern Negro*, 1926.

291 "I know that I run the risk": ZNH, "Characteristics of Negro Expressions," 1934.

"a glorious paean": Rita Dove, foreword to *Jonah's Gourd Vine*, 1990 HarperPerennial edition.

292 "White folks are very stupid": ZNH, "Black Death," *The Complete Stories*.

292 "The characters in the story": ZNH, "Art and Such," essay written in the fall of 1938 for *The Florida Negro*, a project of the WPA's Federal Writers' Project in Florida. The essay was never published in Hurston's time, but was published in Henry Louis Gates, Jr., ed., *Reading Black, Reading Feminist* (New York: Penguin Books, 1990).

292 a biblical story: Book of Jonah, Chapter 4, Verses 6–10.

292 "One act of malice": ZNH to Van Vechten, February 28, 1934. Van Vechten Papers, Yale University.

293 "I have tried to present": ZNH to Johnson, April 16, 1934. JWJ Correspondence, Yale.

293 "scared to death": ZNH to Van Vechten, April 26, 1934. Van Vechten Papers, Yale.

293 "Here is negro folk lore": Fannie Hurst, introduction to *Jonah's Gourd Vine*, enclosed in letter to Hurston, February 14, 1934. Fannie Hurst Collection, Brandeis University.

293 "a very swell novel": Van Vechten to Hughes, undated, around February 21, 1934. Bernard, p. 119.

293 "Seldom have we had an author": Lippincott to Grover, February 5, 1934. ZNH Collection, University of Florida. The novel was recommended by the Book-of-the-Month Club as an alternate, not as a prestigious "main selection," which would have turned it into a cash cow.

294 "*Jonah's Gourd Vine* can be called without fear": Margaret Wallace, "Real Negro People," *The New York Times Book Review*, May 6, 1934.

294 "a credible, human": Martha Gruening, "Darktown Strutter," *The New Republic*, July 11, 1934.

294 "It seems as if Miss Hurston": Estelle Fenton, review of *Jonah's Gourd Vine*, *Opportunity*, August 1934.

294 "quite disappointing and a failure": Andrew Burris, review of *Jonah's Gourd Vine*, *The Crisis*, June 3, 1934.

295 "I do not attempt to solve": ZNH to Fannie Hurst, undated but sometime in late 1933 or early 1934. Fannie Hurst Collection, Brandeis University.

295 "She has captured the lusciousness": Andrew Burris, review of *Jonah's Gourd Vine*, *The Crisis*, June 3, 1934.

295 Gildersleeve did not think as highly: Virginia Gildersleeve to Bertram Lippincott, May 28, 1934. Barnard Archives.

295 "I see Jesus": ZNH, *Jonah's Gourd Vine*, pp. 177–78.

295 "too good": John Chamberlain, "Books of the Times," *The New York Times*, May 3, 1934.

296 "I suppose that you have seen": ZNH to Johnson, May 8, 1934. JWJ Correspondence, Yale University.

296 "To the first and only": ZNH, original dedication, manuscript of *Jonah's Gourd Vine*. For unknown reasons, this dedication never made it to print; apparently, Hurston replaced it with the one that was published, honoring her Rollins College ally, Bob Wunsch.

296 "Hurston's language is superb": Rita Dove, foreword to *Jonah's Gourd Vine*, 1990 HarperPerennial edition.

297 "I have inserted": ZNH to Franz Boas, August 20, 1934. Franz Boas Papers, American Philosophical Society.

297 "I'm too delighted at your nerve": ZNH to Dorothy West, March 24, 1934. Dorothy West Collection, Boston University Library.

297 "horde of murmurers": ZNH, "The Fire and the Cloud," *Challenge*, September 1934. Reprinted in ZNH, *The Complete Stories*.

298 "the idea being": ZNH to Johnson, October 7, 1934. JWJ Correspondence, Yale.

298 "The fascinating Zora Neale Hurston": "Book News," *Daily News* of Chicago, October 25, 1934.

299 "I don't know who": Phone interview with Katherine Dunham, January 27, 2000. Conducted by Eugene B. Redmond as part of the Zora Neale Hurston Festival of the Arts and Humanities in Eatonville, FL. Notes taken by author.

299 "Katherine Dunham loaned us": ZNH, *Dust Tracks*, p. 285.

300 "The vehicle, packed with folklore": Review of *Singing Steel*, unidentified news clipping, Rollins College Archives.

300 "Frankly, I feel flattered": ZNH to Van Vechten, Thanksgiving Day, 1934. Van Vechten Papers, Yale University.

301 "I buried many turkey bosoms": ZNH to Van Vechten, December 10, 1934. Van Vechten Papers, Yale University.

301 "The pictures are swell!": Ibid.

301 "Life has picked me up": ZNH to Edwin Osgood Grover, December 13, 1934. ZNH Collection, University of Florida.

CHAPTER 24

302 "no holiday pleasures": ZNH to Edwin Osgood Grover, undated. ZNH Collection, University of Florida.

302 "continuance of work satisfactory": Edwin Embree to ZNH, December 19, 1934. Rosenwald Fund Papers, Fisk University. Also, Economic History Resources online "How Much Is That?" Conversion Calculator.

303 "Now I realize": ZNH to Boas, December 14, 1934. Franz Boas Papers, American Philosophical Society.

303 "We are glad to cooperate": Embree to ZNH, December 19, 1934. Rosenwald Fund Papers, Fisk University.

303 "Fawn as you will": ZNH, "Race Cannot Become Great Until it Recognizes its Talent," *The Washington Tribune*, week ending December 29, 1934.

304 though Hughes was still writing prolifically: Rampersad, p. 301.

304 "He was our leader": Dorothy West, quoted in Watson, p. 166.

304 "the golden days": Bontemps, quoted in Bruce Kellner, *The Harlem Renaissance: A Historical Dictionary of the Era* (Westport, CT: Greenwood Press, 1984).

305 Harper & Brothers had offered Hurst: ZNH to Van Vechten, February 28, 1934. Also Kroeger, pp. 212–13.

305 "the greatest condemnation": Kroeger, p. 207.

306 "Whenever I pick up": ZNH, "You Don't Know Us Negroes," 1934, unpublished essay written for *The American Mercury*. Manuscript Division, Library of Congress.

307 "Most white people": Ibid.

308 "certainly brilliant": Embree to Boas, January 2, 1935. Rosenwald Fund Papers, Fisk University.

308 Embree claimed Hurston's coursework: Embree to ZNH, January 21, 1935. Rosenwald Fund Papers, Fisk University.

308 "thorough and careful work": Embree to Boas, March 26, 1935. Rosenwald Fund Papers, Fisk University.

309 "Naturally the uncertainty": Boas to Embree, March 20, 1926. Rosenwald Fund Papers, Fisk University.

309 "Miss Hurston said that": "Author Plans to Upbraid Own Race: Zorah Hurston Denies There Is 'Tragedy' in Being Negro," *The New York World-Telegram*, February 6, 1935.

309 "We have been distressed": Embree to Boas, March 26, 1935. Rosenwald Fund Papers, Fisk University.

310 "working like a slave": ZNH to Edwin Osgood Grover, May 14, 1935. ZNH Collection, University of Florida.

310 "Where did you disappear": Fannie Hurst to ZNH, March 28 and April 12, 1935. Fannie Hurst Collection, Brandeis.

310 "Since I don't compose well": "Zora Neale Hurston Success as Author and Scientist," April 6, 1935. *New York Amsterdam News*.

310 "I did not just fall in love": ZNH, *Dust Tracks*, p. 205.

311 A member of his college orchestra: City College of New York, 1934 yearbook. According to the program notes from *The Great Day*, Punter played "the shack rouser" and led the cast in the railroad songs, including "John Henry."

311 "He was tall, dark brown": ZNH, *Dust Tracks*, p. 205. This reconstruction of the Hurston-Punter relationship is based mainly on Zora's account in *Dust Tracks on a Road*, in which she identifies Punter as "P.M.P." Additional details are gleaned from her correspondence of the period. Unfortunately, no letters between the lovers have been located. But Robert Hemenway interviewed Punter for his 1977 Hurston biography. According to Hemenway, Punter acknowledged his close friendship with Hurston, but seemed to want to downplay the intimacy of their relationship. At the same time, though, Punter recalled very intimate details about Hurston, such as how her colorful wardrobe looked as it hung in her bedroom closet.

311 "He began to make shy overtures": ZNH, *Dust Tracks*, pp. 206–7.

311 "You passionate thing!": ZNH, *Dust Tracks*, p. 212.

312 "a maintenance engineer": Notes from Robert Hemenway's interview with Percival Punter, January 14, 1976. REH Files.

312 "nothing to offer": ZNH, *Dust Tracks*, p. 205.

312 Born in 1912: Punter's birthdate comes from the Alumni Federation Index, Columbia University. Also Punter interview, REH Files.

312 "mental youth": ZNH to Charlotte Mason, September 25, 1931. Alain Locke Papers, Howard University.

312 "People waste too much time": ZNH on relationships, in letter to Herbert Sheen, May 7, 1953. REH Files.

312 "the real love affair": ZNH, *Dust Tracks*, p. 207.

312 "Under the spell of moonlight": ZNH, *Dust Tracks*, p. 213.

313 Punter was impressed: Punter interview, 1976, REH Files.

313 "No matter which way": ZNH, *Dust Tracks*, p. 205.

313 "Celebs too numerous": ZNH to Edwin Osgood Grover, May 14, 1935. ZNH Collection, University of Florida.

313 "a flaming white dress": Bertram Lippincott interview, 1971. REH Files.

313 "And didn't our Zora": Fannie Hurst to Anne Nathan Meyer, May 13, 1935. Fannie Hurst Collection, Harry Ransom Humanities Research Center, University of Texas at Austin.

313 "I was hog-tied": ZNH, *Dust Tracks*, pp. 209–10.

314 "He was so extraordinary": ZNH, *Dust Tracks*, pp. 207–8.

314 "No woman on earth": ZNH, *Dust Tracks*, pp. 205–6.

314 "New York is not a good place": ZNH to Edwin Osgood Grover, December 29, 1935, ZNH Collection, University of Florida.

315 "I had things clawing inside of me": ZNH, *Dust Tracks*, pp. 207–8.
"We were alternately": ZNH, *Dust Tracks*, p. 209.
"Something primitive inside": Ibid.

316 "the best informed person": Alan Lomax to Oliver Strunk of the Library of Congress, August 5, 1935. Music Division, Library of Congress. Also, *Dust Tracks*, p. 209.

316 "Through Miss Hurston's influence": Alan Lomax to Oliver Strunk of the Library of Congress, August 5, 1935. Music Division, Library of Congress.

316 "They have thronged our house": Alan Lomax to John Lomax, June 18, 1935. Lomax Papers, Texas Collection, University of Texas.

317 "I am a little tardy": ZNH to Embree, June 28, 1935. Rosenwald Fund Papers, Fisk University. The novel that Hurston had drafted would become, after several revisions, *Moses, Man of the Mountain*.

318 "And leave all this good watermelon": Author interview with Anne Wilder, Fort Pierce, FL, February 1999.

318 "a temperament as big": Alan Lomax interview, 1971. REH Files.

318 "almost entirely responsible": Alan Lomax to Oliver Strunk of the Library of Congress, August 5, 1935. Music Division, Library of Congress.

318 "Our bitterest enemies": ZNH, *Dust Tracks*, pp. 209–10.

318 "I have lived thru a horrible period": ZNH to Van Vechten, September 6, 1935. Van Vechten Papers, Yale University.

319 "Go home and turn": Lewis, p. 283.

319 As a "dramatic coach": Transcript of Employment, U.S. General Services Administration, National Personnel Records Center.

319 "She was very nice": Author interview with Zora Mack Goins, June 30, 2000. See also N. Y. Nathiri, *Zora! A Woman and Her Community* (Orlando: Sentinel Communications, 1991), pp. 63–64.

320 Zora had written it: ZNH to Edwin Osgood Grover, December 29, 1935. ZNH Collection, University of Florida.

320 Hurston's bawdy, all-black version: John Houseman, *Run-Through, A Memoir* (New York: Simon & Schuster, 1972), p. 182.

320 "senior research worker": Transcript of Employment, U.S. General Services Administration, National Personnel Records Center.

CHAPTER 25

321 "A bold and beautiful book": From the book jacket of *Mules and Men*, 1935.

321 "To read *Mules and Men*": Lewis Gannett, "Books and Things," *The New York Herald Tribune Weekly Book Review*, October 11, 1935.

321 "did more than record these tales": Henry Lee Moon, "Big Old Lies," *The New Republic*, December 1, 1935.

322 "an unusual contribution": Franz Boas, preface to *Mules and Men*.

322 "the intimacy she established": Henry Lee Moon, "Big Old Lies," *The New Republic*, December 1, 1935.

322 "She has plunged into": H. I. Brock, "The Full, True Flavor of Life in a Negro Community," *The New York Times Book Review*, November 10, 1935.

322 "a very tricky dialect": Ibid.

322 "There are one or two grousing references": Sterling Brown, "Old Time Tales," *New Masses*, February 25, 1936.

323 "We talk about the race problem": "Zora Neale Hurston," in *Twentieth Century Authors*.

323 "to point out to the world": ZNH, "You Don't Know Us Negroes," unpublished article, 1934.

324 "in the crib of negroism": ZNH, *Mules and Men*, p. 1.

324 "For when a Negro author": Harold Preece, "The Negro Folk Cult," *The Crisis* 43 (December 1936).

325 "It seemed rather shameless": Rampersad, p. 153.

325 "There is certainly more outspoken": ZNH, "You Don't Know Us Negroes," unpublished article, 1934.

326 "I think that the security": Fannie Hurst, "Confidential Report on Candidate for Fellowship," December 11, 1935. Archives of the J. S. Guggenheim Foundation.

326 "Zora Hurston is one of the most important": Carl Van Vechten, "Confidential Report on Candidate for Fellowship," December 6, 1935. Archives of the J. S. Guggenheim Foundation.

326 "Miss Hurston is a thorough": Edwin Osgood Grover, "Confidential Report on Candidate for Fellowship," December 7, 1935. Archives of the J. S. Guggenheim Foundation.

327 "I think it is not saying too much": Melville Herskovits, "Confidential Report on Candidate for Fellowship," December 10, 1935. Archives of the J. S. Guggenheim Foundation.

328 "My ultimate purpose": ZNH, "Plans for Work," Guggenheim application, November 15, 1935. Archives of the J. S. Guggenheim Foundation.

328 "I made no real money": ZNH, *Dust Tracks*, p. 285.

328 "literary science": ZNH, Guggenheim application, November 15, 1935. Archives of the J. S. Guggenheim Foundation.

329 "a study of magic practices": Henry Allen Moe to ZNH, March 16, 1936. Archives of the J. S. Guggenheim Foundation.

329 "Hurrah!": Fannie Hurst to Carl Van Vechten, March 28, 1936. Fannie

Hurst Papers. Harry Ransom Humanities Research Center, University of Texas at Austin.

329 "I received the official announcement": ZNH to Moe, March 30, 1936. Archives of the J. S. Guggenheim Foundation.

329 "To me there was no conflict": ZNH, *Dust Tracks*, p. 206.

329 "As soon as he took his second degree": ZNH, *Dust Tracks*, p. 210.

330 "almost priestly": Percival Punter interview, January 14, 1976. REH Files.

330 "Weather fine": ZNH to Van Vechten, postmarked April 13, 1936. Carl Van Vechten Papers, Yale.

330 "with the eye to a good book": ZNH to Moe, undated, received May 5, 1936. Archives of the J. S. Guggenheim Foundation.

330 "Just squat down awhile": "U.S. Woman on Hoodoo Hunt in Jamaica," April 24, 1936. Kingston *Daily Gleaner*.

331 "I have corrected several": ZNH to Moe, undated, received May 5, 1936. Archives of the J. S. Guggenheim Foundation.

331 "it takes many generations": ZNH, *Tell My Horse* (New York: Harper & Row, Perennial Library Edition, 1990; originally published in 1938), pp. 6–8.

331 "Oh, these wisdom-wise Western women": ZNH, *Tell My Horse*, pp. 16–17.

331 "The wish is to bring": ZNH, *Tell My Horse*, pp. 18–20.

332 "It is a curious thing": ZNH, *Tell My Horse*, pp. 57–58.

333 "a gracious plenty": ZNH to Moe, May 22, 1936. Archives of the J. S. Guggenheim Foundation.

333 "CREDIT LETTER LOST": ZNH, cablegram to Moe, May 21, 1936. Archives of the J. S. Guggenheim Foundation.

334 "I am the most unhappy": ZNH to Moe, May 22, 1936. Archives of the J. S. Guggenheim Foundation.

334 "Visiting Lady Writer": Kingston *Daily Gleaner*, undated typescript of article. Archives of the J. S. Guggenheim Foundation.

334 "I feel that I have no talents": ZNH to Moe, May 28, 1936. Archives of the J. S. Guggenheim Foundation.

334 "Don't feel so sad": Moe to ZNH, June 3, 1936. Archives of the J. S. Guggenheim Foundation.

334 "It has occurred to me": ZNH to Moe, June 10, 1936. Archives of the J. S. Guggenheim Foundation.

335 "so many weird": ZNH to Moe, May 22, 1936. Archives of the J. S. Guggenheim Foundation.

335 "The only thing": ZNH, *Tell My Horse*, pp. 21–22.

335 "She had been there for a month": ZNH to Moe, September 24, 1936. Archives of the J. S. Guggenheim Foundation.

335 "If I do not see a dance": ZNH to Moe, May 22, 1936. ZNH, *Tell My Horse*, p. 22.

335 "ceased chirping": ZNH, *Tell My Horse*, pp. 29–30.

336 "I had never pictured anything": ZNH, *Tell My Horse*, p. 35.

336 "one of the most exciting things": ZNH to Moe, January 6, 1937. Archives of the J. S. Guggenheim Foundation.

336 "worth a year's study": ZNH to Moe, May 22, 1936. Archives of the J. S. Guggenheim Foundation.

336 complex voodoo beliefs of Haiti: Throughout this account, I use spellings current in Hurston's time for the names of the loas (now called lwas), which were modified in 1990 when the new Haitian Creole orthography was introduced. I also use Hurston's spelling of "voodoo," though the religion's adherents today prefer to spell it "Vodou."

337 "I know that thousands": ZNH to Moe, October 14, 1936. Archives of the J. S. Guggenheim Foundation.

337 "The plot was far": ZNH, *Dust Tracks*, p. 175, pp. 210–11.

CHAPTER 26

338 "in the heart of Africa": ZNH to Moe, January 6, 1937. Archives of the J. S. Guggenheim Foundation.

338 "a peace I have never known": ZNH, *Tell My Horse*, p. 135.

339 "the old, old mysticism": ZNH, *Tell My Horse*, p. 113.

339 "It is like explaining": ZNH to Moe, January 6, 1937. Archives of the J. S. Guggenheim Foundation.

339 "Voodoo is a religion": ZNH, *Tell My Horse*, p. 113.

339 "I beg the opportunity": ZNH to Moe, January 6, 1937. Archives of the J. S. Guggenheim Foundation.

340 "Haiti is so thrillingly real": ZNH to Moe, March 20, 1937. Archives of the J. S. Guggenheim Foundation.

340 "with no effort": Lippincott interview, REH Files.

340 "ideal of achievement": ZNH to Moe, March 20, 1937. Archives of the J. S. Guggenheim Foundation.

341 "there have been repercussions": ZNH to Moe, July 6, 1937. Archives of the J. S. Guggenheim Foundation.

341 "drenched in kindliness": ZNH, *Tell My Horse*, p. 259.

341 "his soul and his peace": ZNH, *Tell My Horse*, p. 252.

341 "a religion no more venal": ZNH, *Tell My Horse*, p. 204.

341 After being claimed: Hurston is extremely vague about her own initiation into the mysteries of voodoo, mentioning it only briefly in *Tell My Horse*, pp. 173–74.

342 "You are liable to get involved": ZNH, *Tell My Horse*, p. 189.

342 "Some things are very dangerous": ZNH, *Tell My Horse*, pp. 200–201.

342 "the two offices occupy the same man": ZNH, *Tell My Horse*, pp. 189, 204.

343 "Perhaps it will cost you": ZNH, *Tell My Horse*, pp. 205–6.

343 "It seems that": ZNH to Moe, July 6, 1937. Archives of the J. S. Guggenheim Foundation.

344 "I am sleeping and eating": Ibid.

344 "I am <u>extremely pleased</u>": Ibid.

344 "You have complete liberty": Moe to ZNH, July 9, 1937. Archives of the J. S. Guggenheim Foundation.

344 "It is swelling up in me": ZNH to Moe, August 26, 1937. Archives of the J. S. Guggenheim Foundation.

345 "a lovely book": Sheila Hibben, "Vibrant Book Full of Nature and Salt," *The New York Herald Tribune Weekly Book Review*, September 26, 1937.

345 "This is Zora Hurston's third novel": Lucille Tomkins, untitled review, *The New York Times Book Review*, September 26, 1937. Actually, it was Hurston's second novel, but her third published book.

347 "you got tuh *go* there": All quotes in this summary are taken from ZNH, *Their Eyes Were Watching God* (New York: HarperPerennial, 1990). Originally published by J. B. Lippincott, 1937.

348 a book of transcendent appeal: *Their Eyes Were Watching God* has received an abundance of critical attention. Various interpretations on all aspects of the story abound. Among the critical treatments that have influenced my own reading of the novel, as reflected in this discussion: Hemenway, *Zora Neale Hurston: A Literary Biography*; Deborah G. Plant, *Every Tub Must Sit on Its Own Bottom: The Philosophy and Politics of Zora Neale Hurston*; Sherley Anne Williams, foreword to 1978 University of Illinois Press edition of *Their Eyes Were Watching God*; Cheryl A. Wall, "Zora Neale Hurston: Changing Her Own Words"; Mary Helen Washington, "'I Love the Way Janie Crawford Left Her Husbands': Emergent Female Hero"; Henry Louis Gates, Jr., "*Their Eyes Were Watching God*: Hurston and the Speakerly Text"; Cynthia Bond, "Language, Speech, and Difference in *Their Eyes Were Watching God*"; Maria Tai Wolff, "Listening and Living: Reading and Experience in *Their Eyes Were Watching God*." Many of the essays mentioned here have been collected in *Zora Neale Hurston: Critical Perspectives Past and Present*, edited by Henry Louis Gates, Jr,. and K. A. Appiah (New York: Amistad Press, 1993). Also see Barbara Johnson, "Metaphor, Metonymy and Voice in *Their Eyes Were Watching God*," in *Black Literature and Literary Theory*, edited by Henry Louis Gates, Jr. (New York: Methuen, 1984.)

349 "most successful": June Jordan, "On Richard Wright and Zora Neale Hurston: Notes Toward a Balancing of Love and Hatred," *Black World*, August 1974.

349 protest literature: I am grateful to Lucy Hurston, Zora's niece, for our discussions about this aspect of the novel. I would argue that "Sweat" and 1933's "The Gilded Six-Bits" could be read as protest literature as well, for similar reasons. For further discussion of this idea, see David Headon, "'Beginning to See Things Really': The Politics of Zora Neale Hurston," in Glassman and Seidel, eds., *Zora in Florida*.

350 "The author does not dwell": Sterling Brown, "Luck Is a Fortune," *The Nation*, October 16, 1937.

350 "They's mighty particular": ZNH, *Their Eyes Were Watching God*, p. 163.

350 "Only a few self-conscious Negroes": ZNH, "You Don't Know Us Negroes," unpublished article, 1934.

350 "These sitters had been": ZNH, *Their Eyes Were Watching God*, p. 1.

351 "affirmation of black values": June Jordan, "On Richard Wright and Zora Neale Hurston: Notes Toward a Balancing of Love and Hatred," *Black World*, August 1974.

351 "Miss Hurston seems": Richard Wright, "Between Laughter and Tears," *New Masses*, October 5, 1937.

351 "a very fine American novel": Sterling Brown interview, April 29, 1971. REH Files.

351 Hurston wrote a playful profile: ZNH, "Fannie Hurst: By Her Ex-Amanuensis," *The Saturday Review of Literature*, October 9, 1937.

352 "I must look": ZNH to Edwin Osgood Grover, October 23, 1937. ZNH Collection, University of Florida.

352 "God does love": ZNH to Hurst, October 15, 1937. Fannie Hurst Papers. Harry Ransom Humanities Research Center, University of Texas at Austin.

352 "Not because I didn't want to": ZNH, *Dust Tracks*, p. 211.

352 "good singing": ZNH to Van Vechten, November 5, 1937. Van Vechten Papers, Yale.

352 "My publishers insist": ZNH to Van Vechten, December 1, 1937. Van Vechten Papers, Yale.

353 "gift for poetic phrase": Alain Locke, untitled review, *Opportunity*, January 1938.

353 "I wish that I could write it": ZNH, *Dust Tracks*, p. 175.

354 "in his eagerness to attract attention": ZNH, "The Chick with One Hen," unpublished essay, early 1938. James Weldon Johnson Correspondence, Yale.

354 "I get tired of the envious": ZNH to Johnson, undated. James Weldon Johnson Correspondence, Yale.

354 "a dyed-in-the-wool": Claude McKay to Locke, quoted in Lewis, p. 153.

354 "failure as a writer": Jessie Fauset to Locke, quoted in Lewis, pp. 274–75.

354 "So far as the young writers are concerned": ZNH to Johnson, undated. James Weldon Johnson Correspondence, Yale.

355 "I dislike cold weather": ZNH, quoted in *Twentieth Century American Authors*, 1942,

355 "too hurried before": ZNH to Edwin Osgood Grover, October 23, 1937. ZNH Collection, University of Florida.

CHAPTER 27

356 "When will the Negro novelist": Alain Locke, untitled review, *Opportunity*, January 1938.

356 "Can the black poet": ZNH, "Art and Such," essay written for the Florida Federal Writers' Project, 1938. (Published posthumously in *Hurston: Folklore, Memoirs & Other Writings*, edited by Cheryl Wall. Also published in Gates, ed., *Reading Black, Reading Feminist*.)

356 "the maximum degree": Richard Wright, "Blueprint for Negro Writing," originally published in *New Challenge*, 1937. Reprinted in *The Portable Harlem Renaissance Reader*, edited by David Levering Lewis.

357 "love and hate and fight": ZNH, "Art and Such," essay written for the Florida Federal Writers' Project, 1938.

357 "Can the black poet sing": Ibid.

358 "to give a true picture": ZNH to Moe, January 6, 1937. Archives of the J. S. Guggenheim Foundation.

358 "I have so much material now": ZNH to Edwin Osgood Grover, October 23, 1937. ZNH Collection, University of Florida.

358 "It was to be half and half": ZNH to Moe, January 6, 1937. Archives of the J. S. Guggenheim Foundation.

358 *Uncle Tom's Children*: Hazel Rowley, *Richard Wright: The Life and Times* (New York: Henry Holt, 2001), p. 139.

359 "This is a book about hatreds": ZNH, "Stories of Conflict," *The Saturday Review of Literature*, April 2, 1938.

359 "so vivid": Eleanor Roosevelt, "My Day," *New York World-Telegram*, April 1, 1938. Quoted in Rowley.

359 "The U.S. has never had": "White Fog," *Time*, March 28, 1938.

359 Hurston declined: For a comprehensive account of Hurston's work with the Federal Writers' Project, see biographical essay in Bordelon, *Go Gator and Muddy the Water*.

360 "Most of the entire population": Stetson Kennedy interview, "The WPA Guide to Florida," *Florida Forum*. Undated clipping from the ZNH Collection, Rollins College Archive.

360 "housewives with a high school education": Stetson Kennedy, "Florida

Folklife and the WPA, An Introduction," in *A Reference Guide to Florida Folklore from the Federal WPA*. Florida State Archives, Department of State.

360 "one person of writing and editorial ability": Henry Alsberg, quoted in Bordelon, *Go Gator*, p. 15.

361 the Florida FWP hired: Transcript of Employment, U.S. General Services Administration, National Personnel Records Center.

361 "Manuscripts from the Negro Unit": Stetson Kennedy, "Florida Folklife and the WPA, An Introduction," in *A Reference Guide to Florida Folklore from the Federal WPA*. Florida State Archives, Department of State.

361 "Unaccustomed as we were": Ibid.

361 "We were sort of bemused": Stetson Kennedy interview, "The WPA Guide to Florida," *Florida Forum*. Undated clipping from the ZNH Collection, Rollins College Archive.

362 "great verve": Carita Dogget Corse interview, conducted by Robert E. Hemenway. February 25, 1971. REH Files.

362 "We sat in the back": Ibid.

362 "dance-possible": ZNH, "The Sanctified Church," 1938. Published in *Hurston: Folklore, Memoirs & Other Writings*, edited by Cheryl Wall. Also published in Bordelon, *Go Gator*.

362 "a very dynamic": Corse interview, REH Files.

363 some five hundred participants: "Zora Hurston's Chanters Offer Concert Sponsored by Rollins Folk-Lore Group," *Sentinel Star*, May 1, 1938.

363 he wrote to Corse: Alsberg to Corse, June 21, 1938, Central Correspondence, FWP, National Archives.

363 "Although Zora was frequently": Stetson Kennedy, "Florida Folklife and the WPA, An Introduction," in *A Reference Guide to Florida Folklore from the Federal WPA*. Florida State Archives, Department of State.

364 "The man is just full": ZNH, *Dust Tracks*, p. 238. This essay, "My People, My People!" was written as a stand-alone piece, dated July 2, 1937. It was printed in recent editions of *Dust Tracks* in the appendix, as part of the restored text established by the Library of America.

365 "When she wanted to dress": Winifred Hurston Clark, quoted in Bordelon, "New Tracks on Dust Tracks." Also see Bordelon biographical essay on Hurston, *Go Gator*.

365 one photograph from 1938: Beyond the photograph, no information has been found about this performance. I am grateful to historian/archivist Herman "Skip" Mason for bringing this photograph to my attention and for granting me permission to publish it in this book.

365 "Every now and then": ZNH to Corse, December 3, 1938, ZNH Collection, University of Florida.

365 "In response to my letters": Stetson Kennedy, "Florida Folklife and the WPA, An Introduction," in *A Reference Guide to Florida Folklore from the Federal WPA*. Florida State Archives, Department of State.

366 Hurston told the story: ZNH, "The Ocoee Riot," 1938. Published in *Hurston: Folklore, Memoirs & Other Writings*, edited by Cheryl Wall.

366 "The white/black relationship": Stetson Kennedy, "Florida Folklife and the WPA, An Introduction."

366 "businesslike" prayers and songs: ZNH, "The Sanctified Church," 1938.

366 "a nine-page diatribe": Kennedy, "Florida Folklife and the WPA, An Introduction."

367 "the boiled-down juice": ZNH, "Go Gator and Muddy the Water," 1938. Published in Bordelon, *Go Gator*.

367 "all unpleasant doings": ZNH, "Negro Mythical Places," 1938. Published in Bordelon, *Go Gator*.

367 "Jim Crow kept watch": Kennedy, "Florida Folklife and the WPA, An Introduction."

367 "she'd come back": Corse interview, REH Files.

368 "The South has no interest": ZNH, "The 'Pet Negro' System," *The American Mercury*, May 1943.

368 "the deification of": ZNH, *Tell My Horse*, pp. 219–24.

369 "This work does not pretend": ZNH, *Tell My Horse*, p. 131.

370 "disorganized but interesting": Untitled review in *The New Yorker*, October 15, 1938. *The New York Times* review quoted on *Tell My Horse* book jacket.

370 "That Miss Hurston loves": Elmer Davis, "Witchcraft in the Caribbean Islands," *The Saturday Review of Literature*, October 15, 1938.

370 "Seldom has there been": Carl Carmer, untitled review, *The New York Herald Tribune*, October 23, 1938.

370 when the book was published in England: ZNH to Edwin Osgood Grover, October 12, 1939. The book was published in London on May 4. ZNH Collection, University of Florida.

371 "the most exquisite things": Corse interview, REH Files.

371 "Those were the days": Stetson Kennedy, "Florida Folklife and the WPA, An Introduction."

372 Hurston finally got a raise: Transcript of Employment, U.S. General Services Administration, National Personnel Records Center.

372 "There is a grave": Stetson Kennedy, "Florida Folklife and the WPA, An Introduction."

372 "The terrorism was real": Ibid.

374 "I just get in a crowd": From the 1939 Jacksonville recording session, audio-tape copy from the Library of Congress. Transcription by author.

374 On the marriage license: Marriage License, Albert Price III and ZNH,

June 27, 1939. Marriage Book 10, p. 148 (Court Records, Nassau County, FL).

374 "a smooth brown": Author interview with Hortense Williams Gray, Jacksonville, FL, February 5, 1999.

374 "Aunt Zora doesn't": Winifred Hurston Clark, quoted in Bordelon, "New Tracks on *Dust Tracks*," *African American Review*.

375 "an average-size": Author interview with Hortense Williams Gray, Jacksonville, FL, February 5, 1999.

375 "all that she wanted": Zora Neale Hurston Price vs. Albert Price, Answer and Counter Claim, April 1, 1940. Circuit Court of Duval County, FL.

375 "I was compelled": Zora Neale Hurston Price vs. Albert Price, Special Master's Report, November 9, 1943. Circuit Court of Duval County, FL.

375 "obscene language": Zora Neale Hurston Price vs. Albert Price, Bill for Divorce, February 9, 1940. Circuit Court of Duval County, FL.

375 she left her job: Transcript of Employment, U.S. General Services Administration, National Personnel Records Center.

CHAPTER 28

376 "a one-horse religious school": ZNH, "The 'Pet Negro' System," *The American Mercury*, May 1943.

377 "We are going to try": ZNH, quoted in "Drama Group Concludes Meet; Zora Neale Hurston Featured: Noted Negro Author Outlines Plans for Native Drama," *The Daily Tar Heel*, October 8, 1939.

377 "Hi, nigger!": Don Pope to Robert E. Hemenway, undated letter. REH Files. Paul Green also recalled this story in an interview, April 6, 1971. REH Files.

377 "We want to follow": ZNH, quoted in "Drama Group Concludes Meet; Zora Neale Hurston Featured: Noted Negro Author Outlines Plans for Native Drama," *The Daily Tar Heel*, October 8, 1939.

377 "She had serious points": Don Pope to Robert E. Hemenway, undated letter. REH Files.

378 "As a child I couldn't see": Paul Green interview, April 6, 1971. REH Files.

378 "I think that is": ZNH to Edwin Osgood Grover, October 12, 1939. ZNH Collection, University of Florida.

378 "Green, with his Carolina country drawl": Don Pope to Robert E. Hemenway, undated letter. REH Files.

378 "very funny, ironic": Ibid.

378 "It still doesn't say": ZNH to Edwin Osgood Grover, October 12, 1939. ZNH Collection, University of Florida.

379 "a remarkable book": Lippincott to Van Vechten, October 4, 1939. Van Vechten Papers, Yale.

379 "I fell far short": ZNH to Van Vechten, October 12, 1939. Van Vechten Papers, Yale.

380 "Wherever the children of Africa": ZNH, Introduction to *Moses, Man of the Mountain*, 1939.

380 Hurston's Moses: Though this novel has received scant critical attention, my analysis of *Moses* has been influenced by several important sources: Deborah G. Plant, *Every Tub Must Sit on Its Own Bottom*; Robert E. Hemenway, *Zora Neale Hurston: A Literary Biography*; Deborah E. McDowell, "Lines of Descent/Dissenting Lines," published in Gates and Appiah, *Zora Neale Hurston: Critical Perspectives*.

380 merely a good joke: Darwin Turner, in a particularly hostile essay on Hurston, praises *Moses* for its humor and calls it Hurston's master work. Still, he says the novel "does not comment significantly on life or people," adding "a good joke, at best, is merely a joke." Turner, *In a Minor Chord: Three Afro-American Writers and Their Search for Identity* (Carbondale: Southern Illinois University Press, 1971).

381 "Ho, ho! Pharaoh": ZNH, *Moses, Man of the Mountain*, 1939 (New York: HarperPerennial, 1991), p. 78. All quotes in this plot summary are from that edition of the novel.

386 "It is not a logically projected work": Louis Untermeyer, "Old Testament Voodoo," *The Saturday Review of Literature*, November 11, 1939.

386 "It is warm with friendly personality": Percy Hutchison, untitled review, *The New York Times Book Review*, November 19, 1939.

387 "a fine Negro novel": Carl Carmer, untitled review, *The New York Herald Tribune*, November 26, 1939.

387 "caricature instead of portraiture": Alain Locke, "Dry Fields and Green Pastures," *Opportunity*, January 1940.

387 "For Negro fiction": Ralph Ellison, "Recent Negro Fiction," *New Masses*, August 5, 1941.

387 "I have the feeling": ZNH to Edwin Osgood Grover, October 12, 1939. ZNH Collection, University of Florida.

388 North Carolina College for Negroes: This institution is now called North Carolina Central University.

388 "She had the president": Arna Bontemps interview, December 18, 1970. REH Files.

388 "She gave me a wonderful time": Arna Bontemps to Langston Hughes, November 29, 1939. Nichols, pp. 43–44.

389 "Have you heard": Van Vechten to Hughes, December 3, 1939. Bernard, p. 158.

389 "Just in your last letter": Hughes to Van Vechten, December 15, 1939. Bernard, p. 165.

389 "the meek and humble type": Zora Neale Hurston Price vs. Albert Price, Bill for Divorce, February 9, 1940. Circuit Court of Duval County, FL.

389 "power both in spirits": Zora Neale Hurston Price vs. Albert Price, Answer and Counter Claim, April 1, 1940. Circuit Court of Duval County, FL.

389 granted her petition: Special Master's Report, November 9, 1943. Final Decree of Divorce, November 9, 1943. Circuit Court of Duval County, FL. The divorce was not finalized until three years after Hurston filed for it; this, along with a statement she makes in the Special Master's Report, indicates that she and Price may have reconciled temporarily and that he accompanied her on a summer research trip to Beaufort, SC.

389 "the perfect man": ZNH, *Dust Tracks*, p. 212.

391 "Well, to tell you the truth": ZNH to Jane Belo, March 20, 1940. Margaret Mead Papers, Manuscript Division, Library of Congress.

391 "she was as cute": Paul Green interview, April 6, 1971. REH Files.

391 "staid and tyrannical": Author interview with Alex Rivera, March 13, 1998.

391 "certain things would not": Author interview with Brooklyn T. McMillon, March 13, 1998.

391 "social intercourse": Undated letter from Dr. James E. Shepard addressed to faculty. Library of North Carolina Central University (formerly North Carolina College for Negroes).

391 "She was a bit advanced": Adelle Ferguson Lafayette to Robert Hemenway, March 25, 1971. REH Files.

392 "she upset things": Author interview with Alex Rivera, March 13, 1998.

392 "These courses are not only basic": ZNH to James E. Shepard, December 14, 1939. Paul Green Papers, UNC–Chapel Hill.

393 "If you have decided": ZNH to Paul Green, January 24, 1940. Paul Green Papers, UNC–Chapel Hill.

393 "When those two personalities": Author interview with Alex Rivera, March 13, 1998.

393 "Then I will tell you": ZNH to Fannie Hurst, February 6, 1940. Harry Ransom Center, University of Texas, Austin.

CHAPTER 29

395 "In this church": ZNH, field notes, "Ritualistic Expression From the Lips of the Communicants of the Seventh Day Church of God, Beaufort, South Carolina." Manuscript Division, Library of Congress.

395 "We got some perfectly grand stuff": Jane Belo to Carl Van Vechten, July 7, 1940. Van Vechten Papers, Yale.

395 "On the Fourth of July": ZNH, field notes, "Ritualistic Expression From the

Lips of the Communicants of the Seventh Day Church of God, Beaufort, South Carolina." Manuscript Division, Library of Congress.

396 "God knows": Belo to Van Vechten, July 7, 1940. Van Vechten Papers, Yale.

396 "by two very enthusiastic Jews": ZNH to Paul Green, May 3, 1940. Paul Green Papers, UNC–Chapel Hill.

396 "We can't let": ZNH to Green, May 3, 1940. Paul Green Papers, UNC–Chapel Hill.

396 "Good going": Green to ZNH, undated wire. Paul Green Papers, UNC–Chapel Hill.

396 "Please send the men": ZNH to Belo, May 2, 1940. Margaret Mead Papers, Library of Congress.

397 "a nice little Jewish boy": Belo to ZNH, April 29, 1940. Margaret Mead Papers, Library of Congress.

397 Hurston participated fully: ZNH footage, May 1940. From the Norman Chalfin Collection, Library of Congress.

397 "Without Zora": Norman Chalfin to Jane Belo, May 20, 1940. Margaret Mead Papers, Library of Congress.

397 various projects: Norman Chalfin to Bess Hawes, October 31, 1989. Library of Congress.

398 "a blend of disingenuousness": Arnold Rampersad, *The Life of Langston Hughes*, vol. 1, p. 388.

398 "Girls are funny creatures!": Hughes, *The Big Sea*, p. 332. ZNH to Fannie Hurst, August 4, 1940. Fannie Hurst Papers, Harry Ransom Center, University of Texas.

398 *Native Son* sold 215,000 copies: Rowley, pp. 179–94.

398 "I have the uncomfortable feeling": ZNH to Green, March 21, 1940. Paul Green Papers, UNC–Chapel Hill.

399 "God's image of a friend": ZNH, in dedication for *Tell My Horse*.

399 "I was so conditioned": Paul Green interview, April 6, 1971. REH Files.

399 "a nice quiet place to work": ZNH to Fannie Hurst, August 4, 1940. Fannie Hurst Papers, Harry Ransom Center, University of Texas.

400 "That made me happy": ZNH, *Dust Tracks*, p. 211.

400 "She fed me well": ZNH, *Dust Tracks*, p. 273.

401 "Cock Robin Beale Street": ZNH, "Cock Robin Beale Street," 1941. *The Complete Stories*, pp. 122–26.

401 "To my notion": ZNH, *Dust Tracks*, p. 274.

401 "a writer and technical adviser": Paramount contract, as summarized by Barbara Hall, Research Archivist, Margaret Herrick Library, Academy of Motion Picture Arts and Sciences.

401 Equivalent to $1,200 today: Economic History Resources, "How Much Is That?" Conversion Calculator.

402 "This job here at the studio": ZNH to Edwin Osgood Grover, December 30, 1941. ZNH Collection, University of Florida.

402 "I see that the high principles": ZNH, *Dust Tracks*, pp. 258, 261.

403 "the best presented by television": Eva Jessye and Charlie Spears, "Mamba's Daughters Star Repeats Her Success in New Role," *Pittsburgh Courier*, July 8, 1939.

403 "just like watching": ZNH, *Dust Tracks*, p. 199.

403 "You know I can give a guy": Ethel Waters, quoted in Ted Poston, "The Musical Comedy Audience Gets Blue When a Singer Goes Into a High Hat Show: Harlem Thinks Ethel Was Just as Hot as a Torch," *New York Post*, January 12, 1939.

404 "I don't lament the prejudice": Ethel Waters, *Current Biography*, 1942.

404 "Don't care how good": ZNH, *Dust Tracks*, pp. 199–202.

404 "dynamic informality": "Zora Hurston at Tuskegee; Tells of Haitian Customs," *Afro-American* (Baltimore), April 18, 1942.

404 "keep on eating": ZNH to Moe, June 25, 1942. Archives of the J. S. Guggenheim Foundation.

404 "Oh, my God, I've done": Norton Baskin interview, February 27, 1971. REH Files.

405 "She really was just sensational": Norton Baskin interview, February 27, 1971. REH Files.

405 "a lush, fine-looking": Marjorie Kinnan Rawlings to Norman Berg, July 7, 1942. Gordon E. Bigelow and Laura V. Monti, ed., *Selected Letters of Marjorie Kinnan Rawlings* (Gainesville: University Press of Florida, 1983), pp. 222–23.

406 "an older woman": Author interview with Hortense Williams Gray, February 5, 1999.

406 "Some of them bound": ZNH, "Story in Harlem Slang," *The American Mercury*, July 1942. Reprinted in *The Complete Stories*.

407 "You crazy in the head?": ZNH, "Now You Cookin' with Gas" and "Harlem Slanguage," 1942. Published in *The Complete Stories*.

408 "a distinguished Negro novelist": ZNH, "Lawrence of the River," *Saturday Evening Post*, September 5, 1942.

408 "She has lived in primitive simplicity": Flap copy from first edition, *Dust Tracks on a Road*, J. B. Lippincott Company, 1942.

408 "The worst thing Ah ever knowed": ZNH, *Their Eyes Were Watching God*, p. 3.

409 "no lurid tales to tell": ZNH, *Dust Tracks*, p. 139.

409 "Now, women forget all those things": ZNH, *Their Eyes Were Watching God*, p. 1.

410 "Memoir writers must manufacture": William Zinsser, Introduction,

Inventing the Truth: The Art and Craft of Memoir (Boston, New York: Houghton Mifflin, 1998), p. 6.

410 "imaginative autobiography": I am grateful to Dr. Jerry Ward for discussions about Wright's concept of an "imaginative autobiography."

411 "I did not want to write it all": ZNH to Hamilton Holt, February 11, 1943. ZNH Collection, University of Florida.

411 "What will be the end?": ZNH, *Dust Tracks*, p. 211.

411 "the theory behind our tactics": ZNH, *Mules and Men*, p. 3.

412 "a great American success story": Mary Margaret McBride, in radio interview with ZNH, January 25, 1943. Library of Congress.

412 "What do I want, then?": ZNH, *Dust Tracks*, pp. 230–31.

413 "I wrote a chapter": ZNH to Van Vechten, November 2, 1942. Hurston Collection, Yale.

413 "Now, I look like a hog": ZNH to Hamilton Holt, February 11, 1943. ZNH Collection, University of Florida.

413 "Popes and Prelates": ZNH, *Dust Tracks*, p. 256. Restored text established by the Library of America.

413 "good laxatives for heathens": ZNH, *Dust Tracks*, p. 259.

413 "Anyone would be a liar": ZNH, *Dust Tracks*, pp. 262–63.

414 "And how can Race Solidarity be possible": ZNH, *Dust Tracks*, p. 251.

414 "I just think it would be": ZNH, *Dust Tracks*, pp. 261–62.

414 "If you are better than I": ZNH, *Dust Tracks*, p. 253.

414 "Miss Hurston deals": Arna Bontemps, "From Eatonville, Florida to Harlem," *The New York Herald Tribune*, November 22, 1942.

415 "There were book buyers": Bertram Lippincott interview, undated. REH Files.

415 "I know that there is race prejudice": ZNH, *Dust Tracks*, p. 253.

416 "I have no race prejudice": ZNH, *Dust Tracks*, pp. 231–32.

416 "charming practicality": Phil Strong, "Zora Hurston Sums Up," *The Saturday Review of Literature*, November 28, 1942.

417 "an encouraging and enjoyable one": Beatrice Sherman, "Zora Hurston's Story," *The New York Times Book Review*, November 29, 1942.

417 "a masterpiece of understanding": Edwin Osgood Grover to ZNH, November 12, 1942. ZNH Collection, University of Florida.

CHAPTER 30

418 "working harder and more consistently": ZNH to Edwin Osgood Grover, December 10, 1942. ZNH Collection, University of Florida.

418 "Do you think": ZNH to Van Vechten, November 2, 1942. Hurston Collection, Yale.

419 "a galaxy of socialites": *New York Age*, November 28, 1942, quoted in Bernard, p. 212.

419 "I ached in my heart": ZNH to Locke, January 10, 1942. Alain Locke Papers, Howard University.

419 "Isn't it grand!": Van Vechten to Harold Jackman, November 1942, Countee Cullen Collection, Atlanta University.

419 "Zora Neale Hurston's books": George Pfeiffer III to Edwin Osgood Grover, November 4, 1942. ZNH Collection, University of Florida.

419 "the best book": Grover to Pfeiffer, November 12, 1942. ZNH Collection, University of Florida.

420 "Don't serve any more time": Grover to ZNH, November 22, 1942. ZNH Collection, University of Florida.

420 "I cannot forbear to write": Hamilton Holt to ZNH, January 27, 1943. ZNH Collection, University of Florida.

420 "Born so widely apart": ZNH, *Dust Tracks*, p. 268.

420 "You will never know": ZNH to Locke, January 10, 1943. Alain Locke Papers, Howard University.

421 "I wanted macaroni": ZNH in radio interview with Mary Margaret McBride, January 25, 1943. Library of Congress.

421 "The lot of the Negro": Douglas Gilbert, "When Negro Succeeds, South Is Proud, Zora Hurston Says," *The New York World-Telegram*, February 1, 1943.

422 "Miss Hurston is a bright person": Roy Wilkins, "The Watchtower," *Amsterdam News*, February 27, 1943.

423 "the genius Millay": ZNH to Van Vechten, February 15, 1943. Hurston Collection, Yale.

423 "The article is untrue": "Zora Hurston Denies Saying Race Better Off in South," *Atlanta Daily World*, March 3, 1943.

425 "slippery word": ZNH, "A Negro Voter Sizes Up Taft," *Saturday Evening Post*, December 8, 1951.

425 "individualist": For further discussion of Hurston's "individualist" politics, see Deborah G. Plant, *Every Tub Must Sit On Its Own Bottom*.

426 "any means necessary": Malcolm X, December 3, 1964, quoted in *By Any Means Necessary: Speeches, Interviews, and a Letter by Malcolm X*. Edited by George Breitman (New York: Pathfinder, 1970).

426 "My stand is this": ZNH to Countee Cullen, March 5, 1943. Hurston Papers, Tulane.

426 "No man may make another": ZNH, *Moses*, p. 282.

426 "they had songs and singers": Ibid., pp. 259, 283.

427 "Liberate the self": David Headon, "'Beginning to See Things Really': The Politics of Zora Neale Hurston," in Glassman and Seidel, eds., *Zora in Florida*.

427 "an admirable autobiography": *Saturday Review*, February 20, 1943.

427 "The minute I have": ZNH to Hamilton Holt, February 11, 1943. ZNH Collection, University of Florida.

427 "I want my residence": ZNH, *Twentieth Century American Authors*, 1942.

427 "All the other boat-owners": ZNH to Marjorie Kinnan Rawlings, August 21, 1943. ZNH Collection, University of Florida.

427 "as broke as a he-hant": ZNH to Ben Botkin, July 25, 1943. Archive of Folk Song, Library of Congress.

428 "I have that solitude": ZNH to Rawlings, August 21, 1943. ZNH Collection, University of Florida.

428 "Literary secret": ZNH to Rawlings, May 16, 1943. ZNH Collection, University of Florida.

428 "a falsely morbid picture": ZNH to Edwin Osgood Grover, November 7, 1943. ZNH Collection, University of Florida.

428 "You have written the best thing": ZNH to Rawlings, May 16, 1943. ZNH Collection, University of Florida.

428 "He was top-superior": ZNH, "High John De Conquer," *The American Mercury*, October 1943.

429 "sugared up to flatter": ZNH to Locke, July 23, 1943. Alain Locke Papers, Howard University.

429 "Freedom's Plow": Langston Hughes, quoted in Arnold Rampersad, *The Life of Langston Hughes, Volume II: I Dream a World* (New York, Oxford: Oxford University Press, 1988), pp. 56–58.

429 "have put our labor and our blood": ZNH, "High John De Conquer," *The American Mercury*, October 1943.

430 "a fixed idea": ZNH to Locke, July 23, 1943. Alain Locke Papers, Howard University.

430 "I was glad to see": ZNH to Edwin Osgood Grover, November 7, 1943. ZNH Collection, University of Florida.

431 "In those days": Interview with Mary Holland, undated. REH Files.

431 "Z. Hurston to Wed": *Amsterdam News*, Feb. 5, 1944.

431 she married Pitts: Information on Hurston's third and previously unknown marriage is taken from records provided by the Clerk of the Court, Volusia County, Deland, Florida.

432 "Who is Dorothy Waring": Carl Van Vechten to Harold Jackman, Aug. 3, 1944. Countee Cullen Collection, Atlanta University.

432 "a sort of Gershwinesque feeling": Dorothy Waring interview, May 21, 1971. REH Files. "Polk County" was never produced in Hurston's lifetime. A shortened adaptation of the four-hour play received its world premiere at the Arena Stage in Washington, D.C., in the spring of 2002.

433 "the various natural expressions": ZNH to Henry Allen Moe, September 8, 1944. Archives of the J. S. Guggenheim Foundation.

CHAPTER 31

434 "even if I have to toe-nail it": ZNH to Henry Allen Moe, September 8, 1944. Archives of the J. S. Guggenheim Foundation

434 Her plan was to collect folklore: Ibid.

435 "Have you a motion picture camera": ZNH to Jane Belo, October 1, 1944. Margaret Mead Papers, Library of Congress.

435 "I have sold my car": Ibid.

436 "I must hoard every penny": ZNH to Ben Botkin, October 6, 1944. Archive of Folk Song, Library of Congress.

436 "this boat is rearing": ZNH to Belo, October 18, 1944. Margaret Mead Papers, Library of Congress.

436 "I went away feeling the pathos": ZNH, "My Most Humiliating Jim Crow Experience," *Negro Digest*, June 1944.

436 "These do be times": ZNH to Botkin, October 6, 1944. Archive of Folk Song, Library of Congress.

437 "I love sunshine": ZNH, *Twentieth Century American Authors*, 1942. Also, ZNH to Jane Belo, October 18, 1944. Margaret Mead Papers, Library of Congress.

437 "I have been sick": ZNH to Van Vechten, July 15, 1945. Hurston Collection, Yale.

437 "No, I have not tried any of it": ZNH to Van Vechten, July 24, 1945. Hurston Collection, Yale.

438 "the publishers seem frightened": ZNH to W.E.B. Du Bois, June 11, 1945. Tulane.

438 "little else besides its FOUNDER": ZNH, "The Rise of the Begging Joints," *The American Mercury*, March 1945.

439 "There is over-simplification": "Zora Neale Hurston Reveals Key to Her Literary Success," *Amsterdam News*, November 18, 1944.

439 "a serious one on the upper stata": ZNH to Van Vechten, September 12, 1945. Hurston Collection, Yale.

439 "Zora was a natural writing genius": Bertram Lippincott interview, 1970s. Also Lippincott to Robert E. Hemenway, October 27, 1970. REH Files.

440 She stayed afloat: ZNH, "The Negro in the United States," *Encyclopedia Americana*, 1947. And ZNH, "Negroes," in Charles Earle Funk and Henry Wysham Lanier, eds., *The New International Year Book* (New York: Funk & Wagnalls, 1946).

440 "I am crazy about the idea": ZNH, "Crazy For This Democracy," *Negro Digest*, December 1945.

441 "depressed and distressed": ZNH to Tracy L'Engle, October 24 and November 4, 1945. Tracy L'Engle Papers, University of Florida.

441 "It was tough and rough": ZNH to Tracy L'Engle, February 19, 1946. Tracy L'Engle Papers, University of Florida.

442 "favorite poet": ZNH to Countee Cullen, March 5, 1943, Tulane.

442 "trade, profession, or particular kind of work done": Charlotte Mason death certificate. Alain Locke Papers, Howard University.

443 with a royalty check: ZNH to Whit Burnett, June 15, 1946. Archives of *Story* magazine and Story Press, Princeton University Library.

443 in the 1944 presidential election: "Presidential Vote and Party Identification of Black Americans, 1936–92," Joint Center for Political and Economic Studies.

443 "a solid kind of a man": ZNH to Tracy L'Engle, November 4, 1945. ZNH Collection, University of Florida.

443 "the finest man": Hugh Conway, "Author Quits Houseboat to Beat Powell in Harlem," *The New York World-Telegram*, undated clipping.

443 "little cubby hole": Grant Reynolds interview, undated. REH Files.

444 "It's the old idea": "Fighter Against Complacency and Ignorance," *Barnard College Alumnae Magazine*, Autumn 1946.

444 "something of a women's lib attitude": Sterling Brown interview, April 29, 1971. REH Files.

444 two intriguing essays: I discovered these previously unknown, unpublished essays in the Helen Worden Erskine Collection, Rare Book & Manuscript Library, Columbia University.

445 "basement to Hell": ZNH to Carl Van Vechten, July 30, 1947. Hurston Collection, Yale.

445 "Except for the waters": ZNH to Maxwell Perkins, May 20 1947. Archives of Charles Scribner's Sons, Princeton University.

446 "a grand job": Ann Watkins to ZNH, June 20, 1947. Scribner Archives, Princeton.

446 "It is useless to repeat": ZNH to Burroughs Mitchell, July 31, 1947. Scribner Archives, Princeton.

446 "A drab terror": Ibid.

446 "I hope that tells you": Mitchell to ZNH, August 18, 1947. Scribner Archives, Princeton.

446 "No use in having": ZNH to Mitchell, September 3, 1947. Scribner Archives, Princeton.

447 "Please remember": ZNH to Mitchell, late October 1947. Scribner Archives, Princeton.

447 "Being what they call here": ZNH to Mitchell, September 3, 1947. Scribner Archives, Princeton.

447 "gnaw finger-nails": ZNH to Mitchell, January 14, 1948. Scribner Archives, Princeton.

447 "a fine and unusual book": Mitchell to ZNH, February 9, 1948. Scribner Archives, Princeton.

447 "Having been down here": ZNH to Mitchell, February 14, 1948. Scribner Archives, Princeton.

448 "Have you been working": Mitchell to ZNH, September 9, 1948. Scribner Archives, Princeton.

CHAPTER 32

449 Zora soon learned: The incidents in this chapter have been reconstructed from a large file of court documents obtained from the New York Municipal Archives, as well as from Hurston's correspondence of the period. Specific documents are cited only when quoted directly.

450 Hurston also faced her accusers: The nicknames of the boys are used throughout this account, but their full names have been withheld for reasons of privacy.

450 "Then the horror took me": ZNH to Carl Van Vechten and Fania Marinoff, October 30, 1948. Hurston Collection, Yale.

450 Scribner's hired Waldman: Charles Scribner to Louis Waldman, October 27, 1948. Scribner Archives, Princeton.

451 "absolutely fearless": Louis Waldman interview, undated. REH Files.

452 "vile charge": ZNH to Van Vechten and Marinoff, October 30, 1948. Hurston Collection, Yale.

452 "I am not laughing": Transcript of testimony from the preliminary hearing, undated document, New York Municipal Archives.

452 "has a hundred meanings": ZNH, *Mules and Men*, p. 62.

452 "Jerry said it was nature": Transcript of testimony from the preliminary hearing, undated document, New York Municipal Archives.

453 Hurston was arraigned: "The People Vs. Zora Hurston," Court of General Sessions in and for the County of New York, undated document. New York Municipal Archives.

453 the publisher offered her: Scribner's interoffice memo, October 5, 1948. Scribner Archives, Princeton.

453 "Miss Hurston's astonishing": Worth Tuttle Hedden, "Turpentine and Moonshine," *New York Herald Tribune Weekly Book Review*, October 10, 1948.

454 Within a few days of publication: N. H. Snow to Burroughs Mitchell, October 14, 1948, office memorandum. Scribner Archives, Princeton.

454 "I have to stay": All quotes from this plot summary and discussion are taken from the HarperPerennial edition of *Seraph on the Suwanee*, 1991. The book was originally published in 1948 by Charles Scribner's Sons.

455 "About the idiom of the book": ZNH to Marjorie Kinnan Rawlings and Norton Baskin, December 22, 1948. ZNH Collection, University of Florida.

456 "Have you ever been tied": ZNH to Burroughs Mitchell, October 2, 1947. Scribner Archives, Princeton.

457 "I get sick of her": Ibid.

457 "I have hopes": ZNH to Van Vechten, November 2, 1942. Hurston Collection, Yale.

457 "Her days had nothing in them": ZNH, *Seraph on the Suwanee*, p. 268.

458 "The author knows": Frank G. Slaughter, "Freud in Turpentine," *The New York Times Book Review*, Oct 31, 1948.

458 "Reading this astonishing novel": Worth Tuttle Hedden, "Turpentine and Moonshine," *New York Herald Tribune Weekly Book Review*, October 10, 1948.

458 the "impossible accusation": Bill Chase, "Noted Novelist Denies She 'Abused' 10-Year-Old Boy," *The New York Age*, October 23, 1948.

459 "Boys, 10, Accuse Zora": *The Afro-American*, national edition, October 23, 1948.

459 "I feel and believe": ZNH, *Seraph on the Suwanee*, p. 262.

459 "The reviewer noted": Front page, *The Afro-American*, national edition, October 23, 1948.

459 "I intend to fight": Bill Chase, "Noted Novelist Denies She 'Abused' 10-Year-Old Boy," *The New York Age*, October 23, 1948.

460 "That is the blow": ZNH to Van Vechten and Marinoff, October 30, 1948. Hurston Collection, Yale.

460 "124th St. is in a state of horror": Ibid.

460 "I think the people": Arna Bontemps interview, December 18, 1970. REH Files.

460 "Have you heard": Langston Hughes to Arna Bontemps, September 21, 1948. Quoted in Rampersad, Vol. II, p. 163.

461 "I care nothing": ZNH to Van Vechten and Marinoff, October 30, 1948. Hurston Collection, Yale.

461 "West Hell is the hottest": ZNH, "Negro Mythical Places," 1938.

461 "All that I have ever tried to do": ZNH to Van Vechten and Marinoff, October 30, 1948. Hurston Collection, Yale.

462 "I love courage": ZNH, *Twentieth Century American Authors*, 1942.

462 "To be brave": ZNH to Annie Nathan Meyer, January 15, 1926. Annie Nathan Meyer Papers, American Jewish Archives.

462 "It is the AFRO's belief": "Publicity Where It's Needed," *The Afro-American*, November 6, 1948.

462 "inconceivable horror": ZNH to Van Vechten and Marinoff, October 30, 1948. Hurston Collection, Yale.

462 Richard Rochester: The Rochester incident has been reconstructed from a series of Hurston letters: ZNH to Helen Worden Erskine, February 4, 1949, and May 2, 1949. Helen Worden Erskine Papers, Columbia. And ZNH to Fannie Hurst, February 10, 1949. Harry Ransom Center, University of Texas. Also, Hurston apparently enlisted Langston Hughes as a potential character witness in the Rochester case, though he never had to testify; see Rampersad, vol. II, pp. 163–64.

463 "threatened me": ZNH to Fannie Hurst, February 10, 1949. Harry Ransom Center, University of Texas.

463 "spiteful and untrue charges": Ibid. Also "Zora Hurston Pens New Court Chapter," *The New York Age*, January 29, 1949.

463 "a professional frame": Louis Waldman interview, undated. REH Files.

463 "This man Rochester": Louis Waldman to Burroughs Mitchell, January 25, 1949. Scribner Archives, Princeton.

463 "I am now strapped": ZNH to Fannie Hurst, February 10, 1949; also an undated followup letter. Harry Ransom Center, University of Texas.

464 "a good man": Louis Waldman interview, undated. REH Files.

464 the district attorney's office submitted: Recommendation for Discharge, undated document. New York Municipal Archives.

465 On March 14, 1949: Louis Waldman to Charles Scribner's Sons, March 21, 1949. Scribner Archives, Princeton.

465 "We have had official notification": Burroughs Mitchell to ZNH, March 23, 1949. Scribner Archives, Princeton.

465 "I haven't heard from her": Burroughs Mitchell to Jean G. Parker, April 25, 1949. Scribner Archives, Princeton.

465 "I haven't anything": Mitchell to ZNH, July 13, 1949. Scribner Archives, Princeton.

466 "I am feeling fine": ZNH to Mitchell, undated (fall 1949). Scribner Archives, Princeton.

466 "I feel that I have come to myself": Ibid.

CHAPTER 33

467 "I have regained": ZNH to Carl Van Vechten and Fania Marinoff, postmarked December 22, 1949. Hurston Collection, Yale.

467 "Day by day in every way": ZNH to Burroughs Mitchell, January 24, 1950. Scribner Archives, Princeton.

467 "Hurston writes well": Helga H. Eason to Charles Scribner's Sons, January 17, 1950, and Barbara J. Mousley to Helga H. Eason, January 19, 1950. Scribner Archives, Princeton.

468 "a fascinating study": ZNH to Mitchell, January 24, 1950. Scribner Archives, Princeton.

468 "It means work": Mitchell to ZNH, March 14, 1950. Scribner Archives, Princeton.

468 "Nagged by the necessity": This was a phrase Hurston used in a 1943 letter. "I know so tragically what it means to be trying to concentrate and being nagged by the necessity of living," she wrote. ZNH to Marjorie Kinnan Rawlings, August 21, 1943. ZNH Collection, University of Florida.

469 "I have been amazed": ZNH, "What White Publishers Won't Print," *Negro Digest*, April 1950.

469 "It was a difficult few hours": Zora's employer, quoted in James Lyons, "Successful Author Working as a Maid," *St. Louis Post-Dispatch Sunday Magazine*, April 24, 1950.

469 "You can only use your mind": ZNH, quoted in Lyons, "Famous Negro Author Working as Maid Here Just 'To Live a Little,'" *Miami Herald*, March 27, 1950.

470 "Although Miss Hurston": "Famous Author Working as Maid for White Folks Down in Dixie!"*Amsterdam News*, April 1, 1950.

470 "I tried to avoid the publicity": ZNH to Mitchell, undated (sometime in early April). Scribner Archives, Princeton.

470 "What I want to know is": Mitchell to ZNH, April 10, 1950. Scribner Archives, Princeton.

471 "a humility the likes of which": Quoted in James Lyons, "Famous Negro Author Working as Maid Here Just 'To Live a Little,'" *Miami Herald*, March 27, 1950.

471 Hurston presents Laura Lee : ZNH, "The Conscience of the Court," *Saturday Evening Post*, March 18, 1950.

472 "For various reasons": ZNH, "What White Publishers Won't Print," *Negro Digest*, April 1950.

472 "Under our Constitution": ZNH, "I Saw Negro Votes Peddled," *American Legion Magazine*, November 1950.

473 "I wanted the money": ZNH to Mitchell, July 21, 1950. Scribner Archives, Princeton.

473 "the extravaganza of summer": ZNH, "What White Publishers Won't Print," *Negro Digest*, April 1950. Also ZNH to Mitchell, Aug 23, 1950. Scribner Archives, Princeton.

473 "Zora in person": Carl Van Vechten to Harold Jackman, October 26, 1950. Countee Cullen Collection, Atlanta University.

473 "I hate snow!": ZNH to Charles S. Johnson, December 5, 1950. Amistad Research Center, Tulane.

474 "literature about the higher emotions": ZNH, "What White Publishers Won't Print," *Negro Digest*, April 1950.

474 "Somehow, the reader": Mitchell to ZNH, October 3, 1950. Scribner Archives, Princeton.

475 "with a year's work gone": ZNH to Jean Parker Waterbury, March 7, 1951. Armitage Watkins Papers, REH Files.

475 "Being under my own roof": ZNH to Waterbury, Sunday morning [late February or early March] 1951.Watkins Papers, REH Files.

475 "telling how the Communists": Joseph C. Keeley to Jean Parker Waterbury, January 5, 1951. Watkins Papers, REH Files.

475 "I keep telling her": ZNH to Henry Allen Moe, September 8, 1944. Archives of the J. S. Guggenheim Foundation.

476 "The dear peasant": ZNH, "Why the Negro Won't Buy Communism," *American Legion Magazine*, June 1951. Hurston's full title for the piece was "Mourner's Bench, Communist Line: Why the Negro Won't Buy Communism."

476 While she awaited payment: ZNH to Waterbury, February 13, 1951. Watkins Papers, REH Files.

476 "I would pray": ZNH to Waterbury, Sunday morning [late February or early March] 1951. Watkins Papers, REH Files.

476 "novel material": Waterbury to ZNH, March 5, 1951. Watkins Papers, REH Files.

476 "But the very mention of 'novel'": ZNH to Waterbury, March 7, 1951. Watkins Papers, REH Files.

477 "I am all too weary": Ibid.

477 "I had exactly four pennies": ZNH to Waterbury, March 18, 1951. Watkins Papers, REH Files.

477 "Never have I been so ill": ZNH to Waterbury, undated, received April 9, 1951. Watkins Papers, REH Files.

477 "truly indigenous Negro novel": ZNH to Waterbury, May 1, 1951. Watkins Papers, REH Files.

478 "take a good look at the man": ZNH to Waterbury, May 1 and June 4, 1951. Watkins Papers, REH Files.

478 Her article: ZNH, "A Negro Voter Sizes Up Taft," *Saturday Evening Post*, December 8, 1951.

478 "It looked like a jungle": ZNH to Waterbury, July 9, 1951. Watkins Papers, REH Files.

478 "Somehow, this one spot on earth": Ibid.

479 "Living the kind of life": ZNH to Mitchell, July 15, 1951. Scribner

Archives, Princeton.

479 "A serene and happy aura": ZNH to Waterbury, July 15, 1951. ZNH Collection, University of Florida.

479 "a fine, warm, attractive character": Mitchell to ZNH, July 9, 1951. Scribner Archives, Princeton.

480 "Digging in my garden": ZNH to Mitchell, July 15, 1951. Scribner Archives, Princeton.

480 "The tropical water": ZNH to Waterbury, August 8, 1951. ZNH Collection, University of Florida.

480 "I am bunching my muscles": ZNH to Waterbury, September 13, 1951. ZNH Collection, University of Florida.

480 Zora proposed several magazine pieces: ZNH to Waterbury, August 19, 1951. ZNH Collection, University of Florida.

481 "You and Tay Hohoff": ZNH to Waterbury, September 13, 1951. ZNH Collection, University of Florida.

481 "Keeping outdoors": ZNH to Waterbury, October 25, 1951. ZNH Collection, University of Florida.

481 "Too much work": ZNH to Waterbury, March 6, 1952. ZNH Collection, University of Florida.

482 "She could write like an angel": Jean Parker Waterbury interview, undated. REH Files.

482 "I try to get down to work": ZNH to Waterbury, June 15, 1952. ZNH Collection, University of Florida.

483 "I watched her for": ZNH, "Victim of Fate!" *Pittsburgh Courier*, October 11, 1952.

484 "At times I have wished": ZNH to Mitchell, August 12, 1955. Scribner Archives, Princeton.

485 "She wanted beauty and poetry": ZNH, "The Life Story of Mrs. Ruby J. McCollum!" third installment, *Pittsburgh Courier*, March 14, 1953.

485 "By nature, Ruby": ZNH, "The Life Story of Mrs. Ruby J. McCollum!" fourth installment, *Pittsburgh Courier*, March 21, 1953.

485 "As she said, she does not know": ZNH, "The Life Story of Mrs. Ruby J. McCollum!" tenth installment, *Pittsburgh Courier*, May 2, 1953.

486 In 1956, Huie would publish: Huie to ZNH, September 1, 1954, and April 19, 1955. University of Florida.

CHAPTER 34

487 "Mumble a prayer for me": ZNH to Herbert Sheen, March 13, 1953. REH Files.

488 The largest royalty payment: Royalty figure from Hemenway, p. 5.

Hemenway got this figure from correspondence from the J. B. Lippincott Company listing sales and royalty figures for ZNH books.

488 "I don't know any more": ZNH, *Dust Tracks*, p. 231.

489 nine dollars in his bank account: Rampersad, *The Life of Langston Hughes, Vol. II*, p. 204.

489 "with her feeling": Hughes to Bontemps, February 18, 1953, in Nichols, p. 302.

490 "The spirit is willing": ZNH to Burroughs Mitchell, January 24, 1950. Scribner Archives, Princeton.

491 "When I get old": ZNH, *Dust Tracks*, p. 231.

491 "It is interesting to see": ZNH to Herbert Sheen, March 13, 1953. REH Files.

491 "the most loved man on earth": ZNH to Sheen, March 31, 1953. REH Files.

491 "I have one to send you": ZNH to Sheen, March 13, 1953. REH Files.

492 "You wouldn't think": Leo Schumaker, "Zora Hurston Sees King Herod Play As Her 'Greatest Work,'" *All-Florida Magazine*, August 8, 1953. African American File, Florida Collection, Jacksonville Public Library.

492 "If I can only carve him out": ZNH to Mitchell, October 2, 1953. Scribner Archives, Princeton.

492 "I remember": Mitchell to ZNH, October 5, 1953. Scribner Archives, Princeton.

492 "under the spell": ZNH to Mitchell, October 2, 1953. Scribner Archives, Princeton.

493 "deep in creative mood": ZNH to Sheen, January 7, 1955. REH Files.

493 "a very hard and continuous grind": Ibid.

493 "It is a hard, tough assignment": ZNH to Mary Holland, June 13, 1955. ZNH Collection, University of Florida.

493 "In spite of your knowledge": Mitchell to ZNH, July 21, 1955. Scribner Archives, Princeton.

493 "Please, please": ZNH to Mitchell, August 12, 1955. Scribner Archives, Princeton.

494 "If there are not adequate Negro schools": ZNH, "Court Order Can't Make Races Mix," *Orlando Sentinel*, August 11, 1955.

494 "as one of those": Ibid.

494 "Physical contact means nothing": ZNH to Margrit Sabloniere, December 3, 1955. ZNH Collection, University of Florida.

495 "As a Negro": ZNH to Sabloniere, March 15, 1956. ZNH Collection, University of Florida.

495 "something that looks like": ZNH to Mitchell, July 15, 1951. Scribner Archives, Princeton.

496 "terribly distressed": ZNH to Sabloniere, March 15, 1956. ZNH Collection, University of Florida.

496 "the foremost Negroes": Richard Bardolph to ZNH, September 1, 1955. ZNH Collections, University of Florida.

496 "education and human relations": Richard Moore to ZNH, May 18, 1956. Also, untitled clipping, *Daytona Beach Morning Journal*, May 24, 1956.

496 Zora reported to: P. H. Goddard of Pan American World Airways to ZNH, June 13, 1956. ZNH Collection, University of Florida.

496 "If I can set it down": ZNH to Guggenheim Foundation, handwritten note on letter to her dated July 1, 1957. Archives of the J. S. Guggenheim Foundation.

497 "That is suicide": ZNH to Sheen, June 28, 1957. REH Files.

497 "too well educated": ZNH to Holland, June 27, 1957. ZNH Collection, University of Florida.

497 "This is not the South": ZNH to Holland, July 2, 1957. ZNH Collection, University of Florida.

497 "I have no sentimental": ZNH to Sheen, June 28, 1957. REH Files.

498 "I wanted a long life": ZNH, *Moses, Man of the Mountain*, p. 58.

498 "You are alive": ZNH, sketchbook. ZNH Collection, University of Florida.

498 "some very good articles": Bolen quoted in untitled article by John Hicks, in Nathiri, pp. 38–39. Article originally published in *Florida* magazine.

498 "A lot of times": C. E. Bolen interview, undated. REH Files.

499 "My name as an author": ZNH to M. Mitchell Ferguson, March 7, 1958. ZNH Collection, University of Florida.

499 "criticized by some teachers": Dr. Leroy C. Floyd, quoted in John Hicks article in Nathiri, p. 39. Also ZNH to M. Mitchell Ferguson, March 7, 1958. ZNH Collection, University of Florida.

499 "She was an incredible woman": Alice Walker, "Looking for Zora," *In Search of Our Mothers' Gardens* (New York: Harcourt Brace Jovanovich, 1983), p. 110.

499 "The first afternoon": John Hicks article in Nathiri, pp. 39–40.

500 "Zora was very secure": Author interview with Anne Wilder, Fort Pierce, FL, February 2, 1999.

500 "She didn't carry any air": Author interview with Zanobia Jefferson, Fort Pierce, FL, February 2, 1999.

501 "I wish I had": Dr. C. C. Benton, quoted in John Hicks article in Nathiri, p. 42.

501 "She was a typical artist": Author interview with Arlena Benton Lee, Fort Pierce, FL, February 3, 1999.

501 "The things that were precious": Marjorie Silver, in John Hicks article in Nathiri, pp. 41–42.

501 "I am very fond": ZNH, *Twentieth Century Authors*, 1942.

501 "I have always had": George Beebe to Doug Silver, July 9, 1958. ZNH Collection, University of Florida.

502 "strong interest": John Scott Mabon to ZNH, September 15, 1958. ZNH Collection, University of Florida.

502 "This is to query you": ZNH to Harper Brothers, January 16, 1959. ZNH Collection, University of Florida.

502 "manage herself": Dr. C. C. Benton, in John Hicks article in Nathiri, p. 44.

503 "Sometimes she would run out": Quoted in Walker, p. 111.

503 On October 12: Hospital records cited in John Hicks article in Nathiri, p. 44. Hemenway reports that Hurston's stroke was in "early 1959," and that she went home and deteriorated there. But interviews with Fort Pierce residents seem to confirm Hicks's account: that she was transferred to the nursing home soon after the stroke. The earlier deterioration seems to have been from her illness, rather than from a stroke. Fort Pierce Memorial Hospital no longer exists.

503 "She couldn't really write much": Benton, quoted in Walker, pp. 110, 112.

503 "She didn't focus": Author interview with Anne Wilder, Fort Pierce, FL, February 2, 1999.

503 "she was fine": Vivian Hurston Bowden, quoted in Nathiri, p. 62.

503 "I have known the joy": ZNH, *Dust Tracks*, p. 231.

504 "Why fear?": ZNH, *Dust Tracks*, p. 226.

504 "They said they had": John Hicks article, Nathiri, p. 45.

504 having lived three years longer: The average length of life for black women in the United States in 1960 was 66.3 years. *National Vital Statistics Report*, vol. 47, no. 13, 1998.

504 $661.87 was raised: "Many at Services for Mrs. Hurston," undated clipping from the *Fort Pierce Chronicle*.

504 "a nice funeral": Author interview with Curtis E. Johnson, February 2, 1999.

504 an "impressive" funeral: February 1960 clippings from the *Fort Pierce Chronicle*.

505 "There were so many folks": Author interview with Curtis E. Johnson, February 2, 1999.

505 "you could hardly see the casket": C. E. Bolen interview. REH Files.

505 "a pale pink": Silver, quoted in John Hicks article, Nathiri, p. 46.

505 "They said she couldn't": Jennings, quoted in Theodore Pratt, "Zora Neale Hurston," *Florida Historical Quarterly*, July 1961.

505 "The local Negro population": Theodore Pratt, "Zora Neale Hurston," *Florida Historical Quarterly*, July 1961.

505 "a pauper's funeral": Quoted in Walker, p. 112.

506 "I know that nothing": ZNH, *Dust Tracks*, p. 226.

POSTSCRIPT

507 "a gift to both": Fannie Hurst, "Zora Neale Hurston: A Personality Sketch," *Library Gazette*, Yale University, 1961.

507 "You make all the girl's faults": Van Vechten to Hurst, July 5, 1960, quoted in Kroeger, p. 340.

507 "I LOVED Zora": Van Vechten to Harold Jackman, February 10, 1960. Countee Cullen Collection, Atlanta University.

508 "a weird postlude": Marjorie Silver, quoted in Hicks article in Nathiri, p. 46.

508 "around dusk-dark": Author interview with Patrick Duval, February 2, 1999.

508 "Condemned to a deserted island": Alice Walker, "Zora Neale Hurston: A Cautionary Tale and a Partisan View," foreword to Hemenway, *Zora Neale Hurston: A Literary Biography*, p. xiii.

509 "Let no Negro celebrity": ZNH to W.E.B. Du Bois, June 11, 1945. Tulane.

509 The picture apparently became mixed up: See series of notes at the Library of Congress in Lomax Visual Image Collection, Prints and Photographs Division.

511 "God balances the sheet in time": ZNH to Herbert Sheen, June 28, 1957. REH Files.

Published Works by Zora Neale Hurston

BOOKS

(This list refers to first publications; reprint editions cited in Notes are given last.)

Jonah's Gourd Vine. Philadelphia: J. B. Lippincott, 1934. Reprinted, with a foreword by Rita Dove, New York: HarperPerennial, 1990.

Mules and Men. Philadelphia: J. B. Lippincott, 1935. Reprinted, with a foreword by Arnold Rampersad, New York: HarperPerennial, 1990.

Their Eyes Were Watching God. Philadelphia: J. B. Lippincott, 1937. Reprinted, with a foreword by Mary Helen Washington, New York: HarperPerennial, 1990.

Tell My Horse. Philadelphia: J. B. Lippincott, 1938. Reprinted, with a foreword by Ishmael Reed, New York: HarperPerennial, 1990.

Moses, Man of the Mountain. Philadelphia: J. B. Lippincott, 1939. Reprinted, with a foreword by Deborah E. McDowell, New York: HarperPerennial, 1991.

Dust Tracks on a Road. Philadelphia: J. B. Lippincott, 1942. Reprinted, with restored text and foreword by Maya Angelou, New York: HarperPerennial, 1996.

Seraph on the Suwanee. New York: Charles Scribner's Sons, 1948. Reprinted, with a foreword by Hazel V. Carby and afterword by Henry Louis Gates, Jr., New York: HarperPerennial, 1991.

BOOKS PUBLISHED POSTHUMOUSLY

The Complete Stories. Introduction by Henry Louis Gates, Jr., and Sieglinde Lemke. New York: HarperCollins, 1995.

Every Tongue Got to Confess: Negro Folk-Tales from the Gulf States. Edited by Carla Kaplan, foreword by John Edgar Wideman. New York: HarperCollins, 2001.

Folklore, Memoirs, & Other Writings. Edited and with notes by Cheryl A. Wall. New York: Library of America, 1995.

Go Gator and Muddy the Water: Writings by Zora Neale Hurston from the Federal Writers' Project. Edited and with a biographical essay by Pamela Bordelon. New York: W. W. Norton, 1999.

I Love Myself When I Am Laughing . . . & Then Again When I Am Looking Mean and Impressive: A Zora Neale Hurston Reader. Edited by Alice Walker, introduction by Mary Helen Washington. Old Westbury, N.Y.: The Feminist Press, 1979.

Mule Bone: A Comedy of Negro Life. Written with Langston Hughes. Edited and with introductions by George Houston Bass and Henry Louis Gates, Jr. New York: HarperPerennial, 1991.

Novels and Stories. Edited and with notes by Cheryl A. Wall. New York: Library of America, 1995.

The Sanctified Church. Foreword by Toni Cade Bambara. Berkeley, Calif.: Turtle Island Foundation, 1981.

Spunk: The Selected Short Stories of Zora Neale Hurston. Berkeley, Calif.: Turtle Island Foundation, 1985.

OTHER PUBLISHED WORKS (IN CHRONOLOGICAL ORDER)

"John Redding Goes to Sea." *Stylus* 1 (May 1921), pp. 11–22. Reprinted in *Opportunity* 4 (January 1926), pp. 16–21.

"O Night." *Stylus* 1 (May 1921), p. 42.

"Poem." *Howard University Record* 16 (February 1922), p. 236.

"Drenched in Light." *Opportunity* 2 (December 1924), pp. 371–74.

"Spunk." *Opportunity* 3 (June 1925), pp. 171–73. Reprinted in *The New Negro*, edited by Alain Locke (New York: Albert and Charles Boni, 1925), pp. 105–11.

"Magnolia Flower." *Spokesman*, July 1925, pp. 26–29.

"The Hue and Cry About Howard University." *Messenger* 7 (September 1925), pp. 315–19, 338.

"Under the Bridge." *X-Ray: Journal of the Zeta Phi Beta Sorority*, December 1925.

"The Ten Commandments of Charm." *X-Ray: Journal of the Zeta Phi Beta Sorority*, December 1925.

"On Noses." *X-Ray: Journal of the Zeta Phi Beta Sorority*, December 1925.

"Muttsy." *Opportunity* 4 (August 1926), pp. 246–50.

"Possum or Pig." *Forum* 76 (September 1926), p. 465.

"The Eatonville Anthology." *Messenger* 8 (September–November 1926), pp. 261–62, 297, 319, 332.

Color Struck: A Play. *Fire!!* 1 (November 1926), pp. 7–15.

"Sweat." *Fire!!* 1 (November 1926), pp. 40–45.

The First One: A Play. Ebony and Topaz. Edited by Charles S. Johnson (New York: National Urban League, 1927), pp. 53–57.

"Cudjo's Own Story of the Last African Slaver." *Journal of Negro History* 12 (October 1927), pp. 648–63.

"Communication." *Journal of Negro History* 12 (October 1927), pp. 664–67.

"How It Feels to Be Colored Me." *World Tomorrow* 11 (May 1928), pp. 215–16.

"Dance Songs and Tales from the Bahamas." *Journal of American Folk-Lore* 43 (July–September 1930), pp. 294–312.

"Hoodoo in America." *Journal of American Folk-Lore* 44 (October–December 1931), pp. 317–418.

"The Gilded Six-Bits." *Story* 3 (August 1933), pp. 60–70.

"Characteristics of Negro Expression." *Negro: An Anthology*. Edited by Nancy Cunard (London: Wishart, 1934), pp. 39–46.

"Conversations and Visions." *Negro: An Anthology*, pp. 47–49.

"Shouting." *Negro: An Anthology*, pp. 49–50.

"The Sermon." *Negro: An Anthology*, pp. 50–54.

"Mother Catharine." *Negro: An Anthology*, pp. 54–57.

"Uncle Monday." *Negro: An Anthology*, pp. 57–61.

"Spirituals and Neo-Spirituals." *Negro: An Anthology*, pp. 359–61.

"The Fire and the Cloud." *Challenge* 1 (September 1934), pp. 10–14

"Race Cannot Become Great Until It Recognizes Its Talent." *Washington Tribune*, December 29, 1934.

"Full of Mud, Sweat and Blood." Review of *God Shakes Creation* by David M. Cohn. *New York Herald Tribune Books*, November 3, 1935, p. 8.

"Fannie Hurst by Her Ex-Amanuensis." *Saturday Review*, October 9, 1937, pp. 15–16.

"Star-Wrassling Sons-of-the-Universe." Review of *The Hurricane's Children* by Carl Carmer. *New York Herald Tribune Books*, December 26, 1937, p. 4.

"Rural Schools for Negroes." Review of *The Jeanes Teacher in the United States* by Lance G. E. Jones. *New York Herald Tribune Books*, February 20, 1938, p. 24.

"Stories of Conflict." Review of *Uncle Tom's Children* by Richard Wright. *Saturday Review*, April 2, 1938, p. 32.

"Now Take Noses." *Cordially Yours* (Philadelphia: J. B. Lippincott, 1939), pp. 25–27.

"Cock Robin Beale Street." *Southern Literary Messenger* 3 (July 1941), pp. 321–23.

"Story in Harlem Slang." *American Mercury* 55 (July 1942), pp. 84–96.

"Lawrence of the River." *Saturday Evening Post*, September 5, 1942, pp. 18, 55–57. Condensed in *Negro Digest* 1 (March 1943), pp. 47–49.

"The 'Pet Negro' System." *American Mercury* 56 (May 1943), pp. 593–600. Condensed in *Negro Digest* 1 (June 1943), pp. 37–40.

"High John de Conquer." *American Mercury* 57 (October 1943), pp. 450–58.

"Negroes Without Self-Pity." *American Mercury* 57 (November 1943), pp. 601–3.

"The Last Slave Ship." *American Mercury* 58 (March 1944), pp. 351–58. Condensed in *Negro Digest* 2 (May 1944), pp. 11–16.

"My Most Humiliating Jim Crow Experience." *Negro Digest* 2 (June 1944), pp. 25–26.

"The Rise of the Begging Joints." *American Mercury* 60 (March 1945), pp. 288–94. Condensed in *Negro Digest* 3 (May 1945).

"Crazy for This Democracy." *Negro Digest* 4 (December 1945), pp. 45–48.

"Bible, Played by Ear in Africa." Review of *How God Fix Jonah* by Lorenz Graham. *New York Herald Tribune Weekly Book Review*, November 24, 1946, p. 5.

"Jazz Regarded as Social Achievement." Review of *Shining Trumpets* by Rudi Blesh. *New York Herald Tribune Weekly Book Review*, December 22, 1946, p. 8.

"The Negro in the United States." *Encyclopedia Americana*, 1947 edition.

"Thirty Days Among Maroons." Review of *Journey to Accompong* by Katharine Dunham. *New York Herald Tribune Weekly Book Review*, January 12, 1947, p. 8.

"The Transplanted Negro." Review of *Trinidad Village* by Melville Herskovits and Frances Herskovits. *New York Herald Tribune Weekly Book Review*, March 9, 1947, p. 20.

Review of *Voodoo in New Orleans* by Robert Tallant. *Journal of American Folk-Lore* 60 (October–December 1947), pp. 436–38.

"At the Sound of the Conch Shell." Review of *New Day* by Victor Stafford Reid. *New York Herald Tribune Weekly Book Review*, March 20, 1949, p. 4.

"Conscience of the Court." *Saturday Evening Post*, March 18, 1950, pp. 22, 23, 112–22.

"I Saw Negro Votes Peddled." *American Legion Magazine* 49 (November 1950), pp. 12–13, 54–57, 59–60. Condensed in *Negro Digest* 9 (September 1951), pp. 77–85.

"Some Fabulous Caribbean Riches Revealed." Review of *The Pencil of God* by Pierre Marcelin and Philippe Thoby Marcelin. *New York Herald Tribune Weekly Book Review*, February 4, 1951, p. 5.

"What White Publishers Won't Print." *Negro Digest* 8 (April 1950), pp. 85–89.

"Mourner's Bench, Communist Line: Why the Negro Won't Buy Communism." *American Legion Magazine* 50 (June 1951), pp. 14–15, 55–60.

"A Negro Voter Sizes Up Taft." *Saturday Evening Post*, December 8, 1951, pp. 29, 150.

"Zora's Revealing Story of Ruby's First Day in Court." *Pittsburgh Courier*, October 11, 1952.

"Victim of Fate." *Pittsburgh Courier*, October 11, 1952.

"Ruby Is Sane; Trial Date Set." *Pittsburgh Courier*, October 18, 1952.

"Ruby McCollum Fights for Life." *Pittsburgh Courier*, November 22, 1952.

"Justice and Fair Play Aim of Judge Adams as Ruby Goes on Trial." *Pittsburgh Courier*, November 29, 1952.

"Ruby's Lawyer Disqualified; Plot Reported." *Pittsburgh Courier*, November 29, 1952.

"McCollum-Adams Trial Highlights." *Pittsburgh Courier*, December 27, 1952.

"Ruby Bares Her Love." *Pittsburgh Courier*, January 3, 1953.

"Doctor's Threats, Tussle Over Gun Led to Slaying." *Pittsburgh Courier*, January 10, 1953.

"Ruby's Troubles Mount." *Pittsburgh Courier*, January 17, 1953.

"The Life Story of Mrs. Ruby J. McCollum!" *Pittsburgh Courier*, February 28, March 7, 14, 21, and 28, April 4, 11, 18, and 25, and May 2, 1953.

"The Trial of Ruby McCollum," in *Ruby McCollum: Woman in the Suwanee Jail*, by William Bradford Huie (New York: E. P. Dutton, 1956), pp. 89–101.

"This Juvenile Delinquency." *Fort Pierce Chronicle*, December 12, 1958.

"The Tripson Story." *Fort Pierce Chronicle*, February 6, 1959.

"The Farm Laborer at Home." *Fort Pierce Chronicle*, February 27, 1959.

"Hoodoo and Black Magic." Column in *Fort Pierce Chronicle*, July 11, 1958–August 7, 1959.

Selected Bibliography

Anderson, Jervis. *This Was Harlem: A Cultural Portrait, 1900–1950*. New York: Farrar, Straus & Giroux, 1982.

Awkward, Michael, ed. *New Essays on* Their Eyes Were Watching God. Cambridge: Cambridge University Press, 1990.

Baker, Houston A., Jr. *Workings of the Spirit: The Poetics of Afro-American Women's Writing*. Chicago: Chicago University Press, 1991.

Banks, William M. *Black Intellectuals: Race and Responsibility in American Life*. New York: W. W. Norton, 1996.

Berg, A. Scott. *Max Perkins: Editor of Genius*. New York: Riverhead Books, 1978.

Bernard, Emily, ed. *Remember Me to Harlem: The Letters of Langston Hughes and Carl Van Vechten, 1925–1964*. New York: Alfred A. Knopf, 2001.

Bontemps, Arna. *The Harlem Renaissance Remembered*. New York: Dodd, Mead, 1972.

Bordelon, Pamela. "New Tracks on Dust Tracks," *African American Review*, vol. 31, no. 1.

Bundles, A'Lelia. *On Her Own Ground: The Life and Times of Madam C. J. Walker*. New York: Scribner, 2001.

Dahl, Linda. *Morning Glory: A Biography of Mary Lou Williams*. New York: Pantheon Books, 1999.

Davis, Angela Y. *Blues Legacies and Black Feminism*. New York: Pantheon Books, 1998.

Davis, Rose Parkman. *Zora Neale Hurston: An Annotated Bibliography and Reference Guide*. Westport, Conn.: Greenwood Press, 1997.

Davis, Thadious M. *Nella Larsen, Novelist of the Harlem Renaissance: A Woman's Life Unveiled*. Baton Rouge: Louisiana State University Press, 1994.

Dodson, Howard, Christopher Moore, and Roberta Yancy. *The Black New Yorkers: The Schomburg Illustrated Chronology*. New York: John Wiley & Sons, 1999.

Douglas, Ann. *Terrible Honesty: Mongrel Manhattan in the 1920s*. New York: The Noonday Press, 1995.

Duberman, Martin. *Paul Robeson: A Biography*. New York: The New Press, 1989.

Edelman, Hope. *Motherless Daughters: The Legacy of Loss*. New York: Delta Trade Paperbacks, 1994.

Faderman, Lillian. *Odd Girls and Twilight Lovers: A History of Lesbian Life in Twentieth-Century America*. New York: Penguin Books, 1992.

Gates, Henry Louis, Jr. "Zora Neale Hurston and the Speakerly Text," in *The Signifying Monkey: A Theory of Afro-American Literary Criticism*. New York and Oxford: Oxford University Press, 1988.

Gates, Henry Louis, Jr., and K. A. Appiah, eds. *Zora Neale Hurston: Critical Perspectives Past and Present*. New York: Amistad, 1993.

Genovese, Eugene D. *Roll, Jordan, Roll: The World the Slaves Made*. New York: Vintage Books, 1976.

Giddings, Paula. *When and Where I Enter: The Impact of Black Women on Race and Sex in America*. New York: William Morrow, 1984.

Glassman, Steve, and Kathryn Lee Seidel, eds. *Zora in Florida*. Orlando: University of Central Florida Press, 1991.

Griffin, Farah Jasmine. *If You Can't Be Free, Be a Mystery: In Search of Billie Holiday*. New York: The Free Press, 2001.

Haygood, Wil. *King of the Cats: The Life and Times of Adam Clayton Powell, Jr.* Boston: Houghton Mifflin, 1993.

Heilbrun, Carolyn G. *Writing a Woman's Life*. New York: Ballantine Books, 1988.

Hemenway, Robert E. *Zora Neale Hurston: A Literary Biography*. Urbana: University of Illinois Press, 1977.

Hill, Lynda Marion. *Social Rituals and the Verbal Art of Zora Neale Hurston*. Washington, D.C.: Howard University Press, 1996.

Hine, Darlene Clark, Elsa Barkley Brown, and Rosalyn Terborg-Penn, eds. *Black Women in America: An Historical Encyclopedia*, vols. I and II. Bloomington and Indianapolis: Indiana University Press, 1994.

Hine, Darlene Clark, and Kathleen Thompson. *A Shining Thread of Hope: The History of Black Women in America*. New York: Broadway Books, 1998.

Holloway, Karla. *The Character of the Word: The Texts of Zora Neale Hurston*. Westport, Conn.: Greenwood Press, 1987.

Howard, Lillie P. *Zora Neale Hurston*. Boston: Twayne Press, 1980.

Hughes, Langston. *The Big Sea*. New York: Alfred A. Knopf, 1940. Reprinted, New York: Hill and Wang, 1993.

Huggins, Nathan Irvin. *Harlem Renaissance*. New York: Oxford University Press, 1971.

Hutchinson, George. *The Harlem Renaissance in Black and White*. Cambridge, Mass.: The Belknap Press of Harvard University Press, 1995.

Jordan, June. "On Richard Wright and Zora Neale Hurston: Notes Toward a Balancing of Love and Hatred," *Black World*, August 1974.

Kaplan, Carla, ed. *Zora Neale Hurston: A Life in Letters*. New York: Doubleday, 2002.

Kellner, Bruce. *The Harlem Renaissance: A Historical Dictionary of the Era*. Westport, Conn.: Greenwood Press, 1984.

Kennedy, Stetson. "Florida Folklife and the WPA, An Introduction," in *A Reference Guide to Florida Folklore from the Federal WPA*. Florida State Archives, Department of State.

Kramer, Victor. *The Harlem Renaissance Re-Examined*. New York: AMS Press, 1987.

Kroeger, Brooke. *Fannie: The Talent for Success of Writer Fannie Hurst*. New York: Times Books, 1999.

Lewis, David Levering. *When Harlem Was in Vogue*. New York: Vintage Books, 1979.

———, ed. *The Portable Harlem Renaissance Reader*. New York: Viking Penguin, 1994.

Lowe, John. *Jump at the Sun: Zora Neale Hurston's Cosmic Comedy*. Urbana and Chicago: University of Illinois Press, 1997.

Nathiri, N. Y., ed. *Zora! Zora Neale Hurston: A Woman and Her Community*. Orlando: Sentinel Communications, 1991.

Newson, Adele S. *Zora Neale Hurston: A Reference Guide*. Boston: G. K. Hall, 1987.

Nichols, Charles H., ed. *Arna Bontemps–Langston Hughes Letters, 1925–1967*. New York: Paragon House, 1990.

Otey, Frank M. *Eatonville, Florida: A Brief History*. Winter Park, Fla.: Four-G Publishers, 1989.

Parker, Idella, with Bud and Liz Crussell. *Idella Parker: From Reddick to Cross Creek*. Gainesville: University Press of Florida, 1999.

Parker, Idella, with Mary Keating. *Idella: Marjorie Rawlings' "Perfect Maid."* Gainesville: University Press of Florida, 1992.

Pierpont, Claudia Roth. *Passionate Minds: Women Rewriting the World*. New York: Alfred A. Knopf, 2000.

Plant, Deborah G. *Every Tub Must Sit on Its Own Bottom: The Philosophy and Politics of Zora Neale Hurston*. Champaign: University of Illinois Press, 1995.

Radway, Janice A. *A Feeling for Books: The Book-of-the-Month Club, Literary Taste, and Middle-Class Desire*. Chapel Hill: University of North Carolina Press, 1997.

Rampersad, Arnold. *The Life of Langston Hughes, Volume I: 1902–1941—I, Too, Sing America*. New York and Oxford: Oxford University Press, 1986.

———. *The Life of Langston Hughes, Volume II: I Dream a World*. New York and Oxford: Oxford University Press, 1988.

Roses, Lorraine Elena, and Ruth Elizabeth Randolph. *Harlem Renaissance and Beyond*. Cambridge, Mass.: Harvard University Press, 1990.

Rowley, Hazel. *Richard Wright: The Life and Times*. New York: Henry Holt, 2001.

Rymer, Russ. *American Beach*. New York: HarperCollins, 1998.

Taylor, Frank C., with Gerald Cook. *Alberta Hunter: A Celebration in Blues*. New York: McGraw-Hill, 1987.

Thurman, Wallace. *Infants of the Spring*. New York: Macaulay, 1932. Reprinted, Boston: Northeastern University Press, 1992.

Walker, Alice. *In Search of Our Mothers' Gardens*. New York: Harcourt Brace Jovanovich, 1983.

Wall, Cheryl A. *Women of the Harlem Renaissance*. Bloomington: Indiana University Press, 1995.

Waters, Ethel. *His Eye Is on the Sparrow*. New York: W. H. Allen, 1951.

Watson, Steven. *The Harlem Renaissance: Hub of African-American Culture, 1920–1930*. New York: Pantheon Books, 1995.

Williams, Susan Millar. *A Devil and a Good Woman Too: The Lives of Julia Peterkin*. Athens: University of Georgia Press, 1997.

Zinsser, William, ed. *Inventing the Truth: The Art and Craft of Memoir*. Boston and New York: Houghton Mifflin, 1998.

Acknowledgments

It's nothing short of a blessing to have had an opportunity to investigate, contemplate, and articulate a life—especially one as fully lived as Zora Neale Hurston's. *Wrapped in Rainbows* truly has been a communal endeavor; scores of people have helped me make this journey.

I must give thanks to:

My parents, Laura and Roger Boyd, for my first books, for my first typewriter, and for setting the best possible example through their lives of hard work and quiet, steady love.

Mignon Goode and Kamela Eaton, for an auspicious beginning, and for keeping the faith.

Kelley Alexander, for her openhanded and openhearted support.

Norma Clarke, for her bountiful friendship.

Dale and Lee Marshall, for their unceasing goodwill and benevolence.

Rudolph Byrd, for gallantly providing me with a room of my own at a most crucial time.

Lisa C. Moore, for serving as my second pair of hands and feet on the research trail.

Lylah Salahuddin, for her enthusiastic and valuable assistance with research and other necessary tasks.

Joseph Blount, for helping me to organize mounds of documents, and for making it enjoyable.

Tiajuana Malone, for the photos, and for being the first to know.

Lucy Hurston, Lois Hurston Gaston, and the entire Hurston family, as well as the Victoria Sanders Literary Agency, for graciously opening the door to Zora's life.

Robert E. Hemenway, for a remarkable road map, and for his uncommon generosity.

Alice Walker, for loving Zora first—and fiercely.

Cheryl Wall, for reading the manuscript with loving regard and rigorous candor, and for peppering me with provocative questions and pushing me to dig deeply for the answers.

Pearl Cleage, Robert Kanigel, and Teresa K. Weaver, for reading parts of the manuscript and offering invaluable feedback and insight.

My agent, John McGregor, for his tireless advocacy and unremitting encouragement.

My editor, Lisa Drew, for her patient support, thoughtful editing, and eternal optimism. Thanks also to her assistants, Jake Klisivitch and Erin Curler, and to top-notch attorney Emily Remes.

I also wish to thank the following people and resources:

Attorneys Elsie O'Laughlin and Ron Jayson, for offering their Hurston files.

The George A. and Eliza Gardner Howard Foundation of Brown University, for financial assistance.

My supportive colleagues at *The Atlanta Journal-Constitution.*

My friends from the MFA program in creative nonfiction at Goucher College.

The Zora Neale Hurston/Richard Wright Foundation and its visionary leader, Marita Golden.

When I began working on this book in 1996, only a few of Hurston's peers remained. I tried to interview them all, and anyone else who had firsthand knowledge of Hurston's life. I am thankful to the following people, some of them now deceased, for sharing their memories of Zora: Margaret Benton, Valerie Calhoun, John Henrik Clarke, Katherine Dunham, Patrick Duval, Zora Mack Goins, Hortense Williams Gray, Zanobia Jefferson, Curtis E. Johnson, Adelle Ferguson Lafayette, Cleo Leath, Arlena Benton Lee, Brooklyn T. McMillon, Margaret Paige, Louise Thompson Patterson, Grant Reynolds, Alex Rivera, and Anne Wilder.

I am deeply indebted to the administrators and staff members of the following libraries and institutions: Atlanta's Auburn Avenue Research Library on African American History and Culture; the State of Alabama Department of Archives and History; the Beinecke Rare Book and Manuscript Library, Yale University; the Moorland-Spingarn Research Center, Howard University; the Library of Congress; the Schomburg Center for Research in Black Culture; Rare Books and Manuscripts, Library of the University of Florida at Gainesville; the George A. Smathers Library, Department of Special Collections, University of Florida; the Florida Historical Society; the University of South Florida Library; the National Archives; the American Philosophical Society; the Archives of the John Simon Guggenheim Memorial Foundation; Charles Scribner's Sons Archives, Princeton University Library; Clark Atlanta University Library; the

Harry Ransom Humanities Research Center, University of Texas at Austin; Amistad Research Center, Tulane University; Special Collections, Fisk University Library; Columbia University Rare Books and Manuscripts Library; the American Jewish Archives at Hebrew Union College; Joan Nestle and Amy Beth of the Lesbian Herstory Archives; the Library of the University of North Carolina at Chapel Hill; North Carolina Central University Library; Boston University Library; Dr. Kenneth J. Hernden of the Rush Medical Center Archives; Barbara Hall of the Margaret Herrick Library, Academy of Motion Picture Arts and Sciences; the Office of the Chancellor, University of Kansas. Though much of Hurston's correspondence is scattered at the above-cited archives, and elsewhere, her known letters have now been collected in Carla Kaplan's book *Zora Neale Hurston: A Life in Letters*.

Many friends, family members and supporters have given of themselves unselfishly, offering places to stay, conversations to cherish, and so much more. At the risk of leaving someone out, I wish to thank: Jabari Asim; BarbaraO; Joye Mercer Barksdale; Amy Belkin; Timothy Boyd; Linda, Steve, Stephanie, and Joseph Blount; Michael, Venetta, and Kaylisha Boyd; Louise, Harold, Robyn, and Camille Brittain; A'Lelia Bundles; Nancy Chase; Eileen Drennen; Ralph B. Fielder; the late Leon Forrest; the late Egypt Freeman; Marcia Ann Gillespie; Uldine "Red" Goler; Farah Jasmine Griffin; Beverly Guy-Sheftall; Kimberly Harding; Bernitta Harris; Charsie Herndon; Tamara Jeffries; B. Lamont Jones; Sonya Jones; Kim Kuncl and Dena Smith; Roy LaGrone; Thonnia Lee; Alexa Maat; Louis Massiah; Dianne McIntyre; Cricket Mena and Brenda Brown; Sara Minnifield; Marcia, Daniel, and Azari Minter; Debb Moore; Swasti Kozue Oyama; Phyllis Alesia Perry; Eugene B. Redmond; Sheila Reed; Sara Lomax Reese; Craig Seymour; Ellen Sumter; Dorrie Toney; Elizabeth Van Dyke; Iyanla Vanzant; Mike Weaver; Laura Wexler; Cynthia, Sherman, Malik, and Kenya Wheeler; Evelyn C. White; Shay Youngblood; and all my friends at SYMCA.

And finally, but not least, I thank my best friend and *sadhana* partner, Veta Goler, for believing in this calling as much as I did, and for propping me up on every leaning side.

Index